W0232684

The Rays before Satyajit

The Rays before Satyajit

*Creativity and Modernity
in Colonial India*

CHANDAK SENGOOPTA

OXFORD
UNIVERSITY PRESS

OXFORD
UNIVERSITY PRESS

Oxford University Press is a department of the University of Oxford.
It furthers the University's objective of excellence in research, scholarship,
and education by publishing worldwide. Oxford is a registered trademark of
Oxford University Press in the UK and in certain other countries.

Published in India by
Oxford University Press
YMCA Library Building, 1 Jai Singh Road, New Delhi 110 001, India

First Edition published in 2016

ISBN-13: 978-0-19-946475-3
ISBN-10: 0-19-946475-8

Typeset in ScalaPro 10/12.4
by The Graphics Solution, New Delhi 110 092
Printed in India at Rakmo Press, New Delhi 110 020

In memory of Nirmalya Acharya, *Ekshan*,
and those Coffee House days

Contents

Acknowledgements

This book emerged unexpectedly while I was working on a biography of Satyajit Ray funded by the Leverhulme Trust, UK, and supported by my colleagues at Birkbeck College, especially Miriam Zukas, Julian Swann, Naoko Shimazu, Sunil Amrith, and John Arnold. Henriette Bruun and Dan Todes gave me wise advice and Partha Chatterjee, Partha Mitter, and Suranjan Ganguly provided much support. I shall be forever in their debt.

I am deeply grateful to the editors at Oxford University Press for the interest they took in the project, to the two anonymous reviewers who offered many suggestions for improving the manuscript, to Pinaki De for the excellent cover, and to Indrani Majumdar for making it all possible. As the book goes to press, I think of Nirmalya Acharya, whose untimely death robbed me of an inspiring and affectionate mentor, Bengal of an exponent of the highest type of *adda*, and the world of a scholar-editor of the kind they just do not seem to make any more. *The Rays before Satyajit* is dedicated to his memory and that of *Ekshan*, the magazine to which he dedicated his very life and which has never had an equal.

It has been an exciting book to write and I was helped along constantly by colleagues and friends, often through email or Facebook but also directly, during three long trips to Kolkata. Punam Zutshi and Ujjal Chakraborty had, at different times, encouraged me to write a biography of Satyajit Ray and the idea was warmly supported by Sandip, Lolita, and Souradeep Ray. They allowed me full access to the Ray family archives and I was guided through it first by Ujjal himself and then by Kaushik Ghosh and the incomparable

Ramesh (Punu) Sen. Working in Satyajit Ray's famous study—which I had had the good fortune to visit in Ray's lifetime for some brief but unforgettable conversations—was as exciting as it was nostalgic, and the archival discoveries that awaited me there were truly extraordinary. My thanks, too, to Arup K. De and the Ray Society for their support.

Those who have worked on any aspect of Indian or Bengali history would know that published sources are often as hard to find as archival material but thanks to the generosity of Debasis Mukhopadhyay, Riddhi Goswami, Biswajit Mitra, Indrani Majumdar, Debjani Ray, Sourit Dey, Debasish Deb, Amit Das, Anikendra Home, Syamantak Chattopadhyay, Sarbajit Mitra, and Arunkumar Roy, the task was less arduous than it might have been. I would also like to salute the work of the late Siddhartha Ghosh—his research on the Ray family was path-breaking in its time and it is lamentable that his essays and books have never been translated into English. Those who look at my notes will realize how indebted I am to his pioneering work and if, in my analyses, I differ from him, I do so with the most profound respect.

Paroma Maiti, an exemplary research assistant, worked harder on the project than I ever did, and even subjected herself and her ever-cheerful partner, Sourya Deb, to an agonizing trip in order to locate a particularly scarce periodical. My own travels were rather more pleasant, especially a trip to Santa Cruz, California, where Dilip Basu and Dayani Kowshik Basu guided me through the remarkable Lethbridge Collection of the Ray Film and Study Center at the University of California, Santa Cruz. I am thankful also to my sister, Anuradha (Bula), for sending many books and references from Kolkata.

I owe very special thanks to Soumen Paul for presenting me with innumerable books, periodicals, and photocopies that I could never have found by myself and for being such an unfailingly reliable source of information on graphic design, publishing, and every aspect of the book-world of Kolkata. He reminds me often of the late, greatly missed Indranath Majumdar, who had lightened the loads of generations of scholars and who passed away just as I was beginning to work on this project. Barun Chattopadhyay, who is himself working on a comprehensive biography of Dwarakanath and Kadambini Ganguli, led me to sources and issues that were new to me, providing me with beautifully scanned electronic copies of innumerable essential but scarce documents. Addas with him taught me more about historical research, Bengali society, human warmth, and collegial generosity than I could ever hope to list, and the chapters on Dwarakanath in this book could not have been written without his help.

Many colleagues, from near and far, offered encouragement, support, and intellectual inputs over the years it took me to finish the study. Satadru Sen alerted me to topics I had been utterly ignorant of; Ben Zachariah taught me not to turn everything into the history of nationalism; Manjita Mukharji, Sunil Khilnani, Jon Wilson, Ranjan Ghosh, Mark Mazower, Paul Lay, and the late Christopher Bayly got me to write or present papers that helped me clarify my ideas about the Rays; Behroze Gandhy and the British Film Institute invited me to teach a four-week course on Satyajit Ray's cinema that gave me an opportunity to test out my arguments on a diverse and articulate group of students; Madhubanti Bhattacharyya showed me how to edit my 'imperishable' prose; Pam Cullen, Kitty Cooper, Devika Banerjee, Shyamal Choudhury, and others at the Satyajit Ray Foundation helped me understand the intricacies of doing film history in the UK; Anindita Ghosh showed me how to find the hidden gems of the British Library's Bengali collections, and the staff of the Rare Books and Music Reading Room put up cheerfully with the endless book requests that I then proceeded to place; and Saumitra SenGupta and Ilana Glaun, with characteristic wit, warmth, and panache, took me on an enthralling ride in San Francisco and Santa Cruz.

Swati Ganguly, Jayita Sengupta Sen, Shoubhik Sen, Sagnik Chatterjee, Alakananda Bhattacharya, Anuradha Chaudhuri, Sarbari Ghosal, Sayantani Adhikary, Arnab Dutta, Anirban Bandyopadhyay, Titas De Sarkar, Amit Das, Sanghita Nath, Sriparna Barman Bhattacharya, Kaushik Majumdar, Debajyoti Guha, Natsu Hattori, Misa Hanrath, and Sreeparna Mitra kept up my spirits with banter, books, drinks, laughter, gifts, food, and adda, while Priyamvada Gopal earned my undying gratitude by introducing me to Grumpy Cat. My warm thanks, too, to Madhab Mondal, the staff of Fanindra Guest House and of La Zeez (especially Pranab Chanak) for making my Kolkata trips so comfortable.

Over the last two decades, Jane Henderson has lit up my life and filled it with joy. Neither this book nor, I sometimes fear, its author would have existed had it not been for her and our cats—Harry and Sally, then Barney and Bella—and I still feel amazed that I was lucky enough to have stumbled into their lives.

Introduction

The Rays and the History of Modernity in India

This book tells the story of a remarkable family of
nineteenth-century India—the Rays of Calcutta—and uses it
to illuminate the larger history of Indian modernity.
Although some of the Rays, especially Upendrakishore Ray
(1863–1915) and his son Sukumar (1887–1923), are iconic figures in their home province of Bengal, it is only Sukumar's
son, the filmmaker, writer, graphic artist, and composer
Satyajit (1921–1992), who is well known beyond the Bengali-
speaking world. The diverse endeavours of this family
deserve, however, to be better known, not only for their
intrinsic interest but also because they can illuminate the
history of cultural modernity in India from unusual angles.
From printing technology to religious reform, from children's literature to nationalist politics, from painting to
sound recording, from the education of women to the emancipation of indentured labourers, from book design to
cricket, the Rays were at the leading edge of a whole range of
key reforms, debates, and cultural adventures, a surprising
number of which remain unaddressed in the ever-growing
scholarly literature on Indian modernity. This book uses the
Rays and their work to extend, complicate, and revise some
of the contentions of that literature.

The little that is available in English on the history of the
Ray family is to be found in the earlier sections of Satyajit
Ray's biographies, but these accounts are necessarily brief
and do not seek to situate the earlier Rays in their own

historical contexts.[1] Understandably, much more has been written in Bengali on them and their work but except for the inspirational research of Siddhartha Ghosh on the technological interests of Upendrakishore Ray and his brother-in-law, Hemendramohan Bose (from the empirical riches of which I have drawn extensively), Bengali historiography is almost exclusively concerned with the family's contributions to children's literature. The Rays, certainly, were pre-eminent in children's literature, so much so that the poet, novelist, and critic Buddhadev Bose commented in 1948 that they seemed to 'hold a monopoly' in that trade.[2] But for all their literary eminence, the Rays were not merely a family of writers.

They were involved, individually or collectively, with virtually every reformist project of the nineteenth century and beyond. In her study of visual culture in Maharashtra, Kajri Jain has shown how Indian modernity involved the formation of unpredictable but productive links between such ostensibly separate spheres as art, business, and film.[3] The story of the Ray family reveals many similar links. Technology and religion, in particular, were of great importance to the Rays, as were art, literature, nationalism, and social reform. The Rays, Ashis Nandy once remarked, had a predilection for 'odd', even 'eccentric', careers. Nandy offered only a psychological analysis of this pattern, but as we shall see, what it demands is comprehensive historical exploration. When fully contextualized, the Rays' seemingly 'odd' endeavours reveal the unruly, ad hoc, and inchoate nature of India's experiments with the modern.[4]

The Cast of Characters

The earliest known Rays established themselves in Bengal in eastern India during the Mughal period. Despite the ruling order being Muslim, they prospered, like many other Bengali Hindus, as scribes or legal professionals. After the establishment of British rule, one member of the family, Harikishore Ray, entered the new landed gentry brought into being by the land reforms of the East India Company and adopted Kamadaranjan Ray, the five-year-old son of a cousin from the scribal branch of the family. The boy was given the new and aristocratic-sounding name of Upendrakishore Raychaudhuri (1863–1915).

Shuttled between two different social identities from childhood, the artistically gifted Upendrakishore embraced neither in full. At

INTRODUCTION   3

odds with the mainstream Hindu faith of his adoptive as well as biological families and not keen on living as a rural landowner or a scribe, in 1879 he moved to Calcutta—then the capital of British India and the nearest thing to a world city in South Asia. Such a journey was only too common for aspirational young men of the colonial era but unlike most of them, Upendrakishore did not pursue a career in law, medicine, or the colonial bureaucracy. Although he graduated with a BA, he became an artisan and entrepreneur. Simultaneously, he converted to the Brahmo faith, a monotheistic variety of Hinduism that not only opposed idolatry and polytheism but also rejected the caste system, championed the education of women, propagated the virtues of reason and science, and sought to create a whole new ethos and politics that combined nationalism with a cosmopolitan and universalist outlook. Upendrakishore's affiliation with this radical group was formalized when he married Bidhumukhi, the daughter of Dwarakanath Ganguli (1844–1898), a remarkable Brahmo crusader against traditional Hindu as well as modern colonial injustices.

Born into a conservative Brahmin family and milieu in a village near Dhaka (now the capital of Bangladesh), Dwarakanath Ganguli had received little formal education, but even when working as an itinerant schoolteacher in the villages of East Bengal, he had begun to publish a journal for and about women. Shocked by the consequences of polygamy—the highest-ranking Brahmins of the time (such as Dwarakanath himself) were encouraged to marry as many women as they could—he dedicated himself to fighting the custom through his journal. Predictably, Dwarakanath moved to Calcutta in 1870, converted to Brahmoism, and threw himself into diverse campaigns for reform. He and his radical associates were the moving spirits behind two pioneering boarding schools for girls, where Dwarakanath himself did most of the teaching.

Girls' schools had begun to emerge in mid-nineteenth-century Calcutta but even the best provided no more than elementary education, that too of the kind appropriate for future housewives. Dwarakanath, however, wanted his students to go to university; one of them, Kadambini Basu (1861–1923), eventually became one of the first two women graduates of Calcutta University and, subsequently, one of the first women doctors in India. Just before commencing her medical studies, she married her mentor Dwarakanath Ganguli, who was nearly twenty years her senior and a widower with two children. Needless to say, traditionalists disapproved of the match—less predictably, many supposedly radical Brahmos were displeased too—but it turned out to be a happy and largely progressive match. Dwarakanath supported Kadambini in all her professional ambitions, including a voyage to England that involved leaving their young children with her mother.

Dwarakanath Ganguli's reformism was not confined to the domestic sphere. Along with many of his Brahmo associates, he worked energetically to build up one of the earliest nationalist bodies in British India, the Indian Association. Founded in 1876, it predated the Indian National Congress by some ten years and, although it was heavily Bengali in its membership, it fought for political reforms which would have benefited all Indians. The Association, like all 'moderate' nationalist bodies of the time, wanted India to remain within the British Empire but was sharply critical of the day-to-day government of British India and one of its primary objectives was to ensure that India was ruled mostly by Indians themselves. Today, the Indian Association is often regarded as little more than a bourgeois talking shop but at the time, it was regarded by many as a radical, pro-peasant, and anti-elite organization. That image was exaggerated but not entirely fictitious. The Association's support for land reforms and its campaign against the ill-treatment of indentured labourers in the tea plantations of Assam revealed the distinctiveness of its position. The latter campaign, in particular, is of the utmost importance for us, since it was led almost single-handedly by Dwarakanath Ganguli. In an era when nationalists were preoccupied with opening up the hallowed portals of the Indian Civil Service for Indians, Dwarakanath's grass-roots activism was unusually radical. Even though it failed to achieve immediate results, its revelation of 'slavery in British dominion' embarrassed the Raj far more profoundly than any of the Indian Association's more genteel 'constitutional' campaigns.

Although immersed in the pursuit of art, music, technology, and literature, and showing little overt interest in larger social or cultural questions, Upendrakishore Ray, too, was a reformer, albeit of a very different kind from his father-in-law. Musically inclined from childhood, Upendrakishore, whose conversion to Brahmoism had endangered his inheritance and income, first set up in business as a photographer—scarcely the kind of profession chosen by other young men from the landowning class. He did not even pursue conventional prosperity by photographing the rich and famous—a route taken by many Bengali photographers of the time in Calcutta—and gradually came to concentrate on the question of the *printing* of photographs. The print culture of nineteenth-century Bengal was booming but as far as illustrations were concerned, all that Bengali periodicals and books could offer were woodcuts. Upendrakishore may well have sensed an untapped business opportunity here but he was also motivated by his disappointment with the quality of wood-engravings in his first book, a retelling of the Ramayana for children. Thus commenced his lifelong involvement with half-tone photography—a new technology to print photographs or paintings without robbing them of their tonality.

The production of half-tone blocks was a complicated business and the whole process was still new and incompletely understood even in the West. It is remarkable, then, that Upendrakishore mastered it only with the help of imported books and equipment, quickly becoming the premier block-maker for Calcutta's leading illustrated periodicals. Simultaneously, he published original research articles on the theoretical and practical aspects of half-tone processes in British technical journals, acquiring a significant global reputation as an expert. His metropolitan prominence, however, was transient, not because of any deficiencies in his research or, as believed in Bengal even today, because his innovations were 'stolen' by a Western block-maker. As we shall see, research on photomechanical reproduction was moving at a breakneck pace across the West and soon went far beyond what Upendrakishore could achieve with his limited resources. Also, his recognition in the metropole was dependent largely on the support of one well-connected British printing expert, William Gamble. Whatever Gamble could not (or would not) do for Upendrakishore—such as help him patent his innovations—never got done and as the half-tone technology itself was outshone by newer processes such as photogravure, Upendrakishore's work became less and less relevant.

Upendrakishore's brother-in-law, Hemendramohan Bose (1864–1916), revealed yet another kind of modernist sensibility. A very successful perfumer, Bose's innovative advertising campaigns for his cosmetic products—especially the literary competition named after his hair oil Kuntalin, which pioneered product placement in India—deserve a place in any history of modern advertising in South Asia. But Bose was also an avid technophile and started pioneering ventures selling phonographs, wax cylinders for phonographic recordings, bicycles, and motor cars to the Calcutta gentry. He never tried, however, to reshape these European technologies into indigenous forms or improve them by means of his own research. Even the one thing he did manufacture—wax cylinders for phonographic recordings—merely replicated the Western product with indigenous material. Upendrakishore's half-tone research was of a wholly different kind—although starting with imported ideas, he went on to make original contributions to the field, while Bose remained a mere importer and distributor of Western technology.

The two were also very different in their approaches to literature. Bose patronized literature quite effectively with his Kuntalin prize but Upendrakishore was a prolific and talented writer who wrote for children from his undergraduate days, contributing to the new children's magazines emerging in nineteenth-century Bengal. This, too, was an area where Brahmos were prominent and their involvement in children's literature complemented their commitment to women's education. The historian R. H. Tawney once observed that nothing revealed the 'true character of a social philosophy' more than its treatment of the poor and children.[5] The extensive historical literature on the Brahmo Samaj has much to say on its treatment of the poor but contains little real analysis of the place of children and childhood in Brahmo social ideology. A contextual study of the career of Upendrakishore helps us understand the latter.

The overarching aim of Brahmo reform was to create a true civil society in India, where reformed, refined, and regenerate men and women would participate equally (though not identically) and the ranks of which would be constantly replenished by young people who had been inculcated with the right values from childhood and were, therefore, likely to be morally superior to their elders. Satadru Sen has argued that the Bengali middle-class child, from the nineteenth century onwards, came to be seen variously as 'modern, masculine, scientific, authentic' and contrasted to 'colonized, effeminate, inauthentic, unscientific' adults in children's literature.[6] Sociologist Norbert Elias remarked that the progress of civilization in Europe had gradually created a gulf between 'refined' adults and children that had to be bridged by teaching the child to be 'civilized'.[7] For Bengali reformers, too, there was a gulf between children and adults, except that, to them, colonized adults seemed to have few virtues that children needed to acquire—the point was to bring up children to be different from, and better than, their adult contemporaries.

The Ray family's literary and editorial work was implicitly guided by such a contrast and the drive to 'modernize' the child by enlarging its intellectual universe and (gently) shaping its moral identity. The reform of adults was, of course, considered vital for the improvement of contemporary society. However, not only was reforming children easier because of the inherent plasticity of their minds but it was of paramount importance for ensuring that the future nation would be populated by *better* adults than the colonial present.[8] Traditional fairy tales or ghost stories were deemed acceptable in moderation but much more was needed to groom India's children for their future responsibilities. Overt didacticism and religious propaganda, including Brahmo propaganda, had to be avoided, needless to say, but the blend had to be 'improving' as well as entertaining, and the target audience was almost entirely middle-class and non-Muslim.[9] Perhaps the most famous vehicle for this invigorating brew was the magazine *Sandesh*, which was founded by Upendrakishore in 1913.

Initially written and illustrated entirely by Upendrakishore and printed with his own blocks, *Sandesh* represented the culminating achievement of his career, combining his literary gifts, artistic abilities, technological wizardry, and artisanal insistence on doing everything with his own hands. Above all, however, it aimed to create a new kind of child. As Upendrakishore's son, Sukumar, wrote in *Sandesh* after its founder's death: 'Driven by the deepest affection for you, he laboured hard and applied all his intelligence and subtlety to improve you while entertaining you.' There was a strong emphasis on science in the magazine although exemplary tales of virtue, nobility, and courage from the Hindu epics and Sanskrit classics were also included—but only after their sexual, scatological, and socially retrogressive elements had been carefully eliminated. When purified, the traditional tales would sustain modern children, giving them a secure Indian identity and thereby providing them with a firm national base from which to embrace the cultural and intellectual riches of the entire world. Little of this was explicitly nationalistic but in founding *Sandesh*, Upendrakishore sought ultimately to build the *future* nation. This project to create tomorrow's citizens was the perfect, if understated, match for his father-in-law's more high-profile involvement with nationalism and women's education.

Upendrakishore's eldest son, Sukumar (1887–1923), is remembered today mostly for his incomparable nonsense writings, some of them inspired by Lewis Carroll and Edward Lear but all of them utterly Bengali in tone and ambience. Although he trained in printing technology in Britain and was shaping into a worthy successor of his father, his enduring fame was to come from literature. From taking over the editorship of *Sandesh* after Upendrakishore's death in 1915 and until his own early death at thirty-six, Sukumar flowered into one of Bengal's most original and captivating writers. His nonsense writings extended the family's hegemony over children's literature and despite being clearly inspired by Lewis Carroll, Edward Lear, and other Western sources, they were wholly indigenous in their characters, allusions, and style. Sukumar's best works—notably the *Alice*-like *Haw-Jaw-Baw-Raw-Law*—defy simplistic categorization as 'derivative' or 'original'. They assimilated the foreign while remaining so thoroughly rooted in their native cultural soil that attempts to translate them into English have never quite succeeded in capturing their essence. Compelling us to reconsider conventional understandings of creativity, inspiration, and originality, Sukumar's work can serve as a literary analogue for Indian modernity itself.

With Sukumar's death in 1923, the Ray family story seemed to head for a premature, depressing conclusion. The family business went bankrupt within a few years and Upendrakishore's house on Garpar Road was auctioned off with all its belongings. Sukumar's widow, Suprabha, and their son Satyajit—delivered by Kadambini Ganguli, the boy was not even three years old at the time of his father's death—faced a calamitous situation, from which they were saved by a combination of old values and new identities. Suprabha and Satyajit found a home with Suprabha's brother, Prasantakumar Das, and the future filmmaker grew up in the kind of large and traditional joint family that is often blamed for stifling creativity and individuality. Suprabha took up a job, which was uncommon even among progressive Brahmo women of the time, taught her son at home (he was sent to school when he was over eight), sculpted (often selling her work for good money), and took charge of the kitchen (her cooking was universally regarded as superlative) of her brother's large household. She was also an excellent singer of Rabindranath Tagore's songs and the poet, a family friend since Upendrakishore's time, often personally taught her his new songs. The epitome of the Brahmo ideal of womanhood, Suprabha Ray combined creativity and domesticity with the kind of consummate skill that may be rare even in the twenty-first century. Her modernity was indubitable but so was her loyalty to certain aspects of Hindu tradition. Not only did she appreciate the security and conviviality of the joint-family environment but she also chose to don the marks of Hindu widowhood—especially the plain white sari known as *thaan*—even though Brahmos were not under any compulsion to do so.

Her son, however, did not seem to share her attachment to tradition. A quiet boy fond of Western classical music, Hollywood films, and English popular fiction, the young Satyajit showed little obvious interest in anything Indian. This changed when, after graduating with an economics degree, he went, at his mother's insistence, to Tagore's university at Santiniketan to train as a painter even though he thoroughly disliked the kind of showily Indian art that he had always associated with Santiniketan. The two and a half years he spent there were to transform his very soul. The wide open spaces and their natural beauty awed him and he discovered the true depths of Indian aesthetics from his mentors Nandalal Bose and Binodebihari Mukhopadhyay. Other acquaintances deepened his appreciation of music (Western as well as Indian), the library proved to be a treasure house of the world's knowledge (it even had several books on the art of the film), and two trips with three of his classmates to the Ajanta caves (in western India) and elsewhere opened his eyes to the sheer extent of India's artistic and architectural heritage. By the time he returned to Calcutta in 1941 (without completing his painting course), he had turned into a cosmopolitan youth, aesthetically sensitive but level-headed, neither deracinated nor narrowly indigenist, and ready to carry on the modernist endeavours of his forefathers—though not, as we shall see, their entrepreneurial experiments.

The Rays and the Story of Modernity in India

The Ray family's protean initiatives and accomplishments can be— and, indeed, often have been—recounted simply as a dramatic, multi-generational tale of heroic creativity. While seeking to capture that drama and creativity, this book, however, uses the Rays to illuminate the larger history of their age and their complex, changing society. The vast network formed by the extended Ray clan, their connections by marriage and all their respective offspring, was shaped by and, in turn, shaped the social processes transforming Bengal and India in the nineteenth century. The biographical narrative of the book, therefore, is entwined with an analysis of what the saga of the Rays can tell us about the character and ambiguities of colonial modernity. The latter, of course, has been extensively studied in recent years and it is essential to indicate how this book builds on and diverges from the available approaches.[10]

Modernity, like light, is easy to recognize but hard to define. Historian Prathama Banerjee provides a daunting list of its diverse connotations: modernity is

> now a set of ideas (reason, enlightenment, progress); now a set of norms (equality, liberty, secularity); now an orientation of the self (secular, rational, individual, modernist, schizophrenic); now institutions and technologies (public sphere, governmentality, democracy); now capital; now an epoch (with a beginning but no end); and now an empty placeholder (filled with content by various peoples in various times and places).[11]

But it is this multiplicity of meanings that makes modernity such a useful organizing concept for a book on the polymathic Rays. As Banerjee rightly observes, the modern condition *was* multidimensional and whether we chart the history of individual freedom, rationalism, the rule of law, religious reform, capitalism, industrial development, literary experimentation, technological advancement, gender equality, social liberalism, consumerism, nationalism, democracy, or cosmopolitanism with most of which the Rays were directly involved—they 'all seem to flow into the singular and capacious story of the modern'.[12]

For historians of the non-Western world, however, there is an additional layer of complexity to negotiate. Even if Marshall Berman's speculation, based entirely on his survey of nineteenth-century Russia, that modernity beyond Western Europe was 'truncated and warped ... shrill, uncouth and inchoate' is dismissed as over-generalized, we have to contend with the tenacious notion that Indian modernity was delivered virtually fully formed by the West through the subcontinent's British rulers.[13] As the celebrated Bengali historian Sir Jadunath Sarkar proclaimed in 1928, 'the modernization of India is the work of the English, and it has affected the entire Indian continent'.[14] Historian after historian, not to mention countless general writers and commentators, have presented the story of Indian modernity as the tale of 'western wisdom poured into an oriental void'.[15] Such narratives, as historian Brian Hatcher has justly remarked, are based on 'a model of cultural encounter that envisions European ideas being unloaded and distributed in Calcutta like so many commodities'—and India's indigenous reformers have thus been implicitly regarded as imitators or, at best, translators, 'mimic men' who merely disseminated Europe's gifts among their benighted compatriots.[16]

The oppressive aspects of colonial subjugation are not necessarily denied in these accounts but the emphasis, almost always, is on the benefits bestowed, even if unwittingly, by British colonial rule. The 'processes of empires and colonies, race and genocide, resurgent faiths and reified traditions' that are now recognized to be 'at the core of modernity' are simply left out.[17] Even when recognized, the brutishness of colonialism is seen to be compensated by its beneficent gifts. As one fairly recent scholar of women's history put it pithily, 'if by its colonial rule England robbed Bengal of her legendary wealth, in its turn it gave her its liberal education and ideas and transformed her into a modern society'.[18] Often in the same breath, however, these traditional historians list how Indian modernity failed to live up to its Western models. If anything looks modern at first sight—say, campaigns for women's rights in colonial India—but, upon examination, reveals a disinclination to emulate the West in every detail, then it is dismissed as an instance of incomplete or failed modernization. The history of modernity in India, from this perspective, invariably represents 'a sad figure of lack and failure'.[19]

This conventional history of Indian modernity—rather like the modernization theory that was so popular with social scientists in Cold War America—does not only assume that there was one single path to modernity, the Western industrial–capitalistic one.[20] It is also usually intertwined with a heroic reading of the cultural history of one particular region—Bengal. Since the modern is taken to be Western by definition and because Bengal was exposed to colonial influence for much longer than the rest of India, Bengali modernity has come to be regarded as the prototype of Indian modernity and the experiences of nineteenth-century Bengal have long been graced with the grandiose label of the 'Bengal Renaissance'. Bengal during the British period, observed Jadunath Sarkar, illuminated the rest of India 'with a borrowed light, which it had made its own with marvellous cunning ... new literary types, reform of the language, social reconstruction, political aspirations, religious movements and even changes in manners that originated in Bengal, passed like ripples from a central eddy, across provincial barriers to the furthest corners of India'.[21] Countless historians have endorsed this interpretation, in which modernity, born in Europe, travels to Bengal with British colonists and is then transmitted to the rest of India by Bengalis.[22]

This so-called renaissance in Bengal is supposed to have commenced with Rammohan Roy (1772[?]–1833) and his efforts to improve the lives of women and also to uncover the pure monotheistic heart of Hinduism.[23] The drama speeds up from the mid-nineteenth century, with a succession of remarkable figures like the educator and philanthropist Iswarchandra Vidyasagar (1820–1891), the novelist Bankimchandra Chattopadhyay (1838–1894), and the religious reformer Keshabchandra Sen (1838–1884), climaxing with Rabindranath Tagore (1861–1941), whose Nobel Prize in 1913 seemed to salute not only his own achievements, but the entire Bengal Renaissance.[24] All of these great Bengalis, we have long been told, were inspired by the new (Western) knowledge to rethink old (Indian) orthodoxies, and their valiant efforts to synthesize the East and the West awakened (some) Indians from their long cultural slumber. The notion of 'synthesis' was crucial: the heroes of the Bengal Renaissance, it is still held by many, created 'an integrated culture—the product of a fusion of East and West'.[25]

It is evident with hindsight that the Bengal Renaissance concept was especially popular during Bengal's mid-twentieth-century descent into 'war, famine, communal riots, and Partition' and provided some nostalgic solace for a present that was unbearable.[26] But few educated Indians—or, for that matter, Westerners—questioned the myth until the 1970s, when a group of young Marxist scholars began to emphasize the very limited and even deformed nature of the modernity that had emerged in colonial Bengal.[27] Acknowledging the often great merits of the standard heroes of the Renaissance narrative, they sought to clarify the 'objective constraints' of a colonial society that so often prevented the reformers from reaching their goals.[28] They, however, remained at one with the traditional champions of the Renaissance concept in accepting the European Renaissance and, more broadly, Western modernity as a yardstick with which to judge the cultural efflorescence in nineteenth-century Bengal. The R-word, some of the critics argued, was inapplicable to Bengal because the actual phenomenon failed to measure up to its Western analogues.[29]

Decades ago, historian Charles Heimsath had warned that India's contact was 'with a civilization ... which itself was experiencing in the 19th century a far-reaching social reformation, based on political reforms and economic changes, which excited Europeans and

Americans with its revolutionary implications no less than it did Indians'.[30] This awareness of the global, roughly concurrent nature of the emergence of modernity is generally absent from the classic histories of the Bengal Renaissance and Indian modernity.[31] To take one particularly relevant example, traditional Indian historians—and not a few revisionists—have always tended to overestimate the opportunities available to nineteenth-century Western women. To be sure, an English middle-class woman did not live in seclusion and she was not denied elementary education. But in Britain at least, universal free education did not exist before 1870 and even after that, an Englishwoman could not ordinarily aspire to higher education or to a professional identity.[32] As for medical education, the first *university* medical schools to admit women were in Zurich in 1864 and in Paris in 1867; there was no scope for British women to obtain university medical qualifications at home until after the First World War.[33] The record of Calcutta University in awarding its BA degree to Kadambini Basu and Chandramukhi Basu in 1883 and its medical degree to Bidhumukhi Basu (younger sister of Chandramukhi) and Virginia Mary Mitter in 1890 seems rather impressive when situated in this international context.[34]

As Sanjay Joshi reminds us, the tensions, contradictions, and limitations of middle-class modernity in colonial India were by no means unique to the subcontinent.[35] Modernities *everywhere* were 'built with a variety of resources, including much that modernity labels either tradition or non-modern, whether it is in the form of patriarchal ideas, racism, notions of patronage and deference, or religion'.[36] The ideal type of Western modernity was never realized *anywhere*—'paradoxes and fractures ... inhabit the heart of modernity'.[37] To say this is not, of course, to deny the very substantial differences between nineteenth-century Europe and India, but simply to emphasize that the standard practice of comparing India's admittedly incomplete and even misshapen modernity with the West's supposedly perfectly formed version is based on idealized readings of European history.

More recently, some scholars have attempted to jettison the European analogy altogether (or, at least, to 'provincialize' it), giving us many inspiring studies—based mostly on 'high' literary sources or works of what we would call social theory today—of the character and nuances of 'our modernity'.[38] (This trend, of course, parallels sociological reconceptualizations of global modernities as plural, heterogeneous, or, in Shmuel Eisenstadt's oft-quoted formulation, multiple.)[39] If India's reformers were less heroic than we expect them to be, then we should remember how greatly they were constrained by the weaknesses of the colonial bourgeoisie as a class, and also by the reluctance of the colonial state, especially after the Sepoy Rebellion of 1857, to yield to demands for social legislation from indigenous reformers. The latter could never aspire to more than what historian Tanika Sarkar has called 'minimalist' programmes— 'nothing else would have the remotest chance of acceptability either with the legislative authorities or in Hindu society'.[40] Also, many of the limitations and dilemmas of nineteenth-century Bengali middle-class culture cannot be fully explained from exclusively individualist perspectives. Ultimately, the differences between individual reformers, creators, and activists are less important than the vulnerabilities of their entire class, the fundamental cause of which was economic.

Economic historians have shown that whatever other benefit the British may have bestowed on Indians, large-scale, nationwide industrial capitalism was not one of them. The character of Indian modernity—especially that developing in Bengal—was crucially shaped by this absence. For a short period in the first half of the nineteenth century, a few socially mobile Indians (like the fabled Dwarakanath Tagore) had started business enterprises of substantial size, often with British partners, but these ventures had all failed by 1850, and from then until the Second World War, India was a source of raw materials for Western manufactures and, in an age of tariff restrictions in the US and many European nations, an increasingly important market for British exports, especially cotton textiles, steel, and engineering products.[41] While cheap cotton textiles made in Lancashire clothed poorer Indians, their wealthier compatriots read about and admired the industrial might of Manchester and Leeds, used imported cosmetics, sent telegrams or travelled by rail and steamer. None, regardless of personal wealth, could, however, aspire to be railway barons or owners of large chemical factories.[42]

Indeed, the English education to which so many historians have attributed the cultural glories of nineteenth-century India may even have distanced people from whatever remained of the traditional trades and crafts. Technical education, even if available and patronized, would not have helped since there would have been little demand for the graduates in the largely unindustrialized economy. The representatives of Indian modernity, by and large, came from a uniquely skewed colonial middle class that, in Bengal, has traditionally been labelled as *bhadralok* or genteel folk, and which was created by the changes brought about by colonial rule. It had no authentic pre-colonial past to draw upon and as Benjamin Zachariah has pointed out, the criteria for inclusion in it have always been unclear and elusive.[43] Nobody who earned his bread through manual labour or petty trade would ever be considered *bhadra*, but, as Nirad Chaudhuri pointed out, there were many levels within the category and the definition of the bhadralok had nothing to do with wealth.[44] The vast majority of the bhadralok were high-caste Hindus but lower-caste individuals could be admitted as long as they fulfilled some educational and socio-moral requirements and the occasional Muslim, too, may have been admissible, at least in principle.[45]

The bhadralok, S.N. Mukherjee has rightly pointed out, were 'all agents of "modernity"' in their economic as well as sociocultural actions.[46] Whether it was the establishment of modern banking, the introduction of English education and modern science, or raising funds for famine relief in Ireland, the Bengali bhadralok were always in the vanguard of reform. But not all bhadralok had such agency. As Sumit Sarkar has emphasized, this was a highly differentiated group and while some bhadralok were rich, highly educated, well-travelled, and professionally successful, vast numbers of others spent their lives as poorly paid clerks.[47] The Europeans were socially and economically superior to both groups, of course, and even the best-placed bhadralok, for all their volubility, lofty ideas, and often sincere efforts, simply did not possess the socio-economic prowess of the nineteenth-century European bourgeoisie, and their social hegemony was always balanced by their lack of state authority.[48]

The Bengali bhadralok were almost invariably reliant on white-collar (though not necessarily well-paid) jobs, professional and/or rent income and this has traditionally been regarded as a kind of character-flaw of Bengalis.[49] As John McGuire has shown, few Indians could enter the hallowed 'covenanted' ranks of the Indian Civil Service but the lower-paid 'uncovenanted' posts in the civil service as well as government posts below them were staffed by 'natives', making the colonial state 'the greatest employer in British India'.[50] The fundamental cause of this phenomenon, however, was economic, not psychological or racial. Examining the careers of all those who graduated from Calcutta University in the first quarter-century of its existence, Krishnachandra Roy remarked: 'If there is *chakri* [modest desk-jobs] to be had, educated men will go in for it, whether they are Bengalis or Englishmen, as that appears to be the easiest way of earning one's livelihood.'[51] It was not just the availability of chakri that was responsible for the Bengali fondness for it but, more importantly, the relative *un*availability of other secure career options to individuals of average talent and little property.[52]

For those with actual capital, too, the options were far from extensive.[53] As Surendranath Banerjea's newspaper *The Bengalee* reflected ruefully in 1891, 'if capital can be invested in land with the certainty of yielding a return of six to seven per cent, people will not incur the risk of investment in industrial undertakings, which may give them a higher return, but which may also involve them in ruin'.[54] Big technology or big business, in any case, were unrealistic goals for most Indians and even the most enterprising had to aim lower. As Rajat Kanta Ray reminded us long ago, the history of big business or heavy industry in India, on which historians have focused so intently, tells 'less than half the story'. Right up to the outbreak of the Second World War, 'unorganized industry with a strong component of rural artisan manufacture' remained, apart from agriculture, the most important sector of the Indian economy.[55] Even here, however, opportunities had shrunk in British times with the end of the Mughal practice of establishing large imperial workshops or court studios (*karkhanas*) where craftsmen could produce handcrafted goods for the delectation of the wealthy.[56] One reason why the Rays repay study is because they managed to break free of this economic prison-house without any help from the state and without damaging their status as bhadralok.

The Rays as 'Small Masters'

The Rays were bhadralok but not of the conventional kind.[57] There were no lawyers, doctors, or clerks among them and only one—Upendrakishore's youngest brother Pramadaranjan—who worked for the government, though not in the kind of high-status administrative post that was sought after by middle-class Bengalis. Also, although many of the Rays wrote a lot, they were not exclusively writers or thinkers. Some of them (such as Upendrakishore) received some income from landed property but it was not their chief source of subsistence. Most of them, instead, chose to be artisans or traders—but not of the traditional kind. They evolved atypical and often small-scale ways of being emphatically modern and technologically advanced in an economy that was neither industrialized nor fully capitalistic.[58]

In fully developed capitalism, wrote Karl Marx, the capitalist is able to devote all his working time 'to the appropriation and therefore control of the labour of others, and to the selling of the products of this labour'. If, however, the capitalist took part 'directly in the process of production', then he was 'only a hybrid between capitalist and labourer, a "small master"'.[59] Full-blown industrial capitalism of the British variety being absent in British India, this kind of semi-capitalistic form was to be found in many indigenous businesses of the time but they have yet to be studied in detail. Its socio-economic distinctiveness has not been fully addressed even in the best histories of Indian technology, such as Christopher Pinney's studies on photography or David Arnold's recent, insightful work on 'everyday technology'.[60] Amiya Bagchi is right, of course, to point out that 'these small capitalists did not start an industrial revolution' but his comment that they 'did not pioneer any new methods of production or any new industries' cannot be fully endorsed.[61] In any case, as Andrew Sartori has recently emphasized, it is less productive to ask *whether* India underwent an industrial revolution in the nineteenth century—since the answer is obviously 'no'—than to study *how* colonial India was integrated with 'global structures' of capitalism.[62] When we turn to that latter question, Marx's 'small masters' emerge as important figures.

A government investigation of the industrial situation in Bengal found in 1908 that although Indian big capital (or what there was of it) was usually not invested in industrial enterprise, there *were* some commendable indigenous efforts to set up industries run by 'the small capitalist or by small syndicates' and all realistic hopes for the industrial development of Bengal lay in this sector. J.G. Cumming, the author of the report, considered the Bengal Chemical and Pharmaceutical Works, established by the chemist Prafullachandra Ray and specializing in producing drugs from indigenous sources, to be exemplary in its 'resourcefulness and business capacity'.[63] And Bengal Chemical was not alone for very long. Between 1912 and 1928, '423 small and middle entrepreneurs and researchers applied to the government for patent rights' and many more, of course, innovated without patenting. These entrepreneurs sometimes sought to regenerate traditional crafts but more often, they concentrated on new technologies, especially those that did not require a huge outlay of capital.[64]

As Dwijendra Tripathi has pointed out, around 1900 and especially during the years of *swadeshi*, the rising interest of Bengalis in business and industry was relatively unconcerned with traditional industries like cotton textiles: 'They expressed their entrepreneurial zeal in promoting enterprises based on advanced scientific knowledge and involving more sophisticated manufacturing processes.' The fields they chose—pharmaceuticals, chemicals, cosmetics, pottery, electrical items—faced little indigenous competition, which, of course, was profoundly ironic given the indigenist aspirations of the swadeshi movement.[65] The list provided by historian Amit Bhattacharyya includes not only textiles and leather goods, but pottery, paper, tobacco, shipping, and insurance.[66] Often, the innovations of these companies consisted of replicating an imported technology with indigenous material, perhaps with some minor modifications for the local context.[67]

In his 1908 report, Cumming had called for the revitalization of India's artisanal traditions by 'the teaching of improved methods, and also the assistance of the educated upper-middle classes in a more organized system of production and distribution'.[68] The report, of course, was still thinking of *improving* traditional handicrafts. Upendrakishore, however, took from the artisanal tradition only its small-scale and largely manual working-style and used it to practise the most modern of technologies, which Cumming had not even considered to be of relevance to Indian conditions. Upendrakishore realized that while colonialism had led to the relative eclipse of older crafts, it had opened possibilities of cultivating new ones by connecting British India with Europe. It was now *possible* (though, of course, not usual and certainly not easy) for an Indian with only modest amounts of capital to gain significant access to European technical knowledge and instruments. The emerging technology of half-tone photography and block-making, in which he was personally interested and for which there was significant potential demand in Bengali print-culture, could still be cultivated at a very high level in a semi-artisanal colonial setting.[69]

Unlike the traditional artisans of early-modern Europe, Upendrakishore's skills were not based in any craft secrets handed down over generations and attested by the membership of a particular guild. But the very novelty and technical complexity of photomechanical reproduction meant that his skills were, in effect, unique in the Bengali context.[70] Moreover, half-tone technology was still in a sufficiently unformed state to enable a moderately resourced colonial entrepreneur to improve it and win metropolitan recognition for his innovations. What Upendrakishore accomplished, in other words, was not simply a 'creative adaptation'—which Dilip Parameshwar Gaonkar considers to be a hallmark of modernities developing beyond the West—or a local application of an imported innovation. He was a colonial contributor to what we would call Western modernity but which Upendrakishore's generation would have thought of as *universal* progress.[71]

For Upendrakishore's brother-in-law Hemendramohan Bose, the pursuit of technological modernity was more a trade or even a hobby rather than a field of serious, sustained research. From phonographs and bicycles to motor cars, Bose sold some of the greatest technological marvels of the age and was a pioneer in advertising. He was an ardent supporter of the swadeshi movement and played a major role in disseminating the patriotic songs that Rabindranath Tagore and Dwijendralal Roy wrote for the movement. But Bose's contributions to indigenous *manufacturing* were confined to cosmetics and wax cylinders for phonographic recordings. The first Indian bicycle manufacturer Sudhirkumar Sen (1888–1959) bought his first bike, a Rover, from Bose's shop but Bose himself was not the first manufacturer of bicycles in India and never seems to have harboured such an aspiration.[72] And as we shall see, neither Bose nor Upendrakishore participated in the national education movement that was a vital part of the swadeshi upsurge and one strand of which, led by the great physician Nilratan Sircar and others, tried to provide artisanal and technical training to young Bengalis.

Upendrakishore, his son Sukumar, and several other Rays were also writers and artists but their literary or artistic activities were not conducted in isolation from their artisanal-technological endeavours.[73] The family magazine *Sandesh* encapsulated the entire artisanal-entrepreneurial ethos of the Rays. The family members did not simply contribute to the magazine's content; the design of the cover, the blocks for the illustrations, the layout of the magazine and, eventually, its printing were all done by the Rays themselves or under their direct supervision. Although produced with the resources of the latest technology and sold like any other magazine in the growing modern, commodified marketplace, *Sandesh* remained, at the same time, a personal statement, an object crafted from start to finish by a master artisan, his kin, and a few associates in a personal workshop. And the overall aim of the magazine was to build the future nation by edifying as well as entertaining the children who would eventually be its citizens.

The Ray family's entrepreneurial activities, therefore, challenge Claude Markovits's argument that there was a total separation between 'the educated Bengali middle class and the "new" commercial middle class' in colonial times.[74] In a structural sense, at least, the Rays belonged to *both* of those categories: they produced literary work of enduring significance and engaged in diverse reformist endeavours, while their primary income came from the family printing and block-making business until the 1920s. They were not just entrepreneurs but cultural entrepreneurs.

Nationalism, Religious Reform, and the Role of the West

Although the colonial context undoubtedly enabled (without necessarily encouraging) the dissemination of many Western innovations in India, the actual shape and trajectory of social and cultural change were determined by Indians, most of whom would have used the Western term 'middle class' to describe themselves. Of late, it has become fashionable to bundle almost every member of the progressive middle classes of South Asia into an undifferentiated 'nationalist elite', erasing the often very significant differences between nationalists and misrepresenting those who did not subscribe to nationalism.[75] It is true, however, that despite countless variations among progressives on the question of nationalism, the fundamental aim of *improving* national life was widely shared and political nationalism, despite the many shades of opinion concealed by the term, did play a significant role in the lives of some of our protagonists. So, although the Rays did not belong to some homogeneous 'nationalist elite', we need to engage with the history of nationalism in India if we wish to understand the contexts of their work.

Non-Western nationalisms, in Benedict Anderson's influential formulation, were no more than applications of Western models of nationhood, national identity, and nationalist agitation.[76] Long before

Anderson, Bruce McCully had declared that nineteenth-century Indian nationalism was an 'exotic growth implanted by foreign hands and influences'; the great nationalist figures of the time 'invented little or nothing in the way of ideology'.[77] Perhaps they did not, but nationalism is a practice as well as an ideology and the attempts to mould a huge, diverse population divided by religion, language, and cultural traditions into a coherent, unified nation were noteworthy in their own right. English education did not magically transform colonial Indians into 'liberal individuals capable of resisting colonial domination'.[78] Strenuous ideological and organizational work was needed before that could come about. If, as Anderson and others have claimed, it was print-capitalism and associations that disseminated Western nationalist ideologies in the non-West, then it was Indians themselves 'who invested in presses, worked as journalists, created civic and political associations, and published and debated their ideas either in the press or in the forums of their associations'.[79]

The growth of voluntary associations and 'associational life' in late-eighteenth- and early nineteenth-century Europe, it has been argued, was 'the primary context of expression for bourgeois aspirations to the general leadership of nineteenth-century society'.[80] Those aspirations were no less real for the colonial Indian middle classes. Civic, political, and religious associations multiplied luxuriantly in nineteenth-century Bengal—'there is hardly any district in Bengal where there is not at least one association', reported the *Brahmo Public Opinion* in 1880.[81] Rajnarayan Basu recalled that he had established so many associations for different projects that he was finally urged by a friend to set up an association to stop the proliferation of associations (*sabha-nibarani sabha*)![82] These associations not only represented the vanguard of modernity but also, as Veena Naregal has pointed out, served to separate the English-educated bilingual elites from the unregenerate masses of native society.[83]

The Ray family's history provides a diverse and beautifully correlated set of examples illustrating this process of indigenous cultural entrepreneurship in the colonial age. Some of them aimed to build the nation of the future by moulding the sensibilities of children, while others played leading roles in the nationalist politics of the present; and virtually all of them participated, directly or indirectly, in the great nineteenth-century project to eliminate the unmodern elements from Hinduism and transform it into a faith fit for modern man— and woman. Partha Chatterjee has argued that Indian nation-builders of the nineteenth century, accepting their political powerlessness against the colonial state, concentrated on building up their own 'inner domain of cultural identity'. It was in this sovereign inner space that they sought to prepare themselves for future political hegemony.[84] As we shall see, the history of the Ray family supports as well as deviates from Chatterjee's model. Although the Rays did tend sedulously to the 'inner' domain of art, literature, and religion, their technological endeavours suggest that they were anything but inactive in the 'outer' domain. Indeed, one cannot but note that the inner/outer distinction sometimes seems to reflect the self-restriction of postcolonial theorists to abstract, literary, and theoretical sources, leaving the 'real' worlds of technology, science, and entrepreneurship to specialists in those fields.[85]

Even in the area of religious reform, the inner/outer division does not quite apply to the Rays. They belonged to the Brahmo faith, which, today, constitutes a small, quiet Hindu sect most of whose members are urban, educated Bengalis. The community was no bigger in the nineteenth century but back then the Brahmos had been regarded—with good reason—as social revolutionaries out to destroy the rigidly ordered universe of orthodox Hinduism. The theological core of Brahmoism was monotheistic Hinduism, which its founder Rammohan Roy had based on his reading of the Upanishads, the interest in Islam and sufism that he is supposed to have acquired in boyhood, and his knowledge of Unitarian Christianity.[86] The polytheistic idolatry of orthodox Hinduism, Roy and his associates argued, was a corruption of 'the pure Upanishadic belief' in the unity of the Godhead and worship, they believed, had to be congregational. Christ was respected, not as a divine figure, but for his ethical teachings. Contemporary Brahmos, remarked a Christian missionary in 1915, had progressed even further along this route and were 'as distinctly outside Hinduism as the Christian is'.[87]

Such misinterpretations were common at the time, especially among self-congratulatory Christians, but as Brian Hatcher explains, what Rammohan and his movement opposed was 'Puranic Hinduism':

> In the immense corpus of the Sanskrit Puranas (narrative texts from the middle of the first through the middle of the second millenium CE), and in the broader range of local and oral religious discourse that flowed from them, the vast majority of Hindus found the legends, myths, and maxims that framed their religious and moral universe. Bolstered by the ritual and legal traditions

associated with orthodox Hindu practice, popular Puranic Hinduism offered a world grounded in the transcendent laws of *dharma*, articulated socially in rules of caste and family law, and punctuated by the regular performance of domestic and temple rituals ... centered on devotion to the deities widely worshiped in Bengal—namely, Krishna, Rama, Shiva, Durga, and Kali. But it was this entire mythic and ritualistic framework that Rammohan had threatened to undermine; his call was for a nonidolatrous, egalitarian mode of worship, centered not on the personal deities of the Puranas but on the transcendent absolute of the Upanishads.[88]

There was a strong trend towards universalism and cosmopolitanism within this group, which, in its mature years, scorned the division of the world into 'ours' and 'theirs'.[89] Brahmos, in general, were always ready to adopt Western mores when they seemed rational or progressive. As Sivanath Sastri (1847–1919), a leading light of the movement's radical strand, declared, 'the mission of the Brahmo Samaj is to combine the East and the West ... our solemn conviction is that the salvation of modern India lies in the combination of the two ideals, i.e., in a new faith that will combine both of them in due measure'.[90] As David Kopf has pointed out, Rammohan Roy's reformist activities in India were closely linked to the global Unitarian movement for socioreligious reform and Rammohan even founded a Calcutta Unitarian Committee and a Unitarian Press. The Indian context obviously shaped Rammohan's reformism; his outlook, however, was anything but narrowly indigenist—or, for that matter, simply imitative of the West.[91]

'One of the noblest characteristics of the Brahmo Samaj', remarked the British Unitarian Sophia Dobson Collet, was its 'endeavour to purify life as a whole, and to regenerate Indian Society *as well as* Indian faith'.[92] Large sections of the Brahmo community regarded religious and social reform as intertwined and of equal importance. Their efforts to reform social customs—for example, the Hindu insistence on denying education to women and marrying them off in childhood—marked them out as radical in the eyes of mainstream Hindus.[93] Not all nineteenth-century Brahmos were social radicals, of course, and even the radicals had their conservative tendencies, but overall, it was within Brahmo ranks that some of the most critical aspects of Bengali (and, indirectly, Indian) modernity took shape. Figures as different as Bipinchandra Pal and Nirad Chaudhuri agreed that all educated Bengalis, whether or not they had formally converted to Brahmoism, were influenced, at least to some extent, by Brahmo ideals and aspirations in the nineteenth century.[94] Also, it was the Brahmo 'reformation' that facilitated, if it did not directly cause, the Hindu 'counter-reformation'—better-known as 'Hindu revivalism'—of the late nineteenth century. As Amiya P. Sen has shown, neo-Hindus of the late nineteenth century were influenced, at least to some degree, by 'the basic principles of Brahmo social and moral ideology' and they emulated Brahmo models of organization and propaganda.[95]

The Brahmos had a turbulent history after Rammohan and the community experienced two major splits, once in the mid-1860s and then in the late 1870s. Each split was precipitated by disagreements between those who wanted the movement to remain purely religious and those who wanted to combine the reform of religion with the reform of society. The latter kind of Brahmos were always ready to collaborate with the colonial state against Hindu orthodoxy and we cannot fully explain such phenomena with Partha Chatterjee's model of a cohesive and undifferentiated 'nationalist elite' absorbed in a sovereign—and undivided—inner domain and leaving the colonial state to its own business.[96] And it was these radical Brahmos who also established the nationalist Indian Association and exposed, in spite of their loyalty to the British Empire, many of the injustices of the British Raj.

The story of the Ray family was entwined with the fortunes of this fascinating community and brought together not only the familiar themes of the history of Indian modernity—English education, nationalism, women's emancipation—but many others that were crucial to that history but which have not been adequately explored by historians or, as with technology, treated in relative isolation. In his recent, fascinating book dealing with the advent of 'small-scale technology in India', David Arnold, for instance, provides welcome studies of the coming of the bicycle, the sewing machine, the typewriter and the rice mill to India, but confines his exploration to 'technological modernity' alone, instead of investigating how, in the larger history of Indian modernity, technological pursuits could be interwoven with literature, politics, and social theory.[97] Similar comments, *mutatis mutandis*, could be made with regard to Christopher Pinney's work on photography or Kajri Jain's work on visual arts and the mass media.[98] This is the kind of disciplinary divide, so characteristic of modern academic research, that we can transcend by focusing on the Rays. Their exuberant, enthusiastic and distinctive endeavours over nearly a century maintained no such boundaries and they can, therefore, help us attain a more variegated understanding of Indian engagements with modernity. Traversing a wide range of themes from literature and religion to technology and nationalist politics, this volume is not simply a study of one Bengali family but an exploration, through the multifarious activities of that family and their contexts, of almost the entire spectrum of modernity as it unfolded in colonial India.

Note on Transliteration

There is no standard system for the transliteration of Indian names in English, especially if one wishes to avoid diacritics. I have followed a common-sense approach in the text, using indigenous spellings and forms most likely to be comprehensible to a twenty-first century reader. The Bengali middle name (as, for instance, Chandra in Ramesh Chandra Dutt) is often printed by itself in English but since it is, in fact, an appendage of the first name, I have followed indigenous usage in joining the two—thus, Rameshchandra Datta instead of Ramesh Chandra Datta, Rammohan Roy instead of Ram Mohan Roy. For citations of English-language works by Indian authors, however, I have retained the spellings used in the original publications— so, the person referred to as Upendrakishore Ray in the text is identical to the cited author Upendrakisor Ray or U. Ray. Since upper-caste Bengali surnames are relatively few in number, referring to people by their surnames can lead to serious confusion. I have, therefore, either used the full name or followed the Bengali convention of referring to individuals by their first names (thus, either Dwarakanath Ganguli or Dwarakanath, but not Ganguli). Place names have usually been left in the most familiar form—Calcutta, not Kolkata; Bombay, not Mumbai; Mymensingh, not Maimansingha. Although the Gregorian calendar has been used for all dates, the Bengali calendar equivalents are sometimes mentioned. These are marked BE (=Bengali Era).

Note on Currency

For the period covered in this book, the Indian rupee was equivalent to 1 shilling and 4 pence and 1 pound amounted to 15 rupees. The rupee was divided into 16 annas, with 1 anna being equal to a penny. There were 4 pice to every anna, each pie being equivalent to a farthing. All of these were coins; paper currency was used only for values above five rupees.[99]

Notes

1. See Marie Seton, *Portrait of a Director: Satyajit Ray*, revised edn (Delhi: Penguin, 2003); and Andrew Robinson, *Satyajit Ray: The Inner Eye*, 2nd edn (London: I. B. Tauris, 2004).

2. Buddhadeva Bose, *An Acre of Green Grass: A Review of Modern Bengali Literature* (Bombay: Orient Longman, 1948), 95.

3. Kajri Jain, *Gods in the Bazaar: The Economies of Indian Calendar Art* (Durham, NC: Duke University Press, 2007), 154.

4. Ashis Nandy, 'Satyajit Ray's Secret Guide to Exquisite Murders: Creativity, Social Criticism, and the Partitioning of the Self', in *The Savage Freud and Other Essays on Possible and Retrievable Selves* (Princeton: Princeton University Press, 1995), 237–66, at 245–6.

5. R.H. Tawney, *Religion and the Rise of Capitalism* (London: John Murray, 1926), 268.

6. See Satadru Sen, 'A Juvenile Periphery: The Geographies of Literary Childhood in Colonial Bengal', *Journal of Colonialism and Colonial History*, 5, no. 1 (2004): 1–29, at 21 (https://muse.jhu.edu/journals/journal_of_colonialism_and_colonial_history/v005/5.1sen.html, accessed on 6 June 2014).

7. This, as Hugh Cunningham has shown, was also the basic argument of Philippe Ariès's well-known study of 1960, *Centuries of Childhood*. See Hugh Cunningham, *Children and Childhood in Western Society since 1500*, 2nd edn (Harlow: Pearson, 2005), 4–5.

8. In the nineteenth century, the idea of the child's plasticity of nature—the possibility of moulding it into an angel or a devil by the right or wrong kind of training—was an article of faith even for reformers in the West but philanthropic measures to improve the lot of children were addressed mostly to children of the labouring classes or those abandoned by their parents. See Cunningham, *Children and Childhood*, 138. The Bengali initiatives, in contrast, were directed at the children of the educated middle classes, the sections most directly affected by British rule.

9. S. Sen, 'A Juvenile Periphery', 5.

10. See, for some influential examples of recent scholarship, Arjun Appadurai, *Modernity at Large: Cultural Dimensions of Globalization* (Minneapolis, MN: University of Minnesota Press, 1996); Dipesh Chakrabarty, *Provincializing Europe: Postcolonial Thought and Historical Difference* (Chicago: University of Chicago Press, 2000); Partha Chatterjee, *The Nation and Its Fragments: Colonial and Postcolonial Histories* (Princeton: Princeton University Press, 1993); Dilip Parmeshwar Gaonkar, ed., *Alternative Modernities* (Durham,

NC: Duke University Press, 2001); Dipankar Gupta, *Mistaken Modernity:*
India between Worlds (Delhi: HarperCollins, 2000); and Saurabh Dube and
Ishita Banerjee-Dube, eds, *Unbecoming Modern: Colonialism, Modernity,*
Colonial Modernities (Delhi: Social Science Press, 2006). For a helpful theo-
retical analysis of theories of modernity and their applicability to India, see
Sudipta Kaviraj, 'An Outline of a Revisionist Theory of Modernity', *Archives*
Européennes de Sociologie 46, no. 3 (2005): 497–526.

11.   Prathama Banerjee, 'Afterword', in *Handbook of Modernity in South*
Asia: Modern Makeovers, edited by Saurabh Dube (Delhi: Oxford University
Press, 2011), 262–74, at 268.

12.   P. Banerjee, 'Afterword', in *Handbook of Modernity*, 269.

13.   Marshall Berman, *All That Is Solid Melts into Air: The Experience of*
Modernity (New York: Penguin, 1988), 232.

14.   Jadunath Sarkar, *India through the Ages: A Survey of the Growth of*
Indian Life and Thought, 2nd edn (Calcutta: S.C. Sarkar & Sons, 1945), 69, 71.

15.   The phrase is Ranajit Guha's. See Ranajit Guha, *Dominance without*
Hegemony: History and Power in Colonial India (Cambridge, Mass.: Harvard
University Press, 1997), 158.

16.   Brian A. Hatcher, *Bourgeois Hinduism, or the Faith of the Modern*
Vedantists: Rare Discourses from Early Colonial Bengal (New York: Oxford
University Press, 2008), 196–7.

17.   Saurabh Dube, 'Makeovers of Modernity: An Introduction', in
Handbook of Modernity, 1–25, at 8–9.

18.   Ghulam Murshid, *Reluctant Debutante: Response of Bengali Women to*
Modernization, 1849–1905 (Rajshahi: Rajshahi University Sahitya Samsad,
1983), 167. Dermot Killingley has even argued that one of the essential features of Indian modernity was the 'tendency to criticize Indian traditions by
foreign standards' and to look for 'elements of tradition which could be valued
highly by those standards'. See D.H. Killingley, 'Vedanta and Modernity', in
Indian Society and the Beginnings of Modernisation, c.1830–1850, edited by C.H.
Philips and Mary Doreen Wainwright (London: School of Oriental and
African Studies, 1976), 127–40, at 128.

19.   D. Chakrabarty, *Provincializing Europe*, 28, 32, 40.

20.   On modernization theory and its contexts, see Michael Latham,
Modernization as Ideology: American Social Sciences and 'Nation-Building' in the
Kennedy Era (Durham, NC: University of North Carolina Press, 2000).

21.   Jadunath Sarkar, ed., *The History of Bengal, Muslim Period 1200–1757*
(Patna: Academica Asiatica, [1948] 1973), 497–8.

22.   See, for instance, the influential views of historian Susobhan Sarkar,
first published in 1946 under the pseudonym Amit Sen:

The impact of British rule, bourgeois economy and modern Western
culture was felt first in Bengal. For about a century, Bengal's conscious awareness of the changing modern world was more

developed than and ahead of that of the rest of India. The role played by Bengal in the modern awakening of India is thus comparable to the position occupied by Italy in the story of the European Renaissance. (Susobhan Sarkar, *On the Bengal Renaissance* [Calcutta: Papyrus, 1979], 13.)

Although Sarkar later emphasized the conflicts and contradictions within the Bengal Renaissance and acknowledged the limitations of the entire movement, he continued to portray pre-British Bengali culture as moribund and the Western influence—comprising 'social reform, liberal rationalism, secular humanism'—as entirely positive, not only in its historical context but also for the 'future progress' of the Indian nation. He even used the term 'Westernism' to signify liberal, reformist, and progressive ideologies. See his 'Conflict within the Bengal Renaissance' (1967), in *On the Bengal Renaissance*, 69–75, at 73, 74–5; and Sumit Sarkar, *A Critique of Colonial India*, 2nd edn (Calcutta: Papyrus, 2000), 73. On the influence of Sarkar's 1946 study, see Tithi Bhattacharya, *The Sentinels of Culture: Class, Education, and the Colonial Intellectual in Bengal (1848–85)* (Delhi: Oxford University Press, 2005), 17–18.

23.   On Rammohan, see Sophia Dobson Collet, *The Life and Letters of Raja Rammohun Roy*, edited by Dilipkumar Biswas and Prabhatchandra Ganguli (Calcutta: Sadharan Brahmo Samaj, 1962); and Amiya P. Sen, *Rammohun Roy: A Critical Biography* (Delhi: Penguin, 2012). On Unitarian engagements with India, see Spencer Lavan, *Unitarians and India: A Study in Encounter and Response* (Boston: Beacon Press, 1977).

24.   Incidentally, the Rays are almost never mentioned in standard accounts of the Bengal Renaissance. Susobhan Sarkar, although a good friend of Sukumar Ray's and aware of the importance of children's literature to the Bengal Renaissance, did not even mention the Rays in his influential studies of the Renaissance. The only children's writers he named were Jogindranath Sarkar and Abanindranath Tagore. See Susobhan Sarkar, *On the Bengal Renaissance*, 68.

25.   Chidananda Das Gupta, *The Cinema of Satyajit Ray*, 2nd edn (Delhi: National Book Trust, 2001), 12.

26.   Sumit Sarkar, *Modern Times: India, 1880s–1950s—Environment, Economy, Culture* (Ranikhet: Permanent Black, 2014), 325–6.

27.   For an excellent review of these shifts, see Brian A. Hatcher, 'Great Men Waking: Paradigms in the Historiography of the Bengal Renaissance', in *Bengal: Rethinking History—Essays in Historiography*, edited by Sekhar Bandyopadhyay (Delhi: Manohar/International Centre for Bengal Studies, 2001), 135–63, at 136, 153–5. For Sumit Sarkar's contributions, see his *Critique of Colonial India*, 2nd edn. Recently, the cognitive scientist Subrata Dasgupta has sought to revive the concept of the Bengal Renaissance. See Subrata Dasgupta, *The Bengal Renaissance: Identity and Creativity from Rammohun Roy to Rabindranath Tagore* (Ranikhet: Permanent Black, 2007); and S. Dasgupta,

Awakening: The Story of the Bengal Renaissance (Delhi: Random House India, 2011). Dasgupta's *Renaissance* is broader in scope than Susobhan Sarkar's and his use of concepts from cognitive science undoubtedly novel, but the colonial context is still mostly ignored and the social character of the phenomenon is left virtually unanalysed.

28. Sumit Sarkar, *Critique of Colonial India*, 72.

29. For a spirited discussion of these critiques, see Partha Chatterjee, 'The Fruits of Macaulay's Poison Tree' [1985], in *Empire and Nation: Selected Essays* (New York: Columbia University Press, 2010), 91–110, at 98–9.

30. Charles H. Heimsath, *Indian Nationalism and Hindu Social Reform* (Princeton: Princeton University Press, 1964), 21.

31.   See Sudipta Kaviraj, 'On the Structure of Nationalist Discourse' [1994], in *The Imaginary Institution of India: Politics and Ideas* (Ranikhet: Permanent Black, 2010), 85–126, at 122–4. Moreover, as Sumit Sarkar has rightly pointed out, the 'West' is too often equated by historians of South Asian modernity with 'rationalism' or 'post-Enlightenment modernity' although rationalism was not unknown in the Indian traditions and of the many gifts brought to India by the West, at least one was scarcely rational: 'Christian missionary propaganda'. See Sumit Sarkar, *Writing Social History* (Delhi: Oxford University Press, 1998), 171.

32.   Women were first offered complete degrees (and full university membership) in 1878 by the University of London but medical degrees were excluded. Although Oxford allowed women to sit for undergraduate examinations from 1875, they could not take degrees or be considered full members of the University until 1920. Cambridge was even more laggardly and excluded women from full membership until 1948. See Carol Dyhouse, *No Distinction of Sex? Women in British Universities 1870–1939* (London: University College London Press, 1995), 2, 11.

33.   Women from Germany, Britain, and the USA travelled to Switzerland to train as doctors; although four separate medical schools for women had been established in the US between 1850 and 1870 and in the UK in 1874, university medical faculties were largely closed to women in both countries until the First World War. See Thomas N. Bonner, *Becoming a Physician: Medical Education in Britain, France, Germany, and the United States, 1750–1945* (Baltimore: Johns Hopkins University Press, 1995), 211–13, 313; and T.N. Bonner, *To the Ends of the Earth: Women's Search for Education in Medicine* (Cambridge, Mass.: Harvard University Press, 1992), 15–16, 24–6, 30.

34.   The Maharashtrian Anandibai Joshi was the first Indian woman to obtain a medical degree (1886), but she trained at the Women's Medical College in Philadelphia. See Meera Kosambi, 'Anandibai Joshee: Retrieving a Fragmented Feminist Image', *Economic and Political Weekly*, 7 December 1996: 3189–97. On Bidhumukhi Basu and Virginia Mary Mitter, see Murshid, *Reluctant Debutante*, 101. Kadambini Basu (Ganguli), who graduated from the

Calcutta Medical College in 1888, was the first woman doctor in Bengal but she had not been able to complete all requirements for the MB degree and was awarded a special diploma. See Chapter 2.

35. Sanjay Joshi, *Fractured Modernity: Making of a Middle Class in Colonial North India* (Delhi: Oxford University Press, 2001), 21–2, 175, 177.

36. S. Joshi, *Fractured Modernity*, 185.

37. S. Joshi, *Fractured Modernity*, 187.

38. Two of the most influential works in this genre are: P. Chatterjee, *Nation and Its Fragments* and D. Chakrabarty, *Provincializing Europe*. See also P. Chatterjee, *Empire and Nation*.

39. For a concise introduction to the sociological debates over modernity, see Peter Wagner, *Modernity: Understanding the Present* (Cambridge: Polity, 2012). On the concept of multiple modernities, see Dominic Sachsenmaier, Jens Riedel, and Shmuel N. Eisenstadt, *Reflections on Multiple Modernities: European, Chinese and Other Interpretations* (Leiden: Brill, 2002). See also Timothy Mitchell, 'The Stage of Modernity', in *Questions of Modernity*, edited by T. Mitchell (Minneapolis, MN: University of Minnesota Press, 2000), 1–34.

40. Tanika Sarkar, 'Conjugality and Hindu Nationalism: Resisting Colonial Reason and the Death of a Child-Wife', in *Women and Social Reform in Modern India: A Reader*, 2 vols, edited by Sumit Sarkar and Tanika Sarkar (Ranikhet: Permanent Black, 2007), 1: 385–419, at 407. Tapan Raychaudhuri has also argued on the same lines. See Tapan Raychaudhuri, 'The Bengal Renaissance: Reconsidering Revisions', in *Europe Reconsidered: Perceptions of the West in Nineteenth-Century Bengal*, 2nd edn (Delhi: Oxford University Press, 2002), 345–62.

41. See Sumit Sarkar, *Modern Times*, 168. Except in western India, where Jews, Parsis, and Gujarati Hindus were prominent in business and industry, the subcontinent was characterized by 'the domination of all the major industries by a small group of European managing agency houses'. See Amiya Kumar Bagchi, *Private Investment in India 1900–1939* (Cambridge: Cambridge University Press, 1972), 176, 420, 425; Christine Dobbin, *Urban Leadership in Western India: Politics and Communities in Bombay City, 1840–1885* (Oxford: Oxford University Press, 1972); and Amiya Kumar Bagchi, *Colonialism and Indian Economy* (Delhi: Oxford University Press, 2010), 13–56.

42. As Rajnarayan Basu was to remark in 1874, 'our exterior glitters with Shakespeare, Milton and differential calculus but we are completely empty inside. We are dependent on the sahibs for everything'. See his 'Sekal aar Ekal' [1874], in *Rajnarayan Basu: Nirbachita Rachana Sangraha*, edited by Baridbaran Ghosh (Calcutta: Dey Book Store, 1995), 286–338, at 320.

43. Benjamin Zachariah, 'The Chemistry of a Bengali Life: Acharya/Sir Prafulla Chandra Ray in his Times and Spaces', in *Beyond Representation: Colonial and Postcolonial Constructions of Indian Identity*, edited by Crispin Bates (Delhi: Oxford University Press, 2006), 322–52, at 344; and Benjamin

Zachariah, *Playing the Nation Game: The Ambiguities of Nationalism in India* (Delhi: Yoda Press, 2011), 120–3, 132–3, 137–8.

44. See Nirad C. Chaudhuri, *The Autobiography of an Unknown Indian* (London: Hogarth Press, [1951] 1991), 370. As long as 'certain values were maintained and certain social proprieties observed', one could be a bhadralok even if one was poor or unemployed. See also J.H. Broomfield, *Elite Conflict in a Plural Society: Twentieth-Century Bengal* (Berkeley: University of California Press, 1968), 13–14; S.N. Mukherjee, 'Bhadralok in Bengali Language and Literature: An Essay on the Language of Class and Status', *Bengal Past and Present*, 95, part 2 (July–December 1976): 225–37, especially 230–2; P. Chatterjee, *Nation and Its Fragments*, 35–75; and John McGuire, *The Making of a Colonial Mind: A Quantitative Study of the Bhadralok in Calcutta, 1857–1885* (Canberra: Australian National University, 1983).

45. Broomfield, *Elite Conflict in a Plural Society*, 15; and McGuire, *Making of a Colonial Mind*, 21–3. The urban bhadralok of Calcutta usually hailed from the three superior castes of Brahman, Baidya, and Kayastha, but high caste alone did not make one bhadra—a Brahmin cook, despite belonging to the highest caste, was not a member of the bhadralok—and it was not unknown for members of low castes to attain bhadralok status. Although Bengali Muslims formed the second largest community in Calcutta, they were radically underrepresented among bhadralok but not entirely absent. See S.N. Mukherjee, 'Class, Caste and Politics in Calcutta, 1815–38', in *Elites in South Asia*, edited by Edmund Leach and S.N. Mukherjee (Cambridge: Cambridge University Press, 1970), 33–78, at 38, 56; and Zachariah, *Playing the Nation Game*, 122. For an excellent analysis of the ideological role of education in maintaining bhadralok identity, see T. Bhattacharya, *Sentinels of Culture*.

46. S.N. Mukherjee, 'Class, Caste and Politics in Calcutta', 61.

47. Sumit Sarkar, *Writing Social History*, 171–2, 285.

48. 'The "middle class" in colonial Bengal', Sumit Sarkar has asserted, 'was not based on properly bourgeois forms of industry, trade or even land management. Its members were only too eager to buy themselves positions in the vast and growing Permanent Settlement hierarchy, through intermediate tenures or superior "raiyat" rights, once they climbed the ladder of success via English education and the liberal professions' (*Critique of Colonial India*, 78).

49. After the First World War, a Commission examining the Calcutta University declared that there was 'no room for doubt that the desire for admission to Government service is one of the most powerful of all the motives which attract students to follow the university course'. That same Commission also noted that although 'an enormously higher proportion of the educated male population of Bengal proceeds to university studies than is the case in the United Kingdom', the vast majority of Bengali students took 'purely literary courses which do not fit them for any but administrative,

clerical, teaching and (indirectly) legal careers'. The Commission attributed the elective affinity between Bengalis and clerical jobs to 'a certain incapacity for practical callings', observing in passing that 'there are, as yet, practically no students of technical science, because the scientific industries of Bengal are in their infancy, and draw their experts mainly from England'. See *Calcutta University Commission, 1917–19: Report*, 13 vols (Calcutta: Superintendent of Government Printing, 1919), 1: 20, 25; 3: 275–6.

    50.   McGuire, *Making of a Colonial Mind*, 19.

    51.   See Krishnachandra Roy, *High Education and the Present Position of the Graduates in Arts and Law of the Calcutta University* (Calcutta: Sanskrit Press Depository, 1882), 23. See also A.K. Bagchi, *Private Investment in India*, 19–25, 165–74.

    52.   See Bruce T. McCully, *English Education and the Origins of Indian Nationalism* (1940; reprint, Gloucester, MA: Peter Smith, 1966), 190–3.

    53.   See J.G. Cumming, *Review of the Industrial Position and Prospects in Bengal in 1908* (Calcutta: Bengal Secretariat Book Depot, 1908), 2; and Rajat Kanta Ray, ed., *Entrepreneurship and Industry in India, 1800–1947* (Delhi: Oxford University Press, 1992), 35–45.

    54.   'The Industrial Conference', *The Bengalee*, 12 September 1891, 435.

    55.   Rajat K. Ray, *Industrialization in India: Growth and Conflict in the Private Corporate Sector, 1914–47* (Delhi: Oxford University Press, 1982), viii–ix.

    56.   Ratnabali Chatterjee, *From the 'Karkhana' to the Studio: A Study of the Changing Social Rules of Patron and Artist in Bengal* (Delhi: Books & Books, 1990), 16–20. See also Jain, *Gods in the Bazaar*, 83.

    57.   Another Bengali clan somewhat similar to the Rays was the Mahalanobis family. Originally from a scribal background—'Mahalanobis', just like 'Ray', was a title bestowed on the clan in early modern times—the Mahalanobis family's history became Calcutta-centred with the arrival of Gurucharan Mahalanobis from East Bengal in 1854. He converted to Brahmoism, married a child widow, and ran a pharmaceutical business. Of his sons, Prabodhchandra Mahalanobis set up a sporting goods and gramophone business in central Calcutta with his brother-in-law, the eminent physician Nilratan Sircar. This shop, named Carr and Mahalanobis, was eventually run by Prafullachandra Mahalanbobis, who played a major role in the lonely childhood of Satyajit Ray. Prafullachandra's brother Prasantachandra (later a famous statistician) had been one of the closest friends of Satyajit's father, Sukumar. On the Mahalanobis family, see Ashok Rudra, *Prasanta Chandra Mahalanobis: A Biography* (Delhi: Oxford University Press, 1996), 1–23.

    58.   By 'artisan', I do not, of course, mean the early-modern European artisan, specializing in one particular craft and organized in guilds. See James R. Farr, *Artisans in Europe, 1300–1914* (Cambridge: Cambridge University Press, 2000). Nor do I mean the kind of *traditional* Indian craftsman

(especially, but not exclusively, the weaver) whose hereditary and often caste-bound crafts some nationalists sought to modernize in the late-nineteenth and early twentieth centuries. See Abigail McGowan, *Crafting the Nation in Colonial India* (New York: Palgrave Macmillan, 2009), 3, 11, 149–86; and Douglas E. Haynes, 'The Logic of the Artisan Firm in a Capitalist Economy: Handloom Weavers and Technological Change in Western India, 1880–1947', in *Institutions and Economic Change in South Asia*, edited by Burton Stein and Sanjay Subrahmanyam (Delhi: Oxford University Press, 1996), 173–205. What the Rays took from artisanal traditions was their *mode* of work: small masters producing specialized commodities in small quantities and in family settings without heavy machinery.

59. Karl Marx, *Capital: A Critique of Political Economy*, vol. 1, translated by Samuel Moore and Edward Aveling, edited by Frederick Engels (London: Lawrence & Wishart, 1970), 308.

60. David Arnold, *Everyday Technology: Machines and the Making of India's Modernity* (Chicago: University of Chicago Press, 2013); Christopher Pinney, *The Coming of Photography in India* (London: British Library, 2008); and Roy MacLeod and Deepak Kumar, eds, *Technology and the Raj: Western Technology and Technical Transfers to India 1700–1947* (Delhi: SAGE, 1995).

61. A.K. Bagchi, *Private Investment in India*, 442.

62. Andrew Sartori, *Bengal in Global Concept History: Culturalism in the Age of Capital* (Chicago: University of Chicago Press, 2008), 71.

63. Cumming, *Review of the Industrial Position*, 4–5, 30–1.

64. See Amit Bhattacharyya, 'Swadeshi Industry and Technology: P.M. Bagchi & Co. (1883–1947)', in *Science, Technology, Medicine and Environment in India: Historical Perspectives*, edited by Chittabrata Palit and A. Bhattacharyya (Calcutta: Bibhasa, 1998), 108–27, at 118–20; and Jayanta Kumar Ray and Shantanu Chakrabarti, 'Science and Technology in India', in *Aspects of India's International Relations, 1700 to 2000: South Asia and the World*, edited by Jayanta Kumar Ray (Delhi: Pearson, 2007), 311–67, at 337.

65. Dwijendra Tripathi, *The Oxford History of Indian Business* (Delhi: Oxford University Press, 2004), 155.

66. It drew its recruits from middle-class people (i.e., engineers, doctors, chemists, school teachers, clerks, and others), the artisans, and some zamindars. See Amit Bhattacharyya, *Business, Politics and Technology: Select Themes in the Economic History of Modern India* (Calcutta: Readers Service, 2005), 12–13.

67. 'When the German Pfaff sewing machines were first introduced in the Indian market in the early twentieth century, four Indian mechanics tore it apart, studied it, modified it and manufactured the first Indian sewing machine. That was the beginning of Usha sewing machines in Jay Engineering Company under Bengali ownership.' See A. Bhattacharyya, 'Swadeshi Industry and Technology', 120–1.

68. Cumming, *Review of the Industrial Position*, 6.

69. Ironically, Cumming, in his report on Bengal's industrial future, had mentioned wood-engraving and lithography (in only one brief sentence) but not half-tone photography and block-making. See Cumming, *Review of the Industrial Position*, 41. Recent historical studies of Indian technology, too, have said little on photomechanical reproduction. See, for example, Arnold, *Everyday Technology*.

70. On the importance of specialized and carefully protected skills for early-modern European artisans, see Farr, *Artisans in Europe*, 284–5.

71. On creative adaptations, see Gaonkar, *Alternative Modernities*, 17–22. On the colonial Indian tendency to define certain progressive aspects of Western culture as 'universal' and, therefore, untouched by the taint of colonial subjugation, see Zachariah, *Playing the Nation Game*, 151–2. Modern science and technology, in particular, were regarded by intellectuals in nineteenth- and early-twentieth-century Bengal as 'common to all humankind'—'the liberal bequests of great minds to every individual of the human race'. See J. Lourdusamy, *Science and National Consciousness in Bengal, 1870–1930* (Hyderabad: Orient Longman, 2004), 18–19.

72. See Baridbaran Ghosh, 'Bhumika', in *Kuntalin Galpa-Satak*, edited by Baridbaran Ghosh (Calcutta: Ananda Publishers, 1989), 11–41, at 13; and Mani Bagchi, *Sudhirkumar Sen: Jiban-Charit* (Calcutta: Shamin Basu, 1964), 30.

73. In its three incarnations—the original series, edited by Upendrakishore and then by Sukumar, the shortlived new series that was published from 1931 to 1933 under the joint editorship of Subinoy Ray and Sudhabindu Biswas, and the still-continuing third series begun by Satyajit Ray and Subhas Mukhopadhyay in 1961—*Sandesh* published writings by virtually every member of the Ray family. While this book will focus only on the major contributors, it is worth remembering that figures like Santilata (Upendrakishore's youngest daughter, who died early), Kuladaranjan Ray's daughters Madhurilata and Ila, or Subinoy Ray's wife Puspalata all contributed to *Sandesh* at different times. For a brief discussion of these contributors, see Bratati Chakravarty, *Bangla Shishu Sahitya Charcha: Ray Paribar* (Calcutta: Dey Book Store, 1997), 209–12.

74. Markovits suggests that the two elements of the middle class drew closer only after Independence as a result of state involvement in industrialization but it was only with the coming of consumerism in the 1990s that there was anything like a proper fusion. See Claude Markovits, 'What about the Merchants? A Mercantile Perspective on the Middle Class of Colonial India', in *The Middle Class in Colonial India*, edited by Sanjay Joshi (Delhi: Oxford University Press, 2010), 118–31, at 125.

75. For a critique of the current nomenclature, see Sumit Sarkar, 'Nationalisms in India', in *India and the British Empire*, edited by Douglas M.

Peers and Nandini Gooptu (Oxford: Oxford University Press, 2012), 135–67, at 142.

76. Benedict Anderson, *Imagined Communities: Reflections on the Origin and Spread of Nationalism*, revised edn (London: Verso, 2006).

77. See McCully, *English Education*, 388–9.

78. See Veena Naregal, *Language Politics, Elites, and the Public Sphere* (Ranikhet: Permanent Black, 2001), 56.

79. S. Joshi, 'Introduction', in *Middle Class in Colonial India*, xix.

80. See Geoff Eley, 'Nations, Publics, and Political Cultures: Placing Habermas in the Nineteenth Century', in *Habermas and the Public Sphere*, edited by Craig Calhoun (Cambridge, Mass.: MIT Press, 1992), 289–339, at 297–9.

81. 'Retrospect of 1879', *Brahmo Public Opinion*, 1 January 1880, reprinted in *Selections from English Periodicals of 19th Century Bengal, 1878–80: Brahmo Public Opinion*, edited by Benoy Ghose (Calcutta: Papyrus, 1978), 90–123, at 123. For a comprehensive survey, see Rajat Sanyal, *Voluntary Associations and the Urban Public Life in Bengal (1815–1876)* (Calcutta: Riddhi-India, 1980).

82. See Rajnarayan Basu, 'Atmacharit', in *Rajnarayan Basu: Nirbachita Rachana Sangraha*, edited by Baridbaran Ghosh (Calcutta: Dey Book Store, 1995), 1–171, at 57. My thanks to Barun Chattopadhyay for this reference.

83. Naregal, *Language Politics*, 234.

84. P. Chatterjee, *Nation and Its Fragments*, 6.

85. This does not simply apply to theorists of South Asian modernities but to most theorists of modernity. As Thomas J. Misa has observed, 'the "modern" society that has emerged in the writings of social theorists and philosophers in the past several decades has been a theoretical construct that is surprisingly devoid of technology', even though virtually all modern societies, whether wealthy or merely aspirational, are 'constituted, in various ways, through technological systems and networks'. See Thomas J. Misa, 'The Compelling Tangle of Modernity and Technology', in *Modernity and Technology*, edited by T.J. Misa, Philip Brey, and Andrew Feenberg (Cambridge, Mass.: MIT Press, 2003), 1–30, at 4, 8.

86. The Unitarians, as Clare Midgley has summed up, 'were heterodox Protestants who dissented from mainstream Christian beliefs in the divinity of Christ and the doctrine of original sin; influenced by Enlightenment thought, they were optimistic about the potential for human perfectibility, stressed the application of reason to religion, promoted both religious and political liberty, and played leading roles in nineteenth-century social reform, anti-slavery and women's rights movements'. See Clare Midgley, 'Mary Carpenter and the Brahmo Samaj of India: A Transnational Perspective on Social Reform in the Age of Empire', *Women's History Review* 22, no. 3 (2013): 363–85, at 366. On the shifting ways in which Brahmos of different

generations engaged with Unitarianism, see David Kopf, 'The Brahmo Idea of Social Reform and the Problem of Female Emancipation in Bengal', in *Bengal in the Nineteenth and Twentieth Centuries*, edited by John R. McLane (East Lansing, Michigan: Asian Studies Center, Michigan State University, 1975), 35–58, especially 35.

87. J.N. Farquhar, *Modern Religious Movements in India* (New York: Macmillan, 1915), 38.

88. Brian A. Hatcher, *Bourgeois Hinduism, or the Faith of the Modern Vedantists: Rare Discourses from Early Colonial Bengal* (New York: Oxford University Press, 2008), 28–9.

89. Founded by Rammohan Roy in 1828 as the Brahmo Sabha (which, in turn, had been preceded by the Atmiya Sabha, another reformist body set up by Roy in 1814), a forum for Vedantic worship, the Brahmo Samaj almost came to an end after the death of Roy in 1833 on a trip to England but was revived in the 1840s by the wealthy zamindar Debendranath Tagore (1817–1905) with the assistance of the rationalist-deist Akshaykumar Datta (1820–1886). See Kenneth W. Jones, *Socio-Religious Reform Movements in British India* (Cambridge: Cambridge University Press, 1989), 33; Ajitkumar Chakrabarty, *Maharsi Debendranath Thakur* (Allahabad: Indian Press, 1916), 289; and Sophia Dobson Collet, ed., *The Brahmo Year-Book for 1876: Brief Records of Work and Life in the Theistic Churches of India* (London: Williams and Norgate, 1876), 9. In absolute terms, however, the Brahmo movement remained tiny and, in Debendranath's time, its members hailed largely from the affluent classes. Even in 1870, the number of Brahmos in Calcutta did not exceed 6,000. See Kanailal Chattopadhyay, *Brahmo Reform Movement: Some Social and Economic Aspects* (Calcutta: Papyrus, 1983), 60. Many of these Brahmos probably declared themselves to be Hindus in official contexts. The 1921 Census found the entire population of Calcutta to be 1,327,547 and of these, only 1,821 (i.e., 14 per cent) were Brahmo. See *Census of India 1921* (Calcutta: Bengal Secretariat Book Depot, 1923), 6, pt 1: 40. Compare with the figures of 1891 (708 Brahmos in a total population of 681,560, i.e., 11 per cent) in *Report on the Census of Calcutta* (Calcutta: Bengal Secretariat Press, 1891): 20.

90. Sivanath Sastri, *History of the Brahmo Samaj* [1911–12], 2nd edn, 2 vols in 1 (Calcutta: Sadharan Brahmo Samaj, 1974), 370–1.

91. Orthodox Christians and missionaries often thought that Rammohan had become a Unitarian Christian. The Unitarian Committee faded away after Rammohan established the Brahmo Sabha in 1829 but the Unitarian influence continued to act on radical Brahmos long after Rammohan's time. From the mid-1850s, Unitarian missionaries and visitors in Calcutta (notably C.H.A. Dall but also Mary Carpenter in the 1860s) and younger Brahmos (in particular, Keshab Sen) pushed the Brahmo Samaj towards social reform and a greater assimilation of some Christian teachings. The writings of the socially committed American Unitarian Theodore Parker, which were

translated into Bengali in the 1860s, also had a major impact. See David Kopf, *The Brahmo Samaj and the Shaping of the Modern Indian Mind* (Princeton: Princeton University Press, 1979), 9–10, 12, 15, 27–31.

92. Collet, *Brahmo Year-Book for 1878*, 77–8, emphasis added.

93. Nirad C. Chaudhuri, 'Srestha Bangali Key?' [1994], in *Nirbachita Prabandha*, edited by Dhruvanarayan Chaudhuri (Calcutta: Ananda Publishers, 1997), 112–27, at 124.

94. Bipinchandra Pal, *Nabajuger Bangla* (Calcutta: Yugajatri, [1921–4] 1955), 245; Nirad C. Chaudhuri, 'Srestha Bangali Key?', 124. Indeed, the Brahmo movement, with all its transformations and dissensions, is often 'taken as a shorthand for the history of the entire [Bengal] Renaissance'. See Brian A. Hatcher, 'Great Men Waking', 140.

95. Farquhar, *Modern Religious Movements in India*, 26. For the Counter-Reformation analogy, see N.C. Chaudhuri, *Autobiography of an Unknown Indian*, 195–202. In the nineteenth century, the Brahmo Samaj and the broader Brahmo-inspired movements were often regarded as manifestations of a Hindu Protestantism. See, for example, Manoharlal Zutshi, *Hindu Protestantism* (Allahabad: Hindustan Review, 1907), especially 24. Regarding the Brahmo impact on mainstream Hindus, see Amiya P. Sen, *Hindu Revivalism in Bengal, 1872–1905: Some Essays in Interpretation* (Delhi: Oxford University Press, 1993), 36, 406–7.

96. With regard to elites, it is still worth recalling Barun De's decades-old observation that

> the subjects of British India, even the urban intelligentsia, should not ... be called 'elites.' *Vis-à-vis* the poor or the petty bourgeoisie, some members of the more cultivated urban intelligentsia might have harboured a mentality which is called 'elitist' in the simplistic sense of that term. But *vis-à-vis* the British *Herrenvolk*, they felt racially inferior or counterdependent, were discriminated against, even when possessed of equal talents for advancement in careers in official service, and faced metropolitan commercial protection when they sought to build up their fortunes in production or mercantile activity.

See Barun De, 'A Historiographical Critique of Renaissance Analogues for Nineteenth-Century India', in *Perspectives in Social Sciences, I: Historical Dimensions*, edited by Barun De (Calcutta: Oxford University Press, 1977), 178–218, at 211. De makes the additional, important point (De, *Perspectives in Social Sciences, I*, 212) that the majority of nineteenth-century Indian social activists and reformers hailed from 'petty bourgeois, and sometimes well-to-do peasant social and economic roots' and were 'closer to the common man' than historians tend to assume.

97. Arnold, *Everyday Technology*, 3–4.

98. See Pinney, *The Coming of Photography in India*; and Jain, *Gods in the Bazaar*.

99. Charles Watney and Herbert Lloyd, *Motoring in India: A Guide for the Tourist and Resident* (London: The Car Illustrated, 1909), 50–1.

1

From the Old World to the New

A Family in Transition

The earliest history of the Ray family—like that of most Indian families—is almost entirely anecdotal and unverifiable. Nevertheless, it reflects the transition in Bengal from the rule of sultans and Mughal satraps to the reign of the East India Company.[1] The genealogy begins with Ramsundar Deb, who, in the middle of the sixteenth century, moved from Chakdaha in the Nadia district of western Bengal to Sherpur, and then to Yasodal in eastern Bengal. The King of Yasodal, we are told, was so impressed by the clever and handsome Ramsundar that after having gifted him substantial tracts of land, he made him his son-in-law—or, according to an alternate tradition, his brother-in-law.[2] In the early eighteenth century, Ramsundar's descendant Ramnarayan Deb, accompanied by his son Krishnajiban, moved to a village called Masua. Located on the banks of the Brahmaputra River, this village was part of what, after 1787, would be the district of Maimansingha or, in the more familiar anglicized spelling, Mymensingh.

Mymensingh was the largest district in the Bengal Presidency and one of the largest districts in India. More

than three-quarters of its population was Muslim; this was an unusually high proportion in comparison to other districts in eastern
Bengal—the population of Dhaka, for instance, was fairly evenly
divided. Mymensingh had never been the seat of old feudal families
and its Hindus were mostly professionals (especially lawyers) and
traders, who, in subsequent years, would be active in 'progressive'
endeavours of all kinds.[3] The Brahmaputra changed its course during
the time of Ramnarayan's grandchildren and swept Masua away; the
Debs moved to the nearby village of Khukurpara which was renamed
in memory of their original domicile as Baro Masua (Masua Major)
but inevitably came to be called Masua.[4]

The Rays were Kayastha by caste and, like most of their caste-
mates, belonged to the old scribal community of lower-level administrators, clerks, and judicial officials.[5] The scribal classes of pre-colonial
India, historian Hayden Bellenoit has remarked, 'could be more critical to Mughal authority than the sword' and one Mughal-era writer
called them the 'pillars of the citadel of empire'.[6] Although the highest posts in the government and criminal justice were usually held by
Muslims in Mughal times, revenue administrators were almost
always Hindu.[7] Traditional historical portraits of 'Muslim tyranny'
tend not to highlight the Hindu employees of the sultans and Mughals,
who were not just adept in Farsi (Persian), the administrative language of the era, but Persianized in their attire and lifestyle as well.[8]
At the same time, they learnt Sanskrit, revered Brahmins, and built
Hindu temples.[9] This was not unique to Bengal, and Hindu Kayastha
scribes serving Muslim courtly elites in north India lived similarly.[10]
No matter how orthodox their background, Hindu boys often learnt
Farsi with Muslims in special schools and recited the formula 'there
is no God but Allah and Mohammed is his prophet' at the commence-
ment of every lesson without any qualms.[11]

Although professional contact between high-caste Hindus and
their Muslim employers could generate considerable anxiety about
pollution among the former—one such 'polluted' Brahmin family
being that of the Tagores—the total polarization of Hindu and Muslim
communities was not characteristic of the times.[12] Hindu scribes
often received honorific titles from the Muslim notables they worked
for and these titles were often adopted as surnames.[13] The Debs
received various titles, being known over time as Majumdar,
Khasnabis, and Ray, but by the time of Krishnajiban's two sons,
Brajaram and Vishnuram, the family name had stabilized as Ray.[14]

Brajaram's son Lokenath Ray was an archetypal scribe and fluent in Farsi, Arabic, and Sanskrit. Family legend credited him with the near-incredible ability to take up any text in one of those languages and, while reading it out, to translate it instantaneously and impeccably into the other two. He was also a skilled land surveyor but gave up the profession because of the bribes he was offered by rival claimants, reportedly declaring: 'A job so full of financial temptation is to be avoided like poison.'[15] Something of a yogi and mystic, Lokenath preferred to spend his time in tantric worship and married only because his father begged him to leave an heir.[16] When a son had been born to him, his father, fearing that Lokenath might now renounce family life and become a *sannyasi*, quietly consigned his son's religious books and accessories to the depths of the Brahmaputra. The thirty-two-year-old Lokenath was so shaken by this that, we are told, he entered into a deep trance and was dead within three days.[17]

Lokenath's only son, Kalinath (d. 1879), who was also known as Shyamsundar Munsi, seems to have inherited all his father's talents but not his mystical bent.[18] Kalinath was as fluent as Lokenath in Persian, Sanskrit, and Arabic but the times having changed, he learnt English late in life.[19] When he served as a court assistant (*sirastadar*) for the deputy magistrate of Mymensingh, the latter needed to raise a significant sum for building a school house, and Kalinath's speech in Persian induced Muslims to contribute lavishly to the fund.[20] Muslims came to him for interpretations of Persian documents and although a Kayastha, he was invited to Brahmin conclaves to discourse on arcane aspects of Sanskrit poetics.[21] One story claims that once, while debating the interpretation of the Bhagavad Gita with another Sanskritist, Kalinath developed his points over an entire week, stopping only when his interlocutor was too exhausted to continue. Kalinath also ran a *tol* (a Sanskrit 'secondary' school for boys usually conducted by Brahmins) and his pupils, it is said, feared him so greatly that when passing his home, they crossed to the other side of the road.[22] Appointed an examiner for Bengali grammar and literature at a school, he set such tough questions that even the teachers of the school were stumped by them.[23]

Kalinath was as deeply religious as his father but the nature of that religiosity remains ambiguous. Those of his descendants who embraced Brahmoism portrayed Kalinath almost as a proto-Brahmo. The Brahmins of his village, observed his grandson Sukumar Ray, had tried to prevent him from reading the Vedas because he was not a Brahmin and persecuted him because he had dined with a family that had lost caste when one of its members had married a widow.[24] Accounts of the same Kalinath/Shyamsundar by his orthodox Hindu descendants do not mention any of these incidents, however. Instead, we are told quite emphatically that the Kayastha Shyamsundar was so learned and so pure-hearted that everybody spontaneously showed him the respect they would show a Brahmin and his study of Sanskrit and occasional performance of Brahminical duties were welcomed by Brahmins.[25] Neither account is verifiable but they illustrate how the religious divisions of the nineteenth century affected not only the lives of actual converts and their relatives but also shaped the way they perceived their ancestors.

Kalinath and his wife Joytara had five sons—Saradaranjan (1858–1925), Kamadaranjan (1863–1915), Muktidaranjan (1867–1934), Kuladaranjan (1873–1950), and Pramadaranjan (1875–1947)—and three daughters, Giribala, Sarasibala, and Mrinalini.[26] We know relatively little about Giribala and Sarasibala but Mrinalini, the youngest daughter and the last of Kalinath's children, is a slightly more familiar name because of her marriage to the entrepreneur Hemendramohan Bose.[27] The sons of Kalinath Ray were the first of the Rays to feel the full force of British rule and they proved highly imaginative in adapting to the new age. This was a common pattern with the old scribal communities. After the hegemony of the Persian language ended in 1838 with its replacement in the law courts by English, the old scribal classes—*not* the native aristocracy or what passed for it—swiftly mastered English, the new language of command, and filled the East India Company's army of clerks and subordinate officials. As Veena Naregal has emphasized, however, English was not just of bureaucratic or political importance—it was also the 'language of the imperious discourses of modernity'. The scribal classes' embrace of this potent language, as the story of the Ray family shows, reflected as well as facilitated their embrace of modernity.[28]

Mymensingh, as a whole, was regarded by the British as 'the most backward in education among the districts of West Bengal' but the professional classes were keen on English education and the Rays took full advantage of it.[29] The Hindu middle classes of Mymensingh were regarded by British officials as being so obsessed with getting government jobs for their children that they could be blamed for 'the slow progress of commercial and industrial enterprise in Bengal', but the Rays, ironically, were to avoid the stifling world of chakri with remarkable consistency.[30] Only one of Kalinath Ray's sons—Pramadaranjan—was to work directly for the government but even he was a surveyor travelling to far-flung places, not a desk-bound administrator. In their professional choices, the Rays were atypical for their age and class—Ashis Nandy has described their careers as 'odd'—and preferred to be independent in whatever they did; their avoidance of the three independent professions beloved of aspirational Bengalis of the time (law, engineering, and medicine) is especially striking.[31]

Cricket, Mathematics, Fishing, and Sanskrit:
The Many Worlds of Saradaranjan Ray

Among all of Kalinath's children, Saradaranjan and Kamadaranjan (better known as Upendrakishore) illustrated two completely different ways of coming to terms with modernity without severing their cultural roots. According to family tradition, Saradaranjan inherited all the brilliance of his father Kalinath and possessed such a perfect memory that he could master all his lessons just by listening. A music-loving uncle who was good at picking up tunes but hopeless at memorizing lyrics would take young Sarada along to village concerts or plays (jatra) and the boy would learn all the lyrics for his uncle. Although he spent his days playing or, as he got a little older, fishing, he always did well in his examinations because of his phenomenal memory. And when memory failed, he received psychic help. On the night before an examination for which he had not sufficiently prepared, he had an extraordinary dream in which he saw himself walking into the examination hall, taking his seat, and reading the question paper. When he went to take the examination, he discovered that his dream had been wholly accurate and he did well enough to be awarded a scholarship.[32]

After entering college in Dhaka, Saradaranjan discovered one of the enduring passions of his life: the very modern—and then very British—game of cricket. But although he spent much time on sport, his academic work did not greatly suffer and he graduated with a second-division BA in 1878. Two of his biggest interests were Sanskrit and mathematics.[33] Moving to Calcutta, he completed his MA in 1879 and subsequently joined the Anglo-Oriental College in Aligarh (a district town to the south of Delhi) as a mathematics lecturer.[34] The

Mohammedan Anglo-Oriental College, established in 1875 by Sir
Syed Ahmad Khan (1817–1898) in the image of Cambridge, was part
of a broader programme to bring Western education, hitherto virtually monopolized by Hindus, to the Muslims of India.[35] Saradaranjan
would always be known, as we shall see, for his unswerving allegiance
to orthodox Hinduism and it is ironic that he commenced his teaching
career at an institution that admitted non-Muslim students but was
Islamic in its fundamental purpose, orientation, and culture—
common dining, for instance, was the norm and no allowances were
made for caste differences.[36]

While working in Aligarh, Saradaranjan also taught some
Sanskrit, law, English, and history and became, according to his son
Kumudranjan, very popular with the students. When the college
asked him to take over all the teaching in Sanskrit, Saradaranjan
insisted on being paid (in addition to his current salary) the entire
amount that would be paid to a full-time Sanskrit lecturer.[37] The
authorities refused to do so and Saradaranjan immediately resigned.
According to official records, his service at Aligarh was only 'for some
months'.[38] It is said that Saradaranjan was responsible for introducing cricket in Aligarh and for the Aligarh cricket team's enormous
fame. This is unlikely to be correct.[39] The College Cricket Club had
been established in 1878 (a year before Saradaranjan joined the university) and the cricketing prowess of the members could not have
had very much to do with Saradaranjan, given the brevity of his
employment in Aligarh. The enthusiasm of the college's principals
H.G.I. Siddons and, later, Theodore Beck is likely to have been far
more important in ensuring the College's prominence in cricket.[40]

After Aligarh, Saradaranjan moved to Berhampore College and
then to his alma mater, Dhaka College, where he seems to have had a
happy and intellectually fulfilling time until disputes with the British
Principal led to his transfer to Cuttack College in Orissa.[41] At that
point, he had another one of his celebrated dreams, this one warning
him not to go to Cuttack. He, therefore, resigned from his government
job and accepted the great reformer and educationist Iswarchandra
Vidyasagar's invitation to join the Metropolitan Institution, the first
university-affiliated college in Calcutta to be staffed and managed
entirely by Indians.[42] Starting as a lecturer in 1888, Saradaranjan
became the Vice-Principal of the college in 1892; promoted to
Principal in 1909, he occupied that post until his death in 1925.[43]
When the College entered into dire financial difficulties after

Vidyasagar's death in 1891, Saradaranjan and some of his senior colleagues took over the management of the institution; their salaries went into a college fund to pay the salaries of their junior colleagues and other staff.[44]

Probably because of this decision to sacrifice his salary to save the institution, Saradaranjan was compelled to look for extramural sources of income. A classified advertisement from 1895 reveals that he tutored students privately in Sanskrit and mathematics. For six hours of coaching per week, he charged between 100 and 200 rupees—considerable sums at the time—and special rates were available for 'whole time engagement'.[45] He also earned significant amounts from his mathematics and Sanskrit textbooks. His annotated editions of the Sanskrit classics acquired considerable popularity—at least one remained in print into the 1960s—and he was awarded the titles of Vidyabinod and Siddhanta Vachaspati for his expertise in Sanskrit.[46] He started a publishing firm of his own, which issued some of these textbooks, and the venture was profitable enough for him to use some of the income to manufacture and sell sporting goods and angler's requisites, an initiative that reminds one more of Upendrakishore and even more, of their brother-in-law Hemendramohan Bose. S. Ray & Co., founded in 1898, became quite well-known, with customers across Bengal. Nirad Chaudhuri recalled that when a child in Mymensingh, his family would order sporting goods from Saradaranjan's shop.[47]

Although the shop sold products imported from Europe, Saradaranjan also manufactured cricket bats, footballs, and other items, often from his own designs.[48] His cricket bat and tennis racquet won gold medals at the Indian Industrial and Agricultural Exhibition held at Calcutta in 1906–7 and a fishing tackle and reel received a silver medal.[49] 'We got the highest prize,' boasted Saradaranjan in his subsequent advertisements. 'Others also exhibited but none got a prize or even honourable mention for cricket bats. Please note this for the ensuing cricket season.'[50] His son Kumudranjan also recalled his father designing a special type of football called the Iron Duke and fish hooks that did not require to be baited.[51] For those who preferred to fish in the old-fashioned way, a special bait was also available under the wonderful name of Idharao (come here!).[52]

Saradaranjan's own love for fishing bordered on obsession. Kinsman Hitendrakishore Raychaudhuri, in his boyhood, often saw

Saradaranjan fishing in the ponds of Calcutta's central park (*maidan*) with brother Muktidaranjan holding an umbrella over his revered elder's head.[53] Saradaranjan's youngest daughter, Suhasa, also recalled that Saradaranjan was regularly accompanied by brother Kuladaranjan on his many fishing expeditions to the outskirts of Calcutta and even to relatively distant regions like Burdwan.[54] After an incomplete recovery from pleurisy two years before his death, Saradaranjan's doctor advised him to move to a drier climate and he went to Deoghar, 'not forgetting to take his angling equipment with him' and made arrangements for fishing at a nearby lake. He fell ill again shortly thereafter and passed away.[55] But fishing was far from being Saradaranjan's sole passion. He attained his greatest fame as a cricketer, coming to be known as the 'WG Grace of Bengal' and the 'father of Bengali cricket'.[56] Cricket, needless to say, came to India with the British and stayed with them until the mid-nineteenth century, when it became popular in Parsi and, subsequently, Hindu circles in Bombay. In Bengal, the game remained British until the 1870s, attracting the Hindu middle classes and native princes only when they decided that traditional methods of physical culture would not accomplish their project of making Bengali youth 'manly'.[57]

As one admirer put it, Saradaranjan had been born with a book in one hand and a cricket bat in the other.[58] Saradaranjan helped expand the sporting facilities at the Metropolitan Institution and inspired his students to take up cricket as well as other games like hockey or football.[59] Along with his brothers Kuladaranjan and Muktidaranjan, and the zamindar Brajendrakishore Raychaudhuri, he founded the Town Club in the early 1880s—it soon became the leading 'native' cricket club in Bengal and from 1895, played every year against the all-European Calcutta Cricket Club.[60] Muktidaranjan, Kuladaranjan, and Pramadaranjan along with Muktidaranjan's six sons were all enthusiastic cricketers and hockey players.[61] Even Upendrakishore, not a person one usually associates with sport, was quite an enthusiastic cricket player in his youth.[62] Saradaranjan's nephews Ganesh (Hirendramohan) and Kartik (Nripendramohan) Bose—the sons of Mrinalini Ray and Hemendramohan Bose—also excelled at cricket but it is not known to what extent they were influenced by Saradaranjan himself. (Ironically, however, not one of Saradaranjan's own four sons shared their father's sporting abilities or interests.)[63]

Saradaranjan quickly became a prominent member of Calcutta's world of sport and held many posts in different athletic clubs. Many regular fixtures—such as the University League match or the Indian Schools vs European Schools game—were founded either by him or at his instigation.[64] His efforts to encourage sports among students were certainly innovative. The students of Calcutta's many colleges 'conformed', Nirad Chaudhuri recalled (about a slightly later period), 'to a common type, the citizen-student, for in their existence, politics, both open and secret, studies, gadding about, and interminable talk formed almost equal ingredients. There was, however, practically nothing of sport'.[65] Saradaranjan, in contrast, believed that the healthy body was the indispensable preliminary for a healthy mind. Strengthening the body by exercise and maintaining physical health with a sensible diet were an individual's prime duties. (Next came, quite predictably, the duty to cultivate spirituality and religion.)[66] This stress on physical fitness, however, was not simply a matter of bodily health for him. He had a positively Victorian notion of sport as a builder of character and an Englishman's conviction of the moral value of cricket. 'He did not look on cricket as a pastime but as a serious subject for study and culture,' observed one admirer after his death. 'The three maxims of his life were to be straight, strong and honest ... as we should always deal in a straightforward way so we should play straight balls with a straight bat.'[67] Nor was he alone in such views. His brother Upendrakishore wrote that being good at cricket meant cultivating all the skills needed for doing any kind of great work in life. Referring to an English newspaper's sarcastic remark that the only 'native' who was fit for a high administrative post was the cricketer Ranjitsinhji, he admitted that proficiency in cricket was likely to indicate the level of expertise in any demanding task.[68]

It would not do, however, to regard all this simply as a wholesale mimicry of English ways. There was a local or, more specifically, colonial context too. The colonial idea that the Bengalis were a feeble and effete race had a profound impact on nineteenth-century nationalists and many of them (for example, Nabagopal Mitra, the founder of the *National Paper* and the Hindu Mela) tried to bring about the physical regeneration of the race by establishing gymnasia and encouraging young men to take up sport and exercise.[69] As we saw earlier, it was the failure of this movement that led to the popularization of cricket, which, as Boria Majumdar has shown, was also connected with a nationalist or proto-nationalist desire to meet and excel the colonial rulers at their own game.[70] We know nothing about Saradaranjan's views on colonial rule and it would be rash to label him a nationalist in the conventional sense. The advertisements for his sporting goods business, for instance, emphasized that 'the giant bat-makers of England ... alone know how to turn out high class bats'.[71] Everything we do know about him, however, suggests that he believed in the greatness of Hindu culture and he would undoubtedly have shared the prevalent notion that the physical weakness of present-day Hindu Bengalis was a great obstacle to national regeneration. The fervent espousal of cricket by many of the Rays as a force of physical and moral improvement was intimately associated with the Bengali 'self-image of effeteness' that historian John Rosselli analysed in his well-known essay.[72]

A huge man with a personality to match, Saradaranjan awed his entire family.[73] His temper was as legendary as his stern ethical sense. His niece Leela Majumdar could not recall ever having chatted with him but one of his declamations—'What do you mean by compromise? One can never compromise with what's wrong'—remained with her for life.[74] His brothers, to whom he had been a virtual father after the death of Kalinath Ray, were equally in awe of the man and his son Kumudranjan recalled that while his father occasionally showed affection for other people's children, his own sons and daughters rarely saw that side of his personality.[75] Saradaranjan's temper could be literally murderous. Once, Saradaranjan's son Manoranjan had brought a goat home; when the goat bleated incessantly and disturbed him at work, Saradaranjan was so enraged that he beat it to death with his stick.[76] His students were petrified in his presence and even insolent Europeans, it was proudly reported, were no match for him. Once, when travelling on a tram, a British soldier kept putting his feet up on the seat next to Saradaranjan's. After the soldier ignored several requests to take his feet off the seat, Saradaranjan and his companion, his equally hefty brother Muktidaranjan, grabbed his feet and simply pulled him off his seat. Dropping shamefacedly on the floor, the European did not even think of attacking these 'two bold Aryan-like Bengalis' (the phrase is Kumudranjan's) and got out at the next stop.[77]

Even if these tales of prowess are exaggerated, there is no doubt that Saradaranjan was a man of robust health. When in his mid-sixties, a European stopped him while he was jogging to the Ganges for his morning dip and asked him his age. 'Guess,' responded Saradaranjan. 'Forty-five,' said the European and raised his estimate by five years when Saradaranjan chuckled. After several such exchanges, the European was staggered to learn that his strapping interlocutor was actually sixty-seven years old. 'I have never seen a middle-aged Bengali who was so physically fit,' he is reported to have declared. A couple of years before that, an ayurvedic physician had declared that Saradaranjan was still fit enough to be a soldier.[78] Saradaranjan himself, incidentally, was well known as an amateur homoeopathic and ayurvedic physician—his son Kumudranjan recalled that all the common maladies of the household were treated by Saradaranjan himself; a doctor trained in Western medicine—or, as colloquially known in Bengal, an allopath—was consulted only if a surgical intervention was required. He also prescribed for himself; even a month before his own death, he was relying solely upon his own medical skills to treat his ailments.[79]

Saradaranjan was a staunch Hindu—every morning, he walked to the Ganges to bathe and although he educated his daughters at home, he did not send them to school and married them off by the time they were fifteen or sixteen. Earlier, as soon as his brother Kamadaranjan had converted to Brahmoism, Saradaranjan, in fear that the nineteen-year-old Muktidaranjan (1867–1934) might follow suit, arranged for his marriage and domestication into the lifestyle of a good traditional Hindu.[80] The polytheism and idolatry of conventional Hinduism were essential for Saradaranjan. Discussing the formless Absolute *Brahman*, which Brahmos worshipped instead of idols, he remarked that 'this *Brahman* is altogether unconditioned, and, as such, cannot be the subject matter of the devotee's meditation. The mind hankers after something conditioned, a personal god ... Shiva, Vishnu, etc. are the objects of their daily worship ... [and] manifestations of *Brahman* himself'.[81]

Saradaranjan's views on caste, too, were quite conventional. He is said to have had a dream that in some past life he had been a devout Brahmin living in the holy city of Benaras but was born as a Kayastha as a punishment for his vanity.[82] His son, in his memoir of Saradaranjan, repeatedly portrays him as a Kayastha who, although the equal of Brahmins in his learning, acknowledged Brahminical authority in all applicable spheres because of his innate reverence for the Hindu social order.[83] It is likely that Saradaranjan shared the Hindu belief that one lost one's caste by crossing the oceans because when Kumudranjan wanted to go to Britain to take the entrance examination for the Indian Civil Service, Saradaranjan refused to entertain the idea. A man of integrity, with the help of God, could build his fortune without needing foreign qualifications, he told his son, adding that there was nothing so valuable for a human being as his moral/religious sensibility (*dharmabhab*) and it was vital to protect it from being corrupted by Western influence.[84] While Kamadaranjan (Upendrakishore)'s descendants portrayed him as the prophet of modernity and the new learning, the descendants of his elder brother lionized Saradaranjan as the epitome of all that was great in orthodox Hinduism. Stoical, abstemious, and profoundly religious, Saradaranjan was presented, as it were, as living refutation of the Brahmo charge that mainstream Hindus were decadent, superstitious, and licentious. Anger, Kumudranjan stated, was his father's only failing and fishing his sole addiction.[85]

As entrepreneur, sportsman, and academic, Saradaranjan engaged confidently with the modern world but as a Sanskritist and Hindu householder, he held firmly to the religious and social practices of his ancestors. These apparently contradictory orientations do not seem to have precipitated any turmoil in his soul; nor, however, did they fuse at any point. What we find in Saradaranjan is the compartmentalization of potentially contradictory impulses—what Ashis Nandy, in a different context, has called the 'partitioning of the self'—rather than the harmonious 'synthesis' of East and West that is supposed to have been the defining feature of the Bengal Renaissance.[86] With his brother Kamadaranjan, we encounter an approach to modernity that was very different but equally insistent, in its own way, on staying true to one's cultural roots.

The Transformation of Kamadaranjan

Kalinath and Joytara's second son Kamadaranjan would reunite the family line of Brajaram Ray with that of Vishnuram Ray.[87] Vishnuram's great-grandson Harikishore Ray was a sirastadar in the Diwani Adalat, the civil court of the East India Company, which, in the earlier decades of the nineteenth century, administered Mughal laws. Although he was reportedly incorruptible—he is even said to have refused a bribe of 50,000 rupees, a princely sum at the time—Harikishore made enough money to buy a *zamindari* estate and subsequently expanded his surname to the aristocratic-sounding Raychaudhuri.[88] He was a pious Hindu and became worried when he remained childless in middle age, despite being two years into his third marriage. Dying without having fathered a son, conventional

Hindus believed, ensured eternal damnation because only a son could perform the ritual oblations a soul needed to enter heaven.[89] Adoption seemed to be the best option but Harikishore did not want his eventual inheritor to be the child of a total stranger.[90] So he asked his cousin Kalinath Ray to let him adopt one of his three sons. Refusing to part with his eldest, Saradaranjan, Kalinath asked Harikishore to adopt either Muktidaranjan or Kamadaranjan. Harikishore chose Kamadaranjan, reportedly because he was the fairest among Kalinath's three sons or, as another tradition claims, because young Kamada came and spontaneously sat on his lap. The five-year-old was formally adopted in 1868 and given the grand new name of Upendrakishore Raychaudhuri.[91]

The adoptive parents were besotted with the boy and he grew so accustomed to being spoilt that the slightest rebuke for any kind of naughtiness would lead to tantrums. One of his favoured strategies, Upendrakishore later told his children, was to stand between Kalinath and Harikishore's neighbouring houses and wail loudly. This had the predictable result of his biological as well as adoptive relatives rushing out to calm him.[92] Ironically, a couple of years after his adoption, Harikishore and his third wife, Rajlakshmi—who was only about ten years older than Upendrakishore—were to have their own son, Narendrakishore (1870–1930) and, subsequently, two daughters, Manorama and Surobala.[93] The birth of Harikishore's biological son did not, as far as we know, lead to any displacement of Upendrakishore from the family's affections or, indeed, from his position as Harikishore's heir.

The young Upendrakishore was a bright student, but instead of burying his nose in books, he preferred to play the flute or the violin or to paint. In most of the stories that have come down to us about the Rays, their lack of the usual Bengali bookishness is a recurrent theme and so it is for Upendrakishore, but with additional emphasis on his ability from childhood to master demanding arts without instruction. His son Sukumar recalled, for instance, how Upendrakishore, without ever having received any formal training, had acquired remarkable drawing skills. In July 1877, Sir Ashley Eden (1831–1887), the Lieutenant-Governor of Bengal, came to visit Mymensingh.[94] While gazing upon the Lieutenant-Governor, Upendrakishore sketched a likeness of him in his notebook and as luck would have it, Eden happened to pass his desk at that moment. Upon noticing his own visage in the boy's notebook, Eden was so impressed by the quality of the sketch that he reportedly encouraged Upendrakishore to choose art as his career.[95] 'Alone and unaided,' declared Ramananda Chatterji in Upendrakishore's obituary in *Modern Review*, 'he mastered the mysteries of light, shade, and perspective. The drawings which he lavished upon his books and papers in his school-boy days excited the admiration of his teachers.'[96] Despite the hyperbole of these tributes and reminiscences, 'teach yourself' does seem to have been Upendrakishore's motto and, indeed, that of most of his descendants. One is almost surprised not to find an account of the Rays in Samuel Smiles's bestselling guide for aspirational Victorians, *Self Help* (1859)!

Upendrakishore's teachers, however, did not quite see things that way. Because of the multiplicity of his interests he would not, they feared, perform well at the entrance examination.[97] After a serious conversation with his headmaster—the same man had previously asked Saradaranjan Ray to give up fishing until after the examination—Upendrakishore realized how much the school was counting on him and (literally) smashing his violin, sat down with his school books. Having done very well in the examination and having obtained a government scholarship for further study, he used his scholarship money not to buy college textbooks but a violin and other musical instruments. He also hosted a celebratory feast at a well-known Mymensingh institution, the so-called Brahmo Shop.[98]

The owner of this shop, which he had established in 1872 in partnership with Saratchandra Chaudhuri, was Saratchandra Ray (1846–1901), one of the leading lights of the Brahmo community of Mymensingh. Located on the bank of the Brahmaputra River, the Brahmo Shop sold all kinds of goods, many of which were brought over from Calcutta—no easy feat since there was no railway link to Mymensingh at the time—but its fame did not stem from its inventory.[99] Thanks to Saratchandra Ray's ability to inspire local youths into social service, the shop became a philanthropic landmark of Mymensingh. In the words of one observer, 'all the weapons of social reform were sharpened here and every idea to improve the life of Mymensingh was born here'.[100] Ray and his band of young associates regularly nursed the sick (including those suffering from cholera), even when the patients or their relatives were staunchly anti-Brahmo.[101] They also started a night school for the working classes, established a school for girls, brought out *Bangali*, the first literary monthly to be published in Mymensingh, and then, from 1875, the weekly newspaper *Bharat Mihir*, which, according to Bipinchandra

Pal, was a 'powerful organ of educated Bengalee opinion that commanded universal respect'.[102] Ray, who had never had much formal
education himself, took particular interest in helping students, not
just with advice and encouragement but also with financial assistance.
Ratnamani Gupta, the headmaster of the Zillah School—who, like
many other schoolmasters of Mymensingh, was a Brahmo—considered Ray's shop to be virtually a wing of the higher classes of his
school.[103]

Despite holding a feast at the Brahmo Shop, Upendrakishore, at
this point in his life, was fairly resistant to the Brahmo faith and
unlike many of his peers, he was not involved with Saratchandra Ray's
philanthropic initiatives. Upendrakishore's close friend and distant
relative Gaganchandra Home (1857–1929), who had begun in his
teens to attend Brahmo services against the wishes of his parents and
had run away from home to live with the Brahmos, recalled how
Upendrakishore used to taunt him for his Brahmo convictions.
'Occasionally,' Home recorded in his memoirs, 'he even spat at me.'
Home liked Upendrakishore so much that he did not usually react to
these attacks but one day, he could not control his temper and hit
Upendrakishore with a stick, crying: 'You just wait—I shall not rest
until I have made you a Brahmo too.'[104] Upendrakishore would
indeed convert and spend his life as a devout Brahmo but not until
after he had left Mymensingh and distanced himself from his adoptive father and the zamindari that awaited him.[105] But why was
Brahmoism so controversial in Mymensingh and what made it so
important to mere schoolboys?

A New Faith for a New Age

Hinduism being a way of life rather than a well-defined religion,
movements for its reform have always involved some element of
social reform.[106] The Brahmo movement illustrated this perfectly.
While it sought to end polytheism and idol-worship by returning to an
Upanishadic conception of the Absolute, many younger Brahmos led
by the charismatic Keshabchandra Sen (1838–1884) were inspired by
Unitarian Christianity in the 1860s to take up projects of social and
moral reform.[107] Sen's electrifying oratory drew younger, middle-class
and rural members into the movement, transforming it into a larger
campaign for social reform and cultural reorientation.[108] Much has

been written on the history of Brahmoism but its impact on the rural hinterland (especially eastern Bengal) is still not fully appreciated. In the late nineteenth century, it spread across the villages and district towns of East Bengal like 'a conflagration', despite intense persecution from conventional Hindus.[109] The Dhaka Brahmo Samaj, established in 1846, and the Mymensingh Brahmo Samaj, established in 1853, were two of the oldest and most important centres of Brahmo activities.[110]

It is not too much to claim that the Hindu communities of East Bengal first encountered modernity because of the Brahmo dissenters. They campaigned for women's education and the remarriage of widows, opposed child-marriage, and encouraged philanthropic drives without discriminating against mainstream Hindus. Today, the Brahmos of the nineteenth century are often derided—justifiably— for their puritanical quirks. True religiosity, for them, began with the cleansing of the self, proceeded to the cleansing of religion, and culminated with the cleansing of society.[111] Devout Brahmos sought not only to rise above their own fleshly cravings but also to shun the corrupt and the dissolute. Although the Brahmos could descend into narrow-minded puritanism—for instance, in their inflexible opposition to the theatre because prostitutes played female roles on the professional Bengali stage—their puritanism, in its time, was not entirely irrational. 'The Brahmo Samaj began its moral crusade with a practical programme,' observed the Mymensingh boy Nirad Chaudhuri. 'It attacked four vices ... sensuality, drunkenness, dishonesty, and falsehood', which, according to Chaudhuri, 'overlay Hindu society like a coat of slime'.[112] As the historian Sumit Sarkar has pointed out, the puritanism was also 'a defence mechanism for a movement which could—and often did—incur charges of licentiousness' on account of the social freedoms enjoyed by Brahmo women.[113]

Puritanism notwithstanding, the years of Brahmo ascendancy would come to be seen as a golden age by many East Bengalis. Nirad Chaudhuri, a great admirer of Gibbon's *Decline and Fall of the Roman Empire*, would echo its celebrated lines on the Antonine utopia in hailing the achievements of the Brahmos:

> Perhaps there never was any period in the last two hundred years of the history of the Hindu middle class in which it showed greater probity in public and private affairs, attained greater happiness in family and personal life, saw greater fulfilment of cultural aspirations, and put forth greater creativeness in every field, than the fifty

years between 1860 and 1910 dominated by the moral ideals of Brahmo and new Hindu puritanism.[114]

Although the community of Brahmos in Mymensingh remained small—even in 1915, the total number (counting all three branches the movement had divided into) did not cross 200—the orthodox Hindus were sufficiently worried by their stance against idolatry and their call for educating women to subject them to various degrees of social ostracism and, in 1867, they established a society for the 'protection' of the Hindu faith, in which Upendrakishore's adoptive father, Harikishore, was a prominent figure.[115]

Harikishore was so paranoid about Brahmos that he even tried to prevent Upendrakishore, who was then quite hostile to Brahmoism, from associating with Gagan Home.[116] Since the two boys liked each other at an individual level, they had to meet in secret.[117] Many of Upendrakishore's biographers claim that the two, during their clandestine meetings, discussed the nature of the godhead and the Brahmo faith.[118] Home's memoirs, however, suggest nothing of the kind; even if the two boys did discuss religious or spiritual matters, those obviously did not have the major, immediate impact on Upendrakishore that his standard biographies imply.[119] And small wonder. Upendrakishore's very identity, at this point, was tied up with Harikishore's and an allegiance to conventional Hinduism was essential to it. Upendrakishore would rethink that identity only when he embraced a life of greater toil and uncertainty in Calcutta.

From *Zamindar* to Artisan

After finishing school in their villages or district towns, most East Bengal students had to move to a major city like Calcutta or Dhaka if they wished to study further. As Benedict Anderson has observed with reference to the similar situation in the Dutch East Indies (colonial Indonesia), brighter rural youths seeking higher education had to embark on a 'pilgrimage' after completing primary school; in the East Indies, 'the Rome of these pilgrimages was Batavia' but in colonial Bengal, it was Calcutta.[120] Of the thousands of college students in Calcutta, only a relatively small proportion came from the city itself; most came from rural regions of Bengal or from other parts of India.[121] Like those ambitious boys from rural Bengal, the sixteen-year-old Upendrakishore, armed with a scholarship for higher study,

trekked to Calcutta in 1879 in pursuit of university education, travelling, as was typical at the time for most East Bengalis, for three days
by elephant, boat, steamer, and rail.[122]

He first joined Calcutta's Presidency College, established in 1855
by the Viceroy Lord Dalhousie as the new incarnation of the famous
Hindu College, the fountainhead of English education in Bengal and
the site of the young professor Henry Derozio's alleged transformation of good Hindu youth into beef-eating, beer-drinking infidels. The
rebranded institution was funded entirely by the government and
opened to all communities, not just Hindus. From 1857, the year of
the Great Rebellion, the College lost its institutional independence
and was affiliated with the brand-new University of Calcutta. Modelled
on the University of London, Calcutta University was neither a
teaching institution nor a research centre. It was simply an examining body providing the degree—BA—that was the basic requirement for white-collar jobs. The University's reach was vast in its early
years, covering not just Bengal but the North-West Provinces, the
Central Provinces, Assam, British Burma, and Ceylon but its actual
social impact was limited.[123] University education was mainly patronized by the middle and professional classes and, as a commission
investigating it in the early twentieth century was to note, it was little
more than 'a means of obtaining marketable qualifications'.[124]

Upendrakishore, however, did not fit this pattern. Before one
could get the coveted BA, one had to pass the First Arts course, which
he did in 1881 (in the second division) but he then did something
rather strange. Leaving the elite Presidency College, he moved to the
Metropolitan Institution, from where he graduated with a BA in 1884
in the third (the lowest) division.[125] Upendrakishore was always
proud of his BA degree, using it in advertisements of his block-making business and on the cover of his magazine *Sandesh*, but why did a
boy passing his entrance examination with flying colours do so poorly
in his BA? And why exactly did he quit the prestigious Presidency
College—the 'centre and heart' of Calcutta University—and opt for
the Metropolitan, which was not a government institution and had
none of the cultural mystique of Presidency College?[126] His elder
brother Saradaranjan Ray could have had nothing to do with the
move, because Saradaranjan did not commence working at the
Metropolitan until four years after Upendrakishore's graduation.
Although we do not have sufficient information for definitive answers,
it is important to address these questions, for they can help us explore

Upendrakishore's maverick personality a little more thoroughly than existing accounts have sought to do.

Led by Iswarchandra Vidyasagar, the Metropolitan Institution was a fully indigenous alternative to Presidency College, charging lower fees and providing bursaries to the poorest students.[127] Naturally, students from modest backgrounds flocked to the Metropolitan, as did those with a nationalist bent. In 1891, Presidency had 415 students while the Metropolitan had 577.[128] Prafullachandra Ray chose to study at the Metropolitan not only because it was 'a national institution' but also because his father had recently suffered financial reverses and could not afford the high fees charged by Presidency College.[129] Upendrakishore's choice may also have been determined by financial stringency. His obituary in the *Modern Review* mentioned that his plans for higher study had been 'cut short by ... domestic troubles' and his refusal to compromise with his adoptive father.[130] What, however, caused the dispute?

One possible reason had to do with Harikishore's desire that Upendrakishore study law. Law was one of the most popular and lucrative professions for middle-class Hindu gentry and Presidency College, in particular, had become 'a veritable seminary of deputy magistrates and government pleaders'.[131] Harikishore had himself made a fortune as a lawyer and he would have rightly thought that a legal training would be the ideal preparation for the task of managing the estate.[132] Upendrakishore's refusal to study law would obviously have irritated Harikishore but there was a much bigger cause for discord. During his stay in Calcutta, Upendrakishore, as we shall see, was very close to young, radical Brahmos and after hearing rumours about his adoptive son's possible conversion, Harikishore spent sleepless nights fretting about the future of his heir and estate.[133] Shortly before his death in 1883, Harikishore even made a new will leaving only one-fourth of his estate to Upendrakishore and the rest to his biological son, Narendrakishore.[134] In a desperate effort to bring Upendrakishore back to the straight and narrow, Harikishore may well have stopped—or reduced—his allowance previously, compelling the young man to quit Presidency College for the cheaper Metropolitan.

Upendrakishore's life was seriously unstable at this point, but his steely determination to repudiate the life of a rural zamindar does not seem to have wavered despite the sudden shortage of funds. His poor BA result, surprising in its own right, may have been brought about by the seventeen-year-old college student's decision to take up the unusual—and, for the Bengali gentry, socially inferior—job of repairing damaged musical instruments, possibly for Dwarkin's, a prominent indigenous dealer in musical instruments. He also did some musical tutoring and planned to write a book on science for children.[135] Upendrakishore's biographers usually recount these episodes merely to illustrate the teenager's technological and musical gifts. Those talents are, of course, beyond dispute but we should also ask *why* he chose to express them in such socially incongruous ways at a time when they would interfere seriously with his studies. Was it, perhaps, his stomach, rather than his irrepressible genius, that drove him to work as an artisan?

Whatever the answer to that question, it is clear that Upendrakishore was determined not to be a rural zamindar. When requested by family and friends to return to Masua and run the estate after Harikishore's death in 1883, he promised to do so only if he could run the estate without ever lying or performing a single unethical act. These surreal stipulations were interpreted quite correctly by his family, who accepted the inevitable, and it was Harikishore's biological son, Narendrakishore—fifteen years old and still in school—who was compelled to give up his studies and take charge of the estate. Upendrakishore caused further difficulty by declining to perform the orthodox Hindu funeral rites, which involved feeding Brahmins and distributing alms. Although he had not formally converted yet, his religious sensibilities had already been reshaped by his close encounters with Brahmos and he found it impossible to participate in such orthodox, casteist rites.[136] Again, it was the young Narendrakishore who had to step in.[137]

Passing his BA in 1884, Upendrakishore worked as an artist and photographer—interesting occupations no doubt, but far from socially prestigious, especially for a zamindar's heir.[138] The business was simply named 'U. Ray, Artist'. The tag 'Chaudhuri', which Upendrakishore's adoptive father had added to his name to denote his high social and economic status, was dropped by the young artisan for his business and for the technical articles that he would publish in English.[139] Upendrakishore's embrace of private enterprise, no doubt, was primarily because of his personal circumstances and preferences. One must not forget, however, that it was entirely consonant with the Brahmo approach to national regeneration. As Debendramohan Bose once remarked, Brahmos, although not always talented businesspeople, often 'risked their earnings in starting tea gardens and other industries' to fulfil their 'plan for the economic growth of the country through indigenous agencies'.[140] It was certainly fitting, then, that shortly after starting his own business, Upendrakishore completed his secession from Hariki-shore's orthodox universe by formally converting to Brahmoism in 1884.

The Brahmo Fortress

Students from East Bengal, it was widely believed at the time, tended to be drawn into Brahmoism and various kinds of 'political' work after coming to Calcutta.[141] Upendrakishore, certainly, fit this stereo-type and began to lose his resistance to the Brahmo faith once he settled in the big city. The distance from Harikishore Raychaudhuri's Hindu household probably helped in his transformation but more important was the company of the dynamic young Brahmos with whom he shared a house on Sitaram Ghosh Street.[142] Gaganchandra Home lived there with other young Brahmos and Brahmo sympa-thizers, including Hemendramohan Bose, Upendrakishore's future brother-in-law, and Pramadacharan Sen, in whose magazine *Sakha* Upendrakishore would commence his career as a writer for children. Dwarakanath Ganguli, one of the most radical figures in the Brahmo movement, was a regular visitor—Home called him 'our leader'—and spent much time discussing politics and religion with the young men. Such Brahmo luminaries as Sivanath Sastri or Bijoykrishna Goswami would also drop in from time to time and Home was not being too hyperbolic when he described their house as a 'Brahmo fortress'.[143]

The Brahmo fortress was not only filled with prayer and lofty dis-cussions but gave birth to some noted publications. The newspapers *Indian Messenger* and *Sanjibani* began to be published from here in 1883.[144] Founded by Dwarakanath Ganguli, Krishnakumar Mitra, Herambachandra Maitra, Kalisankar Sukul, and others, *Sanjibani* was a cooperative venture and would eventually publish Ganguli's own investigations of the mistreatment of coolies in Assam.[145] Edited by Krishnakumar Mitra from 1883 until his own death in 1936, the paper was broadly nationalistic in its politics and became the unofficial mouthpiece of radical Brahmos and their sympathizers.[146] From the remarriage of widows to the suppression of the opium trade, the paper was consistently progressive, albeit always in a typically Brahmo way: it refused to accept advertisements for tobacco, alcoholic drinks, stage plays, and medicines for sexually transmitted diseases.[147]

As far as Upendrakishore was concerned, however, the most important publication to emerge from the fortress was *Sakha*, a children's magazine edited by the frail but spirited Pramadacharan Sen (1859–1885). Sen had fallen into bad company in his childhood and it was only after he became a student of Calcutta's Hare School and was taken under Sivanath Sastri's wings that he had begun to reform. Eventually, he was to do so well in his studies that he aspired to go to Britain for higher education but when this proved impossible, he joined the City Collegiate School as a teacher. He converted to Brahmoism (for which he was disowned by his father) and devoted his life to the improvement and entertainment of children.[148] Finding it hard to raise funds for the publication of *Sakha*, he saved money by eating only one meal a day and cutting back on every personal expense.[149] The first issue, published in January 1883, was sixteen pages long and, although less obviously didactic than earlier Bengali magazines for children, the magazine was driven by its editor's conviction that young people needed good advice to prevent them from going astray.

'*Sakha*,' he declared in his first editorial, 'would seek to fill the role of the teacher as well as the parent in providing its readers with instruction as well as advice.' The contributors would do their utmost to help children grow into 'real human beings' (*bastabik manush*). In the first year, *Sakha* had 600 subscribers—at the cost of one rupee per year—but the magazine was soon in such demand that the first volume had to be reprinted and the number of subscribers rose to 1,000 from its second year.[150] Pramadacharan Sen wrote virtually everything published in the magazine's first issue but from the second number, he was joined by Upendrakishore Ray, who contributed an article on the housefly, his first known piece for children.[151] Such informative pieces were accompanied by moral exhortations on the evil effects of drinking and smoking (the latter co-authored by Upendrakishore) and the undesirability of women wearing too much jewellery.[152] Slightly more subtle was the editor's serialized novel *Bhimer Kapal*.[153] Generally recognized as the first Bengali novel for children, it was not based on English or classical Indian sources. In over ten instalments, it charted out the painful experiences and consequent moral improvement of a Bengali boy called Bhimchandra.[154] Indirectly autobiographical, the novel concluded with the declaration that there was no need for its young readers to suffer like its hero: 'Truly wise people educate themselves about their duties before they get into trouble. Bhimchandra's story is at an end—I hope that my readers will begin to educate themselves now.'[155]

Sen declared in an editorial in *Sakha* that since today's boys and girls would be tomorrow's citizens, to improve their minds was to brighten the nation's future. He wanted *Sakha* to serve simultaneously as the child's playmate, teacher, friend, and mentor.[156] Patriotism was as vital to *Sakha* as moral integrity. The magazine published what was probably the first political article in a Bengali children's magazine: a piece by Bipinchandra Pal about the imprisonment of the nationalist leader Surendranath Banerjea.[157] It ended with the peroration: 'Readers! Learn to shed a tear for your unfortunate motherland! One day, you too might sanctify India's prison, one day your nation's misfortunes will be ended by your efforts, and your fame will cover your nation in glory.'[158] This explicit nationalism was largely absent from the children's literature of the time. When political or national issues were raised at all, openly anti-colonial sentiments were carefully avoided and it was only at the end of the 1930s that Bengali children's literature began to talk about imperialist oppression or the Indian nationalist movement.[159]

Sen died of tuberculosis in 1885, when he was twenty-seven and his magazine barely two years old, but *Sakha* was kept running under the editorship of Sivanath Sastri until 1886 and then of Pramadacharan's brother Annadacharan Sen. In 1894, *Sakha* merged with another magazine called *Sathi* to form *Sakha-o-Sathi*. Upendrakishore contributed prolifically to *Sakha* as well as *Sakha-o-Sathi* and made something of a speciality of articles on scientific as well as other topics, often illustrated with photographs taken by him.[160] From then until the end of his life, Upendrakishore, in spite of his many other interests, would remain utterly committed to entertaining and elevating Bengali children and his prolific output would embrace science along with fairy tales, poetry as well as graphic illustrations, culminating with the magazine, *Sandesh*, which he would establish two years before his death. But although he had cut his literary teeth on *Sakha*, he would not emulate its nationalism when he founded his own magazine, *Sandesh*. As we shall see, the only remotely 'political' piece that Upendrakishore published was a homage to George V on his accession to the throne.

The Faith of Reformers

Today, Upendrakishore is remembered primarily on account of his contributions to children's literature and they have come to over-shadow the rest of his polymathic accomplishments and the broader reformist projects of the Rays in general. The latter were conducted largely under the aegis of the Brahmo Samaj. When Upendrakishore converted to Brahmoism in 1884, the Brahmo Samaj had already undergone two splits and it was the socially radical Sadharan Brahmo Samaj that he joined. The next year, he married the daughter of the Brahmo firebrand Dwarakanath Ganguli, a leading light of virtually every major reform initiative of the late nineteenth century—from nationalism to women's emancipation.[161] By marrying a girl who was not only Brahmo but, in orthodox Hindu terms, Brahmin by caste, Upendrakishore removed himself definitively from the traditional Hindu universe of his adoptive father, Harikishore. More importantly, the story of the Rays now became entwined with the life and work of Upendrakishore's father-in-law, one of the feistiest reformers in the annals of the Brahmo Samaj.

Brahmo reformism was but one chapter in the pan-Indian his-tory of Hindu social reform and had been preceded—occasionally, even surpassed—by the work of others.[162] Any history of social reform in India would highlight figures such as Dayananda Saraswati, Khwaja Altaf Husain Hali, R. Venkata Ratnam Naidu, Behramji Malabari, Dhondo Keshav Karve, and Mahadev Govind Ranade.[163] Some of these figures were Brahmos (or associated with the cognate Prarthana Samaj of western India) but by no means all.[164] Even within Bengal, the Brahmos had been preceded by other Bengali reformers in emphasizing the importance of women's issues but such efforts had remained largely theoretical.[165] Even the legislation resulting from Iswarchandra Vidyasagar's celebrated crusade to allow Hindu widows to remarry remained a dead letter. Brahmo pro-jects were more practical and, generally speaking, more successful, even though confined in the beginning to their own small community. Perhaps the greatest Brahmo success was in facilitating women's access to education, and not just their right to basic literacy. As Sivanath Sastri, a prominent radical Brahmo, proclaimed in 1882, 'All attempts at social reformation without educating and elevating our females are futile.'[166] The early history of Indian nationalism also reveals a strong Brahmo presence and in both of these areas,

Upendrakishore's father-in-law, Dwarakanath Ganguli, was a colossal and ever-active presence.

Notes

1. The Turkish conquest of large parts of Bengal and Bihar in the early thirteenth century had led to the establishment of the so-called Bengal Sultanate, ruled by various Indo-Islamic dynasties until the Mughal conquest of Bengal in the late sixteenth century. In the late seventeenth century, Bengal came to be ruled by the Nawabs of Murshidabad, who acknowledged the paramountcy of the Mughals but ran a near-autonomous government. See Jadunath Sarkar, ed., *The History of Bengal, Muslim Period 1200–1757* (Patna: Academica Asiatica, [1948] 1973).

2. Upendrakishore Ray, 'Amader Bansa-Parichay', reproduced in *Masuar Moudgalya Gotriya Kayastha Bansabali* by Purnachandra Bhattacharya, (Masua, Mymensingh, no pub., 1933), section 2 ('Masuar Itihas'), 1–10, at 1. Full family trees are available in P. Bhattacharya, *Masuar Moudgalya Gotriya Kayastha Bansabali*, section 1 ('Masuar Moudgalya Gotriya Kayasthaganer Bansabali o Parichoy'), 1–7. The original family name was Deo and it is surmised that Ramsundar's own ancestors had moved to Bengal from Bihar. See Leela Majumdar, *Upendrakishore* (Calcutta: Newscript, 1963), 14.

3. See F.A. Sachse, *Bengal District Gazetteers: Mymensingh* (Calcutta: Bengal Secretariat Book Depot, 1917), 1, 35; Kedarnath Majumdar, *Maimansingher Itihas* (Calcutta: Sanyal & Co., 1906), 102; and Amarchandra Dutta, *Saracchandra: Jibani* (Mymensingh: The Author, 1915), 46–7 (my thanks to Sourit Dey for this scarce volume).

4. U. Ray, 'Amader Bansa-Parichay', 2.

5. Although the scribal trade was virtually a 'hereditary enterprise' of the Kayasthas, Brahmans and Baidyas were also prominent in scribal communities. See Kumkum Chatterjee, 'Scribal Elites in Sultanate and Mughal Bengal', *Indian Economic and Social History Review*, 47, no. 4 (2010): 445–72, especially 447–8 and 455.

6. Hayden Bellenoit, 'Paper, Pens and Power between Empires in North India, 1750–1850', *South Asian History and Culture*, 3, no. 3 (July 2012): 348–72, at 355. Many artists of Mughal court ateliers were also Kayasthas—see Dinkar Kowshik, *Nandalal Bose: The Doyen of Indian Art* (Delhi: National Book Trust, 1985), 2.

7. See S.N. Mukherjee, 'Class, Caste and Politics in Calcutta, 1815–38', in *Elites in South Asia*, edited by Edmund Leach and S.N. Mukherjee (Cambridge: Cambridge University Press, 1970), 33–78, at 39.

8. Sumit Sarkar, *A Critique of Colonial India*, 2nd edn (Calcutta: Papyrus, 2000), 40. Although the cultivation of Persian in India commenced in the

thirteenth century, it became 'something approaching a first language for many Indians' after it became the language of administration during Akbar's reign. See Muzaffar Alam, 'The Culture and Politics of Persian in Precolonial Hindustan', in *Literary Cultures in History: Reconstructions from South Asia*, edited by Sheldon Pollock (Berkeley: University of California Press, 2003), 131–98, at 166. On the different roles of Arabic and Persian, see Kumkum Chatterjee, *The Cultures of History in Early Modern India: Persianization and Mughal Culture in Bengal* (Delhi: Oxford University Press, 2009), 216–17.

9. Ramesh Chandra Mitra, 'Education', in *The History of Bengal (1757–1905)* edited by Narendra Krishna Sinha (Calcutta: University of Calcutta, 1967), 429–71, at 432–3.

10. See Sanjay Joshi, *Fractured Modernity: Making of a Middle Class in Colonial North India* (Delhi: Oxford University Press, 2001), 104.

11. Bipinchandra Pal, *Sattar Vatsar: Atmajibani* (Calcutta: Kalpan, [1927–8] 2005), 27–8, 55. Earlier, Bhudev Mukhopadhyay had also made a similar observation. See Sudipta Kaviraj, 'The Reversal of Orientalism: Bhudev Mukhopadhyay and the Project of Indigenist Social Theory' [1995], in *The Imaginary Institution of India: Politics and Ideas* (Ranikhet: Permanent Black, 2010), 254–89, at 260. On Farsi schools in Bengal as providers of a quasi-secular education, see Paramesh Acharya, *Banglar Deshaja Sikshadhara* (Calcutta: Anustup, 1989), 170–6.

12. See K. Chatterjee, 'Scribal Elites', 464–5; and S.N. Mukherjee, 'Class, Caste and Politics in Calcutta', 42.

13. See K. Chatterjee, 'Scribal Elites', 453.

14. P. Bhattacharya, *Masuar Moudgalya Gotriya Kayastha Bansabali*, section 2, 11.

15. Kumudranjan Ray, ed., *Adhyaksha Saradaranjan Ray* (Calcutta: Kamalranjan Ray, 1958), 2–4 (my thanks to Sarbajit Mitra and Sourit Dey for this pamphlet). For a slightly different version, see U. Ray, 'Amader Bansa-Parichay', 3.

16. The tantric tradition in Hinduism was centred on the Goddess, notionally the consort of Siva but conceptualized as his inherent power or *sakti*. Characterized by esoteric, sometimes magical or even erotic, rites and divided into many sects, much of tantrism, by the time of Kalinath Ray, had coalesced with classical Hinduism and many of its transgressive practices had been domesticated. See Alexis Sanderson, 'Saivism and the Tantric Traditions', in *The World's Religions*, edited by Stewart Sutherland, Leslie Houlden, Peter Clarke, and Friedhelm Hardy (London: Routledge, 1988), 660–704; and André Padoux, 'Tantrism', in *Encyclopedia of Religion*, edited by Mircea Eliade, 16 vols (New York: Macmillan, 1987), 14: 273–80.

17. K. Ray, *Adhyaksha Saradaranjan Ray*, 4; U. Ray, 'Amader Bansa-Parichay', 3.

18. Hemantakumar Adhya, *Sukumar Ray: Jibankatha* (Calcutta: Pustak Bipani, 1990), 7. 'Munsi' was the typical honorific title bestowed in Mughal-era Bengal on those literate in Persian. See K. Chatterjee, *Cultures of History*, 226. Dates of birth and death are not available for most of the earlier Rays but Kalinath is known to have died in 1879. See K. Ray, *Adhyaksha Saradaranjan Ray*, 30, 65–6.

19. See Kalikrishna Ghosh, *Sekaler Chitra* (Calcutta: A.K. Ghosh, 1918), 27–8.

20. K. Ray, *Adhyaksha Saradaranjan Ray*, 9. On the judicial system of the early British period and the role of the sirastadar, see B.B. Misra, *The Indian Middle Classes: Their Growth in Modern Times* (London: Oxford University Press, 1961), 162–75, especially 170.

21. U. Ray, 'Amader Bansa-Parichay', 5.

22. P. Bhattacharya, *Masuar Moudgalya Gotriya Kayastha Bansabali*, section 2, 11. On tols in Mymensingh, see Kedarnath Majumdar, *Maimansingher Itihas*, 184–5.

23. K. Ghosh, *Sekaler Chitra*, 27.

24. Sukumar Ray, 'Upendrakishore Ray' [1916], in *Sukumar Sahityasamagra*, edited by Satyajit Ray and Partha Basu, 3 vols (Calcutta: Ananda Publishers, 1989), 3: 77.

25. K. Ray, *Adhyaksha Saradaranjan Ray*, 7.

26. Hemantakumar Adhya, *Upendrakishore Raychaudhuri* (Delhi: Sahitya Akademi, 1997), 4.

27. History is almost silent on Sarasibala, who died young, but Giribala seems to have been a woman of spirit and intelligence. Although she had not received an English education and lived mostly in Masua, she had strong—and very Victorian—views on art. In the 1920s, the artist Hemendranath Mazumdar (1898–1948), a distant relative of the Rays, had made a name for himself with his lush female nudes. Giribala, scandalized by the reproduction in a magazine of Mazumdar's painting of a bathing beauty, produced a pen and commanded one of her nieces to draw a blouse on the model. When the niece protested that the painting reflected contemporary tastes and the artist could not be blamed for it, she retorted: 'Nonsense! The artist's job is to foster good taste, not pander to the public's bad taste.' See Leela Majumdar, *Aar Konokhaney* (Calcutta: Mitra and Ghosh, 1968), 92. In another version of the story recounted later by the same author (Leela Majumdar, *Pakdandi* [Calcutta: Ananda, 1986], 109–10), we hear of Giribala subjecting the artist himself to the same homily. On Mazumdar and his context, see Partha Mitter, *The Triumph of Modernism: India's Artists and the Avant-garde, 1922–1947* (Delhi: Oxford University Press, 2007), 134–40; and Kamal Sarkar, *Bharater Bhaskar o Chitrasilpi* (Calcutta: Jogmaya, 1984), 240–2.

28. See A.F. Salahuddin Ahmed, *Social Ideas and Social Change in Bengal 1818–1835* (Calcutta: Papyrus, 2003), 200–26; Bellenoit, 'Paper, Pens', 357–8,

362; Bruce T. McCully, *English Education and the Origins of Indian Nationalism* (1940; reprint, Gloucester, MA: Peter Smith, 1966), 184–93; S.N. Mukherjee, 'Class, Caste and Politics in Calcutta', 41; and Veena Naregal, *Language Politics, Elites, and the Public Sphere* (Delhi: Permanent Black, 2001), 69.

29. Only 4.6 per cent of the entire population of Mymensingh were literate according to the Census of 1911, and the Muslim communities were reported to be particularly 'backward'. Among the chief purveyors of English education in the district was the Mymensingh Zillah School (established in 1853), where Saradaranjan and Upendrakishore studied. See Sachse, *Bengal District Gazetteers*, 137–8. It was only in 1866, three years after Upendrakishore's birth and nearly a decade after the establishment of Calcutta University, that Mymensingh had its first two university graduates and the next year, its first MA. People travelled from distant villages to behold these pioneers. See Kedarnath Majumdar, *Maimansingher Itihas*, 186–7.

30. See Sachse, *Bengal District Gazetteers*, 62.

31. Ashis Nandy, 'Satyajit Ray's Secret Guide to Exquisite Murders: Creativity, Social Criticism, and the Partitioning of the Self', in *The Savage Freud and Other Essays on Possible and Retrievable Selves* (Princeton: Princeton University Press, 1995), 237–66, at 245–6.

32. Subimal Ray, 'Saradaranjan Ray-er Kathha', in *Pretsiddher Kahini o Anyanya Rachana* (Calcutta: Asha Prakasani, 1978), 83–5, at 83–4 (my thanks to Indrani Majumdar for this text); and K. Ray, *Adhyaksha Saradaranjan Ray*, 27–9, 44, 62.

33. K. Ray, *Adhyaksha Saradaranjan Ray*, 31; and *Calcutta University Calendar, 1879–80* (Calcutta: Thacker, Spink, 1879), 219.

34. The Master of Arts degree of Calcutta University was granted at the time to any graduate who had passed a further Honours examination in one of five subjects. Saradaranjan's Honours examination was in Mathematics and he passed it in the second division. See *Calcutta University Calendar, 1879–80*, 38–41, 203.

35. Founded as a 'progressive' residential school for Muslims in 1875, the institution began to offer lower-level university courses from 1878 and, from 1881, degree courses. Before its affiliation with the University of Allahabad in 1885, it was affiliated with Calcutta University. In 1920, the College became the Aligarh Muslim University. See Safi Ahmad Kakorwi, ed., *Morison's History of the MAO College Aligarh* (Lucknow: Markaz-e-Adab-e-Urdu, 1988); and David Lelyveld, *Aligarh's First Generation: Muslim Solidarity in British India* (Princeton: Princeton University Press, 1978). On the question of Muslim 'indifference' to English education, see McCully, *English Education*, 180–4.

36. On the Muslim ambience of the College, see L.S.S. O'Malley, ed., *Modern India and the West: A Study of the Interaction of Their Civilizations* (London: Oxford University Press, 1941), 400.

FROM THE OLD WORLD TO THE NEW 67

37. Siddhartha Ghosh, 'Saradaranjan Ray o Cricket-ey Bangalir Haatey-
khori', in *Cricket Elo Banglaye*, edited by Siddhartha Ghosh (Calcutta: Subarnarekha, 2002), 57–67, at 60; and K. Ray, *Adhyaksha Saradaranjan Ray*, 21–2.
38. On the shortness of his stay at Aligarh, see Kakorwi, *Morison's History*, 81.
39. See the reminiscences of Jagadindranath Roy, the Maharaja of Natore,
in K. Ray, *Adhyaksha Saradaranjan Ray*, 54–5; and on the fame of Aligarh's
cricketers 'through India and beyond', see O'Malley, *Modern India and the West*, 400.
40. See Kakorwi, *Morison's History*, 19–20; and for an excellent analysis of
the importance of cricket in the Aligarh model, see Lelyveld, *Aligarh's First Generation*, 254–61.
41. The Principal, reportedly, had asked Saradaranjan to join the cricket
team pretending to be a student so that it could win a match against the students of a rival college. Saradaranjan, always known for his hot temper and
moral integrity, offended the principal by protesting against this deception
and, allegedly in retaliation, the principal subsequently forced him to teach
physics. It was not a subject that Saradaranjan was comfortable with and the
results, as his son put it delicately, were 'not satisfactory'. See K. Ray, *Adhyaksha
Saradaranjan Ray*, 31–2; S. Ghosh, 'Saradaranjan', 60–1; and Boria Majumdar,
Cricket in Colonial India, 1780–1947 (London: Routledge, 2008), 93.
42. The Metropolitan Institution grew out of the Calcutta Training School,
which had been founded in 1859 to provide English education to Hindu youth.
Vidyasagar took over the management in 1861, renamed the school as the
Metropolitan Institution, and, by 1879, converted it into a degree-level college
without employing any European lecturers. Within a few years, the excellent
performance of its students in the University examinations attracted many and
it became the largest college in Bengal. Vidyasagar invested a lot of his own
money in the College and provided free studentships to many poor students.
Saradaranjan's brother Muktidaranjan also worked at the Metropolitan as a pro-
fessor of mathematics. See Subalchandra Mitra, *Isvar Chandra Vidyasagar: A
Story of His Life and Work* (Calcutta: New Bengal Press, 1902), 430–59;
Santoshkumar Adhikari, *Vidyasagarer Sesh Swapna: Jatiya Sikshayatan
Metropolitan* (Calcutta: Vidyasagar Gabesana Kendra, 1992); Subodh Chandra
Sengupta, 'History of the College', in *Presidency College, Calcutta: Centenary
Volume, 1955* (Calcutta: West Bengal Government Press, 1956), 1–35, at 17;
Calcutta University Calendar, 1878–79 (Calcutta: Thacker, Spink, 1878), 140;
Bipinchandra Pal, *Memories of My Life and Times* (Calcutta: Bipinchandra Pal
Institute, 1973), 165; Asok Sen, *Iswar Chandra Vidyasagar and His Elusive
Milestones* (Calcutta: Riddhi-India, 1977), 73, 138–9; and Radharaman Mitra,
Kalikata Darpan, 2 vols (Calcutta: Subarnarekha, 1980–2004), 2 (2004), 57–60.
43. S. Ghosh, 'Saradaranjan', 61; and K. Ray, *Adhyaksha Saradaranjan
Ray*, 34–5, 44.

44.   S. Ghosh, 'Saradaranjan', 61.

45.   August 1895 advertisement in *The Statesman*, reproduced in Ranabir Ray Choudhury, *Early Calcutta Advertisements 1875–1925* (Bombay: Nachiketa, 1992), 309.

46.   K. Ray, *Adhyaksha Saradaranjan Ray*, 16–17. For an example of Saradaranjan's annotated editions of Sanskrit classics, see Saradaranjan Ray, *Bhavabhuti's Uttaracharitam with Sanskrit Commentary, English Translation, Critical and Explanatory Notes and Introduction*, 2nd ed., revised and enlarged by Kumudranjan Ray (Calcutta: The Editor, 1926). This annotated edition remained in print for years and the last known reprint was in 2008 from Bharatiya Kala Prakashan, Delhi.

47.   K. Ray, *Adhyaksha Saradaranjan Ray*, 17; and Nirad C. Chaudhuri, *The Autobiography of an Unknown Indian* (London: Hogarth Press, [1951] 1991), 109.

48.   For advertisements of the 'very best' footballs, 'all hand-made in our premises', and priced between four rupees six annas and nine rupees eight annas, see *The Bengalee*, 12 May 1909, 6. Imported footballs were also available: see *The Bengalee*, 17 June 1909, 7.

49.   See Hitendrakishore Raychaudhuri, *Upendrakishore o Masua Ray Paribarer Galpasalpa* (Calcutta: Firma K.L. Mukhopadhyay, 1984), 37; Siddhartha Ghosh, 'Upendrakishore: Shilpi o Karigar', *Ekshan*, 16, no. 6 (1984): 92; S. Ghosh, 'Saradaranjan', 63–4; and *A Report of the Indian Industrial and Agricultural Exhibition, Calcutta, 1906–07* (Calcutta: 'Industrial India' Office, n.d.), 156. For advertisments of 'our' fishing reels and the 'best reels from the best English makers', see *The Bengalee*, 17 June 1909, 7. See also S. Ghosh, 'Saradaranjan', 63–4. Beginning with the 1901 session of the Indian National Congress, a non-political exhibition of indigenous industrial and agricultural goods, funded largely by wealthy Indian donors, was held simultaneously with the annual Congress sessions. The December 1906–February 1907 exhibition in Calcutta covered a site of nearly 22 acres, hosted nearly a thousand exhibitors, and was visited by more than 300,000 Europeans and 'natives'. Despite its non-political nature, this exhibition gained from the impetus provided to Indian manufactures by the concurrent swadeshi movement. The winning entries were chosen by European as well as Indian judges, with 'the more important branches of indigenous industry' being submitted 'to European judgment' in the conviction that the 'just opinion of other people is always more valuable to us than our own good opinion of ourselves'. For the history of industrial and agricultural exhibitions in India, see Glyn Barlow, *Industrial India*, 2nd ed. (Madras: Natesan, 1911), 62–80.

50.   *The Bengalee*, 8 January 1908, 6, repeated in many subsequent issues (e.g., 30 January 1908, 7).

51.   Some of the more sophisticated fish-hooks designed by him had to be produced, however, in Britain. See K. Ray, *Adhyaksha Saradaranjan Ray*, 17.

52. Satyajit Ray, Introduction to Siddhartha Ghosh, 'Jantrarasik H. Bose', *Ekshan*, 16, nos 3–4 (1983): 53.

53. H. Raychaudhuri, *Upendrakishore*, 34.

54. See S. Ghosh, 'Saradaranjan', 64.

55. K. Ray, *Adhyaksha Saradaranjan Ray*, 46.

56. S. Ghosh, 'Upendrakishore', 54.

57. See B. Majumdar, *Cricket in Colonial India*, 74–104; and on the Bengali preoccupation with physical feebleness, see John Rosselli, 'The Self-Image of Effeteness: Physical Education and Nationalism in Nineteenth-Century Bengal', *Past and Present*, 86 (February 1980): 121–48; Mrinalini Sinha, *Colonial Masculinity: The 'Manly Englishman' and the 'Effeminate Bengali' in the Late Nineteenth Century* (Manchester: Manchester University Press, 1995); and Indira Chowdhury, *The Frail Hero and Virile History: Gender and the Politics of Culture in Colonial Bengal* (Delhi: Oxford University Press, 1998).

58. K. Ray, *Adhyaksha Saradaranjan Ray*, 57.

59. In 1911, Vidyasagar College even established six fairly substantial monetary prizes for excellence in cricket. See B. Majumdar, *Cricket in Colonial India*, 87.

60. K. Ray, *Adhyaksha Saradaranjan Ray*, 55; B. Majumdar, *Cricket in Colonial India*, 84.

61. Bratati Chakravarty, *Bangla Shishu Sahitya Charcha: Ray Paribar* (Calcutta: Dey Book Store, 1997), 34. At least one commentator, the journalist Ramananda Chatterji's son Kedarnath, thought that Kuladaranjan, who was a member of the Natore team, acquired greater fame than his brothers in the cricketing world. See Kedarnath Chattopadhyay, 'Satabarshik Sraddhhanjali: Upendrakishore', *Vishwa Bharati Patrika*, 20, no. 2 (1963 [Kartik-Poush 1370 BE]): 117. Kuladaranjan was also pioneering in taking some of his female relatives to watch a game of cricket. Imagining that brother Saradaranjan, who was playing, would object to this he had refrained from informing him about it. See B. Chakravarty, *Bangla Shishu Sahitya Charcha*, 91.

62. 'The Late Mr U. Ray', *Modern Review*, 19, no. 1 (January 1916): 105; and Kedarnath Chattopadhyay, 'Satabarshik Sraddhhanjali', 117.

63. B. Chakravarty, *Bangla Shishu Sahitya Charcha*, 32–3.

64. K. Ray, *Adhyaksha Saradaranjan Ray*, 39–40.

65. N.C. Chaudhuri, *Autobiography of an Unknown Indian*, 295.

66. K. Ray, *Adhyaksha Saradaranjan Ray*, 49.

67. K. Ray, *Adhyaksha Saradaranjan Ray*, 58.

68. Upendrakishore Raychaudhuri, 'Ranjit Sinhaji', in *Cricket Elo Banglaye*, 18. On Ranjitsinhji (1872–1933) and his multiple contexts, see Satadru Sen, *Migrant Races: Empire, Identity and K. S. Ranjitsinhji* (Manchester: Manchester University Press, 2004). On Ranjitsinhji's visit to Calcutta in 1895, when he was feted by thousands of spectators, see B. Majumdar, *Cricket in Colonial India*, 86.

69. L. Majumdar, *Pakdandi*, 115; and Rosselli, 'Self-Image of Effeteness'.

70. See B. Majumdar, *Cricket in Colonial India*, 82–3, 88–9.

71. November 1899 advertisement reproduced in Ghosh, *Cricket Elo Banglaye*, 126.

72. Rosselli, 'Self-Image of Effeteness'.

73. It is not known when he married but he and his wife, Sasimukhi, were to have four sons: Manoranjan, Rohiniranjan, Sudhiranjan, and Kumudranjan; and four daughters: Susama, Surama, Suprabha, and Suhasa. Kumudranjan Ray became an ayurvedic physician and seems to have served as his father's literary executor. Scarcely anything is known about the other three sons and the four daughters. See P. Bhattacharya, *Masuar Moudgalya Gotriya Kayastha Bansabali*, section 1, 3.

74. L. Majumdar, *Aar Konokhaney*, 93; and L. Majumdar, *Pakdandi*, 159.

75. K. Ray, *Adhyaksha Saradaranjan Ray*, 41–2.

76. H. Raychaudhuri, *Upendrakishore*, 34.

77. K. Ray, *Adhyaksha Saradaranjan Ray*, 19. Muktidaranjan was devoted to his elder brother but he was of a far more genial temperament than Saradaranjan. He was very approachable and spent hours chatting with his child-relatives, even at Upendrakishore's Brahmo household. It is not known, however, whether he ate with them. See H. Raychaudhuri, *Upendrakishore*, 36–7.

78. Subimal Ray, 'Saradaranjan Ray-er Kathha', 83–5, at 85; and K. Ray, *Adhyaksha Saradaranjan Ray*, 25.

79. K. Ray, *Adhyaksha Saradaranjan Ray*, 38–9; and B. Chakravarty, *Bangla Shishu Sahitya Charcha*, 32. When his brother Upendrakishore fell terminally ill in Giridi in 1915, Saradaranjan was also in the neighbourhood and prescribed homoeopathic medicines for his brother. See Adhya, *Upendrakishore*, 33.

80. L. Majumdar, *Pakdandi*, 136, 155–6. Muktidaranjan was married to Kundalini Dutta and they had six sons (Sailajaranjan, Haimajaranjan, Neerajaranjan, Indujaranjan, Khirajaranjan, and Nripajaranjan) and four daughters (Pritilata, Charulata, Asrulata, and Snehalata). Sailajaranjan was an advocate and both Haimajaranjan and Neerajaranjan were engineers. All three were good cricket and football players. See P. Bhattacharya, *Masuar Moudgalya Gotriya Kayastha Bansabali*, section 1, 4. Saradaranjan and Muktidaranjan initially lived under the same roof with their families but their wives did not get along and ultimately, Saradaranjan advised Muktidaranjan to set up his own household. See Mitra, *Kalikata Darpan*, 1: 99. Of Saradaranjan's brothers, only Kamadaranjan (Upendrakishore) and Kuladaranajan (1873–1950) formally embraced Brahmoism but Pramadaranjan (1874–1947), although he did not formally convert, married in the Brahmo way and lived like a fairly strict Brahmo. See Adhya, *Upendrakishore*, 35.

81. See S. Ray, *Bhavabhuti's Uttaracharitam*, vii–viii.

82. K. Ray, *Adhyaksha Saradaranjan Ray*, 22.

83. K. Ray, *Adhyaksha Saradaranjan Ray*, 45.

84. K. Ray, *Adhyaksha Saradaranjan Ray*, 48–9.

85. K. Ray, *Adhyaksha Saradaranjan Ray*, 46.

86. See Ashis Nandy, 'Satyajit Ray's Secret Guide to Exquisite Murders: Creativity, Social Criticism, and the Partitioning of the Self', in *The Savage Freud and Other Essays on Possible and Retrievable Selves* (Princeton: Princeton University Press, 1995), 237–66.

87. S. Ghosh, 'Upendrakishore', 49–50; and Marie Seton, *Portrait of a Director: Satyajit Ray*, expanded edition (Delhi: Penguin, 2003), 13.

88. U. Ray, 'Amader Bansa-Parichay', 5.

89. Meredith Borthwick, *The Changing Role of Women in Bengal, 1849–1905* (Princeton: Princeton University Press, 1984), 151. It was such a potent threat that it was not unknown for childless wives to encourage their husbands to take a second wife. The first, childless wife of Bipinchandra Pal's father, for example, persuaded her husband to marry for a second time and even found an appropriate bride for him. See B. Pal, *Sattar Vatsar*, 29.

90. His first two wives had both died without giving him a son (H. Raychaudhuri, *Upendrakishore*, 7). A British official of the early 20th century observed that the bulk of the land in Mymensingh district was 'held by a few big zamindars' and 'the most striking feature in the histories of these families is the large part played by adoption in providing heirs'. See Sachse, *Bengal District Gazetteers*, 61.

91. Adhya, *Sukumar Ray*, 8–9; and H. Raychaudhuri, *Upendrakishore*, 4.

92. Leela Majumdar, *Upendrakishore Raychaudhuri*, translated by Syed Kausar Jamal (Delhi: National Book Trust, 1993), 10.

93. H. Raychaudhuri, *Upendrakishore*, 7.

94. On Eden's Mymensingh trip, see Kedarnath Majumdar, *Maimansingher Itihas*, 224.

95. Sukumar Ray, 'Upendrakishore Ray', 77.

96. 'The Late Mr U. Ray', 103. Although unsigned, the obituaries in this magazine were all written by the magazine's editor Ramananda Chatterji.

97. The entrance examination was conducted by the Calcutta University and held once a year in Calcutta and various other centres across the Bengal Presidency. Candidates were examined in English, one vernacular language, History, Geography and Mathematics. See *The Calcutta University Calendar 1877–78* (Calcutta: Thacker, Spink, 1877), 31–2.

98. Sukumar Ray, 'Upendrakishore Ray', 78; and 'The Late Mr U. Ray', 103.

99. See A. Dutta, *Saracchandra*, 1–2, 12, 31, 75–6, 87, 90, 124, 131.

100. See Srinath Chanda, *Brahmo Samajey Challis Batsar* (Dhaka: Bharat Mahila Press, 1913), 76–7, 104–6, 237; and K. Ghosh, *Sekaler Chitra*, 48–51. Sivanath Sastri remarked: 'Newcomers found shelter there; persecuted people found refuge; and Samaj workers held their conversation meetings in his

room.' See Sivanath Sastri, *History of the Brahmo Samaj* [1911–12], 2nd ed., 2 vols in 1 (Calcutta: Sadharan Brahmo Samaj, 1974), 416.

101. Their selfless labours, we are told, convinced many orthodox Hindus to give up some of their prejudices against Brahmos. See Gaganchandra Home, *Jiban-Smriti* (Calcutta: Privately Published, 1929), 21–2; and S. Chanda, *Brahmo Samajey*, 106–7. I am deeply grateful to Gaganchandra Home's grandson Anikendra Home for providing me with a copy of Home's autobiography.

102. S. Chanda, *Brahmo Samajey*, 108–9, 117, 140–2, 155–7; B. Pal, *Memories of My Life*, 226; A. Dutta, *Saracchandra*, 81–2 and appendix. But Ray was not simply a philanthropist—even if in a small way, he was an entrepreneur of integrity and vision. Apart from running the Brahmo Shop, he also started an ink-manufacturing business in Calcutta in 1877. See A. Dutta, *Saracchandra*, 83.

103. On the prevalence of Brahmoism among schoolteachers of Mymensingh, see S. Chanda, *Brahmo Samajey*, 137, 222, 237. For vivid accounts of the Brahmo efflorescence in Mymensingh, see Krishnakumar Mitra, *Atmacharit*, 2nd ed. (Calcutta: Sadharan Brahmo Samaj, 1975), 47–72; and Kedarnath Majumdar, *Maimansingher Itihas*, 190–4.

104. Home, *Jiban-Smriti*, 3–9. Such stories are not to be heard from Upendrakishore's hagiographers or even his son Sukumar, who merely state that Home had been asked to draw Upendrakishore into the Brahmo fold by Saratchandra Ray, who had been greatly impressed by Upendrakishore and thought that the boy would be a great man one day. See Sukumar Ray, 'Upendrakishore Ray', 78; and Kedarnath Chattopadhyay, 'Satabarshik Sraddhhanjali', 117.

105. Home, *Jiban-Smriti*, 9.

106. As a western Indian judge would observe, 'The Hindu religion has intertwined itself with the customs of the people in almost every phase of life's activity from the cradle to the grave. Every action is prescribed or proscribed with the sanction of religious merit or demerit ... those who are social reformers are at the same time more or less religious and political reformers.' See C.V. Vaidya, *On the History of Hindu Social Reform—Agitation and the Proper Methods of Carrying It On* (Poona: Arya-Bhushan Press, 1890), 18–19, 68.

107. On Rammohan's interest in Unitarianism and his active involvement with Unitarian ministers, see Sastri, *History of the Brahmo Samaj*, 22–4. Dipesh Chakrabarty has attributed 'the growth of something like a "social conscience"' among the younger Brahmos of the 1860s to their 'own private sense of sin' and their consequent urge to save fallen souls. Dipesh Chakrabarty, 'Sasipada Banerjee: A Study in the Nature of the First Contact of the Bengali Bhadralok with the Working Classes of Bengal', *Indian Historical Review*, 2, no. 2 (January 1976): 339–64, at 342 (my thanks to Barun Chattopadhyay for referring me to this article).

108. Kanailal Chattopadhyay, *Brahmo Reform Movement: Some Social and Economic Aspects* (Calcutta: Papyrus, 1983), 163–4. Sen's lecture tours around India spread the Brahmo message very effectively and although Brahmoism

would eventually come to be confined largely to Bengal, his efforts led to a brief period of Brahmo influence across the subcontinent. See Kenneth W. Jones, *Socio-Religious Reform Movements in British India* (Cambridge: Cambridge University Press, 1989), 35; Sophia Dobson Collet, ed., *Brahmo Year-Book for 1876* (London: Williams and Norgate, 1876), 13–14; B. Pal, *Memories of My Life*, 380–1; and S. Natarajan, *A Century of Social Reform in India*, 2nd ed. (Bombay: Asia Publishing House, 1962), 10–11.

109. Sastri, *History of the Brahmo Samaj*, 397; and Muntasir Mamun, *Unish Satakey Purbabanger Samaj (1857–1905)* (Dhaka: Samaj Nirikshan Kendra, 1986), 159–90. For personal accounts of the growth of the movement in East Bengal and its persecution by Hindus, see Bangachandra Roy, *Amar Jiban-Alekhya* (Dhaka: Umeshchandra Sen, 1910); S. Chanda, *Brahmo Samajey*; K. Ghosh, *Sekaler Chitra*; and A. Dutta, *Saracchandra*. The influence of East Bengali Brahmos was not confined to their home region. As Sivanath Sastri acknowledged, 'much of the strength of Calcutta Brahmoism has been due to the presence of East Bengal men amongst us'. See Sastri, *History of the Brahmo Samaj*, 391.

110. Collet, *Brahmo Year-Book for 1876*, 27–8, 31; Collet, *Brahmo Year-Book for 1881*, 104–8. Propagated in the mid-1850s by schoolmasters and a handful of lawyers and low-ranking civil servants with the support of a liberal zamindar, Mymensingh Brahmoism was initially confined mainly to worship according to the conservative rites of Debendranath Tagore's Adi Brahmo Samaj. But after Keshab Sen's visit to Dhaka and Mymensingh in 1865–6 Mymensingh Brahmos gravitated towards Sen's radical group, the Brahmo Samaj of India. A group of older schoolboys formally established a 'Branch' Samaj in 1867, probably the first to be established by students and more interested in the typically Brahmo projects of character-building and self-improvement than its parent, the Mymensingh Brahmo Samaj. See S. Chanda, *Brahmo Samajey*, 39, 41.

111. See Bipinchandra Pal, *Nabajuger Bangla* (Calcutta: Yugajatri, 1955), 184.

112. N.C. Chaudhuri, *Autobiography of an Unknown Indian*, 210–11.

113. See Sumit Sarkar, 'The "Women's Question" in Nineteenth-Century Bengal', in *Women and Culture*, edited by Kumkum Sangari and Sudesh Vaid (Bombay: SNDT Women's University Research Centre for Women's Studies, 1985), 157–72, at 164.

114. N.C. Chaudhuri, *Autobiography of an Unknown Indian*, 217.

115. 'Fathers have solemnly vowed to desert their sons [in rural East Bengal],' reported the *Indian Mirror*, 'brothers to forsake brothers, and relations to disown their nearest kinsmen.' Excerpted in Collet, *Brahmo Year-Book for 1876*, 26–7. The ostracism was so serious that many Brahmos decided to return to the orthodox faith. In some families, converts were secretly given roots and herbs with a reputation for bringing recalcitrant minds under control and stories were told of young men who had been driven insane by such 'remedies'. See S. Chanda, *Brahmo Samajey*, 24–5, 28–36, 85, 95–8; A. Dutta,

Saracchandra, 49–51; and Bijaykrishna Goswami, *Brahmo Samajer Bartaman Abastha ebang Amar Jibaney Brahmo Samajer Parikshita Bisay* [1872] (Calcutta: Indo-Overseas Publications, 1982), 18–21. On Harikishore Raychaudhuri's prominence in the orthodox campaign against Brahmoism, see Kedarnath Majumdar, *Maimansingher Itihas*, 191–2. On the size of the Mymensingh Brahmo community, see A. Dutta, *Saracchandra*, appendix.

116. U. Ray, 'Amader Bansa-Parichay', 5. Harikishore's biological son, Narendrakishore, although very close to Upendrakishore, does not seem to have felt any attraction towards Brahmoism and remained a staunch Hindu like his father. See Manasi Dasgupta, *Upendrakishore Raychaudhuri (1863–1915)* (Calcutta: Bangiya Sahitya Parishat, 2004), 5.

117. Once Harikishore had retired for the night, Upendrakishore would play his flute to indicate that the coast was clear for Home to visit. On many occasions, however, the family discovered Home's presence and turfed him out. See Home, *Jiban-Smriti*, 9.

118. See, for instance, Adhya, *Upendrakishore*, 10.

119. Home, *Jiban-Smriti*, 9.

120. Benedict Anderson, *Imagined Communities: Reflections on the Origin and Spread of Nationalism*, 2nd ed. (London: Verso, 1991), 121.

121. *Calcutta University Commission, 1917–19: Report*, 13 vols (Calcutta: Superintendent of Government Printing, 1919), 1: 413.

122. L. Majumdar, *Upendrakishore*, 10. Upendrakishore passed his entrance examination in 1879 in the first division. See Calcutta University Calendar (UCC), 1881–82, 260. That was also the year when his father Kalinath passed away—it is known that Saradaranjan Ray, then doing his MA in Calcutta, went to Masua for a last glimpse of his father and for conducting the funerary rites. There is no evidence that Upendrakishore was present. On Kalinath Ray's death, see K. Ray, *Adhyaksha Saradaranjan Ray*, 30, 65–6.

123. See Krishna Chandra Roy, *High Education and the Present Position of the Graduates in Arts and Law of the Calcutta University* (Calcutta: Sanskrit Press Depository, 1882), 1; and McCully, *English Education*, 131–75.

124. See *Calcutta University Commission, 1917–19: Report*, 1: 48.

125. Candidates for the First Examination in the Arts (which could be taken after two years of approved study after passing the entrance examination) were examined on English and one other non-vernacular language, history, mathematics, logic, and either psychology or chemistry. A candidate who had studied for another two academic years after the 'First Arts' at an affiliated institution was eligible to sit for the University's Bachelor of Arts (BA) examination. For details, see UCC, 1881–82, 33–7. For Upendrakishore's 'First Arts' result, see UCC, 1882–83, 95; and for his BA result, UCC, 1884–85, 97 (the lists of graduates were separately paginated with the page numbers in bold). A candidate obtaining between 180–230 marks (out of 500) was placed in the third division; to be placed in the first

division, one needed a minimum of 280 marks. See Krishna Chandra Roy, *High Education*, 10.

126. Presidency College was described as the 'centre and heart' of the University in *Calcutta University Commission, 1917–19: Report*, 1: 415.

127. See Subalchandra Mitra, *Isvar Chandra Vidyasagar*, 455.

128. S.C. Sengupta, 'History of the College', 17.

129. Prafullachandra Ray, *Life and Experiences of a Bengali Chemist* (Calcutta: Chuckervertty, Chatterjee & Co., 1932), 47.

130. 'The Late Mr U. Ray', 104.

131. Dasgupta, *Upendrakishore*, 14–16. Of the 1589 students who graduated from Calcutta University with an arts degree between 1857 and 1882, 526 entered government service, 581 trained in law, and 470 were 'largely employed as teachers in the colleges and high schools'. See *Calcutta University Commission, 1917–19: Report*, 1: 49; 3: 24–6. Nationalism in India, it has often been observed, was largely the creation of lawyers. Bipinchandra Pal, a nationalist but not a lawyer, thought that the dominance of legal professionals in early nationalism had created a veritable 'Vakil Raj'. See B. Pal, *Memories of My Life*, 395. On the popularity of legal courses at Presidency College, see Benjamin Zachariah, Subhas Ranjan Chakraborti and Rajat Kanta Ray, 'Presidency College, Calcutta: An Unfinished History', in *Knowledge, Power and Politics: Educational Institutions in India*, edited by Mushirul Hasan (Delhi: Roli Books, 1998), 304–88, at 316. This was not unique to Bengal. In nineteenth-century Bombay, too, university law courses were very popular and it was widely recognized that 'a legal career offered the best prospects to a young man aspiring to rise in the world'. See Christine Dobbin, *Urban Leadership in Western India: Politics and Communities in Bombay City, 1840–1885* (Oxford: Oxford University Press, 1972), 44–6.

132. Dasgupta, *Upendrakishore Raychaudhuri*, 14–16. It is harder, however, to find support for Dasgupta's subsidiary claim that Upendrakishore left Presidency College because he wanted to study science. Early in the history of the Hindu College, the Government had established a chair in experimental philosophy 'and by 1824, funds had been released for the purchase of necessary scientific apparatus. The instruction, however, was in the form of lecture-demonstrations, not hands-on practical classes'. See Zachariah et al., 'Presidency College', 309–10 and 312. The BA curriculum at Presidency College included chemistry, zoology, and geology from 1863 and from 1875, practical classes in chemistry were offered by Alexander Pedler. See Prafullachandra Ray, *Life and Experiences of a Bengali Chemist*, 83; and Roy M MacLeod, 'Pedler, Sir Alexander (1849–1918)', *Oxford Dictionary of National Biography* (Oxford: Oxford University Press, 2004) (http://www.oxforddnb.com/view/article/48706, accessed on 1 September 2014). Upendrakishore did study chemistry at Presidency College with Pedler but all we know about his activities is confined to his popularity as a singer. Ruchi Ram Sahni, a student

from the Punjab who attended the same classes, recalled Upendrakishore's musical voice and charming personality in his memoirs, adding that as soon as Pedler's class was over, the students would press Upendrakishore to sing: 'Sometimes quite for a quarter of an hour the laboratory used to be thrilled with his songs.' See Narender K. Sehgal and Subodh Mahanti, eds, *Memoirs of Ruchi Ram Sahni: Pioneer of Science Popularisation in Punjab* (Delhi: Vigyan Prasar, 1994), 10–11. My thanks to Soumen Paul for this reference. The other sciences do not seem to have received comparable attention, however. Physics had been taught at the College from 1856 but it was only in 1897 that 'a photographic and magnetic laboratory' was set up for use by the physics department. See *Presidency College: Centenary Volume*, 15–18, 19–20, 53, 57–8. Jagadischandra Bose, who was appointed in 1885 as the first 'native' Professor of Physics at Presidency College, recalled how, in his initial years at the College, he had no laboratory worth the name, no sophisticated equipment, and no colleague with whom he could collaborate in his research. See J.C. Bose, 'The Uphill Way' [undated], in *J.C. Bose Speaks*, edited by Dibakar Sen and Ajoy K. Chakraborty (Calcutta: Puthipatra, 1986), 38–43, at 39–40; and Subrata Dasgupta, *Jagadis Chandra Bose and the Indian Response to Western Science* (Oxford: Oxford University Press, 1999), 55, 71–2. Nevertheless, the scientific training at Presidency was far better than at any other nineteenth-century college and unlikely to have been matched, let alone surpassed, by the Metropolitan Institution.

133. H. Raychaudhuri, *Upendrakishore*, 10–11.

134. Harikishore's widow, Rajlakshmi, reportedly disregarded the will and divided the estate equally between Upendrakishore and her own son, Narendrakishore. The latter, too, agreed to this. See H. Raychaudhuri, *Upendrakishore*, 10–11.

135. This was reported by his son Sukumar Ray on the basis of Upendrakishore's diary for 1880. The diary is now lost but see Sukumar Ray, 'Upendrakishore Ray', 78. Dwarkin's had been established by Dwarakanath Ghosh in 1875. Ghosh, a music-lover and formerly an instrument restorer for the British firm Harold & Co., had met and befriended Upendrakishore early on and it was, in fact, Upendrakishore who had suggested the name 'Dwarkin' for the business—because, reportedly, he thought that a Western-sounding name would suggest high quality to the Calcutta elite. Initially concentrating on selling and repairing imported instruments, Ghosh gradually went into manufacturing and the 'Dwarkin-Flute', a hand-operated harmonium introduced in 1887, won high praise from the cognoscenti and became extremely popular with professional musicians as well as amateurs. Upendrakishore gradually became Ghosh's close friend and advisor and provided Dwarkin's with a testimonial in 1889, offering 'every praise for the successful manner in which you have been trying to meet the want of an instrument really suited to the Indian climate'. See Jnanprakash Ghosh, 'Dwarkiner Katha', *Desh*, Annual

Binodan Number (1980): 143–50, at 145–7 (my thanks to Debasis Mukhopadhyay for this article); and Michael S. Kinnear, *The Gramophone Company's First Indian Recordings, 1899–1908* (London: Sangam, 1994), 35–6. On the propensity of Indian businesses to use English-sounding names, see Barlow, *Industrial India*, 201. Upendrakishore, incidentally, also appeared as a model in a Dwarkin's advertisement that showed him playing the 'India Dulcetina (Harmonium)'. See *The Hindoo Patriot*, 17 March 1894, 4.

136. Dasgupta, *Upendrakishore Raychaudhuri (1863–1915)*, 6; and B. Chakravarty, *Bangla Shishu Sahitya Charcha*, 41.

137. Narendrakishore, his son later wrote, 'always regretted that he could not go to college' but he does not seem to have harboured any lasting resentment towards Upendrakishore. In adult life, Narendrakishore, an orthodox Hindu like his father Harikishore, would never dine with his Brahmo brother—although he permitted his children to do so—but in every other respect, the two were on excellent terms. Upendrakishore's friends would sometimes taunt Narendrakishore for his orthodox ways but Upendrakishore would always defend his brother's right to choose his faith and lifestyle. See H. Raychaudhuri, *Upendrakishore*, 19–21, 27–8, 115–16. Upendrakishore seems to have had an innate capacity to sail through turbulence and controversy without permanently antagonizing his critics. His son Sukumar attributed this to his unshakeable integrity and sweet personality, while the obituary in the *Modern Review* remarked upon the combination of 'a very affectionate heart' and 'a retiring disposition' with 'a sturdy independence of character'. See Sukumar Ray, 'Upendrakishore Ray', 79; and 'The Late Mr U. Ray', 105.

138. Few of Upendrakishore's photographs have survived. Some were printed in the *Penrose Annual* from his own blocks to illustrate his articles. See, for example, the photographs entitled 'I'm Here' and 'Storm and Sunshine', unpaginated plates accompanying William Gamble, 'The Editor's Notes', *Penrose's Pictorial Annual: The Process Year Book*, 1904–5, 1–4; and Siddhartha Ghosh, *Chhabi Tola: Bangalir Photography Charcha* (Calcutta: Ananda, 1988), 132. The two little girls in these pictures, incidentally, were the two daughters of Kuladaranjan Ray. Upendrakishore's photograph of the fiery nationalist Arabinda Ghosh—freshly acquitted from a terrorist charge—was commissioned by Ramananda Chatterji and published in *Probasi*, 9 (1316 BE [1909]), no. 2 (Jaistha), facing p. 140 (http://archiv.ub.uni-heidelberg.de/savi-fadok/volltexte/2009/953, accessed on 25 August 2014). On other existing photographs by Upendrakishore, see Siddhartha Ghosh, *Karigari Kalpana o Bangali Udyog* (Calcutta: Dey's, 1988), 65–6.

139. The name of the business was changed in 1910 to U. Ray & Sons. Typically, however, Upendrakishore never completely severed his roots. In many of his Bengali writings, he continued to call himself Upendrakishore Raychaudhuri. See S. Ghosh, *Karigari Kalpana*, 60, 87, 101. Later, this use of two surnames, which persisted among his children, would cause problems

for Sukumar Ray when he visited England for training in printing technology. See Satyajit Ray and Partha Basu, eds, *Sukumar Sahityasamagra*, 3 vols (Calcutta: Ananda Publishers, 1989), 3: 222.

140. D.M. Bose, 'Abala Bose: Her Life and Times', *Modern Review*, 119, no. 6 (June 1966): 441–56, at 442.

141. See Saratchandra Raha, 'Kalikatar Chhatrabas', *Bharati*, 22 (1305 BE/1898): 598–611, at 602.

142. After moving to Calcutta, Upendrakishore had lodged briefly at a house on Ratu Sarkar Lane. Many young men from Mymensingh, including Saradaranjan Ray, lived there during their student days and the house had come to be known as the 'Mymensingh mess'. See Adhya, *Upendrakishore*, 10; and K. Ray, *Adhyaksha Saradaranjan Ray*, 64. When they came to Calcutta, students from the interior often resided with others from their community or region in a 'mess'. Nirad Chaudhuri, who had himself lived in a Calcutta mess in the years leading up to the First World War, considered the messes to be 'little colonies in Calcutta of the different districts of East Bengal'. See N.C. Chaudhuri, *Autobiography of an Unknown Indian*, 296. For an obviously incomplete list of such messes, see B. Pal, *Memories of My Life*, 162–3; and for a vivid picture of mess life, see Dwijendranath Basu, 'Students' Mess', *Bharati* 22 (1305 BE [1898]): 773–97.

143. Home, *Jiban-Smriti*, 13–14.

144. At some point, *Sanjibani* became a daily—the precise date is unknown because most issues of the paper have perished—but reverted to weekly publication from January 1906. See Kanailal Chattopadhyay, ed., *Samayikpatrey Samajchitra: Krishnakumar Mitra Sampadita 'Sanjibani'* (Calcutta: Dey's, 1989), 412.

145. See the advertisement of *Sanjibani* in *The Bengalee*, 26 May 1883, 249; and the description in Home, *Jiban-Smriti*, 13–14. The advertisement supports the view of Bipinchandra Pal that Krishnakumar Mitra and Dwarakanath Ganguli had been regular contributors to *Bangabasi* (founded 1881) and founded *Sanjibani* after falling out with the proprietor of *Bangabasi* for ideological reasons. See B. Pal, *Memories of My Life*, 349–50, 359; R.L. Ghosh, 'The Late Babu Dvarakanath Ganguli', *Amrita Bazar Patrika*, 3 July 1898, 6 (my thanks to Barun Chattopadhyay for a copy of this obituary); and Amiya P. Sen, *Hindu Revivalism in Bengal, 1872–1905: Some Essays in Interpretation* (Delhi: Oxford University Press, 1993), 255–6. *Bangabasi* eventually turned into a hugely popular Hindu revivalist paper while *Sanjibani* came to represent the radical voice of the Sadharan Brahmo Samaj.

146. Bipinchandra Pal, 'Krishna Kumar Mitra', in *Character Sketches* (Calcutta: Yugajatri, 1957), 234–43, at 235; and B. Pal, *Memories of My Life*, 350. It supported the Indian National Congress when it was established in 1885 and played a prominent role in the movement against the partition of Bengal in 1905. *Sanjibani* had been calling for the regeneration of Indian industry from the 1880s and it was Krishnakumar Mitra who, at the time of the 1905

partition, first suggested on the pages of *Sanjibani* that Bengalis boycott British products in protest. Historian Bipan Chandra described it as the 'most important and consistent champion' of the swadeshi movement in Bengal. See Bipan Chandra, *The Rise and Growth of Economic Nationalism in India: Economic Policies of Indian National Leadership, 1880–1905* (Delhi: People's Publishing House, 1966), 134; and Sumit Sarkar, *The Swadeshi Movement in Bengal 1903–1908*, new ed. (Ranikhet: Permanent Black, 2010), 32, 219, 244.

147. *Sanjibani*'s support of the swadeshi cause, too, was tempered by Brahmo propriety. While supporting Rabindranath Tagore's call for all Bengalis, regardless of religion or caste, to tie *rakhis* (wristbands) on one another as a symbolic refusal to accept the partition of Bengal, *Sanjibani* emphasized that men should tie rakhis only on men and women only on other women. See Kanailal Chattopadhyay, appendix to Krishnakumar Mitra, *Atmacharit*, 2nd ed. (Calcutta: Sadharan Brahmo Samaj, 1975), 330–4.

148. See Sastri, *History of the Brahmo Samaj*, 288–9, 534–9. Sastri would edit *Sakha* for two years (1885–7) after Pramadacharan Sen's untimely death at 27, and then start *Mukul*, his own magazine for children and adolescents in 1895. For a description of Pramadacharan Sen's last days, see Home, *Jiban-Smriti*, 19–20.

149. See Sunil Das, 'Pramadacharan: Sakha o Bhimer Kapal', in *Bhimer Kapal*, edited by Sunil Das (Calcutta: Ananda, 1981), 7–21; and Sivanath Sastri, 'Swargiya Pramadacharan Sen', *Sakha*, 3, no. 7 (July 1885): 97–102 (http://archiv.ub.uni-heidelberg.de/savifadok/volltexte/2009/895, accessed on 7 June 2013).

150. Sunil Das, 'Pramadacharan', 13–14; and 'Patrikar Katha', in *Sakha, Sakha o Sathi*, edited by Aruna Chattopadhyay (Calcutta: Kallol, 2002), 3–8, at 6.

151. Kedarnath Chattopadhyay, 'Satabarshik Sraddhhanjali', 108. Upendrakishore's first contribution was an essay on the house fly, which came out in 1883 when he was still in college. Even at this early stage, Upendrakishore revealed a gift for explaining difficult subjects lucidly, a skill that won him much admiration in his later life. See Punyalata Chakrabarti, *Chhelebelar Dinguli* (1958; reprint, Calcutta: Newscript, 1981), 50. From the fifth issue onwards, the magazine began to publish the work of other contributors and gradually, a distinct group of writers coalesced around *Sakha*. Upendrakishore remained a vital presence, often contributing multiple pieces to the same issue. See Amal Pal, 'Kishorpathhya Patrikar Suchana o *Sakha*', in *Kishorpathhya Patrikapanchak: Suchi-Sankalan*, edited by Amal Pal (Calcutta: Dey's, 2007), 13–41, at 15, 18–19.

152. See 'Singha o Matal', *Sakha* 1, no. 9 (September 1883): 138–40; 'Khola-Bhaatir Phol', *Sakha*, no. 11 (November 1883): 165–7; 'Dhumpaan', *Sakha*, no. 3 (March 1883): 45–7; 'Poshak', *Sakha*, no. 6 (June 1883): 950. Although not outwardly religious, some readers suspected *Sakha* of harbouring Brahmo propagandist ambitions. After one boy cancelled its subscription in 1885 on

those grounds, Sivanath Sastri, who was then the editor, forcefully denied the allegation, declaring that the magazine's sole aim was to 'benefit boys and girls' of all faiths. See Editorial, *Sakha*, 3, no. 1 (January 1885): 1–3, at 2. All available at http://archiv.ub.uni-heidelberg.de/savifadok/view/schriftenreihen/sr-61.html?lang=en (accessed on 7 June 2013).

153.   For a discussion of previous attempts at writing novels for children in Bengali, see Sunil Das, 'Pramadacharan', 18–20.

154.   The novel was serialized in *Sakha*, 1 (1883): 2–4, 21–4, 39–40, 60–1, 66–9, 81–3, 97–100, 113–15, 129–32 and 145–9 (http://archiv.ub.uni-heidelberg. de/savifadok/volltexte/2009/893, accessed on 7 June 2013).

155.   *Sakha-o-Sathi*, 1, no. 10 (October 1883): 149 (http://archiv.ub.uni-heidelberg.de/savifadok/volltexte/2009/893, accessed on 7 June 2013).

156.   '*Sakha* Poribar Kayekti Niyam' (1884), reprinted in A. Chattopadhyay, *Sakha, Sakha o Sathi*, 276–8, at 277–8.

157.   See Bipinchandra Pal, 'Surendrababur Karabaas', *Sakha* 1, no. 6 (June 1883): 88–91 (http://archiv.ub.uni-heidelberg.de/savifadok/volltexte/2009/ 893, accessed on 7 June 2013). Banerjea was found guilty of contempt of court for an editorial he had written for his newspaper *The Bengalee* and imprisoned in May 1883 for two months. The imprisonment triggered many public protests across Bengal and other parts of India. See Surendranath Banerjea, *A Nation in Making: Being the Reminiscences of Fifty Years of Public Life* (London: Oxford University Press, 1927), 74–84.

158.   Khagendranath Mitra, *Satabdir Shishu Sahitya, 1818–1960*, 2nd ed. (Calcutta: Vidyodaya, 1967), 15–16. In his autobiography, Bipinchandra Pal wrote warmly about his friendship with Pramadachaan Sen but claimed that he had never contributed to *Sakha*. See B. Pal, *Memories of My Life*, 425. After Banerjea's release from prison, Pramadacharan Sen even organized a celebratory reception for him at their Sitaram Ghosh Street 'fortress'. Among the guests were Banerjea himself, the eminent Brahmo Anandamohan Bose, and the Christian priest and man of letters Krishnamohan Bandyopadhyay. See Home, *Jiban-Smriti*, 14.

159.   See Nabendu Sen, *Bangla Shishu Sahitya: Tattwa, Tathya, Rup o Bisleshan* (Calcutta: Puthipatra, 1992), 29–31.

160.   See Amal Pal, 'Kishorpathhya Patrikar Suchana o *Sakha'*, 18–19; and S. Ghosh, 'Upendrakishore', 51–2, 55.

161.   L. Majumdar, *Upendrakishore*, 29.

162.   The Bombay Presidency was particularly progressive. The Students' Literary and Scientific Society, established in Bombay in 1848, had, by 1852, established four girls' schools with financial help from the Parsi businessman Kharshedji Nasarvanji Kama (Cursetji Nasserwanji Cama) and staffed initially by student volunteers from the prestigious Elphinstone College. No comparable initiative was ever undertaken by the much-idolized students of Calcutta's Hindu College or its later incarnation, Presidency College. The

Cama family also sponsored two journals, one for women (*Stri Bodh*, founded in 1857) and *Rast Goftar*, a newspaper for reformers established in 1851 and edited by Dadabhai Naoroji. See Dobbin, *Urban Leadership*, 55–7, 60; Charles H. Heimsath, *Indian Nationalism and Hindu Social Reform* (Princeton: Princeton University Press, 1964), 13–14, 64; Naregal, *Language Politics*, 234–9; and Natarajan, *A Century of Social Reform*, 41, 54–5.

163. Geraldine Forbes, *Women in Modern India* (Cambridge: Cambridge University Press, 1996), 20; and Heimsath, *Indian Nationalism and Hindu Social Reform*, 190, 196; and more generally, 176–204.

164. Heimsath, *Indian Nationalism and Hindu Social Reform*, 14.

165. In the 1830s and 1840s, the students of Henry Derozio had criticized the polygamous practices of *kulin* Brahmins and had even called for the remarriage of widows; the practical outcome of those critiques, however, was negligible. See Sumit Sarkar, *A Critique of Colonial India*, 38, 74.

166. Sivanath Sastri, 'Some Practical Suggestions regarding Female Education in Bengal', *Journal of the National Indian Association*, no. 138 (June 1882): 309–30, at 310. See also David Kopf, *The Brahmo Samaj and the Shaping of the Modern Indian Mind* (Princeton, NJ: Princeton University Press, 1979), 10, 14–15. The Brahmo project to improve the lot of women, however, was grounded in a problematic reading of Indian history derived ultimately from British orientalist scholarship. The appalling state of Hindu women in the nineteenth century was contrasted with their supposedly high status in ancient India and the decline attributed to the evil effects of Islamic rule. See Forbes, *Women in Modern India*, 14–17.

2

New Faith, New Woman, New Society*

The condition of Indian women, Western observers often argued, 'proved' the degraded status of contemporary Indian civilization and justified colonial rule. Many of India's own reformers accepted the connection between women's status and the health of a civilization, arguing that improving the lives of Indian women would lead to the regeneration of the nation itself.[1] The ideology was practised with some sincerity and, as the life and work of Dwarakanath Ganguli demonstrates, at a substantial personal cost. Nor did the reformers receive much support or assistance from the colonial state which was never more than an enabler of reform, and that too only on occasion.

Although everybody knows that the lives of Indian women were constrained by countless rules and conventions during the nineteenth century, it is not often realized that the situation in Bengal during the very period of its

---

* This chapter could not have been written without the help of Barun Chattopadhyay, who provided me with copies of virtually all the writings of Dwarakanath Ganguli—including extant copies of *Abalabandhab*—and innumerable other sources. I am profoundly in his debt but he is not, of course, responsible for my interpretations and arguments.

much-hyped Renaissance was, in fact, among the worst. Bengali visitors to the Bombay Presidency were often amazed by the freedom of
movement women seemed to possess there.[2] Conversely, the
Maharashtrian Anandibai Joshi, later the first Indian woman to hold
a medical degree, was dismayed when, on a visit to Calcutta, she was
'stared at and laughed at' when out on the street with her husband.[3]
In Bengal, women in wealthier families lived in seclusion in a separate interior wing—known as zenana or, in Bengali, antahpur—but
even in poorer families, it was mandatory to observe as much separation as possible from men.[4] Even their dress—a sari wrapped around
the body without any undergarments and no footwear of any kind—
ensured that venturing out of the antahpur would be impossible, even
if it were permissible.[5] This secluded life commenced at marriage and
since Hindu girls were married before reaching puberty, they could
never go to school.[6] Home education was not acceptable either, since
the majority of Hindus believed that literate women ended up invariably as widows.[7]

By the end of the nineteenth century, however, many of these
seemingly enduring features of Bengali society had changed significantly and the Brahmos had played an enormous role in the transformation. Meredith Borthwick has justly remarked that 'wherever a
Brahmo was posted, he would set up—often with the help of his
wife—a Brahmo Samaj, a boys' school, a charitable dispensary, and a
school for girls'.[8] Brahmo 'feminism', of course, had its limits. Even
the self-consciously progressive Sadharan Brahmo Samaj did not do
more than give women occasional seats on their Executive Committee.
Although there were occasional examples of a woman serving as
acharya (that is, leading public worship at a Brahmo temple and deliv-
ering the sermon), they remained exceptional.[9] Moreover, Brahmo
reforms are often dismissed by today's scholars because they are
thought to have had no impact beyond the small confines of the
Brahmo community.[10] Now, while it is true that the Brahmos were
never numerous—the Sadharan Brahmo Samaj, at the end of twenty-
five years of existence in 1903, could boast of only about 800 enrolled
members—their social influence far exceeded their numbers.[11] A
Unitarian preacher once told Sivanath Sastri that there were 'more
Brahmos outside the Brahmo Samaj than within it' and there was a
grain of truth in that remark.[12] By educating their women in defiance
of orthodox opposition and facilitating their free movement in society,
the Brahmos, as we shall see, ultimately inspired many mainstream

Hindus to change *some* of their views on women's education and seclusion. This was not a revolution but given the context of the times, it was a significant achievement.

The reform of women's lives came to be of central importance to Brahmos after Keshab Sen's trip to England in 1870. Inspired by the example of British Unitarians and other reformers, he set up the Indian Reform Association (IRA), which had separate sections devoted to temperance, mass education, inexpensive books and periodicals, charity, and 'female improvement'.[13] Aided by a two-hundred-rupee donation from the British Unitarian reformer Mary Carpenter and subsequent gifts from across the subcontinent, the Association established a normal school for training women teachers (of all creeds) in 1871.[14] The trainee teachers from this school started the Bama Hitaisini Sabha (Women's Welfare Society), an organization with male and female members, presided over by Sen and meeting every Friday to discuss topics ranging from 'true modesty', 'sisterly love', and 'charity' to 'false refinement' and 'female liberty'. The *Bamabodhini Patrika*, a pioneering women's magazine founded in 1863 by Umeshchandra Datta, was taken over by the IRA in 1871 and it began to publish essays by members of the Bama Hitaisini Sabha.[15]

The IRA declined into relative insignificance by the year 1875 but by then, Sen and his associates had brought about at least one major social reform of enduring importance by persuading the government to legislate for civil marriage.[16] Ironically, Sen himself was to infringe the Act in arranging the marriage of his thirteen-year-old daughter Suniti to the seventeen-year-old Hindu prince of Cooch Bihar in 1878, compelling his radical associates to secede and form their own church: the Sadharan Brahmo Samaj, with the barrister Anandamohan Bose (1847–1906) as its president.[17] Keshab Sen's cousin and close colleague Pratapchandra Mazumdar had declared at the height of the Cooch Behar marriage dispute that Keshab Sen was not interested in social reform and the Brahmo Samaj had 'no "social ideal", apart from its religion'.[18] Many of the founders of the Sadharan Brahmo Samaj, however, had been attracted to the Brahmo movement precisely because of its rational approach to social questions and saw no clear distinction between religious and social reform.[19] The Sadharan Brahmo project, Bipinchandra Pal emphasized, was far more than merely religious: the new church was concerned with freedom in all its forms—'personal, social as well as political'.[20]

The Making of a Reformer

The Sadharan Brahmo Samaj was not short of radicals but even among such firebrands, Dwarakanath Ganguli easily stood out as the kind of 'courageous, unbending, fearless and heroic' individual one rarely encountered.[21] Today, he is remembered largely for his efforts to expand educational opportunities for women, although, as we shall see in the next chapter, he did much else besides that.[22]

Born in Magurkhanda village near Dhaka in a Brahmin family in 1844, Dwarakanath's father, Krishnapran, was often away on work and the boy was brought up mostly by his mother, Udaytara, and educated at ordinary village schools. The Gangulis were not just Brahmins, but kulins, the highest-ranking members of the highest caste.[23] The kulin system, supposedly established in Bengal in the twelfth century during the reign of the Hindu king Ballal Sen, persisted until the twentieth century and its chief social manifestation was polygamy.[24] A kulin girl could not marry just any Brahmin but only another kulin and kulin grooms were also in demand among non-kulin Brahmins. Kulin men, therefore, made a living out of polygamy, receiving substantial dowries from the parents of each bride at the time of marriage and large presents whenever they visited their 'wives'.[25] In the early nineteenth century, William Ward had reported that married kulin women, who hardly ever saw their so-called husbands, often lived 'in adultery; in some cases, with the knowledge of their parents' and many drifted into prostitution.[26]

Even as a schoolboy, Dwarakanath Ganguli, some of whose relatives had married forty times or more, was revolted by polygamy and along with his school friends, all of them kulins, pledged to be strictly monogamous.[27] A tragic personal experience was partly responsible for this. An unmarried girl from his village, whom he had known and later described as 'exquisitely beautiful' (*paramasundari*), was killed by her own family because, while her family was looking for an appropriate husband, she had had an affair and become pregnant.[28] Dwarakanath, who was only seventeen at the time, was shocked to discover that such deaths—sometimes murders, sometimes suicides—were only too common.[29] But Dwarakanath's lifelong devotion to women's causes was not inspired solely by the tragedy of a girl he had personally known. In school, he had encountered the works of the early unorthodox Brahmo Akshaykumar Datta (1820–1886), who had been one of the first in

Bengal to condemn polygamy and child-marriage and to urge people to marry outside their caste.[30] Datta did not even consider it worthwhile to pray to God for personal benefits, a view that Dwarakanath later defended with gusto.[31]

Datta, whom historian Sumit Sarkar calls 'a lone deist' among Brahmos, was appointed in 1843 by Debendranath Tagore to edit the Brahmo Samaj's newsletter, the *Tattvabodhini Patrika*. Datta transformed it into a leading magazine of the era, packed with essays on social reform and a broad range of scientific topics.[32] Debendranath Tagore was often irritated by Datta's 'secular' preoccupations but they endeared him to young radicals such as Dwarakanath Ganguli and his classmates.[33] It was doubtful, Dwarakanath once declared, if anybody had exerted a greater influence on Bengali youth than Datta, especially through his two books *Bahyabastur Sahit Manabprakritir Sambandhabichar* (1851–2) and *Dharmaneeti* (1856).[34] Neither was an original work.[35] *Sambandhabichar*, perhaps the more influential of the two, was an abridged, Indianized, and occasionally critical translation of Scottish lawyer George Combe's celebrated bestseller, *The Constitution of Man Considered in Relation to External Objects* (1828).[36] It endorsed Combe's message that the surest path to happiness, health, and fulfilment was to live in accordance with the beneficent laws of nature but was sprinkled liberally with Datta's own observations on Bengali and Indian transgressions of the natural laws—child marriage, refusing to educate women, lack of understanding of the principles of good sanitation, disinclination for physical exercise—and their unhappy outcomes.[37]

Inspired by Datta's teachings and driven by his own tragic experience, the kulin Dwarakanath stuck to his refusal to practise polygamy.[38] Other kulin families were so offended by the young man's stance that it became impossible to find grooms for his two sisters. The names of those two women, who may well have died as spinsters, are lost to history and their sacrifice at the altar of their brother's feminism is barely mentioned in biographies.[39] Dwarakanath himself married in 1862 or 1863 and had two children, daughter Bidhumukhi and son Satischandra.[40] In the light of the Ganguli family's virtual elimination from the kulin Brahmin community, one wonders how and where a match was found for Dwarakanath and what she may have felt about her husband's activism. It is unlikely, though, that we shall ever find answers to these questions. Although reams have been written on Dwarakanath's second wife, Kadambini, the first wife of this great campaigner for women's rights has been virtually erased from history. Even her name—Bhabasundari—cannot be found in Dwarakanath's biographies and it is often incorrectly claimed that she had died before Dwarakanath moved to Calcutta in 1870.[41]

Nor do we know much about Dwarakanath's own life and work before then. He failed to pass his entrance examination, never went to college, and was compelled, in the earlier decades of his life, to earn his living by teaching in obscure village schools.[42] It was while teaching at Lonsingha village in East Bengal in 1869 that he started publishing a fortnightly paper called *Abalabandhab* (a literal translation of the title would be 'Friend of the Weak') which has been described by David Kopf as 'the first in the world devoted solely to the "liberation of women"'.[43] *Abalabandhab* certainly was not the first paper for and about women in Bengal, let alone the world. The first Bengali magazine for women was Pyarichand Mitra's *Masik Patrika*, founded in 1854, and in 1863, Umeshchandra Datta (1840–1907) and his Bamabodhini Sabha began to publish *Bamabodhini Patrika*, which, as we have seen, was later adopted by the IRA and supported women's education and social liberation, albeit not very radically.[44] *Abalabandhab* may not have been particularly radical either. Although its first numbers have perished, an overview of its contents reported by the *Brahmo Public Opinion* in January 1870 mentions articles on home economics, the telephone, the phonograph, the microphone, a biographical essay on Thomas Alva Edison and a piece on the knowledge of Sanskrit among Muslims. *Abalabandhab* seems, in fact, to have tried to liberate women by providing them with at least some of the general education that its women readers could not obtain elsewhere.[45]

One year after starting the magazine, Dwarakanath moved to Calcutta, reportedly because of worsening difficulties with his family, and it was only then that he formally became a Brahmo. Although, unlike many conventional Brahmos, he was never too outspoken about his faith, he, like his mentor Akshay Datta, held that God had designed the universe to provide for all legitimate needs of humans and one could lead a godly life simply by obeying the laws of nature.[46] This calm faith did not, however, entail an acceptance of social injustice and his radicalism endeared him to the young turks of the Brahmo Samaj.[47] The latter, however, may not have been of much direct help to his work. In Dhaka, Dwarakanath had received considerable assistance from several Brahmo young men in bringing out his magazine but after coming to Calcutta, he not only had to write the articles and correct the proofs but also distribute the magazine himself and even write each mailing label for postal subscribers.[48] The lawyer Durgamohan Das

(1841–1897), who moved to Calcutta from Barisal at the end of 1870 and became a firm ally of Dwarakanath, reportedly provided some funds but the paper, which was turned into a monthly in 1874, did not thrive, primarily because of subscribers not paying their dues.[49]

One issue of this monthly version has survived, however, and its contents repay study.[50] The opening article, surprisingly, is an account—in English—of an English winter by an unknown, presumably British, author.[51] The Bengali contents are a mixed bag and include a translation of John Stuart Mill's tribute to his wife Harriet, shorter pieces on scholarships available to women students in Calcutta, the management of the Hindu Mahila Vidyalaya (which is discussed later) and the difficulties of publishing *Abalabandhab* regularly.[52] But the most fascinating piece in this issue is a long essay on beauty. Women considered to be beautiful, it declares, were treated far better by their in-laws and human happiness could be enhanced if only human beauty could be enhanced. One obvious way to do it was for unattractive people not to marry or if they did, not to have children but the essay proffered an even more radical proposal. Extreme physical traits such as the African's jet-black skin or the Laplander's milky-white complexion, it argued, were inimical to true beauty. If people from different races intermarried freely, then such extreme traits would be blended away over generations, not only improving the physical appearance of the entire human species but putting an end to conflicting notions of beauty among different races.[53] This quasi-eugenic approach was balanced up to a point by the author's evident passion to improve the lives of women and to end racial discrimination but its eagerness to re-design humans so as to fit in with social prejudices, fortunately, was absent from the reforming campaigns of Dwarakanath Ganguli.

The Pedagogy of Emancipation

Keshab Sen, along with some young Brahmos, had established a programme of home education for women (*antahpur stri-siksha* or zenana instruction) in 1862.[54] Reading lists were drawn up by the programme directors and the enrolled women read the books at home, sending in quarterly reports on their studies and the best of these receiving prizes.[55] Sen, however, did not believe that women needed any more than a purely elementary education.[56] When the young Sivanath Sastri, then teaching at the women's school run by the IRA, proposed teaching geometry, logic, and metaphysics to his students, Sen scoffed at the idea and advised Sastri to restrict his teaching to the 'elementary principles of science'.[57] Long before their secession from Sen's Brahmo Samaj of India, Dwarakanath and his fellow radicals were already calling for a far more intensive programme in which women would receive essentially the same education as men, albeit with additional training in the feminine arts.

For a time, it seemed as if they had found an ally in Annette Akroyd (1842–1929), a thirty-year-old British Unitarian, alumna of London's Bedford College and a trained governess. Moved by Keshab Sen's appeal for 'English sisters' to come out to India and help provide an 'unsectarian, liberal, sound, useful education', Akroyd arrived in Calcutta in 1872.[58] Akroyd's ideas on female education turned out, however, to be very different from Sen's and, as her son William Beveridge recorded, she lost faith in Sen 'almost from her first days in India'.[59] Akroyd now gravitated towards his radical critics within the Brahmo Samaj, to whom she was introduced by Manamohan Ghosh (1844–1896), a progressive Brahmo barrister, 'the first Bengali who regularly practised in the Courts of Bengal as a member of the English Bar' and the co-founder with Keshab Sen of the newspaper *Indian Mirror*.[60] Her new friends warmly endorsed Akroyd's intention of starting a full-fledged, English-style boarding school for girls and they helped her found the Hindu Mahila Vidyalaya in 1873.[61]

The first girls' school in Bengal had been established in 1818 in the small town and former Dutch colony of Chunchura or Chinsurah (about thirty miles from Calcutta) by the London Missionary Society and subsequently, other missionaries had founded various girls' schools across Bengal and especially in Calcutta. Because they often taught (or were suspected of teaching) Christian doctrine, the higher classes of Hindus did not patronize them.[62] Apart from a small school founded in 1847 in Barasat (about ten miles from Calcutta) by the well-known professor and temperance activist Pyaricharan Sarkar, the first major non-missionary institution for girls in Bengal was established in Calcutta in 1849 by John Elliot Drinkwater Bethune (1801–1851), the Legal Member in the Governor General's Council, in collaboration with wealthy, progressive Indians.[63] Iswarchandra Vidyasagar was appointed the Secretary of the School and the school had some eighty students, mostly from middle-class families, on its books by 1851.[64] The curriculum was designed only to provide basic education along with needlework and sewing but even that modest ambition was thwarted because the girls were usually married off around the age of ten and removed from school.[65] The same issue affected all the private girls' schools that began to be established after Bethune's school.[66]

Annette Akroyd's Hindu Mahila Vidyalaya was designed very differently. Its students would be given the same kind of education that boys received and without excluding the possibility of further study or professional training.[67] Not many Bengalis of the time would have supported such an approach. Even a notable reformer like Sasipada Banerji, who was involved with the management of the Hindu Mahila Vidyalaya, thought that it was fine for women to pursue the highest knowledge if they wished to do so, but it would destroy their finer attributes if they were subjected to competitive examinations and professional tests.[68] Notwithstanding such reservations even among its own patrons, the school began well. Manamohan Ghosh and Durgamohan Das provided the finance and Akroyd supervised the teaching.[69] The British judge John Budd Phear (1825–1905) and his wife, Emily (1836–1897), were also loyal allies. The school began with only five students. Dwarakanath Ganguli and Durgamohan Das admitted their own daughters to the school and Durgamohan's wife Brahmamoyee also sent several of the young widows she was sheltering.[70]

Ultimately, however, it was Dwarakanath Ganguli who, in the words of Sivanath Sastri, 'was the principal organiser' and 'the chief executive agent on whom rested the whole practical work' of the school.[71] He taught every subject except English and his student Abala Bose (née Das) remembered his indomitable energy and total dedication to the school.[72] As a historian noted more recently, Dwarakanath 'served that school simultaneously as headmaster, teacher, dietician, darwan [gateman], and maintenance man'. He 'even swept up daily after class'.[73] Since Dwarakanath did not like existing textbooks in mathematics, geography, and health science, he wrote his own. He also edited several collections of poetry for use as textbooks.[74] These received good reviews and also brought him a 'tolerably decent income'.[75] A coherent moral vision of childhood and what was proper to it was evident in these ventures. In the most popular of his poetry collections, *Kabigatha*, he expressed his shock on seeing that many comparable collections were careless enough to include poems that were obscene or did not sufficiently encourage the necessary virtues: love for learning, patriotism, sense of duty, courage, and truthfulness.[76] In addition to the usual 'academic' subjects, the girls were taught cooking, sewing, and other domestic arts; 'national music' was also an important part of the curriculum and since there was no appropriate collection of national songs, Dwarakanath compiled his own *Jatiya Sangeet*, which was the first such collection in Bengali.[77]

Despite her grand ambitions, Akroyd found the Hindu Mahila Vidyalaya very hard to run. She complained about Bengali students being unmanageable and her relations with her Brahmo allies quickly degenerated. Some of her colleagues and associates found her to be too rigidly 'English' and difficult to relate to.[78] Her relations with Dwarakanath Ganguli, arguably the most important member of the school's staff, soon soured. By 1874, we find Akroyd declaring in letters to her sister Fanny that one should have 'as little to do with Bengalis as possible' and by the middle of that year, Dwarakanath had severed all connections with the school.[79] In an ill-tempered correspondence from August 1874, he told Akroyd that he did not even wish to recall that he 'ever had any connection' with the Hindu Mahila Vidyalaya and warned her that he was planning to criticize the school's current management in the press.[80] No such publication can be traced but earlier, in the June 1874 issue of *Abalabandhab*, Dwarakanath had strongly criticized the ways in which people were being appointed to the management committee of the school.[81] Despite Ganguli's departure, however, the Hindu Mahila Vidyalaya continued to function for another year, and no information is available on that phase of its history. It closed only in 1875, when Akroyd married the thirty-eight-year-old widower Henry Beveridge, a member of the Indian Civil Service, and moved away from Calcutta. She would later describe her voyage to India 'as a mad venture and of her time in Calcutta as semi-suicide'.[82]

The idea of an advanced school for girls, however, survived Akroyd's departure. With financial assistance from Anandamohan Bose, Durgamohan Das, and his wife Brahmamoyee (1845–1876), a new school called the Banga Mahila Vidyalaya was established on 1 June 1876 and Dwarakanath Ganguli, once again, gave it his all.[83] Located on Old Ballygunge Road, it had fourteen students to begin with, including nine unmarried girls and four widows, and they were taught in English. Although all the students were Brahmos, the School was open to all creeds—there was no religious instruction and the boarding did not recognize any caste rules. The school was run by a Lady Superintendent (an Englishwoman) and employed a British 'second mistress' and Dwarakanath Ganguli as pandit.[84] For the first year, it was financed entirely by donations and fees (which, at ten rupees per month, was quite high) but then received municipal and government grants. The teaching followed the syllabus for Calcutta University's entrance examination. In other words, the curriculum was conventionally 'academic'.[85]

Ironically, this kind of conventional higher education for women was not in fact regarded as ideal by Dwarakanath Ganguli. In a revealing essay of 1878, he attacked the tendency to cram young heads with facts and figures that had no connection to the students' lived experience and future needs. Teachers of history, he urged, should stop concentrating on kings, queens and wars, and try to show students how to be socially and politically responsible citizens. Geography lessons, instead of listing the minutiae of lands the students would never see, should provide a richer picture of the region and the nation. At the same time, however, Dwarakanath rejected the notion that girls were incapable of learning mathematics and science. If indeed the female mind was lacking in the penetration and rigour demanded by mathematics, then, he argued, the study of mathematics was all the more essential for correcting those deficiencies. A basic scientific training, he emphasized, was vital not just for males or for those who wanted to be scientists but for *everybody*, regardless of gender, class, or occupation.[86]

One authority invoked repeatedly in the essay was Herbert Spencer (1820–1903), who, before becoming known for his voluminous writings on evolutionary biology, sociology, and psychology, had published several influential critiques of Victorian pedagogy, calling for teachers to work with children's innate tendencies instead of force-feeding them with information they could not understand or care for.[87] Indian progressives were greatly inspired by Spencer's conviction that since every individual was organically linked to society, the development of one affected all and even a small number of progressive individuals could make a significant difference to the larger society. Reformers like Dwarakanath Ganguli, whose campaigns were rarely backed by the masses or even by every so-called progressive, would have found this an especially appealing prospect.[88] The Banga Mahila Vidyalaya, however, could not possibly have given Dwarakanath the opportunity to practise a fully Spencerian pedagogy. The institution wanted its students to pass the entrance examination of Calcutta University and then, hopefully, to 'finish their education at the new college for women at Cambridge', that is, Girton. The government's *Report on Public Instruction for 1876–77* described it as 'in every sense the most advanced school in Bengal' but this was more because of its compliance with the academic standards of the University—unequalled by any existing school for girls—than for any Spencerian departure from them.[89]

It is not unlikely that Dwarakanath, despite his own different educational ideals, embraced this strategy because it could open the portals of the university to women and thereby bring about a big enough social reform to compensate for the compromise with conventional pedagogy. Unfortunately, we do not have any details about the actual teaching at the school but a solitary student essay does survive. Written in 1876 by Kadambini Basu (who would later play a pivotal role in Dwarakanath's life and the history of Bengal), it was considered impressive enough to be published by the *Bamabodhini Patrika*. As the editor explained, the essay was notable because the student, instead of following the usual safe practice on writing on God or education, had chosen to write on something as ordinary as a coconut tree.[90] In its focus on the everyday and the utilitarian, one can perhaps detect the influence of Dwarakanath's pedagogical philosophy but its author, as we shall see, would make a name for herself by entering a profession that, although not previously open to women, was considered entirely conventional for men.

Dwarakanath's involvement with the 'academic' education of girls from progressive, urban, and relatively wealthy families was soon complemented by an initiative to provide elementary education to the girls of rural Bengal, who could not even dream of a university education. Convinced that these women could be freed from their captivity only by a basic, practical education equipping them for rational thought, Dwarakanath founded a committee that set up several girls' schools in villages in his home district of Bikrampur in eastern Bengal. Unlike the Banga Mahila Vidyalaya, these schools were run on the Spencerian conviction that it would be 'more beneficial for the students if they learnt a bit of anatomy' instead of the names of rivers running through the 'distant plains of Siberia'.[91] Hardly anything, however, is known about this effort at mass education and the reputation of Dwarakanath continues to be rooted primarily in his commitment to higher education for urban elites.

The Banga Mahila Vidyalaya acquired such a high reputation so quickly that it is surprising to see in an 1877 government report that it was going to be closed temporarily 'for certain causes'.[92] Those causes, although left unspecified, were probably financial, since John Phear, the Chairman of the management committee of the Bethune School, suggested that instead of funding the poorly performing Bethune, the Government should extend its support to the Banga Mahila Vidyalaya.[93] What actually happened, however, was a merger of the two institutions.[94] Two prominent Brahmos—Anandamohan Bose and Durgamohan Das—joined the revamped management committee of the Bethune School and the merged school was run as a Brahmo institution, although open to all.[95] Dwarakanath Ganguli was not on the committee but may well have taught there.[96] Expectedly enough, the orthodox Hindu press protested at the merger of a Hindu institution with a 'notoriously un-Hindu' one and even in 1890, *Sahachar*, a Calcutta weekly, wrote that Hindu parents were now reluctant to send their daughters to the Bethune School because of the preponderance of Brahmos and Christians in its management, teaching staff, and student body.[97] Despite such controversies, however, the merged institution went from strength to strength.

Originally, students of Bethune School had simply been given a basic education. None of them was expected to take the entrance examination, let alone study further. The merger with the Banga Mahila Vidyalaya, with its '15 grown girls boarding at the school', changed all that.[98] One of the institution's students, Kadambini Basu, passed the entrance examination in the year of the merger and went on to achieve greater things. Brought up in Bhagalpur in Bihar, Kadambini (1861–1923) was the daughter of Brajakishore Basu, a Brahmo schoolmaster and co-founder of a women's society in Bhagalpur.[99] There was then a small but significant Bengali community in Bhagalpur; it had many Brahmos, who founded a girls' school called the Bhagalpur Institution in 1868. Kadambini, who had already started her education at home, was one of the eight students with whom the school commenced its journey.[100] In 1875, she was taken to Calcutta, where she lodged with her cousin, the barrister Manamohan Ghosh. Ghosh encouraged Kadambini's parents to send her to the new school he had helped establish, the Hindu Mahila Vidyalaya. When it closed, she moved to the Banga Mahila Vidyalaya, and then, after the merger, to Bethune, from where she sat for her entrance examination in 1878.

Before she could sit for the examination, however, the University had to change its policy of admitting men alone. It is sometimes claimed that the regulations were changed only because of Dwarakanath Ganguli's energetic lobbying of the vice-chancellor Sir Arthur Hobhouse but the University, in fact, had already allowed Chandramukhi Basu, a Bengali Christian from Dehradun, not to sit for the official examination but to be 'privately examined in the Entrance papers'.[101] Similar caution was adopted for the two Calcutta students. Kadambini Basu and Sarala Das had to sit for a preliminary test in 1877 in English, mathematics, history, and Bengali and it was only after they had passed this test that they were permitted to appear at the entrance examination, though at 'a separate place, under the supervision of ladies'.[102] The University, in other words, was offering a half-open door to women, whom the Vice-Chancellor described as 'the predominating influence' within households in all societies. The nation that did not educate its women was refusing, he asserted, to develop all its available strength.[103]

This, of course, was a common liberal (and imperialist) mantra at the time, but the Vice-Chancellor's pious words were at least backed by some genuine action. Although Sarala Das did not appear at the examination—rather shockingly for the daughter of Brahmo radical Durgamohan Das, she was married off at sixteen and her formal education was left incomplete—Kadambini did and performed very well in Bengali, history 'and even in the exact sciences—a subject which', the Vice Chancellor remarked in his convocation address, 'is not usually considered to be congenial to the female intellect'. Her aggregate marks fell short of the first division by a single mark.[104] Apart from receiving a gold medal, a book-prize, and a commendation from the Viceroy, she was also awarded a special scholarship, which would pay her fifteen rupees per month as long as she continued to study for two more years.[105]

But study where? There were no colleges in Bengal that admitted women. The Lieutenant-Governor Sir Ashley Eden, therefore, decided to start a special college-level class at the Bethune School, where Kadambini was, at first, the only student.[106] By 1881, Kadambini had passed her First Arts, albeit only in the third division, and was studying for the BA in the same college class.[107] She graduated in January 1883—along with Chandramukhi Basu—becoming one of the first women in India to hold a BA degree.[108] H.J. Reynolds, the Vice-Chancellor of Calcutta University, hailed

their graduation as the 'most memorable event' of the year. Educating
India's women, he declared with all the ardour of a liberal imperialist, was the best way to 'grapple with and efface the two great
national sins of India, the sin of child-marriage, and the sin of
enforced widowhood'. Lest orthodox Hindus be too unnerved by the
prospect, Reynolds quickly added that the progress of female education in India was going to be slow and the ensuing social transformation would occur 'as gently and imperceptibly as the morning twilight
melts into day'.[109]

For Brahmos of the more progressive variety, however, the
changes could not come fast enough and they took full advantage of
the new, expansive approach to women's education.[110] A full decade
after the merger with the Banga Mahila Vidyalaya, there were only 44
mainstream Hindus among Bethune's 136 students and 87
Brahmos.[111] Not all Brahmos were on board, however. In 1883, the
year of Chandramukhi and Kadambini's graduation, Keshab Sen
established the Victoria College with the goal of training girls 'to be
good Hindu wives and Hindu mothers.'[112] Almost in riposte to Sen's
move, the two women graduates set out to achieve even more than
they already had. Chandramukhi Basu went on to be the first woman
to hold a master's degree from Calcutta University and when the
college class at Bethune School matured into a full-fledged college in
1888, she became its first principal.[113] Kadambini, meanwhile,
shocked even radical Brahmos by marrying her long-time mentor, the
thirty-nine-year-old widower Dwarakanath Ganguli on 12 June 1883,
and then embarking on the study of medicine.[114]

Doctor, Housewife, Mother

Since women living in seclusion could not consult male doctors, the
need for female doctors, many reformers argued, was especially acute
in Indian society.[115] When the first medical schools for women were
established in Boston, Philadelphia, New York, and Chicago between
1850 and 1870, their founders, too, had emphasized the inappropriateness of women being treated by male doctors.[116] The process of opening medical schools for women may have been difficult in Bengal but
it had not been easy *anywhere*.

In nineteenth-century Europe, a woman could train as a doctor
on the same terms as men only in Zurich and from the end of the

1860s, in Paris. In Austria and Germany, two of the leading medical centres of the period, women were not admitted to medical schools until the end of the nineteenth century. As for the United States (US), the admission of Elizabeth Blackwell into the Geneva Medical School of New York state in 1847 was an experiment that the School decided never to repeat. In the latter decades of the nineteenth century, American women could study medicine only in institutions meant exclusively for women or in 'sectarian' medical schools following homoeopathic or other unorthodox systems of medicine. Real medical co-education commenced in the US only in 1893 at the Johns Hopkins University School of Medicine in Baltimore. In Britain, Sophia Jex-Blake and four other women faced endless obstruction and persecution from the faculty and students when they sought clinical training at the University of Edinburgh in the 1870s. Denied their degrees, Jex-Blake and her fellow-students had to go to Europe to qualify while British medical schools remained all-male for twenty more years. Although Scottish medical schools introduced co-education in the 1890s, it would be 1948 before medical schools in London routinely admitted both sexes. Before 1877, there were only two officially recognized women doctors in Britain—Elizabeth Blackwell (who had trained, of course, in America) and Elizabeth Garrett, who did not have a full medical degree but only an apothecary's license to practise.[117]

Also, we must not forget that as women's demands for entry to higher education and medicine grew more insistent in the West, 'scientific experts' began to warn that women, whose bodies and minds were biologically inferior to men's, were wholly unsuited to *any* kind of academic study.[118] The earthy realities of the human body, moreover, were too indelicate for the genteel lady to cope with.[119] For reasons that we shall examine, however, such views were not argued in Bengal with anything like the same force and women received the right to study medicine in co-educational institutions rather earlier than in the US or Europe.

The first attempts to provide medical education to Indian women were small-scale, short-lasting initiatives by missionaries such as the school established in Nainital in 1869 by a medical member of the American Methodist Episcopal Church Mission to India. It lasted for only about three years and other initiatives of this type had similar histories.[120] The first appeal to the government for allowing a Hindu woman to study at a medical school was made in January 1875 by

Nilkamal Mitra, a wealthy Calcutta businessman who had himself spent three years at the Calcutta Medical College without completing his course. He wanted to find out whether his fifteen-year-old grand-daughter, Birajmohini (married to a doctor and living in seclusion), would be given the medical diploma if she studied mostly at home and attended lectures, dissections, and midwifery practicals under purdah or in the company of her husband.[121]

The Principal of the Calcutta Medical College, Surgeon-Major Norman Chevers, declined to open the 'very difficult and debatable' question of women's fitness for medical study on account of 'one solitary candidate, especially considering that she is a *purdah-nashin* female'.[122] The Government of Bengal's Director of Public Instruction as well as the Lieutenant-Governor Richard Temple, however, opposed Chevers, declaring that 'this lady, or any other lady who may qualify herself by a proper course of study, may be permitted to go in for examination, and if she can pass the examination, will be entitled to obtain a diploma'.[123] This decision, incidentally, was taken in 1875, two years *before* the Royal Free Hospital in London became the first traditional teaching hospital in England to allow women to train in its wards.[124] For unknown reasons, however, Birajmohini never enrolled in medical school and the whole question of women's medical study was forgotten in Bengal for some years.[125] Meanwhile, in 1875, the Madras Medical School admitted Mary Scharlieb (1845–1930), an Englishwoman married to a barrister who qualified as a licentiate of medicine, surgery, and midwifery in 1878.[126] Within a few years of Scharlieb's graduation, the Madras Medical School admitted Abala Das (who had passed her entrance examination from Bethune School in 1880) and Ellen D'Abreu (who passed her First Arts from the spe-cial college class at Bethune in 1881), both of whom had been refused admission in Calcutta.[127]

In 1882, the Director of Public Instruction reminded the Principal of the Medical College that the number of women passing university examinations was bound to rise in the coming years and a medical career should not be closed to them.[128] Although the majority of the College's faculty remained opposed to admitting women, the sands were shifting under them. Durgamohan Das, the father of Abala, had applied to J.M. Coates, the Principal of the Calcutta Medical College, for a transfer of his daughter from the Madras Medical School and Kadambini Basu had herself written to Coates asking to be admitted. Coates, who seems to have been far more open-minded than his

colleagues, made inquiries in Switzerland, France, and Madras, discovering that the presence of women in medical classes had actually
'had a refining influence on all present'.[129] The medical professoriate
still refused to budge and the matter was placed for adjudication
before Augustus Rivers Thompson, the Lieutenant-Governor of
Bengal, who had nothing but contempt for the intelligence and ability
of 'natives'.[130]

With regard to medical education for Indian women, however,
Rivers Thompson proved unexpectedly liberal.[131] Refusing to let
women study medicine was dangerous, he asserted, because most
'native' women 'would prefer death to treatment by a male physician'.
This typically colonial view of benighted natives, however, was complemented by an impatience with professorial objections to women's
admission to the Medical College. The only way to decide on that
question, he remarked, was to try it out and see what happened: 'The
ladies who apply for admission to the College will be the only losers if
they fail in the trial; the community will be great gainers if they succeed.' Personally, the Lieutenant Governor 'had no doubt that they
will succeed far beyond the expectations of their most sanguine supporters' and he looked forward to a time 'when Calcutta hospitals
shall be partly officered by lady doctors'.[132] After this, nobody could
keep Kadambini out of medical school and by 1884, she had been
joined by Virginia Mary Mitter and Bidhumukhi Basu (the younger
sister of Chandramukhi), all of them receiving a new government
scholarship of twenty rupees a month.[133]

Keshab Sen, in keeping with his new conservative incarnation,
opposed the idea of women doctors. 'To us Indians, in the present
state of Native Society, lady MDs are an expensive luxury,' he remarked.
'Indian women do not die because of the absence of female doctors
possessed of high University honors, but deaths, miserable and hor-
rible, have actually resulted from the want of good midwives.'[134] Sen's
concern was misplaced. There was no great rush among women for
medical training. Even in 1907, the number of Bengali Hindu women
medical students was small. As late as in 1912, 'when there were two
and three Hindu women students respectively at medical colleges in
Madras and Bombay, there was none in Calcutta'.[135] And, as we shall
see, the few women doctors tended to be treated merely as midwives
by their patients.

Sadly, almost nothing is known about Kadambini's experiences as
a medical student. Although at least one of her peers—Amritalal

Sircar, the son of the founder of the Indian Association for the Cultivation of Science—had his private doubts about the wisdom of teaching men and women in the same class, there is no record of any persecution comparable to that experienced by Sophia Jex-Blake and four other women at the University of Edinburgh Medical School in the 1870s.[136] Kadambini's academic performance, however, was disappointing.[137] She failed the first part of the MB (Bachelor of Medicine) examination, which had to be taken at the end of a student's third year of study and in 1886, she switched to the lower-level LMS (Licence in Medicine and Surgery) course.[138] In the final examination for the LMS in 1888, however, disaster struck again and she failed her medicine paper. Principal Coates endorsed Kadambini's petition to the University to reconsider her result, but the examiner refused to change the mark.[139] Having given up on the MB and failing to obtain even the lower-grade Licentiateship, Kadambini, it seemed, would never be able to practise medicine.

But Principal Coates still had a card up his sleeve. Before the establishment of Calcutta University in 1857, the Medical College used to award its own diploma GMCB (Graduate of the Medical College, Bengal). This had long been discontinued but finding that the College still had the prerogative to award it, Coates arranged to confer it on Kadambini.[140] It gave her the right to practise medicine and her reputation as the first Indian woman medical practitioner to have trained in an Indian medical school is perfectly legitimate.[141] The Maharashtrian Anandibai Joshi had qualified as a doctor before Kadambini but she had trained in the US, and Bidhumukhi Basu and Virginia Mary Mitter, the first Calcutta women to acquire MB degrees, graduated two years after Kadambini.[142]

Kadambini was eager for a hospital appointment but found it hard to obtain a permanent post. Racial discrimination was almost certainly at play, especially in that curious form whereby European women doctors, facing sexual discrimination at home, came out to the colonies and were preferred, simply because of their race, over Indian women. The latter, as Meredith Borthwick rightly commented, 'were left to labour under the oppressive effects of dual discrimination on grounds of both sex and race'.[143] It is not as if there was the slightest evidence that Indian women doctors were unfit for responsible hospital posts since, as Kadambini pointed out, none had ever been appointed to one. 'Without giving Indian medical women opportunities to prove their capabilities, it is not fair to them to pronounce that they are not competent to hold first class appointments,' she pointed out.[144] It was a fine argument but such arguments rarely worked in the racially hierarchical world of British India. She did teach gynaecology at the Campbell Medical School and it was noted at the time that she was probably the first woman lecturer at an Indian medical school but it was as a private practitioner that she shone.[145]

Kadambini went into private practice in July 1888, specializing in the diseases of women and children.[146] Most of her clinical work, inevitably, was confined to obstetrics.[147] Kadambini was a confident practitioner who could, when necessary, oppose the (male) professional consensus. Gaganchandra Home recalled that when various well-known doctors had advised his wife to terminate her pregnancy because of dangers to her health, Kadambini persuaded her to ignore that advice and eventually delivered her of a healthy girl.[148] Despite her clinical skills and university qualification, however, Kadambini was often treated simply as a midwife. Once, after conducting a delivery at a wealthy household, Kadambini and her assistant—who *was* a midwife—were not only asked to eat separately from the family but asked to clear away after themselves because the maids could not be expected to touch the leavings of unclean midwives.[149]

Although she did fairly well as a practitioner, Kadambini seemed to have realized that her status as the first woman doctor in Bengal would not guarantee professional pre-eminence for very long. Although the number of women doctors was not high, the few that were emerging had more impressive degrees than she did.[150] But those degrees were all indigenous and one obvious way in which Kadambini could maintain her professional uniqueness would be to become the only Bengali woman doctor with a Western qualification. That would also allow her to be favoured by 'native' patients over European women doctors.[151] It was, of course, quite common by the 1890s for wealthier Bengali men to go to England, whether for legal or medical training or to compete for entry into the Indian Civil Service.[152] Nor was it unknown for women to travel abroad: one thinks of the poet Toru Dutt and her sister Oru (who were Christian), Rajkumari Devi (the first wife of Sasipada Banerji, who accompanied him to England in 1871), Gyanadanandini Devi (married to the first 'native' member of the Indian Civil Service, Satyendranath Tagore), or the housewife and writer Krishnabhabini Das.[153] All of these women, however, were accompanied by their husbands (or even families) and none, as far as we know, had any personal, academic, or professional motive for their voyage.

Kadambini may well have been the first Bengali woman to go to England entirely alone and solely in quest of professional advancement. Perhaps because of the unprecedented nature of her decision, she proceeded in a puzzlingly indirect manner. In 1892, entries were invited from all over the world for an international exhibition to be held in Chicago to celebrate the 400th anniversary of Columbus's discovery of America.[154] Kadambini wrote to *The Bengalee* proposing to collect the finest specimens of handicrafts made by Indian women and exhibit them in Chicago. It would, she argued, dispel the idea 'that Indian women are devoid of cultural and artistic skill'.[155] Government help in the shape of 'a decent pecuniary grant' was, of course, essential but given the improbability of obtaining one, the ever-dynamic Dwarakanath Ganguli wrote to *The Bengalee* a fortnight later with a proposal for 'a profitable business' to transport, exhibit, and sell 'Indian art-work, jewellery and other indigenous articles of commerce' at the Exposition or even to distribute 'trade circulars, handbills and catalogues ... among the visitors to the Exhibition and the American people generally'.[156] The capital needed was about thirty thousand rupees and it was proposed to sell three hundred shares worth a hundred rupees each. The business, Dwarakanath revealed, was not only supported by the editors of *The Bengalee* (Surendranath Banerjea) and the *Indian Mirror* (Narendranath Sen), but would gain from the 'most valuable suggestions' and other assistance from Trailokyanath Mukhopadhyay, who, apart from being a famous writer, was the pre-eminent expert on Indian handicrafts and natural resources.[157]

It is not known whether this business venture was successful but Kadambini's appeal did receive a good response. In February 1892, she left for Chicago (via England) with a large collection of samples. The *Bamabodhini Patrika* reported that after helping with the exhibition of the material she had collected, Kadambini would stay on in the US and seek to obtain an American medical degree. Wishing her all success, the magazine urged her to work towards 'uniting the sisters of the New World with those of India'.[158] Once she was in London, however, Kadambini seemed to have given up the idea of going to the US. She arranged for the exhibits she had collected to be transported safely to Chicago through the good offices of Princess Christiana and decided to seek a British medical qualification.[159]

Although residing in Maida Vale in London, Kadambini did not pursue any kind of training at the many famous hospitals and medical schools in London. Instead, she went for so-called 'triple qualification' (TQ) offered by the three medical corporations of Scotland—the Royal College of Physicians (Edinburgh), the Royal College of Surgeons (Edinburgh), and the Faculty of Physicians and Surgeons (the predecessor of the Royal College of Physicians and Surgeons) of Glasgow. Envisaged as a three-year course, the TQ had been offered from 1884 as an alternative to medical study at universities and was open to women from its inception.[160] The candidates could study at any recognized hospital or at an 'extra-mural' medical school and were examined by a conjoint board of the three Royal Colleges at the end of the first, second, and third years. If the candidate already had a medical degree from abroad, then the only requirement was for one year's clinical training at a British hospital.[161] The latter was rarely waived but Kadambini seems to have been given an exemption. Nor, it seems, did she appear for the three scheduled examinations.[162] No official record is available that explains these waivers but one assumes that training in the Calcutta Medical College was accepted as equivalent to that in a British hospital. Passing her final examination on her birthday (18 July 1893) she returned to Calcutta forthwith.[163]

A Licentiateship of the three Royal Colleges was an impeccably Western qualification, although not the most prestigious. Crucially, however, no other woman doctor of Calcutta could boast of anything similar, let alone higher.[164] 'Foreign-returned' Kadambini applied for a job at the Dufferin Hospital for Women in Calcutta and although she was turned down for it—no doubt for racial reasons—she was appointed to be in charge of the outpatients' department at the Eden Hospital and she also gave lectures on midwifery and gynaecology at the Campbell Medical School.[165] But she soon seemed to have tired of these jobs and gave them up for full-time private practice.[166] She attracted many prosperous patients, including the Queen Mother of the Kingdom of Nepal, and practised literally until the last day of her life. Details of her practice, again, are unavailable and one does not know if she still had to concentrate on obstetrics. Even if she did, it is likely that her new status would have prevented her from being treated as an 'unclean' midwife.[167]

What, however, of Kadambini's private life? On the whole, she seems to have been fairly successful in maintaining what we would call a work–life balance but it was never very easy. Her marriage to

Dwarakanath had been deeply controversial, even to radical Brahmos. Dwarakanath was pushing forty at the time, while Kadambini was barely twenty-one. Many felt that he had taken unfair advantage of a devoted former student. Kadambini, it was rumoured, had several well-placed suitors who were deeply disappointed by her choice and fomented much opposition, nearly causing, remarked a leading newspaper, 'another schism in the continually divided Brahmo community'.[168] It is not known whether Kadambini's father Brajakishore, who died in 1885, approved of the match and whether he was at his daughter's wedding. But we do know that some of Dwarakanath's closest friends and radical allies—Sivanath Sastri, Anandamohan Bose, Durgamohan Das—did not attend.[169] Reportedly, however, there were many European guests—although we do not know their identities—and the religious service was conducted by Ramkumar Vidyaratna, whose fascinating life and labours will feature in the next chapter.[170] Despite the concerns of friends and foes, however, the marriage turned out to be very successful and the couple not only stayed together but had eight children.[171]

Dwarakanath was as committed to his wife's independence as he was to the emancipation of all women. He supported Kadambini consistently and strongly in all her professional endeavours, including the trip to Britain. The latter must have caused much anxiety, since the couple's children were still very young—the youngest (Prabhatchandra, 1889–1973) was barely three years old—and had to be left with Kadambini's mother. The decision could not have been taken lightly and Kadambini had to pay an emotional price for it. When she returned, Prabhatchandra did not recognize who she was and refused to come near her, causing his mother to break down in tears.[172] But although traumatized by this incident, Kadambini was not a clingy or a sentimental mother. One acquaintance was surprised to find how bluntly she spoke to her children and Leela Majumdar recalled her as a stern, aloof woman whom children feared to approach.[173] Kadambini's step-granddaughter Punyalata Chakrabarti, who lived in the same house and saw much more of Kadambini than either of them, remembered her, however, as a woman of extraordinary charm, whose great courage and strength of character did not prevent her from keeping children 'entranced with witty, hilarious stories'.[174]

Punyalata Chakrabarti also observed that Kadambini was not a single-minded professional—she was as adept at cooking and the domestic arts as any housewife of her class. At the same time, she led a very busy professional life, dressing at the height of contemporary fashion and speaking English so fluently that one might imagine it was her mother tongue.[175] She never wasted a minute: travelling in horse-drawn carriages for consultations across Calcutta, she utilized the travelling time by making fine lace.[176] We shall never know how Kadambini Ganguli saw her own life and what she thought of her challenges, achievements, and aspirations, but there is no evidence that she experienced much of a conflict between her professional and domestic obligations or neglected either for the sake of the other.

The Conservative Assault

Not many Indian women entered the public sphere in the nineteenth century but the very fact that *any* did was sufficient to cause consternation among traditionalists. Would the literate woman still be a good wife and mother, wondered some, while others shuddered at the prospect of good Hindu women turning into licentious *memsahibs*.[177] Those fighting for women's education were ostracized, lampooned, threatened, and persecuted.[178] Inevitably, Kadambini and her husband were pulled into this maelstrom. In 1891, the conservative Bengali journal *Banganibasi* (not *Bangabasi*, as often claimed, but a rival seeking what a liberal newspaper of the time described as 'diseased popularity') abused the couple—and all Brahmos following in their footsteps—in the vilest terms but without actually naming them.[179] The paper is no longer available but one report of the ensuing libel trial noted that the piece, appearing on 17 April 1891, had described an unnamed man, fitting the description of Dwarakanath, who was the slave of his wife, a prostitute, 'and ... illumined by her light'.[180]

The summaries available in the *Report on Native Papers* do not include anything identical but the following passage from one of *Banganibasi*'s many tirades indicates the paper's stance on educated women and those who supported them:

> You [the British government] have introduced female education in our country in order to ruin us ... You make no distinction between respectable women and prostitutes; you place the *devi* (goddess) and the *rakshasi* (female demon) on an equal footing.... It was only the other day, on the occasion of the distribution of prizes to the girls of the Entally female school, that a prostitute was invited and

brought to witness the ceremony which was graced by the presence
of the wife of the Lieutenant-Governor. It is in this way that our
goddess-like Hindu girls are insulted at your places of instruction.
The prostitute whom we hate with all our heart, who is ostracised
from family and society alike, and with whom society hates to sit
on the same seat, is allowed by you to come to the school, and it is
thus that you insult our goddesses. This is the result of your
education![181]

The libellous piece on Kadambini and Dwarakanath is unlikely to
have been more temperate.

Dwarakanath Ganguli sued *Banganibasi* for libel at the Calcutta
Police Court before the Chief Presidency Magistrate. Two other prosecutions were started simultaneously by Sivanath Sastri (on behalf of
the Sadharan Brahmo Samaj) and by the physician Nilratan Sircar,
representing the Samaj's Calcutta congregation.[182] The paper pleaded
guilty to the Brahmo Samaj charges and Sastri and Sircar declared
themselves satisfied with the admission, possibly touched by the
defence counsel's admonition that Sastri, as a religious preacher,
should 'accept the apology and ... not show any vindictiveness by
pressing the charge'.[183] It was Dwarakanath Ganguli's libel suit that
was argued fully in court. The defence—conducted by Taraknath
Palit, a leading Bengali barrister—argued that the article had not
named anybody and if Dwarakanath and his wife 'chose to fit the cap
on themselves, the accused could only be sorry for it'.[184] The magistrate, however, decided otherwise; the proprietor of *Banganibasi*
Maheshchandra Pal was fined a hundred rupees and sent to prison
for six months while the publisher and printer were punished more
lightly.[185]

Banganibasi was not the only paper that attacked educated women
like Kadambini. On another occasion, an unidentified paper published a cartoon showing Kadambini Ganguli in men's clothes,
smoking a cigar. Dwarakanath Ganguli, never a man to take such
taunts lightly, is reported to have stomped over to the paper's office
with a cutting of the offending cartoon and, using his walking stick,
rammed the piece of paper into the editor's mouth until the man had
literally eaten his words.[186] Despite the virulent opposition from
mainstream Hindus, however, the reformers' job was, on the whole,
easier in Bengal, where their opponents could, with some justification, be dismissed as ignorant, bigoted, or simply incapable of
engaging with modernity. This was very different from the West,

where the forces of science and modernity were mobilized against women's education and reformers needed not only to combat traditionalists but also biologists, physicians, and psychologists who pronounced, with all the authority of modern science, that the laws of biology (including that of Darwinian evolution) made women unfit for higher study.[187] The situation would gradually change in Bengal too, but in Dwarakanath's lifetime, the modernist, 'scientific' opposition to women's education or emancipation was negligible.[188]

For all the objections of the opponents and the doubts and equivocations of the reformers themselves, the campaigns for educating women were far from unsuccessful. Initiatives to educate women at home—zenana education—not only continued but even gained in popularity at the end of the nineteenth century.[189] More surprisingly, even traditionalists started their own girls' schools where education was tempered by 'tradition'. In Calcutta, Hindus established the hugely popular Mahakali Pathshala in 1893, where students were taught only the basics of reading, writing, and arithmetic and schooled extensively in Hindu ideals of womanhood and religious rituals.[190] The Irish Hindu activist and devotee of Swami Vivekananda, Margaret Noble—known in Bengal as Sister Nivedita—started another school in 1898 mostly for adult women where, too, the curriculum was explicitly Hindu and the students were allowed to maintain *purdah*. In 1911, the Muslim reformer Begum Rokeya Sakhavat Husain (1880–1932), herself a Bengali and critical of purdah, established a school in Calcutta for Muslim girls where the language of instruction was Urdu and purdah was mandatory.[191]

Much more research needs to be done on these orthodox attempts to tame modernity, but it is clear that they could not entirely do without Brahmo skills and resources. Much of the teaching at Nivedita's staunchly Hindu school, for instance, was done by Labanyaprabha Bose, a Brahmo alumna of Bethune College and sister of the scientist Jagadischandra Bose. Brahmo girls fluent in English were employed as interpreters in Nivedita's own classes.[192] And Rokeya Sakhavat Husain, before starting her conservative Muslim school for girls, personally visited Brahmo institutions for pedagogical and administrative guidance.[193] William Adam, if he had come back in the early twentieth century to write another of his reports, would have been amazed at the change that had occurred in the six decades since his earlier investigations and he would surely have commended the Brahmos for their role in this transformation.

A New Patriarchy?

The emergence of a broad consensus on the legitimacy of educating
girls did not, however, lead to any widespread recognition of women's
right to lead their lives in their own way. This has often been blamed
on the fact that the reformers were all men, and women were the
objects of reform, not its agents.[194] In the words of Himani Bannerji,
Hindu progressive males of the nineteenth century 'took on the role
of Pygmalion and sought to fashion for themselves a Galatea'.[195] For
Ghulam Murshid, the male activists who fought for women's emancipation did so only in order 'to exploit them further'.[196] The 'new
woman' of nineteenth-century Bengal, Partha Chatterjee has suggested in a more sophisticated argument, was 'subjected to a *new
patriarchy*' that, while opposing many gender norms of Hindu society,
continued to uphold the social authority of husbands over their wives
and of the 'new men' over the 'new women'.[197]

Certainly, the project for emancipating women was designed, in
many ways, to serve male interests. In *Stree-Siksha Bidhayak* (1822),
the first Bengali treatise supporting women's education, Gourmohan
Vidyalankar, a Sanskrit *pandit* working for the Calcutta School Society
and the Calcutta School Book Society, argued with a host of examples
from classic Sanskrit texts that it was essential to educate women
because illiterate girls were no good as wives or mothers.[198] Akshay
Datta's influential autobiographical account from the 1850s of the torments of educated men married to illiterate wives is well known and
in the 1860s, the reformer Sasipada Banerji personally educated his
unlettered wife Rajkumari because he was convinced that 'either he
must help her up or himself go down to her level'.[199] Barrister
Manamohan Ghosh, after marrying a 'normal' (that is, uneducated)
Hindu girl, sent her to the Loreto Convent in Calcutta—a Catholic
missionary institution—and agreed to live with her only after her education had been completed.[200] At least one goal of the reformers, as
Dipesh Chakrabarty has argued, was to transform the Hindu woman
into a modern version of Lakshmi, the goddess of prosperity and the
ideal-type of the good wife.[201]

But it was not just a Hindu aspiration. Mary Carpenter, who had
herself been given a boy's education by her Unitarian father and who
had met Rammohan Roy in her youth, remarked that the purpose of
women's education in India was to produce 'fit and useful helpmates'
for men.[202] The Bishop of Calcutta urged that women 'ought to receive

feminine training' and the *Indian Christian Herald* declared that 'India wants her ... daughters to be *daughters* and *not* sons'.[203] Nor was this concern with domesticity a purely Indian affair. Judith Walsh has shown how 'bourgeois, European ideas on home and family life' were 'naturalized in this period as a transnational, hegemonic discourse on domestic life'. This 'global domesticity' was as evident in 'prescriptive domestic literatures from England and America' as in those from India.[204] The new Indian home, in other words, was not an actualization of Partha Chatterjee's 'inner' domain presided over by Dipesh Chakrabarty's *grihalakshmi* but a transnational construct that was anything but isolated from global currents.

But just as 'feminine training' was the fundamental aspiration for some supporters of women's education and emancipation, a stress on domesticity could also be strategic. Ideological critiques of the male reformers of nineteenth-century Bengal often overlook their social context. Before the cause of women's education could prosper, Hindus had to be convinced that the educated woman was not only at no risk of widowhood but was the perfect housewife and ideal companion. Thanks to the widespread custom of child marriage, helped along by the kulin Brahmin practice of an aged man marrying multiple young women, one in three Hindu women in the 1890s was a widow and in 1931, one in four.[205] The Hindu widow had never been integrated into mainstream Bengali society, in spite of Vidyasagar's hard-won Widow Remarriage Act of 1856, and her life was almost unimaginably hard, joyless, and marginal.[206] Ordinary parents would never want to educate their daughters if they even suspected it of increasing the potential for widowhood or that for memsahib-like behaviour. Small wonder, then, that so many reformers and quite a few New Women themselves constantly stressed the domestic happiness resulting from women's education and criticized any perceived lack of domestic skills among educated women.[207]

Much more importantly, not all reformers equated women's emancipation with the construction of perfect housewives. As Sivanath Sastri declared, 'to deny woman the blessings of education and the chance of using her faculties for the furtherance of general good ... goes against the will of God and contravenes the Divine purpose'.[208] The views of Dwarakanath Ganguli were even more radical. Malavika Karlekar has argued that Dwarakanath did not wish to 'challenge the basic tenets of feminine socialization' but simply to create 'the modern, enlightened helpmate'.[209] To be sure, Dwarakanath's ideal of the

emancipated woman could not fully satisfy twenty-first century progressive tastes. His novel *Suruchir Kutir* is, among other things, a
paean to modern domesticity and companionate marriage. The heroine Suruchi is educated and emancipated—she founds and runs several businesses—but she is also the perfect (though far from
subservient) spouse, mother, and housewife.

But it is not at all clear that Dwarakanath regarded conjugality
and domesticity as *more* important than education, rationality, or
moral autonomy. In an essay in *Abalabandhab*, he criticized the
emerging trend of giving girls some education simply to improve
their marital prospects. He wrote,

> Married women are learning to read and write in order to please
> their husbands and to win their love. Unmarried girls are educating
> themselves in the hope of finding good husbands, of living well.
> They are also eager to find recognition in society. None of these
> aspirations deserve to be summarily condemned, but *they are cer-
> tainly not indicative of genuine humanity ... the moment they enter the
> mind, they produce a meretricious glitter that obscures the beautiful, the
> sweet and the universal.* The glitter, it is true, dazzles many but I have
> seen enough to realize that it impoverishes national life.[210]

Education, he added, was real only when it inculcated rationality,
sympathy, morality, social responsibility, and humanity. Such qualities, he acknowledged, were only too rare among men but the deficiencies of one sex, he commented, need not be emulated by the
other.[211] Dwarakanath also condemned prevalent Hindu notions of
female devotion to husbands (*satitva*). Urging women not to give up
their personal autonomy, he called upon them to be equals of men,
showing the world that the strength and potential of women were no
less than those of men.[212] In yet another essay, he declared that the
lives of women would change only when society was forced to allow
women to act on their own and think independently on all issues.[213]
These are scarcely the sentiments of a patriarch, whether old or new.

Dwarakanath, in fact, *opposed* those reformers who preferred
women to be guided by men towards a slow and gradual emancipation. Umeshchandra Datta, the editor of *Bamabodhini Patrika*, was
such a gradualist and argued that too much liberty for women might
produce injurious social consequences and encourage immorality.
When this argument was ridiculed in Dwarakanath's *Abalabandhab*,
Bamabodhini hit back by arguing that the women of India were still,

like children, 'under our guardianship'. Just as one harmed children if one freed them from parental supervision too early, Indian women would be harmed if emancipation were to be thrust upon them before they were strong enough to cope with it. The relations between the two editors, hitherto fairly cordial, soured permanently after this spat.[214] It is worth recalling, too, that in an 1879 lecture, Dwarakanath had asserted that since 'the capabilities of women have not yet been sufficiently tested to determine their aptitude or disability in the pursuit of any particular subject, no limit can at the present state of their progress be set beyond which they are not to proceed'. Although he was all for women being 'trained to perform all the domestic duties', he wanted the Brahmo Samaj to champion ways of educating women so that 'they may earn *an independent livelihood*, in order to mitigate many of their miseries and ills incident on a life of destitution'.[215]

The education that Dwarakanath worked so hard to provide to women might not seem to have been of revolutionary potential but as Tanika Sarkar has remarked, education, in the long run, was no 'liberal mirage' but the foundation for 'an authentic, autonomous female selfhood'.[216] Or, as Judith Walsh has put it more pithily, 'ultimately, what women learned when men gave them advice was this: they learned to read' and to use their literacy 'to open their own explorations of agency and self-identity'.[217] By the 1920s, as Mrinalini Sinha has demonstrated, Indian middle-class women formed a distinct constituency of their own; they (or, at least, some of them) were now the agents as well as the objects of their reform.[218] While no single individual, of course, can be credited with that change and although Indian women, even today, do not possess an adequate degree of social power, none, arguably, worked harder than Dwarakanath Ganguli to arm women with the basic tool to undermine the patriarchy: education.

Imagining Utopia

Dwarakanath's campaign for women's education was not just a pedagogical project. It was the central strand of a comprehensive programme for national regeneration. His only substantial work of fiction, the two-volume didactic novel *Suruchir Kutir* (Suruchi's Cottage, 1880–4), gives us a detailed picture of the utopia he was working towards.[219] Meredith Borthwick called it 'an archetypal middle-class moralistic novel', but while it is certainly that, it is indispensable for understanding the man and the breadth of his reformist vision.[220]

Published in the 'Mary Carpenter Series' of books designed for use in zenana teaching, *Suruchir Kutir* was dedicated to Dwarakanath's daughter (and Upendrakishore's wife) Bidhumukhi and promised to teach its readers how to lead 'a comfortable and philanthropic life on a low income'.[221] The reviewer for the *Brahmo Public Opinion* described it as 'an attempt to impress on the Bengali mind the necessity and advantages of thrift' and today's reader may well be surprised by Dwarakanath's relentless stress on everyday economics and the importance of saving.[222] At the time, however, thrift was an issue of huge importance for reformers across the world. From the late eighteenth century, governments and reformers in Europe had sought to create 'prudent, self-reliant citizens', encouraging poorer people to acquire the saving habit. Banks and institutions offering 'safety, convenience, and attractive interest rates' to ordinary savers, including children, were established. Frugality and thrift, along with discipline, industriousness, and orderliness, came to be regarded as cardinal virtues by the European middle classes.[223] Perhaps the greatest publicist for those virtues was Samuel Smiles (1812–1904), the bestselling author of *Self-Help* (1859) and *Thrift* (1875).[224]

That global trend was no less marked in colonial India, even though the majority of ordinary Indians did not have access to savings bank facilities until the establishment of Post Office banks in 1882.[225] Thrift became a major subject of didactic literature in the later nineteenth century, both among Hindus and Muslims. Middle-class incomes in India could rarely ensure a proper bourgeois lifestyle; education, especially good education, was costly and even the best-educated men could have trouble generating enough income to live respectably.[226] Much of the burden of maintaining a bourgeois lifestyle, needless to say, fell on women and, consequently, nineteenth-century thrift literature was largely about women as well as addressed to them.[227] *Suruchir Kutir* was no exception. Thrift, for Dwarakanath, was not simply a matter of being careful with money but central to a whole constellation of bourgeois virtues and although the name of Samuel Smiles was not mentioned in *Suruchir Kutir*, the novel was imbued with the Smilesian conviction that hard work not only brought wealth but built character and by forming the moral, upstanding individual, improved society at large. In Smiles's Victorian utopia, there was as little room for idle aristocrats as for dole-seeking paupers and Dwarakanath's ideal society was no different.

The narrative of *Suruchir Kutir* commences in 1860. After his father dies and the family's meagre possessions are confiscated by creditors, the sixteen-year-old Mymensingh boy Sureshchandra Ghosh moves to Calcutta with just two rupees in his pocket. His hopes of finding work in the big city are disappointed and he finally finds shelter at a Brahmo students' mess. One of the inmates finds Suresh a tutoring job and the ambitious young man resumes his own studies. After passing his entrance examination in the first division, Suresh, like most other Bengalis of his station, takes up a clerical job at a British firm but instead of reconciling himself to a life of genteel poverty, saves a part of his salary every month. After eight years of work, he possesses five thousand rupees and begins to lend money out on interest, like many Indians of his time.[228]

We then meet the heroine Suruchi, the only daughter of Iswarchandra Bhattacharya, a *vansaja* Brahmin of Kalighat. Being lower in status than kulin Brahmins, vansaja parents usually sought to marry their daughters to kulins and vansaja men often had to pay for the hand of a girl belonging to their own order.[229] When Suruchi is three, her father marries her off to a man of forty for a bride-price of five hundred rupees. The groom dies within a year from tuberculosis; Suruchi returns home to her repentant parents, who both die by the time their daughter is twelve. The family's doctor Dharmadas Basu, a progressive and philanthropic soul—his Brahmo identity is hinted at but not confirmed—then welcomes Suruchi into his home and brings her up with his own daughters.

Since she starts her education relatively late in life, Suruchi is considered unsuited for conventional 'academic' studies and learns Bengali, some arithmetic, English, domestic science, hygiene, basic home medicine, and nursing. She reads English works on thrifty living, learns sewing from an old tailor, and is soon making clothes for the entire family.[230] When Suruchi is old enough for marriage, her foster father begins to invite various Brahmo young men regularly. Suresh—who has come to be known as Brahmo by associating with Brahmos and has refused to marry a twelve-year-old widow because she was too young—is one of them and eventually, the two are drawn to each other, especially after Suruchi declares that she would never do his bidding unless her own conscience approved of the action.[231] They have a simple wedding (much to the disappointment of friends who expected a grand feast) and Suruchi advises Suresh to lend out the saved money on interest.[232] Suruchi redecorates the old house that Suresh has bought, displaying all her innate refinement—in Bengali, *suruchi* means good taste—and proves to be an excellent housewife. She cooks twice a day, grows her own vegetables in a tiny garden and buys a cow, not only for the milk but because the animal would consume food waste.[233]

So far, Suruchi fits the *grihalakshmi* ideal that, according to Dipesh Chakrabarty, the Bengali New Woman was enjoined to emulate.[234] But Suruchi is much more than that. True, she does not go out to work but she *creates* businesses and institutions from home, extending her domestic management skills into areas having little to do with conventional domesticity. Suruchi challenges the presumption—widely shared by middle-class Bengalis of her time as well as by many of their recent historians—that the only work that counts is office work. Having discovered that the neighbourhood women had little productive work through the day, Suruchi teaches them to sew and starts a sewing cooperative that makes substantial money by selling its products. The portrayal of Suruchi's business activities suggests how the bourgeois imagination of nineteenth-century Bengal was not entirely incapable of harnessing nascent capitalism in innovative, even unexpected ways. Throughout the novel, moreover, middle-class characters show none of the characteristic Bengali bourgeois disdain for working with their hands and here, Dwarakanath's social philosophy is identical to his son-in-law Upendrakishore's, revealing the same aspiration to enlarge middle-class lives, attitudes, and incomes by embracing manual labour. But this positive attitude had its own limits—it was not just any form of manual work that was celebrated but only the more artisanal kind requiring technical dexterity, imagination, and, ideally, an aesthetic instinct.

Suruchi, unsurprisingly, is a thrifty businesswoman. She keeps a quarter of the profits from her business and distributes the rest among her associates, which they deposit with Suruchi in a bank-like arrangement.[235] Here, Dwarakanath may have been paying tribute to Sasipada Banerji, whose many efforts to improve the lives of the working classes in the industrial suburb of Baranagar included teaching them to weave in their spare time and to save their additional income in a savings bank that he persuaded the government to set up in 1871.[236] (It is worth pointing out in this context that despite much talk about the benefits of the cooperative principle by Indian nationalists and government officials, the colonial state was to introduce legislation for cooperative credit societies—analogous to the friendly societies of Britain—only in 1904.)[237] Suresh then starts a school for the men, encourages them to start saving and offers to hold their savings as deposits. Soon, many of the men have enough to buy their own buggies and horses.[238] Within three years, the residents buy up the entire land of their neighbourhood and dividing it among themselves, establish a colony with proper drains, toilets, streets, gardens, a library for men, and a library for women, recreation clubs and even a press, run entirely by women and printing only morally worthy works.[239]

A school is founded for the children as well as a savings bank where the parents pay in small sums for each child and the deposits reinvested so that each child would have a substantial sum to its name upon reaching adulthood. Suruchi and Suresh contribute substantial sums for each of these projects but never the full cost. The new institutions are not philanthropic gifts but built with the resources of the entire community and managed by themselves. The library or the press are financed by subscriptions from every resident of the neighbourhood and the press is run by the women of the community, who do everything from composing type to operating the press. Profits are shared equitably and workers receive productivity-related bonuses. The thorough and lasting improvement of society, it is implied, can occur only when entire communities are involved with the endeavour and have literal ownership of it: 'Suruchi's excellent system, if instituted across all of India, could produce tremendous benefit,' reflects the narrator.[240]

Suruchi and Suresh eventually have five children—three sons and two daughters. The education of children is one of the major themes of the novel and the narrative is held up by long disquisitions—some of them taken word for word from essays in *Abalabandhab*—on the deficiencies of conventional pedagogy and the right way to prepare children for life.[241] Suruchi refuses to send her children to school at a young age and teaches them at home, following the principles of Friedrich Froebel (1782–1852), the founder of kindergarten education. Dwarakanath himself was a great admirer of Froebel and wrote two long and appreciative articles on his pedagogical ideas for *Abalabandhab* in 1878.[242] Again, there may have been a link here with Sasipada Banerji, who, on a trip to England, had been so impressed by the Froebel system that he had set up a kindergarten in 1873 at Baranagar. It is far from unlikely that Dwarakanath, who is known to have visited Baranagar several times to lecture at a night school for labourers set up by Banerji, had heard of Froebel from him.[243]

Froebel's fundamental pedagogical principle, diametrically opposed to conventional ideas of primary education in the nineteenth century, was to use 'children's constant activity and interaction with the physical world' to awaken their minds. As Norman Brosterman has summed up, play was 'the engine that propelled the [kindergarten] system' and the goal was to create a child who was sensitive, curious, imaginative, and able to integrate diverse kinds of knowledge and experience into a life that was 'unified and supple'.[244] The idea of following the child's natural inclinations was taken up by Dwarakanath but often interpreted too liberally. Even the fondness of the child for sweet things, he insisted in *Suruchir Kutir* as well as in articles in *Abalabandhab*, should not be discouraged. As physiologists had shown, sugar was a source of energy and children craved sugar because they needed more energy than grown-ups.[245] Similarly, parents should not try to curb children's natural restlessness. Enforced inactivity was pernicious for development, and the ordinary play of children, Dwarakanath argued, was far more beneficial than the supervised games and gymnastics that were beginning to be introduced in schools. Suruchi sends her children to the maidan in Central Calcutta every day to play unsupervised.[246] She countermands none of their legitimate desires but firmly resists any effort by the children to wheedle something out of her by crying.[247] Morals and religion are taught by example rather than precept. The probity and decency with which Suresh and Suruchi lead their lives are considered to be the best lessons for the children, but they are also taught to perform daily worship (*upasana*) and place their complete faith in God.[248]

As soon as they are a little older, Suruchi and Suresh push their children beyond the conventional boundaries of the Bengali middle classes. One son, Ramesh, learns carpentry and ironwork, while another, Jogesh, becomes interested in chemistry and then in the dyeing industry.[249] The two daughters, Surama and Sushama—named, one assumes, after the daughters of Dwarakanath's friend Ramkumar Vidyaratna—are first taught at home (cookery and domestic management are not neglected) and then sent to a small, informal school run by an educated Englishwoman.[250] Sushama reveals a bent for science and eventually goes off to study medicine with a medical missionary in north-western India since, the narrator pointedly adds, no medical school in India was willing to admit women. Surama marries a rich man of dubious character, leaves him soon but returns to nurse him when he is terminally ill. The repentant husband dies leaving all his money to her, which she uses to build a clinic for her doctor sister and to finance the Brahmo proselytizing campaigns of Sushama's husband Mahananda.[251]

As a novel, *Suruchir Kutir* is unlikely to find many readers today. Although the prose is supple enough, the tone is heavily didactic and the plot no more than a vehicle—at times, a rather insubstantial vehicle—for its many social, moral, and economic messages. Although many would be tempted to describe it as a profoundly Victorian screed, the novel was in fact very Indian in addressing a society that lacked Victorian England's industrial capitalism. The ideal society of the novel was based on a cooperative model utilizing whatever modern resources were available in colonial Bengal— printing, chemistry, modern medicine, Froebelian education—and evolved home-grown versions (such as domestic savings banks) of modern institutions that did not yet exist in colonial India. But the success of this social project depended, ultimately, on human beings and the novel emphasized the need for new kinds of pedagogy, family life, and what one may call 'life-management' to ensure that the citizens of the future, regardless of their gender, were diligent, morally upright, thrifty, rational, cosmopolitan, and socially responsible. That Dwarakanath's characters also ended up wealthy was a welcome by-product of their exertions and provided resources for fresh initiatives, but it was never the fundamental purpose or objective of their lives.

Although obviously influenced by Victorian British and other contemporary currents of reformist thought, *Suruchir Kutir* did not seek to turn Bengal into a miniature version of England. One is startled to discover, for instance, that the community institutions of Suruchi's neighbourhood are not gender-blind. The library has separate reading rooms for men and women and the press has no male staff. Even more strikingly, Suresh warns emancipated Bengali women to be more discriminating in their socializing than their British sisters. Any association with disreputable people, he believes, would give the New Woman an undeservedly bad reputation in the hidebound society of Bengal. 'Mindless imitation [of the West],' he warns, 'can cause immense harm.'[252] These are not just the views of a fictional character. In an essay in *Abalabandhab*, Dwarakanath himself had written that it was vital for India's women to free themselves from their domestic prisons but they must not endanger their reputation by associating with immoral people or with those hypocritical men who had a salacious interest in meeting emancipated women but who would not dream of allowing the women of their own families out of seclusion.[253] These concerns would seem quaint today and might even suggest an uncharacteristic loss of nerve. During a period when the New Woman was being vilified in countless commentaries, novels and farces as no better than a whore, the warning was not, however, inappropriate. Emancipated women, Dwarakanath Ganguli knew only too well, would lose whatever support they had in bhadralok society if they appeared to substantiate the conservative equation of emancipation with immorality. The contradiction, if there was one, was between the emancipatory project and its social context, rather than within the former alone.

Notes

1. Geraldine Forbes, *Women in Modern India* (Cambridge: Cambridge University Press, 1996), 30. India, as a well-known song by Dwarakanath Ganguli asserted, would never be regenerated until its women awoke: 'Na jagiley saba Bharata-lalana, e Bharat aar jagey na, jagey na.' See his anonymously published *National Song Book: Jatiya Sangeet* (Calcutta: G.P. Roy, 1876), 40–1. Another song, 'Smariley purber katha, asrujoley ankhi bhasey', lamented the decline of Hindu women from their high social position in ancient times and called on the moderns to dedicate themselves to reviving that lost glory. See Durgadas Lahiri, ed., *Bangalir Gaan* (Calcutta: Natabar Chakravarti, 1905), 908. On the unjustifiable glorification of ancient Indian gender relations and the concurrent condemnation of Muslim influence, see Sumit Sarkar, *Modern Times: India, 1880s–1950s—Environment, Economy, Culture* (Ranikhet: Permanent Black, 2014), 352.

2. On the surprising degree of freedom enjoyed by women in Bombay, see Mary Carpenter, *Six Months in India*, 2 vols (London: Longmans, Green, 1868), 1: 20; and Mary Carpenter, *Letters to the Rt Hon the Marquis of Salisbury, Secretary of State for India, on Female Education in India, Prison Discipline, and the Necessity for a Factory Act in India, being a Report of her Fourth Journey to India in 1875–76* (Bristol: Arrowsmith, 1877), 9; and Bipinchandra Pal, *Memories of My Life and Times* (Calcutta: Bipinchandra Pal Institute, 1973), 318. Many Brahmos explained the freedom of women in Bombay as a consequence

of relatively light Muslim influence. See, for instance, Sitanath Tattvabhushan, *Social Reform in Bengal: A Side Sketch* (Calcutta: City Book Society, 1904), viii.

3. Although she had been taunted by an occasional passer-by when going to school in Bombay, Joshi found the treatment she received in Bengal to be much worse. See Meera Kosambi, 'Anandibai Joshee: Retrieving a Fragmented Feminist Image', *Economic and Political Weekly*, 7 December 1996, 3189–97, at 3190 and 3194.

4. Dagmar Engels, *Beyond Purdah? Women in Bengal 1890–1939* (Delhi: Oxford University Press, 1996), 19–20. Meredith Borthwick points out that the zenana was a complex, closed world in which women exerted considerable social power not only over themselves but also over their husbands, male relatives, and the family as a whole. It is also worth remembering that most middle-class British and American women of the period, although not formally secluded, also spent much of their time in female company. See Meredith Borthwick, *The Changing Role of Women in Bengal, 1849–1905* (Princeton: Princeton University Press, 1984), 25, 34–5, 148–9.

5. It was Brahmo women who changed this. They introduced a hybrid dress, the bottom half of which was derived from the European gown and the upper portion from the Indian sari and subsequently, Gyanadanandini Devi, then in Bombay with her civil servant husband Satyendranath Tagore, proposed a style of draping the sari that was inspired by western Indian (especially Parsi) styles and came to be known as the *Brahmika* style. See Borthwick, *Changing Role of Women in Bengal*, (Princeton: Princeton University Press, 1984), 248–50, 254–5; and Prabhatchandra Gangopadhyay, *Banglar Nari-Jagaran* (Calcutta: Sadharan Brahmo Samaj, 1997), 71–2. For the Foucauldian argument that these sartorial reforms constituted a new 'textile prison, fashioned by male tailors and fathers of Bengal's social reform', see Himani Bannerji, *Inventing Subjects: Studies in Hegemony, Patriarchy and Colonialism* (London: Anthem Press, 2001), 99–134, especially 129–30.

6. During the 1830s, the Unitarian minister William Adam had gloomily noted that 'early marriages, juvenile widowhood, the interdiction of second marriages, and consequent vice and degradation' were the biggest obstacles to the amelioration of women's lives. See William Adam, *Reports on the State of Education in Bengal (1835 and 1838)*, edited by Anathnath Basu (Calcutta: University of Calcutta, 1941), 452.

7. Except for the daughters of some zamindars (who were given some education so that they could look after the family estates if widowed) and many ordinary women of the socially marginal Vaishnava community (who were expected to read the scriptures by themselves), Bengali women were largely illiterate. See Adam, *Reports*, 187–8. On the marginality of the Vaishnavas, see Tattvabhushan, *Social Reform in Bengal*, 39–40.

8. See Borthwick, *Changing Role of Women in Bengal*, 85. This link with heterodoxy was prominent in other parts of India too—in Madras, the

Theosophical Society pushed for women's education while in the Punjab, it was the Arya Samajists. See Forbes, *Women in Modern India*, 44.

9. Borthwick, *Changing Role of Women in Bengal*, 288. The few instances of women leading Brahmo prayers are detailed in P. Gangopadhyay, *Banglar Nari-Jagaran*, 78–9.

10. Sumit Sarkar, 'The "Women's Question" in Nineteenth-Century Bengal', in *Women and Culture*, edited by Kumkum Sangari and Sudesh Vaid (Bombay: SNDT Women's University Research Centre for Women's Studies, 1985), 157–72, at 163–5.

11. See Sivanath Sastri, *History of the Brahmo Samaj* [1911–12], 2nd edn, 2 vols in 1 (Calcutta: Sadharan Brahmo Samaj, 1974), 358.

12. Sastri, *History of the Brahmo Samaj*, 546.

13. On Sen's suggestion, Mary Carpenter set up an organization in Britain to promote the regeneration of India and to ensure better communication between Indian and British reformers. Commencing as the Bristol Indian Association in 1870, it eventually grew into the National Indian Association in Aid of Social Progress. Although established as a forum for reformers, it eventually became little more than an information bureau for Indian visitors to Britain, especially students. See 'The First Annual Report of the National Indian Association' (Bristol: Arrowsmith, 1871) [bound with *Journal of the Indian Association*, 1 (1871), British Library ST 182]; Norman C. Sargant, *Mary Carpenter in India* (Bristol: A.J. Sargant, 1987), 100–1, 105–13; and J. Estlin Carpenter, *The Life and Work of Mary Carpenter* (London: Macmillan, 1881), 298–9.

14. Charles H. Heimsath, *Indian Nationalism and Hindu Social Reform* (Princeton: Princeton University Press, 1964), 91; Sargant, *Mary Carpenter in India*, 74–6, 105; and the 'Annual Report of the Indian Reform Association, 1870–71', in Prosanto Kumar Sen, *Biography of a New Faith*, 2 vols (Calcutta: Thacker, Spink, 1950–1954), 2: 277–84.

15. P.K. Sen, *Biography of a New Faith*, 2: 290–2; and Sivanath Sastri, *Atmacharit*, edited by Gautam Neogy (Calcutta: Sadharan Brahmo Samaj, 1982), 471–6. For a sharp critique of the male domination of the Bama Hitaisini Sabha and a call for women to conduct their own activities without advice from men, see the unsigned essay (almost certainly by the editor Dwarakanath Ganguli) 'Narisamaj o Bratabidhi', in *Abalabandhab*, new ser., 1, no. 8 (Jaistha 1286/May 1879): 53–7, at 53–4.

16. Sen persuaded a dozen well-known doctors to declare that a girl younger than fourteen was not physiologically ready for marriage, and presented this evidence to the government. For the medical evidence—some of which was quasi-eugenic, arguing that the children of child-mothers tended to be weak and biologically deficient—see 'Annual Report of the Indian Reform Association, 1870–71', in P.K. Sen, *Biography of a New Faith*, 2: 310, 319, 321–2.

After much lobbying by Sen and many revisions, the Native Marriage Act or Act III went on in the statute books in 1872, stipulating 14 as the minimum marriageable age for girls and 18 for boys, forbidding polygamy, and legalizing inter-caste marriage and divorce, both impossible in a traditional Hindu marriage. Those wishing to marry under the Act had to declare, however, that they did not profess Hinduism or *any* other recognized faith, a requirement that offended even some radical Brahmos. See 'Brahmo Marriages: Their History and Statistics', in *The Brahmo Year-Book for 1879*, edited by Sophia Dobson Collet (London: Williams and Norgate, 1879), 36–9; Nandini Chatterjee, 'English Law, Brahmo Marriage, and the Problem of Religious Difference: Civil Marriage Laws in Britain and India', *Comparative Studies in Society and History*, 52 (2010): 524–52; and Jogananda Das, 'The Brahmo Samaj', in *Studies in the Bengal Renaissance*, edited by Atulchandra Gupta (Calcutta: National Council of Education-Bengal, 1958), 479–508, at 494–5.

17.   Not only was Suniti underage by Brahmo criteria but the marriage ceremony itself did not follow Brahmo rites. See Collet, *Brahmo Year-Book for 1878*, 31–4; Sastri, *Atmacharit*, 162–4, 189–91, 205–19, 495–500, 518–27. Once Suniti's engagement was announced, the radicals rose in furious protest, publishing two new weekly journals—the *Brahmo Public Opinion* in English and a Bengali paper called *Samalochak*—to challenge Sen's actions. Funded by the wealthy, socially radical barristers Durgamohan Das and Anandamohan Bose, *Samalochak* was first edited by Sivanath Sastri, but his style was found to be too mild and he was replaced as editor by the fiery Dwarakanath Ganguli. See Sastri, *History of the Brahmo Samaj*, 177. On Anandamohan Bose, who played major roles in virtually every radical or nationalist initiative of the time, see Sastri, *History of the Brahmo Samaj*, 277–8 and Hemchandra Sarkar, *A Life of Anandamohan Bose* (Calcutta: A.C. Sarkar, 1910), xii.

18.   Meredith Borthwick, *Keshub Chunder Sen: A Search for Cultural Synthesis* (Calcutta: Minerva, 1977), 153–4.

19.   Collet, *Brahmo Year-Book for 1878*, 78.

20.   B. Pal, *Memories of My Life*, 277. This stance was influenced greatly by the radical egalitarianism of the American Unitarian Theodore Parker, whose call for 'the harmonious development of all the faculties of our manhood' had influenced many Brahmos. See Sastri, *History of the Brahmo Samaj*, 288; and David Kopf, 'The Brahmo Idea of Social Reform and the Problem of Female Emancipation in Bengal', in *Bengal in the Nineteenth and Twentieth Centuries*, edited by John R. McLane (East Lansing, Michigan: Asian Studies Center, Michigan State University, 1975), 35–58, at 38–41. The lawyer Durgamohan Das (1838–1897) and his wife Brahmamoyee (1845–1876), for instance, had almost converted to Christianity in their youth but desisted only after reading Parker's works. Fiercely radical in their later life, Das and his wife faced brutal social persecution in Barisal for arranging remarriages of several young

widows—most notably, that of Durgamohan's own widowed stepmother. See Dwarakanath Ganguli's anonymously published *Jibanalekhya: Srijukta Durgamohan Daser Paralokgata Sahadharmini Brahmamoyee-r Sankhhep Jiban Brittanta*, 2nd edn (Calcutta: B.M. Ghose, 1879), 6–13, 19–25; and for a description of the persecution faced by Das after arranging his stepmother's wedding, see Sivanath Sastri, *Ramtonu Lahiri o Tatkalin Bangasamaj* (1909; reprint, Calcutta: New Age, 1977), 297–8.

21.   Sastri, *Ramtonu Lahiri o Tatkalin Bangasamaj*, 302, 306.

22.   He was, of course, not alone in working for women's emancipation—several Brahmos of his time, including some of his associates, were sincerely devoted to the cause and often took great risks. See, for instance, the case of the kulin girl Bidhumukhi Mukhopadhayay who refused to marry an elderly groom with eleven wives and escaped to Calcutta with Brahmo assistance in 1870, in Collet, *Brahmo Year-Book for 1879*, 59–62.

23.   For an account of the kulin system by a Baptist missionary, see William Ward, *A View of the History, Literature, and Mythology of the Hindoos including a Minute Description of their Manners and Customs, and Translations from their Principal Works*, 3rd edn, 4 vols (London: Black, Kingsbury, Parbury and Allen, 1817–20), 3: 78–83.

24.   For the complex details of Ballal Sen's system and its subsequent modifications, see H.H. Risley, *The Tribes and Castes of Bengal: Ethnographic Glossary*, 2 vols (Calcutta: Bengal Secretariat Press, 1891), 1: 145–8.

25.   S.N. Mukherjee, 'Raja Rammohun Roy and the Status of Women in Bengal in the Nineteenth Century', in *Women in India and Nepal*, edited by Michael Allen and S.N. Mukherjee, 2nd edn (Delhi: Sterling, 1990), 155–78, at 159.

26.   Ward, *A View of the History*, 3: 82–3. Many indigenous reformers, including Iswarchandra Vidyasagar, had called for legislation against polygamy but to no avail. See Subalchandra Mitra, *Isvar Chandra Vidyasagar: A Story of his Life and Work* (Calcutta: New Bengal Press, 1902), 554–71; Asok Sen, *Iswar Chandra Vidyasagar and His Elusive Milestones* (Calcutta: Riddhi-India, 1977), 63–6; and Malavika Karlekar, 'Reflections on Kulin Polygamy: Nistarini Debi's *Sekeley Katha*', *Contributions to Indian Sociology* 29, nos 1–2 (1995): 135–55.

27.   Mahendranath Roy, *Srijukta Babu Akshaykumar Datter Jiban-Brittanta* (Calcutta: Sanskrita Yantra, 1885), 118–19.

28.   'Abar e Durmati Keno?', *Abalabandhab*, new ser. 1, no. 1 (Kartik 1285/ October 1878): 1–4, at 3; and Brajendranath Bandyopadhyay, *Dwarakanath Gangopadhyay* (Calcutta: Bangiya Sahitya Parishat, 1950), 9.

29.   Narayan Dutta, *Abalabandhab-Dwarakanath o Kadambini* (Calcutta: Karuna, 2006), 17–23. Another Brahmo activist, Sasipada Banerji (who would later suffer public humiliation for arranging the marriage of a widowed niece)

had experienced something similar when he was about nine years old. A child-widow related to him was beaten to death for having an affair and her death declared to be a suicide. Banerji's second wife, Girijakumari, was a widow and in 1887, he founded a widows' home and school, the first of its kind in India. See Kuladaprasad Mallik, *Nabajuger Sadhana*, 2nd edn (Calcutta: A.C. Sarkar, 1913), 334–5, 344–62, 374; Sitanath Tattvabhushan, *Indubala: A Domestic Picture* (Calcutta: A.C. Sarkar, 1908), 4; and Sunita Bandyopadhyay, *Brahmarsi Sasipada: Samoy, Samaj, Sadhana* (Calcutta: Dolphin/Dey's, 2007), 124.

30.   B. Bandyopadhyay, *Dwarakanath Gangopadhyay*, 9. Married and the father of a child while he was still a student, Datta had a difficult relationship with his wife and was to become a great critic of child-marriage and polygamy. See Swapan Basu, ed., *Akshaykumar Datta Rachana Sangraha* (Calcutta: Paschimbanga Bangla Akademi, 2008), 466–70, 474, 552–4, 639–46; Annapurna Biswas, *Akshaykumar Datta: Samaj, Bigyan o Dharmachinta* (Calcutta: Radical Impression, 1998); and Muhammad Saiful Islam, ed., *Akshaykumar Datta: The First Social Scientist in Bengal* (Calcutta: Renaissance, 2009).

31.   Nakurchandra Biswas, *Akshay-Charit* (Calcutta: Adi Brahmo Samaj, 1887), 39–40.

32.   Sumit Sarkar, *A Critique of Colonial India*, 76; M. Roy, *Srijukta Babu*, 82–9, 106–8; and Biswas, *Akshay-Charit*, 18–19. On the importance of Datta's scientific essays, see Buddhadev Bhattacharya, *Bangasahitye Bigyan: Bangla Bhasa o Sahitye Bigyancharchar Itihas* (Calcutta: Paschimbanga Bangla Akademi, 2004), 45–62.

33.   See *The Autobiography of Maharshi Devendranath Tagore*, translated by Satyendranath Tagore and Indira Devi (London: Macmillan, 1914), 71–2. In a letter to a close associate, Debendranath once fumed that his beloved *Tattvabodhini* had been taken over by 'a bunch of atheists'. See Priyanath Sastri, ed., *Maharsi Debendranather Patrabali* (Calcutta: Hitabadi Library, 1909), 10–11.

34.   For Dwarakanath's tribute, see 'Akshaykumar Datta', in *Nababarshiki* (Calcutta: Roy Press Depository, 1880), 185–91, at 189. See also Rajnarayan Basu, 'Bangala Bhasa o Sahitya Bisayak Baktrita' [1878], in *Rajnarayan Basu: Nirbachita Rachana Sangraha*, edited by Baridbaran Ghosh (Calcutta: Dey Book Store, 1995), 209–54, at 225; and Ar Cy Dae [Rameshchandra Datta], *The Literature of Bengal* (Calcutta: I.C. Bose, 1877), 172–3.

35.   Both are available in S. Basu, *Akshaykumar Datta*, 431–527 (*Dharmaneeti*) and 113–315 (*Sambandhabichar*). *Dharmaneeti*, which David Kopf described as 'the culmination of an ideological quest to apply his notion of natural law to ethics, with the end of harmonizing social relationships and promoting progress', was heavily influenced by the Scottish lawyer George Combe's

Moral Philosophy (1840) and other Western sources. See David Kopf, *The Brahmo Samaj and the Shaping of the Modern Indian Mind* (Princeton: Princeton University Press, 1979), 51–2.

36. Today, the *Constitution* is often taken to be a phrenological tract because its author was pre-eminent in popularizing phrenology, but in fact the *Constitution* was 'a philosophical treatise—a new secular scientistic bible of natural laws' and influenced many Victorian works including Samuel Smiles's 1859 bestseller *Self Help* (London: John Murray, 1859). See John van Wyhe, *Phrenology and the Origins of Victorian Scientific Naturalism* (Aldershot: Ashgate, 2004), 52–6 and 96–166. Datta had long been interested in phrenology but his version of Combe's *Constitution* contained even less on phrenology than the original. See M. Roy, *Srijukta Babu*, 28–9, 260–1; and S. Basu, *Akshaykumar Datta*, 34–41.

37. He also added appendices arguing for vegetarianism and temperance—Keshab Sen became a vegetarian after reading *Sambandhabichar* while Debendranath Tagore gave up drinking and started a gymnastics class in his mansion. See M. Roy, *Srijukta Babu*, 120–2. Interestingly, Datta himself was never a teetotaller and practised vegetarianism only when he was writing *Sambandhabichar*. See Biswas, *Akshay-Charit*, 51.

38. N. Dutta, *Abalabandhab-Dwarakanath o Kadambini*, 12–13.

39. R.L. Ghosh, 'The Late Babu Dvarakanath Ganguli', *Amrita Bazar Patrika*, 3 July 1898, 6.

40. Bidhumukhi, of course, was to marry Upendrakishore Ray. Satischandra, who was disabled from childhood, composed hymns for the Brahmo Samaj and lived in Upendrakishore and Bidhumukhi's household. See N. Dutta, *Abalabandhab-Dwarakanath o Kadambini*, 161–2; Hemantakumar Adhya, *Upendrakishore Raychaudhuri* (Delhi: Sahitya Akademi, 1997), 13; and Leela Majumdar, *Pakdandi* (Calcutta: Ananda, 1986), 100.

41. See, for example, B. Bandyopadhyay, *Dwarakanath Gangopadhyay*, 37. Partha Basu discovered Bhabasundari's name in the document drawn up at Sukumar Ray's naming ceremony. (Brahmos conducted a formal naming ceremony for their children and a 'deed' was drawn up on the occasion naming the child's grand- and great-grandparents.) See Partha Basu, *Satyajit Ray* (Calcutta: Paschimbanga Bangla Akademi, 2006), 18–19. Sukumar Ray's 'naming deed' appears to be lost today and could not be found despite the unstinting efforts of Lolita and Sandip Ray. Bhabasundari was obviously alive during Dwarakanath's early days in Calcutta because her daughter Bidhumukhi recalled her planting a tree in the garden of the first house they had lived in. See Punyalata Chakrabarti, *Chhelebelar Dinguli* (1958; reprint, Calcutta: Newscript, 1981), 108. It is not known, however, when Bhabasundari died.

42. B. Bandyopadhyay, *Dwarakanath Gangopadhyay*, 8. Despite his lack of formal education, Dwarakanath was well-known for the breadth of his reading

and the depth of his knowledge. See Sivanath Sastri, 'Swargiya Dwarakanath Gangopadhyay', *Mukul* 4, no. 4 (1898–9): 49–51, at 51.

43. Kopf, *The Brahmo Samaj*, 123; Sastri, *Ramtonu Lahiri o Tatkalin Bangasamaj*, 269–70, 304; and N. Dutta, *Abalabandhab-Dwarakanath o Kadambini*, 23. The use of the word *abala* (feeble or weak) to refer to women was not, to my knowledge, criticized in Bengal. See Sanjay Joshi, *Fractured Modernity: Making of a Middle Class in Colonial North India* (Delhi: Oxford University Press, 2001), 84, for a sharp attack in a Lucknow journal on the practice of referring to women as abalas in 1930. Despite its title, however, *Abalabandhab* often published pieces illustrating the valour of Indian women of the past. See, for instance, 'Bharater Birangana', *Abalabandhab*, new ser., 1, no. 6 (Chaitra 1285/March 1879): 168–71.

44. *Bamabodhini* survived, with several interruptions, up to 1923 and was quite popular, usually having more than 500 subscribers, not all of them Brahmo or even Calcuttans. See Ghulam Murshid, *Reluctant Debutante: Response of Bengali Women to Modernization, 1849–1905* (Rajshahi: Rajshahi University Sahitya Samsad, 1983), 233–4, 237–9.

45. N. Dutta, *Abalabandhab-Dwarakanath o Kadambini*, 31–2. Some of these articles may have been reprinted in later runs of the magazine. See, for example, the essay on Sanskrit-learning among Muslims in *Abalabandhab*, new ser., 1, no. 2 (Agrahayan 1285/November 1878): 44–7; on Edison, *Abalabandhab*, new ser., 1, no. 2, 51–6; and on the telephone, microphone, and phonograph, *Abalabandhab*, new ser., 1, no. 2, 56–9.

46. Dwarakanath like his mentor Akshay Datta, was not a believer in praying to God for the fulfilment of *particular* desires, although he believed pro-foundly in the importance of daily worship (*upasana*), considering it essential for building human character and maintaining mental peace. See Dwarakanath Gangopadhyay, 'Prarthanar Ouchityanuchitya Bichar', *Samadarsi*, 1 (1874–5): 130–9; 'Prakriti o Abhyas Sugathan', *Abalabandhab*, new ser., 1, no. 4 (Magh 1285/January 1879): 105–8, at 107; and 'Upasana', *Abalabandhab*, new ser., 1, no. 6 (Chaitra 1285/March 1879): 177–81. God's will had to be accepted wholeheart-edly at all times (including at the point of death), he advised young readers in his little book of moral tales, *Shishur Sadachar* (Calcutta: Sadharan Brahmo Samaj, 1946), 25–6 (my thanks to Amit Das for a copy of this scarce booklet).

47. B. Bandyopadhyay, *Dwarakanath Gangopadhyay*, 35; Sastri, *Atmacharit*, 147.

48. Sastri, *Ramtonu Lahiri o Tatkalin Bangasamaj*, 304.

49. See 'Abar e Durmati Keno?', *Abalabandhab*, new ser., 1, no. 1 (Kartik 1285/October 1878): 1–4. *Abalabandhab* closed permanently after only nine issues had been published in the new series.

50. This is the June 1874 issue of *Abalabandhab*—the first to appear as a monthly—and was found by Barun Chattopadhyay in the collections of the Dhaka Bangla Akademi (Bangladesh).

51. 'An English Winter: Part II', *Abalabandhab*, [June 1874], 1–6.

52. See the untitled pieces on women's education in Calcutta and Barisal in *Abalabandhab*, [June 1874], 6–10. For the translation of Mill on Harriet Taylor, see *Abalabandhab*, [June 1874], 26–40; on the management committee of the Hindu Mahila Vidyalaya, *Abalabandhab*, [June 1874], 11–13; and on the difficulties of publishing the magazine and the decision to convert it into a monthly, *Abalabandhab*, [June 1874], 13–15.

53. 'Soundarya', *Abalabandhab*, [June 1874], 15–26.

54. Zenana education programmes, in which 'lady-teachers, both European and native, go out visiting native houses, and giving instruction in reading, writing and needlework' had first been introduced by Christian missionaries and, according to Sivanath Sastri, the standard of education they provided was, with occasional exceptions, 'worthless'. See Sivanath Sastri, 'Some Practical Suggestions regarding Female Education in Bengal', *Journal of the National Indian Association*, no. 138 (June 1882): 309–30, at 319.

55. See Jogesh C. Bagal, 'History of the Bethune School & College (1849–1949)', in *Bethune School & College Centenary Volume*, edited by Kalidas Nag (Calcutta: no pub., 1951), 26–7; Lotika Ghose, 'Social and Educational Movements for Women and by Women, 1820–1950', in *Bethune School & College Centenary Volume*, edited by Kalidas Nag (Calcutta: no pub., 1951), 132–3; Borthwick, *Changing Role of Women in Bengal*, 81–2.

56. Borthwick, *Changing Role of Women in Bengal*, 274–5.

57. Sastri, *Atmacharit*, 162.

58. Borthwick, *Keshub Chunder Sen*, 114. On Akroyd's time in Calcutta, see the memoir by her son: Lord Beveridge [William Beveridge], *India Called Them* (London: George Allen & Unwin, 1947), 73–93.

59. Beveridge, *India Called Them*, 89–90. Sen began to remind her of Savonarola and she predicted that he would land 'some day—not in an ordeal of fire, but in an ordeal of disrespect and ridicule. Even now the most educated Brahmos hold aloof or remain with him only as helpers of the good of the Church, which they desire not to diminish by disunion' (Beveridge, *India Called Them*).

60. On Ghosh's pioneering status as barrister, see E.J. Trevelyan's 1897 tribute in *University of Calcutta: Convocation Addresses*, 2 (1880–8): 807–20, at 808.

61. On Akroyd and her dispute with Sen, see M.A. Scherer, 'A Cross-Cultural Conflict Re-Examined: Annette Akroyd and Keshub Chunder Sen', *Journal of World History* 7, no. 2 (1996): 231–59.

62. On the history of the missionary schools for girls, see Bagal, 'History of the Bethune School', 3–7; and Adam, *Reports*, 46–9, 311. In South India, the girls' schools run by the Scottish Church Society and other missionary bodies were far more successful. See Forbes, *Women in Modern India*, 39. As late as in 1890, the conservative paper *Bangabasi* declared that Christian

missionaries had 'laid a trap for Hindu girls, and the Hindus should beware'. See *Report on Native Papers—Bengal*, 10 May 1890, 443.

63. Mallik, *Nabajuger Sadhana*, 278. Among the first students of this school were Soudamini, the eldest daughter of the supposedly conservative Debendranath Tagore. See Ajitkumar Chakrabarty, *Maharsi Debendranath Thakur* (Allahabad: Indian Press, 1916), 227–8.

64. No government assistance was asked for initially. The land was donated by the Derozian Dakshinaranjan Mukherjee, who also provided a thousand rupees to help towards the cost of constructing a building, and Bethune himself contributed substantially towards the cost of running the school. After Bethune's death in 1851, the costs of running the School were paid by the Governor General Lord Dalhousie from his own funds and the Government finally took charge of the institution after Dalhousie left India in 1856. No fees were charged until 1866, books were supplied without cost, and for students living far away, the school provided free transport by carriages or palanquins. See Bagal, 'History of the Bethune School', 13–25, 111; and Borthwick, *Changing Role of Women in Bengal*, 81.

65. See Bagal, 'History of the Bethune School', 24.

66. There were as many as thirty-five by 1863, all founded by 'natives'. See Bagal, 'History of the Bethune School', 14–25; and Borthwick, *Changing Role of Women in Bengal*, 73.

67. Borthwick, *Changing Role of Women in Bengal*, 85.

68. Mallik, *Nabajuger Sadhana*, 290–2. The young Rabindranath Tagore also expressed similar views in 1885—see his essay 'Lathir upar Lathi', in Anathnath Das and Amal Pal, eds, *Balak: Baisakh 1292–Chaitra 1292* (Calcutta: Dey's, 2010), 54–6.

69. B. Bandyopadhyay, *Dwarakanath Gangopadhyay*, 12; and P. Gangopadhyay, *Banglar Nari-Jagaran*, 64–5.

70. See Borthwick, *Changing Role of Women in Bengal*, 89; and [Dwarakanath Ganguli], *Jibanalekhya*, 51–3.

71. Sastri, *History of the Brahmo Samaj*, 164.

72. For Abala Bose's recollections and tributes by others on the occasion of Dwarakanath's birth centenary, see 'Dwarakanath Gangopadhyayer Janmasatabarsiki', *Probasi* 44, no. 2 (Jaistha 1351/June–July 1944): 92–3, http://archiv.ub.uni-heidelberg.de/savifadok/volltexte/2009/1018 (accessed on 26 September 2014). On Abala Bose's own life and her contributions to social reform, see D.M. Bose, 'Abala Bose: Her Life and Times', *Modern Review* 119, no. 6 (June 1966): 441–56.

73. Kopf, *The Brahmo Samaj*, 124; N. Dutta, *Abalabandhab-Dwarakanath o Kadambini*, 69.

74. He also published *Nababarshiki* (first pub. 1880 and probably followed by at least one new edition), an innovative yearbook-almanac containing, apart from basic information about the different regions of India,

128   THE RAYS BEFORE SATYAJIT

biographies of important personalities of the time that had been vetted for accuracy by their subjects themselves. See N. Dutta, *Abalabandhab-Dwarakanath o Kadambini*, 68, 172–82.

75. The *Brahmo Public Opinion* recommended the adoption of his arithmetic textbook by all vernacular schools, commending 'the author's powers of clear exposition and his facility in teaching'. See Collet, *The Brahmo Year-Book for 1882*, 75. On the income from his textbooks, see R.L. Ghosh, 'The Late Babu Dvarakanath Ganguli', 6.

76. Dwarakanath Gangopadhyay, ed., *Kabigatha*, 13th edn (Calcutta: Metcalfe Press, 1895), unpaginated preface, http://www.dli.ernet.in/ (accessed on 27 November 2013).

77. Collet, *Brahmo Year-Book for 1878*, 88–9; and P. Gangopadhyay, *Banglar Nari-Jagaran*, 66.

78. Borthwick, *Changing Role of Women in Bengal*, 90; and B. Ghosh, *Rajnarayan Basu: Nirbachita Rachana Sangraha*, 153–4.

79. See Akroyd's letters to Fanny Mowatt, 14 May 1874 and 17 May 1874 (British Library, India Office Records and Private Papers, Beveridge Collection, MSS Eur C176/160). In one of his earliest letters to Akroyd, her future husband Henry Beveridge had written: 'The besetting sin of Bengalees is that they will think and talk and talk and think for ever but that they will not act. But then that is the very reason we are here, for if Bengalees could only act half as well as they talk there would be no need for us westerns [sic] to rule over them' (letter of 13 March 1873, reprinted in Beveridge, *India Called Them*, 96).

80. There is no reply from Akroyd in the file but a strongly worded letter from Emily Phear reproving Dwarakanath for the 'tone and tenor' of his correspondence. See Dwarakanath Ganguli, letter to Annette Akroyd, 31 August 1874; and Emily Phear, letter to D.N. Ganguli, 2 September 1874 (British Library, India Office Records and Private Papers, Beveridge Collection, MSS Eur C176/160).

81. He recalled how the Bengali judge Dwarakanath Mitra (Dwarkanath Mitter, 1833–1874) had been put on the committee even though many thought that Mitra was against the very idea of educating women and after Mitra's departure, two new Bengali members were inducted into the committee even though they had never supported the education of women. See *Abalabandhab*, [June 1874], 11–13.

82. Ironically, the irreligious Beveridge persuaded his Unitarian bride to get married at a Registrar's office under Act III of 1872, perhaps the greatest achievement of her *bête-noire* Keshab Sen. Akroyd's only objection, eventually withdrawn, was to being married by a *native* Registrar. See Beveridge, *India Called Them*, 108–12, 128.

83. Borthwick, *Changing Role of Women in Bengal*, 90; Collet, *Brahmo Year-Book for 1878*, 88; and P. Gangopadhyay, *Banglar Nari-Jagaran*, 65–6.

Brahmamoyee was an especially valuable ally for Dwarakanath and even more progressive than her husband. When Durgamohan Das wanted to marry his daughters off early because educating them would be too expensive, it was Brahmamoyee who forced him to relent. See [Dwarakanath Ganguli], *Jibanalekhya*, 4, 6–7, 75–7, 102–6. For another moving tribute to Brahmamoyee by a progressive Brahmo, see Sastri, *Atmacharit*, 183–6.

84. The Lady Superintendent was paid one hundred rupees a month while Dwarakanath received only forty rupees. See Collet, *Brahmo Year-Book for 1878*, 88–9. There was at least another 'native' teacher: Dwijadas Datta, who later turned into a violent opponent of the Sadharan Brahmo Samaj and its leaders. See Dwijadas Datta, *Behold the Man or Keshub and the Sadharan Brahmo Samaj* (Comillah: Dwijadas Datta, 1930), 117–18.

85. Collet, *Brahmo Year-Book for 1876*, 49; Tattvabhushan, *Social Reform in Bengal*, 68; and [Dwarakanath Ganguli], *Jibanalekhya*, 102–3.

86. 'Siksha o Sikshitabya Bishay', *Abalabandhab*, new ser., 1, no. 2 (Agrahayan 1285/November 1878): 33–44, at 43. Krishna Kumar has argued that Indian as well as British educational reformers cited the importance of teaching modern science in justifying English education but little was actually done to facilitate the teaching of science in schools and colleges. See Krishna Kumar, *Political Agenda of Education: A Study of Colonialist and Nationalist Ideas* (Delhi: SAGE, 1991), 41–3.

87. See Herbert Spencer, *Essays on Education, etc.* (London: Dent, 1911); and on the contexts and influence of Spencer's ideas, Stephen Tomlinson, 'From Rousseau to Evolutionism: Herbert Spencer on the Science of Education', *History of Education*, 25 no. 3 (1996): 235–54; and David Wiltshire, *The Social and Political Thought of Herbert Spencer* (Oxford: Oxford University Press, 1978).

88. See Kumar, *Political Agenda of Education*, 37–8.

89. See *General Report on Public Instruction in Bengal* (1876–7): 77. After the merger of the Banga Mahila Vidyalaya with Bethune School, the institution was often referred to as the Girton of the East. See Borthwick, *Changing Role of Women in Bengal*, 95.

90. Kadambini Basu, 'Narikel Brikkha', *Bamabodhini Patrika*, no. 143 (Ashar 1282/June 1875): 95–6.

91. B. Bandyopadhyay, *Dwarakanath Gangopadhyay*, 14–15; and L. Ghose, 'Social and Educational Movements', 136–7. There were several similar societies, often called Unions, each dedicated to spreading women's education in a particular district. Most of them, however, concentrated on home education. See B. Pal, *Memories of My Life*, 295–6, 300; Srinath Chanda, *Brahmo Samajey Challis Batsar* (Dhaka: Bharat Mahila Press, 1913), 117–19; and Sivanath Sastri, 'Some Practical Suggestions regarding Female Education in Bengal', 323–4.

92. *General Report on Public Instruction in Bengal* (1876–7): 74.

93. Since Bethune students were mostly withdrawn as soon as they reached marriageable age, Phear recommended that instead of supporting that institution, the government should 'take up and carry on the work of the Banga Mahila Bidyalaya, an institution for the education of grown women'. See *General Report on Public Instruction in Bengal* (1876–7): 74.

94. The two institutions began to operate as one from 1 August 1878—a great merger to complement that year's momentous split in the Brahmo Samaj—but, as the Director of Public Instruction noted in his annual report, without informing him about 'the manner of this amalgamation, or the organization of the joint school'. See *General Report on Public Instruction in Bengal* (1877–8): 77. There was considerable criticism of the merger in the press, including sections of the Brahmo press loyal to Keshab Sen, on account of the alleged Western dress and diet of the Banga Mahila Vidyalaya's students. See P. Gangopadhyay, *Banglar Nari-Jagaran*, 70–2.

95. The government promised that there would be a weekly Brahmo worship at the School and on Sundays, the students would join the prayers at the Sadharan Brahmo Samaj temple. It was also promised that the board of governors would include members nominated by the Brahmo Samaj. See the list of members of the Bethune School Committee (1856–1908) in Bagal, 'History of the Bethune School', 117–18; and Krishnakumar Mitra, *Atmacharit*, 2nd edn (Calcutta: Sadharan Brahmo Samaj, 1975), 172–3.

96. Unfortunately, however, the names of teaching staff are not available for that period. Dwarakanath had also assisted a short-lived teacher-training ('normal') school attached to Bethune to find students willing to train as teachers. See Subalchandra Mitra, *Isvar Chandra Vidyasagar*, 470.

97. See *Report on Native Papers—Bengal*, 18 January 1890, 51; and Borthwick, *Changing Role of Women in Bengal*, 91–4.

98. *General Report on Public Instruction in Bengal* (1878–9): 81.

99. Leela Majumdar (*Pakdandi*, 101) reported the prevalent belief that Kadambini was a child-widow but there is no independent confirmation for this; and the case of Keshab Sen notwithstanding, it seems implausible that a progressive Brahmo like Brajakishore would have married off an underage daughter. On Brajakishore's background, see Soma Basu, *Kadambini Ganguly: A Portrait of a Doctor at Dawn* (Chandannagar: Rupali, 2012), 36–40.

100. On the history of this school, which was the first indigenous girls' school in Bihar and among the founders of which was the doctor Krishnadhan Ghosh (father of the radical swadeshi leaders Aurobindo and Barindra Ghosh), see Sumanta Niyogi, *Brahmo Samaj Movement and Development of Education, 1870–1975: A Case Study of Bihar* (Patna: Janaki Prakashan, 1986), 77–84.

101. See N. Dutta, *Abalabandhab-Dwarakanath o Kadambini*, 72; Bagal, 'History of the Bethune School', 36–7; and *University of Calcutta: Minutes*, 56–7.

102. See P. Gangopadhyay, *Banglar Nari-Jagaran*, 68–9; and *University of Calcutta: Minutes* (1877–78): 8. In April 1878, all University examinations were opened to women. See *University of Calcutta: Minutes* (1878–79): 2–3.

103. See *University of Calcutta: Minutes* (1876–77): 97–8.

104. See Borthwick, *Changing Role of Women in Bengal*, 334; and the Vice-Chancellor Sir Alexander Arbuthnot's convocation address of 15 March 1879, in *University of Calcutta: Minutes* (1878–79): 110–11.

105. *General Report on Public Instruction in Bengal* (1878–79): 81–2.

106. Sasibhushan Datta, a lecturer at the Cuttack College, was transferred to Bethune and took charge of this class. See *General Report on Public Instruction in Bengal* (1878–79): 82. Kadambini was soon joined by Ellen D'Abreu, who had passed the entrance examination in December 1879. The college class, since then, could admit non-Hindu women but the School continued to be for Hindus alone. See *General Report on Public Instruction in Bengal* (1879–80): 82.

107. Bagal, 'History of the Bethune School', 39. Kadambini was joined by Chandramukhi Basu—both were awarded special monthly scholarships for further study and both, of course, progressed to the BA degree. See *General Report on Public Instruction in Bengal* (1880–81): 87–8.

108. Malavika Karlekar, 'Ganguly, Kadambini (c.1862–1923), *Oxford Dictionary of National Biography*, http://www.oxforddnb.com/view/article/58727 (accessed on 22 August 2011). The new paper *Sanjibani*, launched by Dwarakanath Ganguli and other Brahmos, announced that Kadambini would be contributing to its columns. See the advertisement in *The Bengalee*, 26 May 1883, 249. Most issues of *Sanjibani* have been lost, however, and there is no trace of any contribution by Kadambini in the extant numbers. See Kanailal Chattopadhyay, ed., *Samyikpatrey Samajchitra: Krishnakumar Mitra Sampadita 'Sanjibani'* (Calcutta: Dey's, 1989).

109. H.J. Reynolds, Convocation Address, 10 March 1883, in *University of Calcutta: Convocation Addresses*, 2 (1880–1898): 457–78, at 464, 466–9. The Director of Public Instruction remarked that the graduation of Chandramukhi and Kadambini was 'the most notable event in the history of female education in Bengal'. See *General Report on Public Instruction in Bengal* (1882–83): 70.

110. Kamini Sen and Subarnaprabha Basu both passed the entrance examination in 1880 and Kamini, who passed the entrance in the first division and was later to win some fame as a poet, went on to study towards the First Arts. See *General Report on Public Instruction in Bengal* (1880–81): 88; and Bagal, 'History of the Bethune School', 40–1.

111. See Bagal, 'History of the Bethune School', 47.

112. L. Ghose, 'Social and Educational Movements', 144; and Collet, *Brahmo Year-Book for 1882*, 12–14.

113. See Bagal, 'History of the Bethune School', 45–6; and Punyalata Chakrabarti, *Ekal Jakhhan Shuru Holo* [1964], edited by Jayeeta Bagchi, Abhijit Sen, and Anindita Bhaduri (Calcutta: Dey's, 2007), 23, 71–2.

114. It is often thought that she married Dwarakanath only after admission into medical school. Citing contemporary news reports of the wedding, Narayan Dutta has shown that the marriage preceded her registration at medical school by eleven days. See N. Dutta, *Abalabandhab-Dwarakanath o Kadambini*, 125–6.

115. Usually, the male doctor never saw the secluded female patient and heard about her complaints from a male member of the family and prescribed on that basis. See Borthwick, *Changing Role of Women in Bengal* 321–2. For an excellent survey of women's medical education in India, see S.N. Sen, *Scientific and Technical Education in India, 1781–1900* (Delhi: Indian National Science Academy, 1991), 510–17.

116. See Thomas N. Bonner, *Becoming a Physician: Medical Education in Britain, France, Germany, and the United States, 1750–1945* (Baltimore: Johns Hopkins University Press, 1995), 211–13.

117. Thomas N. Bonner, *To the Ends of the Earth: Women's Search for Education in Medicine* (Cambridge, Mass.: Harvard University Press, 1992), 6–10, 75, 135–7, 161–3.

118. On the American situation, see Rosalind Rosenberg, *Beyond Separate Spheres: Intellectual Roots of Modern Feminism* (New Haven: Yale University Press, 1982), especially 1–27; and for Britain and continental Europe, Katharina Rowold, *The Educated Woman: Minds, Bodies, and Women's Higher Education in Britain, Germany, and Spain, 1865–1914* (New York: Routledge, 2010).

119. Bonner, *To the Ends of the Earth*, 123–4, 127–31.

120. S.N. Sen, *Scientific and Technical Education in India*, 511–12.

121. Chitra Deb, *Mahila Daktar: Bhin Graher Basinda* (Calcutta: Ananda, 1994), 43–5. Lest Mitra's insistence on a medical student maintaining purdah seem too outlandish even for nineteenth-century Hindu society, it may be worth recalling that even in France in the late 1860s, the young American Mary Putnam (later the celebrated Dr Mary Putnam Jacobi) not only had to pull many strings to be allowed into the Paris Ecole de Médicine—she was the very first woman to be admitted there—but had to agree to sit separately from the male students at lectures and to enter the lecture hall through a side door. See Bonner, *To the Ends of the Earth*, 1. On the general history of co-education in the West, see Christine D. Myers, *University Coeducation in the Victorian Era: Inclusion in the United States and the United Kingdom* (New York: Palgrave Macmillan, 2010), 17.

122. *Proceedings of the Lieutenant-Governor of Bengal, Education Department,* April 1875, 104.

123. See Letter of H.J. Reynolds, Officiating Secretary to the Government of Bengal, of 5 April 1875, in *Proceedings of the Lieutenant-Governor of Bengal, Education Department,* April 1875, 104–5.

124. In October 1874, Sophia Jex-Blake, Elizabeth Garrett, and Elizabeth Blackwell had established the London School of Medicine for Women since

no regular medical school was willing to admit women. See Bonner, *To the Ends of the Earth*, 131–3.

125. Deb, *Mahila Daktar*, 45.

126. Scharlieb then returned to Britain to obtain an MBBS degree from the London School of Medicine for Women and returned to Madras where she set up a hospital for the treatment of 'native' women. In 1887, she left India for reasons of health and was to have a long medical career in Britain. See Mary Scharlieb, *Reminiscences* (London: Williams and Norgate, 1924), especially 29–48 and 95–122; and S.R. Collinson, 'Mary Ann Dacomb Scharlieb: A Medical Life from Madras to Harley Street', *Journal of Medical Biography*, 7 (1999): 25–31.

127. See letters of J.M. Coates, dated 12 May and 18 May 1883, in *Proceedings of the Lieutenant-Governor of Bengal, General Department—Education*, July 1883, 11. Abala had to discontinue her medical studies because of illness, however. See Bagal, 'History of the Bethune School', 41–2. Incidentally, the Cooch Behar royal family, before selecting Keshab Sen's daughter as the prince's bride, had shown interest in Abala. But although she was over fourteen, her mother Brahmamoyee had refused to let her daughter marry a teenager (the prince was about seventeen); moreover, she thought that marrying a prince would isolate her daughter from her brothers and sisters. Abala was later to marry the scientist Jagadischandra Bose. See Sastri, *Atmacharit*, 207; N. Dutta, *Abalabandhab-Dwarakanath o Kadambini*, 46–7, 51; and Dwijadas Datta, *Behold the Man*, 117–18.

128. See *Proceedings of the Lieutenant-Governor of Bengal, General Department—Education*, July 1883, 3–4. Elsewhere, Croft declared that the demand for women's entry into medicine was 'one of those movements which no amount of opposition will finally succeed in overcoming'. See *General Report on Public Instruction in Bengal* (1881–82): 92.

129. Letter of J.M. Coates, dated 31 October 1882, and of J. Keess, Principal of Madras Medical College, dated 24 October 1882, in *Proceedings of the Lieutenant-Governor of Bengal, General Department—Education*, July 1883, 9–10.

130. See letters of J.M. Coates, dated 12 May and 18 May 1883, in *Proceedings of the Lieutenant-Governor of Bengal, General Department—Education*, July 1883, 11. Rivers Thompson, along with most Europeans resident in India, had strongly opposed the Ilbert Bill of 1883, which had proposed to allow Indian magistrates to try criminal cases involving Europeans, declaring that 'natives' lacked 'independent force of character' and differed radically from Europeans 'as regards moral standards, social customs, and political status'. See C.E. Buckland, *Bengal under the Lieutenant-Governors*, 2 vols (Calcutta: S.K. Lahiri, 1901), 2: 768–91; Edwin Hirschmann, *White Mutiny: The Ilbert Bill Crisis in India and Genesis of the Indian National Congress* (Delhi: Heritage, 1980); and W.S. Blunt, *India under Ripon: A Private Diary* (London: T. Fisher Unwin, 1909), 85, 96–7, 109.

131. See letter from A.P. MacDonnell, Officiating Secretary to the Government of Bengal to the Director of Public Instruction, dated 29 June 1883, in *Proceedings of the Lieutenant-Governor of Bengal, General Department—Education*, July 1883, 15–17, at 15. In its report of the Lieutenant-Governor's decision, *The Bengalee* (edited by Surendranath Banerjea) applauded Rivers Thompson's 'clear-sighted statesmanship', while acknowledging that Thompson headed 'the most unpopular government that we can recall to mind'. See 'Admission of Women to the Calcutta Medical College', *The Bengalee*, 7 July 1883, 317.

132. Letter from A.P. MacDonnell, Officiating Secretary to the Government of Bengal to the Director of Public Instruction, dated 29 June 1883, in *Proceedings of the Lieutenant-Governor of Bengal, General Department—Education*, 16.

133. Ellen D'Abreu and Abala Das, although studying in Madras, were also given the same scholarship. See Bagal, 'History of the Bethune School', 44.

134. Borthwick, *Changing Role of Women*, 327–8.

135. See D. Engels, *Beyond Purdah?*, 137.

136. For Amritalal Sircar's comment, see Soma Basu, *Kadambini Ganguly: A Portrait of a Doctor at Dawn*, 81. On Bengali medical women's relative freedom from persecution and its possible reasons, see Deb, *Mahila Daktar*, 37–42. On Jex-Blake's experience in Edinburgh, see Bonner, *To the Ends of the Earth*, 125–9.

137. There is a possibility that she was treated unfairly in examinations by the Bengali doctor Rajendra Chandra. See N. Dutta, *Abalabandhab-Dwarakanath o Kadambini*, 128–32.

138. Her incomplete 'First MB' result was accepted by the University as the equivalent of a pass in the 'First LMS' examination. See *University of Calcutta: Minutes* (1886–87): 84.

139. The examiner, however, was the same Dr Rajendrachandra Chandra who is rumoured to have been hostile to Kadambini. See *University of Calcutta: Minutes* (1888–89): 13, 15.

140. N. Dutta, *Abalabandhab-Dwarakanath o Kadambini*, 129.

141. Malavika Karlekar, *Voices from Within: Early Personal Narratives of Bengali Women* (Delhi: Oxford University Press, 1991), 177.

142. Married at the age of nine and pregnant at thirteen, Anandibai Joshi had received staunch support from her physically abusive but socially liberal husband Gopalrao Vinayak Joshi. Funding for her studies came from American philanthropists. After qualifying from the Women's Medical College in Philadelphia in October 1886, Joshi returned to India to practise but, tragically, died before she could commence her career. See Meera Kosambi, 'Anandibai Joshee: Retrieving a Fragmented Feminist Image'; and on Bidhumukhi Basu and Virginia Mary Mitter, see Murshid, *Reluctant Debutante*, 101.

143. Borthwick, *Changing Role of Women*, 326; and D. Engels, *Beyond Purdah?*, 140–1.

144. N. Dutta, *Abalabandhab-Dwarakanath o Kadambini*, 136–7.

145. N. Dutta, *Abalabandhab-Dwarakanath o Kadambini*, 153.

146. In her initial years as a practitioner, she set aside an hour each afternoon for the free treatment of poor patients. See her advertisement in *The Bengalee*, 14 July 1888, 333. After a few years, however, her advertisements omitted the offer, merely stating that her terms were 'moderate'. See, for example, the advertisement in *The Bengalee*, 4 April 1891, 166.

147. Malavika Karlekar, 'Kadambini and the Bhadralok: Early Debates over Women's Education in Bengal', *Economic and Political Weekly* 21, no. 17 (26 April 1986), WS25–WS31, at WS27.

148. Gaganchandra Home, *Jiban-Smriti* (Calcutta: Privately Published, 1929), 39.

149. L. Majumdar, *Pakdandi*, 102.

150. Generally, it seems that medical studies did not prove too popular with Bengali Hindu women. As late as in 1912, 'when there were two and three Hindu women students respectively at medical colleges in Madras and Bombay, there was none in Calcutta'. See D. Engels, *Beyond Purdah?*, 137.

151. N. Dutta, *Abalabandhab-Dwarakanath o Kadambini*, 140–1.

152. See Simonti Sen, *Travels to Europe: Self and Other in Bengali Travel Narratives, 1870–1910* (Delhi: Orient Longman, 2005).

153. On Indian women who travelled to England in the nineteenth century, see the introduction to Simonti Sen, ed., *Krishnabhabini Daser Englandey Bangamahila* (Calcutta: Stree, 1996), xi–xxxii; and Sunita Bandyopadhyay, *Brahmarsi Sasipada: Samoy, Samaj, Sadhana* (Calcutta: Dolphin/Dey's, 2007), 35.

154. A massive fair covering six hundred acres of land and visited by 28 million people, the World's Columbian Exposition was opened in April 1893 and ran for six months. Almost 65,000 exhibits were sent to it from across the world and they were housed in pavilions that were architectural and technological marvels of their time. See Norman Bolotin and Christine Laing, *The World's Columbian Exposition: The Chicago World's Fair of 1893* (Urbana: University of Illinois Press, 1992).

155. See *The Bengalee*, 16 July 1892, 344.

156. See Dwarakanath Ganguli's letter in *The Bengalee*, 30 July 1892, 367.

157. Trailokyanath had represented India at the Colonial and Indian Exhibition of 1886 in London and the 1887 Glasgow International Exhibition. See 'Abstract of Services of Babu Trailokyanath Mukharji, FLS, 1866 to 1896', in *Trailokya Rachanasamagra*, edited by Satyanarayan Bhattacharya, Nirmal Das, Shyamal Sengupta, Dibyajyoti Majumdar, and Nepalpada Das, 2 vols (Calcutta: Granthamela, 1973–74), 1 (1973): 551–75, at 560–5.

158. *Bamabodhini Patrika*, no. 337 (February 1892): 319.

136   THE RAYS BEFORE SATYAJIT

159. *Bamabodhini Patrika*, no. 342 (July 1893): 158.

160. The first women to receive the TQ were Janet Hunter and Sarah Gray in 1888. See Andrew Hull and Johanna Geyer-Kordesch, *The Shaping of the Medical Profession: The History of the Royal College of Physicians and Surgeons of Glasgow, 1858–1999* (London: Hambledon Press, 1999), especially 13, 17, 27, 42–3, 46–7.

161. On the curriculum for the TQ and the rarity of exemptions from the training requirement (often requested by foreign candidates), see H.M. Dingwall, 'The Triple Qualification Examination of the Scottish Medical and Surgical Colleges, 1884–1993', *Journal of the Royal College of Physicians Edinburgh*, 40 (2010): 269–76, at 270–2.

162. See Kadambini Ganguli's 'Schedule of the Course of Study for the Joint Qualifications in Medicine and Surgery of the Royal Colleges of Physicians and Surgeons of Edinburgh, and the Faculty of Physicians and Surgeons of Glasgow', Royal College of Surgeons of Edinburgh Library. My thanks to Steven Kerr and the RCSE Library for providing me with this source.

163. For the date of the examination and the names of the successful candidates, see the College Records of 18 July 1893. Copy provided by Steven Kerr and the RCSE Library. Kadambini's date of birth (18 July 1861) is recorded in Kadambini Ganguli's 'Schedule of the Course of Study'.

164. At least one male obstetrician and gynaecologist with foreign qualifications (including the Scottish 'double' licentiateship, a predecessor of the 'triple qualification' Kadambini had obtained) advertised in Calcutta in the 1880s. He had also worked as an obstetrician in Dublin. See the advertisement of Dr U.K. Dutt in *The Bengalee*, 4 August 1883, 370.

165. N. Dutta, *Abalabandhab-Dwarakanath o Kadambini*, 153.

166. N. Dutta, *Abalabandhab-Dwarakanath o Kadambini*, 156.

167. Karlekar, 'Ganguly, Kadambini (c. 1862–1923)'.

168. *Reis and Rayyet*, 7 July 1883, 315.

169. N. Dutta, *Abalabandhab-Dwarakanath o Kadambini*, 122–4.

170. *The Bengalee*, 23 June 1883, 291.

171. They had four sons (Nirmalchandra; Prafullachandra, nicknamed Monglu because he was born on Tuesday or *mangalbar*; Prabhatchandra, nicknamed Jang and then Janglu or Jangli because Shamser Jang Bahadur, the ruler of Nepal, had presented him with a miniature court dress; and Amalchandra) and four daughters (Nirupama, Jyotirmoyee, Jayanti, and Himani). See N. Dutta, *Abalabandhab-Dwarakanath o Kadambini*, 161, 163. The Queen Mother of Nepal also presented Kadambini with a pony, which delighted her own children as well as Upendrakishore's. See Karlekar, 'Ganguly, Kadambini (c. 1862–1923)'.

172. L. Majumdar, *Pakdandi*, 101.

173. Santa Nag, *Purbasmriti* (Calcutta: Papyrus, 1986), 56; L. Majumdar, *Pakdandi*, 101.

NEW FAITH, NEW WOMAN, NEW SOCIETY 137

174. Hitendrakishore Raychaudhuri, *Upendrakishore o Masua Ray Paribarer Galpasalpa* (Calcutta: Firma KLM, 1984), 11–12; and P. Chakrabarti, *Chhelebelar Dinguli*, 109.

175. P. Chakrabarti, *Ekal Jakhhan Shuru Holo*, 19–20.

176. P. Chakrabarti, *Chhelebelar Dinguli*, 109. Kadambini had always been deft with her hands. At the annual prize distribution at Bethune School in 1882, the chief guest, the Marchioness of Ripon, was presented with 'a very prettily worked paper basket' made by Kadambini. See 'The Bethune School, Calcutta', *Journal of the National Indian Association*, no. 137 (May 1882): 269–75, at 275.

177. Borthwick, *Changing Role of Women*, 141. Calcutta's playwrights, in particular, excelled in satires on women masculinized by education. See Tanika Sarkar, 'Strishiksha and Its Terrors: Re-Reading Nineteenth-Century Debates on Reform', in *Literature and Gender: Essays for Jasodhara Bagchi*, edited by Supriya Chaudhuri and Sajni Mukherjee (Delhi: Orient Longman, 2002), 153–84, at 169, 179–80.

178. Tanika Sarkar and Sumit Sarkar, 'Introduction', in *Women and Social Reform in Modern India: A Reader*, edited by Sumit Sarkar and Tanika Sarkar, 2 vols (Ranikhet: Permanent Black, 2007), 1: 1–18, at 9.

179. *Reis and Rayyet*, 2 May 1891, 209. The offending article in *Banganibasi* was actually about the murder of a Brahmo woman by her lover in Calcutta— the paper had used the tragedy to abuse Brahmos and educated women. See N. Dutta, *Abalabandhab-Dwarakanath o Kadambini*, 139.

180. *Reis and Rayyet*, 25 July 1891, 356; and 'The Brahmo Defamation Case', *The Bengalee*, 18 July 1891, 340–1.

181. *Banganibasi*, 13 March 1891, summary in *Report on Native Papers— Bengal*, 21 March 1891, 346–8, at 347.

182. *Tattvakaumudi*, 1 Sravan 1813 Sak (23 July 1891), 82.

183. *The Hindoo Patriot*, 1 June 1891, 261.

184. *Reis and Rayyet*, 6 June 1891, 269. Simultaneously, Kadambini Ganguli filed a suit in the High Court claiming 100,000 rupees as damages from *Banganibasi*. The judge described her claim as 'extravagant' (*Reis and Rayyet*, 6 June 1891) and ultimately, she received 3,000 rupees and costs. See *The Hindoo Patriot*, 25 May 1891, 247.

185. 'The Brahmo Defamation Case', *The Bengalee*, 18 July 1891, 340–1. The publisher Nabakumar Basu was imprisoned for three months and fined fifty rupees, while the printer Girischandra Ray was simply fined fifty rupees. See the reports of the trial in *Bamabodhini Patrika*, August 1891, 97; and *Reis and Rayyet*, 25 July 1891, 356. It is likely, however, that none of them was the real culprit. The actual author of the offending article may have been the former editor of *Banganibasi*, who had died and was succeeded to the editorship by the proprietor Maheschandra Pal less than a month before the publication of the offending article. See 'The Brahmo Defamation Case', *The Bengalee*, 18

July 1891, 340–1; and *The Hindoo Patriot*, 1 June 1891, 261. The *Dainik-o-Samachar Chandrika*, a conservative paper, commented: 'Even the victorious Ganguli will admit that Mahesh Chandra was not the real culprit, and that the offence was committed by someone else' (*Report on Native Papers—Bengal*, 25 July 1891, 754).

186. Parimal Goswami, *Aami Jnader Dekhechhi* [1969] (Calcutta: Pratikshan, 1995), 151; and Parimal Goswami, *Adhunik Byanga Parichoy* (Calcutta: Nabagranthana, 1969), 14–15.

187. On the battles over women's higher education in nineteenth-century Europe, see Katharina Rowold, *The Educated Woman*, especially 24–35.

188. In 1917, when the Calcutta University Commission investigated Bengali views on women's education, many respondents (including the scientist Prasantachandra Mahalanobis and the physician and future politician Bidhanchandra Roy, both of them Sadharan Brahmos) opined that girls and boys should receive different *kinds* of education, in conformity with the biological, psychological, and social differences between males and females. By then, younger Bengalis had mastered their Darwin and Havelock Ellis and their views carried echoes of the 'scientific' opposition to women's education in Victorian Britain. See M. Karlekar, 'Kadambini and the Bhadralok', WS29–WS30.

189. Karlekar, 'Kadambini and the Bhadralok', WS28–WS29.

190. In the early twentieth century, the Mahakali Pathshala had more students than any other girls' school in Bengal. See L. Ghose, 'Social and Educational Movements', 146.

191. Forbes, *Women in Modern India*, 46–57; and Heimsath, *Indian Nationalism*, 238–41. On attempts to emancipate and educate Bengali Muslim women in the nineteenth and twentieth centuries, see Sonia Nishat Amin, 'The Early Muslim *Bhadramahila*: The Growth of Learning and Creativity, 1876 to 1939', in *From the Seams of History: Essays on Indian Women*, edited by Bharati Ray (Delhi: Oxford University Press, 2005), 107–48.

192. Bagal, 'History of the Bethune School', 54; and L. Ghose, 'Social and Educational Movements', 145–7.

193. Gail Minault, *Secluded Scholars: Women's Education and Muslim Social Reform in Colonial India* (Delhi: Oxford University Press, 1998), 258.

194. Forbes, *Women in Modern India*, 27.

195. Himani Bannerji, *Inventing Subjects: Studies in Hegemony, Patriarchy and Colonialism* (London: Anthem Press, 2001), 101.

196. Murshid, *Reluctant Debutante*, 160–1.

197. Partha Chatterjee, 'Colonialism, Nationalism, and Colonialized Women: The Contest in India', *American Ethnologist* 16, no. 4 (November 1989): 622–33, at 627; and Judith E. Walsh, *Domesticity in Colonial India: What Women Learned When Men Gave Them Advice* (Lanham, MD: Rowman & Littlefield, 2004), 3–5. Partha Chatterjee has acknowledged, however, that

the patriarchal elements in the campaigns for women's education made it *easier* for women, and not just Brahmo women, to bridge the home and the world. 'Once the "essential" femininity of women was fixed in terms of certain culturally visible "spiritual" qualities', Chatterjee argues, it became socially permissible for women to educate themselves, travel on their own and, gradually, take up paid work. See Partha Chatterjee, 'The Nationalist Resolution of the Women's Question', in *Recasting Women: Essays in Colonial History*, edited by Kumkum Sangari and Sudesh Vaid (Delhi: Kali for Women, 1989), 233–53, at 244, 246–7.

198. Gourmohan Vidyalankar, *Stree-Siksha Bidhayak*, reprinted in Swapan Basu, ed., *Unish Satakey Stree-Siksha* (Calcutta: Bangiya Sahitya Parishat, 2005), 47–68, especially 58–68. Sixty years after Vidyalankar, Sivanath Sastri remarked that an illiterate woman could not be a 'rational and moral' companion for the modern Bengali man. Their marriage would lack 'that elevating power and moral influence which true marriage always exercises on the mind'. See Sivanath Sastri, 'Some Practical Suggestions regarding Female Education in Bengal', 311–12.

199. See S. Basu, *Akshaykumar Datta*, 467; and Mallik, *Nabajuger Sadhana*, 74–6, 103, 285–6. In the early 1860s, a lecture at the Bethune Society argued that the Hindu woman needed education in order to be 'an agreeable companion, a good mother, an intellectual and loving wife and an excellent housewife' providing 'solace to her husband in his brightest and darkest moments' and an ideal upbringing for her children. See Kumar Harendra Krishna, *A Lecture on Female Education in Bengal Delivered at the Bethune Society* (Calcutta: Bengalee Press, 1863), 15.

200. See Ramgopal Sanyal, *A General Biography of Bengal Celebrities, Both Living and Dead* (1889), edited by Swapan Majumdar (Calcutta: Rddhi, 1976), 15–32; and Sastri, *Ramtonu Lahiri o Tatkalin Bangasamaj*, 307–10.

201. Dipesh Chakrabarty, 'Limits of the Bourgeois Model?', in *The Middle Class in Colonial India*, edited by Sanjay Joshi (Delhi: Oxford University Press, 2010), 178–201, at 183–4.

202. Borthwick, *Changing Role of Women*, 32–3, 39, 83–4. Carpenter visited India in 1866, 1868, 1869, and 1875, with three main objectives: the establishment of 'normal' (institutions to train female teachers) schools for the training of female teachers, the improvement of the condition of female prisoners, and the foundation of reformatory schools. See Carpenter, *Six Months in India*; Sargant, *Mary Carpenter in India*; J. Estlin Carpenter, *Life and Work of Mary Carpenter*, 275, 340–1; and Clare Midgley, 'Mary Carpenter and the Brahmo Samaj of India: A Transnational Perspective on Social Reform in the Age of Empire', *Women's History Review* 22, no. 3 (2013): 363–85, at 372.

203. Borthwick, *Changing Role of Women*, 96–9.

204. Walsh, *Domesticity in Colonial India*, 2, 11–14.

205. See D. Engels, *Beyond Purdah?* 80–1.

206. Even the sight of a widow was supposed to be unlucky for beholders and some commentators declared that the custom of burning widows to death on their late husband's pyre (*sati*) was in fact kinder than the fate of living widows. Among Muslims, however, the remarriage of widows was permitted and only about one in eight Bengali Muslim women lived in widowhood. See Borthwick, *Changing Role of Women*, 35–6; and D. Engels, *Beyond Purdah?*, 40, 56–61, 94. On Vidyasagar's reform and its failure, see Asok Sen, *Iswar Chandra Vidyasagar and His Elusive Milestones*, 53–66, 78–83; and Heimsath, *Indian Nationalism*, 85.

207. T. Sarkar, 'Domesticity and Middle-Class Nationalism in Nineteenth-Century Bengal', in *Middle Class in Colonial India*, edited by Sanjay Joshi, 157–77, at 168.

208. Sivanath Sastri, 'Some Practical Suggestions regarding Female Education', 313, 328.

209. M. Karlekar, *Voices from Within*, 180–1.

210. 'Kayekti Katha', *Abalabandhab*, new ser., 1, no. 6 (Chaitra 1285/March 1879): 171–7, at 173–4 (emphasis added).

211. 'Kayekti Katha', 175–6, 177.

212. 'Jagatey Satitver Adarsa', *Abalabandhab*, new ser., 1, no. 8 (Jaistha 1286/May 1879): 33–9, at 38–9.

213. 'Narisamaj o Bratabidhi', in *Abalabandhab*, new ser., 1, no. 8 (Jaistha 1286/May 1879): 53–7, at 57.

214. See *Bamabodhini Patrika*, no. 95 (Ashar 1278/June 1871): 96–7, http://archiv.ub.uni-heidelberg.de/savifadok/volltexte/2010/1249 (accessed on 25 November 2013). See also N. Dutta, *Abalabandhab-Dwarakanath o Kadambini*, 35–8.

215. *Brahmo Public Opinion*, 5 June 1879, excerpted in Collet, *Brahmo Year-Book for 1879*, 82, emphasis added.

216. Tanika Sarkar, '*Strishiksha* and its Terrors', 153, 176. Examining the north Indian evidence, Sanjay Joshi has reached a broadly similar conclusion. See S. Joshi, *Fractured Modernity*, 61, 94.

217. Walsh, *Domesticity in Colonial India*, 5.

218. Mrinalini Sinha, *Specters of Mother India: The Global Restructuring of an Empire* (Durham, NC: Duke University Press, 2006), 191.

219. Dwarakanath Gangopadhayay, *Suruchir Kutir*, vol. 1 (Calcutta: Roy Press Depository, 1880); vol. 2 (Calcutta: Bhubanmohan Ghosh, 1884). Digital versions available at http://hdl.handle.net/10689/6677 (vol. 1); and http://hdl.handle.net/10689/5943 (vol. 2).

220. Borthwick, *Changing Role of Women*, 189. As Sophia Dobson Collet, a sympathetic observer of Brahmo activities, observed, 'the author's zeal for the improvement of his countrymen must have a beneficial effect, and is in itself a sign that the process of improvement has already begun'. See Collet, *Brahmo Year-Book for 1880*, 97.

221. D. Gangopadhayay, *Suruchir Kutir*, 1: unpaginated dedication. After Mary Carpenter's death, the Bengal branch of the National Indian Association had decided, at the suggestion of its founder Sasipada Banerji (1840–1924), to start a book-series named after her. The authors of books selected for the series received 'handsome prizes'. Dwarakanath Ganguli was awarded Rs 200 for *Suruchir Kutir*. See Tattvabhushan, *Social Reform in Bengal*, 66; and 'Annual Report of the Bengal Branch of the National Indian Association', *Journal of the National Indian Association in Aid of Social Progress in India* (1881): 264–7, at 265.

222. Quoted in Collet, *Brahmo Year-Book for 1880*, 97.

223. See Sheldon Garon, *Beyond Our Means: Why America Spends While the World Saves* (Princeton: Princeton University Press, 2012), 4–5, 24–5; and Dipesh Chakrabarty, 'The Difference-Deferral of (A) Colonial Modernity: Public Debates on Domesticity in British Bengal', *History Workshop Journal*, 36 (1993): 1–34, especially 4–5, 21–2.

224. Apart from being read by thousands in Europe and America, Smiles's *Thrift* moulded opinion across Asia. See Samuel Smiles, *Thrift* (London: John Murray, 1875); Garon, *Beyond Our Means*, 48–9; Tim Travers, *Samuel Smiles and the Victorian Work Ethic* (New York: Garland, 1987); and J.C. Ghosh, *Bengali Literature* (London: Oxford University Press, 1948), 123.

225. In 1870, the government had set up District Savings Banks but these were few and far between. See Richard Burn, J.S. Cotton, W.W. Hunter, W.S. Meyer, and H.H. Risley, eds, *The Imperial Gazetteer of India*, 3rd edn, 26 vols (Oxford: Clarendon Press, 1907–9), 3 (1907): 434. See also Amiya Kumar Bagchi, *The Evolution of the State Bank of India: The Roots, 1806–1876*, 2 parts (Bombay: Oxford University Press, 1987), 1: 31, 48; and *Indian Central Banking Enquiry Committee 1931: Report and Evidence*, 4 vols (Calcutta: Government of India, 1931), 1, pt i (Majority Report): 432–47; and 1, pt ii (Minority Report by Manu Subadar): 349–68 (British Library, Asia and Pacific Collection, IOR V/26/331/5; my thanks to Benjamin Zachariah and Anirban Bandyopadhyay for their help with this resource.)

226. Sanjay Joshi, *Fractured Modernity*, 69–70, 72.

227. See S. Joshi, *Fractured Modernity*, 70.

228. Moneylending seems to have been common and far from disreputable among Indians possessing even modest amounts of surplus wealth and was, no doubt, encouraged by the paucity of savings banks. See Glyn Barlow, *Industrial India*, 2nd edn (Madras: Natesan, 1911), 15.

229. On the marriage of vansaja Brahmins, see 'The Kulin Brahmins of Bengal', *Calcutta Review*, 2, no. 3 (1844): 1–31, at 27–8. (http://books.google.co.uk/books/about/Calcutta_review.html?id=SpNHAAAAYAAJ&redir_esc=y, accessed on 5 July 2013).

230. D. Gangopadhayay, *Suruchir Kutir*, 1: 24–8.

231. D. Gangopadhayay, *Suruchir Kutir*, 1: 7–22, 30–1, 33–4.

232. D. Gangopadhayay, *Suruchir Kutir*, 1: 34–7.

233. D. Gangopadhayay, *Suruchir Kutir*, 1: 44–5, 51–3, 67–8.

234. D. Chakrabarty, 'Difference-Deferral', 1–34; but see also Walsh, *Domesticity in Colonial India*.

235. D. Gangopadhayay, *Suruchir Kutir*, 1: 58–60. Suruchi gives up her share some years later when she is too busy bringing up her children; it is divided between three of the most productive members of the cooperative. See D. Gangopadhayay, *Suruchir Kutir*, 2: 60.

236. See Mallik, *Nabajuger Sadhana*, 172–5, 228; and Tattvabhushan, *Indubala*, 13. For Dwarakanath's own biography of Sasipada, which mentions the bank, see 'Sasipada Bandyopadhyay', in *Nababarshiki* (Calcutta: Roy Press Depository, 1880), 262–5.

237. One does not know whether—or to what extent—Dwarakanath was familiar with the history of the cooperative movement that commenced in Britain in 1844 with the Equitable Pioneers of Rochdale or the slightly later attempts in Germany to start co-operative societies for various tasks from sickness relief to the distribution of food to the poor. See Eleanor M. Hough, *The Co-operative Movement in India: Its Relation to a Sound National Economy* (London: P.S. King, 1932), 50–8; and C.F. Strickland, *Studies in European Co-operation*, 2 vols (Lahore: Government of Punjab, 1922–5).

238. D. Gangopadhayay, *Suruchir Kutir*, 1: 62–4. Yet again, these events are reminiscent of Baranagar jute-mill labourers prospering under the guidance of Sasipada Banerji. See Mallik, *Nabajuger Sadhana*, 198.

239. D. Gangopadhayay, *Suruchir Kutir*, 1: 66–8; 2: 61–4.

240. D. Gangopadhayay, *Suruchir Kutir*, 1: 72–3. Dwarakanath also urged the introduction of savings accounts for children in 'Shishur Sanchay Bhandar', *Abalabandhab*, new ser., 1, no. 9 (Ashar 1286/June 1879): 65–8.

241. Compare D. Gangopadhayay, *Suruchir Kutir*, 2: 51–3 with 'Siksha o Sikshitabya Bishay', *Abalabandhab*, new ser., 1, no. 2 (Agrahayan 1285/November 1878): 33–44.

242. 'Shishur Udyan', *Abalabandhab*, new ser., 1, no. 1 (Kartik 1285/October 1878): 11–17; and 'Shishur Udyan (Kindergarten): Dwitiya Prastab', *Abalabandhab*, new ser., 1, no. 2 (Agrahayan 1285/November 1878): 59–64. On Froebel, the kindergarten concept and their contexts, see Norman Brosterman, *Inventing Kindergarten* (New York: Abrams, 1997); and Roberta Wollons, ed., *Kindergartens and Cultures: The Global Diffusion of an Idea* (New Haven: Yale University Press, 2000).

243. See Mallik, *Nabajuger Sadhana*, 439–41; and Kopf, *The Brahmo Samaj and the Shaping of the Modern Indian Mind*, 121–2. For a list of Banerji's numerous projects and a brief description of the Baranagar of the time, see Tattvabhushan, *Indubala*, 40–1.

244. See Brosterman, *Inventing Kindergarten*, 32–3, 39.

245. See D. Gangopadhayay, *Suruchir Kutir*, 2: 36–7; and D. Gangopadhyay, 'Sarir Palan', *Abalabandhab*, new ser., 1, no. 3 (Poush 1285/December 1878): 65–75. Although a misinterpretation of Froebel, this approach was radical for the period when the need to *control* children's natural cravings was emphasized by most authorities. See D. Chakrabarty, 'Difference-Deferral', 6.

246. Dwarakanath does not tell us exactly where the family lives or how the children travel to the maidan every day, even though the distance between the centrally located maidan and northern Calcutta (the native parts of the city) was too great for daily trips. Even the government's efforts in the 1890s to encourage colleges to send their students to play on the maidan had failed because of this. See Buckland, *Bengal under the Lieutenant-Governors*, 2: 926.

247. Nor do they have unquestioned rights over their parents' attention. The period when Suresh returns from work and rests is reserved strictly for husband and wife and the children are taught to leave their parents at peace. The narrator declaims: 'Many unfortunate husbands, who come home from work only to be set upon by their children, go out again searching for peace and enjoyment. They would not do so if Suruchi's regulations were enforced in every home.' See D. Gangopadhayay, *Suruchir Kutir*, 2: 31–4, 40–4, 66.

248. D. Gangopadhayay, *Suruchir Kutir*, 2: 58–9. Again, this was radically opposed to the standard child-rearing advice of the time. See Pradip Kumar Bose, 'Sons of the Nation: Child Rearing in the New Family', in *Texts of Power: Emerging Disciplines in Colonial Bengal*, edited by Partha Chatterjee (Calcutta: Samya, 1996), 118–44.

249. From a young age, Ramesh starts earning money by selling his carpentry products and cutlery, while Jogesh manufactures his own ink and sells it to his fellow students. Suresh sets up savings accounts for each of them. See D. Gangopadhayay, *Suruchir Kutir*, 2: 65–9. Sasipada Banerji had attempted something similar for his own children. See Mallik, *Nabajuger Sadhana*, 444. It is interesting to note, by the way, that an early twentieth-century Government report on the industrial prospects of Bengal stated that the dyeing trade offered many opportunities to Indian entrepreneurs, especially if they modernized the industry and its techniques. See J.G. Cumming, *Review of the Industrial Position and Prospects in Bengal in 1908* (Calcutta: Bengal Secretariat Book Depot, 1908), 32–3.

250. Suruchi gets them to take turns at cooking the family dinner. See D. Gangopadhayay, *Suruchir Kutir*, 2: 70–3.

251. D. Gangopadhayay, *Suruchir Kutir*, 2: 94–116.

252. D. Gangopadhayay, *Suruchir Kutir*, 2: 5–6.

253. 'Paramarsha', *Abalabandhab*, new ser., 1, no. 3 (Poush 1285/December 1878): 89–96, especially 93. Even the *Brahmo Public Opinion*, the newspaper of the Sadharan Brahmo Samaj and a strong supporter of women's emancipation, warned in 1880: 'It won't do for us to imitate exactly European

manners, and let loose our women upon society, by giving them unlimited liberty to go wherever they please, and to mix with any person they like, in the present state of our society.' See 'Education and Emancipation of Hindu Women', *Brahmo Public Opinion* (9 September 1880), reprinted in Benoy Ghose, ed., *Selections from English Periodicals of 19th-Century Bengal, 1878–80: Brahmo Public Opinion* (Calcutta: Papyrus, 1978), 220–3, at 222–3.

3

Empire, Nation, Women

Dwarakanath Ganguli's campaigns for women's education
and social emancipation were complemented by his engagements, friendly as well as critical, with the British Raj. The
nineteenth century was a period of imperial realities and
nationalist dreams.[1] Although the concept of 'nation' has
always been ambiguous to scholars, the 'national idea' was a
driving force, perhaps the driving force, of modern European
history.[2] Non-Europeans, including Indians, also fell under
its spell, although the goal of a sovereign, independent
nation state did not feature on Indian agendas until the
twentieth century.[3] Dwarakanath lived and died before the
radicalization of Indian nationalism and although he
attacked certain aspects of colonial rule with great fervour,
he happily cooperated with the Raj when its policies, even
when contemptuous of 'native' customs and traditions,
seemed to him to be rational or progressive.

Today, Indian nationalism is often described as a
'derivative discourse' and its early practitioners, indeed,
proudly proclaimed their ideological affinity with European
nationalists.[4] Nevertheless, even this loyalist variety of
Indian nationalism was vastly different from European
models and it could not be otherwise.[5] For India, needless to
say, was still securely ensconced within the British Empire
and no Indian nationalist of any importance wanted that
imperial connection to be severed until the twentieth

century. The nineteenth-century nationalist demand was for India to be a 'self-governing colony', free of the bureaucratic despots of the Raj and their colonial racism, but not a sovereign nation. 'These men spoke highly of British justice,' remarked the historian Anil Seal. 'They asked God to bless the British Queen. They had friends inside the British parliament. But they spoke of the 'Un-Britishness of British Rule in India'.[6] Their agitations were 'constitutional', which meant they were loyal, peaceful, law-abiding, and conducted mainly in the form of petitions and memorials to the Government of India or the British Parliament about Indian grievances with the firm conviction that the fair-minded, freedom-loving British race would be open to correcting the deficiencies of their Indian regime once their subjects had pointed them out.[7]

To take just one typical example, when Viceroy Lytton introduced the Vernacular Press Act of 1878 to control 'seditious' Indian-language periodicals, the Indian Association not only organized protest meetings in Calcutta but sent a memorial to William Gladstone in London.[8] Gladstone, then in Opposition, raised the issue in the House of Commons in July 1878 but unwilling to embarrass the Viceroy, called only for very minor changes.[9] Even that mild proposal, however, was defeated and nothing changed in India until the Liberal Lord Ripon replaced Lytton as Viceroy.[10] No wonder that the British diplomat Wilfrid Scawen Blunt, who visited India in the early 1880s and met many leading nationalists of the time, lamented their 'too naive confidence ... in the good faith of English political action' and their confidence that 'when they should have proved their griefs to be well-founded, relief would thereupon be given'.[11]

These early nationalists would be derided, quite rightly, as 'mendicants' in the twentieth century, when Indian nationalism had become more radical but for the period we are concerned with, this so-called moderate nationalism was the only variety on offer.[12] The aspiration to be a 'self-governing colony' was to become associated most closely with the Indian National Congress in its early decades but long before the establishment of Congress in 1885, moderate nationalist ideas were flourishing within voluntary associations and even before that, in literature and the arts.[13] Dwarakanath Ganguli was involved deeply with all of these phases. He was writing, teaching, and crusading for women at the same time as he was engaging enthusiastically in nationalist campaigns. Sumit Sarkar has claimed that middle-class interest in women's issues declined in the late nineteenth century because of the rise of nationalism.[14] This generalization, like so many others, is inapplicable to Dwarakanath Ganguli and some of his fellow Brahmos.

Brahmos played a prominent role in the history of nationalism, although historians have paid more attention to their cosmopolitanism. It was not simply individual and religious freedom that the more radical Brahmos fought for: many of them also aspired for national freedom, to the dismay of Keshab Sen, a loyal supporter of British rule.[15] Dwijadas Datta, who defected to the Keshabite rump after the split of 1878, asserted that the Sadharan Brahmos were 'politicians first and men of religion after' and had destroyed 'the self-effacing spirit of true religion' by injecting 'the political poison of self-assertion' into the Brahmo movement.[16] In fact, the radicals believed that that there could be no spiritual freedom without political freedom and vice versa.[17] Born from the controversy over Keshab Sen's personality cult, the Sadharan Brahmos had aspired to make their church truly democratic and insisted on the Samaj framing a formal constitution providing for the annual election of officials and representative committees drawn from Calcutta as well as the outlying areas.[18] The constitution of the Sadharan Brahmo Samaj, Bipinchandra Pal observed, was framed so as to 'furnish a model for the constitution of the future national state of India'.[19] The Brahmo Samaj's encouragement of individual conscience and reason and its readiness to battle against social oppression or theological commandments, Pal argued, gave birth to the Indian freedom struggle.[20]

Of course, it was not just Brahmos who were embracing nationalism in the 1870s. The educated youth of Calcutta, inspired by Surendranath Banerjea's lectures on Mazzini and Italian nationalism, were beginning to form small secret societies in emulation of the Carbonari, although their patriotic sentiments were more impressive than their revolutionary capabilities.[21] Sivanath Sastri conducted a remarkable series of secret initiation ceremonies in late 1877, in which willing young Brahmos, Bipinchandra Pal, Sundarimohan Das, Saratchandra Ray (the owner of Mymensingh's famous 'Brahmo Shop') and three others, slit their chests and then, with their own blood, wrote out on banyan leaves what they would renounce—lust, anger, greed, jealousy, idolatry, caste-belief, and colonial subjection—and the leaves were then consigned to the sacrificial fire.[22] The last renunciation was explicitly political—although acknowledging that there was no current alternative to British rule, the young men pledged never to work for the colonial state, no matter how great their need for economic security. The ultimate goal was national self-government, which was 'the only form of political government ordained by God'.[23] But only a physically strong population, they believed, could attain self-government. The British held Bengalis in contempt for their physical weakness and lack of courage; the Bengali intelligentsia, concurring with this negative evaluation, emphasized that the cultivation of physical strength was indispensable to national regeneration.[24] The initiates, therefore, also took a pledge to cultivate physical prowess and attain proficiency in horse-riding and shooting. These scattered and often short-lasting initiatives were given organizational focus by the Indian Association, one of the first bourgeois nationalist bodies in India.[25] It was established in 1876 almost entirely by Sadharan Brahmos and the Association 'linked the Brahmo Samaj's liberal quest for individual freedom with the new quest for political freedom'.[26]

Recent historical work has strongly emphasized the many exclusions and injustices involved in the quest to build a unitary Indian nation from a vast subcontinent of infinite diversity.[27] Virtually every nineteenth-century British expert on India would have endorsed those critiques. In *India* (first published in 1888), which was a Bible for generations of Indian Civil Service officers, John Strachey (1823–1907) declared: 'There is not, and never was an India, or even a country of India, possessing, according to European ideas, any sort of unity, physical, political, social or religious.'[28] Indian nationalism was always an uneven combination of what Amalendu Guha felicitously called 'great' and 'little' nationalisms, the first pan-Indian in vision and the second rooted in regional identities.[29] It was never easy to coordinate the two, and then as now, 'great nationalism' was undermined more by religious differences than by the many 'little nationalisms'. English-educated Indians tended—often unconsciously—to equate 'Indian' with 'Hindu' or, even more mythically, with 'Aryan', portraying the centuries of Muslim rule as an age of despotism that was infinitely worse than the British Raj.[30] The nationalists of his time, remarked Bipinchandra Pal, might criticize the Raj but they never forgot that the pax Britannica had ended the 'universal anarchy and disorder' of late Mughal rule. The British, they all agreed, had 'replaced that reign of terror by a new reign of law'.[31]

Muslim Invaders = British Colonialists?

The emphasis on India's 'Hindu' and 'Aryan' character and depictions of the nation's history as a series of heroic struggles with the invading foreigner, Anuradha Roy has pointed out, were ways of imagining the culturally diverse subcontinent as a unitary, powerful nation. Without some such device, she argues, it would have been impossible to conceive of, say, Bengalis as having much in common with Rajputs or the Marathas. As for the bravery of Indians, it could, of course, have been established by celebrating the 1857 Mutiny-Rebellion but the Bengali intelligentsia had never supported the Rebellion and, even if they had resolved to swallow their objections in the national interest, they would have attracted unwelcome attention from the colonial state.[32] So, it was the Muslims who became the prototypical foreigners for most nationalist literati—and not, as one might assume, simply for conservative Hindus among them—and the unrelenting negativity with which they portrayed Muslim rule, while it might have cemented the bonds between otherwise very different Indians, impeded their goal by splitting Hindu from Muslim.[33]

The tendency of non-Muslim nationalists to emphasize Muslim tyranny, however, was not necessarily one-dimensional. Often, the figure of the 'Muslim invader' was used to symbolize all foreign rulers, including the British, in forms that would not attract the hostile attention of the colonial state. One example of such a nationalist text was Dwarakanath Ganguli's play *Vira Nari: The Heroine of Scinde*. Published anonymously in 1875, it depicted an incident from the war in AD 712 between Dahir, the King of Sind, and the Muslim invader Muhammad Ibn Kasim.[34] The sources were Mountstuart Elphinstone's *History of India* (first published in 1841) and James Tod's hugely popular *Annals and Antiquities of Rajasthan* (1829–1832).[35] Long before Gandhi quoted Tod at the 1931 Round Table Conference in London, nationalists had used Tod's accounts of Rajput battles with Muslim invaders to encourage contemporary Hindus to rediscover the martial prowess and patriotism of their ancestors.[36]

The history of medieval India, generally regarded then as one of subjugation and 'foreign' conquest, seemed to offer only one example of Hindu (that is, 'Indian') valour—that of the fiercely independent Rajputs.[37] For Bengalis, whom the British considered to be effeminate, duplicitous, and physically feeble and who themselves regarded their history as one of centuries of defeat and subjection, the Rajputs were the kind of Indians the nation needed and they read Tod with fascination.[38] Historic Rajasthan became emblematic for what they wished Bengal to be in the India of the future and thus, a 'symbiotic relationship' came to be forged between Bengal and Rajasthan, places that were poles apart in terms of geography, ethnography, and history.[39] 'Two-thirds of the national ideas now in Bengal', remarked Swami Vivekananda in 1898, were derived from Tod's account of Rajputs and writers as different as Michael Madhusudan Dutt (1824–1873), Bankimchandra Chatterji (1838–1894), Girischandra Ghosh (1844–1911), Dwijendralal Roy (1863–1913), and four of the famous Tagores—Jyotirindranath (1848–1925), Swarnakumari (1855–1932), Rabindranath (1861–1941), and Abanindranath (1871–1951)—all produced works that retold, or were at least inspired by, stirring episodes from Tod.[40]

Rajasthan did not entrance Bengalis simply because of the valour of Rajput men. As the poet Rangalal Bandyopadhyay (1827–1887), the first of Tod's Bengali appropriators, pointed out in 1858, Tod had also highlighted the 'chastity, gentleness, and courage' of the women of Rajputana.[41] Even progressives who considered the banning of sati to be one of the greatest benefits of British rule admired Rajput women burning themselves to death in mass immolations (jauhar) to avoid surrendering to the invading Mughals.[42] The Rajput woman, combining the purity of the eternal (Hindu) feminine and the courage of warriors, came to represent the new Indian woman, 'the symbolic center around which the "nation" coalesced'.[43] Together with the idealization of Rajput women, Rajput–Mughal wars were glorified as the authentic Indian nation's response to the alien faith of Islam and to imperialism tout court.

For some nationalistically inclined Bengalis, there is little doubt that the stereotype of the invading Muslim also symbolized the British imperialist but there were good reasons why such identifications were never overt.[44] At least from the time of Dinabandhu Mitra's 1860 play Nil-Darpan (The Indigo Planter's Mirror) about the oppression of peasants by European indigo planters, Bengali drama had acquired a radical reputation and there was a proliferation of anti-British plays after the establishment of professional theatres in Calcutta in the 1870s. Realizing that the stage was being used by nationalists to disseminate their criticism of British rule, the colonial state promulgated the Dramatic Performances Act in 1876, which made it impossible for the British to be attacked explicitly.[45] Dramatists, therefore, began to convey their anticolonial messages through ostensibly remote tales of Rajput or Maratha struggles against the Mughal or earlier Muslim rulers.[46] Such explanations did not, of course, convince Muslims and around 1900, as Ramya Sreenivasan has shown, they began to publish works 'asserting the glories of pre-modern Islam' and of Muslim rule in India.[47] But non-Muslim nationalists broadly agreed, as Bipinchandra Pal was to put it, that when dramatists 'abused the Muslims, they actually meant the English'.[48]

All this is the indispensable context for Dwarakanath Ganguli's *Vira Nari*. His involvement with the stage is curious since Brahmos condemned the theatre as an agent of immorality, largely because of the use of prostitutes as actresses.[49] Keshab Sen's newspaper *Indian Mirror* even welcomed the prosecution (under an ordinance preceding the Dramatic Performances Act) of theatre personalities Amritalal Bose and Upendranath Das for obscenity.[50] This kind of moral vigilantism was not unique to Brahmos or Bengalis—the Lucknow middle classes, for instance, sought to marginalize the celebrated courtesan culture of the city during the same period—but the Brahmos became identified with it in the popular imagination.[51] The fabled puritanism of the Brahmos, John Rosselli has speculated, may have stemmed from their urge to counter the British charge that Hinduism encouraged licentiousness and immorality but the 'social boycott' of the theatre by Brahmos may have impeded the development of the Bengali stage.[52] And Dwarakanath not only wrote for the theatre, but his play was staged at the Bengal Theatre, which was the first to employ actresses and reviled for that very reason by Brahmos.[53]

It is possible that any immoral associations of the stage were outweighed for Dwarakanath by its ability to convey his message to a far wider audience than he could otherwise reach. His play was not simply a piece of entertainment but a programmatic text, pervaded by its author's lifelong interest in women's emancipation and nation-building. Dahir, the king of Sind, is killed in war with Muhammad Ibn Kasim and when Dahir's cowardly son escapes from the battlefield, the widowed queen emerges to lead the army. Kasim places the capital under siege and when the food runs out, the queen and all the women of the city decide to perform jauhar, while the men throw themselves on the enemy knowing that death was certain. The play ends with a song lamenting that 'golden India' was now occupied by infidels—*sonar Bharat aaj jabanadhikarey*—and calling upon all

Indians to fight the invaders to death, just like the heroes and heroines of Sind. The play, and especially the concluding song, may well
have inflamed more perceptive audiences against British colonists
but there is no denying the overt anti-Muslim thrust of the text and its
assumption that India was a land of Hindus alone.

Dwarakanath's views on Muslims were always rather ambiguous.
In 1880, he expressed 'disquiet'—*ashanka*—about the rapid growth of
the Muslim population of India with a pointed question: 'Who can say
that India would not some day become a nation of Muslims?'[54] He
did express some admiration for the puritanical Wahabi Muslims
who opposed the decadent Muslim rulers of eighteenth-century
Bengal but the Wahabi campaign to purify Islam might have seemed
to him to complement Brahmo attempts to purify Hinduism.[55] But
he could be pro-Muslim in a far more direct way too. In his brief
speech at the 1886 Congress in Calcutta, he spoke up for the right of
Bengali Muslims to be appointed to the Indian Civil Service. 'We
know that our Mahomedan friends, so far as Bengal is concerned, are
not duly represented,' he observed. 'So in justice to them ... a certain
proportion of the appointments [to the ICS] should be reserved for
Mahomedans who are qualified.' Dadabhai Naoroji, the President of
the Congress for that year, rejected the proposal, however, remarking
that 'the interests of the country demanded that the best men should
get the appointments irrespective of nationality, caste or creed'.[56] But
even if Dwarakanath himself was not wholly anti-Muslim and even if
we assume that the anti-Muslim rhetoric of *Vira Nari* was no more
than a ploy, the play cannot be taken as a straightforward allegory
about Indian opposition to British colonial rule.

Dwarakanath was deeply critical of some aspects of Raj
administration and he was not reluctant to get into physical alterca-
tions with Europeans whom he had caught trying to exploit or insult
Indians.[57] But neither he nor his 'moderate' nationalist peers ever
called for the kind of mass uprising against the British that the Rajputs
had resorted to against the Mughals. Dwarakanath's criticism of
British rule was always tempered by his conviction that for all its faults,
it was still the best available option for India. In the preface to
Kabigatha, a poetry collection for children, he explained that while
India's subjection to a foreign power was to be regretted, '*at the
moment*, we cannot hope to find better rulers' and since the flaws in
the British government of India were not inherently British—notice
the typically moderate distinction between the despots of the Raj and

the 'real' British—they could be corrected by bringing the injustices to the attention of the London government by 'constitutional' agitation.[58] And it was not as if the many problems of India could be reformed simply by improving its governance or even by independence. National independence, he wrote in an essay in *Abalabandhab*, was desirable because it enhanced human freedom and dignity but independence alone could not guarantee national improvement until the people's moral development had progressed significantly.[59] India could not be regenerated until Indians had corrected those 'deficiencies in our character that have made us so inferior and useless'.[60] It would, therefore, be rash to take the extreme nationalism of *Vira Nari* to be a faithful representation of his attitude towards British rule.

The anthology of nearly thirty patriotic songs titled *Jatiya Sangeet* that he published one year later reflected his ideological stance rather more clearly.[61] As Anuradha Roy has shown, the number of 'nationalist verse-books' was 'overwhelming' in late-nineteenth-century Bengal and Dwarakanath's collection, which was probably meant for use at the Banga Mahila Bidyalaya, was one of many available.[62] It commenced with Satyendranath Tagore's song 'Miley sabey Bharatasantan, ektan manapran, gao Bharater jashagan' (Sing the glory of India in unison, all you children of India) and ended with two songs from Dinabandhu Mitra's *Nildarpan* denouncing indigo planters. Apart from Satyendranath, two other Tagores, Gunendranath and Dwijendranath, featured among the authors. Several of Dwarakanath's own compositions were included but printed without credit and described simply as 'previously unpublished'. Among these were 'Na jagile saba Bharatalalana, e Bharat aar jagey na jagey na' (India will never awaken until all of India's women waken), a song that fused its author's two great ideological projects and was popular enough to find a place in other collections of the time.[63]

Most of the songs in *Jatiya Sangeet* lamented the present state of India but avoided condemning the British explicitly. The Mughals, again, were represented as aggressors, and the anthology included the last song from *Vira Nari* and another based on the legend of Maharashtrian Brahmin-minstrel Madhavacharya inspiring his fellow-Marathis to fight the Mughals. The latter reflected the wider nationalist trend of supplementing tales of Rajasthan with accounts of the Maratha Kingdom's battles with the Mughals. Since the Marathas had not only fought with the Mughals but also with the British, their glorification could, of course, imply an anti-British position.[64] At an explicit level, however, the collection offered nothing overtly critical of British rule. Chancing upon the volume nearly three decades after its publication, Bipinchandra Pal admired the 'exquisite and inspiring' songs Dwarakanath had collected, recalling how they had once been 'in the mouth of everybody who could, or thought he could sing'. Over time, however, the very character of patriotism had changed, Pal observed, and these old songs, whose nationalistic spirit stemmed from 'an intense longing to emulate, to rise up to, to be even like the British' had lost their appeal.[65]

A Loyal Opposition

All the songs collected in *Jatiya Sangeet* were about India (*Bharat*), not Bengal, and this was eminently compatible with the ideology of the Indian Association, a pioneering association of nationalists founded in the very year of publication of the collection by, among others, Anandamohan Bose, Sivanath Sastri, Dwarakanath Ganguli, and Surendranath Banerjea. Except for Surendranath Banerjea, the Association's founders came mostly from the ranks of those Brahmos who, two years after the establishment of the Indian Association, would form the socially radical Sadharan Brahmo Samaj, which a critic would describe, not entirely without justification, as a 'half-religious and half-political' body.[66]

The Indian Association was not the first formal association of nationally minded 'natives'. The British Indian Association, founded in 1851, had, in its earlier years, been ready to criticize the government when necessary but after the Sepoy Rebellion of 1857, it turned into a cosy club of fairly conservative zamindars charging astronomical membership fees (fifty rupees a year) that no ordinary person could afford. Perhaps more important were the various non-political—or, to use Anil Seal's terminology, proto-political—organizations and initiatives of the 1860s.[67] The Hindu Mela—an annual fair organized by Nabagopal Mitra from 1867 that celebrated Indian achievements and heritage, with which the Tagore family was deeply involved—had triggered small-scale projects to establish national schools, national gymnasia, and national newspapers.[68] Although Mitra's nationalism was entirely cultural and co-existed happily with a profound loyalty to the British Empire, it prepared the ground for more political but equally pro-British forms of nationalism.[69] Bipinchandra Pal declared that it was from Nabagopal Mitra that young Bengalis had received their first lessons in nationalism and Dwarakanath Ganguli was also a great supporter of Mitra's initiatives. Abala Bose recalled how, when she was nine, Dwarakanath had taught her a patriotic poem and had then taken her to the Hindu Mela where she had recited it in public.[70]

This kind of cultural nationalism came to be complemented by a more politically aware variety with the formation of the Students' Association in 1875 by Anandamohan Bose, freshly returned from Cambridge and acclaimed locally as the 'first Indian Wrangler'.[71] Modelled upon a similar association in Bombay, the Student Association's members were regaled with lectures on great European nationalists as well as noble figures from Indian and Bengali history—Mazzini, Garibaldi, Sri Chaitanya, the Sikhs—by Surendranath Banerjea, then a young academic just dismissed, allegedly on unfair grounds, from the Indian Civil Service.[72] The politicization of nationalism was further reinforced by the formation of the Indian League in 1875 by the brothers Hemantakumar and Sisirkumar Ghose, publishers of the newspaper *Amrita Bazar Patrika*.[73] Banerjea as well as Bose joined the Indian League but did not get on too well with the Ghose brothers and launched the Indian Association in July 1876.[74] The Indian Association was proudly middle-class and critical of the aristocratic British Indian Association. 'If there were anything like a Parliament here,' remarked the *Brahmo Public Opinion*, 'the British Indian Association would form the House of Lords and the Indian Association the House of Commons.'[75]

The Indian Association's name was carefully chosen so as to indicate its aspiration 'to be the centre of an all-India movement' that would bring the entire nation 'upon the same common political platform'.[76] Branches were set up throughout northern India—although these were often controlled by expatriate Bengalis—and the Association pursued alliances with the associations of the south.[77] In December 1883, the Association organized a full-scale National Conference in Calcutta, hailing it as the first step towards 'that unification of the Indian races', which, dependent as it was on the English language and owing its relevance to British political paramountcy in the subcontinent, would 'constitute the brightest glory of British rule'.[78] Delegates came from all over India and two visitors from Britain: the Liberal MP John Seymour Keay (1839–1909) and the anti-imperialist poet, diplomat, and man-of-the-world Wilfrid Scawen Blunt (1840–1922).[79] Anandamohan Bose described the conference

as 'the first stage toward a national Parliament' and although Blunt
found the Conference to be rather a Bengali affair, it did include representatives from all parts of India, ranging from Delhi and Lahore to
Ahmedabad and Madras.[80] Their numbers might not have been particularly impressive but the Indian Association's national aspirations
were real enough and it was only after the establishment of the Indian
National Congress in 1885 that it came to concern itself more with
Bengali issues.[81]

Dwarakanath Ganguli was one of the founding members of the
Indian Association and served as its Assistant Secretary from 1882 to
1898. His work for the Association won high praise from Surendranath
Banerjea. Describing him as 'my indefatigable friend' and 'an ardent
lover of what he believed to be the truth', Banerjea recalled that 'he
threw his whole soul' into the Association and worked for it 'with an
energy and devotion, the memory of which, now that he is dead, his
friends cherish with affectionate gratitude'.[82] As we have seen,
Dwarakanath broadly shared the Association's aim to serve as the
Raj's loyal opposition but there is no reason to think that he would
have disagreed too violently with Surendranath Banerjea's idealization of 'England' as 'our political guide and our moral preceptor'.[83]
Neither he nor the more active members of the Indian Association
ever forgot, however, that an opposition, no matter how loyal, was also
required to oppose.

Their oppositional initiatives, moreover, were not exclusively
concerned with urban middle-class grievances. The Association succeeded in organizing unions of peasants (rayats) across rural Bengal
and while it stressed the need for 'mutual amity' between zamindars
and their tenants, it collected much information on oppression of peasants.[84] Famines were fairly regular events at the time and the Association
not only sent its agents to collect information during the food shortages
of the 1880s and 1890s but, during the famine of 1884–5, it opened
relief centres in distressed villages in collaboration with the Sadharan
Brahmo Samaj, and Lieutenant-Governor Augustus Rivers Thompson
thanked the Samaj and the Association formally for 'their charitable
and patriotic exertions ... in the relief of distress'.[85] Assistant Secretary
Dwarakanath Ganguli was particularly keen on such initiatives and
after his death, the Association seems to have retreated from them.[86]
Ganguli was also responsible for the Association's greatest attempt to
champion the cause of the poor and oppressed: the campaign against
the ill-treatment of the tea coolies of Assam.

The Unquiet Hills

Annexed by the East India Company from the local Ahom kings in 1826 after the First Anglo-Burmese War and incorporated with the Bengal Presidency up to 1874, Assam was 'a wild—almost unknown—tract of jungle' for most of the nineteenth century.[87] Despite its inaccessibility, it became important as a tea-growing area from 1833, when the East India Company, having lost its monopoly of tea imports from China, decided to grow tea in India. The discovery of a tea plant which was native to Assam—as well as cheap land made available by the government—led to the proliferation of tea gardens, most of them run by European planters.[88] By 1901, India was supplying more than 40 per cent of the world tea market while China, once the largest supplier, was contributing a mere 26 per cent.[89] The tea planters were treated with deference by the officials of the Raj and became the virtual rulers of Assam.[90]

The planters had one problem, however: a shortage of labour. Assam was not heavily populated and lacked a large body of agricultural labourers; whatever labour was available locally was too expensive and, allegedly, lazy and addicted to opium.[91] Hence, indentured labourers were imported from other parts of India.[92] Originally designed by the British to find a replacement for slave labour across the entire empire, the indenture system was theoretically based on a voluntary, fixed-term contract but in practice, most indentured labourers were persuaded to sign up by false promises of idyllic, well-paid lives in beautiful climes and indenture came to constitute what historian Hugh Tinker has called 'a new system of slavery'.[93] The case of Assam was no different.[94] At first, tea garden coolies were supplied by European contractors working through Indian recruiters or *arkattis* who 'did the actual recruiting in districts of Bengal and Bihar' and were paid for each worker they obtained.[95] This process was subject to some government regulation—recruiters, for instance, needed to be licensed—but a new Inland Emigration Act removed even those limited safeguards in 1882.[96] Numerous unregistered recruiters now entered the trade and because they were rewarded much more lavishly, thousands could be active in the same district.[97] Abduction of village people was rife, as was the practice of enticing young men with promises of alcohol and women.[98]

The 1882 Act came to be known in Indian nationalist circles as the 'Slave Act of British India'.[99] The high cost of recruitment—caused largely by the enhanced fees demanded by the recruiters—was compensated by using every means to keep wages low and extracting the maximum amount of labour from the workers. Living conditions for tea garden coolies were abysmal and the punishments for insufficient productivity brutal. From 1882 to 1901, one of every four labourers recruited under the 1882 Act died before completing the contract, the deaths being explained by the planters as due to the coolies being already diseased or failing to adjust to the climatic conditions of Assam. Desertion was rife and some 5 per cent of workers absconded every year. Countless more *tried* to abscond but were tracked down by the planters and subjected to merciless floggings or imprisonment in dungeons.[100] 'They are literally roasted there,' Dwarakanath Ganguli would report, 'and when they appeal for water to quench their thirst, not even a drop of water is given to them, and when their sufferings become unbearable, there is none to listen to their piteous cries.'[101]

Dwarakanath was not the first to reveal the ill-treatment of coolies in Assam, rumours about which had been circulating from the 1860s.[102] 'We hereby warn the tea planters again not to behave like indigo planters,' the Bengali paper *Somprakash* had asserted in 1862. 'If they continue oppressions like that of indigo planters, they will have to leave India soon.'[103] A five-act play *Cha-Kar Darpan* (The Tea Planter's Mirror), modelled on Dinabandhu Mitra's anti-indigo planter play *Nil Darpan*, had been written by the obscure playwright Dakshinacharan Chattopadhyay in 1875.[104] But the first detailed exposé was by the Brahmo missionary Ramkumar Bhattacharya, known as Ramkumar Vidyaratna ([1836?]–1901), one of whose daughters, incidentally, was brought up by Upendrakishore Ray and later married Upendrakishore's brother Pramadaranjan.[105] Ramkumar, although born in a family of Brahmin priests, was a founding member of the Sadharan Brahmo Samaj and was appointed the Samaj's missionary in Assam.[106] He travelled there several times between 1878 and 1887, discovering by chance the ill-treatment of plantation coolies and published his findings in *Brahmo Public Opinion*, the *Indian Messenger*, and other Brahmo newspapers of Calcutta.[107]

One of the cases exposed by Ramkumar concerned a fourteen-year-old boy coolie named Umesh. He had been kicked to death and trampled on by one Mr Gordon, the British manager of a tea garden in Kalajola. Gordon was arrested and tried at the District Court, only to be acquitted. Another notorious case reported by Vidyaratna was that of Charles Webb, who worked for a steamer company in Assam.

Coolies arrived by steamer and were housed briefly under Webb's charge and then sent off to the various plantations. Webb raped a married female coolie, Sukurmani, who was beaten severely for resisting and died shortly afterwards. At Webb's trial, the medical witness declared that Sukurmani had died naturally. But there had been many eyewitnesses and the coolie population, normally so sub-servient, grew agitated after the tragedy. Webb was now tried by the Assistant Commissioner of Assam but let off with a modest fine. The case was referred to the Calcutta High Court, which upheld the verdict. But the controversy did not die down and some Calcutta men went on a deputation to Lord Ripon. Ripon agreed with them that Webb's trials had been 'incomplete and unsatisfactory' but the Governor General had no authority to intervene in the judicial process.[108]

The full details of the Webb trial were put together by Dwarakanath Ganguli and others in an 1884 pamphlet with the graphic title *Justice Murdered in India: The Papers of the Webb Case Recording the Sacrifice of a Daughter of India to the Lust of an Anglo-Indian, Presented to the Electors of Great Britain and Ireland.* Printed and published by the Sadharan Brahmo Samaj, it was sent to Wilfrid Scawen Blunt to be presented to the British Parliament.[109] I have found no record that it was actually placed before the House of Commons but even if it was, it did not lead to any action, illustrating the fallacy of the nationalist conviction that the metropolitan British would correct the failings of the Raj if only they were informed about them. Ironically, it was Lord Ripon, the head of the Raj, who paid more attention to Vidyaratna's reports and the Indian Association's memorial, mentioning them in 1882 when the Assam Emigration Bill was being debated in the Viceroy's Council. But the law nevertheless went on the statute books without any second thoughts.[110]

After the foundation of *Sanjibani* in 1883, Vidyaratna kept its readers informed on the appalling conditions in the tea plantations and the leniency with which the magistrates treated planters charged with oppressing their coolies. Such reports put Vidyaratna at consid-erable personal risk. He reported to *Sanjibani* that it was being said in Assam that he would be a 'victim of the planters' gun'.[111] Nothing, however, happened to the missionary and he continued to visit Assam, sometimes, it is said, visiting tea plantations disguised as a coolie.[112] By 1886, his reports had shaken the Calcutta elite and in July, Dwarakanath Ganguli decided to examine the situation on behalf of the Indian Association.[113] Sivanath Sastri also visited Assam around the same time and recalled how profoundly government officials were agitated about the presence of the Indian Association's Assistant Secretary in Assam. Dwarakanath was constantly followed by the police and information collected on him from local Bengali families. Since Sastri was travelling with him, mystified government agents often sat through his religious lectures in the hope of collecting some incriminating evidence. At one of Sastri's lectures, held during bad weather, hardly anybody turned up except for the Deputy Commissioner himself! The rough terrain of Assam posed its own difficulties: once, Dwarakanath was almost drowned while trying to cross a monsoon-swollen river.[114]

Nothing, however, could persuade him to suspend his mission or to keep his findings to himself. Combining his own eyewitness testimony with data culled from court records and government reports, Dwarakanath published horrifying accounts of coolie-life in *Sanjibani* and *The Bengalee*. The *Sanjibani* reports, unfortunately, are lost, since most issues of the paper have perished but those in *The Bengalee* (published between September 1886 and April 1887) are available.[115] The reports were prefaced by a message from the Indian Association declaring: 'It may be a useful thing to reclaim the wilds of Assam, but surely it would be a heavy price to pay, if such a result were to be obtained by the adoption of a qualified form of slavery in British India.' It was not, the Association emphasized, a political question: 'It appeals to the deepest feelings of the Christian and of the philanthropist; and to them we appeal for help and sympathy in this work.'[116]

In his first report, Dwarakanath showed how perfunctorily the Registering Officer and others were enforcing the 1882 Act's stipulation that the labourers be aware, at the time of recruitment, of the nature of their work and their rights. The labourers were trained to give 'correct' answers to the questions asked by the Registration Officer and those who were unwilling to do so were 'either kept back in depots and there shut up like prisoners' till they consented. The really refractory cases were not even presented to the Registration Officer—'other people personify them and answer to their names'. The Registration Officer never enquired whether a coolie had been recruited by coercion or fraud by the agents.[117] Even the coolies who willingly gave the 'right' answers were usually unaware of the true meaning of the words they had been taught to speak. One question, for example, asked whether they knew where they were going. The correct answer was Assam but 'it is doubtful whether one in a thousand knows what Assam really is', let alone whether the place was 'good or bad, healthy or unhealthy'. Another question asked whether the coolie knew what he would have to do. For males, the right response was 'to hoe' but, observed Dwarakanath, 'for how many hours and whether he will have to do any other work, he does not know'. The employer was free 'to exact as much of task-work from his employees as he [thought] ... fit'.[118]

The British claim that the indenture system was based on free and informed consent was, therefore, false, at least as far as tea garden recruitment was concerned. But the coolies' real troubles commenced only after they reached Assam. Apart from the harsh climate and terrain, there was the brutal discipline to contend with. Even an ill coolie was forced to work—'otherwise', as one coolie put it, 'the severe lashes of the whip will cut my flesh into inch-pieces'—and poor as they had been in their former abodes, the gardens of Assam reduced the migrants to a level lower than animals. Since wages varied according to the ability to work, some of the newer coolies earned too little to eat. Suicide was common and one starving coolie killed his wife with her consent and then turned himself in so that he could be put to death, thus ending all their troubles. Instead of investigating the case, the Magistrate simply sentenced the coolie for 'murder'.[119]

Even worse was the condition of children—Dwarakanath quoted a report by the Civil Surgeon of Dibrugarh:

A coolie woman gets a variable amount of leave for her confinement. After that, if the infant is not strangled at birth, she must either take it out to her work or leave it behind, with no one to look after it. In the former cases, tied to its mother's back or left in the nearest drain, it is exposed to extremes of heat and cold, to wind and to rain; in the latter the child gets half starved and so paves its way to a death from some bowel disorder or succeeds in cutting short its career by a fall or a roll into the open fire.[120]

Those too old or infirm to work were also forced to labour and all were subject to the whip if their performance was below par.[121] Many coolies actually deserted so that they could get into jail, which, for all its horrors, was still superior to their 'normal' living conditions.[122] And all this, Dwarakanath remarked, was being tolerated by 'our Christian Government', which was so humane that it patronized 'societies for the prevention of cruelty to animals!'[123]

Few coolies, however, complained officially about the ill-treatment or sought legal remedies. This, Dwarakanath pointed out, was not only because of their ignorance and poverty but also because of their belief 'which is unhappily too well-founded, that it is very difficult to get a European offender punished'.[124] The law provided for inspectors who would periodically visit the gardens and assess whether the coolies were being overworked but inspection visits took place only about once a year and many gardens did not even receive an annual visit.[125] Few inspections were rigorous—'the Inspectors when they visit the gardens generally dine and peg with the planters, play and exchange with them the social amenities of life'—and since the planters knew when the inspector would visit, they had no trouble in reducing the coolies' workload before the visit and raising it as soon as the inspector left. 'The daily task has lately been raised by 50 per cent, all around, and in some gardens it has nearly been doubled. Has any Inspector as yet brought this matter to the notice of the Government?' Dwarakanath asked.[126]

Then there was the question of the planters' morals and their attitudes towards women. Many of the planters were unmarried and lived with local concubines, most of whom were young girls sold to the planters by their parents. 'Although no traffic in human flesh is allowed by law, and slavery is strictly prohibited, yet in Assam women were freely bought and sold for a more heinous purpose than that of slavery,' remarked Ganguli.[127] But more informal means of obtaining sexual partners were also used: attractive coolie women were 'invited to dance in their masters' houses' and then plied with strong drink and taken advantage of.[128] Citing several other instances of the immorality of the planters, Dwarakanath concluded that a comprehensive collection of such cases 'would form another sensational chapter of Mr Stead's pamphlet on Modern Babylon'.[129] Unsurprisingly, labourers whose contracts had expired rarely re-contracted and the planters often resorted to violence, kidnap of spouses, or fraud to make them sign fresh contracts.[130] Dwarakanath charged that 'the most dishonest and dishonourable practice of forging documents for the renewal of agreements is carried on with shameless impunity'. Very few coolies, he observed, possessed 'sufficient intelligence' to see through the ruses of the planters and they 'must therefore live in bondage for life'.[131]

The government's response to Dwarakanath's graphic reports merely insisted that 'the coolie is better off in Assam than he would

be probably anywhere else'.[132] The Calcutta middle classes, however, were outraged. Many ordinary people were so appalled that
they stopped drinking tea. As one correspondent declaimed in
Sanjibani, 'drinking Assam tea is nothing more or less than drinking
the blood of the poor persecuted coolie'.[133] Bipinchandra Pal wrote
in his memoirs: 'We readily compared the condition of tea garden
labourers in Assam to that of Negro labour in America before the
Emancipation.'[134] The Sadharan Brahmo Samaj, obviously, was
equally concerned about the situation but many Brahmos, unlike
Dwarakanath, blamed the victims more than they blamed the
planters. A correspondent writing from the same residential address
as Dwarakanath Ganguli's pointed out on the pages of the Sadharan
Brahmo Samaj paper *Tattvakaumudi* that if Assam tea were to be
chemically analysed, 50 per cent of it would be shown to consist of
the blood of coolies, 25 per cent of their sexual infidelities, and the
last quarter of their irreligion. Calling upon all Brahmos to devote
themselves to the cause of the coolies, the writer warned that simply
ending their oppression by the planters would not suffice. It was
essential to provide the ignorant labourers with moral and social
education. Only when their current lack of sexual morals, spiritual
knowledge, and family bonds had been reformed could Brahmos
rest from their labours.[135]

Fortunately for historians, at least one tea garden—Monai in
Sibsagar, Assam—was owned by two radical Brahmos: Durgamohan
Das and Anandamohan Bose. Although we have no details about the
condition of coolies there, an 1890 report in *Sanjibani* suggests that
the *Tattvakaumudi* correspondent may have been speaking for the
majority of Brahmos. The report congratulated this Brahmo plantation for discovering the perfect solution to the labour problems plagu-
ing other tea gardens: religion. Maghotsava, the annual festival of the
Brahmos in January, had just been celebrated at the plantation and
after sermons had been delivered to the coolies, they were given
hearty meals of '*dadhi* (curd milk) and *cheera* (beaten rice)'. It would
be a 'happy day ... when the managers of all the tea-gardens will
endeavour in this way to ameliorate the *moral condition* of the poor
unlettered coolies'. If the Monai model had been universally followed,
then, claimed *Sanjibani*, 'the country would have by this time heard
the last about coolie oppression'.[136] This almost exclusive stress on
the religious and moral reformation of those who, from a secular perspective, might seem to be the victims of colonial exploitation, was a

fairly typical Brahmo 'humanitarian' response and by no means limited to the travails of plantation coolies.[137]

Politicians and journalists did, of course, criticize the planters but with little effect and not always with much zeal. The Indian Association continued to memorialize the government regularly but not necessarily with any of the fervour or indignation of its Assistant Secretary's reports.[138] Surendranath Banerjea even observed in 1888 that the Indian Association's coolie campaign was not directed against planters, who had 'converted the howling jungles of Assam into a smiling garden', but simply against an unjust law. The amendment of the latter would not only benefit the coolies, but also the planters because a contented workforce would be far more productive.[139] Even this mild stance was unacceptable for the Indian National Congress. At the 1886 Congress in Calcutta—only the second in its history— Banerjea wanted to ask a question on labour emigration to Assam but the President Dadabhai Naoroji pronounced it to be too regional for consideration by the 'present National Assemblage'.[140] Dwarakanath Ganguli correctly pointed out that the President was mistaken: Assam coolies were not regionally recruited but from places as distant from Assam as the Punjab, Bombay, and Madras; their problems, therefore, were a national question. That did not, however, persuade Naoroji to reconsider his decision.

The coolie question was first formally debated at the Bengal Provincial Conference in 1888, which was organized by the Indian Association and its many branch associations and independent from the Congress.[141] At that meeting, Bipinchandra Pal called for the investigation of tea gardens by a commission that had at least some independent (that is, non-government) members 'with a view to early legislation for the redress of such grievances as may be proved'.[142] Recalling his encounter in childhood with a coolie who had been thrown out of his plantation because he was too ill to work, Pal remarked: 'Hard-worked, ill-paid, poorly fed, untended and uncared for in sickness and in sorrow, the sparks of whatever of manhood might be in them, stamped out by inhuman oppression, deprived of the enjoyments of this world, and the consolations of the next, the coolie leads the life of a veritable beast of burden in the tea-plantations of Assam.'[143]

Dwarakanath Ganguli then spoke, seconding Pal's resolution and reminding the delegates of the appalling illustrations of cruelty and oppression that he had gathered during his own travels in Assam, and of the routine use of fraud in obtaining the consent of coolies. His speech was especially interesting in its use of government reports and Anglo-Indian newspapers to support his own arguments about the 'pernicious' system of coolie recruitment and the 'barbarous' practices the coolies were subjected to.[144] Other speakers with personal knowledge of the recruitment process also contributed horrifying details.[145] The Chairman of the conference, the eminent physician Mahendralal Sircar, declared that 'this coolie business' was 'an East Indian edition of the West Indian slave trade' and if the conference did not pass a resolution calling for an independent investigation and legislative redressal, then he would conclude that 'Bengal has no heart'.[146] Nevertheless, Sircar could not sacrifice his characteristically 'moderate' faith in the British. The West Indian slave trade, he asserted, had been 'abolished by Christian England at an enormous sacrifice, and you need not feel doubtful as to the result of your petition, when you remember that you are under the same ruling power here'. The British Government of India, he added for good measure, was 'in reality the most civilised, the most enlightened, the most generous and therefore, the most liberal in the world' and would undoubtedly end this glaring injustice.[147]

The Raj, however, did not justify Sircar's faith in its Christian magnanimity. The year after the resolution and Sircar's appeal, the Government of India claimed that the 1882 Inland Emigration Act was working satisfactorily. Infuriated by this announcement, Dwarakanath Ganguli and the other proprietors of *Sanjibani* published a long, detailed pamphlet showing with figures that 'the state of things in a large number of gardens is such as to lead to a mortality which culminates in a larger ratio than *one man in every four*, and, *at its lowest, amounts literally to a decimation*'.[148] The pamphlet was treated with no greater respect than the many memorials that had preceded it. In 1891, the government described the agitation Ganguli had spearheaded as the work of 'perambulating philanthropic Babus' and 'a mere handful of obscure and disreputable men representing nobody but themselves'.[149] The Assamese elite were not too happy with the Calcutta critics either, and in one of the few discussions of the issue, Bolinarayan Bora sneered at 'our newspaper writing friend of the coolie, the Bengali babu'.[150] From the Assamese middle-class perspective, the tea industry seemed to offer the best available route to economic and social 'progress' for the region and they preferred to look away from the oppression of coolies.[151] An occasional Assamese

Brahmo like Lakshminath Bezbaruah did assail the planters but on the whole, the tea-coolie issue excited Calcuttans much more than the Assamese middle classes.[152]

The Bengali babus, however, were not easy to silence. In 1888, Ramkumar Vidyaratna published *Kulikahini* (Coolie-Story), a fictionalized account of the torments suffered by plantation coolies in Assam.[153] It was dedicated to Dwarakanath Ganguli, whose labours in Assam were gratefully mentioned in the dedicatory epistle, and the book became known as Bengal's *Uncle Tom's Cabin*.[154] Even Christian missionaries entered the debate. In *Tea Garden Coolies in Assam* (1894), the missionary Charles Dowding repeated many of Dwarakanath's criticisms, without, however, referring to him or his newspaper reports.[155] 'If you cannot open out Assam without this frightful waste of life,' Dowding wrote to the Secretary of State for India, 'you had better leave it unopened.... A coolie is not a pawn but a living man with wife and children depending on him. He is not to be classed with livestock.'[156]

Finally in 1896, even the Indian National Congress got around to discussing the coolie issue. On the last day, in a crowd of resolutions waiting to be passed, there was a call for the repeal of the 1882 Inland Emigration Act and its 1893 amendment, sandwiched between a resolution asking for Universities to be given 'teaching functions' and another demanding the inclusion of a non-civil service member in the Governors' Councils. One delegate expressed 'surprise that the British, who had abolished slavery, allowed this disgraceful Act on the Statute Book' but there does not seem to have been any extended discussion.[157]

It was only in 1899, a year after Dwarakanath Ganguli had passed away, that the Chief Commissioner of Assam, Henry Cotton (1845–1915), launched an investigation that showed how poorly the workers were paid.[158] In 1901, a new law was introduced, restricting the arkatti system and providing for the licensing of recruiters.[159] Nothing more radical was attempted and historians agree that the changes failed to effect any significant improvements.[160] At the time, too, it was seen to be inadequate: Sivanath Sastri felt that despite the new legislation, nothing had changed. But, he remarked, now that Dwarakanath Ganguli was gone, there was 'nobody left to weep for the coolies'.[161] Later, Cotton was often given the credit for ending the indenture system, even by Dwarakanath Ganguli's son Prabhatchandra.[162] In fact, Cotton's record was more ambiguous. When appointed Chief

Commissioner of Assam in 1896, he had been convinced that the tea industry was vital for Assam and helped the planters in every way, including in 'the recovery of their coolies who were alleged to have absconded', and not hesitating at 'straining the law for this purpose'.[163] It was, in fact, the much-reviled Lord Curzon who refused to accept Cotton's pro-planter stance and compelled him to look into specific cases.

As he delved more deeply into them, Cotton came to appreciate that European magistrates did tend to acquit—or simply fine— planters who had abused or killed coolies.[164] Curzon now inducted him into his Council as an expert on Assam and during debates on a new Assam Labour and Emigration Bill, Cotton, surrounded by bureaucrats sympathetic to the tea industry, felt obligated to represent the interest of the coolies. The fraud, abduction, and brutality resorted to in the recruitment of coolies, he observed, constituted 'a tale of crime and outrage which would arouse a storm of public indignation in any civilised country'.[165] The fiercest indignation Cotton's remarks aroused, however, was among the planters and their supporters in the Anglo-Indian press, who charged him with 'malignity, inveracity, and dishonesty' and called for his dismissal. Curzon lost his nerve and declared that he was 'reluctant to believe' Cotton's findings.[166] Cotton resigned and rather like Lord Ripon, left India reviled by his fellow-Europeans but lionized by Indians.[167]

In 1904, he was offered the Presidency of the Twentieth Session of the Indian National Congress in Bombay and received a red-carpet welcome.[168] Ironically, the issue of indentured labour was not raised at all at the Congress over which he presided and there was no change in legislation until 1915, despite a Labour Commission report advocating the termination of the indenture system in 1906.[169] It was only in 1915 that new legislation expressly forbade recruitment by arkattis and entrusted the plantation sardars with the responsibility of recruiting coolies. It was still possible, however, to lure labourers into signing a fresh contract under a different act after their original contract had expired—and any breach in that contract could be punished by imprisonment. This final loophole was closed only in 1920, more than two decades after the death of Dwarakanath Ganguli. It is unlikely, however, that he would have been satisfied by it and he would probably have agreed with Sumit Sarkar's assertion that the labour 'catchment areas' remained identical and the recruitment methods of so-called 'free labour' were not radically different.[170]

He would also have noted that whatever might be the legislative picture, ground-level reality in the tea plantations continued to be unacceptable. In 1919, N.C. Bardaloi, an Assamese lawyer, politician, and owner of a small tea plantation reported, for instance, that 'a manager may assault a labourer, insult him, and take girl after girl from the lines as his mistress, yet there will be none to dispute his action or authority'. It was only the greater fire-power of the planters and their government allies that, said Bardaloi, prevented the coolies from rioting. In 1921, a European planter, in order to get a coolie woman to be his mistress, shot her father but was acquitted by a European-majority jury. The only real difference from the old days was that there was a strike in the tea estate in protest.[171]

What exactly, then, did Dwarakanath's campaign for the coolies achieve? At the time of his birth centenary, one admirer described him as the leader of India's very first labour movement.[172] This, of course, was far from true. Although Dwarakanath fought with sincerity and courage *for* labourers, he saw himself as an investigator exposing misdeeds rather than as the leader of a movement *of* labourers. Where women's issues were concerned, Dwarakanath frequently expressed his opposition to male reformers who thought that the extent and degree of women's emancipation should be regulated by men. The liberation of coolies, however, was quite another matter. It was up to middle-class reformers like him to represent their cause and rescue them from oppression. There was no question of organizing labourers' movements or calling for short-term strikes.[173] Here, we not only perceive the political limits of middle-class reformism but the fundamental contradictions of a nationalist ideology that expected the colonial masters to correct their misdeeds as soon as they had been brought to their attention through petitions and newspaper reports.

Although Dwarakanath was not as naive as those Brahmos who imagined that the moral reformation of the coolies was more important than disciplining the planters, even he could not break out of the iron cage of constitutionalist agitation. Indian nationalists would gradually come to appreciate the need for more radical forms of protest—most markedly in Bengal during the swadeshi movement and then after the First World War—but for Dwarakanath, who died in 1898, moderate nationalism and its mendicant procedures were the only options available and he never even tried to move beyond them despite their obvious impotence.[174] In the end, his fire-breathing reports and his Bengali middle-class readers' outraged reactions were simply words, and words alone could not hurt the planters or the Raj. Henry Cotton's realization of the iniquities of the planters was induced not by nationalist protests but by his own investigations, which were triggered by the demands of an imperious but ultimately craven Viceroy.

While analysing the failures of the reformers and nationalists, however, we must not overlook the sheer clout of their adversaries. Neither the good-hearted imperialists like Cotton nor nationalists appreciated that the exploitation of coolies could not simply be addressed as an instance of man's inhumanity to man. It was, in essence, an instance of the exploitation of labour by capital, worsened unimaginably by racial arrogance and political acquiescence. Dwarakanath did perceive many of the links between capital and empire that enabled the perpetuation of the abuses but they were not his primary concerns. There was a very obvious reason for this blindness—his 'moderate' faith in the fundamental fairness of British rule. He charged the planters with inhumanity but said little about the vast, impersonal forces that created and perpetuated the planting enterprise and many others of its type—imperialism and capitalism. Like so many humane but politically superficial campaigns of our time, Dwarakanath's campaign was easily contained by the combined forces of Empire and Capital and very little changed for the coolies whose cause he had taken up with such sincere determination.

Feminizing Nationalism?

Despite the presence of such an outstanding supporter of women's emancipation in its higher echelons, the Indian Association remained a predominantly male organization and we have no evidence that Dwarakanath ever tried to change this. Indeed, Indian nationalism, as a whole, attracted few women until the early twentieth century; in Bengal, it was only during the swadeshi movement that women began to engage in open political activity and even then in very small numbers.[175] Nevertheless, the names of Dwarakanath and Kadambini were associated with what little representation that women did have in the early days of the Indian National Congress.

In 1889, when the Indian National Congress met for its annual session in Bombay, its founding father Allan Octavian Hume wanted women to attend it as official delegates.[176] Ten finally did, including three from Bengal: Kadambini Ganguli, the now-untraceable Mrs G.N. Das, and Swarnakumari Devi (1855–1932), sister of Rabindranath Tagore, novelist, and founder of the Sakhi Samity, an organization for sheltering and giving vocational education to female destitutes. There were two European women, both doctors, and the rest were from the Bombay Presidency. Among the latter was Pandita Ramabai.[177] The inclusion of women delegates was all that the Congress was prepared to accept at this point and they were asked to 'be seen and not heard'.[178]

Dwarakanath Ganguli put up with this but when, in the course of a debate on the reform of the Legislative Councils, it was proposed to give the vote to 'all males above twenty-one years of age', he tabled an amendment calling for the replacement of the word 'males' with 'persons'. India, he remarked, was 'somewhat in advance of the English people' in opening universities to women and it would be ironic if a Congress session including women delegates were not to call for women to be given voting rights. 'Would it not be inconsistent', he asked, 'if they did not allow Pandita Ramabai to be a voter?'[179] Congressmen, however, remained implacable and the amendment was rejected. The proposal was also ridiculed in some newspapers. 'The Congress will make itself the laughing stock of all if it goes to such lengths as this,' wrote *Pratikar*, a weekly newspaper of Bengal. 'It is considered the height of impudence in Indian women to be even present at public meetings. And it must be too much to demand for them rights which have not yet been granted to their more advanced sisters in England and America.'[180]

Nationalist women, predictably, were disappointed by the Congress's half-hearted attempt to include them. As Allan Octavian Hume wrote, the 'dear ladies' invited to the Bombay session of the Congress had 'resented' the commandment to be silent and when approached for the next Congress in Calcutta, asked the organizers to put 'some pretty wax figures, nicely dressed, on the platform'.[181] Finally, four did agree to be delegates but only after Pherozeshah Mehta (the President of the session), Manamohan Ghosh (the Chairman of the Reception Committee), and the jurist Sir Romesh Mitter had ensured that 'a woman was not only allowed to speak, but was selected for the honourable post of proposing the vote of thanks to the President'.[182] That woman was Kadambini Ganguli. She had, in fact, wanted to speak on a resolution regarding the Salt Tax but was

EMPIRE, NATION, WOMEN 171

'suppressed by some busybody' and persuaded to accept the innocuous task of thanking the President.[183]

The magazine *Bharati* (edited by Swarnakumari Devi) reported that Kadambini's 'sweet' and concise speech—prefaced with the apology that 'a woman's voice was not strong enough to make itself audible in this enormous hall'—was cheered loudly by the audience.[184] Mehta declared it to be a historic event, Hume considered it to be among the greatest achievements of the Congress, and, Annie Besant declared that the speech symbolized how 'India's freedom would uplift India's Womanhood'.[185] Such jubilation, however, was premature. At the next annual session of the Congress, held in Nagpur, Hume expected at least six women delegates but there was only one, an Anglo-Indian or, in the terminology of that period, Eurasian. For the next quarter century, no Congress session had more than a couple of women delegates. It was only after 1915 that the numbers rose.[186]

Meredith Borthwick argues that Kadambini and Swarnakumari found a place in the Congress sessions as 'token representatives rather than full political participants'. They were invited more because of their husbands' prominence than as genuine representatives of India's women.[187] Borthwick is correct in a narrow sense—Dwarakanath Ganguli as well as Swarnakumari Debi's husband Janakinath Ghosal (1840–1913) were prominent Congressmen, not to mention Kadambini's cousin Manamohan Ghosh—but uncharacteristically blind to the historical context.[188] The Indian Association, the greatest nationalist organization before the coming of the Congress, had been virtually oblivious to women's existence and concerned with matters of little direct relevance to women's lives or problems. Given this historical lineage and the fact that women did not have much political representation in Britain, the model nation for this generation of nationalists, the fact that the Indian National Congress invited *any* women delegates at all was a significant advance.

Dwarakanath Ganguli's proposal that the Congress should ask for women to be given the vote was even more remarkable and it is hardly surprising that it was not endorsed by his *bien-pensant* contemporaries. The baby steps the Congress took towards greater gender equality are unlikely to impress us today but even if they had been taken simply to please some influential men, they were still noteworthy in the dispiriting history of the inclusion of women in Indian civil society. The author of *Suruchir Kutir* undoubtedly wanted much more than Congress was willing to grant and the rejection of his amendment must have caused his well-known temper to flare. However, he was also a pragmatic reformer, generally welcoming even the smallest change in the right direction while refusing to be content with it, and he is unlikely to have dismissed the admission of women delegates as an insignificant cosmetic act.

A Second Mutiny?

Dwarakanath Ganguli criticized the Raj when necessary but he was perfectly prepared to cooperate with it when government initiatives were in line with his own mission of reforming Hindu society and in particular, the position of Hindu women. Unlike many of his nationalist colleagues, such as Surendrananth Banerjea, Dwarakanath refused to tone down his support for progressive measures even if they infuriated the majority of Hindus. Such a situation arose with the Age of Consent Bill of 1890–1, which proposed to raise the age of consent for girls from ten (as set by the Indian Penal Code of 1860) to twelve.[189] The legislation would end the Hindu upper caste practice of marrying a girl off long before she was twelve.

Hindus across the country were appalled by the Bill and rose in protest. Hindu religious law, it was held, decreed that a girl must have intercourse immediately after her first menstruation. Without this ritual consummation, known as *garbhadhan*, any child born to the woman would be tainted. When sati had been banned in the 1820s or the remarriage of widows permitted in the 1850s, there had been controversies, to be sure, but confined to relatively elite levels. The Hindu masses had then been disorganized and the media too undeveloped to incite any large-scale protests.[190] By the 1890s, however, the rise of nationalism, the revival of mainstream Hinduism, and the proliferation of newspapers all combined to make this legislation one of the most hotly contested in the history of British India. It was not simply conservatives who were affronted by the bill. Many liberals, as we shall see, opposed it too, not least because it seemed to violate Queen Victoria's promise in 1858 that the British would never interfere with the religious beliefs of their Indian subjects.[191]

The history of the age of consent legislation went back to the campaign against child marriage conducted from the 1880s by the Parsi reformer Behramji Malabari (1853–1912).[192] After failing to convince the Government of India to legislate against child marriage, Malabari moved to London and worked with Mary Carpenter's National Indian Association to raise British awareness of the issue.[193] A committee was set up that included former viceroys, current governors of Indian provinces, British aristocrats, and intellectuals such as Herbert Spencer and Max Müller, and it demanded legislation to fix the minimum age of marriage for a girl at twelve.[194] As a result of this metropolitan pressure and the 1889 case of the child-bride Phulmani dying after her husband Hari Maiti forced her to have intercourse, the Government of India produced a bill to raise the age of consent for girls from ten to twelve.[195] Intercourse with girls younger than twelve, it stipulated, would be punishable by imprisonment for ten years or transportation for life.[196] As Himani Bannerji has pointed out, the legislation merely stipulated a minimum age for experiencing sexual penetration and none of the debates over the measure highlighted the need for women's willing consent to sexual intercourse.[197] Even the ordinary Hindu women the bill was purporting to aid were scarcely to be heard in the controversy that ensued: the debate was conducted almost entirely by males.

The protests were particularly intense in Bengal.[198] The campaign was 'organized on a scale that had not previously been attained' and the rally held in the Calcutta Maidan on 25 February 1891 was the 'largest that had ever been held to protest against any measure of the government'.[199] *Bangabasi*, a conservative Hindu newspaper with a huge circulation, played a leading role in organizing and disseminating objections to the bill. 'Assuming that Phulmani died from the effects of her husband's inconsiderate act, does it follow that a social custom should be abolished because it has produced a bad result in one case?' it thundered.[200] In September 1890, it dismissed the Indian supporters of the proposal as 'a few dozens of ill-educated pseudo-patriots' and warned: 'A slighter cause than this kindled the fire of the Sepoy Mutiny in 1857, and though thirty-three years have elapsed since that event, and the Indians have become still more emasculated during that period, yet it should be remembered that even the most contemptible worm will sting the man that treads upon it.'[201]

It was not just conservative Hindus who opposed the legislation. *Sulabh Samachar*, which had begun as a Brahmo paper and was still run by a member of Keshab Sen's family, urged the government not to ride rough-shod over the objections of the Hindus in order to please 'a handful of Brahmos, Christians, and others whom the Bill will in no way affect'.[202] Muslims also protested, though they were necessarily overshadowed in Calcutta by the Hindu majority.[203] The great reformer Iswarchandra Vidyasagar pointed out that many girls reached puberty after twelve and the proposed legislation would offer 'an invitation and encouragement to husbands to consummate marriage' regardless of their wives' biological maturity. The simplest way out of the dilemma without offending religious sensibilities, Vidyasagar pointed out with impeccable logic, was to make it an offence to consummate marriage before the beginning of menstruation.[204] Barrister Manamohan Ghosh, a doughty supporter of women's education, observed that the Government had merely legislated on intercourse instead of prohibiting the 'custom which strikes at the very root of the well-being of the people'—child marriage. One would still be able to give one's children in marriage at a tender age, as long as the couple refrained from having intercourse.[205]

Most of the 'native' supporters of the bill in Bengal were Sadharan Brahmos.[206] *Sanjibani*, the voice of radical Brahmos, was the only consistent defender of the legislation and Kadambini Ganguli was the first among 150 women who signed a petition to the government calling for an end to child-marriage. (This was probably the only occasion when significant numbers of women entered the controversy.) Brahmos were attacked—even physically assaulted—for their support of the bill but they did not really pose much of a threat to the forces of orthodoxy.[207] While *Sanjibani* had a circulation of a mere 4,000, *Bangabasi* (which was prosecuted in 1891 for sedition on account of some of its inflammatory writings against the Bill) was read by five times that number.[208] The nationalist weekly *Amrita Bazar Patrika* became so popular on account of its opposition to the consent bill that it was relaunched as a daily from February 1891 onwards.[209] The issue was particularly difficult for nationalists— opposing the bill would mark them out as social reactionaries while supporting it wholeheartedly would decimate their support among Hindus. Understandably, therefore, the Indian National Congress refused to comment and even Surendranath Banerjea, writing on behalf of the Indian Association, did not extend wholehearted support to the government.[210]

The Association's Assistant Secretary, Dwarakanath Ganguli, however, was not the man to equivocate and sent in a personal letter of support to the government.[211] Although he felt that the bill, in its present form, was not strong enough to 'grapple with all the evils which premature sexual intercourse with physically immature girls involve', he supported it, characteristically, as 'a partial measure of reform in the most necessary direction'.[212] The argument that the government should not interfere in religious matters, even if true, was outweighed by the government's duty to protect all its subjects from harm, especially children and the defenceless. 'It would be recognizing a most dangerous principle if Government were to allow one class of its subjects to tyrannise over another, the oppressor claiming religious custom as his right for doing so.' It was not a question of abstract rights alone, but also of the biology of human development. He reminded the government that during the campaign for Act III of 1872, most doctors had testified that girls younger than fourteen were not physiologically ready for intercourse.[213]

The Hindu religious law, he pointed out, was too full of contradictory prescriptions to be taken seriously on the right age of marriage and sexual intercourse. While some interpreters averred that intercourse was mandatory at the first menstrual period, no less an authority than Manu, the ancient lawgiver, had allowed parents to keep their daughters unmarried up to three years beyond puberty. Even in the present day, it was common for kulin Brahmin girls to remain unmarried long after puberty because the families of many brides could not afford to satisfy the economic demands of the groom's family. Moreover, since girls younger than sixteen were not legally permitted to change their religion or to dispose of their property, it was surely 'preposterous' that they were taken to be fit for marriage and procreation at a substantially lower age.[214]

Despite the intensity of the opposition, the government was sufficiently confident to put the law on the statute book in March 1891. The Viceroy grandly declared that 'in all cases where demands preferred in the name of religion would lead to practices inconsistent with individual safety and the public peace, and condemned by every system of law and morality in the world, it is religion and not morality which must give way'.[215] The opponents of the bill, predictably, were incandescent. 'We have now learnt,' said the Navayuga, a Calcutta weekly, 'that the British flag has been posted not only upon the soil of Hindustan, but also upon the Sastras of the Hindus, upon the customs of the country, upon their life, religion, joys and hopes.'[216] A correspondent in Bangabasi even called for a boycott of British-made products including salt and sugar, a tactic that would re-emerge during the early-twentieth-century swadeshi movement and which, then, would be proposed by Krishnakumar Mitra, the long-serving editor of *Sanjibani*, the paper that was the most consistent opponent of *Bangabasi*'s orthodox position.[217] The Act, in any case, remained a dead letter since it was almost impossible to enforce, especially after an executive order that removed the provision of prosecutions for 'marital rape'.[218] But the intensity of 'native' opposition to it ensured that the government did not attempt any major social reform legislation for nearly four decades.[219]

The End of an Era

Although he played a prominent role in the controversy around the Age of Consent Bill, Dwarakanath was already seriously ill with a liver disease that cannot be precisely identified. A major operation at the onset of his disease is said to have saved his life but he remained weak and was periodically incapacitated.[220] Despite the pressures of her own professional life, Kadambini cared for him with a devotion that surprised a British doctor who had been called in for a consultation.[221] Dwarakanath, of course, was not the man to lie quietly in his sickbed. Apart from the consent bill, there were other matters demanding his attention and in one of the last public engagements of his life, he led a Brahmo-organized movement to popularize the plague vaccine.

Bubonic plague first broke out in Calcutta in April 1898 and the high mortality frightened many people, especially labourers, into leaving the city. The government took strong, invasive measures. Patients were removed to hospitals and their contacts segregated in special camps; affected houses were disinfected and all clothes and bedding destroyed. It was hard, however, to persuade people to accept the recently introduced plague vaccine. Even the enlightened objected to it because it was very painful and caused fever and malaise and at the popular level, rumours were rife about its toxicity.[222] Many believed that the vaccine was a lethal poison, made from the blood of the sacred cow and was being used on the Queen's order to thin out the Indian population. People panicked and individuals suspected of being plague inoculators—almost anybody wearing European clothes could be suspected of being an inoculator—were beaten up.[223] Few believed what the government was saying about the disease and even a responsible newspaper like *The Bengalee* doubted that there was genuine plague in Calcutta. The condition being identified as bubonic plague, it pointed out, was not as infectious or as lethal as the plague that had recently affected Bombay.[224] The Sadharan Brahmo Samaj formed a Plague Suppression Committee to persuade the people to rise above such fears and paranoia. Dwarakanath and Kadambini Ganguli were the prime movers and they organized a mass inoculation of more than sixty Brahmos (including children) a day after the official announcement of the epidemic. Soon, other notables of the city, Hindus as well as Muslims, also volunteered to get vaccinated.[225]

Shortly after this, Dwarakanath's liver disease took a turn for the worse and he died on 27 June 1898, virtually, as the *Dacca Gazette* remarked, 'in harness'.[226] The Executive Committee of the Sadharan Brahmo Samaj, recording its 'profound sorrow', described him as 'ever a friend of the suffering and the oppressed; whose zeal as a reformer was a source of great strength to the progressive movements of this country'.[227] Recalling his involvement with the Indian Association since its inception, *The Bengalee* saluted Dwarakanath's 'zeal and devotion', which had 'largely contributed' to the Association's success. But it was not just the Indian Association that owed him a debt of gratitude. 'He was the very soul of honesty, and was uncompromising in his opposition to all that savoured of wrong and injustice'—the death of 'such a man is not only a loss to the circle of his immediate friends but to the wider community which he sought to benefit by his public-spirited labours,' the paper declared.[228] *Amrita Bazar Patrika*'s long obituary, while noting that even his friends did not always agree with him and that he could be downright offensive in his attempts to change their views, acknowledged that the entire nation had been galvanized by his social and political radicalism.[229]

Even those at the receiving end of his attacks ended up respecting the man's integrity and courage. 'Few of us had not been stung by Ganguli's words or actions, but I have never met anybody who did not respect this man from the depth of his heart,' Sivanath Sastri remarked.[230] Many years later, Dwarkanath's son Prabhatchandra described his father as 'no visionary idealist but really a practical worker'.[231] This laconic, understated tribute truly captured the essence of the man. Dwarakanath did, of course, have a clear vision of a just society as we saw in our discussion of his novel *Suruchir Kutir*. But he was not a theorist, nor a demagogue. Well aware of the formidable power of the traditions he had resolved to oppose, he worked indefatigably and with incomparable determination, often for gains that could seem minute to twenty-first century eyes. At the time, however, these were far from insignificant and if they seem less impressive today, that itself is a reflection of the changes in Indian society that Dwarakanath and the radical Brahmos, among others, worked to bring about.

As an individual of courage, integrity, and vision, Dwarakanath Ganguli had few equals but he also had his limitations. Although he did an enormous amount of practical, ground-level work in all his areas of interest, he preferred to act alone—albeit often with the aid of close associates like Brahmamoyee and Durgamohan Das—to change the social and cultural convictions of the masses, instead of trying to create a movement of like-minded people. In nationalist circles, he stood out for his fearless criticism of the Raj as well as for his attempts to highlight the problems of the rural poor, but he never led a team that shared his goals and which could perpetuate his legacy. Perhaps this was impossible for a man who was primarily a reformer. As Bipinchandra Pal once pointed out, reformers were concerned more with ending 'the darkness, the ugliness, the evil and the ignorance' they saw around them than with loving the nation, warts and all, right or wrong. The reforming drive being necessarily critical, it never attracted as many followers as an uncritical, emotionally coloured patriotism.[232] Pal's either/or formula is far too schematic but if we imagine the reformist and nationalist orientations as co-existing in different proportions in every individual, then Dwarakanath, we could argue, was a nationalist *and* a reformer, but rather more of the latter than the former.

Small wonder, then, that today, most people remember Dwarakanath solely as the husband of Bengal's first woman doctor. Of course, his steadfast support for his wife Kadambini's professional and public work was exemplary in its time and perhaps not entirely unremarkable even in the twenty-first century. And Kadambini Ganguli, needless to say, was not just the wife of Dwarakanath but a living, breathing manifestation of his life's work. She lived on for years after her husband's death but did not remarry and tried as best as she could, in spite of her busy professional life and domestic obligations, to participate in some of the progressive causes Dwarakanath had favoured.[233] She became the president of the Indian branch of the Transvaal Indian Association—a body established by Henry Pollack, an associate of Gandhi—and raised funds for it. In 1922, she and the poet Kamini Roy travelled through the coal mining

EMPIRE, NATION, WOMEN 179

areas of Bihar to investigate the working conditions of female and child labourers.[234] Suffering from hypertension towards the end of her life, she reduced some of her medical workload but did not entirely retire. Even on the day of her death, she is reported to have performed a major surgical operation and the fifty rupees she had received as her fee was used to pay for her funeral.[235] For us, however, one of her other late-life medical engagements might be of greater interest. Two years before her death, on 2 May 1921, in a house on Calcutta's Garpar Road, she supervised the birth of Suprabha and Sukumar Ray's only child, a son who was first called Prasad but later renamed Satyajit.[236] Herself the product of one great cycle of Bengali engagements with modernity, she was surely the most appropriate obstetrician for the birth of the man who would be a towering exemplar of another.

Notes

1. For comprehensive overviews, see John Breuilly, ed., *Oxford Handbook of the History of Nationalism* (Oxford: Oxford University Press, 2013).

2. See Eric Hobsbawm, *Nations and Nationalism since 1780: Programme, Myth, Reality*, 2nd edn (Cambridge: Cambridge University Press, 1992); Anthony D. Smith, *Nationalism and Modernism: A Critical Survey of Recent Theories of Nations and Nationalism* (London: Routledge, 1998); and Peter Burke, 'Nationalisms and Vernaculars, 1500–1800', in *Oxford Handbook of the History of Nationalism*, edited by Breuilly, 21–35. On the growth of nationalisms in Europe, see Eric Hobsbawm, *The Age of Empire, 1875–1914* (London: Abacus, 1987), 142–64.

3. Early nationalists in Europe, too, sought 'various kinds of autonomy' rather than sovereign states of their own. See Hobsbawm, *Nations and Nationalism*, 37.

4. See Partha Chatterjee, *Nationalist Thought and the Colonial World: A Derivative Discourse* (Minneapolis: University of Minnesota Press, 1993). Benedict Anderson, in a celebrated analysis, has even argued that European ideas of nationalism served as ready-made, plug-and-play modules across the non-Western world. See his *Imagined Communities: Reflections on the Origin and Spread of Nationalism*, revised edn (London: Verso, 2006).

5. On this point, see, especially, Joya Chatterji, 'Nationalisms in India, 1857–1947', in *Oxford Handbook of the History of Nationalism*, 242–62.

6. See Anil Seal, *The Emergence of Indian Nationalism: Competition and Collaboration in the Later Nineteenth Century* (Cambridge: Cambridge University Press, 1968), 15.

7.   See Sanjay Seth, 'Rewriting Histories of Nationalism: The Politics of "Moderate Nationalism" in India, 1870–1905', *American Historical Review*, 104, no. 1 (February 1999): 95–116; Daniel Argov, *Moderates and Extremists in the Indian Nationalist Movement, 1883–1920* (London: Asia Publishing House, 1967); and Bipinchandra Pal, *Swadeshi and Swaraj: The Rise of New Patriotism* (Calcutta: Yugayatri, 1954), 134.

8.   On the provisions of the Act and its impact, see Jogesh Chandra Bagal, *History of the Indian Association, 1876–1951* (Calcutta: Indian Association, 1953), 33–9; and Sukumar Mitra, 'The Newspaper Press', in *Studies in the Bengal Renaissance*, edited by Atulchandra Gupta (Calcutta: National Council of Education-Bengal, 1958), 423–38, at 432. On the Indian Association's response, see Prabhatchandra Gangopadhyay, *Bharater Rastriya Itihaser Khasra*, 2nd edn (Calcutta: Jignasa, 1965), 89–93.

9.   See *Hansard's Parliamentary Debates*, 3rd ser., 142 (23 July–16 August 1878): 48–66, at 54.

10.   *Hansard's*, 3rd ser., 142 (23 July–16 August 1878): 64–6, 123–33; and C.E. Buckland, *Bengal under the Lieutenant-Governors*, 2 vols (Calcutta: S.K. Lahiri, 1901), 2: 719–20.

11.   Wilfrid Scawen Blunt, *Ideas about India* (London: Kegan Paul, Trench, 1885), 40.

12.   On the shift from 'moderate' to more radical approaches, see Sumit Sarkar, *Modern India 1885–1947* (Houndmills, UK: Macmillan, 1989), 97–100.

13.   On the pre-Congress associations, see Seal, *Emergence of Indian Nationalism*, 194–244; S.R. Mehrotra, *The Emergence of the Indian National Congress* (Delhi: Vikas, 1971), 146–229; and Leonard Gordon, *Bengal: The Nationalist Movement, 1876–1940* (New York: Columbia University Press, 1973), 15–37.

14.   Sumit Sarkar, 'The "Women's Question" in Nineteenth-Century Bengal', in *Women and Culture*, edited by Kumkum Sangari and Sudesh Vaid (Bombay: SNDT Women's University, 1985), 157–72, at 162.

15.   In his famous 1866 lecture 'Jesus Christ: Europe and Asia', Sen had declared: 'It is to the British Government that we owe our deliverance from oppression and misrule, from darkness and distress, from ignorance and superstition'. See *Keshub Chunder Sen's Lectures in India*, 2 vols (London: Cassell, 1901–1904), 1: 20.

16.   Dwijadas Datta, *Behold the Man, or Keshub and the Sadharan Brahmo Somaj: A Confession* (Comilla: Dwijadas Datta, 1930), 222–3, 263–4. It is worth pointing out that even in the days of Debendranath Tagore, the Brahmo movement attracted some who were more interested in national regeneration than in religion. Apart from Akshay Datta, there was the physician Durgacharan Bandyopadhyay (the father of Surendranath Banerjea), a religious sceptic who supported the Brahmo movement for its socially progressive ideology. See Baridbaran Ghosh, ed., *Rajnarayan Basu: Nirbachita Rachana Sangraha* (Calcutta: Dey Book Store, 1995), 34.

17. Bipinchandra Pal, *Memories of My Life and Times* (Calcutta: Bipinchandra Pal Institute, 1973), 256.

18. Sivanath Sastri, *History of the Brahmo Samaj* [1911–12], 2nd edn, 2 vols in 1 (Calcutta: Sadharan Brahmo Samaj, 1974), 361–2; and Sivanath Sastri, *Atmacharit*, edited by Gautam Neogy (Calcutta: Sadharan Brahmo Samaj, 1982), 222.

19. See B. Pal, *Memories of My Life*, 277–8; and Jogananda Das, 'The Brahmo Samaj', in *Studies in the Bengal Renaissance*, 479–508, at 499.

20. Bipinchandra Pal, *Brahmo Samaj and the Battle for Swaraj in India* (Calcutta: Brahmo Mission Press, 1926), 4–7.

21. B. Pal, *Memories of My Life*, 199–200.

22. Sastri, *Atmacharit*, 205–7, 505–12.

23. B. Pal, *Memories of My Life*, 252; and Gaganchandra Home, *Jiban-Smriti* (Calcutta: Privately Published, 1929), 25–6. No other member was ever inducted but none of the initiates ever worked for the government. See Sastri, *Atmacharit*, 507–8; and Bipinchandra Pal, *Sattar Vatsar: Atmajibani* (Calcutta: Kalpan, [1927–8] 2005), 145–6. Home's great friend Upendrakishore Ray, incidentally, was not even a Brahmo at this point and would convert only some six years later in 1884.

24. Bengali attempts to pursue physical fitness were encouraged by the British, until many gymnastic clubs were taken over by militant nationalists. See John Rosselli, 'The Self-Image of Effeteness: Physical Education and Nationalism in Nineteenth-Century Bengal', *Past and Present*, 86 (February 1980): 121–48. Bipinchandra Pal recalled how Nabagopal Mitra, the organizer of the Hindu Mela, had devoted 'not only his time and energy but also practically the whole of his financial resources' to run a full-scale gymnasium for young men, where the standard exercises were supplemented by 'our national exercises of wrestling, *lathi*, dagger and sword-play' (B. Pal, *Memories of My Life*, 213–14).

25. Supporters of the Indian Association hailed 'mainly from the non-zamindar professional intelligentsia' and in the early days of the Association, its stance on agrarian issues was markedly pro-peasant and anti-zamindar. See Sumit Sarkar, *A Critique of Colonial India*, 2nd edn (Calcutta: Papyrus, 2000), 59–60, 63.

26. B. Pal, *Sattar Vatsar*, 129–30; and B. Pal, *Brahmo Samaj*, 4–7. Later, many Brahmos would be attracted to more radical kinds of nationalism. Bipin Pal himself became an 'extremist' and Bhupendranath Datta, brother of Swami Vivekananda and an early member of the underground terrorist movement of the early twentieth century, recalled that most of his peers were either Brahmos or members of its western Indian cognate, the Prarthana Samaj. See Bhupendranath Dutta, *Bharater Dwitiya Swadhinata Sangram* [1926] (Calcutta: Nababharat, 1983), 7; and Sumit Sarkar, *The Swadeshi Movement in Bengal, 1903–1908*, new edn (Delhi: Permanent Black, 2010), 410–11. On the Prarthana Samaj, see Christine Dobbin, *Urban Leadership in Western India:*

Politics and Communities in Bombay City, 1840–1885 (Oxford: Oxford University Press, 1972), 249–54.

27.   See Benjamin Zachariah, *Playing the Nation Game: The Ambiguities of Nationalism in India* (Delhi: Yoda Press, 2011).

28.   John Strachey, *India* (London: Kegan Paul, 1888), 5–8; and on the contemporary importance of this book, see Eric Stokes, *The English Utilitarians and India* (Oxford: Clarendon Press, 1959; reprint, Delhi: Oxford University Press, 1982), 137, 305. In the twentieth century, Winston Churchill would famously proclaim that India was a mere 'geographical term' and 'no more a united nation than the Equator'. See his speech at the Constitutional Club, 26 March 1931, in Winston S. Churchill, *India: Speeches and an Introduction* (London: Thornton Butterworth, 1931), 134–41, at 136.

29.   Amalendu Guha, *Planter-Raj to Swaraj: Freedom Struggle and Electoral Politics in Assam 1826–1947* (Delhi: Indian Council of Historical Research, 1977), 334.

30.   See Partha Chatterjee, *The Nation and Its Fragments: Colonial and Postcolonial Histories* (Princeton: Princeton University Press, 1993), 76–106. Not that all Hindus were necessarily united—the lower middle classes, especially in Bengal, often found the nationalists of Banerjea's type to be elite, deracinated, and motivated by their own narrow interests. On the differences in social character and ideological orientation that separated the Bengali lower and upper middle classes in the nineteenth century, see Sumit Sarkar, *Writing Social History* (Delhi: Oxford University Press, 1998), 190–1, 303–6. The reformers and nationalists of the nineteenth century, therefore, had to fight on two fronts: 'The "manly" Sahib looked down upon the "cowardly" Bengali from above and the clerk of his own race carped at him from below.' See Rajat Kanta Ray, 'Bengal: An Overview, 1800–2000', in *Art of Bengal: Past and Present, 1850–2000* (Calcutta: Centre of International Modern Art, 2000), 13–21, at 16.

31.   B. Pal, *Memories of My Life*, 236.

32.   Anuradha Roy, *Nationalism as Poetic Discourse in Nineteenth-Century Bengal* (Calcutta: Papyrus, 2003), 48–9.

33.   Chatterji, 'Nationalisms in India, 1857–1947', 248; and A. Roy, *Nationalism as Poetic Discourse*, 49–52.

34.   *Vira Nari, or The Heroine of Scinde* (Calcutta: Jogeshchandra Bandyopadhyay, 1875). *Bengal Library Catalogue of Books Registered in the Presidency of Bengal: Appendix to the Calcutta Gazette*, 2nd quarter (1875), 22–3, identifies the copyright owner as 'Dwarkanath Sen Gupta of Musalmanparah'. Dwarakanath Ganguli, however, acknowledged his authorship shortly before his death in a letter, for which see 'Bangla Bhasar Lekhak', *Janmabhumi*, 8, no. 1 (December 1897/Poush 1304), 8, http://archiv.ub.uni-heidelberg.de/savifadok/volltexte/2009/567 (accessed on 21 December 2013).

35.   James Tod (1782–1835) was appointed the East India Company's Political Agent for the western Rajput states in 1818. He was convinced that the Rajputs were racial cousins of the British and, if treated with dignity,

would form 'one of the strongest pillars of our empire'. The *Annals* were published in two volumes in 1829 and 1832. Although not very popular in Europe, they electrified Indian nationalists. See Jason Freitag, *Serving Empire, Serving Nation: James Tod and the Rajputs of Rajasthan* (Leiden: Brill, 2009), especially 33–50, 76, 91, 107, 111, 125–7, and 194–5.

36. Freitag, *Serving Empire, Serving Nation*, 19, 171.

37. Barunkumar Chakrabarty, *Toder Rajasthan o Bangla Sahitya* (Calcutta: Pustak Bipani, 1981), 34; Meenakshi Mukherjee, 'History and Imagined History: Romesh Chunder Dutt's Construction of the Past', in *Elusive Terrain: Culture and Literary Memory*, edited by M. Mukherjee (Delhi: Oxford University Press, 2008), 138–53; M. Mukherjee, 'Tod's Rajasthan and the Bengali Imagination', in *Elusive Terrain*, 154–68.

38. On the negative self-image of Bengalis in this period, see Rosselli, 'Self-Image of Effeteness'; Mrinalini Sinha, *Colonial Masculinity: The 'Manly Englishman' and the 'Effeminate Bengali' in the Late Nineteenth Century* (Manchester: Manchester University Press, 1995); and Indira Chowdhury, *The Frail Hero and Virile History: Gender and the Politics of Culture in Colonial Bengal* (Delhi: Oxford University Press, 1998).

39. M. Mukherjee, 'History and Imagined History', 145–6; and Ramya Sreenivasan, *The Many Lives of a Rajput Queen: Heroic Pasts in India, c. 1500–1900* (Seattle: University of Washington Press, 2007), 181.

40. Sister Nivedita, *Notes of Some Wanderings with the Swami Vivekananda*, edited by Swami Saradananda (Calcutta: Udbodhan, 1913), 161; and Sreenivasan, *Many Lives of a Rajput Queen*, 182.

41. Rangalal Bandyopadhyay's poem 'Padmini Upakhhyan' was published in 1858. See B. Chakrabarty, *Toder Rajasthan o Bangla Sahitya*, 119.

42. Mukherjee, 'Tod's Rajasthan and the Bengali Imagination', 164–5; and Sreenivasan, *Many Lives of a Rajput Queen*, 184–5. Jyotirindranath Tagore's play *Sarojini*, staged in 1875, was among the most famous Bengali celebrations of jauhar. See Hemendra Nath Das Gupta, *The Indian Stage*, 4 vols (Calcutta: M.K. Das Gupta, 1938–44), 2 (1938): 252–3.

43. See M. Mukherjee, 'Tod's Rajasthan and the Bengali Imagination', 158–61.

44. Joya Chatterji, *Bengal Divided: Hindu Communalism and Partition, 1932–1947* (Cambridge: Cambridge University Press, 1994), 160–1; and Freitag, *Serving Empire, Serving Nation*, 171–96.

45. This Act was soon followed by the Vernacular Press Act (1877), another attempt to curb nationalist propaganda. On the history of these acts, see Das Gupta, *The Indian Stage*, 2: 91–101, 243–88; and Pramila Pandhe, ed., *Suppression of Drama in Nineteenth-Century India* (Calcutta: India Book Exchange, 1978), ii.

46. Partha Chatterjee, *The Black Hole of Empire: History of a Global Practice of Power* (Princeton: Princeton University Press, 2012), 231.

47.   See Sreenivasan, *Many Lives of a Rajput Queen*, 172.

48.   B. Pal, *Memories of My Life*, 205; and Bipinchandra Pal, *Nabajuger Bangla* [1921–24] (Calcutta: Yugajatri, 1955), 215–17, 250. Benjamin Zachariah points out that the authors of anti-Muslim plays also 'wrote poetry about the glories of the Mughal court, or of Siraj-ud-Daulah as the legitimate monarch betrayed by his perfidious underlings'. See Zachariah, *Playing the Nation Game*, 130.

49.   Even religious plays were not exempt from their disapproval. See, for instance, *Sanjibani* (29 August 1891), summary in *Report on Native Papers— Bengal*, 5 September 1891, 946. Not all young Brahmos, of course, paid heed to the puritanical precepts of their elders. Bipinchandra Pal recalled that he and many of his friends went to the theatre frequently and many great plays staged in the 1860s and 1870s were 'indirectly doing the very work to which the Brahmo Samaj had consecrated itself' by encouraging patriotism and a broader quest for freedom. See B. Pal, *Sattar Vatsar*, 111, 113; and B. Pal, *Memories of My Life*, 203, 244–5.

50.   See Das Gupta, *The Indian Stage*, 2: 281.

51.   See Sanjay Joshi, *Fractured Modernity: Making of a Middle Class in Colonial North India* (Delhi: Oxford University Press, 2001), 61–2, 68–9.

52.   See Rosselli, 'Self-Image of Effeteness', 125; and Amiya P. Sen, *Hindu Revivalism in Bengal, 1872–1905: Some Essays in Interpretation* (Delhi: Oxford University Press, 1993), 304–5.

53.   See Brajendranath Bandyopadhyay, *Bangiya Natyasalar Itihas, 1795– 1876*, 2nd edn (Calcutta: Bangiya Sahitya Parisat Mandir, 1939), 156–8, 163, 211.

54.   *Nababarshiki 1287 BS* (Calcutta: Ray Press Depository, 1880), 77.

55.   See 'Wahabi Dharma ebang Dharmabir Rafik Mandal o Amiruddin', *Abalabandhab*, 1, no. 2 (Agrahayan 1285/November 1878): 47–51.

56.   *Report of the Second Indian National Congress Held at Calcutta on the 27th, 28th, 29th and 30th December 1886* (Calcutta: no pub., 1887), 96–7.

57.   Punyalata Chakrabarti, *Chhelebelar Dinguli* (1958; reprint, Calcutta: Newscript, 1981), 62–3. One such sahib, according to Dwarakanath's son Prabhatchandra, had subsequently become such an ardent admirer of his father that he had broken down in tears when Dwarakanath died. See Narayan Dutta, *Abalabandhhab-Dwarakanath o Kadambini* (Calcutta: Karuna, 2006), 82.

58.   Dwarakanath Gangopadhyay, ed., *Kabigatha*, 13th edn (Calcutta: Metcalfe Press, 1895), unpaginated preface, emphasis added, http://www.dli. ernet.in/ (accessed on 27 November 2013).

59.   'Jatiya Unnati', *Abalabandhab*, new ser., 1, no. 9 (Ashar 1286/June 1879): 83–8.

60.   *Kabigatha*, unpaginated preface.

61.   *National Song Book: Jatiya Sangeet* (Calcutta: G.P. Roy, 1876). For identification of the editor, see *Bengal Library Catalogue of Books*, 2nd quarter (1876), 10–11.

62. A. Roy, *Nationalism as Poetic Discourse*, 26.

63. See, for instance, Mahimchandra Gupta, ed., *Sangit-Sangraha* (Dhaka: Isanchandra Sil, 1876), 13–14.

64. See Aniruddha Ray, *Adventurers, Landowners and Rebels: Bengal, c.1575–c.1715* (Delhi: Munshiram Manoharlal, 1998), 202.

65. Bipinchandra Pal, *The New Spirit* (Calcutta: Sinha, Sarvadhikari, 1907), 18, 23, 26.

66. Although not a Brahmo, Surendranath worked closely with the radicals of the Brahmo Samaj. See P. Gangopadhyay, *Bharater Rastriya Itihaser Khasra*, 61. Writing late in his life, Banerjea remarked that the Brahmos were to be commended for their reforms but added immediately that he found them too radical. See Surendranath Banerjea, *A Nation in Making: Being the Reminiscences of Fifty Years of Public Life* (London: Oxford University Press, 1927), 397. For the comment on the Sadharan Brahmo Samaj being only 'half-religious', see Datta, *Behold the Man*, 255.

67. Seal, *Emergence of Indian Nationalism*, 15.

68. On the history of the Hindu Mela, see Jogeshchandra Bagal, *Hindu Melar Itibritta* (Calcutta: Maitri, 1968); and B. Ghosh, *Rajnarayan Basu*, 57.

69. In 1868, at a meeting of the Bethune Society, Mitra gave 'an animated speech' arguing that the contact between Britain and India was benefiting Indians and the latter might one day come to match 'their great model'. See *Proceedings and Transactions of the Bethune Society from November 10th 1859 to April 20th 1869* (Calcutta: Bishop's College Press, 1870), cxxii–cxxiii. On another occasion, when asked to display works of indigenous art at the Hindu Mela, Mitra commissioned a huge painting of Indians supplicating before Britannia. See the recollections of Dwijendranath Tagore in Bipinbihari Gupta, *Puratan Prasanga* (Calcutta: Vidya Bharati, 1967), 280–98, at 298.

70. See B. Pal, *Sattar Vatsar*, 170–3; and Abala Bose (née Das)'s recollections in 'Dwarakanath Gangopadhyayer Janmasatabarsiki', *Probasi*, 44, no. 2 (Jaistha 1351/June–July 1944): 92–3, http://archiv.ub.uni-heidelberg.de/savifadok/volltexte/2009/1018 (accessed on 26 September 2014).

71. B. Pal, *Sattar Vatsar*, 121.

72. See Bagal, *History of the Indian Association*, 5–7; and B. Pal, *Nabajuger Bangla*, 276–91.

73. See Bagal, *History of the Indian Association*, 10.

74. The new body soon became influential, while the League collapsed. See P. Gangopadhyay, *Bharater Rastriya Itihaser Khasra*, 78–9.

75. 'Retrospect of 1879', *Brahmo Public Opinion*, 1 January 1880, in *Selections from English Periodicals of 19th Century Bengal, 1878–80: Brahmo Public Opinion*, edited by Benoy Ghose (Calcutta: Papyrus, 1978), 90–123, at 120. Anil Seal (*Emergence of Indian Nationalism*, 216) has argued that that despite its middle-class identity, the Indian Association did not attract 'traders, industrialists and ... landowners of substance'. Although Seal's observation is

correct, few 'native' industrialists existed in nineteenth-century Bengal and most 'landowners of substance' would recoil from an association that was critical of the Raj and, as Seal himself points out (Seal, *Emergence of Indian Nationalism*, 224–6), which was generally regarded as pro-peasant.

76. Greatly influenced by the Italian nationalist Giuseppe Mazzini (1805–1872), Banerjea declared: 'Mazzini had taught Italian unity. We wanted Indian unity.' Mazzini's 'revolutionary teachings', however, he rejected as 'unsuited to the circumstances of India'. See Banerjea, *A Nation in Making*, 41, 43. On Mazzini's influence on Indians, see C.A. Bayly, 'Liberalism at Large: Mazzini and Nineteenth-Century Indian Thought', in *Giuseppe Mazzini and the Globalisation of Democratic Nationalism 1830–1920*, edited by C.A. Bayly and Eugenio F. Biagini (Oxford: Oxford University Press, 2008), 355–74; and Gita Srivastava, *Mazzini and His Impact on the Indian National Movement* (Allahabad: Chugh, 1982), 212, 245, 247.

77. One of the consequences of the enthusiasm for English education in Bengal was the appointment of Bengalis to many government and other posts across the subcontinent during the nineteenth century. Bengali 'colonies' developed in Allahabad, Kanpur, Lucknow, Agra, Aligarh, Mirat, Jabbalpore, and Delhi. See Bruce T. McCully, *English Education and the Origins of Indian Nationalism* (1940; reprint, Gloucester, MA: Peter Smith, 1966), 196–7.

78. See *The Bengalee*, 29 December 1883, 595; and 'The National Conference', *The Bengalee*, 5 January 1884, 4.

79. Wilfrid Scawen Blunt, *India under Ripon: A Private Diary* (London: T. Fisher Unwin, 1909), 114–18; and P. Gangopadhyay, *Bharater Rastriya Itihaser Khasra*, 84. On Blunt, who was often erroneously described as a Member of Parliament in Indian newspapers of the time, see Elizabeth Longford, *A Pilgrimage of Passion: The Life of Wilfrid Scawen Blunt* (London: Weidenfeld and Nicolson, 1979); and for Blunt's own description of his background in the Conservative squirearchy and later as a diplomat, see W.S. Blunt, *Ideas about India* (London: Kegan Paul, Trench, 1885), xiii–xiv. On Keay, see Charles Welch, 'Keay, John Seymour (1839–1909)', rev. H.C.G. Matthew, *Oxford Dictionary of National Biography* (Oxford: Oxford University Press, 2004), http://www.oxforddnb.com/view/article/34253 (accessed on 27 April 2014).

80. Blunt, *India under Ripon*, 118; Bagal, *History of the Indian Association*, 64–6; and S.R. Mehrotra, *A History of the Indian National Congress, 1885–1918* (Delhi: Vikas, 1995), 3–4. A second National Conference was held in 1885 by the Indian Association in Calcutta and received more extensive support: the zamindars of the British Indian Association participated in it, as did members of the National Mohammedan Association. See Amvikacharan Mazumdar, *Indian National Evolution: A Brief Survey of the Origin and Progress of the Indian National Congress and the Growth of Indian Nationalism* (1917; reprint, Calcutta: Frontpage, 2010), 29, 37; and P. Gangopadhyay, *Bharater Rastriya Itihaser Khasra*, 115.

81. See Bimanbehari Majumdar, *Indian Political Associations and Reform of Legislature (1818–1917)* (Calcutta: Firma K.L. Mukhopadhyay, 1965), 157.

82. Banerjea, *A Nation in Making*, 41, 53. Dwarakanath did not hesitate to oppose or criticize Banerjea when needed. Bipinchandra Pal, who was present at one confrontation, remarked that Dwarakanath 'was a sturdy opponent of all forms of autocracy, whether in the Brahmo Samaj ... or in politics'. See B. Pal, *Memories of My Life*, 436.

83. See *Speeches by Babu Surendra Nath Banerjea*, 6 vols in 2 (Calcutta: S.K. Lahiri, 1894–1908), 5 (1896): 1–86, at 82–3, 85.

84. David Kopf, *The Brahmo Samaj and the Shaping of the Modern Indian Mind* (Princeton: Princeton University Press, 1979), 124; Dutta, *Abala-bandhhab-Dwarakanath o Kadambini*, 83–6, 90. On the extensive support for the Association's rural campaigns among peasants, see Kanailal Chattopadhyay, *Brahmo Reform Movement: Some Social and Economic Aspects* (Calcutta: Papyrus, 1983), 144–5.

85. See N. Dutta, *Abalabandhhab-Dwarakanath o Kadambini*, 113; and Bagal, *History of the Indian Association*, 78.

86. John R. McLane, *Indian Nationalism and the Early Congress* (Princeton, NJ: Princeton University Press, 1977), 149.

87. Elizabeth Kolsky, *Colonial Justice in British India* (Cambridge: Cambridge University Press, 2010), 146. On the topographical and climatic barriers between Assam and the rest of India, see Jayeeta Sharma, *Empire's Garden: Assam and the Making of India* (Durham, NC: Duke University Press, 2011), 2–3. Before 1874, 'Assam' included the present-day states of Assam, Nagaland, Meghalaya, and Mizoram. See Guha, *Planter-Raj to Swaraj*, ix, 27–9, 70–1.

88. There was some Indian elite involvement in the early days of the tea trade. The fabled merchant 'Prince' Dwarakanath Tagore was one of those who tried to get into the business in the 1830s. Such indigenous elements, however, were pushed out when the Assam Company was formed in 1839 to exploit the natural resources of Assam, primarily tea but also oil, timber, and coal. It remained the sole planter in Assam until the 1850s, when other European companies entered the scene. See Sharma, *Empire's Garden*, 28–32; and Guha, *Planter-Raj to Swaraj*, 9.

89. See Rana P. Behal and Prabhu P. Mohapatra, '"Tea and Money versus Human Life": The Rise and Fall of the Indenture System in the Assam Tea Plantations 1840–1908', in *Plantations, Proletarians and Peasants in Colonial Asia*, edited by E. Valentine Daniel, Henry Bernstein, and Tom Brass (London: Frank Cass, 1992), 142–72, at 147–50.

90. See Kolsky, *Colonial Justice in British India*, 148.

91. Sharma, *Empire's Garden*, 61–5.

92. Behal and Mohapatra, 'Tea and Money versus Human Life', 145–6. In the early years of the tea industry, Chinese labourers had been brought to Assam from Singapore and Malaya but little is known about them and they

had disappeared by the 1860s. See Sharma, *Empire's Garden*, 36–8. See also Rana P. Behal, 'Power Structure, Discipline, and Labour in Assam Tea Plantations under Colonial Rule', in *Coolies, Capital, and Colonialism: Studies in Indian Labour History*, edited by R.P. Behal and Marcel van der Linden (Cambridge: Cambridge University Press, 2006), 143–72, especially 156–8.

93. Tirthankar Roy, *India in the World Economy: From Antiquity to the Present* (New York: Cambridge University Press, 2012), 142; and Hugh Tinker, *A New System of Slavery: The Export of Indian Labour Overseas, 1830–1920* (London: Oxford University Press, 1974).

94. It is only fair to add that prior to British annexation, 'slaves and bondsmen' had comprised about 5–9 per cent of the population of Assam. This was abolished by the British in 1845 but indentured labour was scarcely more humane. See Guha, *Planter-Raj to Swaraj*, 10–11. As historian Ranajit Guha has rightly argued, it was 'one of the characteristic paradoxes of colonialism that such feudal practices, far from being abolished or at least reduced, were in fact reinforced under a government representing the authority of the world's most advanced bourgeoisie'. See Ranajit Guha, *Dominance without Hegemony: History and Power in Colonial India* (Cambridge, Mass.: Harvard University Press, 1997), 26–7.

95. Coolies for the tea gardens of Assam came from various parts of the subcontinent. Most were 'tribals', especially from allegedly violent groups 'pacified' by the British and their Indian allies. Some, such as the so-called Kolarians from the Chotanagpur-Santal Hill area of Bengal, were particularly favoured in colonial racial lore for their supposed industriousness and obedience. See Sharma, *Empire's Garden*, 6, 71–5.

96. Not that the life of labourers had been pleasant under the old regulations. The Government of Bengal estimated that of 85,000 labourers had been brought to Assam to work on tea plantations between 1863 and 1866, at least 35,000 had died or deserted. See Guha, *Planter-Raj to Swaraj*, 17. Except for some small changes in 1893, the 1882 Act remained in force until the early twentieth century. See Behal and Mohapatra, 'Tea and Money versus Human Life', 147–50.

97. See Behal and Mohapatra, 'Tea and Money versus Human Life', 150–3.

98. See Kolsky, *Colonial Justice in British India*, 152.

99. Bipan Chandra, *The Rise and Growth of Economic Nationalism in India: Economic Policies of Indian National Leadership, 1880–1905* (Delhi: People's Publishing House, 1966), 364. The phrase 'Slave Act of British India' was attributed by Bipinchandra Pal to the journalist Kristodas Pal. See *Report of the Proceedings of the Bengal Provincial Conference held at Calcutta on the 25th, 26th and 27th October, 1888* (Calcutta: N.G. Goswamy, 1888), 6.

100. Behal and Mohapatra, 'Tea and Money versus Human Life', 158–9, 163, 169–70. See also Henry Cotton, *Indian and Home Memories* (London: T.

EMPIRE, NATION, WOMEN   189

Fisher Unwin, 1911), 263; and Dvaraka Nath Ganguli, Krishna Kumar Mitra, Kali Sankar Sukul, and Heramba Chandra Maitra, *A Note on the Present System of Inland Emigration with Special Reference to the Despatch of the Government of India, Dated the 22nd of January, 1889, by the Proprietors of the 'Sanjibani'* (Calcutta: 'Sanjibani' Office, 1889), 19–20.

101. Dwarakanath Ganguli, *Slavery in British Dominion*, edited by Sris Kumar Kunda and Kanailal Chattopadhyay (Calcutta: Jijnasa, 1972), 40–1, 44.

102. Dipankar Banerjee, *Brahmo Samaj and North-East India* (Delhi: Anamika, 2006), 106–7.

103. Quoted by Dipankar Banerjee, *Brahmo Samaj and North-East India*, 107.

104. See Amar Dutta, *Assamey Cha-Kuli Andolan o Dwarakanath* (Calcutta: Swantana Dutta, 1978), 25–6, 29. The play *Cha-Kar Darpan* is reprinted in *Suppression of Drama in Nineteenth-Century India*, edited by Pramila Pandhe (Calcutta: India Book Exchange, 1978).

105. In 1888, Ramkumar lost his wife Gyanada and two years later, became a sannyasi, taking the name Ramananda Bharati and leaving his three daughters in the care of friends. The second daughter, Surama, was brought up by Upendrakishore Ray and married Upendrakishore's youngest brother, Pramadaranjan, in 1905. The author Leela Majumdar was their daughter. See Bratati Chakravarty, *Bangla Shishu Sahitya Charcha: Ray Paribar* (Calcutta: Dey Book Store, 1997), 103; and Durganath Ghosh, *Paribrajakacharya Swami Ramananda* (Calcutta: Sourindranath Roy, 1927), 115–18.

106. Ramkumar also played a major role in organizing relief during a famine in Birbhum in 1885, along with Dwarakanath Ganguli, Gaganchandra Home, and members of the Indian Association. See Durganath Ghosh, *Paribrajakacharya Swami Ramananda*, 23, 80–93.

107. See D. Banerjee, *Brahmo Samaj and North-East India*.

108. Kanailal Chattopadhyay, 'Introduction', in D. Ganguli, *Slavery in British Dominion*, vii–ix.

109. The pamphlet has been reprinted in D. Ganguli, *Slavery in British Dominion*, 57–96. On its contexts, see Kanailal Chattopadhyay, appendix to Krishnakumar Mitra, *Atmacharit*, 294–9; and P. Gangopadhyay, *Bharater Rastriya Itihaser Khasra*, 68–9.

110. See Bagal, *History of the Indian Association*, 53.

111. P. Gangopadhyay, *Bharater Rastriya Itihaser Khasra*, 65–6.

112. D. Banerjee, *Brahmo Samaj and North-East India*, 108.

113. Brajendranath Bandyopadhyay, *Dwarakanath Gangopadhyay* (Calcutta: Bangiya Sahitya Parishat, 1950), 18.

114. Sastri, *Atmacharit*, 298–301.

115. See Kanailal Chattopadhyay, ed., *Samyikpatrey Samajchitra: Krishnakumar Mitra Sampadita 'Sanjibani'* (Calcutta: Dey's, 1989), 7–8; and Dwarkanath Ganguli, *Slavery in British Dominion*.

116. 'An Appeal by the Indian Association' (25 September 1886), reprinted in D. Ganguli, *Slavery in British Dominion*, xiii.

117. D. Ganguli, *Slavery in British Dominion*, 2–6.

118. D. Ganguli, *Slavery in British Dominion*, 48–52.

119. D. Ganguli, *Slavery in British Dominion*, 14–15.

120. D. Ganguli, *Slavery in British Dominion*, 18.

121. D. Ganguli, *Slavery in British Dominion*, 40–1, 44.

122. D. Ganguli, *Slavery in British Dominion*, 6–8.

123. D. Ganguli, *Slavery in British Dominion*, 19.

124. D. Ganguli et al., *A Note on the Present System of Inland Emigration*, 11.

125. D. Ganguli, *Slavery in British Dominion*, 32–5. For the number of gardens that were not inspected, see D. Ganguli et al., *A Note on the Present System of Inland Emigration*, 14–15.

126. D. Ganguli, *Slavery in British Dominion*, 10–11, 33.

127. D. Ganguli, *Slavery in British Dominion*, 47.

128. D. Ganguli, *Slavery in British Dominion*, 47.

129. D. Ganguli, *Slavery in British Dominion*, 48. 'Modern Babylon' was an allusion to a sensational investigative report of 1885 on child prostitution in London by the Victorian journalist W.T. Stead (1849–1912). See James Mussell, '"Characters of Blood and Flame": Stead and the Tabloid Campaign', in *W.T. Stead: Newspaper Revolutionary*, edited by Laurel Brake, Ed King, Roger Luckhurst, and James Mussell (London: British Library, 2012), 21–36, at 24–6.

130. Behal and Mohapatra, 'Tea and Money versus Human Life', 164–5.

131. D. Ganguli, *Slavery in British Dominion*, 53, 56.

132. Quoted by Kolsky, *Colonial Justice in British India*, 155.

133. Kanailal Chattopadhyay, appendix to Krishnakumar Mitra, *Atmacharit*, 299; and Bipan Chandra, *Rise and Growth of Economic Nationalism*, 372.

134. B. Pal, *Memories of My Life*, 446–7.

135. Letter of 20 June 1877 from Binodebihari Roy of 13 Cornwallis Street in *Tattvakaumudi*, reproduced in Amar Dutta, *Assamey Cha-Kuli Andolan o Dwarakanath*, 41–3.

136. *Report on Native Papers—Bengal*, 22 February 1890, 176.

137. The educational work of Sasipada Banerji with labourers in European-owned jute mills, for example, was notable for its humanitarianism but it did little to transform the power relationships of the colonial jute mill. See Sumit Sarkar, *A Critique of Colonial India*, 2nd edn, 76, 89. Sasipada's son, Albion Rajkumar Banerji, a knighted member of the Indian Civil Service, remarked that 'the main principle' of his father's work 'was social, educational and religious, and had no political significance whatsoever'. The aim of Sasipada's devotion to the cause of the working classes was to end 'the use of the strike weapon' and to encourage workers 'to look to the interests of their employers, and at the same time to present their grievances in a legitimate manner'. See

Albion R. Banerji, *An Indian Pathfinder: Being the Memoirs of Sevabrata Sasipada Banerji 1840–1924* (Oxford: Kemp Hall Press, 1934), 60, 75.

138. D. Banerjee, *Brahmo Samaj and North-East India*, 116, 120. A detailed memorial sent to the Viceroy in 1888 by the Association is reproduced in Bagal, *History of the Indian Association, 1876–1951*, xxxiii–xlvi.

139. *Proceedings of the Bengal Provincial Conference* (1888), 27–8.

140. *Report of the Second Indian National Congress Held at Calcutta on the 27th, 28th, 29th and 30th December 1886* (Calcutta, no pub., 1887), 95. Bipinchandra Pal (B. Pal, *Memories of My Life*, 446–7) mistakenly placed this exchange in 1887 at the Third Congress in Madras.

141. See *Proceedings of the Bengal Provincial Conference* (1888), 102–3.

142. *Proceedings of the Bengal Provincial Conference* (1888), 5.

143. *Proceedings of the Bengal Provincial Conference* (1888), 3.

144. *Proceedings of the Bengal Provincial Conference* (1888), 16–22.

145. *Proceedings of the Bengal Provincial Conference* (1888), 22–7.

146. The delegates did pass the resolution unanimously and Sircar congratulated them for displaying 'that sympathy, humanity and philanthropy which should be the guiding and animating principle of all men'. See *Proceedings of the Bengal Provincial Conference* (1888), 28, 108.

147. *Proceedings of the Bengal Provincial Conference* (1888), 28, 110.

148. Ganguli et al., 'Note on the Present System of Inland Emigration', 7, emphases in the original.

149. Government of India, *Special Report on the Working of Act I of 1882, for the Years 1886–89*, 239, quoted by Behal and Mohapatra, 'Tea and Money versus Human Life', 156.

150. Sharma, *Empire's Garden*, 167–8.

151. See D. Banerjee, *Brahmo Samaj and North-East India*, 112–13.

152. D. Banerjee, *Brahmo Samaj and North-East India*, 113.

153. It was published anonymously and was in fact co-authored by its publisher Gaganchandra Home—see *Kulikahini: Sketches from Cooly Life* (Calcutta: G.C. Home, 1888).

154. Ghosh, *Paribrajakacharya Swami Ramananda*, 23.

155. See Charles Dowding, *Tea-Garden Coolies in Assam* (Calcutta: Thacker, Spink, 1894).

156. Quoted by Kolsky, *Colonial Justice in British India*, 164–5.

157. See Annie Besant, *How India Wrought for Freedom: The Story of the National Congress Told from Official Records* (Adyar, Madras: Theosophical Publishing House, 1915), 240, 249.

158. Behal and Mohapatra, 'Tea and Money versus Human Life', 169.

159. Behal and Mohapatra, 'Tea and Money versus Human Life', 167.

160. B. Chandra, *Rise and Growth of Economic Nationalism*, 373.

161. Sivanath Sastri, *Ramtonu Lahiri o Tatkalin Bangasamaj* (1909; reprint, Calcutta: New Age, 1977), 306.

162. See P. Gangopadhyay, *Bharater Rastriya Itihaser Khasra*, 78. The same undeserved praise is accorded to Cotton by Kanailal Chattopadhyay, 'Introduction', in D. Ganguli, *Slavery in British Dominion*, xi.

163. Cotton, *Indian and Home Memories*, 246, 258.

164. On the leniency of European magistrates towards planters and the reciprocal severity towards coolies, see Kolsky, *Colonial Justice in British India*, 143–84.

165. He was incredulous when a special correspondent of the London *Times* reported after a visit to Assam that the tea garden coolie 'is protected from famine, from fraud, from violence, from usury, from all manner of external ills'. See Cotton, *Indian and Home Memories*, 263–4.

166. For a survey of the colonial government's futile attempts to bring the planters under control, see B.B. Misra, *The Indian Middle Classes: Their Growth in Modern Times* (London: Oxford University Press, 1961), 377–9.

167. See Cotton, *Indian and Home Memories*, 269–78; and Amvikacharan Mazumdar, *Indian National Evolution*, 60.

168. See Cotton, *Indian and Home Memories*, 287–90. On the Congress, see Besant, *How India Wrought for Freedom*, 393–414.

169. Cotton, *Indian and Home Memories*, 268.

170. A. Guha, *Planter-Raj to Swaraj*, 104–5; and Sumit Sarkar, *Modern Times: India, 1880s–1950s—Environment, Economy, Culture* (Ranikhet: Permanent Black, 2014), 148–51.

171. A. Guha, *Planter-Raj to Swaraj*, 106, 128–9.

172. See the comments of Mrinalkanti Basu in 'Dwarakanath Gangopadhyayer Janmasatabarsiki', *Probasi*, 44, no 2 (Jaistha 1351/June–July 1944): 92–3, http://archiv.ub.uni-heidelberg.de/savifadok/volltexte/2009/1018 (accessed on 26 September 2014).

173. D. Banerjee, *Brahmo Samaj and North-East India*, 111–12.

174. Dwarakanath and Kadambini's daughter Jyotirmoyee and son Prabhatchandra would be far more radical in their nationalism. Around 1908, Prabhatchandra joined a group of violent swadeshi activists and Jyotirmoyee, during Gandhi's Non-cooperation Movement (1920–1), formed a Women's Volunteer Corps and was later jailed for participating in the civil disobedience movement of 1930–2. Elected in 1933 as a municipal councillor, she was to lose her life during a police raid on a procession of students protesting against the trials of members of Subhas Chandra Bose's Indian National Army in 1946. She was also involved in many feminist projects. See Parimal Goswami, *Aami Jnader Dekhechhi* [1969] (Calcutta: Pratikshan, 1995), 153–4; Jogeshchandra Bagal, 'Rastriya Andoloney Bangamahila', in *Bethune School & College Centenary Volume*, edited by Kalidas Nag (Calcutta: no pub., 1951), 228–35, at 231; and Abhijit Sen and Anindita Bhaduri, eds, *Jyotirmoyee Gangopadhyayer Rachana Sankalan* (Calcutta: Dey's/Jadavpur University, 2007).

175. See Meredith Borthwick, *The Changing Role of Women in Bengal, 1849–1905* (Princeton: Princeton University Press, 1984), 346–56, 359–61.

176. Until 1918, the Indian National Congress had no formal members, and delegates were selected for each year's session. See Mehrotra, *History of the Indian National Congress,* 87.

177. See the *Full Report of Proceedings of the Fifth Indian National Congress Held in Bombay, Dec. 1889* (Bombay: Jehangier & Shroff, 1890), 3; A.M. Zaidi, ed., *The Story of Congress Pilgrimage,* 3 vols (Delhi: Indian Institute of Applied Political Research, 1990), 1: 95; and Mehrotra, *History of the Indian National Congress,* 86, 313–14. My thanks to Barun Chattopadhyay for his help with this section.

178. See *Report of the Sixth Indian National Congress Held at Calcutta, on the 26th, 27th, 29th, and 30th December 1890* (London: British Committee of the Indian National Congress, 1891), xl; and Mehrotra, *History of the Indian National Congress,* 86.

179. See *Proceedings of the Fifth Indian National Congress,* 12, 20.

180. See *Report on Native Papers—Bengal,* 60; and Borthwick, *Changing Role of Women in Bengal,* 341–2. It was only in 1917—nearly twenty years after Dwarakanath's death—that the Congress finally demanded that 'the same tests be applied to women as to men in regard to the franchise and the eligibility to all elective bodies'. See B. Pattabhi Sitaramayya, *The History of the Indian National Congress,* 2 vols (Bombay: Padma, 1935–47), 1: 52.

181. See *Report of the Sixth Indian National Congress,* xl; and Mehrotra, *History of the Indian National Congress,* 86.

182. *Report of the Sixth Indian National Congress,* xl.

183. Quoted in Bimanbehari Majumdar and Bhakat Prasad Mazumdar, *Congress and Congressmen in the Pre-Gandhian Era, 1885–1917* (Calcutta: Firma K. L. Mukhopadhyay, 1967), 235.

184. For the full text of Kadambini's short speech, see *Report of the Sixth Indian National Congress,* 74. See also 'Mahajajna', *Bharati-o-Balak,* 15 (1891): 19–30, at 29, http://archiv.ub.uni-heidelberg.de/savifadok/volltexte/2009/392 (accessed on 1 December 2013).

185. Mehrotra, *History of the Indian National Congress,* 87; and Annie Besant, *How India Wrought for Freedom,* 116.

186. As S.R. Mehrotra notes, 'the impact of the First World War, the examples of Mrs Annie Besant and Mrs Sarojini Naidu, and the efforts of Gandhi served to augment the number of ladies attending the sessions of the Congress from 1915 onwards'. Mehrotra, *History of the Indian National Congress,* 87.

187. Borthwick, *Changing Role of Women in Bengal,* 342, 345–6.

188. Ghosal was once described as 'the pivot round which the Congress turns'. See Mehrotra, *History of the Indian National Congress,* 312–13.

189. See Amiya Sen, 'Hindu Revivalism in Action: The Age of Consent Bill Agitation in Bengal', *Indian Historical Review,* 7, nos 1–2 (1980–1):

160–84. Act III of 1872, of course, had specified an even higher minimum age for marriage for girls, but it had not caused much dismay among mainstream Hindus because they had been explicitly excluded from the Act's purview. See M. Sinha, *Colonial Masculinity*, 145, 157.

190. S. Natarajan, *A Century of Social Reform in India*, 2nd edn (Bombay: Asia Publishing House, 1962), 84.

191. D. Engels, *Beyond Purdah?*, 103–4; and Natarajan, *A Century of Social Reform*, 19.

192. See Heimsath, *Indian Nationalism and Hindu Social Reform*, 147–75. As Meera Kosambi has pointed out, Malabari's campaign was somewhat paradoxical because child marriage was virtually unknown in the Parsi community. See Meera Kosambi, 'Girl-Brides and Socio-Legal Change: Age of Consent Bill (1891) Controversy', *Economic and Political Weekly*, 26, nos 31–2 (3–10 August 1991): 1857–68, at 1858.

193. Rajendra Singh Vatsa, 'The Movement against Infant-Marriages in India 1860–1914', *Journal of Indian History*, 49, nos 145–7 (1971): 289–303, at 292–4.

194. 'Child Marriage and Enforced Widowhood in India', *The Times*, 13 September 1890, 8.

195. Padma Anagol, 'Rebellious Wives and Dysfunctional Marriages: Indian Women's Discourses and Participation in the Debates over Restitution of Conjugal Rights and the Child Marriage Controversy in the 1880s and 1890s', in *Women and Social Reform in Modern India: A Reader*, edited by Sumit Sarkar and Tanika Sarkar, 2 vols (Ranikhet: Permanent Black, 2007), 1: 420–65, at 420. Also relevant was the 1884–8 case of Rakhmabai in Bombay, where Rakhmabai, married in childhood, refused to live with her husband and was taken successfully to court by him for the restitution of conjugal rights. See Kosambi, 'Girl-Brides and Socio-Legal Change', 1858; and Kosambi, 'Gender Reform and Competing State Controls over Women: The Rakhmabai Case (1884–1888)', *Contributions to Indian Sociology*, ns 29, nos 1–2 (1995): 265–89.

196. Vatsa, 'Movement against Infant-Marriages in India', 294–5; and Tanika Sarkar, 'Conjugality and Hindu Nationalism: Resisting Colonial Reason and the Death of a Child-Wife', in *Women and Social Reform in Modern India: A Reader*, edited by Sumit Sarkar and Tanika Sarkar, 1: 385–419, at 400–4.

197. Himani Bannerji, *Inventing Subjects: Studies in Hegemony, Patriarchy and Colonialism* (London: Anthem Press, 2001), 77–8.

198. For an eyewitness account of the 'wild spirit' pervading the movement against the Bill and the persecution of Brahmos, see B. Pal, *Memories of My Life*, 484–7; and the report in *Sanjibani* (28 March 1891), in *Report on Native Papers—Bengal*, 4 April 1891, 414–15. For a sample of orthodox objections to the Bill, see 'The Full Proceedings of a Public Meeting Held on the 22nd January, 1891, at the Residence of the late Maharajah Kamal Krishna Deb

Bahadur, Sabhabazar [sic] Rajbati, Calcutta, to Protest against the Age of Consent Bill (Calcutta: Sabhabazar Standing Committee, 1891)', in *Tracts on Indian Marriage Questions* (British Library Asian and Oriental Collections, 8415 G 62). On the protests in Maharashtra, see Anagol, 'Rebellious Wives and Dysfunctional Marriages'.

199. Rajat Kanta Ray, *Social Conflict and Political Unrest in Bengal, 1875–1927* (Delhi: Oxford University Press, 1984), 127. For descriptions of the February meeting from contrasting viewpoints, see the report of the conservative paper *Banganibasi* in *Report on Native Papers—Bengal*, 7 March 1891, 278–9 and that of the liberal *Sanjibani*, in *Report on Native Papers—Bengal*, 285. For a comprehensive list of the mass meetings held against the Bill in Calcutta, outlying districts of Bengal, Punjab, and Bombay, see Amiya P. Sen, *Hindu Revivalism in Bengal*, Appendix A (part 1), unpaginated.

200. *Report on Native Papers—Bengal*, 19 July 1890, 679.

201. *Report on Native Papers—Bengal*, 27 September 1890, 928.

202. *Report on Native Papers—Bengal*, 24 January 1891, 111–12.

203. See Amiya P. Sen, *Hindu Revivalism in Bengal*, 381–3.

204. For Vidyasagar's statement, see *India: Legislative Proceedings, April 1891*, Proceeding 59, Appendix A16. See also Asok Sen, *Iswar Chandra Vidyasagar and His Elusive Milestones* (Calcutta: Riddhi-India, 1977), 143.

205. *India: Legislative Proceedings 1891*, Proceeding 38, Appendix U.

206. Heimsath, *Indian Nationalism and Hindu Social Reform*, 162.

207. Vatsa, 'Movement against Infant-Marriages in India 1860–1914', 296–7; and Amiya P. Sen, *Hindu Revivalism in Bengal*, 390.

208. See Sukeshi Kamra, *The Indian Periodical Press and the Production of Nationalist Rhetoric* (New York: Palgrave-Macmillan, 2011), 99–126; and A. Sen, 'Hindu Revivalism in Action', 171. Graphic descriptions of the prosecution of *Bangabasi*, the police search of its offices, and seizure of documents are available in long reports in the *Dainik-o-Samachar Chandrika* (8 and 10 August 1891)—see *Report on Native Papers—Bengal*, 15 August 1891, 824–7 and 829–32; and for the *Bangabasi*'s own report and analysis, *Report on Native Papers—Bengal*, 22 August 1891, 863–7. The jury was not unanimous in its verdict and the government withdrew the case after *Bangabasi* had apologized to the Lieutenant-Governor Sir Charles Elliott. See Buckland, *Bengal under the Lieutenant-Governors*, 2: 916–19; and *Report on Native Papers—Bengal*, 3 October 1891, 1056–7; and 10 October 1891, 1080–97.

209. S. Mitra, 'The Newspaper Press', in *Studies in the Bengal Renaissance*, 423–38, at 433.

210. Banerjea thought it was far more important to prohibit child marriage. See *India: Legislative Proceedings 1891*, Proceeding 38, Appendix U; and M. Sinha, *Colonial Masculinity*, 164–5.

211. Sinha, *Colonial Masculinity*, 154, 156, 175.

212. For Ganguli's letter, see *India: Legislative Proceedings, April 1891,* Proceeding 38, Appendix U. My thanks to Barun Chattopadhyay for the reference.

213. *India: Legislative Proceedings, April 1891,* Proceeding 38, Appendix U.

214. *India: Legislative Proceedings, April 1891,* Proceeding 38, Appendix U.

215. 'Speeches in the Supreme Legislative Council at the Time of Passing the Age of Consent Bill, on the 19th March, 1891', in *Tracts on Indian Marriage Questions* (British Library Asian and Oriental Collections, 8415 G 62), 65.

216. *Navayuga* (2 April 1891), in *Report on Native Papers—Bengal,* 11 April, 1891, 427–8.

217. *Bangabasi* (21 March 1891), in *Report on Native Papers—Bengal,* 28 March 1891, 381. The *Banganibasi* followed suit, as did other papers: see *Report on Native Papers—Bengal,* 4 April 1891, 403; and *Report on Native Papers—Bengal,* 11 April 1891, 428, 435–6. Even though *Bangabasi* was socially conservative and ostensibly apolitical, the paper was a consistent supporter of economic nationalism and what would come to be known after 1905 as swadeshi enterprise. See Amiya P. Sen, *Hindu Revivalism in Bengal,* 264–5; and Shyamananda Banerjee, *National Awakening and the 'Bangabasi'* (Calcutta: Amitava-Kalyan, 1968).

218. See M. Sinha, *Colonial Masculinity,* 166; and Tanika Sarkar, 'Conjugality and Hindu Nationalism', 408–9.

219. Until 1929 to be precise, when the minimum age for marriage was raised by the Child Marriage Restraint Act (Sarda Act). It had a smoother passage largely because women themselves were prominent in calling for such legislation. See Heimsath, *Indian Nationalism and Hindu Social Reform,* 174; D. Engels, *Beyond Purdah?,* 44–5; and Mrinalini Sinha, *Specters of Mother India: The Global Restructuring of an Empire* (Durham, NC: Duke University Press, 2006).

220. R.L. Ghosh, 'The Late Babu Dvarakanath Ganguli'.

221. N. Dutta, *Abalabandhhab-Dwarakanath o Kadambini,* 156.

222. Punyalata Chakrabarti, *Chhelebelar Dinguli* (1958; reprint, Calcutta: Newscript, 1981), 61.

223. See Amal Das, 'Plague and People in Calcutta', in *Explorations in History: Essays in Honour of Prof. Chittabrata Palit,* edited by Abhijit Dutta, Keka Dutta Roy, and Sandeep Sinha (Calcutta: Corpus Research Institute, 2003), 117–37.

224. *The Bengalee,* 25 June 1898, 305.

225. Amal Das, 'Plague and People in Calcutta', 132–3.

226. Home, *Jiban-Smriti,* 13; and N. Dutta, *Abalabandhhab-Dwarakanath o Kadambini,* 185–6, 190.

227. Sastri, *History of the Brahmo Samaj,* 341.

228. *The Bengalee,* 2 July 1898, 317.

229. R.L. Ghosh, 'The Late Babu Dvarakanath Ganguli'.

230. Sastri, *Ramtonu Lahiri o Tatkalin Bangasamaj,* 302, 306.

EMPIRE, NATION, WOMEN 197

231. Prabhatchandra Ganguli, Foreword to Dwarkanath Ganguli, *Slavery in British Dominion* (Calcutta; Jijnasa, 1972), n.p.

232. See Pal, *New Spirit*, 202–3.

233. After her husband's death in 1898, Kadambini moved out of the Cornwallis Street house and into a house on Guruprasad Chowdhury Lane that had been gifted to Dwarakanath by a debtor. See Radharaman Mitra, *Kalikata Darpan*, 2 vols (Calcutta: Subarnarekha, 1980–2004), 1 (1980): 99–100.

234. Bagal, 'Rastriya Andoloney Bangamahila', 228.

235. See N. Dutta, *Abalabandhhab-Dwarakanath o Kadambini*, 158–9.

236. Kalyani Karlekar, 'Satyajit's Childhood and the Child in Satyajit', in *Satyajit Ray: An Intimate Master*, edited by Santi Das (Delhi: Allied, 1998), 1–5, at 1.

4

The Polymathic Artisan

While Dwarakanath Ganguli is remembered today mainly on account of his labours for women, his son-in-law Upendrakishore is known primarily as a children's writer. But just as Dwarakanath was not just concerned with women's issues, Upendrakishore, too, did much more than write for the young. As his grandson, Satyajit, observed,

> Upendrakishore embodied a remarkable fusion of science and art, of East and West. He played the *pakhwaj* as well as the violin, conducted original research in printing technology whilst composing Brahmo devotional hymns, studied the heavens with a telescope from the roof of his house, retold the epics and rural tales in inimitably lucid prose for children, and also used oil and watercolour, or pen and ink, to produce pictures that were consummately Western in style.[1]

This lusty versatility compels admiration but it also demands historical analysis, which Upendrakishore's work has never attracted. Siddhartha Ghosh's pioneering research on his contributions to printing technology and related areas is empirically rich but analytically somewhat too uncritical, and while there are many other articles and books on Upendrakishore in Bengali, they do not address the non-literary dimensions of his work with any thoroughness. Scholarly works on Indian modernity—including studies of the Bengal Renaissance—do not even mention Upendrakishore and he is absent, too, from the few studies we have of colonial-era technology and entrepreneurship. This is not only unfortunate but inexplicable, because Upendrakishore's multifaceted career could help us comprehend the character and contradictions of creativity in a colonial setting rather more clearly than the literary and political figures upon whom most theorists of Indian modernity rely so exclusively.

A Progressive Householder

Early in his college days in Calcutta, Upendrakishore, as we know, had become close to Dwarakanath Ganguli and on 15 June 1885, he married Ganguli's daughter, Bidhumukhi (1865[?]–1927), following Brahmo rites.[2] Upendrakishore's marriage was doubly offensive to his Hindu adoptive family. The Gangulis were not only Brahmo but Brahmins too.[3] Upendrakishore's biological mother, Joytara, was a devout Hindu and although she accepted the marriage and treated Bidhumukhi with affection, she would never stay under the same roof with Upendrakishore and Bidhumukhi, lodging on her rare visits to Calcutta with her orthodox Hindu son Saradaranjan.[4]

After their marriage, Upendrakishore and Bidhumukhi moved into the Cornwallis Street residence of Dwarakanath and Kadambini. The building accommodated many tenants who had faced social or family persecution after converting to Brahmoism and because it was the residence of the man famous for editing *Abalabandhab*, it was often referred to by neighbours as the Abala-Barrack.[5] It was also the site of some notable institutions. The Calcutta Training Academy, where Rabindranath Tagore had begun his never-to-be-completed schooling, held its classes here up till 1890 and outside school hours, the Academy's rooms were used by Nabagopal Mitra's National School.[6] After the Training Academy moved away, its place was taken by the Brahmo Girls' School, which also educated boys up to the age of nine and was founded by Sivanath Sastri in 1890.[7] Upendrakishore and Bidhumukhi would live on the first floor of this house for several years and five of their six children—Sukhalata (1886–1969), Sukumar (1887–1923), Punyalata (1889–1974), Subinoy (1891–1945), and Santilata (1893–1919)—were to be born here. The household also accommodated Bidhumukhi's disabled brother, Satischandra, and, at least for a time, her maternal uncle, the unmarried Brahmo missionary

Nabadwipchandra Das (1847–1924).[8] Upendrakishore's daughters Sukhalata and Punyalata and, for a period, his son Sukumar were students of the Brahmo Girls' school, as were the children of Kadambini and Dwarakanath.[9] The Rays would move several times, but until the mid-1920s, they always lived as a classic Hindu joint family, the married sons and their children living under the same roof and accommodating, when needed, relatives or friends in distress.[10]

Upendrakishore, as we have seen, had no interest in being a hands-on landowner, preferring to live in Calcutta and starting his own business. But he did this while continuing to own a share of Harikishore's estate, the management of which he entrusted to Harikishore's biological son Narendrakishore.[11] Upendrakishore was not, however, a typical absentee-landlord living a life of urban luxury financed by rent income from East Bengal.[12] Instead, he used his zamindari income to finance his early research in printing technology as well as his entrepreneurial ventures.[13] These signs of a maverick disposition, along with his conversion to Brahmoism, might have suggested to some that he was shaping up to be a radical reformer like his father-in-law. In fact, however, his life would turn out to be very different. He was never drawn to the high-profile causes dear to Dwarakanath and other progressive Brahmos.[14] An obituarist remarked that he 'had nothing of what is called "push", being of a retiring disposition, and avoiding the glare of fame and publicity'.[15] Upendrakishore's work for children had, as we shall see, their reformist dimensions but this reformism was always quiet and indirect. He was also far more typical in his Brahmo religiosity and puritanism than Dwarakanath. He insisted on the entire family saying Brahmo prayers before meals—much to the irritation of the young Sukumar Ray—and once, when Kuladaranjan Ray returned from a cricket match in Lucknow with embroidered Persian-style shoes for his daughters, Upendrakishore had them thrown away because such shoes, he thought, were fit only for dancing girls.[16]

Upendrakishore's wife, Bidhumukhi, had been educated at home by her father and taught English by an English tutoress.[17] Although, unlike her stepmother Kadambini, she never aspired to a professional identity, she was modern in temperament and lifestyle, and had no qualms about participating in public engagements dressed in the elegant, refined Victorian style of a Brahmo lady.[18] But Brahmo women, of course, were also expected to be domestic goddesses and Bidhumukhi was an excellent cook and superbly efficient at running the large household, nursing the ill, and looking after the children, their friends, and the numerous visiting relatives. 'She was busy the whole day, as if she did not need any comfort or rest,' recalled daughter Punyalata, whose reminiscences portray a household teeming with hordes of energetic, happy, and well-fed children. Upendrakishore was obviously responsible for the prosperity that made it all possible, but it was Bidhumukhi around whom the household revolved.[19] And this was an open-minded, welcoming home. When Upendrakishore's boyhood friend from Mymensingh, the artist Sashi Hesh (1869–?), returned from Europe in 1900 with his French fiancée, Athalie, Flamant, Hesh's family refused to approve of their marriage or to let them stay in the family home. Initially sheltered by Jagadischandra Bose and his wife, the two were married by Brahmo rites and subsequently lived for a while with Upendrakishore and his family.[20] Such hospitality to a mixed-race couple cannot have been common at the time in Bengali households.

Upendrakishore's daughters, too, received the best education possible at the time and all his children were encouraged, not least by their father's endless fund of instructive tales, to read widely and explore all avenues of knowledge and creativity. He took them to museums, exhibitions, and the zoo and showed them the stars with his own telescope.[21] Despite his puritanical bent, he refused to force children to change their fundamental preferences. Narendrakishore Raychaudhuri's son Hitendrakishore, for instance, was left-handed, a habit his father tried to break until Upendrakishore persuaded him to let the boy follow his natural inclinations. Upendrakishore's second son, Subinoy, was also left-handed and had never been urged to be anything else.[22] One does not know if Upendrakishore was influenced by Dwarakanath Ganguli's liberal ideas on child-rearing but it is clear that Bidhumukhi and he rejected the unrelentingly rigorous regime that was supposed to be ideal for children by many Bengali experts.[23] Upendrakishore brought up his children with subtle, friendly guidance, rather than direct commands, lofty pronouncements, and stern punishments; that same approach also characterized all his literary, artistic, and pedagogical work for the children of Bengal.

Teaching, Learning, Doing

Of Upendrakishore's many great passions, the ones that had emerged the earliest were drawing and music. We saw earlier how he had impressed a visiting dignitary with his skill in drawing likenesses and how much he preferred to play the violin instead of concentrating on his studies. 'Words,' he once wrote, 'can only come up to the gateway of life; they cannot reach the heart unless accompanied by music.'[24] He did not only teach his own children to sing or play musical instruments, but many others from neighbouring families, the Brahmo Samaj, and other associations. For a time, he ran a music class as part of a Brahmo Sunday School and then, from 1911, was the chief instructor at a similar class started at the Sadharan Brahmo Samaj temple. He even paid for the instruments and their maintenance. The children sang with their teacher, who accompanied them on his violin.[25] After sixty years, one admirer who had only occasionally attended the class, could still remember how exciting and joyful it was.[26]

Upendrakishore himself composed several Brahmo hymns, of which 'Jago Purobasi' has long been sung at the opening of the Maghhotsava, and Upendrakishore himself provided the violin accompaniment for it during his lifetime.[27] This song and other Brahmo hymns, Nirad Chaudhuri recalled, gave his entire generation an emotional understanding of religion that no intellectual discussion ever could.[28] It was fitting, therefore, that when the British music critic Arthur H. Fox Strangways wanted to include examples of Rabindranath Tagore's compositions in his treatise on the music of India, three of Tagore's devotional lyrics were translated by Upendrakishore, who also compiled for Fox Strangways a list of the thirty *ragas* most commonly found in the music of Bengal.[29] Analysing 'a collection of more than one thousand' popular—as opposed to classical—songs, he not only listed the ragas that were the commonest but, 'with a good deal of diffidence', indicated the emotional qualities associated with each raga. The diffidence, he explained, stemmed from the general emotional inscrutability of Indian music. 'Our gaiety and sadness often merge into each other: our most impassioned passages fail to stir anybody up. There is any amount of enjoyment of the deepest kind, but it is undemonstrative and reposeful; it leads not to action but to abstraction.'[30]

Although he played the flute, the harmonium, the piano, the sitar, the tanpura, the pakhwaj, and, of course, the violin, it was only in the playing of the pakhwaj that Upendrakishore had ever received any professional training.[31] Again and again in the careers of the Rays from Upendrakishore to Satyajit, one notices a family pattern of attaining a high degree of expertise in a craft or art without formal training.[32]

Being self-taught, of course, was not the same thing as being quickly-taught. Upendrakishore gave all his time, concentration, and energy to learning something that seriously interested him, never allowing himself to be discouraged by the difficulties of the subject.[33] The violin was probably his favourite instrument—no other instrument, he once wrote, could express emotions as well as the violin could—and, unusually for the era, he played it in the Western style, holding the instrument on his shoulder and pressing it down with his chin, instead of following the Indian convention of holding the violin pressed to the arm.[34] This, remarked an admirer, allowed him to produce subtler musical effects than would have been possible with the indigenous style of holding the instrument.[35] The young Rabindranath Tagore loved to sing to his accompaniment and even though Upendrakishore belonged to the Sadharan Brahmo Samaj, he was often invited to play the violin at the festivities of the Adi Brahmo Samaj.[36] Very ordinary people, too, were charmed by Upendrakishore's violin-playing. Painter Binodebihari Mukhopadhyay recalled that in his childhood, he had seen crowds thronging outside Upendrakishore's residence, listening to him playing the violin.[37]

Unsurprisingly, the self-taught Upendrakishore did not consider violin-playing to be an esoteric art and wrote a 'teach yourself' manual for the musical instrument dealer Dwarkin's in 1904.[38] This was the second such work that he wrote for the firm. In 1888, they had brought out his *Sikshak Byatirekey Harmonium Siksha* ('Learning the Harmonium without a Teacher'), which was to prove quite popular.[39] Upendrakishore, as we know, may have worked in his student days for Dwarakanath Ghosh, the founder of the firm, but he quickly became a close family friend and business advisor. He drew an oil painting of Ghosh's mother and when Ghosh's elder daughter was dying, came to sing devotional songs at her bedside. He also helped Ghosh disseminate musical knowledge in every possible way. When Dwarkin's began to publish *Veenabadini*, a monthly musical magazine edited by Jyotirindranath Tagore, Upendrakishore designed the cover and it was he who prodded Ghosh into publishing songs with notations.[40]

Upendrakishore's passion for music and the arts was complemented by his technological interests. He was always extraordinarily good with his hands and Marie Seton rightly considered this unusual in a boy brought up in a prosperous Bengali household.[41] During his college days in Calcutta, he had built a working model of a gyroscope from some bits of wood and a ball and when, later, a plaster death-mask of Rammohan Roy had arrived from England in pieces, it was Upendrakishore who had repaired it with 'extraordinary precision'.[42] But he was not simply a good mechanic. His artisanal skills were combined with his keen interest in mastering the latest technologies. As a young man, he became very keen on photography, a craft that allowed him to combine his scientific flair with his passion for art. When he set up in business, his main trade seems to have been pho-tography, especially bromide enlargements. After about a decade as a photographer, however, he moved to half-tone photography, a com-plex new technology of photomechanical reproduction enabling the printing of images without removing their tonal qualities.[43]

By July 1897, Upendrakishore was claiming in advertisements to be able to produce half-tone blocks 'as very few persons in the world have hitherto produced' and which could produce patterns that were 'simply innumerable'.[44] Upendrakishore's switch from conventional photography to photomechanical reproduction was guided not only by his innate interest in technology but had some interesting literary and socio-economic contexts. As we know, Upendrakishore had long been writing for children in magazines and in 1897, he published his first book *Chheleder Ramayan*, an abridged version of the Ramayana for young readers.[45] (The title *Chheleder Ramayan*, incidentally, would be translated as 'The Ramayana for Boys' today but at the turn of the century, the word 'chhele' seems to have been in use as a gender-neutral term for children.)[46] Upendrakishore is said to have been profoundly disappointed by the quality of the printing; his own illustrations, he thought, had been ruined by the wood-engravers.[47] This personal dis-appointment stimulated the self-reliant Upendrakishore to explore ways of improving the reproduction of pictures.

Reading the little that was available on the subject, he ordered equipment for half-tone printing from the Penrose Company in England. Once they had arrived—in huge crates carried by bullock carts, surely not an inappropriate symbol for colonial modernity—he devoted himself to the new craft, heedless of time, expense and, as his son Sukumar recalled, even his own health.[48] In order to have enough space for his experiments, he and his family moved out of the Cornwallis Road house in 1895 and set up their own establishment on north Calcutta's Sibnarayan Das Lane and then, in 1901, moved again to a larger house on Sukea Street.[49] A glass-roofed studio was built on the third storey of the Sukea Street house, where Upendrakishore and his assistants laboured on their tasks, using arc lamps on cloudy days or after sunset.[50] In none of this did Upendrakishore have any guidance except from books, and Rabindranath Tagore was to marvel at the 'mental strength and effort it required to master and then to improve this new craft in India, without any kind of assistance or advice'.[51]

A commercial motivation may also have been at work, however. The European-owned photographic studios in late-nineteenth-century Calcutta attracted the majority of wealthy clients and 'native' photographers often moved into the production of prints and mythological pictures by lithography.[52] Upendrakishore's repositioning of his business may also have been similarly influenced, but instead of specializing in lithography, an old process that now catered to a somewhat downmarket clientele, he went in for the very latest in imaging technology, in which he would face no significant local competition, not even from Europeans.[53] And the shifting cultural politics of fin-de-siècle Bengal created a potential demand for it, which was utilized by Upendrakishore with aplomb.

Printing Pictures: Technology and Society

Even in the middle of the nineteenth century, when photography was becoming almost routine, there was no way to print actual photographs in books, magazines, or newspapers. Engraved wood blocks, when made by a master, could suggest some half-shades and tonal gradations but that was all that was possible.[54] The pioneering investigator Frederic Eugene Ives (1856–1937) realized that the tonality of photographs could be replicated more faithfully in a printed image if one had a block on which printer's ink could be laid 'thickly in the shadows and more or less thinly in the half-shades, whilst no ink at all should be deposited in the whites or highlights'.[55] Ives achieved this by converting the different tones of an image into dots by photographing it through a glass screen embossed with a cross-line grid.[56] Due to lighter and darker parts of the image transmitting different amounts of light, the dots differed in size in accordance with the original tones.[57] A block was made from this dotted image and when printed from, it was not the dots that were reproduced but the continuous tones of the original or a fair approximation of them.[58]

Ives's insights were endorsed and built upon by many researchers scattered across the world and demand from newspapers and magazines for printed pictures reached a critical mass by the 1890s, making the technology, which came to be known as the half-tone process, commercially viable.[59] Producing a glass screen with lines intersecting one another at right angles—as in graph paper—was the key to successful half-tone photography and the first commercially successful screens were introduced only in 1888 by the brothers Louis and Max Levy in Ives's own city Philadelphia.[60] Although half-tone work was quite expensive in the early days—apart from the costly screens, it also needed advanced presses, high-quality printing inks, smooth papers, and generally skilled handling—it became so popular that costs came down quite rapidly.[61] By 1901, a 'process' engraving—'process' was the rather ambiguous term often used for half-tone—could be had for a fraction of the price of a wood-engraving.[62] Reproductions of artistic works, photographs of celebrities and famous sights, scientific illustrations, and, not least, photographic advertisements began to appear everywhere in the print media.[63] By the time of Queen Victoria's Diamond Jubilee in 1897, one commentator declared, all of the major illustrated periodicals had switched to half-tone blocks and wood engravings were virtually passé.[64] The half-tone process was constantly improved and although it faced stiff competition from other, newer techniques of printing images (such as photogravure) from the early twentieth century, it was consigned to history only after the introduction of digital technology towards the end of the century.[65]

Photomechanical reproduction does not simply have a technical, but also a social history. In Britain, 'process' blocks were particularly popular with mass-circulation periodicals which specialized in what Joseph Gleeson White, editor of the art periodical *Studio*, called 'the journalism of pictures, the presentation of ephemeral scenes, and portraits of nobodies'.[66] The populist illustrated magazines of Bengal, however, had vastly fewer resources and catered to a far less solvent readership. They continued, therefore, to rely on wood-engravings for their images and, unlike their Western counterparts, do not seem to have thirsted for the immediacy or vibrancy that half-tone imaging was supposed to evoke.[67] Where the Bengali use of half-tone did resemble that of the West was in the area of art.[68] In the West, the reproduction of fine art in books and periodicals was revolutionized by half-tone technology—even Gleeson White, not a blind fan of 'process', acknowledged that photographic prints of art works had 'educated the ordinary individual far more than Sir Joshua Reynolds or anyone else'.[69] Of course, the printed reproductions removed the art works from their contexts, reduced (or enlarged) their scale, and eliminated their ineffable uniqueness, which Walter Benjamin famously called their 'aura'.[70] But that was hardly an issue for Indians.

In the absence of well-resourced museums and art galleries, Indians with an interest in the world's great art had never had much scope of beholding original paintings or sculptures. Except for the rare individuals who could travel to Europe, the choice was reproductions or nothing at all. Half-tone technology was a godsend and the upmarket sections of Bengali print culture—in particular, Ramananda Chatterji's magazines *Probasi* and *Modern Review*—made good use of it.[71] Their art plates helped enhance the popularity of 'academic' art in the late nineteenth century and helped their readers distance themselves from the world of cheap lithographic prints and engravings associated with the printing district of Battala in Calcutta.[72]

Initially, the finest paintings or sculptures of the entire world were reproduced in *Probasi* and the works chosen reflected (as well as created) that 'infatuation with European Classical and Renaissance art' that characterized the aspirational middle classes of the era.[73] Even before he could read properly, Nirad Chaudhuri recalled, he had encountered Raphael's Madonnas on the pages of *Probasi* and late in life, those prints were still imprinted on his mind.[74] But although Chaudhuri did not mention it, it was not just great Western art that was reproduced in the magazines for Bengal's new bourgeoisie. Noting that Indians were scandalously ignorant about the life and culture of regions other than their own, Ramananda Chatterji decided that one way of resolving this (without expecting every Indian to learn multiple languages) was to publish artworks from every part of India. The universal language of art could help strengthen the bonds between different subcontinental cultures and engender a feeling of national unity.[75] Chatterji's nationalism was initially very cosmopolitan—Indian art was given its due in his magazines but not at the expense of European art—but from the time of the swadeshi movement, it became exclusively indigenist and, as we shall see in the next chapter, the works of Abanindranath Tagore and the so-called Bengal School were all that *Probasi* or *Modern Review* deigned to highlight.[76]

But whether cosmopolitan or narrowly indigenist, the nationalist project could not do without half-tone reproductions and Chatterji, who had a sharp eye for detail, visual appeal, and layout, considered

Upendrakishore's half-tone blocks to be the finest. Even before 1908, when *Probasi* and *Modern Review* were printed and published from Allahabad, the half-tone blocks required by the magazines were supplied from Calcutta by Upendrakishore.[77] Half-tone technology in Bengal, in short, was a tool for cultural enhancement and nation-building, not simply the means to entertain, evoke immediacy, or to encourage consumerism. Although the technology, of course, had come from the West, Bengali print culture did not use it to reproduce 'portraits of nobodies' for a mass readership and reserved it for the dissemination of aesthetic and nationalist values to the upper and middle classes.

The Global, the Peripheral, and the Colonial–Modern

For Upendrakishore, 'process' work was a craft rather than an industry and he regarded himself not merely as the proprietor of his block-making business but as the master craftsman.[78] Such a situation was already unthinkable in Britain. In the large process firms of the late nineteenth century, hordes of anonymous workers laboured under the supervision of foremen who, in turn, reported to managers, who were not expected to have any understanding of the craft itself. No process firm was associated with the name of a master artisan and each piece of work was subdivided into separate tasks and executed by multiple workers. This, of course, enhanced productivity: one well-known company produced 60,000 blocks per year, an output no individual craftsman could ever have matched. Nor did those who actually crafted the blocks have any contact with those who had produced the images or commissioned the blocks. Rarely did a British process firm operate a printing and publishing business in the small-scale, artisanal manner that Upendrakishore and his descendants would do in Calcutta.[79]

Despite the small scale of his enterprise, Upendrakishore aimed to be an innovator rather than a mere purveyor. As Rabindranath Tagore commented in 1898, Upendrakishore 'was the first Bengali who learnt the half-tone process—by himself—and quickly succeeded in improving it'.[80] He was very different from those colonial entrepreneurs (including, as we shall see, his own brother-in-law Hemendramohan Bose) who confined their embrace of modernity to disseminating the latest Western technologies to their compatriots.

When Upendrakishore began his investigations into the half-tone process in the mid-1890s, the technology was still fairly new everywhere but in extensive demand. Many technical and theoretical issues concerning the process, as Sukumar Ray was to remark in a tribute to his father, remained to be resolved.[81] The first English book on half-tone (by William Gamble, writing under the pseudonym Julius Verfasser) had come out only in 1894 and experts remained undecided about the underlying physics of the technology for quite some time.[82] Much research was being done on it all over the world but not in academic institutes and laboratories. It was the trade itself that conducted this research and it was published in what were essentially trade journals.[83] Upendrakishore fit right into this mould. Despite his location in colonial Calcutta and his lack of an academic scientific identity, he became a significant figure in the global history of half-tone research within only a few years of commencing his entirely solitary exploration of the technology, winning praise in Britain for displaying 'not only a clear grasp of the subject' but for suggesting 'new methods of work'.[84]

These encomia came from William Gamble (1864–1933), a pioneer of the half-tone process in Britain and one of its most influential advocates.[85] After publishing his textbook *The Half-Tone Process* in 1894 under the pseudonym Julius Verfasser, Gamble had founded the *Process Work Year Book*, an annual illustrated review of all photomechanical processes that, after several title changes, became *The Penrose Annual*. It was particularly notable for its state-of-the-art coverage— *Penrose* was discussing colour photography and colour printing as early as in 1899—and Upendrakishore was a regular contributor to it.[86] 'The standardizing of half-tone methods in recent years has largely followed the lines indicated by him and many of his suggestions have been adopted in current practice,' remarked Ramananda Chatterji in his obituary of Upendrakishore.[87] That claim was an exaggeration but Upendrakishore's international reputation as an expert on half-tone photography was a fact.

One issue on which his research was pioneering was the ideal distance between the ruled screen and the photosensitive plate recording the dotted image. If the screen and the plate touched each other, then the dots would not vary in size and the gradation of tones in the original would not be captured. The screen had to be placed at a certain distance from the plate, so as to translate the tonality of the original into a variable pattern of dots.[88] The problem was that there was no theoretical explanation of the different effects produced by different screen distances and no universally agreed method of calculating the right distance. Of the methods available, an American handbook of 1907 declared, Upendrakishore Ray's 'automatic screen indicator which, when once set, will indicate all subsequent screen distances', was 'unique'.[89] When the Penrose Company supplied new cameras to the Photographic and Printing Crafts Department of the Manchester Municipal School of Technology—where Sukumar Ray would later be a student—it equipped one of the cameras with Upendrakishore's device.[90] But the screen distance was not the only important determinant of the quality of a half-tone image—the use of proper diaphragms (which determined the size of the lens aperture) was every bit as important. Upendrakishore devoted much time and effort to determine how their use could be optimized and by experimenting with different diaphragms and screen distances, discovered how to split each half-tone dot into four, which led to great improvements in the quality of the printed image.[91] William Gamble marvelled at the 'mathematical exactness' of his insights, declaring that the research on diaphragms and the screen indicator constituted 'the best piece of work Mr Ray has done'.[92]

Also remarkable was Upendrakishore's modified screen. It had become the norm for the lines on the half-tone screen to cross one another at ninety degrees. There was no mathematical rationale for this and, as Gamble remarked, it showed how half-tone workers could 'get into a rut, and keep in it, by accepting a thing because "everyone says so", or "everyone uses it"'.[93] Upendrakishore suggested that if the lines crossed each other at sixty degrees instead, then the tonal variations of the original were captured with greater fidelity. Unfortunately, Gamble revealed, despite Upendrakishore being the first to propose this valuable modification, 'Mr Arthur Schulze of St Petersburg, forestalled him by obtaining German and British patents on it last year [1903].'[94] Upendrakishore himself merely commented that 'to the craft it matters little who gets the credit for a particular invention', while Gamble pointed out that although Schulze had beaten Upendrakishore to the patent, the sixty-degree screen gave its best results only when used with a diaphragm designed by Upendrakishore.[95] Still, it was Schulze's screen that was soon being hailed, even by the very same American handbook that praised Upendrakishore's screen-distance indicator, for allowing 'fifteen per cent more dots in a given area' and thereby improving the tonal quality of the printed image.[96]

There have long been rumours, especially in Bengal, that Schulze had plagiarized Upendrakishore's work.[97] There is no solid evidence to support these rumours—or to disprove them definitively. Leaving aside that undecidable question, it is worth pointing out that even without any plagiarism, simultaneous discoveries and innovations are only to be expected in a rapidly developing and commercially profitable field such as photomechanical reproduction.[98] Quick patenting was essential to establish priority but for somebody in Upendrakishore's location, taking out an international patent was easier said than done. Even in England, Germany, or the US, patent law was complex and unsatisfactory at the time, especially for printing processes.[99] (Within India, patenting was not even an option for Upendrakishore because the Indian Patents and Designs Act was promulgated only in 1911.[100]) There is evidence that he did ask William Gamble for assistance with patenting but for reasons that remain unclear, nothing ever happened and Upendrakishore's work was gradually eclipsed.[101]

After his death, the Penrose Company's monthly *Process Work and Electrotyping* praised his 'scientific mind' and called him 'quite an original investigator of half-tone problems'.[102] Compare that sentence and its eloquent 'quite' with what the same newsletter had written about him more than a decade ago: 'He is far ahead of European and American workers in originality and this is the more surprising when it is considered how far he is from the hub centres of process work, which has necessitated his dependence on reading and experiment.'[103] The latter comment and others like it are often quoted by Upendrakishore's hagiographers to establish the eminence of their hero but Upendrakishore's transient Western reputation deserves deeper analysis for what it can tell us about the non-Western innovator's place in metropolitan discourse and practice. One obviously cannot generalize from the experience of one individual, but certain points emerge from Upendrakishore's encounter with the West that are suggestive of a broader pattern and deserve further exploration by specialists in the transnational history and historical sociology of technology.

The first point to note is that lone researchers in peripheral locations could win Western recognition, but only in certain circumstances. The field of research had to be in a developing but still immature state, with unanswered questions of theoretical or practical relevance that could be successfully resolved with relatively few resources. One cannot easily imagine a nineteenth-century Calcutta artisan being feted in London for his pioneering contributions to, say, shipbuilding or the chemistry of dyestuffs. But half-tone technology, although developing rapidly, still had its mysteries and it was possible for Upendrakishore to elucidate some of them in his workshop without needing a great deal of capital or any institutional support. And because of their own professional and commercial interests, Western practitioners were ready to treat his proposals with respect. What he did not have, however, was any agency over the international dissemination of his work. He was reliant on the patronage of the well-connected William Gamble, who was generous with praise and editorial space but could not (or would not) help him formalize his ownership of his innovations. Even if he had helped, Upendrakishore would have needed professional assistance to navigate the complexities of patent laws and it is not at all certain that he could have done so from Calcutta or been able to afford the costs of engaging an agent in London.

At home, needless to say, his experience was very different. He was awarded a 'Special Gold Medal' as well as a regular one for his half-tone innovations in the 'Mechanical Engravings and Appliances' category of the Indian Industrial and Agricultural Exhibition of 1906–7 and, of course, his local Bengali clients were loyal.[104] His business obviously prospered but probably not as greatly as one might expect from the lack of any local competition.[105] Here again, one may wish to emphasize the man's nobility and lack of greed but it may be more useful to remind ourselves not only of the limited demand for photomechanical reproduction in the Bengali market but also of Upendrakishore's artisanal identity and style. He did not necessarily run a one-man show and there is some truth to Marie Seton's claim that Upendrakishore trained 'a generation of highly skilled craftsmen who would become the finest printers in Bengal'.[106] Writing on the occasion of his birth centenary in 1963, Kedarnath Chatterji asserted that although the business of U. Ray & Sons may have long disappeared, many who now led in the field of printing and engraving in India had been trained there and their current prominence was due entirely to the theoretical and practical training they had received from Upendrakishore and Sukumar.[107]

But despite the availability of assistance from people he had himself trained, Upendrakishore does not seem to have believed that good half-tone blocks could be manufactured on an industrial scale.

As he remarked once, 'it is very easy to make an indifferent half-tone block but really quite difficult to make one that would produce a beautiful, smoothly graded picture'. The difference between the two, he observed, was comparable to that between an educated man and a labourer.[108] Upendrakishore's blocks were commodities, to be sure, but they could not be produced quickly or in large numbers, and certainly not by 'labourers'. This, of course, was entirely opposed to contemporary Western practice where, as we saw earlier, blocks were being produced in their hundreds by workers whose technical or artistic skills were not particularly high.

The history of Upendrakishore's photomechanical innovations also urges us to reconsider the postcolonial consensus that 'our' modernity was largely, or even entirely derivative. Upendrakishore's explorations certainly commenced under foreign tutelage and he could well have conducted a successful half-tone business in Calcutta on the strength of what he had derived from imported resources. Instead, he sought to improve and extend the resources of the craft for the entire world. No matter how briefly or how incompletely, his innovations were recognized as significant from the *metropolitan* perspective, which, for Upendrakishore's generation, was the same as *universal* recognition. In one of the few scholarly explorations of this colonially skewed universalism, Benjamin Zachariah has shown how Indians tended—and perhaps still tend—to regard metropolitan discourses and institutions, especially in science and technology, as untainted by colonialism and, therefore, of universal significance. Regarded as incapable of original intellectual (particularly scientific) work by British colonials, Indians craved recognition from Western institutions, learned societies, scholarly journals, and artists, intellectuals, and scientists. Obviously, only a few succeeded in that quest but for those who did, no matter to how small an extent and for how short a duration, it was the ultimate prize, not only for themselves but for their nation.[109] Universalism, in other words, flowed into nationalism and vice versa. The universalist aspirations of Upendrakishore, as also of Jagadischandra Bose and, for a later period, of Upendrakishore's grandson, Satyajit, can help us appreciate how 'derivative' and 'original' or 'universal' and 'national' were not necessarily mutually exclusive categories but could be dialectically related, with the flow of the dialectic being determined by the realities, perceptions, and, not infrequently, misperceptions of colonial subjection.

The Children of Modernity

Historian R.H. Tawney once remarked that the true character of any social philosophy is evident from its treatment of the poor and of children.[110] Similarly, one could argue that nothing indicates the social priorities of a period better than the literature (and other entertainment) that it produces for its children. Printing came to India only in the nineteenth century and before then, children were reliant on mythological and folk tales narrated by their grandmothers, mothers, aunts, and sisters.[111] Printed books became available only after 1817 and these were mostly textbooks produced by the Calcutta School Book Society (a non-official organization led by the philanthropist David Hare and eminent 'natives' but with funding from the colonial state) for use in the new schools established by the Calcutta School Society.[112] The Society's first publication was the three-volume *Nitikatha* (Moral Tales, 1818), followed by various compendia of great lives, fables, and parables.[113] Magazines for Bengali children appeared soon after the establishment of printing, the earliest of them being missionary publications that naturally concentrated on transmitting Christian values and ideas.[114] The earliest indigenous magazines for children were more secular but their worthy contents—history, moral tales, geography, science, and natural history—and heavily Sanskritized Bengali offered little entertainment to their readers.[115]

Despite their high moral tone, some of these early publications could be startlingly unpuritanical: words like *beshya* or *ganika* (prostitute), for example, appeared in the first volume of *Nitikatha* and even in 1863, a publication of the School Book Society alluded, in a passage derived from Kalidasa, to a lustful woman (*kamuki*) braving a storm for an assignation with her lover. Generally speaking, childhood in premodern agricultural societies was not regarded as qualitatively different from adulthood and the concept of children being innocent and in need of protection from the sordid realities of life emerged only later.[116] The redefinition of childhood was fundamental to the reform of Indian domesticity in the modern era and the reform of children's literature was of central importance.[117] It was not only the obscene that was eliminated. Works such as Madanmohan Tarkalankar's famous primer *Shishu-Siksha* (1849–50) censored anything irrational or superstitious, even geese laying golden eggs or cunning jackals.[118] The moralism and rationalism of the new children's literature reflected the new, 'English-educated' middle class's desire to distance itself from the ribaldries of street culture as well as from the refined eroticism of classical Sanskrit literature.[119]

Child-rearing became a vital issue in bhadralok families, with some encouraging regimes of unrelieved solemnity and moral rigour, and others advocating the encouragement of rationality, gentility, and moral uprightness through eclectic educational programmes that included 'healthy' entertainment.[120] An unregulated exposure to the world and its messy realities was obviously undesirable but a regulated encounter could be brought about by harnessing literature and print culture in the service of children. The project complemented that of educating women, the aim of both being the creation of a true civil society, where men and women would participate equally and which would be constantly replenished by young people inculcated with the 'right' values from childhood. And Brahmos were as prominent in one as they were in the other. Surveying the growth of children's literature in late nineteenth-century Bengal, Partha Mitter noted their predominance not simply as writers for children but as founders of institutions devoted to the 'moral management' of childhood from Sunday schools to children's magazines.[121]

In 1878, Keshab Sen founded *Balakbandhu*, which was the first real magazine for children in Bengali and included stories, poems, and riddles, in addition to more conventional pedagogical material.[122] The magazine, which began as a fortnightly but turned into a monthly from December 1881, was also the first to include pieces by its young readers.[123] This was followed by Pramadacharan Sen's monthly *Sakha* in 1883 and then, in 1885, by the Tagore family's *Balak*, edited by Gyanadanandini Devi (1850–1941), one of the earliest examples of the Bengali New Woman, but actually run by its 'manager', the young Rabindranath Tagore.[124] Convinced that children needed to read *everything* and not only what they could comprehend, Rabindranath filled *Balak* with material that other magazines, then or later, would consider unsuitable for children.[125] While the magazine did feature some child-friendly content, one wonders what average boys or girls would have made of an article on the Gladstone government's Indian policy or on using the income tax to raise money for the many wars of the Raj.[126] Perhaps not surprisingly, *Balak*, after only a year, ended its independent existence.[127]

These were the years when Bengali children's literature was entering into its golden period, albeit guided by the un-Tagorean norm of providing children with age-appropriate material.[128] *Sakha* was still being published and in 1893, it was joined by the new magazine *Sathi*, the two merging in 1894 to become *Sakha-o-Sathi*, which published what may have been the first Bengali 'thriller' for children.[129] A year after *Sakha-o-Sathi* came *Mukul*, a venture conceived by the teachers (all young women) of a Brahmo Sunday school, encouraged by Ramananda Chatterji and Jagadischandra Bose, and edited by Sivanath Sastri, who had also edited *Sakha* for a while.[130] Thus, all the different denominations of the Brahmo community were prominent in the creation of Bengali children's periodicals and it was this tradition that would culminate with the Sadharan Brahmo Upendrakishore's *Sandesh* in 1913.

Most of this new generation of children's writers and editors found Madanmohan Tarkalankar's total rejection of myths and fantasy to be too extreme and evolved a *via media* retaining a great deal of traditional material but cleansed of what they considered to be obscene, transgressive, or socially regressive. 'Tradition', when carefully processed, would sustain today's children and thereby lead to the emergence of a vastly better nation where the riches of modernity would be securely rooted in—and synthesized with—the best elements of indigenous culture.[131] The goal was to help the child grow into a rational, moral, and culturally complete adult—authentically Bengali, deeply Indian, but also confidently cosmopolitan and progressive.[132] Fun and games, poems and tales were as essential to the development of such individuals as were piety, science, and refinement.[133] The literary work of Upendrakishore Ray, his family, and their descendants would be guided by these convictions.

Reflecting on Upendrakishore on his birth centenary, Kedarnath Chatterji (son of Ramananda Chatterji, the editor of *Probasi* and *Modern Review*) remarked that his pen seemed to move with equal felicity from rural legends to distant galaxies, from prehistoric animals to modern science.[134] Upendrakishore, as we saw, commenced his literary career with pieces on science and natural history for Pramadacharan Sen's *Sakha* but his range soon broadened.[135] By 1900, he was contributing folktales, plays, stories, and articles on diverse themes to virtually every children's magazine of the time.[136] Although many of his non-fiction pieces were drawn from foreign sources and others were derived from ancient Indian texts such as the

Mahabharata, Upendrakishore researched each theme diligently and, as the *Modern Review* remarked in its obituary, was not 'a mere compiler or translator'.[137]

His literary work is what most people remember today but it is important to appreciate that for him, it was fully integrated with his other interests. Indeed, as we saw, he may have developed his interest in photomechanical reproduction at least partly because of the disappointing reproduction of the illustrations in his child-friendly version of the Ramayana. His second book was *Sekaler Katha* (Tales of the Past, 1903), an illustrated account of prehistoric animals based on articles on palaeontology that he had published previously in the magazine *Mukul*.[138] In some ways, this book summed up everything that was notable about Upendrakishore's approach to writing for children. Readers, he hoped, would not only enjoy the book but learn from it— the true story of the earth's prehistory, he remarked, was far more entertaining than fiction. The striking frontispiece depicting the Archaeopteryx in colour and the many black-and-white illustrations of dinosaurs had been drawn by the author himself—and not, as he emphasized, lifted from foreign books.[139] Thomas Holland of the Geological Survey of India remarked that Upendrakishore's pictures of dinosaurs were so accurate that they could be used to illustrate science textbooks and Alexander Pedler, the chemist who was now the Bengal Government's Director of Public Instruction, was impressed by the excellence of the printing. Scientific accuracy and good printing aside, the pictures were also praised for their aesthetic qualities by the noted artist Raja Ravi Varma.[140]

The book was no less notable in literary terms. Although Upendrakishore wrote in the formal *sadhu bhasa*, its rigours were compensated by his conversational style, simple phraseology, and humorous analogies. Upendrakishore's translations of the names of dinosaurs—*bajra kumir* for brontosaurus, *trisringanon* for triceratops, *puratan pakhi* for archaeopteryx, or *machh-kumir* for ichthyosaurus— were particularly brilliant in their vernacular simplicity.[141] Scientifically, the book was fairly impressive for its time but although it discussed the successive waves of different species in the history of the earth, there was no mention of Darwin or of evolutionary biology.[142] Although the scientific content of *Sekaler Katha* is now out of date, the book remains interesting for demonstrating how art, literature, science, and book-production signified different sides of a single pedagogical project for Upendrakishore, even though he did not yet have the resources to bring all of it under his exclusive control. He made the blocks for his illustrations, for instance, but he still did not own a press where he could supervise his own printing.[143]

Upendrakishore returned to the epics for his next book, bringing out a lavishly illustrated edition of the children's *Ramayana* in 1907. He had revised his earlier version with the encouragement and assistance of no less a figure than Rabindrananth Tagore, and the text was now almost twice the length of the first edition.[144] There was a great deal of gentle humour in the narrative and it did not leave out anything too crucial but was, perhaps, not as dramatic as it could have been. One could not say that for the brilliant *Chhotto Ramayan*, the Ramayana in verse that he published in 1910 for even younger children. Here, Upendrakishore revealed himself to be a master of different kinds of poetic metre, which he used imaginatively to contrast different episodes.[145] The mauling of enemy forces and the often bloody slaughter of the battlefield were not noticeably diluted but the epic's greatest tragic moment—where Sita forsakes the world and enters into the earth—was left out.[146]

Between the two versions of the Ramayana came *Chheleder Mahabharat* (The Mahabharata for Children), which, again, had gained from the input of Rabindranath Tagore, and *Mahabharater Galpa* (Tales from the Mahabharata).[147] Upendrakishore's language in these books, declared Buddhadev Bose, was in perfect harmony 'with the child's mind, never exceeding its understanding but without omitting anything vital'.[148] But many episodes had in fact been left out of the work, sixty-four of which were presented in *Mahabharater Galpa*. Both books bore the marks of censorship. In his preface to *Chheleder Mahabharat*, Upendrakishore acknowledged that sections of the epic had been 'draped' before being presented to boys and girls, while many of the stories in *Mahabharater Galpa* had been 'simply impossible to recount in full to young boys and girls'.[149] In the tale of Menaka abandoning her daughter (born from illicit congress with a king), Upendrakishore's version simply recounted the discovery of an abandoned baby and commented: 'We have no need to be concerned with the kind of people who could do such a cruel, mean thing to a child.' Stories with scatological elements were also bowdlerized. In a tale that featured an entire army being prevented by a curse from urinating or defecating, Upendrakishore merely mentioned a sudden illness that was not very severe, but still sufficed to drive the soldiers insane in panic and discomfort.[150]

The warrior values of the Mahabharata, however, were left untouched in his adaptations. Bhisma's abduction of the three princesses Amba, Ambika, and Ambalika and the forcible marriage of two of them to his brother Bichitrabirjya were cited as evidence of Bhisma's courage and magnificence. Later, we find Krishna praising the warrior custom of carrying off women as a sign of strength.[151] The barriers of caste (and class) were presented without any overt endorsement but with no criticism either.[152] The text was redolent, too, with the Bengali bhadralok disdain for Hindi-speaking working classes: the man-eating ogre (*rakshasa*) Hirimbo, who threatens to eat the Pandavas, speaks in the mixture of broken Bengali and rustic Hindi that all Bengalis of Upendrakishore's time (and later) associated with upcountry menials working in Calcutta. Hirimbo's sister, Hirimba, however, is allowed to speak in pristine Bengali, no doubt because she is a good rakshasa who tries to save the Pandavas from her brother and eventually marries one of them.[153]

From the later decades of the nineteenth century into the twentieth, many Bengali children's writers would turn repeatedly to the two ancient Indian epics, the Ramayana and the Mahabharata, and the collection of ancient texts known collectively as the Puranas. As Bratati Chakravarty has argued, there was a widespread conviction at the time that children would not discover their innate Indianness unless they were acquainted with the exemplary—and very readable—tales of virtue, nobility, and courage from ancient India that the two epics and the Puranas were crammed with.[154] Other motivations, including Hindu revivalist ones, were at work for some authors.[155] Upendrakishore, however, was not just trying to present the classics to his young Bengali readers as treasured relics from the past. His use of contemporary allusions—when describing Hastinapur, for instance, he felt no hesitation in commenting that it used to be located very near Delhi—suggests that he was seeking to bring about a full integration of the classics with contemporary life.[156] But the past had to be processed for consumption by today's youth. The fact that Upendrakishore censored the epics, however, is less interesting than the nature of what was omitted and what was not. The elimination of erotic and scatological content was, of course, predictable but the retention of casteist and violent content was rather more surprising and inconsistent with the progressive values professed by Upendrakishore and his peers. Perhaps, as a Brahmo writing in an age of resurgent Hinduism and swadeshi-inspired indigenism,

Upendrakishore was anxious not to be accused of disfiguring the great Hindu epics.

Even in the secular sphere, Bengalis of the swadeshi era were growing increasingly concerned with recovering their traditions, especially local and vernacular ones. Perhaps the greatest product of this quest was a text addressed primarily to children: Dakshinaranjan Mitra Majumdar's *Thakurmar Jhuli* (Grandma's Bag of Tales, 1907), an anthology of folk tales that children of the Mymensingh region had been hearing for many generations from their mothers, grand-mothers, and aunts.[157] It was decorated with Mitra Majumdar's own illustrations, which, in keeping with the indigenist spirit, followed patterns used in the decorations (*alpana*) used in rural homes and were reproduced by traditional wood-engravings rather than 'pro-cess' blocks.[158] In his foreword to the anthology, Rabindranath Tagore, still active in the swadeshi movement, welcomed this initiative to recover and preserve the 'ancient simplicity' of these tra-ditional tales.[159] Many other writers followed Mitra Majumdar, whether in making their own collections from current oral traditions or in attempting to replicate the themes, format, and style of the tales in *Thakurmar Jhuli*.[160] One of the most successful of these was Upendrakishore's *Tuntunir Boi* (The Tailor-Bird's Book, 1910). Like *Thakurmar Jhuli*, it presented a series of folk tales from the Mymensingh region but Upendrakishore selected very different kinds of stories and, targeting a much younger readership, he por-trayed a radically different world.[161]

The man-eating monsters of *Thakurmar Jhuli* were absent from *Tuntunir Boi*, as were the adventurous boys braving untold dangers. The stories portrayed the imagined, timeless village of the Bengali imagination, populated by farmers, labourers, and ordinary house-holders, often without specific names and obviously intended to rep-resent types rather than individuals.[162] And there were animals, infused with speech and sentience but also frequently depicted as stupid, greedy, or cowardly.[163] The first few stories of *Tuntunir Boi* describe the antics of a clever little tailor-bird saving itself and its family from fiercer animals, whether cats or humans. Although the tailor-bird was absent from the later stories in the volume, they too highlighted the small defeating the big or the influential purely by their superior intelligence.[164]

The critic Alokeranjan Dasgupta argued that Upendrakishore's fables lacked the ruthless objectivity of Aesop and were pervaded by a

fundamentally Indian conviction of the ultimate fellowship of all crea-
tures.[165] This somewhat orientalist interpretation ignores the possibility that the morals Upendrakishore wished to convey might, unlike
Aesop's, have been subtly political. The tyrannical king's attempts to
control and punish the mischievous tuntuni bird, Supriya Goswami
has recently argued, may well have symbolized the efforts of the
British to suppress swadeshi activism in Bengal, while Majantali
Sarkar, a clever cat who ruled over tigers by pretending to be the king's
minister and tax collector represented the zamindar, 'the oppressive
native intermediary figure and agent of British rule'.[166] Such subtly
anti-colonial themes were not unlikely in a collection published in
1910 but despotic kings and brave animals have been staple ingredients of all fairy tales for centuries and if *Tuntunir Boi* was a swadeshi
text, then it was very successful in conveying its political allusions
through motifs that were ostensibly universal and timeless.

   Tuntunir Boi contained only some of Upendrakishore's folktales.
He wrote many others, some of which were quite complex. In
'Saatmaar Paloan', for example, a rather stupid and cowardly man
acquires an undeserved fame after mistaking a tiger—who had been
scared by somebody else for an unrelated reason—for a horse and
riding on him. It is a story almost worthy of Woody Allen in the way
its simpleton protagonist wins acclaim through a sequence of acci-
dents and serendipitious events. Another story, which was made into
a famous film by his grandson, Satyajit, also had a couple of simple-
minded protagonists but they acquired genuine singing-and-dancing
talents and other magical powers through the kindness of a ghost-
king.[167] Their adventures led them to distant lands and the story
ended with them marrying two princesses. The wish-fulfilment qualities of fairy stories were blended here with adventure and the pica-
resque but nothing too brutal or frightening.

   Upendrakishore was not simply trying to recover and disseminate indigenous traditions but to redefine the past for modern children. The traditional fairy-tales of Bengal and their often bloody
shenanigans were acceptable up to a point but man-eating ogres,
ghosts, and spirits, brutal stepmothers, and all such staples had to be
eliminated. Even when the old folk-tales avoided sexual and scatological themes, their attitude on gender was problematic. Although the
vast majority of these tales were told by women, the female characters, with very rare exceptions, were mere models of 'submission and
docility' or downright evil.[168] The new children's literature aspired to

be much broader, more diverse, and more progressive, without losing their amusing and outlandish qualities.[169] But even renovated folk-tales were insufficient to mould today's children.

They needed some wish-fulfilling entertainment, to be sure, but they also had to be led gently into appreciating the marvels of science, technology, and rationality.[170] From the very beginning of his literary career to the end of his life, Upendrakishore wrote copiously on scientific topics, ranging from physics, chemistry, and biology to geology, palaeontology, and, especially, astronomy.[171] He was himself an enthusiastic amateur astronomer who taught all his children to identify the stars and planets and, even when on holiday in the upcountry town of Giridi, found the time to offer a lecture-demonstration on astronomy.[172] Interestingly, Upendrakishore, in his published essays on astronomy, maintained no hard-and-fast boundary between 'science' and 'myth' or between 'tradition' and 'modernity'. He referred often to ancient mythology—for instance, the notion found in the Mahabharata, that the stars were the congealed souls of the pious and devout, or the Greek myths of Perseus and Andromeda.[173] The pursuit of modernity, for Upendrakishore, was not the pursuit of what was new but rather, a judicious synthesis of the old and the new, the rational and the mythical, the traditional and the contemporary.[174]

Nor was Upendrakishore's literary style overtly modern. Lucid and conversational, it emulated the informality of a kathak—the storyteller of traditional, pre-literate cultures who literally 'told' stories to an assembled audience, often with dramatic or musical flourishes. Often, as in retelling the Mahabharata, Upendrakishore addressed his readers directly, especially in descriptive passages, asking them, for instance, to imagine a scene of splendour that could not be described adequately in words, or to follow a king on a secret expedition. Once, describing a palatial chamber, he confessed: 'and the decorations inside it were so amazing that I cannot even comprehend them, let alone explain them to you'.[175] The narrator also thought nothing of pausing briefly to explain an unfamiliar word, as happened frequently in Upendrakishore's Chheleder Ramayan as well as Chheleder Mahabharat.[176] This was a kathak who was a storyteller as well as, when required, a friendly teacher.

And when words reached their limit, the task of explanation was assumed by illustrations, which, for Upendrakishore, were organic elements of the text and comfortingly familiar.[177] Upendrakishore's gods and demons were all very human and his humans were everyday types, very ordinary but often amusing.[178] The humour of his pictures, remarked his grandson (and trained artist) Satyajit, was very gentle and entirely free of sarcasm or malice.[179] This was not just a reflection of Upendrakishore's own personality but of his larger ideological project. The sacred had to be domesticated, divine horrors had to be diluted, human irrationality had to be fought—but subtly, delicately, gently, and without any wholesale rejection of Hindu tradition. Humour was of paramount importance to this task but not *every* kind of humour. 'A man who can amuse people without hurting them is truly worthy of admiration', Upendrakishore had remarked in a very early article in *Sakha*, and he remained true to that principle for his whole life.[180] To amuse without causing pain and to reform without preaching were two sides of the same coin for Upendrakishore.

Sandesh: Building the Nation of the Future

Upendrakishore was a regular contributor to virtually every children's magazine published in his lifetime. Most of these magazines believed in combining education with entertainment or, perhaps, in educating *by* entertaining. As Sivanath Sastri, who edited *Mukul*, averred, the best way to educate children was to appeal to their imagination, whether in presenting the facts of history or the principles of an ethical life.[181] This idea, like the conviction that children's literature needed to allow for the immature intellects of children, went back to John Locke, who had called for books and games that would entice children into learning.[182] The well-illustrated and attractively laid out magazine—the half-tone blocks were all made by Upendrakishore— was designed to provide what schools and textbooks did not, and to do so in an appetizing and inspiring way. 'Harmless entertainment' (*nirdosh amod*) was part of the blend.[183] Although it carried many pieces by eminent contributors—Rabindranath Tagore, Jagadischandra Bose, Atulprasad Sen, and, of course, Upendrakishore himself— *Mukul* was not too lofty to exclude riddles and puzzles, and its young readers were encouraged to contribute to its pages.[184] The magazine was not narrowly nationalistic and Nirad Chaudhuri recalled how, as a child, he had first read about Theseus and other characters of classical Greek mythology in *Mukul*.[185]

Mukul was the leading children's magazine in the early twentieth century—*Sakha-o-Sathi* had ceased publication in 1898 and many of the new magazines founded in the twentieth century, such as *Prakriti*, published by the New Dispensation wing of the Brahmo Samaj from 1907 to about 1915, or *Toshini*, published from Dhaka, did not have much impact.[186] There was room in the market for another children's magazine and Upendrakishore, now fairly prosperous and pushing fifty, decided to seize that opportunity, putting all he had learnt over his career into the new venture.[187] The name he chose for his magazine was *Sandesh*, a Bengali word meaning news (or information) as well as a much-loved sweet, indicating his allegiance to the Lockean programme of sweetening knowledge so as to make it palatable. In the first editorial, Upendrakishore wrote in 1913: 'The edible *sandesh* benefits us in two ways. It is tasty and it gives us strength. This magazine will justify its name only if it possesses the same two qualities.'[188] The contents, ranging from archaeology to science, from biographies to mythological tales, from translations of European literature to original stories, plays, and riddles, fulfilled the promise of the title and the editorial.[189] *Sakha* and its successors had also aimed for diversity of content but each issue of *Sandesh* included material from many more genres. *Sandesh* was also richer in essays on scientific and related subjects and while it continued to use the formal sadhu bhasa for mythological tales and non-fiction, it was pioneering in using *chalit bhasa* for general fiction.[190]

And, of course, no other magazine for children could compete with the production values of Upendrakishore's magazine. 'Just compare an old copy of *Sakha* with any illustrated magazine of today,' remarked Upendrakishore's anonymous obituarist in *Sandesh* (probably Sukumar Ray). 'You will immediately see the immense difference in pictures. The thick lines in those old pictures are not to be seen in the beautiful illustrations of today. Perhaps you are not aware that it was Upendrakishore who first introduced the methods for printing such pictures in this country.'[191] Leela Majumdar, one of the editors of the third incarnation of *Sandesh*, once ruefully admitted that what Upendrakishore had achieved in the early twentieth century—a magazine printed beautifully on thick, cream-laid paper and accompanied by state-of-the-art half-tone pictures, some of them in colour—was simply unattainable in the 1980s.[192] Most of the contents of *Sandesh's* earliest issues was also provided by Upendrakishore himself. Written and illustrated almost entirely by him and printed with his own blocks, *Sandesh* combined his literary gifts, artistic abilities, techno-logical skill, and artisanal insistence on doing everything with his own hands. Bankimchandra Chatterji had also written virtually every-thing carried by his magazine *Bangadarsan* and Pramadacharan Sen, too, had done the same for the earliest issues of *Sakha*.[193] But neither Bankim nor Pramadacharan had been involved so directly with the design and production of their magazines. *Sandesh* was the product of Upendrakishore's own two hands in an almost literal sense, although, as with his book *Sekaler Katha*, the printing of the magazine's earlier issues had to be entrusted to a neighbourhood press.[194]

Soon, however, Upendrakishore was not writing everything pub-lished in *Sandesh*; almost the entire Ray family—his daughters Sukhalata and Punyalata, sons Sukumar, Subinoy, and, Subimal, and brothers Kuladaranjan and Pramadaranjan—became involved with the project. Any list of eminent children's writers in Bengal would include these names, justifying Buddhadev Bose's comment that the Rays seemed to hold a monopoly in the trade of children's litera-ture.[195] It was the existence of *Sandesh* that enabled—perhaps, com-pelled—this family's involvement with children's literature. Sukumar Ray, who was more interested in writing erudite essays in *Probasi* and other magazines until his father's death, switched almost completely to writing for *Sandesh* when he succeeded Upendrakishore as editor.[196] Decades later in the 1960s, Satyajit Ray, by then a celebrated filmmaker, would emerge as a bestselling writer for children simply because the ancestral magazine, which he had revived, needed new material.[197]

Although the first number of *Sandesh* had a print run of 3500 cop-ies, this proved too ambitious. For the rest of Upendrakishore's edi-torship and the earlier part of Sukumar's, only 3000 copies were printed of each issue. It had an immediate impact on its main rival *Mukul*, which reduced its price in 1914 but to no effect: by 1915, only 400 copies were being printed—ironically, at U. Ray & Sons—and the magazine ceased publication in mid-1919.[198] But *Sandesh*, although popular enough, was not necessarily profitable. The price of 2 annas per copy, Kuladaranjan Ray Leela Majumdar, was too low to recoup the production costs, let alone make a profit.[199] The magazine was subsidized by the other activities of U. Ray & Sons and was, in fact, a reformist project complementing Upendrakishore's father-in-law's feminism and nationalism. As Hitendrakishore Raychaudhuri observed, Upendrakishore's devotion to children's literature expressed his personal vision of swadeshi—a fully indigenous but, unlike the swadeshi movement, a spiritually cosmopolitan initiative to provide Bengali children with the kind of 'healthy' entertainment and subtle edification that would help them grow into ideal citizens.[200]

Aiming, at least in part, to improve the young reader's future is, of course, an almost invariable characteristic of most children's literature. In its first editorial, the British *Juvenile Magazine* (founded in 1788) had hoped that its contents would be 'productive not only of your *present* amusement, but of your *future* welfare'.[201] For Upendrakishore, however, the task was not merely pedagogical or literary but an implicitly nationalistic project of improving tomorrow's society by moulding today's children. He was by no means alone in this ambition but arguably, he practised this challenging art far more subtly and enticingly than, say, the editors of *Sakha* or even *Mukul*. As an anonymous writer (presumably Sukumar Ray) wrote in *Sandesh* after its founder's death: 'Driven by the deepest affection for you, he laboured hard and applied all his intelligence and subtlety to educate and entertain you, to improve you by amusing you (*tomadigakey "phurti" diya bhalo koritey*).'[202]

Little of this was nationalistic in an *explicit* sense—the leading writers for children were rarely involved too deeply in nationalist politics—but the goal, undeniably, was to remake Bengal and India by shaping the characters of children. As Dwarakanath Ganguli had once declared, before demanding national independence, it was essential to correct the flaws that had reduced Indians to their current degenerate condition.[203] *Sandesh* sought to combat that degeneracy at its root—childhood. It aimed to create the perfect citizens of the future by improving children's minds, opening their hearts, deepening their cultural roots, and expanding their cosmopolitan consciousness. Literary critic Saroj Bandyopadhyay has observed that the primary goal of *Sandesh* was 'to arouse the child's mind to an awareness beyond and unpolluted by the mechanical system of a semi-capitalist society' and Leela Majumdar thought the magazine's goal was to make the nation's children into 'fearless, robust and truthful' citizens.[204] Providing Bengal's children with the 'right' kind of spiritual nutrition, combining East and West, art and science, fun, morality, and knowledge, was, for Upendrakishore and his successors, the best way to build the India of the future.[205]

While traditional Bengali folk-tales had been full of fierce monsters, Upendrakishore wrote tales of stupid tigers and benign ghosts.

Having noticed that village children were terrified of ghosts and tigers, he wished to help children overcome such 'irrational' fears and portrayed these fearsome entities in his tales as benign or stupid.[206] Supriya Goswami has suggested that for Upendrakishore, the stupid tiger is 'the symbol of a greatly weakened and emasculated Bengal'.[207] In fact, Upendrakishore's stupid tigers were devices for *regenerating* Bengal by infusing courage into the children who would grow up to take charge of the nation. Improvement, of course, also necessitated strategic omissions. During the short period that he edited *Sandesh* (1913–15) Upendrakishore wrote more than twenty stories drawn from the Puranas and it would be hard to tell from the magazine (or, indeed, from any of his other works) that he was not a mainstream Hindu.[208] But he was no admirer of idolatry and made his attitude clear in his characteristically subtle way. In a long travelogue on the seaside resort of Puri, he devoted a great deal of attention to describing the seaside, the ever-changing appearance of the ocean, and the animals to be found in the sea or on the beach. With his usual gentle humour, he also added some descriptions of bathers floundering in the turbulent sea. But the famous temple of Jagannath, which is at least as important a feature of Puri as the sea for ordinary Hindus, hardly appeared in the narrative. In a second, shorter narrative on Puri, he discussed the religious beliefs of the *nuliya*—the local fishermen and bathing guides—but again, left out the temple and the many who visited it for boons from Jagannath.[209] With Dwarakanath Ganguli, there is no difficulty in identifying what he opposed but to discover what Upendrakishore disapproved of, one needs to study his silences.

There was, of course, nothing uniquely Bengali or even Indian about Upendrakishore's approach to children's literature. In early-nineteenth-century Britain, for example, children's books repeatedly emphasized the possibility of social advancement by cultivating 'diligence, thrift, caution, honesty'; later in the century, the child was increasingly perceived as the key to 'the future of the nation and the race'. British anxieties, however, were mostly related to the physical and moral inadequacies of working-class children: 'If the nation was to survive in a competitive and Darwinian world', Hugh Cunningham explains, 'its children would have to become physically fitter to enable them to carry out their destined roles as male workers and soldiers and female wives and mothers'.[210] In late-nineteenth-century Bengal, however, the middle classes were anxious not so much about working-class children but about their own. Although physical fitness was very much on their agenda, the intellectual stimulation and moral training of children were far more important. 'For better or for worse,' wrote a woman in 1901, 'the future of society and of the nation rests on these children of ours. If they are properly educated then nation will follow the path of progress.'[211] It was not just a matter of cramming and examinations but of expanding the personality and intellect of today's child to create the ideal human being and citizen of the future.

Despite its worthy affiliations and impeccable taste, however, there was nothing too overtly stuffy about *Sandesh* in its early years. Writing some four decades later, Buddhadev Bose declared that the fare offered in *Sandesh* was unrivalled in combining deliciousness with nutritional value.[212] During his childhood in East Bengal, Bose recalled, he would run to accost the postman carrying the monthly envelope of *Sandesh*, so desperate was he to get his hands on a new issue. From the multicoloured cover to the final page of riddles and games, the magazine seemed to contain everything that the child's burgeoning sensibility yearned for and all that was needed for children's mental development. He had learnt much from the magazine, said Bose, but the contents were so enjoyable that it never felt like he was being taught anything.[213] That was perhaps the greatest compliment anybody could have paid to Upendrakishore's beloved project but as the years went by, *Sandesh* would change its character and seek to reinvent itself for a new generation and a new, crueller world.

Notes

1.   Satyajit Ray, 'Bhumika', in *Sukumar Sahityasamagra*, 1: ii. Although Upendrakishore had a strong interest in science, this was mostly that of an amateur and popularizer. His own research, as we shall see, was concerned entirely with a specific kind of technology.

2.   The bride was 20 and the bridegroom 22. See Manasi Dasgupta, *Upendrakishore Raychaudhuri (1863–1915)* (Calcutta: Bangiya Sahitya Parishat, 2004), 27.

3.   The Rays, of course, were Kayasthas and, in traditional Hindu societies, not permitted to marry Brahmins. Siddhartha Ghosh, 'Upendrakishore: Shilpi o Karigar', *Ekshan*, 16, no. 6 (1984): 53; and Partha Basu, *Satyajit Ray* (Calcutta: Paschimbanga Bangla Akademi, 2006), 19.

4. When the Kayastha Joytara was asked by relatives to forbid the Brahmin/Brahmo Bidhumukhi from touching her feet in the traditional *pranam*, Joytara retorted: 'Whether she is a Brahmin's daughter or a Muslim's, she has married my son. How can I refuse her my blessings [*payer dhulo*—literally, the dust of my feet]?' See Dasgupta, *Upendrakishore Raychaudhuri*, 34; Leela Majumdar, *Upendrakishore* (Calcutta: Newscript, 1963), 34; and L. Majumdar, *Pakdandi* (Calcutta: Ananda, 1986), 162. For a comparable experience, where the parents of a convert accepted him and his Brahmo bride with joy but never ate with them, see Rajanikanta Guha, *Atmacharit* (Calcutta: Jatindranath Roy, 1949), 266–7.

5. The large house was located virtually opposite the temple of the Sadharan Brahmo Samaj and the entire neighbourhood had come to be known as *Samaj-para* (Samaj neighbourhood) because of the preponderance of Brahmos in the area. See Radharaman Mitra, *Kalikata Darpan*, 2 vols (Calcutta: Subarnarekha, 1980–2004), 1 (1980): 92–115 and 2 (2003): 24–5.

6. Tagore was a student at the Training Academy only for a few months. See Prasantakumar Pal, *Rabijibani: Pratham Khanda*, 1268–84 (Calcutta: Bhurjapatra, 1982), 63–4; and on the other activities occurring in the building, see Mitra, *Kalikata Darpan*, 2 (2004): 23–5, 57.

7. See Sivanath Sastri, *Atmacharit*, edited by Gautam Neogy (Calcutta: Sadharan Brahmo Samaj, 1982), 373, 376. The curriculum included the standard literary subjects but also science, mathematics, art, and music. The kindergarten system was followed as far as practicable and there were lessons in domestic management, sewing, and handicrafts (only for the girls) and various kinds of drill. Although most students were Bengali Brahmos, there were a few students from other parts of India and even, surely unusually for the era, a handful of Muslims. Although the Bengali students came from respectable and moderately affluent families, the School did not appeal to more 'fashionable' parents, who sent their daughters to the Loreto School run by missionaries near Park Street in Central Calcutta. See Punyalata Chakrabarti, *Ekal Jakhhan Shuru Holo* [1964], edited by Jayeeta Bagchi, Abhijit Sen, and Anindita Bhaduri (Calcutta: Dey's, 2007), 23; and for a description of the curriculum, the School's advertisement in *Tattvakaumudi*, 16 Ashar 1813 sak [July 7, 1891], 72 (my thanks to Barun Chattopadhyay for the latter reference). When the Sadharan Brahmo Samaj decided to close the school in 1895 because of financial difficulties, Dwarakanath Ganguli rescued the institution by cashing in his life insurance policy. See Narayan Dutta, *Abalabandhhab-Dwarakanath o Kadambini* (Calcutta: Karuna, 2006), 79.

8. Hemantakumar Adhya, *Upendrakishore Raychaudhuri* (Delhi: Sahitya Akademi, 1997), 13. The unmarried Das lived in various Brahmo households for extended periods. See Bankabihari Kar, *Brahmarpitachitta Swargiya Nabadwipchandra Daser Jibanbrittanta* (Dhaka: Purbabangla Brahmo Samaj, 1926), 28; and Subimal Ray's reminiscences of Das in Kar, *Brahmarpitachitta*

230 THE RAYS BEFORE SATYAJIT

Swargiya, 139–44. On Satischandra Ganguli, see L. Majumdar, *Pakdandi*, 100.

9. See Hemantakumar Adhya, *Sukumar Ray: Jibankatha* (Calcutta: Pustak Bipani, 1990), 22.

10. In 1904, for instance, when Kuladaranjan Ray was widowed, he moved into Upendrakishore's household with his three young children. Earlier, as we have seen, one daughter of Ramkumar Vidyaratna was not only brought up by Bidhumukhi and Upendrakishore but married Upendrakishore's brother Pramadaranjan. See Punyalata Chakrabarti, *Chhelebelar Dinguli* (1958; reprint, Calcutta: Newscript, 1981), 83; L. Majumdar, *Upendrakishore*, 43; and P. Basu, *Satyajit Ray*, 7. There were several similar moves after the collapse of U. Ray & Sons in the mid-1920s and the sale of the 100 Garpar Road house. See L. Majumdar, *Pakdandi*, 175, 199–200. Although this kind of joint family is widely considered to represent immemorial Hindu tradition, historian Tapan Raychaudhuri has shown that it became the norm for upper-caste Bengalis only at the end of the eighteenth century. See Tapan Raychaudhuri, 'Norms of Family Life and Personal Morality among the Bengali Hindu Elite, 1600–1850', in *Aspects of Bengali History and Society*, edited by Rachel Van M. Baumer (Honolulu: University Press of Hawaii, 1975), 13–25, at 14–15.

11. Around 1905, he formalized the division of the estate with Narendrakishore, retaining only the relatively peripheral, less valuable parts of the estate. See Hitendrakishore Raychaudhuri, *Upendrakishore o Masua Ray Paribarer Galpasalpa* (Calcutta: Firma KLM, 1984), 25–6. Later, he sold parts of his share to pay off debts incurred on his photographic and engraving business. See his undated letter in Siddhartha Ghosh, *Karigari Kalpana o Bangali Udyog* (Calcutta: Dey's, 1988), 93. The remaining portions of the estate continued to be owned by the Rays but seem to have been mismanaged. See H. Raychaudhuri, *Upendrakishore*, 89–91.

12. The Permanent Settlement, instituted by the British in the late eighteenth century with the hope that zamindars would become 'improving landlords' if revenue demands were fixed in perpetuity, actually created a class of landowners who lived off the fat of the land without ever significantly investing in it. Generally on the history and socio-economic consequences of the Permanent Settlement, see Ranajit Guha, *A Rule of Property for Bengal: An Essay on the Idea of Permanent Settlement* (Durham, NC: Duke University Press, 1996), especially xiii, xv.

13. See L. Majumdar, *Upendrakishore*, 46.

14. L. Majumdar, *Upendrakishore*, 10.

15. 'The Late Mr U. Ray', 105; Dasgupta, *Upendrakishore Raychaudhuri*, 35–6.

16. Madhurilata Mahalanobis, 'Dada Sukumar Ray', *Korak*, Special issue on Sukumar Ray (2003): 206–9, at 206. Kuladaranjan himself could be puritanical too. When his daughter Madhurilata passed her BA and wanted to

study further, he refused because postgraduate classes of Calcutta University were co–educational. See Mahalanobis, 'Dada Sukumar Ray', 209.

17. P. Chakrabarti, *Ekal Jakhhan Shuru Holo*, 21.

18. Dasgupta, *Upendrakishore Raychaudhuri*, 44.

19. P. Chakrabarti, *Chhelebelar Dinguli*, 84; P. Chakrabarti, *Ekal Jakhhan Shuru Holo*, 21.

20. See Dasgupta, *Upendrakishore Raychaudhuri*, 49; and P. Chakrabarti, *Chhelebelar Dinguli*, 64–5. Hesh, who had trained in Rome, Munich, and Paris, began his career in Calcutta quite auspiciously. He was commissioned to draw portraits of eminent people (among them Debendranath Tagore, Sivanath Sastri, and Sir William Wedderburn) but things must have gone badly wrong at some point, since Hesh soon disappeared from Calcutta under mysterious circumstances. He eventually migrated to Canada but little is known of his life there. Even the date of his death is unknown. See Partha Mitter, *Art and Nationalism in Colonial India, 1850–1922: Occidental Orientations* (Cambridge: Cambridge University Press, 1994), 114–17; and Kamal Sarkar, *Silpi-Saptak* (Calcutta: Banga Sanskriti Sammelan, 1960), 56–66 (many thanks to Sourit Dey and Indrani Majumdar for sharing the latter). For Upendrakishore's analysis of a painting by Hesh of the Mahabharata characters Karna and his mother Kunti, see 'Karna-Kunti Sangbad', *Pradip*, 4 (1308 BE [1901]): 409, http://archiv.ub.uni–heidelberg.de/savifadok/volltexte/2009/878 (accessed on 5 September 2014).

21. Bratati Chakravarty, *Bangla Shishu Sahitya Charcha: Ray Paribar* (Calcutta: Dey Book Store, 1997), 43.

22. Dasgupta, *Upendrakishore Raychaudhuri*, 46.

23. On nineteenth-century parenting advice, see Pradip Kumar Bose, 'Sons of the Nation: Child Rearing in the New Family', in *Texts of Power: Emerging Disciplines in Colonial Bengal*, edited by Partha Chatterjee (Calcutta: Samya, 1996), 118–44.

24. S. Ghosh, 'Upendrakishore', 56–7, 60–2.

25. S. Ghosh, *Karigari Kalpana*, 75–6. Music was only one of the Sunday School's activities. Occasionally, scientist Jagadischandra Bose would conduct classes on science and the children were sometimes taken on trips to the zoo or the botanical gardens. See Adhya, *Upendrakishore Raychaudhuri*, 14. For a description of Upendrakishore's teaching style, see Santa Nag, *Purbasmriti* (Calcutta: Papyrus, 1986), 82–3.

26. Kedarnath Chattopadhyay, 'Satabarshik Sraddhhanjali: Upendrakishore', *Vishwa Bharati Patrika*, 20, no. 2 (1963 [Kartik–Poush 1370 BE]):112. The only pupil Upendrakishore seems to have failed with was young Prasantachandra Mahalanobis, who would later become a close friend of Sukumar Ray's. After it proved impossible to teach young Prasanta 'to sing tunefully', Upendrakishore simply patted the child on his head and asked him to go and play outside. See Shyamasree Lal, '"Sandesh" and the Child's

World of Imagination', *India International Centre Quarterly* 10, no. 4 (1983): 433–42, at 440.

27.   B. Chakravarty, *Bangla Shishu Sahitya Charcha*, 45–6; Hirankumar Sanyal, *Parichoy-er Kuri Bachhar o Anyanya Smritichitra* (Calcutta: Papyrus, 1978), 159.

28.   Niradchandra Chaudhuri, *Atmaghati Bangali: Aji Hotey Satobarsa Agey* (Calcutta: Mitra o Ghosh, 1989), 180–1.

29.   Fox Strangways included several songs by Tagore, of which 'Pratidina taba gathha', 'Prathhama adi taba sakti', and 'Dukhera beshey esechho boley' were translated by Upendrakishore, and the rest by Tagore himself. See A.H. Fox Strangways, *The Music of Hindostan* (Oxford: Clarendon Press, 1914), 161–2, 166. On Fox Strangways and the larger contexts of his project, see Bennett Zon, *Representing Non-Western Music in Nineteenth-Century Britain* (Rochester: University of Rochester Press, 2007), 249–90; and Bob van der Linden, *Music and Empire in Britain and India: Identity, Internationalism, and Cross-Cultural Communication* (New York: Palgrave Macmillan, 2013), 7–13.

30.   Fox Strangways, *Music of Hindostan*, 152 and for the list of ragas, chart facing 151.

31.   'The Late Mr U. Ray', 105. His instructor was Murari Gupta, a well-known pakhwaj player of the time. See B. Chakravarty, *Bangla Shishu Sahitya Charcha*, 46. It is interesting that the only musical instrument Satyajit Ray ever tried to learn systematically was the pakhwaj, although he could not continue because of the pressure of work. See Abhijit Dasgupta, 'Political Film Amader Deshey Bodh Hoy Kara Jay Na: Satyajit', *Anandalok* (Calcutta), 25, no. 8 (1 May 1999): 6–18 and 67–74, at 72.

32.   The Rays may have excelled as autodidacts, but they did not have a monopoly on it. As Sumit Sarkar has noted, there was a proliferation of 'do-it-yourself' manuals on a wide range of subjects in late-nineteenth-century Bengali print culture. Although their actual impact on their readers remains unexplored, it is clear that there was a substantial audience for them. See Sumit Sarkar, *Modern Times: India, 1880s–1950s: Environment, Economy, Culture* (Ranikhet: Permanent Black, 2014), 347.

33.   Kedarnath Chattopadhyay, 'Satabarshik Sraddhhanjali', 112, 115.

34.   For Upendrakishore's views on the expressive qualities of the violin, see Upendrakishore Ray, 'Behala', pt. 2, *Pradip*, 3, no. 10 (Ashwin 1307 [September–October 1900]): 336–9, at 337, http://archiv.ub.uni–heidelberg. de/savifadok/volltexte/2009/877 (accessed on 21 August 2014).

35.   Kedarnath Chattopadhyay, 'Satabarshik Sraddhhanjali', 112. Upendrakishore himself pointed out that the current European practice of holding the violin had evolved over the years, implying that there was nothing sacrosanct about it. See U. Ray, 'Behala', pt. 2, 337.

36.   P. Chakrabarti, *Chhelebelar Dinguli*, 93; and the anonymous obituary in *Tattvabodhini Patrika*, Falgun 1322 sak (February 1916), reprinted in Adhya,

Upendrakishore Raychaudhuri, 43. The obituarist hailed this as an instance of Upendrakishore's unsectarian attitude.

37. See Satyajit Ray, 'Binode-da' [1971], in Ray, *Bishoy Chalachchitra* (Calcutta: Ananda, 1982), 118–23, at 120.

38. Dasgupta, *Upendrakishore Raychaudhuri*, 64.

39. A second edition was published in 1898 and a third in 1904. For bibliographic information see Dasgupta, *Upendrakishore Raychaudhuri*, 64; and S. Ghosh, 'Upendrakishore', *Ekshan*, 56, 60. The manual included notations for many well-known songs of the period and, for that reason alone, it could be a valuable historical resource today if copies were not so scarce. But it was never reprinted after 1904 because Upendrakishore, by then, had come to agree with nationalist critics that the harmonium was inappropriate for Indian music. See 'The Late Mr U. Ray', 105. On nationalist objections that the harmonium removed 'microtonal subtleties' from Indian melodies, see Gerry Farrell, *Indian Music and the West* (Oxford: Oxford University Press, 1997), 54–5.

40. See Jnanprakash Ghosh, 'Dwarkiner Katha', *Desh*, Binodan Annual (1980): 143–50, at 144, 148, 150. My thanks to Debasis Mukhopadhyay for this article.

41. Marie Seton, *Portrait of a Director: Satyajit Ray*, expanded edition (Delhi: Penguin, 2003), 22–3.

42. 'The Late Mr U. Ray', 103; and [Ramananda Chatterji], 'Raja Rammohan Roy-er Rajneeti', *Probasi*, 1, no. 3 (Ashar 1308/June–July 1901): 108–12, at 111–12, http://archiv.ub.uni-heidelberg.de/savifadok/volltexte/2009/946 (accessed on 17 January 2015). My thanks to Soumen Paul for this reference.

43. As his half-tone business prospered, Upendrakishore's brother Kuladaranjan took over his routine photographic work. See S. Ghosh, *Chhabi Tola: Bangalir Photography Charcha* (Calcutta: Ananda, 1988), 133.

44. S. Ghosh, '*Abol Tabol*: The Making of a Book', in *Print Areas: Book History in India*, edited by Abhijit Gupta and Swapan Chakravorty (Delhi: Permanent Black, 2004), 243–4.

45. See the editorial notes in *Upendrakishore Rachanasamagra*: 1, edited by Anathnath Das and Amal Pal (Calcutta: Ananda, 2001), 491–2. On earlier adaptations of the Ramayana for children, see Chitra Deb, 'Bangla Shishusahitya', in *Dui Sataker Bangla Mudran o Prakashan*, edited by Chittaranjan Bandyopadhyay (Calcutta: Ananda, 1981), 258; and Khagendranath Mitra, *Satabdir Shishu-Sahitya, 1818–1960*, 2nd edn (Calcutta: Vidyodaya, 1967), 122–5, 203–4.

46. In his 1912 autobiography, Rabindranath Tagore repeatedly referred to his elder brother Satyendranath Tagore's son Surendranath and daughter Indira as *chhele* or *chhelera* and not, as would be common today, as *chhelemeye* or *chhelemeyera*. See Rabindranath Tagore, *Jiban-Smriti* (1912), in *Rabindra Rachanabali*,

Sulabh Sanskaran, 18 vols (Calcutta: Vishwa-Bharati, 1990), 9: 468–9. Over the first half of the twentieth century, however, the usage seems to have changed, so that 'chhele' came to be used exclusively for boys. When writing a second memoir in 1940, Tagore used the word *chhelemeye* to describe the same children. See Rabindranath Tagore, *Chhelebela* (1940), in *Rabindra Rachanabali*, 13: 735, 737.

47.   He also felt that he had abridged the Ramayana too drastically. The first edition was 72 pages long, while the second edition, published by the City Book Society in 1907, was almost double the length and had completely new pictures printed from half-tone blocks by his brother-in-law Hemendramohan Boses's Kuntalin Press. Rabindranath Tagore was thanked by Upendrakishore (in both editions) for encouraging the project, reading the manuscript, and (for the second edition) even correcting the proofs. See S. Ghosh, 'Upendrakishore', 67–8; and Das and Pal, *Upendrakishore Rachanasamagra*, 3–4, 491. The City Book Society, which published the second edition, was a specialist publisher of children's books established by Jogindranath Sarkar, an iconic figure in the history of Bengali children's literature. For biographical information on Sarkar, see Parthajit Gangopadhyay's preface to the new edition of Jogindranath Sarkar (comp.), *Bande Mataram* [orig. 1905] (Calcutta: Parul Prakasani, 2007), unpaginated [19–34].

48.   See P. Chakrabarti, *Chhelebelar Dinguli*, 46; and Sukumar Ray, 'Upendrakishore Ray' [1916], *Sukumar Sahityasamagra*, 3 vols, edited by Satyajit Ray and Partha Basu (Calcutta: Ananda Publishers, 1989), 3: 77–81, 79.

49.   See Mitra, *Kalikata Darpan*, 1 (1980): 97.

50.   P. Chakrabarti, *Chhelebelar Dinguli*, 70; Subimal Ray, *Pretsiddher Kahini o Anyanya Rachana* (Calcutta: Asha Prakasani, 1978), 78–9 (my thanks to Indrani Majumdar for the latter reference).

51.   Rabindranath Tagore, 'Samayik Sahitya', *Bharati*, 22 (1305 BE/1898): 762–6, at 764.

52.   Tapati Guha-Thakurta, *The Making of a New 'Indian' Art: Artists, Aesthetics and Nationalism in Bengal, c.1850–1920* (Cambridge: Cambridge University Press, 1992), 82–3. Lithography came to India in the 1820s and was initially used by the British for the reproduction of maps and charts. It spread quickly into non-official domains and was being used for portraits by mid-century. Colour lithography (chromolithography) was available in India by the 1860s and was extensively used for mythological and religious images. See Jaya Appasamy, 'Early Calcutta Lithographs', *Lalit Kala Contemporary*, 31 (April 1981): 13–16.

53.   At that time, one of the few places where photoengraving work was done was in the Surveyor-General's Department of the Government of India by the self-taught photographer A. Wellesley Turner. See 'The Late A. Wellesley Turner', *Process Work and Electrotyping: Penrose & Co's Monthly Circular*, February–March 1907, 9. Later, some Bengali artists and engravers (including

the well-known wood-engraver Priyagopal Das) also attempted to produce half-tone pictures, but with little success. See S. Ghosh, *Karigari Kalpana*, 90–1, 109.

54. A wood block could be used to produce a crude, cheap wood cut, or the vastly more refined wood engraving. On this point, see Gerry Beegan, *The Mass Image: A Social History of Photomechanical Reproduction in Victorian London* (Basingstoke: Palgrave, 2008), 43, 49, 65. The eagerness to use photographs in printed material was so great that for a time, actual photographs were pasted in to books in the spaces left for their insertion. See James Moran, ed., *Printing in the 20th Century: A Penrose Anthology* (London: Northwood, 1974), 35. See also William Gamble, 'A Wonderful Process', *Penrose's Pictorial Annual*, 1901, reprinted in Moran, *Printing in the 20th Century*, 85–96, at 86–7.

55. Gamble, 'A Wonderful Process', 87–8.

56. In the 1850s, the photographic pioneer William Henry Fox Talbot had used layers of muslin or lace as a 'photographic veil' to capture intermediate tones in a photograph; he had even taken out a patent in 1852 for a glass screen that could produce this effect. He does not seem to have pursued the idea and 'the scientific principle and method of breaking up the dots' remained very imperfectly understood until Ives. See William Gamble, 'The History of the Half-Tone Dot', *Photographic Journal*, new ser., 21, no. 6 (February 1897): 126–36, at 127; Carl Hentschel, 'Process Engraving,' *Journal of the Society of Arts*, 48 (April 20, 1900): 461–74, at 463–6; Anne Kelsey Hammond, 'Aesthetic Aspects of the Photomechanical Print', in *British Photography in the Nineteenth Century: The Fine Art Tradition*, edited by Mike Weaver (Cambridge: Cambridge University Press, 1989), 163–79, at 165–6; and Josef Maria Eder, *History of Photography* [1945], translated by Edward Epstean (New York: Dover, 1978), 626–38.

57. Julius Verfasser, *The Half-Tone Process: A Practical Manual of Photo-Engraving in Half-Tone on Zinc and Copper*, 2nd edn (Bradford: Percy Lund, 1896), 12–13.

58. Later, screens became available in different orders of fineness: from 85–100 lines to the inch for 'rough newspaper printing' to much finer ones (even up to 400 lines per inch) for high-quality work. The finer screens, however, produced good results only when the image was printed on high-quality paper. See Amstutz, *Amstutz' Hand-Book of Photoengraving*, 3rd edn (Chicago: Inland Printer, 1907), 137–9; and Estelle Jussim, *Visual Communication and the Graphic Arts: Photographic Technologies in the Nineteenth Century* (New York: R.R. Bowker, 1983), 69.

59. Gamble, 'A Wonderful Process', 92–3; and Moran, *Printing in the 20th Century*, 36–7. The expression 'half-tone' was derived from the phrase 'mezzo-tinto', which was in common use by artists. See John Southward, *Progress in Printing and the Graphic Arts during the Victorian Era* (London: Simpkin, Marshall, Hamilton, Kent & Co., 1897), 77.

60.   Gamble, 'A Wonderful Process,' 88–9; Louis E. Levy, 'Forty Years of Process Work: Reminiscences', *Process Work and Electrotyping: Penrose's Monthly*, January 1913, 233–4; and Eder, *History of Photography*, 633–4.

61.   See Beegan, *Mass Image*, 78–9; and Southward, *Progress in Printing and the Graphic Arts*, 78.

62.   On the term 'process' and its use to describe half-tone technology, see Amstutz, *Amstutz' Hand-Book*, 13; and Hentschel, 'Process Engraving', 463. In the discussion following Hentschel's paper (471), one respondent declared that 'process' was 'a most absurd title and meant nothing'. Other virtual synonyms were photoengraving, photo-process and graphic process. See S. Ghosh, *Karigari Kalpana*, 57. See also Michael Twyman, *Printing 1770–1970: An Illustrated History of Its Development and Uses in England* (London: British Library, 1998), 32.

63.   Gamble, 'A Wonderful Process', 95. Of course, the older technologies did not completely die out. Fine-screen process engravings did not print well on poor quality paper and wood engravings remained preferable. See Twyman, *Printing 1770–1970*, 33. Also, pen-and-ink sketches were often preferred to photographs for sensitive subjects like 'poverty, carnage or sex' and printed by the halftone process's close cousin, the so-called line process. Even for photographs reproduced by half-tone, retouching the photo before subjecting it to the half-tone process was virtually the norm. See Beegan, *Mass Image*, 19–21, 131, 139–40, 168, 179.

64.   Southward, *Progress in Printing and the Graphic Arts*, 21.

65.   Beegan, *Mass Image*, 37–8, 207–8.

66.   While praising half-tone technology for providing a truer version of pictures than ordinary engravings, White lamented 'the plethora of unnecessary pictures of people and incidents' that it had led to. See Gleeson White, 'Some Aspects of Modern Illustration', *Photographic Journal*, new ser., 19, no. 11 (July 1895): 347–55, at 350, 353; and Beegan, *Mass Image*, 6–7, 9, 203–5, 208.

67.   See Guha-Thakurta, *The Making of a New 'Indian' Art*, 86.

68.   For an excellent survey of European art magazines, see John Tagg, 'Movements and Periodicals: The Magazines of Art', *Studio International*, 193 (September–October 1976): 136–44, especially 142–3. See also Anthony J. Hamber, *'A Higher Branch of the Art': Photographing the Fine Arts in England, 1839–1880* (Amsterdam: Gordon & Breach, 1996).

69.   White, 'Some Aspects of Modern Illustration', 355. See also Gamble, 'A Wonderful Process', 95.

70.   See the famous title essay in Walter Benjamin, *The Work of Art in the Age of Its Technological Reproducibility and Other Writings on Media*, edited by Michael W. Jennings, Brigid Doherty, and Thomas Y. Levin, translated by Edmund Jephcott (Cambridge, Mass.: Belknap/Harvard University Press, 2008), 19–56, especially 21–5; and Frances Robertson, *Print Culture: From Steam Press to Ebook* (London: Routledge, 2013), 85.

71. *Probasi*, over the first three decades of the twentieth century, was the leading general-interest periodical for Bengali bhadralok across the entire subcontinent. See Samarpita Mitra, 'Periodical Readership in Early Twentieth Century Bengal: Ramananda Chattopadhyay's *Prabasi*', *Modern Asian Studies* 47, no. 1 (2013): 204–49, 215–18, 224, 227, 231, 236; and Guha-Thakurta, *The Making of a New 'Indian' Art*, 213–15, 321. *Pradip*, a magazine Ramananda Chatterji had edited briefly before starting *Probasi*, had been so full of pictures—made from blocks by Upendrakishore—that Rabindranath Tagore had advised Chatterji not to risk bankruptcy by spending so much money on illustrations. See Rabindranath Tagore, 'Samayik Sahitya', *Bharati*, 22 (1305 BE/1898): 762–6, at 766; and S. Ghosh, *Karigari Kalpana*, 91. Not every Bengali art connoisseur was happy, however, with the results of half-tone printing, as we shall see in the next chapter.

72. Guha-Thakurta, *The Making of a New 'Indian' Art*, 28.

73. Guha-Thakurta, *The Making of a New 'Indian' Art*, 68. *Probasi* also provided its readers with translations of European literary classics. See S. Mitra, 'Periodical Readership', 242–3.

74. N. Chaudhuri, *Atmaghati Bangali*, 38.

75. Editorial, *Modern Review*, January 1907, reprinted in Santa Devi, *Bharat-Muktisadhak Ramananda Chattopadhyay o Ardhasatabdir Bangla* (Calcutta: Dey's, 2005), 135.

76. Chatterji turned to his friend Nivedita (the Irishwoman Margaret Noble, who took the name of Nivedita after becoming a disciple of Swami Vivekananda) for assistance in selecting examples of European art and for contributing analytical notes on them. See O.C. Gangoly, *Bharater Silpa o Amar Katha* (Calcutta: A. Mukherjee, 1969), 169.

77. Only the blocks for the first year of *Probasi* had been made by a different company. See Devi, *Bharat-Muktisadhak*, 210. The first block that Upendrakishore made for *Probasi* was for a picture of Sita by Raja Ravi Varma, which was published in October 1901; in 1903, *Probasi* carried the first three-colour reproduction of a painting in any Indian publication; the painting was again by Ravi Varma and the block by Upendrakishore. See S. Ghosh, 'Upendrakishore', 79–80. *Probasi* (along with its editor and his family) moved from Allahabad to Calcutta in 1908; the magazine was subsequently printed at Hemendramohan Bose's Kuntalin Press. See S. Mitra, 'Periodical Readership', 220–1.

78. In this sense, his grandson was no different. One possible reason for Satyajit Ray's interest in controlling as many dimensions of a film as possible—script, dialogue, casting, camera, lyrics, costumes, music, titles, and publicity—was his aspiration to get as far away as possible from the working methods of the modern film *industry*. As we know from the research of Sharmistha Gooptu, we must be careful not to exaggerate Ray's distance from the Bengal film industry but the brand-identity of a Ray film was that of a

complete work of art shaped by the hands of a single omnicompetent craftsman who, in aesthetic terms, resided far above the banal world of the film
industry.

79. See Beegan, *Mass Image*, 56, 82–93.

80. Rabindranath Tagore, 'Samayik Sahitya', 764. Some fifteen years
later, when Tagore published his autobiography *Jiban-Smriti*, it was illustrated
with two dozen illustrations by Gaganendranath Tagore, the blocks for which
were made by Upendrakishore. See the plates in Rabindranath Tagore, *Jiban-
Smriti* (Silaidaha: N. Gangopadhyay/Calcutta: Adi Brahmo Samaj, 1912) and
on the provenance of the blocks, see Ray and Basu, *Sukumar Sahityasamagra*,
3: 205; and S. Ghosh, *Karigari Kalpana*, 101–2.

81. Sukumar Ray, 'Upendrakishore Ray' [1916], 79.

82. Historian Gerry Beegan remarks that 'practice had preceded theory;
process workers knew how the screen worked, even though they didn't know
why'. See Beegan, *Mass Image*, 79; and William Gamble, 'The Last Word on
Half-Tone', *British Journal of Photography*, 51 (June 1904): 501–3, at 501.

83. Beegan, *Mass Image*, 79–80.

84. Gamble, 'A Wonderful Process', 93–4.

85. Gamble had first gone into business in partnership with the chemist
A.W. Penrose in 1893 to supply the requirements of photoengravers. See R.B.
Fishenden, 'William Gamble: An Appreciation' (1933), reprinted in Moran,
Printing in the 20th Century, 141–4. In 1894, the Penrose Company became the
exclusive agents in Britain for Max Levy's 'epoch-making' screens. See
Gamble, 'The History of the Half-Tone Dot', 130.

86. Moran, *Printing in the 20th Century*, 35, 38, 40.

87. 'The Late Mr U. Ray', 104.

88. For a discussion of the effects of changing the distance of the screen,
see *Photographic Journal*, new ser., 19, no. 9 (May 1895): 298–9; and Eder,
History of Photography, 634.

89. Amstutz, *Amstutz' Hand-Book*, 146. On the contemporary influence
of this handbook, see 'The Amstutz Handbook of Photo-Engraving', *Process
Work and Electrotyping*, October–November 1907, 9.

90. [William Gamble], 'A Visit to the Municipal School of Technology,
Manchester', *Penrose's Pictorial Annual*, (1903–4): 129–36, at 132.

91. 'Trade Notes', *Process Work and Electrotyping: Penrose & Co's Monthly
Circular*, June–July 1905, 4–6, at 5.

92. Gamble, 'Last Word on Half-Tone', 503; Gamble, 'The Editor's Notes',
Penrose's Pictorial Annual: The Process Year-Book for 1904–5, 2.

93. Gamble, 'Last Word on Half-Tone', 503.

94. Gamble, 'Last Word on Half-Tone', 503.

95. Upendrakisor Ray, 'The 60° Cross-Line Screen', *Penrose's Pictorial
Annual: The Process Year-Book for 1905–6*, 97–102, at 98; and Gamble, 'The
Editor's Notes', *Penrose's Pictorial Annual: The Process Year-Book for 1904–5*, 2.

All of Upendrakishore's papers in *Penrose* have recently been reprinted in Upendrakishore Raychowdhury, *Essays on Half-Tone Photography* (Calcutta: Jadavpur University Press, 2014) but I have used the original versions.

96. Amstutz, *Amstutz' Hand-Book*, 107.

97. Several Rays are supposed to have had their work plagiarized by Westerners. Upendrakishore's brother Muktidaranjan was known to solve mathematical theorems as a hobby. His niece Leela Majumdar wrote in her memoirs (*Pakdandi*, 115) that he had once sent some of those exercises to a British expert who had sent a routine reply but incorporated Muktidaranjan's equations in the next edition of his own book without any acknowledgement. Yet another incident of this kind happened to Satyajit Ray on his first trip to Britain, but unlike his grandfather or great uncle, he, by his own testimony, stood up for his rights, losing his temper for the first time in his life. See Seton, *Portrait of a Director*, 56–7.

98. For a classic account of scientific simultaneity, see Thomas S. Kuhn, 'Energy Conservation as an Example of Simultaneous Discovery', in *Critical Problems in the History of Science*, edited by Marshall Clagett (Madison: University of Wisconsin Press, 1959), 321–56. See also Susan E. Cozzens, *Social Control and Multiple Discovery in Science: The Opiate Receptor Case* (Albany: State University of New York Press, 1989), especially 1–44.

99. For a discussion of the difficulties, see 'A Point in Patent Law', *Process Work and Electrotyping*, February 1915, 12; and a chartered patent agent's comment on the article in *Process Work and Electrotyping*, March 1915, 21–2.

100. Amit Bhattacharyya, *Business, Politics and Technology: Select Themes in the Economic History of Modern India* (Calcutta: Readers Service, 2005), 55–6.

101. Gamble, 'The Editor's Notes', *Penrose's Pictorial Annual: The Process Year-Book for 1904–5*, 2. Later, Upendrakishore became far more careful about patenting his work and when his son Sukumar was training in printing technology in Britain, he sent him the design for a three-colour process camera that he wanted to patent. Unfortunately, as Sukumar reported, virtually every 'possible variation' on that design had already been patented. See Sukumar's letter to his father in Ray and Basu, *Sukumar Sahityasamagra*, 3: 222.

102. 'Death of Mr U. K. Ray', *Process Work and Electrotyping*, January 1917, 77. See also 'The Late Mr U. Ray', *Process Work and Electrotyping*, December 1919–February 1920, 122.

103. 'Trade Notes', *Process Work and Electrotyping*, June–July 1905, 4–6, at 5.

104. *A Report of the Indian Industrial and Agricultural Exhibition, Calcutta, 1906–07* (Calcutta: 'Industrial India' Office, n.d.), 137.

105. See P. Mitter, *Art and Nationalism*, 124.

106. Seton, *Portrait of a Director*, 30–1. He was a thoughtful and generous employer. The staff, for instance, were paid 10 per cent of the company's

profits in addition to their salary and Upendrakishore believed in training his employees to do more than they had been appointed to do, although the most demanding jobs were reserved, of course, for the master artisan himself. A boy from Bihar called Ramdahin, for instance, had been appointed to be an office-boy but Upendrakishore himself taught him to operate the process camera. See S. Ghosh, *Karigari Kalpana*, 116–18.

107. Kedarnath Chattopadhyay, 'Satabarshik Sraddhhanjali', 114. One of Upendrakishore's senior employees, Lalitmohan Gupta, was once attracted to a higher-paying job at the Geological Survey of India and Upendrakishore, after some anxiety about the future of his own business if Gupta left, not only allowed him to apply but gave him an unequivocal testimonial when, in a piquant turn of events, the Survey asked him to serve as an expert on the appointments panel. Gupta got the job, worked for about a year but then returned to Upendrakishore, in spite of the latter's inability to match the high salary of the Survey. See S. Ghosh, *Karigari Kalpana*, 118. Not all his staff were so loyal, however: some left to start their own businesses and at least one is reported to have embezzled money from Upendrakishore's firm. See Seton, *Portrait of a Director*, 30–1.

108. See Upendrakishore Raychaudhuri, 'Half-Tone Chhabi', *Pradip*, 1, nos 10–11 (Ashwin–Kartik 1305/October–November 1898): 335–8, at 338, http://archiv.ub.uni-heidelberg.de/savifadok/volltexte/2009/875 (accessed on 13 May 2014), 338.

109. See Zachariah, *Playing the Nation Game*, 151–2. On Indian convictions that modern science and technology were 'the liberal bequests of great minds to every individual of the human race' and 'common to all humankind', see J. Lourdusamy, *Science and National Consciousness in Bengal, 1870–1930* (Hyderabad: Orient Longman, 2004), 18–19.

110. R.H. Tawney, *Religion and the Rise of Capitalism* (London: John Murray, 1926), 268.

111. See Shyamasree Lal, '"Sandesh" and the Child's World of Imagination', *India International Centre Quarterly* 10, no. 4 (1983): 433–42, at 433.

112. On the complicated history of the East India Company's involvement in popular education, see Bruce T. McCully, *English Education and the Origins of Indian Nationalism* (1940; reprint, Gloucester, MA: Peter Smith, 1966), 17–18. Between 1817 and 1825, the School Book Society printed more than a hundred thousand textbooks and sold them at very low prices to schools in Calcutta and surrounding regions. See Nikhil Sarkar, 'Adi Juger Pathhyapustak', in *Dui Sataker Bangla*, 165–76, at 166; and Bipinchandra Pal, *Sattar Vatsar: Atmajibani* (Calcutta: Kalpan, [1927–8] 2005), 94–5.

113. The first volume of *Nitikatha* was by Radhakanta Deb, a leading figure in 'native' education and a partly conservative, partly modernist luminary of Bengal's 'age of reform'. Deb also authored primers of the Bengali language and manuals of arithmetic for the School Book Society. See Nikhil

Sarkar, 'Adi Juger Pathhyapustak', 167. On the proliferation of textbooks of morals for children in nineteenth-century Bengal, driven by Christian missionaries as well as indigenous religious reformers, see Ashish Khastagir, *Bangla Gadye Nitisiksha* (Calcutta: Pustak Bipani, 2004). The genre, as Khastagir points out, was based substantially on traditional Sanskrit texts, such as the *Hitopodesa* or the *Panchatantra*, but also drew upon Western sources (Khastagir, *Bangla Gadye Nitisiksha*, 14–15).

114. See Nabendu Sen, *Bangla Shishu Sahitya: Tattwa, Tathya, Rup o Bisleshan* (Calcutta: Puthipatra, 1992), 9. In Britain, the Religious Tract Society's magazines, *Boy's Own Paper* (founded 1879) and *Girl's Own Paper* (founded 1880), enthralled large, secular readerships for many decades but none of the Bengali children's magazines published by missionaries ever captured such a broad readership. On the Religious Tract Society's magazines, profits from which were used to finance the Society's missionary work across the empire, see Kirsten Drotner, *English Children and Their Magazines, 1751–1945* (New Haven: Yale University Press, 1988), 115–30.

115. One of the best-known magazines of this period was the monthly *Abodh-Bandhu*, which was edited for a time by the poet Biharilal Chakrabarty. Rabindranath Tagore remembered it with great affection in his autobiography. See Mitra, *Satabdir Shishu-Sahitya*, ix–x, 5–12.

116. See Peter N. Stearns, *Childhood in World History* (New York: Routledge, 2006), 58; and Harry Hendrick, *Children, Childhood and English Society, 1880–1990* (Cambridge: Cambridge University Press, 1997), 12.

117. See Dipesh Chakrabarty, 'Limits of the Bourgeois Model?' in *The Middle Class in Colonial India*, edited by Sanjay Joshi (Delhi: Oxford University Press, 2010), 178–201, at 182; Sumit Sarkar, *Modern Times: India, 1880s–1950s— Environment, Economy, Culture* (Ranikhet: Permanent Black, 2014), 372; and Meredith Borthwick, *The Changing Role of Women in Bengal, 1849–1905* (Princeton: Princeton University Press, 1984), 178–81. Iswarchandra Vidyasagar published a free translation of the north Indian work *Vetal Pachchisi* in 1847, declaring that he had eliminated the many obscenities in the original text. When he translated parts of the Mahabharata for use in schools, he either excised what he considered to be obscene or altered the content. See Mitra, *Satabdir Shishu-Sahitya*, 48–9, 55–6, 58–9; and N. Sen, *Bangla Shishu Sahitya*, 48.

118. Khastagir, *Bangla Gadye Nitisiksha*, 116–17. In seventeenth-century England, the philosopher John Locke had asserted that a child growing up with 'notions of spirits and goblins' would be a fearful, superstitious adult. See Samuel F. Pickering, Jr, *John Locke and Children's Books in Eighteenth-Century England* (Knoxville, TN: University of Tennessee Press, 1981), 41, 42–3, 69; and Peter Hunt, ed., *Children's Literature: An Illustrated History* (Oxford: Oxford University Press, 1995), 137–8. In Bengal, too, progressives could frown on fairy tales. In 1932, Ramananda Chatterji urged authors to

eliminate ghosts and demons, which, he said, frightened children and prevented them from developing into the kind of bold, fearless adults the nation needed. See 'Probasi Sampadaker Ekti Baktabya', Probasi (Poush 1339/ December–January 1932), 432, http://archiv.ub.uni-heidelberg.de/savifadok/ volltexte/2009/994/ (accessed on 17 November 2011).

119. See Sumanta Banerjee, The Parlour and the Streets: Elite and Popular Culture in Nineteenth-Century Calcutta (Calcutta: Seagull, 1989).

120. P.K. Bose, 'Sons of the Nation', 122–3, 137.

121. P. Mitter, Art and Nationalism, 126.

122. See N. Sen, Bangla Shishu Sahitya, 11.

123. N. Sen, Bangla Shishu Sahitya, 9–10.

124. Married to Satyendranath Tagore, an elder brother of Rabindranath and the first Indian to enter the racially exclusive 'covenanted' ranks of the Indian Civil Service, she went to Britain in 1877 with her three children and spent nearly three years there. See Gyanadanandini Devi, Puratani (Calcutta: Ananda, 2012), 33–7. On Rabindranath and Balak, see Rabindranath Tagore, Rabindra Rachanabali, 9: 409–514, at 502–3; and Parthajit Gangopadhyay's introduction (unpaginated) to the reprint of the magazine's entire run: Balak (Calcutta: Parul, 2008).

125. In his autobiography, Rabindranath wrote: 'What they [children] understand drives them forward but so does what they do not fully comprehend.' See Rabindranath Tagore, Rabindra Rachanabali, 9: 451–2. In his classroom teaching at Santiniketan, too, Tagore never hesitated to confront students with material which they could not possibly comprehend at their age. See Sita Devi, Punyasmriti (Calcutta: Jignasa, 1964), 172; and Pramathananth Bisi, Rabindranath o Santiniketan (Calcutta: Vishwa-Bharati, 1944), 144–5.

126. These pieces were by Sitalakanta Chattopadhyay (the editor of the Lahore Tribune and related by marriage to the Tagores), who also described the strong abuse showered on Indians by a British judge. The words allegedly used by the judge and reproduced in full by Chattopadhyay—haramjada and suyar (roughly translatable as swine)—would be considered unprintable in a Bengali children's magazine even today. See Das and Pal, Balak, 401–5, 500–4. Nor could the average child be expected to grasp the cultural importance of Tagore's essay on libraries, in which he urged Bengalis to reject English, 'the language of clerical work' (keranigirir bhasa), or, for that matter, follow the struggle between rival visions of the divine in his novel Rajarshi, the earlier chapters of which were serialized in Balak. See 'Library', Das and Pal, Balak, 388–92; and for Rajarshi, Rabindranath Tagore, Rabindra Rachanabali, 1: 699–783, 961–2.

127. Balak merged with Bharati, another Tagore family magazine that had been founded in 1877. See Brajendranath Bandyopadhyay, 'Sahitye Bangamahila', in Bethune School & College Centenary Volume, edited by Kalidas Nag (Calcutta: no pub., 1951), 195–211, at 202.

128. The idea that children were not miniature adults and needed 'easy, pleasant books' tailored to their developing intellect was popularized by John Locke and became institutionalized across the world very quickly. See Andrea Immel, 'Children's Books and Constructions of Childhood', in *The Cambridge Companion to Children's Literature*, edited by M.O. Grenby and Andrea Immel (Cambridge: Cambridge University Press, 2009), 19–34, at 30–1.

129. The work was 'Ascharjya Hatyakanda' (Astounding Murder) by Harisadhan Mukhopadhyay. Despite its many strengths, *Sakha-o-Sathi* did not have a long life and closed in 1898. See Mitra, *Satabdir Shishu-Sahitya*, 15, 19, 21; and Amal Pal, ed., *Kishorpathhya Patrikapanchak: Suchi-Sankalan* (Calcutta: Dey's, 2007), 23–7.

130. A. Pal, *Kishorpathhya Patrikapanchak*, 29; Sastri, *Atmacharit*, 289; and Kamal Chaudhuri, 'Sampadak Ramananda', in *Probasi: Nirbachita Sankalan*, edited by Kamal Chaudhuri (Calcutta: Mitra o Ghosh, 2004), 14–36, at 15. If for no other reason, *Mukul* deserves to be remembered for publishing the first poem of the eight-year-old Sukumar Ray in 1896. Ten years later, *Mukul* was to publish Sukumar's first piece of published prose, a scientific essay on the sun. See Ray and Basu, *Sukumar Sahityasamagra*, 2: 327, 331–3, 364.

131. Even Rabindranath Tagore asked his wife, Mrinalini, to prepare a children's version of the Ramayana from the original Sanskrit, but she died before she could complete the work. His nephew Surendranath Tagore was tasked with preparing a similar edition of the Mahabharata and later, Rabindranath used to read from it to the students of Santiniketan. See Rathindranath Tagore, *On the Edges of Time* (Calcutta: Orient Longman, 1958), 25.

132. Introduction to Jogindranath Sarkar (comp.), *Bande Mataram* [1905], edited by Parthajit Gangopadhyay (Calcutta: Parul Prakasani, 2007), 28–9.

133. For similar ideas in Britain, see Robert J. Kirkpatrick, *From the Penny Dreadful to the Ha'Penny Dreadfuller: A Bibliographic History of the Boys' Periodical in Britain 1762–1950* (London: British Library, 2013), 261–3.

134. Kedarnath Chattopadhyay, 'Satabarshik Sraddhhanjali', 110.

135. Dasgupta, *Upendrakishore Raychaudhuri*, 26. Such articles on scientific and natural historical topics were also common in British children's magazines. See Drotner, *English Children and Their Magazines*, 101.

136. Bratati Chakravarty, *Bangla Shishu Sahitya Charcha: Ray Paribar* (Calcutta: Dey Book Store, 1997), 16.

137. 'The Late Mr U. Ray', 104. Indeed, Upendrakishore, unlike his brother Kuladaranjan (1869–1948), never went in for straightforward translations. On Kuladaranjan Ray and his many popular translations, see B. Chakravarty, *Bangla Shishu Sahitya Charcha*, 89–100; N. Sen, *Bangla Shishu Sahitya*, 173–8; Satyajit Ray, *Jakhan Chhoto Chhilam* (Calcutta: Ananda, 1982), 39–40, 14; C. Bandyopadhyay, *Dui Sataker Bangla*, 161; and Kalyani Karlekar, 'Sukumar Ray', in *Sukumar Samagra Rachanabali*, edited by Punyalata

244 THE RAYS BEFORE SATYAJIT

Chakrabarti and Kalyani Karlekar, 2 vols (Calcutta: Asia Publishing, 1960), 1: 1–18, at 2. My thanks to Sourav Bagchi for the last reference.

138. S. Ghosh, 'Upendrakishore', 67; and B. Chakravarty, *Bangla Shishu Sahitya Charcha*, 75.

139. *Sekaler Katha*, in Das and Pal, *Upendrakishore Rachanasamagra*, 155–91, at 157, 166.

140. See the entry on *Sekaler Katha* in Gargi Gangopadhyay's website, http://bengalichildrensbooks.org/SekalerKatha.php (accessed on 8 November 2011), where Pedler's note is reproduced, along with the full-colour illustration of the Archaeopteryx and the title page of the book. For Varma's comment, see Adhya, *Upendrakishore Raychaudhuri*, 24; and for Holland's praise, Sukumar Ray, *Upendrakishore Ray*, 80.

141. *Sekaler Katha*, in Das and Pal, *Upendrakishore Rachanasamagra*, 155–91, at 174 (ichthyosaurus), 176 (brontosaurus), 179 (triceratops), 182 (archaeopteryx).

142. One does not know whether Upendrakishore knew of Darwin's work but *Sekaler Katha* was published at a time when Western scientists were moving away from Darwinian theory due to difficulties of explaining biological evolution with Darwin's mechanism of 'natural selection'. These issues were resolved gradually over the early twentieth century, leading to the reinstatement of Darwin and Darwinism. See Peter Bowler, *The Eclipse of Darwinism: Anti-Darwinian Evolution Theories in the Decades around 1900* (Baltimore, MD: Johns Hopkins University Press, 1983).

143. Before he acquired a press, he set up his own publishing company and the first title to be brought out by it was *Tuntunir Boi* (The Tailor-Bird's Book, 1910). See S. Ghosh, 'Upendrakishore', 68, 86. Although Ghosh says that *Tuntunir Boi* was the first title to be published under the imprint of U. Ray & Sons, the title page of the first edition says that it was published by Sukumar Raychaudhuri (that is, Upendrakishore's son) from 22 Sukea Street, and printed by Kantik Press on Cornwallis Street. See *Tuntunir Boi* (Calcutta: S. Raychaudhuri, 1910; facsimile reprint, Calcutta: Subarnarekha, 2002).

144. See Upendrakishore's prefaces to the different editions in Das and Pal, *Upendrakishore Rachanasamagra*, 3–4.

145. See *Chhotto Ramayan*, in Das and Pal, *Upendrakishore Rachanasamagra*, 97–154.

146. Buddhadev Bose, who loved the *Chhotto Ramayan* as a child and knew it almost entirely by heart, always regretted this omission. Upendrakishore, he felt, had not appreciated that children did not simply want to be amused by a book; they enjoyed feeling sad too and it was 'unfair to deprive them of those tears'. See Buddhadev Bose, 'Upendrakishore Raychaudhuri', *Desh*, Annual Literary Issue (Sahitya Sankhya), 11 May 1963, 133–8, 137. My thanks to Soumen Paul for this article.

147. Again, a literal translation of the first book's title would be 'The Mahabharata for Boys' but the usage, as we have seen, was different in the

early twentieth century and in his preface, Upendrakishore specifically mentioned that the book was for both boys and girls (*balakbalikadiger upajogi*). See Upendrakishore Raychaudhuri, *Chheleder Mahabharat*, 5th edn (Calcutta: City Book Society, 1915), unpaginated preface; and S. Ghosh, *Karigari Kalpana*, 83.

148. Bose, 'Upendrakishore Raychaudhuri', 137–8.

149. *Mahabharater akhhyankey balakbalikadiger upajogi karitey giya uhar sthane-sthaney abaraner prayojon hoyiachhey*. See Raychaudhuri, *Chheleder Mahabharat*, unpaginated preface.

150. B. Chakravarty, *Bangla Shishu Sahitya Charcha*, 68–70.

151. Raychaudhuri, *Chheleder Mahabharat*, 16–17, 68.

152. See, for examples, the unglossed presentation of Draupadi's refusal to consider Karna for marriage because he was the son of a charioteer or the comment that Brahmins must be forgiven even if they have committed a thousand crimes, in Raychaudhuri, *Chheleder Mahabharat*, 53, 56, 65–6.

153. Raychaudhuri, *Chheleder Mahabharat*, 37–40. The same argot is used for the malevolent Bok-rakshasa and also for Bok's brother, Kirmir (Raychaudhuri, *Chheleder Mahabharat*, 44–5, 106).

154. B. Chakravarty, *Bangla Shishu Sahitya Charcha*, 63–4.

155. Supriya Goswami, *Colonial India in Children's Literature* (New York: Routledge, 2012), 143.

156. Alokeranjan Dasgupta, 'Upendrakishore', in Alokeranjan Dasgupta, *Silpita Svabhab* (Calcutta: Sanskrit Pustak Bhandar, 1969), 66–74, at 67–8.

157. Mitra Majumdar had collected the tales over many years of fieldwork, sometimes using a phonograph to record them. See Baridbaran Ghosh, 'Dakshinaranjan Mitra Majumdarer Jibanalekhhya', in *Dakshinaranjan Rachanasamagra*, 2 vols (Calcutta: Mitra o Ghosh, 1981), 2: 1–7. His was a far more comprehensive project than that of the Bengali Christian clergyman, Lal Behari Day, whose *Folk Tales of Bengal* had been published in 1883 by Macmillan in London. All such attempts reflected the worldwide interest, inspired by the Brothers Grimm, in collecting folk tales but the swadeshi movement undoubtedly provided an additional impetus to Mitra Majumdar. See P. Mitter, *Art and Nationalism*, 127; Sankar Sen Gupta, *Folklorists of Bengal: Life-Sketches and Bibliographical Notes* (Calcutta: Indian Publications, 1965); and Giuseppe Flora, 'On Fairy Tales, Intellectuals and Nationalism in Bengal (1880–1920)', *Rivista degli Studi Orientali*, 75 (2002), supplemento no. 1. For critical analyses of the tales of *Thakurmar Jhuli*, see N. Sen, *Bangla Shishu Sahitya*, 197–202 and, especially, Sibaji Bandyopadhyay, *Gopal-Rakhal Dwandasamas Uponibeshbad o Bangla Sisusahitya* (Calcutta: Papyrus, 1991), 38–77.

158. On the illustrations of *Thakurmar Jhuli*, see Kamalkumar Majumdar, 'Bangiya Granthachitran', reprinted in K. Majumdar, *Bangiya Silpadhara o Anyanya Prabandha*, edited by Dayamoyee Majumdar and Sandipan Bhattacharya (Calcutta: Dipayan, 1998), 60–82, at 66 and 78–9.

159. Tagore himself had been collecting folk-rhymes from the 1880s, which, in the true Romantic spirit, he considered to represent the oldest

246   THE RAYS BEFORE SATYAJIT

cultural wealth of the nation. See Prabhatkumar Mukhopadhyay, *Rabindrajibani o Rabindra-Sahitya Prabeshak*, 4th edn, 4 vols (Calcutta: Vishwa Bharati, 1970), 1: 406–7.

160. See Chitra Deb, 'Bangla Shishusahitya', 257–8. It has sometimes been argued that these represented the attempt of male, middle-class authors to expropriate 'something that had previously been produced and controlled' by illiterate, rural women. But, as M.O. Grenby has pointed out with reference to similar attempts to collect folk tales in eighteenth-century Britain, it was less a masculinization of those traditions than their commodification for a modern bourgeois audience. See Grenby, 'The Origins of Children's Literature', 11.

161. See Goswami, *Colonial India in Children's Literature*, 141.

162. B. Chakravarty, *Bangla Shishu Sahitya Charcha*, 57–8.

163. Satadru Sen, 'A Juvenile Periphery: The Geographies of Literary Childhood in Colonial Bengal', *Journal of Colonialism and Colonial History*, 5, no. 1 (2004): 1–29, at 12, https://muse.jhu.edu/journals/journal_of_colonialism_and_colonial_history/v005/5.1sen.html (accessed on 6 June 2014).

164. B. Chakravarty, *Bangla Shishu Sahitya Charcha*, 57–8.

165. Alokeranjan Dasgupta, 'Upendrakishore', 68–9.

166. Goswami, *Colonial India in Children's Literature*, 144–6.

167. For a political reading of this story, which seems to me to be somewhat too schematic, see Goswami, *Colonial India in Children's Literature*, 148–9.

168. See Bansari Mitra, *The Renovation of Folktales by Five Modern Bengali Writers* (Calcutta: Anthropological Survey of India, 2002), 28, 31. My thanks to the author for this reference.

169. Of course, there was no single approach to the presentation of folk-tales to children. When Sivanath Sastri, the founding editor of *Mukul*, published his own collection of folk-tales, he drew upon Hans Christian Andersen and the Brothers Grimm. Other contemporary collections looked to north India or to Japan. See B. Chakravarty, *Bangla Shishu Sahitya Charcha*, 23. The unclassifiable work of Abanindranath Tagore combined fantasy (sometimes drawn from foreign sources) and a very refined kind of adventure or antiquarianism with visual beauty, expressed in the artist-author's inimitable prose. Some of Abanindranath's works were inspired by foreign sources, some by mythology. *Khatanchir Khata*, first serialized in *Sandesh* in 1920, drew upon J.M. Barrie's *Peter Pan* and *Buro Angla* (serialized in *Mouchak*) was a free adaptation of Selma Lagerlöf's *The Wonderful Adventures of Nils*. For a discussion, see N. Sen, *Bangla Shishu Sahitya*, 78–102; P. Mitter, *Art and Nationalism*, 129; and S. Sen, 'A Juvenile Periphery', 21. But the exponent of swadeshi art was unlikely to ignore the question of nationalism even in his works for children. One of Abanindranath's most famous works, *Raj-Kahini* (published in 1909, with the swadeshi movement as its real-life backdrop), portrayed the struggles of the (Hindu) Rajputs against Muslim invaders, drawing upon the old Bengali trend of discovering the raw materials for national pride in Tod's *Annals and Antiquities of Rajasthan*. See Barunkumar

Chakrabarty, *Toder Rajasthan o Bangla Sahitya* (Calcutta: Pustak Bipani, 1981), 185–6; and N. Sen, *Bangla Shishu Sahitya*, 100–1.

170. Kedarnath Chattopadhyay, 'Satabarshik Sraddhhanjali', 110.

171. B. Chakravarty, *Bangla Shishu Sahitya Charcha*, 72–4.

172. 'The Late Mr U. Ray', 69–70; Subimal Ray, *Pretsiddher Kahini o Anyanya Rachana*, 79. On Upendrakishore's astronomical lecture in Giridi, at which a young heckler caused him to lose his temper in public, see Sunirmal Basu, *Jiban Khatar Kayek Pata* (1955), in *Sunirmal Rachana Sambhar*, edited by Nirmalendu Goutam and Haribandhu Mukhoti, 3 vols (Calcutta: Forward, 1973–5), 3 (1975): 161–340, at 221–2.

173. B. Chakravarty, *Bangla Shishu Sahitya Charcha*, 74–5.

174. As Dipesh Chakrabarty has observed, Indian champions of modernity tended to retain, even reinforce, those aspects of tradition and custom that they considered to be valuable. See Dipesh Chakrabarty, 'The Muddle of Modernity', *American Historical Review*, 116, no. 3 (June 2011): 663–75, at 674.

175. See, for examples, the descriptions of Draupadi's wedding, the stalking of the disguised Pandavas by Dhristadyumna and the Pandavas' new council chamber, in Raychaudhuri, *Chheleder Mahabharat*, 51, 58–9, 76.

176. For examples of such parenthetic explanations in *Chheleder Ramayan*, see Das and Pal, *Upendrakishore Rachanasamagra*, 8 (where the word *tonkar* is glossed in the narrative as the twanging sound made by the straightening of the bow when an arrow is released), 12 (where the origin of Seeta's name—from the line made on the earth by a hoe—is explained in a footnote), 13 (where the reader is told that the sage Parashuram was so named because he invariably carried an axe, another name for which was *parshu*), and 71 (where the word *abhisek* is explained as a ritual bath taken before a king's investiture). There are quite a few such explanations in *Chheleder Mahabharat*, too. See, for instance, the gloss of the word *angulposh* (a leather protector for fingers) or the explanation of Karna's famous *kabach* as an armour in Raychaudhuri, *Chheleder Mahabharat*, 22, 24. Occasionally, Upendrakishore used footnotes to explain a potentially confusing point—see, for example, Raychaudhuri, *Chheleder Mahabharat*, 50 (where the note explains that Draupadi's father Drupad was also known as Jagnyasena) or 69, where the note clarifies the family name of Krishna's dynasty.

177. This kind of approach had been uncommon in Bengali children's literature before the days of Upendrakishore, Sivanath Sastri, and Jogindranath Sarkar. See Kedarnath Chattopadhyay, 'Satabarshik Sraddhhanjali', 110. Buddhadev Bose found Sukumar Ray's *Abol Tabol* to be marked by the same organic connections between illustrations, text, format, and book-design. See Buddhadev Bose, 'Kabi Sukumar Ray' [1926], in *Buddhadev Basur Rachanasangraha*, 8 vols (Calcutta: Granthalaya, 1974), 1: 467–80, at 479.

178. P. Mitter, *Art and Nationalism*, 133.

179. Satyajit Ray, 'Bhumika', in *Sukumar Sahityasamagra*, 1: ii.

180. B. Chakravarty, *Bangla Shishu Sahitya Charcha*, 79.

181. See 'Prastabana', *Mukul*, 1, no. 1 (1895): 1–2; Sastri, *Atmacharit*, 534–7; and Khagendranath Mitra, *Satabdir Shishu-Sahitya, 1818–1960*, 2nd edn (Calcutta: Vidyodaya, 1967), 22–3.

182. The idea of 'sweetening' lessons by incorporating them into stories may have been even older. See M.O. Grenby, 'The Origins of Children's Literature', 3–18, at 7–8; and Samuel F. Pickering, Jr, *John Locke and Children's Books in Eighteenth-Century England* (Knoxville, TN: University of Tennessee Press, 1981), 9–10, 44, 70–1.

183. A. Pal, *Kishorpathhya Patrikapanchak*, 33; and Adhya, *Upendrakishore Raychaudhuri*, 21. In its earliest years, however, the magazine had to rely on wood-engravings and once, desperate to bring some colour into its pages, the editors had one illustration hand-tinted in every copy of the magazine. See Devi, *Bharat-Muktisadhak*, 94.

184. A. Pal, *Kishorpathhya Patrikapanchak*, 32.

185. N. Chaudhuri, *Atmaghati Bangali*, 38.

186. Debasis Mukhopadhyay, 'Prasangata: Upendrakishore Raychaudhuri-r "Sandesh"', unpaginated appendix in *Sandesh: Chhelemeyeder janya Sachitra Masik Patra, Prathham Barsha (Baisakh–Chaitra 1320)*, facsimile reprint with additional material (Calcutta: Parul, 2008). Several years after *Sandesh* had been launched, however, the market grew considerably. In 1920, the publisher and bookseller Sudhirchandra Sarkar brought out *Mouchak*, which was to become very popular and published many memorable pieces by the foremost authors of the time, including Rabindranath Tagore, Abanindranath Tagore, Bibhutibhusan Bandyopadhyay, and Satyendranath Dutta, while providing space to younger writers—such as Hemendrakumar Roy—who went on to become very famous indeed. *Mouchak* was perhaps the first Bengali children's magazine that carried regular contributions from Muslim writers, such as Nazrul Islam and Jasimuddin. See Mitra, *Satabdir Shishu-Sahitya*, 158–69. In 1921, the iconic magazine *Probasi* began to include a children's section and in 1922, another publishing business began to bring out *Shishusathi*, which, like *Mouchak*, attracted many distinguished contributors and had a long life. Several other magazines for children came and went, but it was only *Rangmashal*, published from 1937, that proved at all lasting. See Mitra, *Satabdir Shishu-Sahitya*, 139–48, 158–69, 189; and Chitra Deb, 'Bangla Shishusahitya', in C. Bandyopadhyay, *Dui Sataker Bangla*, 252–68, at 266–7.

187. For an eyewitness account of the publication of the first issue of the magazine, see L. Majumdar, *Pakdandi*, 21–2.

188. See 'Sandesher Katha', *Sandesh*, 1, no. 1 (Baisakh 1320/April–May 1913): 2–3, in *Sandesh: Chhelemeyeder*.

189. Mitra, *Satabdir Shishu-Sahitya*, 149.

190. See Susmita Dutta, *Prasanga 'Sandesh': Upendrakishore Sampadana Parba (Baisakh 1320–Poush 1322)* (Calcutta: Parul, 2010), 75, 84–5.

191. 'Swargiya Upendrakishore', *Sandesh*, 3, no. 10 (1915–16): 290–5, at 294, http://archiv.ub.uni-heidelberg.de/savifadok/volltexte/2010/1117/ (accessed on 10 November 2011).

192. S. Dutta, *Prasanga 'Sandesh'*, 86.

193. S. Mitra, 'Periodical Readership, 212–13.

194. Up to the Sravan 1321 (July–August 1914) issue, *Sandesh* was printed at Lakshmi Printing Works on 64-1 and 64-2, Sukea Street and published from Upendrakishore's residence at 22, Sukea Street. See *Bengal Library Catalogue of Books Registered in the Presidency of Bengal: Appendix to the Calcutta Gazette*, 3rd quarter (1914): 164. At the end of 1914, Upendrakishore moved into his own large house on Garpar Road where he put in a new press that printed the magazine and the books published by U. Ray & Sons. See S. Ghosh, 'Upendrakishore', 88–9, 96–7.

195. Buddhadeva Bose, *An Acre of Green Grass: A Review of Modern Bengali Literature* (Bombay: Orient Longman, 1948), 95.

196. Ajit Dutta, *Bangla Sahitye Hasyaras* (Calcutta: Jignasa, 1960), 445–6. Among the few pieces Sukumar Ray wrote for grown-ups after taking over as the editor of *Sandesh* was 'Kyabaler Patra', in which he poked fun at the celebrated litterateur Pramatha Chaudhuri and the somewhat affected style he had introduced. See Sanyal, *Parichoy-er Kuri Bachhar*, 163; and B. Chakravarty, *Bangla Shishu Sahitya Charcha*, 165–6.

197. P. Basu, *Satyajit Ray*, 211–12; and 'College-er Dinguli: Satyajit Ray (1936–1940)', in *Nostalgia: An Illustrated History of Hindu-Presidency College (1817–1992)*, edited by Koustubh Panda (Calcutta: Sulagna Mukherjee/Survey Guild, 1993), 113–15, at 115.

198. See *Bengal Library Catalogue*, 1st quarter (1914): 157–8, 163–4; 2nd quarter (1914): 125; 3rd quarter (1914): 157, 164; 4th quarter (1914): 115–16, 121; 3rd quarter (1915): 117, 122; 4th quarter (1915): 83, 86; 2nd quarter (1916): 89; 3rd quarter (1916): 111; 2nd quarter (1917): 103. The final issue of *Mukul* was the Sraban 1326 (July–August 1919) number. See *Bengal Library Catalogue*, 1st quarter (1920): 149.

199. L. Majumdar, *Upendrakishore*, 75; Leela Majumdar, 'Chhotoder Janya Boi', in C. Bandyopadhyay, *Dui Sataker Bangla*, 244. Upendrakishore, Bratati Chakravarty (B. Chakravarty, *Bangla Shishu Sahitya Charcha*, 221) has claimed, did not include advertisements in *Sandesh* but Sunirmal Basu recalled seeing advertisements of H. Bose's cosmetic products on the back cover. See *Sunirmal Rachana Sambhar*, 3: 218. The absence of covers in existing library copies of *Sandesh* preclude easy verification of either claim, but the text of the magazine was certainly free of advertisements.

200. H. Raychaudhuri, *Upendrakishore*, 57, 69–71.

201. Quoted in Drotner, *English Children and Their Magazines*, 21.

202. 'Swargiya Upendrakishore', *Sandesh*, 3 (1915–16): 290–5, at 290–1, http://archiv.ub.uni-heidelberg.de/savifadok/volltexte/2010/1117/ (accessed on

10 November 2011). This piece is largely an adaptation of the memorial address by Sukumar Ray and was, in all probablity, written by him. Compare with Sukumar Ray, 'Upendrakishore Ray'.

203. Brajendranath Bandyopadhyay, *Dwarakanath Gangopadhyay* (Calcutta: Bangiya Sahitya Parishat, 1950), 28–9.

204. See Saroj Bandyopadhyay, 'The Literary Works of Satyajit Ray', in *Satyajit Ray: An Intimate Master*, edited by Santi Das, translated by Samik Bandyopadhyay (Delhi: Allied, 1998), 83–102, at 84; and L. Majumdar, *Upendrakishore*, 75–6.

205. This is broadly comparable to the effort of British children's magazines of the mid-nineteenth century to inspire their readers to be empire-builders by providing them with exotic, colonial adventures, and biographies of imperialist heroes. See Drotner, *English Children and Their Magazines*, 66–7.

206. Hitendrakishore Raychaudhuri, *Upendrakishore o Masua Ray Paribarer Galpasalpa* (Calcutta: Firma KLM, 1984), 77–8; and L. Majumdar, *Upendrakishore*, 12–14, 64–5, 69. In his reminiscences of his nineteenth-century childhood in Jaguria, a village in Mymensingh, Rajanikanta Guha described how tigers were frequent visitors to his home. See Rajanikanta Guha, *Atmacharit* (Calcutta: Jatindranath Roy, 1949), 27–9. In the early twentieth century, a British official recorded that north-western parts of Mymensingh had, in the mid-nineteenth century, 'contained as many tigers as any district in India'. He thought that tigers were 'still numerous' in Mymensingh and, occasionally, villages would be visited by leopards and bears. See F.A. Sachse, *Bengal District Gazetteers: Mymensingh* (Calcutta: Bengal Secreatriat Book Depot, 1917), 11. The Mymensingh boy Nirad Chaudhuri recalled, however, that thanks to 'our general ignorance about animals', any animal 'with a feline look and dashes of yellow and black in it was, and still is, a tiger of some sort or other'. See Nirad C. Chaudhuri, *The Autobiography of an Unknown Indian* (London: Hogarth Press, [1951] 1991), 17.

207. Goswami, *Colonial India in Children's Literature*, 147.

208. The Puranas interested him from a scholarly point of view too. He was particularly interested in analysing how in each of the different books in the Puranas, the same stories often recurred, albeit with interesting modifications. His final illness, however, prevented him from accomplishing this. See B. Chakravarty, *Bangla Shishu Sahitya Charcha*, 70–1.

209. B. Chakravarty, *Bangla Shishu Sahitya Charcha*, 78–9.

210. See Grenby, 'The Origins of Children's Literature', 9; and Hugh Cunningham, *The Children of the Poor: Representations of Children since the Seventeenth Century* (Oxford: Blackwell, 1991), 191–2, 201.

211. Quoted in Borthwick, *Changing Role of Women*, 168–70.

212. Buddhadev Bose, 'Bangla Shishusahitya' (1952), in Buddhadev Bose, *Sahityacharcha* (Calcutta: Dey's, 1976), 38–64, at 39.

213. Bose, 'Upendrakishore Raychaudhuri', 134, 136.

5

Home and the World

Swadeshi *and Its Ambiguities*

In a recent study, Supriya Goswami has suggested that the swadeshi movement inspired Upendrakishore Ray to produce an indigenous literature for Bengal's children.[1] First, says Goswami, the works he produced after the partition of Bengal were 'homespun and rebellious towards all forms of authority', and second, his rejection of the violent and narrowly Hindu temper of the movement was expressed through 'a more secular and humorous vision' of the 'inclusive and earthy world of Bengali folklore'.[2] Although Goswami's arguments are not always sufficiently nuanced, the context of the swadeshi movement can be helpful in illuminating the complex positions that the Rays took on cultural nationalism and cosmopolitanism.

Swadeshi and Empire

Literally meaning 'of one's own country', the word swadeshi entered the political vocabulary when Bengalis protested against Curzon's 1905 division of Bengal into western and eastern segments by launching a movement for the boycott of imported goods and the adoption of indigenous alternatives.[3] Not simply a political or economic crusade, it aspired to regenerate every aspect of national life—to bring about, as one activist put it, 'swadeshism in dress, in diet, in habits, in life, in arts, in litera-ture, in science, in religion and philosophy'.[4] Some of the most creative people in Bengal were drawn to the swadeshi movement, including Rabindranath Tagore, who wrote some of his finest songs on patriotic themes, led processions, and wrote at length about his own ideas for building up the nation's own inner strength (atmasakti) before retreating in 1907 in protest against the growing violence of the movement.[5] Surendranath Banerjea, the doyen of 'moderate' nationalism but wholehearted in his opposition to Curzon's partition, found the swadeshi upsurge to be the nearest thing to a revolution that he had ever experienced.[6] Few historians today would support Banerjea's assessment. Although the ferment he recalled was real, the movement, in the end, was a narrowly Hindu crusade from which the large Muslim population of Bengal stayed aloof and although much good work was done by swadeshi supporters to establish indigenous businesses and industries, few of them succeeded in supplanting imported products enduringly.[7] In cultural terms, too, the nar-row-minded indigenism of hard-core swadeshi supporters did not leave lasting results.

An East Bengal man who had become prominent in Calcutta and across the world for his indigenous innovations, Upendrakishore could have been a poster-boy for the fight against the partition of Bengal. Moreover, he lived like a Bengali gentleman, ate sitting on the floor, dressed invariably in a simple dhoti and kurta, and he and his brothers always spoke in the 'Bangal' dialect of East Bengal, which, then and later, was derided by the people of West Bengal as rustic.[8] And Upendrakishore was not unsympathetic to nationalism. Although we do not know of any involvement with the Indian Association, his daughter Punyalata recalled him leading rehearsals of patriotic songs to be sung at the annual session of the Indian National Congress and he participated in at least one procession led by Rabindranath Tagore protesting the partition of Bengal.[9] When his adoptive brother, Narendrakishore, embraced the swadeshi cause and wanted to set up handlooms on the estate, Upendrakishore readily consented.[10] A rather more striking expression of Upendrakishore's nationalism came in October 1908, when he anonymously published a one-page 'advertisement' satirizing the British propensity to kick 'native' ser-vants to death and then, with the collusion of European medical witnesses and judges, to have the deaths attributed to the rupture of pathologically enlarged Indian spleens.[11]

That kind of criticism of British racial arrogance and aggression, however, was common at the time and did not necessarily indicate a desire for the British to leave India. The second issue of *Sandesh*, in fact, opened with a lovingly done full-colour frontispiece depicting King-Emperor George V, a Bengali translation of 'God Save the King' and, for good measure, an entirely hagiographic article on the life of 'Our Emperor'.[12] (*Sandesh*, incidentally, never mentioned the award of the Nobel Prize in Literature to Rabindranath Tagore in 1913.)[13] If placed side by side, the satirical 'advertisement' for the spleen protector and the paean to George V might strike today's readers as mutually contradictory but such a combination of imperial loyalty with nationalism, as we recall from our examination of Dwarakanath Ganguli's nationalistic activities, was the norm for this era. The nationalist educator Satishchandra Mukherjee, an important figure in the swadeshi movement and the founder of a 'national' university seeking to provide the kind of culturally rooted education that the British-run Calcutta University could not, hailed King-Emperor George V's visit to the Cornonation Durbar in Delhi in 1911 as an event of 'transcendental importance' brought about by the 'beloved and illustrious' Emperor's 'desire to be of signal service to India'.[14]

The coverage of the First World War in *Sandesh* was also unquestioningly loyal. Although the magazine, at this stage of its history, was meant for the very young, it informed its readers about modern destroyers and their guns, recounting the journey of a shell through a soldier's body without trying to evoke the horror of war or even human pain.[15] Even more striking was the Bengali translation of a Sikh soldier's letter to his father from the warfront in Europe. Written in a deadpan style, the letter brimmed over with gory details about heaps of German corpses and shell attacks that not only blew soldiers into smithereens but festooned trees with the fragments of their uniforms. This remarkable piece ended with the King-Emperor's visit to the Indian troops with Christmas presents and perhaps it was the soldier's praise for George V—'I have heard that despite being raised by God to the throne, he does not keep the poor at a distance'—that induced Upendrakishore to publish it.[16]

This display of royalism and militarism, however, was undermined—no doubt unwittingly—by a poem of Sukumar Ray's that was printed immediately before the soldier's letter. In it, Sukumar poked fun at the war by depicting a Bengali madman Jogai who, after an imagined but valiant fight in the course of which he 'kills' two Germans and 'wounds' three, is hit by a shell and carefully records his own death in his notebook.[17] Sankha Ghosh has asserted that the subject of Sukumar's poem was not the First World War but Jogai's absurd antics.[18] This may well have been the author's *intention*, at least as far as the child readers of *Sandesh* were concerned. For the adult reader, however, reading the Sikh soldier's letter after the poem makes the former sound like a real-life Jogai and, perhaps, as insane in his desire to kill—and be killed—for recognition from the Emperor. This kind of ironic deflation of militarism would be repeated in *Sandesh* when Sukumar assumed the editorship in 1916.[19]

An Art of One's Own?

The swadeshi movement called upon Indians to reject the foreign and to celebrate the indigenous. But although virtually all Bengali Hindus (including Brahmos) opposed the partition of Bengal, not all of them wanted to sever their links with European arts and letters. Nothing demonstrates this more clearly than Upendrakishore's uncharacteristically open debate with those who urged Indian artists to shun all Western influences and cultivate a 'spiritual', non-naturalistic style that was supposedly more authentically Indian.

Looking at Upendrakishore's painting of Sita, Marie Seton lamented that Satyajit Ray's grandfather had depicted the heroine of the Ramayana as a 'pale Victorian Miss' and attributed the deracinated style to 'the role of British art education in India at the time'.[20] When Western-style art education had begun in India, the British had considered the 'native artist' to be useless in portraying nature.[21] British art educators, therefore, took it upon themselves to teach 'natives' to observe nature, to depict the real and to revere the style of the European Renaissance.[22] Art, in order to attain universal relevance, had to depict nature with accuracy and the best kind of art was oil painting, in which the true artist revealed himself as the conduit of 'an authentic civilizational essence'.[23] Elite as well as subaltern Indian artists assimilated the lessons readily, cultivating 'photographic, realistic values' in their work, though only the most confident dabbled in oils.[24]

In the late nineteenth century, it was Raja Ravi Varma (1848–1906) who was the pre-eminent exemplar of this new approach to art.[25] His paintings of Hindu mythological subjects in a style that 'measured up to a broad criterion set by Western Academic norms' captivated just about everybody, the middle classes discovering them through reproductions printed in magazines like *Probasi* while the masses were provided for by cheap chromolithographic prints produced at Varma's own art press.[26] Varma's fortunes, however, shifted in Bengal during the swadeshi years when some of his erstwhile champions (most notably, Ramananda Chatterji) began to find his work inauthentic and embraced the emerging Bengal School of art and art criticism. Led by Abanindranath Tagore, these artists and critics called for the rejection of Renaissance naturalism and the adoption of a supposedly authentic Indian style that disregarded *chiaroscuro*, perspective, and anatomical accuracy and was concerned only with the expression of emotional truth and devout piety.[27] Without Chatterji's unstinting support on the pages of *Probasi* and *Modern Review*, Abanindranath declared, the new school would never have made its mark.[28]

The Bengal School's self-conscious search for an authentic national art was part of a global trend. 'Russian Slavophiles, European Theosophists, Japanese, and Indian Pan-Asianists, the leaders of the Irish Literary Revival and members of the Arts and Crafts Movement' all strove to move beyond 'Western rationality, industrial society and academic illusionism'.[29] The popularity of such movements, Dianne Sachko Macleod has suggested, stemmed from their nostalgic evocation of 'the close-knit communities of bygone days'.[30] In early-twentieth-century Bengal, too, such nostalgia was at work but it was a nostalgia not just for the premodern but for the pre-colonial and pre-Muslim. Many accepted the Bengal School's claim of total national authenticity at the time but hindsight reveals its complicated origins and diverse allegiances. As the Marxist sociologist Dhurjati Mukerji once pointed out, its artists were not exclusively Bengali, its greatest fans were 'Englishmen, Germans, Japanese, Indian princes', its themes were Hindu and Buddhist myths, and its style, instead of replicating that of village potters and painters, was 'eclectic, pastiche if you didn't like it; even the pigments and brushes had to be imported'.[31]

Most revealingly, however, the Bengal School's indigenist quest had been triggered, nurtured, and authenticated by four foreigners: an Irish convert to Hinduism, a Japanese art expert and philosopher, a British colonial art educator and administrator, and a Sri Lankan Tamil who had grown up in England. In their own distinctive ways,

they established an opposition between aesthetic realism and idealism and identified the latter with Indian art and culture. The Indian
artist became indistinguishable from a yogi.[32]

The first of the foreign prophets of aesthetic Indianness was
Margaret Noble, who was so devoted to the late-nineteenth-century
Hindu prophet and revivalist Vivekananda that she took the name of
Nivedita and moved to Calcutta. She was to become a great advocate
for every kind of nationalism, supporting secret societies of terrorists
as well as calling for a return to the 'superior realism' of India's own
artistic tradition.[33] Her call was supported by the Japanese art expert
Kakuzo Okakura (1862–1913), who, on two visits to Calcutta, inspired
many elite figures (including the Tagores) to rediscover the 'oriental'
roots of their civilization.[34] Okakura's influence was all the more
potent because Japan's victory in the Russo-Japanese War of 1904–5
had led to Bengalis regarding Japan as a model of how to become
modern without sacrificing one's national roots.[35] The third foreigner
who inspired indigenist artists was a representative of the British Raj,
Ernest Binfield Havell (1861–1934), who arrived in Calcutta in 1896 to
take charge of the Calcutta School of Art with the conviction—shared
by William Morris and the followers of the Arts and Crafts Movement
in Britain—that the West had sold its soul to the machine and for
Indians to emulate Western art and culture was a manifestation of
'Macaulayism'.[36]

At the Calcutta School of Art, Havell made 'oriental' art the cor-
nerstone of the curriculum and decided to sell off the indifferent collection of European art acquired in the late nineteenth century to help
'natives' learn 'the right way of seeing'.[37] Significantly, many Indian
students rose in protest at Havell's actions, and some of them eventually set up a rival institution where the principles of European naturalism were held in high regard.[38] Havell remained unmoved,
declaring that Indians should focus only on their own art, which was
'always striving to realise something of the Universal, the Eternal, and
the Infinite'.[39] The art critic Ordhendra Coomar Gangopadhyay (O.C.
Gangoly, 1881–1974) even described Havell (who was anything but
supportive of Indian political or economic nationalism) as the 'English
prophet of Indian nationalism'.[40] Nivedita, Okakura, and Havell's
contributions to early-twentieth-century debates on Indian art were
complemented by the work of our fourth foreigner—Ananda K.
Coomaraswamy (1877–1947).[41] Being close for a time to the Arts and
Crafts movement in Britain, Coomaraswamy visited Calcutta in 1909

and although he had little interest in the political or economic goals of the swadeshi movement, he eloquently endorsed its cultural indigenism, calling for 'a Swadeshism of ideas, of music, of art'.[42]

Many intellectuals and artists of the early twentieth century assimilated these interpretations of 'Indian tradition' by non-Indians.[43] Even Rabindranath Tagore, who was not a great admirer of indigenism, confessed that his generation had been 'taken in' by Ravi Varma's paintings and thanked Havell 'for having raised us from that inglorious position'.[44] He did not mention his own nephew Abanindranath Tagore but it was, in fact, Abanindranath who had transformed Havell's theory into practice.[45] Abanindranath, whose initial work had been naturalistic and 'Victorian', described the Englishman as his guru and Havell persuaded him to become the Vice-Principal of the Calcutta Art School.[46] Abanindranath, his pupils and his admirers sought to rediscover an authentic Indian style that scorned European naturalism and emphasized spirituality and transcendence. The paintings of this 'Bengal School' complemented the swadeshi spirit but they were also embraced by the Raj, which regarded—and funded—them as examples of a safe and legitimate swadeshi that could entice Bengali youth away from political nationalism.[47]

The Bengal School had its moment in the sun but its philosophy as well as its artistic productions have long been controversial. The greatest problem with its aesthetic indigenism was the conviction that there was one single homogeneous Indian style—spiritual and implicitly Hindu—and that it could be easily identified and practised. The historian and critic Akshayakumar Maitreya (1861–1930) criticized the artists for their ignorance of classical Sanskrit principles of artistic creation while Gurusaday Dutt (1882–1941), an Indian Civil Service officer who spent years collecting and writing on Bengali folk art, pointed out that there was no such thing as *the* Indian artistic tradition, only a mosaic of different regional styles.[48] In the 1930s, the Indian–Hungarian painter Amrita Sher-Gil declared that instead of bringing about a renaissance in Indian art, the Bengal School had exerted 'a cramping and crippling effect on the creative spirit'.[49] Abanindranath Tagore's own uncle Rabindranath, when appointing Abanindranath's student Nandalal Bose as the head of art education in his university, told him that it was not so easy to become 'foreign' and there was no need to subject his students' art to a nationality test.[50] It is rarely remembered, though, that one of the first major critics of Bengal School indigenism had been Upendrakishore Ray.

Upendrakishore versus the Indigenists

Upendrakishore was an enthusiastic painter with a particular interest in landscapes and mythological characters.[51] At least one of his paintings—an unidentified landscape—was awarded a silver medal at the Indian Industrial and Agricultural Exhibition of 1906–7 by a panel of judges that included Abanindranath Tagore.[52] And when *Sandesh* was established in 1913, Upendrakishore filled its pages with innumerable illustrations—many of them of mythological characters—and designed its full-colour covers and frontispieces. Despite generally avoiding organizational involvements, he had joined the executive committee of the Bangiya Kala Samsad, an organization of Bengali artists that was founded in 1905 and named by Rabindranath Tagore. Little, unfortunately, is known about the Kala Samsad except for the fact that Abanindranath Tagore, O.C. Gangoly, and other proponents of swadeshi art were among its leading members.[53] It may be because of Upendrakishore's involvement with this organization that Tapati Guha-Thakurta described him as 'a painter working broadly within the folds of the new art movement'.[54] Within two years of the founding of the Kala Samsad, however, Upendrakishore had turned against artistic indigenism, becoming one of the earliest and most critical interlocutors of the Bengal School.

Upendrakishore's stylistic preferences were of the age of Ravi Varma, and although he did not use live models, he depicted human beings with anatomical accuracy, was entirely European in his use of perspective, and was opposed to the unnatural colour schemes of Indian folk art.[55] 'Just as our indigenous music lacks harmony,' he once observed, 'so do the paintings of our folk-painters lack natural colours: a yellow man dressed in red uses a black mace to beat up a green man.'[56]

Predictably, therefore, Upendrakishore was dismayed when Abanindranath Tagore, in an uncharacteristically abrasive lecture of 1907, declared that the great artistic traditions of the world—classical Greek, Indian, Japanese—had all disdained empirical reality, soaring 'far above the human world', but that ideal state had been disrupted by the Renaissance imperative to portray nature in minute, photographic detail. The 'evil genius' of modern European art, 'smelling of trader's greed and decked with glittering and fashionable costumes' should be rejected by Indians, Abanindranath urged, in favour of their own noble traditions.[57]

In an article published in the very first volume of Ramananda Chatterji's new English magazine *Modern Review*—which, like its stablemate *Probasi*, was one of the greatest patrons of the new swadeshi art—Upendrakishore rejected Abanindranath's call to eschew European art's fidelity to nature. Describing himself as 'an ardent admirer' of classical Indian art, Upendrakishore denied that Indian artists were only capable of drawing in one, supposedly indigenous style. Citing instances of talented Indians excelling at European-style naturalistic art—including his friend Sashi Hesh—he argued that Indian art and European art were not 'two totally different languages'.[58] But although the Indian artist employed the same artistic language as the European artist, the former, he remarked, spoke it 'like a child, and the latter like a man. There is undoubted charm in a child's lisp, but all the same it is necessary that the child should outgrow it'. An Indian artist practising European-style art was not trying to speak in a foreign language but merely improving his 'grammar and rhetoric'. Bengali poets had done the same with great success— modern poetry in Bengal, the excellence of which was surely undoubted, owed as much to Shelley as to Kalidasa, he pointed out.[59]

Holding to what Partha Mitter has called 'a unilinear view of artistic evolution', Upendrakishore rejected the idea of judging different traditions of art by different criteria.[60] As he observed privately to a young friend, there were no national boundaries within the fine arts: 'What we call indigenous today clearly resembles "foreign" art of an earlier age.'[61] As for naturalism, no artist in any tradition could move completely away from nature and reality. Even Hindu religious art of the kind Abanindranath admired was not as distant from nature as he claimed. The figures might have extra arms or eyes but those arms all looked like arms and the eyes, like eyes.[62] Also, the liberal Brahmo Upendrakishore pointedly observed, Abanindranath's idea of Indian religious art was entirely Hindu and seemed to imply that to be Indian was to acquiesce 'in the tenets of idol-worship'.[63] As a committed artisan, he also opposed the lofty contempt Abanindranath had expressed in his lecture for artists who worshipped Mammon.[64] Ultimately, however, the point for Upendrakishore was that Europeans were simply *better* at pictorial art than Indians, just as Indians surpassed Europeans in the decorative arts. Nationalists who refused to recognize this were obstructing national improvement.[65] 'My nationality,' he declared, 'consists of a legitimate and affectionate pride in all that is noble in our national life and tradition, combined with sincere regret for our shortcomings and eagerness to remove them. It is this nationality that prompts me to advocate the study of European art as a means of improving the Art of my country.'[66]

Upendrakishore's conviction that European art could find a true home in India, asserted O.C. Gangoly in a reply, was reminiscent of 'the insane gardener who wanted to graft a camelia bud on a rose tree'.[67] European art excelled in 'forceful, accurate and sometimes photographic realisation of the outer forms and facts of nature' but Indian artists could not—and should not—aspire to do the same.[68] There was room for cosmopolitanism in science, technology, and industry, but not in art.[69] 'All good art,' he proclaimed, 'is the natural utterance of the soul of a people in a voice peculiarly its own. One can imitate the voice, but cannot body forth the soul.'[70] Upendrakishore retorted that the artist's 'primary concern' was to give expression to 'his own feelings and ideals, and these quite as often as not may have nothing to do with the subject of nationality, but still may be fit for the noblest artistic expression'. If he chose to repress his views 'in deference to those of the nation, he would indeed have lost his birthright and perhaps not got the proverbial "mess of pottage" in return'. It was not just a question of aesthetic individualism for him, however. He again stressed the need for artistic indigenists to respect India's inherent diversity. If the Bengal School enshrined Hindu religious art as India's national art, then what was to stop India's many Muslims from insisting that an artist could not be Indian unless he followed the principles of Islamic aesthetics?[71] This was his last public utterance on the subject.[72] In private, the equable Upendrakishore did not give way to rancour, but merely commented that the debate on art was not being conducted in the proper spirit. 'All this heated talk, all this bickering over what is true and what false, what is natural and what unnatural' suggested to him that the debaters had lost their way.[73]

In his overall understanding of pictorial realism, the backwardness of Indian representational art, and the universality of Western naturalism, it is obvious that Upendrakishore remained stuck in a conventional position, unlike Upendrakishore the printing technologist who, in spite of starting with a complicated imported technology, succeeded in adding value to it with his own research. In art, however, a field where a colonial practitioner naturally had much more freedom to experiment and innovate, Upendrakishore revealed a paradoxically different personality. Here, he concentrated only on *learning* from the West and never seriously tried to improve on what he had learnt. Of course, the champions of swadeshi art were inconsistent too, not to mention prejudiced. The idea that Hindu and Buddhist symbols stood for the Indian nation—which, at that point, had far more Muslims in its midst than after the 1947 partition—was majoritarian at best and communal at worst. Nor were the devotees of swadeshi art satisfied with swadeshi resources. O.C. Gangoly, for instance, did not think that half-tone blocks could reproduce the delicate nuances of Indian art and when editing the art journal *Rupam*, devoted exclusively to Indian art but funded by a British grant, he got his plates printed by photogravure in London, Berlin, or Tokyo.[74]

These inconsistencies were not just individual eccentricities but manifestations of fundamental colonial contradictions. The indigenists as well as the cosmopolitans, for all their rationalizations, relied on the West for ideas, resources, or patronage. Upendrakishore, the printing technologist, might have acquired a degree of international recognition for his homemade innovations, but apart from half-tone technology being immature enough to welcome colonial input, he owed much to the supportive publicity of William Gamble. In art, the situation was completely different. European artists might occasionally admire exotic art from the colonies, some of them might even aspire to a 'primitivist' style but it is hard to imagine a situation where an Indian artist's artistic innovations would have been welcomed in, say, Britain as a genuine contribution to 'universal' art. Upendrakishore the technologist was certainly more imaginative and adventurous than Upendrakishore the artist, but even if the two had thought and worked with identical philosophies, they would have experienced very different outcomes in a world where the West set 'universal' standards and only accepted non-Western assistance when it served its own interests.

Hemendramohan Bose: Marketing *Swadeshi*

Upendrakishore's position on indigenism and intellectual cosmopolitanism can be contrasted usefully with his brother-in-law Hemendramohan Bose's very different attempt to be modern and nationalistic at the same time. Businessman, technophile, and entrepreneur, Hemendramohan Bose (1864–1916) was the nephew of the celebrated Brahmo leader Anandamohan Bose.[75] Hemendramohan was a bright but erratic student, with a range of eclectic interests. While studying at the Mymensingh Zillah School, he subscribed to *The Times*—which his elders considered to be pretentious—and digested, like many young intellectuals of the period, the works of Walter Scott and Shakespeare. During his schooldays, he came in touch with Saratchandra Ray of the Brahmo Shop but he does not seem to have been one of Ray's young volunteers.[76] He was also a great enthusiast for sport, especially cricket, and much later, would be one of the founders of the Sporting Union Club.[77]

What seems to have really attracted Bose, however, was technology. He often neglected his school-work to conduct chemical experiments, practise photography, and manufacture various devices and products, ranging from invisible ink to machines for producing carbonated drinks. These activities were frowned upon by his guardians, and so, most of Bose's technological experiments were conducted in secret and late at night. The cameras and other equipment were kept under his bed and hidden by an overhanging bed sheet. Music was also a passion and this interest, too, he had to pursue away from the eyes of his elders. To practise the flute, he went every evening to a local garden and climbed on a tree with foliage dense enough to hide him.[78] At some point in his life, he also learnt to play the violin and once he had made some money, is reported to have acquired a Stradivarius.[79]

Although his technological interests were not popular with his parents, the young man was determined not to compromise. When offered, through family connections, a job as a deputy magistrate— the pinnacle of achievement for most Bengali youth of that time—he refused, declaring that he would rather be a street pedlar than work for anybody else.[80] Unlike many young men making similar resolves, however, Hemendramohan stuck to it for his entire life. Following the usual trajectory, he came to Calcutta for higher studies after finishing school at Mymensingh and lodged at the 'Brahmo fortress', where he came to know Upendrakishore. For unknown reasons but foreshadowing something of a lifelong pattern of restless movement from one activity to another, Hemendramohan did not complete his BA course and enrolled in medical school. He could not complete his medical course either because of an eye injury and, once again, his well-wishers urged him to take up an ordinary job or to study law, the royal road to wealth and renown in colonial Bengal.

He did none of those things, however, and spent all his time producing a fragranced hair oil. As he would later claim in an advertisement, it was made from 'the purest Ceylon coconut oil', which had been 'highly refined and made perfectly odourless (a thing which has been so long deemed an impossibility, by a new and harmless process which is the manufacturer's own)'. The deodorized coconut oil was then 'infused with certain medicinal ingredients which materially increase its efficacy as a Hair Tonic' and perfumed. The product, which would later become iconic under its brand-name Kuntalin, was advertised as 'an excellent preserver and invigorator of the hair', and so sweetly scented as to be particularly welcome to women and children.[81] On other occasions, it was recommended for its effects on the brain: 'Each hair has its own share in the duty of maintaining the temperature of your brain at normal. Without a well-trained head of hair, your brain is apt to get too hot in summer or too cold in winter.' The way to have such brain-friendly hair was, of course, to use Kuntalin, a five ounce bottle of which was available for one rupee.[82] In another inspired advertisement, Bose proclaimed that the sight of one's first grey hair was assumed to indicate the onset of old age and 'you take to sedentary habits, cease to pursue your occupation with vigour and distrust your physical and mental strength'. In fact, of course, all this apparent senescence was the result of 'the improper supply of blood to the hair glands and nerves', for which Kuntalin was the most reliable remedy.[83] Sensitive, as always, to new needs and preferences, he later introduced the Kuntalin Hair Wash, an oil-free hair dressing.[84]

It was with Kuntalin and a capital of nine hundred rupees that Bose started his own business in 1891.[85] Kuntalin was soon followed by the perfume Delkhosh, which, Bose's advertisements promised, was so enduring that once sprinkled on a handkerchief, the scent persisted for a week.[86] Indeed, it was not just a perfume but a preventative against heat exhaustion: 'The fragrance of flowers has very strong influence over the troubles resulting from excessive heat of the season' and those seeking 'a sweet sense of relief' from the heat of the Calcutta summer could do no better than invest in a vial of Delkhosh.[87] Many other products were to join these two over the years—Tambulin (a blend of condiments to be chewed with the betel leaf or *paan*, which Bose himself was very fond of), syrups, the Cocolin bath soap, various dental products, and a range of essences capturing 'the very soul of fresh flowers' (such as Bokool, Chameli, Violets, or Aparajita).[88] Anticipating aromatherapy as well as harking back to early modern European ideas of epidemic prevention, Bose counselled the Bengali

gentry that 'cheerfulness of mind very naturally conduces to good
health' and the 'charming delicacy and sweetness and permanency' of
his flower essences produced 'almost unbounded' delight, while pre-
venting 'germs of diseases from entering the body' and thus protect-
ing lives 'in times of epidemic diseases'.[89]

Once his business prospered, Bose married Upendrakishore's
fourteen-year-old sister, Mrinalini.[90] It is not known how this marriage
came about. Mrinalini belonged to the Hindu branch of the Ray
family and Hemendramohan was Brahmo. It is, of course, likely that
Upendrakishore arranged the match, but one does not know how
Saradaranjan Ray, Mrinalini's guardian, was persuaded to give his
approval.[91] The marriage should also have been problematic from the
Brahmo point of view, since the bride's age fell barely within the limits
set by Act III of 1872, but of course, like many Brahmos of the time,
Bose may not have married in accordance with the Act. It seems, however, to have been an excellent match. The couple would have fourteen children and many of them would later excel in diverse fields,
including sport, music, technology, and cinema.[92] After Bose's death
in 1916, the business was taken over by eldest son, Hitendramohan,
but his mother, Mrinalini, unlike Upendrakishore's widow
Bidhumukhi, also helped out. She even taught herself English for that
purpose, a fact suggesting that in the Hindu branch of the Ray family,
women were provided only with traditional education.[93]

The name of the Kuntalin hair oil remains well known in Bengali
culture but that is largely the outcome of its striking publicity campaigns. As Amit Bhattacharyya has shown, many indigenous firms
were producing hair oil and perfumes from the 1880s. The well-known
Kesharanjan hair oil produced by the ayurvedic manufactory of
Nagendranath Sen (an ayurvedic physician or kaviraj by training) was
particularly popular, as was the Jabakusum oil of Chandrakishore
Sen's company. These brands survived far longer than Kuntalin and
were leading players in the hair oil market even in the late twentieth
century.[94] The Delkhosh perfume, too, faced competition.[95] But
despite facing such rivals, the historical record indicates that Bose
'surpassed them all'.[96] His products were marketed not only across
India but in Persia, Ceylon, China, Japan, Southeast Asia, and, as at
least one advertisement claimed, the United States.[97] This was not
necessarily due to the higher quality of Bose's products. Bose set up
an impressive stall at the Indian Industrial and Agricultural Exhibition
of 1906–7 called Delkhosh House to display his wares and won three

gold medals for various products but *none* for the famous Kuntalin.[98] The official report of the Exhibition mentioned, moreover, that despite the grandeur of Bose's hall, 'the products of certain firms such as the "Souravsar" of Messrs S. Datta & Co. and a Bouquet of Messrs M. L. Bose & Co. are in no way inferior, if not actually superior, to the best scents of Mr H. Bose'.[99] We have no means, of course, of evaluating the quality of Kuntalin or Delkhosh today, but what we can be sure of is the excellence of Bose's marketing methods.

As Siddhartha Ghosh has emphasized, Bose, unlike many of his contemporaries, appreciated that a market for indigenous products could not be created simply by urging the boycott of imported goods. The market would have to be built up not only by producing world-class indigenous products but by bringing them to the consumer's attention by imaginative publicity.[100] Bose spent a lot of time and money on advertising his products as widely and attractively as possible, especially in the Bengali-owned papers of Calcutta.[101] He pioneered conceptually sophisticated, culturally aware, and aesthetically appealing advertising long before anything like a real consumer society had come into being in India and at a time when even a sympathetic observer remarked that 'native Indian firms are very poor advertisers'.[102] Prashant Kidambi has recently urged historians to examine 'the material aspects of middle-class lives', instead of focusing exclusively on 'the intellectual and political strivings of the ... intelligentsia', and Bose should feature prominently in any historical study of the material aspects of Bengali middle-class lives.[103] Products manufactured or imported by him not only supplied the existing needs of an evolving class but generated new consumerist desires.

Douglas Haynes has argued that before 1914, Indian advertisements 'possessed little visual material other than the manipulation of the size of the type font for emphasis ... Some images of people were present, but usually those represented were Europeans'. Although Haynes acknowledges that there were exceptions, the list he proffers is limited to 'safes, cars, watches'.[104] Similarly, Kajri Jain, focusing on the marketing of Babuline gripe water by B.A. Oza of Bombay, suggests that 'native' manufacturing and advertising took off only after 1914 and even then, the products were usually simple and low-tech— 'matches, soap, *beedies*, ink, oils, tonics' advertised in almanacs and downmarket publications, rather than in newspapers and magazines.[105] Perhaps that was the case in the Bombay Presidency, the focus of Haynes's research as well as Jain's, but in eastern India, Bose was already using richly visual advertisements in the Bengali as well as the British-Indian press for his products long before 1914.

There were no gods, goddesses, or avatars in his advertisements and the human figures were mostly Indian, especially women with long and luxuriant hair or 'real' people like nationalist leaders Surendranath Banerjea and Lala Lajpat Rai or iconic celebrities such as Rabindranath Tagore. Bose's advertisements were full of striking illustrations by Bose's eldest son, Hitendramohan (1893–1963), and the trained oil painter Purnachandra Ghosh (1885–1949), who had turned to commercial art to make a living.[106] Nor did Bose advertise only in the print media. His were among the first indigenous products to be advertised by posters on tram-cars and by full-colour slides for cinematic projection.[107] Some of his less dramatic initiatives were also novel in the Bengali context. A newspaper advertisement of the Delkhosh perfume, for instance, included a coupon and readers could get 'two copies (for self and a friend)' of 'a lovely little card exquisitely perfumed with our Delkhosh, the king of perfumes' if they returned the coupon to the firm with postage.[108]

Perhaps above all, Bose's advertisements were path-breaking in their use of rhyming copy. The most famous was the jingle *keshe makhho Kuntalin, rumaletey Delkhosh, paaney khhao Tambulin, dhanya hok H. Bose* (Put Kuntalin on your hair, Delkhosh in your handkerchief, Tambulin in your betel, and bring fulfilment to H. Bose), used extensively—often in variant forms—in print advertisements.[109] It is not known who composed these rhymes—Amit Bhattacharyya has attributed them to Bose himself without citing any evidence, while *Keshey makhho Kuntalin*, it has been claimed, was written by the dramatist and wit Amritalal Bose.[110] Whoever the author might have been, it is unlikely to have been a professional copywriter because the only advertising agencies that existed in Calcutta at this time confined their activities to securing advertisements from (mostly) foreign manufacturers and placing them in Indian newspapers.[111] In Bose's lifetime, Indian firms produced their advertising copy in-house, but nothing is known about the mechanics of the process or the personnel involved.

Bose also used endorsements in his publicity material from Bengali luminaries of the time, ranging from Rabindranath Tagore (who certified that a relative with hair loss had grown new hair after using Kuntalin) to the celebrated chemist Prafullachandra Ray who declared that he had analysed Kuntalin and found it to be prepared from the purest ingredients. The nationalist leader Surendranath Banerjea provided a testimonial for Bose's perfumes, declaring that he used them himself and recommending them to all.[112] This use of celebrity testimonials, however, was not particularly original. Advertisement campaigns for Jabakusum hair oil, too, used endorsements from celebrities of the stature of Bankimchandra Chatterji, Rameschandra Dutt, and, again, Surendranath Banerjea. Prafullachandra Ray's Bengal Chemical and Pharmaceutical Works, arguably the most successful indigenous enterprise of the era, advertised its remedies with endorsements from prominent doctors.[113]

Where Bose truly left his mark, however, was in dreaming up the Kuntalin Prize, which, as far as we know, was the first example of 'product placement' in India.[114] The competition, which began in 1896, was ostensibly a literary one. Entrants were invited to send in short stories which were judged by an expert—not a panel—and the best ones were not only awarded cash prizes but published in an annual volume, printed in thousands of copies at Bose's own Kuntalin Press—established next door to his perfumery works in north Calcutta's Sibnarayan Das Lane, where Upendrakishore also lived up to 1901—and distributed free with purchases from Bose's shops.[115] In order to be eligible for participation in the competition, however, the story had to mention the name of Kuntalin hair oil or the Delkhosh perfume somewhere.[116] (After some entries went overboard with their enthusiasm for the miraculous virtues of Bose's products, they were sternly reminded in 1905 that such exaggerated praise ruined the literary value of the entry and embarrassed the sponsors.[117])

In the early twentieth century, the Kuntalin Prize became quite an institution in Bengal and the volumes of prize stories were very popular.[118] By tickling the Bengali bhadralok's fabled literary sensibility, the Kuntalin Prize not only supported, in a small but not insignificant way, Bengali literature but made Bose's products into household names.[119] The very first story to receive a fifty-rupee prize was by none other than the scientist Jagadischandra Bose. He asked for his story to be published anonymously and the prize money was donated, at his request, to the Brahmo Sunday School with which Bose as well as the manufacturer of Kuntalin were deeply involved.[120] The next year, 1897, the first prize went to Radhamani Devi. Behind that very ordinary female name was the well-known writer Prabhatkumar Mukherjee. In that same 1897 Kuntalin collection, Prabhat Mukherjee got in another story, this one written under a male pseudonym. The tendency to send stories pseudonymously, in fact, became so common that from 1901, the rules expressly forbade males from submitting entries with female names.[121] But the use of male pseudonyms was not explicitly banned and the top prize of 1902 went to one Surendranath Gangopadhyay, actually the pseudonym of the future literary lion Saratchandra Chatterji.[122] Henceforth, *all* pseudonyms, and not just cross-gender ones were prohibited.[123]

Douglas Haynes has argued that 'advertising both shaped, and was shaped by, larger discourses of what it meant to be middle-class during this time'.[124] Judging from the style and rhetoric of Bose's advertisements, he was drawing upon (and no doubt also shaping) an emerging middle-class ethos that was 'literary' and increasingly nationalistic. Many of his advertisements emphasized the swadeshi origin of Kuntalin and remarked on the lack of self-respect of those who used foreign products.[125] Many swadeshi-era advertisements urged what one might call import-substitution and Bose's were no exception.[126] But unlike the majority of those, Bose's advertisements did not simply claim that his products were as good as imported ones: they were *better* than their foreign counterparts *and* substantially cheaper. Arvind Rajagopal has argued that advertising in colonial India was divided into 'a vernacular domain whose moral status varied, depending on its fit with patriotic nationalist values, and an English-language realm catering largely to the colonial elite and to relatively affluent city dwellers'.[127] This is broadly true but Bose straddled this division without necessarily concealing his nationalist convictions. Advertising his 'fresh flower extracts' in 1895 in *The Statesman* (a paper owned, edited, and read primarily by the British), Bose simply inserted the tagline: 'Try Them Against Foreign Makes.'[128] Much more work is needed to establish the exact social reach and depth of penetration of Bose's products—some of them, despite being cheaper than imports, would still have been too expensive for an ordinary clerk or a college lecturer—but one can argue, on the whole, that Bose offered a three-fold advantage to his customers. They would save money, smell better, and look better than those who paid exorbitant sums for imported cosmetics, and help build the national economy.[129]

Bose was a staunch indigenist in his personal life—he refused to wear Western clothes and declined to attend events where a *dhoti* would be inappropriate. He lamented that while most Indians loved their respective national dresses, Bengalis were ashamed of theirs and preferred to dress like sahibs.[130] As a businessman, though, Bose was far more pragmatic, almost paradoxically so. For he was not just an indigenous manufacturer of hair oil and perfumes, but a pioneering importer and distributor of the latest foreign technologies, such as the bicycle, the phonograph, or the automobile. Understandably, Bose's nationalist position became complicated and more than a little ambiguous in his efforts to entice the Bengali middle classes to buy these products. Indeed, for the bicycle, he jettisoned all swadeshi rhetoric and when he obtained an agency for Rover, he proudly claimed in his advertisements (even at the height of the swadeshi movement in 1906) that these British bikes were unequalled in 'speed, durability and finish of construction' and were patronized by the English Royal family.[131] At times, though, he was rather more creative and used an imported technology like the phonograph to spread the message of swadeshi.

Domesticating the Foreign

Bose, as we know, was interested in diverse kinds of technology in his childhood but his mature interests, without ever becoming too narrowly specialized, came to be concerned largely with new means of communication and transport. He founded the Kuntalin Press, which not only printed the volumes of Kuntalin prize stories and the catalogues for Bose's many businesses, but many other publications including the magazine *Probasi*. The blocks needed for Kuntalin Press publications were all made by Upendrakishore's firm.[132] Even closer to Upendrakishore's interests was Bose's passion for photography but Bose, unlike his brother-in-law, was not concerned with process photography or photomechanical reproduction. He was an enthusiastic amateur photographer, developing his own photographic plates as well as those of other enthusiasts (obviously for a fee), and also selling cameras and photographic requisites.[133] He was among the first in India to use the expensive Autochrome process for colour photography, which had been invented in 1907 by the same Lumière brothers who had earlier created the modern motion picture with their *cinematographe*.[134]

Where Bose diverged wholly from the world of his brother-in-law was in his interest in sound recording, or more precisely, in the phonograph, which not only allowed its users to listen to recordings—made on cylinders coated with tinfoil and later with wax—but also to make their own recordings on blank cylinders. Invented by Thomas Alva Edison in 1877 a year or so after the introduction of the telephone by Alexander Graham Bell, the news of the phonograph reached Calcutta within a year and the first demonstration of the machine occurred in December 1878.[135] More demonstrations followed in subsequent years, including many by the well-known Belgian priest, scientist, and enthusiastic evangelist for all things scientific, Father Eugene Lafont, who had purchased his own Edison phonograph on a visit to Paris.[136] In European circles of Calcutta, 'phonograph concerts' were often held at clubs and other private venues, some of them charging quite high admission rates.[137] Until the invention of the disc record and gramophone in 1887 by Emile Berliner, a German living in the US, there was no alternative to the phonograph, especially in India where Berliner's innovations did not make much of a mark until the early twentieth century.[138]

Wealthier Calcuttans had begun to buy phonographs by the end of the nineteenth century while the rural poor were acquainted with the new marvel by itinerant entertainers holding phonograph shows in tents at village fairs, rather like the film exhibitors of the period.[139] By 1892, Jagadischandra Bose was using a phonograph and among his recordings was one by his friend Rabindranath Tagore.[140] O.C. Gangoly recalled in his autobiography that while in college, he had spent almost four hundred rupees to buy a phonograph. He made many recordings, even though he was disappointed by the relatively rapid deterioration of their sound quality.[141] Hemendramohan Bose was actually rather slow in adopting the phonograph—he purchased his only around 1900. By then, there were at least three dealers of phonographs in Calcutta and within a few years, the musical instrument company of Dwarkin's was advertising its own phonographic recordings.[142] It is possible that Hemendramohan was associated with Dwarkin's venture but even if not, he soon made his own recordings of such celebrated figures as Prafullachandra Ray and fellow enthusiast Jagadis Bose, but not for commercial purposes.[143] Bose, at this point, does not seem to have had much more than an amateur's interest in sound technology. Around 1903, he tried to form a partnership with the local agents of Pathé Frères, the French record and film company founded by the four Pathé brothers in 1896 but not with the aim of entering the record business.[144] What interested him then was the cinema.

Established by Charles Pathé, who had begun his career as an exhibitor of Edison's phonograph at fairgrounds, Pathé Frères had acquired the Lumière brothers' original cinematograph patents and had rapidly become one of the largest film companies in the world.[145] Bose was eager to make films in India and imported several movie cameras and other equipment from Pathé.[146] At that time, the Madan family held a virtual monopoly on film exhibition all over the subcontinent and on film production in Eastern India, and they told Bose that his entry into the film business would be 'an unfriendly gesture', especially since the Madans themselves administered Pathé's film business in India.[147] Bose promptly retreated and was rebuked for it by Bengal's near-mythical film pioneer Hiralal Sen (1868–1917) and his brother and business partner, Motilal. 'You have not done the right thing,' they reportedly told him. 'A day will come when you'll have to repent for this decision of yours.'[148]

Even after withdrawing from the film business, Bose did not focus on recorded sound but on a novel form of transportation: the bicycle. Although ancestors of the bicycle had emerged in Europe and America in the early nineteenth century, it was not until the end of the century that bicycles really caught on with the public.[149] As was common at the time, the new technology appeared quickly in India but for some time remained restricted to a small number of enthusiasts.[150] Among the earliest users of the bicycle were some of the usual suspects: Jagadischandra Bose, his wife, Abala, Prafullachandra Ray, the physician Nilratan Sircar (1861–1943) and his wife, Nirmala, and Bose himself.[151] In partnership with his brother Jatindramohan, Bose opened the first Indian-owned cycle shop and repairing business in Calcutta—it is not known exactly when the business was founded but newspaper advertisements show that it was flourishing by the early 1900s.[152] Thus, Bose was among the first in a trade that was to take off in India only in the 1910s, when 'Indian cycle dealers appeared on the streets of almost every town and city'.[153] This, however, was a dealership, not a manufacturing business. The brands sold were Rover, imported from Britain (costing one hundred and thirty rupees), the German Dürkopp ('the strongest and the most durable cycle ever made', ideal for 'rough use on bad mofussil roads'), available for one hundred and fifty rupees, and The Eagle, priced much lower at seventy-eight rupees for the basic model.[154] 'Don't go in for a cheap or a second-hand bicycle', warned an advertisement, '[t]he cheapest cycles are the costliest in the end'.[155]

A great bicycle entrepreneur of India, Sudhirkumar Sen (1888–1959)—a Brahmo, son-in-law of cycle enthusiast Nilratan Sircar, and schoolmate of Sukumar Ray—bought his first bike, a Rover, from Bose's shop and in 1910, himself began to import and sell cycles (along with many other articles, including gramophones) in Calcutta. In his early trading activities, Sen essentially followed the Bose model but unlike Bose, Sen was also interested in manufacturing a swadeshi bicycle. It would take years for the dream to materialize but in the 1950s, Sen established the first modern bicycle factory in Bengal, albeit in collaboration with the British firm Raleigh.[156] Bose, as far as we know, had never even entertained such as a possibility.

It was in his bicycle shop that Bose first began to sell phonographs. (The sale of phonographs in bicycle shops seems to have been a common pattern throughout India.)[157] Noting the growing popularity of the recorder-player, however, he set up a new shop in the central location of Dharmatala Street and named it 'The Talking Machine Hall'.[158] Taking out full page advertisements in the leading Calcutta newspapers, Bose announced in early 1906 that it was now possible 'for a talking machine to take the place of a singer' and admonished the public that 'you shall have to give up the old and take to the new; the sooner you do, the better for your enjoyment'. Among the first batch of records he issued were exclusive performances by artistes associated with the Star Theatre of Calcutta.[159] Within a couple of months, his list had grown to include recordings of the two greatest poets and composers of the time, Rabindranath Tagore and Dwijendralal Roy, and the Bande Mataram choral group, which was regarded by the government as quasi-terrorist.[160] Tagore and Roy, the advertisement emphasized, had 'very kindly allowed us to record their voices and this is a privilege which has not been conferred upon any one else'.[161]

Rabindranath Tagore, who, in the early twentieth century, was known as much for his spirited singing voice as for his poetry, was to make many recordings for Bose and since this was at the height of the swadeshi movement and there was great interest in patriotic songs, Bose's catalogue emphasized Tagore's patriotic compositions.[162] Bose made the recordings himself at the residence of Jagadis Bose or at his own north Calcutta home.[163] Amal Home recalled that on the days when Tagore visited the latter for recording, rows of people would stand on either side of the narrow lane simply to catch a glimpse of the great man.[164] But Bose was nothing if not eclectic in his offerings and by the end of 1906, his catalogue had expanded to include performances of classical music by the most popular artists of the time, including Ramzan Khan and Lalchand Boral.[165] 'Bande Mataram', the hymn from Bankimchandra Chatterji's novel *Ananda Math*, was probably the most popular swadeshi song of the time and Bose issued two versions of it on cylinder records in 1906, one sung by Tagore and another by the group Sebak Sampraday.[166]

This 'literary-cum-political context', Amitabha Ghosh has argued, distinguished Bose's recording endeavours from those of others trying to capture the Indian market in the early twentieth century.[167] Bose's nationalism was certainly on full display in the early days of his phonograph business. 'You have given up using Belati [i.e., British or, more broadly, imported] goods', thundered an advertisement, 'you should give up using Belati records as well', and patronize 'a countryman of yours' has produced records of 'a state of perfection which the foreigners could not achieve'.[168] The swadeshi movement had coincided with the explosion of the record industry in India and Bose was not the only entrepreneur to marry the two. In 1908, for instance, a company called Swadeshi Binapani Records advertised its disc records of the Bande Mataram hymn, pointing out—no doubt with Bose in mind—that 'unlike so-called swadeshi phonographic records of which the songs are recorded in India with foreign materials', their records were 'manufactured by swadeshi brethren with swadeshi materials'.[169] But Bose was far too shrewd a businessman to rely exclusively on Bengali nationalistic material and also advertised 'Hindi, Urdu and Urya [sic] songs of all sorts to suit every taste'.[170] And he reminded his clients that when they had been 'surfeited with sweet songs', they could also use the phonograph to record 'songs and conversations of your friends and relatives and preserve their voices'.[171]

H. Bose's Records had agents all over northern and eastern India and the demand for the recordings was high enough for Bose, who had been acquiring his wax cylinders from Pathé, to start manufacturing them himself in Calcutta—which an obituarist would describe as the foundation of a 'new industry'.[172] Although it was a business decision to produce his own blanks—'there are a thousand dealers but only one manufacturer of cylinder records in India', declared one of his full page advertisements—Bose also gave it a political dimension.[173] Bose's records, the advertisement claimed, provided 'another proof of the great success already achieved by us in our endeavour to supply our own needs'. The recordings were technically

flawless ('you no longer hear a machine but the singer himself') and
offered 'the songs of the most celebrated musicians of the country,
permanently preserved by a countryman of yours in a state of perfection which the foreigners could not achieve'. Unlike foreign records,
the advertisement claimed, Bose's swadeshi records had 'no hissing,
no screeching, no nasal or metallic twang'.[174] 'No More Hoarse Voice!!
No More Indistinctness!!!' promised another.[175] One would be a fool,
the advertisements implied, not to 'Use the Best' and 'Avoid the Rest'
(the 'rest,' obviously, meaning foreign records).[176] Although we have
no quantitative data, it is clear that swadeshi recordings did offer
significant competition to the import trade. Christina Lubinski cites
two 1906 letters from the multinational Gramophone Company's representative in Calcutta reporting that the 'Bengali Trade (i.e. in Bengali
Records) is practically at a standstill. The Bengalis are boycotting us as
much as possible ... our trade is entirely done by Mohommedans [sic]
and a few Europeans'.[177]

Bose remained loyal to the phonograph for as long as he could,
shunning the rival technology of disc records.[178] But these were fast-
changing times and he soon faced stiff competition. In 1902, the
Gramophone Company (then known as the Gramophone and
Typewriter Limited), which had hitherto only been exporting records
of Western music to India, decided to aim for the larger subcontinental market for 'native' music. Their recording engineers Frederick
William Gaisberg (1873–1951) and George Walter Dillnutt (1882–
1936), who went on a world tour to collect recordings of exotic
material, reached India in October 1902 and made many recordings.
Pressed into discs in Germany, these reached Indian shops in early
1903 and sold well enough for other Western companies to send their
own engineers on recording expeditions to Asia.[179] In 1908, the
Gramophone Company—attracted, among other things, by the ready
availability of shellac in India—set up its own record factory in
Calcutta, the products of which soon flooded the market. These
records, made in India and mostly by Indian workmen, could not
even be condemned unequivocally as foreign.[180]

In the initial years of the Gramophone Company's incursion into
the Indian market, Bose sought to compete with them—and other
disc record manufacturers—by emphasizing how the phonograph
had improved over time. A 1907 advertisement acknowledged that
although 'the shrill-voiced disc machines have nearly won the public
heart by their noisy loudness', newer varieties of the phonograph

were 'as loud' and 'more clear', *and* retained the one indubitable advantage they had always had.[181] 'Can you make records with your talking machine?' asked Bose. 'If not then either throw it in the lumber-room or try to dispose of it at any price it can fetch now. Provide yourself with a machine that can talk, sing and write.'[182] Moreover, not only did the needles used on disc machines need frequent replacement but even the best needles were sure to scratch the records. The newer phonographs, however, used 'a sapphire point' that did not produce scratches and lasted for ever.[183] These valiant efforts to keep the phonograph alive probably did not work too well, for in little more than a month, Bose began to sell 'all machines, be your choice a gramophone, a Nicolephone, a new model phonograph or an Edison machine' and recordings in every format.[184] In February 1908, he announced a substantial price-reduction for phonographs and cylinder records, offering a hundred-rupee phonograph for eighty and a standard cylinder record for one rupee.[185]

But although he seems to have accepted that the age of the phonograph was now over, Bose did not immediately give way to the gramophone. He set up a new partnership with Pathé Frères and began to supply their Pathephone player. Pathé discs were double-sided, cost between two rupees and three rupees and twelve annas, and could be played on *any* machine, simply by changing the sound-box (which cost a mere five rupees). While the Pathephone could not make recordings, it did use a permanent stylus and Bose's advertisements continued to emphasize this superiority: 'The Music that Touches the Soul is in Pathé where Needles are Needless.'[186] Bose had all of his phonograph recordings transferred to discs by Pathé.[187] The company was well-experienced in this, having transferred its own cylinder recordings to discs recently, but used a recording system that was different from other disc record manufacturers.[188] Although these discs were sold in India as 'Pathé-H Bose's Records', they were manufactured in Belgium and Bose, therefore, could no longer claim a swadeshi provenance.[189]

Nor was there any exclusivity in Bose's arrangements with Pathé. M.L. Saha and the house of Madan also sold Pathephone machines and Pathé discs in Calcutta, and for the same prices as Bose.[190] His position was further undermined when, in 1908, Pathé launched their own tours of the subcontinent to record new material and then opened a shop in Calcutta selling all their recordings, including many on Bose's list, claiming to have established through their records an 'entente

cordiale between France and India'.[191] Bose was named in an advertisement as *one* of their agents and appointed as their broker for finding
and engaging suitable artists in India. The new recordings were marketed under the Disque Pathé brand, without any mention of Bose.[192]
Bose now had full control only over a handful of his recordings—two
songs by Lalchand Boral, a recitation by Rabindranath Tagore, and a
few others.[193] By the end of 1908, we find Bose holding a discount sale,
offering one Pathephone and a dozen Pathé discs (the regular price of
which would have been more than 112 rupees) for a lump sum of 80
rupees, and from mid-1909, he was even offering to accept returns of
Pathé records and advertising various deals for supplying a new
Pathephone in exchange for old talking machines of any type.[194]

It is difficult to explain why Bose, who manufactured phonographic
cylinders in Calcutta before anybody else, could not do the same for
discs. It is not as if producing disc recordings was technologically
impossible in India. A small business in Bombay, the Wellington Cycle
Company, was issuing discs manufactured on its own hand-presses by
1905 and the firm of Mukharji and Mukherjee in Calcutta were manufacturing their own discs by 1906.[195] It is clear, therefore, that Bose
could well have made his own disc records in Calcutta but whether that
would have saved his business is another matter. Even with an early
lead and exclusive recordings by celebrities, it would have been difficult
for him to compete with the Gramophone Company after its Calcutta
factory began to produce Indian recordings on an industrial scale.[196]
Perceiving the way the wind was blowing, Bose had disengaged from
his recording business—which historians now consider to have been 'a
foundation stone' for the Indian recording industry—around 1911,
moving into automobiles.[197]

The motor car, like so many other new technologies, had arrived
in India by the end of the nineteenth century and Calcutta, the capital
of British India, had its first car dealer by 1900, selling imported
petrol-operated as well as electrical cars.[198] The price of cars ranged
between 2,250 and 20,000 rupees, putting them way beyond the reach
of ordinary Indians.[199] Bose was one of the first people in Calcutta to
own a car.[200] He bought a one-cylinder model of the French car
Darracq in 1903—which cost about 200 pounds—and then a two-cylinder model in 1905, priced at around 265 pounds. These prices,
although substantial, were still on the lower side. A single-cylinder
Speedwell, for instance, would have cost fifty pounds more and for a
two-cylinder Lanchester, Bose would have had to pay more

than 400 pounds.[201] Although Bose was an enthusiastic driver, he also perceived a business opportunity in the motor trade. Around 1910, when his recording business became unviable, he set up the Great Eastern Motor Company with a large showroom and repair shop on Free School Street. This was in the 'European' part of the city, where few, if any, Bengali traders owned big shops at the time. By 1911, the Great Eastern was a thriving business, selling a wide variety of new and second-hand cars imported from Europe, and also bicycles.[202] When there was an opportunity to import from Ford in the US, however, Bose dismissed the car (presumably the Model T) as an 'ugly animal'. In his recorded sound business, Bose had at least manufactured one essential component but with motor cars, he was entirely an importer and even his repair shop was headed by a British engineer. Most of the customers were British too.[203] Unfortunately, the car business did not thrive for very long. The car trade, like all trades in imported goods, suffered during the First World War and after Bose's death in 1916, his successors retreated to the original perfumery business.[204]

Bose had regarded his swadeshi records as a contribution to the nationalist cause, but some of his contemporaries would have disagreed with him. 'Every time you accept a gramophone in place of a man you degrade the musician, take from him his living, and injure the group-soul of your people,' Ananda Coomaraswamy wrote in 1909. 'No man of another nation will come to learn of India, if her teachers be gramophones and harmoniums and imitators of European realistic art.'[205] One does not know if Bose read this essay but he (or, for that matter, Upendrakishore) would surely have scoffed at such objections. For them, the pursuit of swadeshi did not merely amount to the revival of India's timeless artistic traditions. It meant catching up with—and perhaps surpassing—the West in modern ideas, tools, and practices, even if that meant learning from the West in the initial stages. Nor did it imply any tendency to champion the indigenous regardless of quality. Bose, for example, derided 'so-called swadeshi perfumes' as worthless, compared to his own expertly blended (but equally swadeshi) products.[206] As we saw in our discussion of the debate between O.C. Gangoly and Upendrakishore, this kind of cosmopolitan swadeshi was not the most popular of positions in early-twentieth-century Bengal. But the Rays were never to budge from this stance and, despite the massive historical differences between the time of Upendrakishore and of his grandson Satyajit, the latter consistently held to the family tradition of embracing the foreign in order to enrich the indigenous.

Bose's swadeshi endeavours, for all their distinctiveness, did have their limitations, however. Most glaringly, he never really developed any of the technologies he distributed and even the manufacture of phonograph cylinders was no more than the successful replication of an imported product. David Arnold is, no doubt, right to stress that Indian involvement in the import and distribution of new technologies was 'almost as crucial in giving Indians a share in the market and a sense of ownership' as manufacturing them, and we do need to be aware of grades of 'swadeshi-ness' when we explore the history of indigenous enterprise.[207] Bose, from such a perspective, would qualify as a swadeshi entrepreneur, albeit one whose performance never quite lived up to his ambitions or, for that matter, to his rhetoric. That failure was not entirely a consequence of his *personal* limitations. A lone Calcutta entrepreneur who was fascinated by complex and lucrative new technologies but did not possess vast amounts of capital and manpower, he was always vulnerable to competition from powerful rivals, as in his sound recording business. Sometimes, his ambitions could be stifled at inception by powerful monopoly interests, as the Madans did with his plans for making films. Contrast all this with Upendrakishore's involvement with half-tone technology—it was new, it was potentially lucrative, and it was being researched all over the world, but no local or multinational competitor was interested in cornering its Calcutta market. Upendrakishore, of course, was ultimately edged out of the international arena but he remained the leading supplier of half-tone blocks in Calcutta. Bose, however, was far more vulnerable to competition. Add to that Bose's tendency to move restlessly from one technology to another and his disinclination to innovate, and it becomes amply clear why the more adventurous divisions of his business empire did not endure.

The Bose Legacy

Although none of Bose's children managed to run his businesses with their late father's panache, some parts of Bose's legacy were preserved and built upon rather more successfully than Upendrakishore's. One reason for this was the fact that Bose had many more children and none of them was to die as early as Sukumar Ray. While some shared their father's enthusiasm for cricket, two of his sons, Nitindramohan (Nitin) and Manindramohan (Mukul), acquired Bose's technophilia and distinguished themselves in the film industry, Nitin as cameraman and director and Mukul as sound recordist.[208] Nitin Bose (1897–1986) had been inducted into photography by his father: 'He would keep me in the dark room and call out instructions from outside', recalled Nitin in old age.[209] Nitin saw his first film at the Congress session held in Calcutta in 1906 and that experience kindled his strong interest in the cinema. Rather like his nephew Satyajit Ray was to do later, he developed the habit of analysing the films he saw and working out ways in which he could have improved upon them.[210] This, too, was encouraged by Nitin's father, who presented him with a movie camera, a projector, and a developing machine. The young man, who slept with the camera beside him, first made a twenty-foot long film featuring his family, then shot a film on plant life for Jagadischandra Bose and of an elephant hunt for the Maharaja of Tripura.[211] The last film—which Satyajit Ray recalled being shown on the Bose family projector in his childhood—was bought by Fox for more than a thousand dollars.[212]

Nitin Bose's first professional job as cameraman came in 1925, for a film called *Incarnation*, directed by Jai Gopal Pillai. Bose, who had never shot a feature, had much to learn but Pillai, apparently, was a great teacher.[213] Other assignments followed, including an early version of the perennial classic *Devdas* (1927) and in 1930, Bose served as cameraman for the new International Filmcraft Company's first productions, *Chorkanta* directed by Charu Roy and *Chasar Meye* directed by Prafulla Roy.[214] The founder of the company, B.N. Sircar, was already thinking of setting up a sound studio in Calcutta and when International Filmcraft's productions flopped, he established New Theatres, which was to be Bengal's most famous production company until the 1950s, and appointed Bose as the technical director and the head of the camera department.[215] In 1933, Nitin Bose directed his first film for New Theatres—a Hindi version of *Chandidas*, which introduced Kundanlal Saigal, who was to attain great fame as a singer-actor—and was to have a long career as director in Calcutta and subsequently, in Bombay.[216]

Nitin was not the only Bose associated with the glorious years of New Theatres. When the sound studio was established, Sircar brought in the American sound engineer Wilford Deming—who had initially worked in Bombay with Ardeshir Irani for *Alam Ara*, the first Indian talkie—to set up the recording equipment for his new studio.[217]

Deming, who contrasted the professionalism of New Theatres with 'the rushing, haphazard methods of Bombay', was paid 250 dollars per month and expenses, but Mukul Bose, who was then a recent New Theatres appointee, mastered the complicated equipment so swiftly that Sircar could dispense with Deming's expensive services. 'Watching them at work, I often felt that Mukul displayed better efficiency than Mr Deming,' Sircar would later remark.[218] Nitin and Mukul went on to reveal a level of technological imagination that even their father may not have possessed. This was demonstrated most compellingly through the brothers' introduction of the 'playback' system, that is, the pre-recording of songs that the screen actors appeared to be 'singing'.

Indian films were full of songs even in the earliest years of the talkies, but until the coming of the playback system, they had to be recorded while the picture was being shot and needed to be sung by the actor or actress.[219] India's first talkie *Alam Ara* had many songs and all of them had been directly recorded. 'We were asked to sing without allowing time for breathing,' one of Irani's actor-singers reminisced, 'and the camera also ran simultaneously. If by mistake we fumbled or spoke a wrong word, the whole process had to be repeated.'[220] This was not easy but the difficulties multiplied when, in a song sequence, the director wanted to switch back and forth between shots. The New Theatres production *Bhagyachakra* (1934) had such a sequence and with direct recording, it was going to be almost impossible to synchronize the song with the changing shots. At that point, Mukul Bose proposed that the song should be recorded separately in its entirety and then, during the shooting, one could play whichever section of it that was required and the actors would only have to pretend to be singing. Many dismissed it as a wild notion but Sircar had full faith in the brothers and the experiment worked out well, and the playback system ensured that Indian films would for evermore be crammed with songs, all sung by a relatively small number of celebrated singers.[221] Rather like Upendrakishore, however, the Bose brothers did not patent their idea or, lamented an elderly Nitin Bose, 'we could have made a fortune'.[222]

Business, Idealism, *Swadeshi*

Bose, despite making substantial profits during his career, never seems to have invested them in landed property. Except for one large house which he built at the very end of his life, all his dwellings and business places were rented.[223] A lavish spender and philanthropist, he donated countless thousands of rupees to people who had approached him for help. 'A poor student or a needy family,' he used to say, 'have as much right to my wealth as my sons.'[224] Upendrakishore had less money to give away but he invested a lot in *Sandesh* without hoping for pecuniary returns and gave generously of his time for other, smaller projects like the music school for Brahmo children. He, too, lived and worked in rented houses and moved to his own house only at the very end of his life.[225]

Satyajit Ray's comment that his ancestors were 'idealists' and 'not practical men', might, therefore, seem appropriate.[226] Upendrakishore as well as Hemendramohan used their businesses not only to earn a living but to master and disseminate—often at considerable cost to themselves—skills and technologies previously unavailable in Bengal. At some level, they regarded themselves as harbingers of the modern and refused to pursue profit for its own sake. The cost of producing *Sandesh*, for instance, was never fully recouped from subscriptions but Upendrakishore kept on with it regardless, as did his descendants. This commitment to projects that were not likely to be immediately (or, for that matter, ever) profitable may have held the Rays back from conventional success. As Siddhartha Ghosh correctly pointed out, Hemendramohan could have built up a huge indigenous chemical industry had he resisted the allure of new technologies and concentrated exclusively on his perfumery business.[227] All of these points are valid at least up to a point but they posit 'idealism' and 'practicality' as mutually exclusive mindsets. Upendrakishore and some of his contemporaries do not seem to have thought similarly. Upendrakishore might not have been a hard-headed businessman but he did run a successful enterprise and Bose, of course, was a prominent entrepreneur. Dwarakanath Ganguli never made much money but who could deny the social value of his contributions to women's education or nationalism?

In fact, Upendrakishore and Hemendramohan might be criticized for focusing so much time and attention on their own businesses and hobbies that they did not do as much as they could have to provide hands-on training in their fields to coming generations. The Rays, for instance, had absolutely nothing to do with the swadeshi-era national education movement, which, among other things, wanted to make provisions for the technical education of young Bengalis.[228]

Plans for the education of Indians in the sciences had begun in the nineteenth century with Rammohan Roy and continued with the Indian Association for the Cultivation of Science (IACS) founded by Mahendralal Sircar.[229] Sircar's project was emphatically geared towards education and research in 'pure' science, although, even at the time of the establishment of the IACS in 1876, the short-lived Indian League argued that it would be far more useful to train young men in the industrial arts and technologies.[230] The more perceptive members of the Raj agreed. As Henry Cotton remarked in the 1880s, scientific training was less important for the economic regeneration of India than practical technical education, which would 'make existing industries and arts more productive and more perfect'. As with his views on tea planters, however, Cotton's plea was largely ignored by the government.[231]

It was only during the swadeshi movement that things changed. One of the great aspirations of the movement was the replacement of the 'foreign' Calcutta University by a truly national institution. The National Council of Education was founded in 1906 by Satischandra Mukherjee (1865–1948), a lecturer at Upendrakishore's alma mater, the Metropolitan Institution, and some of his bright young students, including Binaykumar Sarkar (1887–1949), later a prominent social scientist and polymathic scholar and writer. The Council aimed to create a full-fledged national university offering technical as well as humanistic education—not only the Harvard of Bengal, in the words of Binay Sarkar, but also the Massachusetts Institute of Technology.[232] Meanwhile, other eminent swadeshi sympathizers such as the physician Nilratan Sircar focused on the less grandiose objective of establishing a national institution that would provide young people with the technical and industrial education that the University was unable or unwilling to impart. They founded the Society for the Promotion of Technical Education, which started the Bengal Technical Institute.[233] Funded by the wealthy barrister Taraknath Palit, the Bengal Technical Institute had large 'mechanical workshops, smithery, electrical engineering shed, and a carpentry shed' and 'arrangements for teaching drawing, chemistry and dyeing'. A government report on technical education praised it for opening 'a direct avenue to industrial employment' that would dissuade its pupils from looking for government posts.[234] Initially, the National Council and the Society saw themselves as rivals, the Society being dismissed, in the words of Binay Sarkar, as being dedicated to 'crude *mistrification* [the training of *mistris* or low-grade mechanics]'.[235] Within four years, however, the two institutions had amalgamated, evolving into an engineering college and, after India's independence, into the full-fledged Jadavpur University.[236]

The dream of turning allegedly sedentary, literature-loving Bengali youth into technicians was an enduring one. In 1932, Binay Sarkar declared that the India of the future would have to be built not around the peasant or the bhadralok but around the ideal labourer, a self-reliant, dynamic, and forward-looking creator of industrial and technological prosperity.[237] Just after India had attained independence, he condemned its industrialists for behaving like a 'feudal landed bourgeoisie' and urged them to emulate the 'mentality, technical-mindedness, machine-sense and work-view of the *mistri* (hand worker or artisan), the foreman, the engineer, and the technical expert'.[238] Upendrakishore, of course, was long dead by this time but he was alive, active, and famous when the technical education movement commenced and he was a remarkable—and virtually unique—example of a man who had *mistrified* himself from a feudal-bourgeois background and built an independent career for himself as a sophisticated artisan. Moreover, some of the early leaders of the national education movement—especially Satischandra Mukherjee—had called for India to secure its industrial future by *avoiding* capital-intensive industries and concentrating on those that could be developed 'on a family-handicrafts basis'.[239] Who could have been a more appropriate mascot for such a programme than Upendrakishore or his brother-in-law? Neither man, however, was involved with it in any capacity, not even as donors.[240]

Upendrakishore's writings for children, of course, often dealt with science and he actually taught music to children under the auspices of the Brahmo Samaj, but he never sought to inspire the young to *mistrify* themselves as he had done in his youth. As for Bose, the technophile's quest for the perfect machine, the businessman's drive to find the most competitive product, and the progressive's passion for modernity were all intertwined and embedded within a liberal, patriotic, and nationalistic framework that evinced little interest in transmitting those values to the coming generations. The limitations of the artisanal, family-enterprise model are most evident here. Upendrakishore, no doubt, trained his eldest son, Sukumar, (and some of his own staff) in the mysteries of half-tone technology but failed to register the potential for the craft outside the confines of his own business and family. The same applies, *mutatis mutandis*, to Bose. Both men had accomplished virtual miracles in breaking out of the bhadralok world of landowning and desk-work, creating new ways of living, learning, and earning in the stunted colonial economy. They were keen, moreover, on the question of swadeshi and national regeneration in their own different ways. What they failed to find, however, was a way to transmit their entrepreneurial values and technological skills across society. Although they had modernized the role of the artisan-trader in a technological sense, they could not—or did not wish to—break out of the traditional family-centred universe of the artisan.

Notes

1. Supriya Goswami, *Colonial India in Children's Literature* (New York: Routledge, 2012), 136.

2. Goswami, *Colonial India*, 144.

3. The nationalistic interest in using indigenous products and avoiding imported articles may have reached its peak during the anti-partition agitation in Bengal but it had emerged much earlier, and not only in Bengal. See Bipan Chandra, *The Rise and Growth of Economic Nationalism in India: Economic Policies of Indian National Leadership, 1880–1905* (Delhi: People's Publishing House, 1966), 122–41; Prabhatchandra Gangopadhyay, *Bharater Rastriya Itihaser Khasra*, 2nd edn (Calcutta: Jignasa, 1965), 130–4; and Bimanbehari Majumdar, *History of Indian Social and Political Ideas from Rammohan to Dayananda* (Calcutta: Bookland, 1967), 111–12. The best overall study of the anti-partition movement is still Sumit Sarkar, *The Swadeshi Movement in Bengal 1903–1908*, new edn (Delhi: Permanent Black, 2010) but see also Manu Goswami, 'From Swadeshi to Swaraj: Nation, Economy, Territory in Colonial South Asia', *Comparative Studies in Society and History*, 44, no. 4 (October 2002): 770–99.

4. D.V. Athalye, *The Life of Lokamanya Tilak* (Poona: Chiploonkar, 1921), 138.

5. Sumit Sarkar, *Swadeshi Movement in Bengal*, 47–8.

6. Surendranath Banerjea, *A Nation in Making: Being the Reminiscences of Fifty Years of Public Life* (London: Oxford University Press, 1927), 197.

7. Nirad Chaudhuri opined that the anti-partition agitation was driven not by 'the liberal political thought of the organizers of the Indian National Congress, but the Hindu revivalism of the last quarter of the nineteenth century'. See Nirad C. Chaudhuri, *The Autobiography of an Unknown Indian* (London: Hogarth Press, [1951] 1991), 222.

8. Among the Rays, only Kuladaranjan dressed consistently in the Western style. See Hitendrakishore Raychaudhuri, *Upendrakishore o Masua Ray Paribarer Galpasalpa* (Calcutta: Firma KLM, 1984), 18, 59. The swains of Calcutta usually regarded East Bengal as 'a damp, marshy, dialect-speaking nest of provincials'—as eminent a figure as the scientist Jagadischandra Bose (1858–1937) remained sensitive about his East Bengal origins and accent for his whole life. His brother-in-law Anandamohan Bose, who would come to be famous for his scholarly excellence, had been taunted (or ignored) as a *Bangal* by some of his professors as well as fellow-students when he was a student at Calcutta's Presidency College. See Ashis Nandy, *Alternative Sciences: Creativity and Authenticity in Two Indian Scientists*, 2nd edn (Delhi: Oxford University Press, 1995), 23; and Srinath Chanda, *Brahmo Samajey Challis Batsar* (Dhaka: Bharat Mahila Press, 1913), 157–8. Bipinchandra Pal was once refused a teaching job because it was thought that a 'Bangal' would be unable to control large classes of Calcutta boys. See Bipinchandra Pal, *Sattar Vatsar: Atmajibani* (Calcutta: Kalpan, [1927–8] 2005), 157.

9. Punyalata Chakrabarti, *Chhelebelar Dinguli* (1958; reprint, Calcutta: Newscript, 1981), 73; and Siddhartha Ghosh, 'Upendrakishore: Shilpi o Karigar', *Ekshan*, 16, no. 6 (1984): 88–91.

10. He also gave a solo violin recital at a large swadeshi meeting held at Calcutta's Town Hall. See H. Raychaudhuri, *Upendrakishore o Masua Ray*, 19, 25–6.

11. The advertisement was for a 'spleen-protector' manufactured by Aprakash Gupta of Ghaebpur, Dhaka (each of these words, even the place name Dhaka, can mean 'secret' or 'hidden' in Bengali), that made 'the art of kicking and being kicked made safe'. See *Modern Review*, 4, no. 4 (October 1908), facing 355. Graphic reports of such cases were published in Bengali papers and even the celebrated writer Trailokyanath Mukhopadhayay (1847–1919), who was entirely loyal to the British regime and a caustic critic of the swadeshi movement, found it appalling that the British forgot their own rules for fair fighting and sportsmanship as soon as they arrived in India. See Kanailal Chattopadhyay, ed., *Samayikpatrey Samajchitra: Krishnakumar Mitra Sampadita 'Sanjibani'* (Calcutta: Dey's, 1989), 166–7; and T.N. Mukharji, *A Visit to Europe* (Calcutta: Newman, 1889), 147. As ardent an imperialist as Lord Curzon privately admitted that if the facts behind this 'Indian classic' were known in England, every Englishman would 'hang his head with shame'. See Rajat Kanta Ray, *Social Conflict and Political Unrest in Bengal, 1875–1927* (Delhi: Oxford University Press, 1984), 23. The theme of sahibs kicking their servants to death recurred in many stories by Upendrakishore's grandson. See, for example, Satyajit Ray, *Robertsoner Ruby* (1992), in Ray, *Feluda Samagra*, 2 vols (Calcutta: Ananda, 2005), 2: 655–97; and 'Nil Atanka' (1968) and 'Conway Castle-er Pretatma' (1982), in Ray, *Galpa 101* (Calcutta: Ananda, 2001), 99–107 and 330–40, respectively. For actual cases virtually identical to Ray's fictional representations, see

Elizabeth Kolsky, *Colonial Justice in British India* (Cambridge: Cambridge University Press, 2010), 136–9, 203–4. See also Jordanna Bailkin, 'The Boot and the Spleen: When Was Murder Possible in British India?', *Comparative Studies in Society and History*, 48 (2006): 462–93.

12. See 'Amader Samrat', *Sandesh*, 1, no. 2 (1913): 34–8, http://archiv. ub.uni-heidelberg.de/savifadok/ volltexte/2010/1115/ (accessed on 31 July 2010). There was another coloured frontispiece the following year, depicting George V dressed as an Indian warrior. See *Sandesh*, 2 (1914), facing 225, http://archiv.ub.uni-heidelberg.de/savifadok/volltexte/2010/1116 (accessed on 20 November 2014). The other great children's magazine of the era, *Mukul*, covered imperial politics and wars even more extensively. See, for instance, the long, illustrated feature by Sivanath Sastri on Queen Victoria's Diamond Jubilee in *Mukul*, 2, no. 10 (1906–7): 153–7; the report on the Boer War in *Mukul*, 6, no. 4 (1900–1901): 50–7; the adulatory piece on Lord Curzon's efforts at famine relief in *Mukul*, 6, no. 5 (1900–1901): 67–8; the obituary of Victoria in *Mukul*, 6, no. 10 (1900–1901): 147–50; and the tribute to Edward VII in *Mukul*, 8, no. 4 (1901–1902): 50–5. Another long, illustrated and reverential article on Victoria was contributed to *Mukul* by none other than Upendrakishore Ray—see *Mukul*, 3, no. 3 (1897–8): 34–48. My warm thanks to Paroma Maiti for providing me with copies of these scarce items.

13. My thanks to Ujjal Chakraborty for emphasizing this point.

14. See Haridas Mukherjee and Uma Mukherjee, *The Origins of the National Education Movement (1905–1910)* (Calcutta: Jadavpur University, 1957), 234–5; and Sumit Sarkar, *Writing Social History* (Delhi: Oxford University Press, 1998), 30. There was some nationalist logic behind George V's popularity with the Bengali Hindu elite. During his visit to India as Prince of Wales in 1905–6, he had concluded that the partition of Bengal had been 'a mistake' and after much difficulty, persuaded his ministers and Viceroy to reunify Bengal, the announcement of which was made during his visit to India as King-Emperor in 1911. See F.A. Eustis II and Z.H. Zaidi, 'King, Viceroy and Cabinet: The Modification of the Partition of Bengal, 1911', *History*, 44, no. 166 (June 1964), 171–84, at 182.

15. 'Gola Gulir Katha', *Sandesh*, 2 (1914–15): 204–6, http://archiv.ub.uni-heidelberg.de/savifadok/volltexte/2010/1116 (accessed on 20 November 2014). See also the description of a dog's devotion to his slaughtered German master, in which the carnage of war is mentioned almost incidentally and the account of plastic surgery on a soldier's damaged face, where the focus is entirely on the expertise of the surgeons—'Germaner Kukur'; and 'Ajob Daktari', *Sandesh*, 3 (1915–16): 80–2 and 219–21, respectively, http://archiv.ub.uni-heidelberg.de/ savifadok/volltexte/2010/1117 (accessed on 20 November 2014).

16. See 'Bilatey Sikh Sainya', in *Sandesh*, 3 (1915–16): 28–9, http://archiv. ub.uni-heidelberg.de/savifadok/volltexte/2010/1117/ (accessed on 28 November 2011).

17. 'Abol-Tabol', *Sandesh*, 3 (1915–16): 27–8, http://archiv.ub.uni-heidelberg.de/savifadok/volltexte/2010/1117/ (accessed on 28 November 2011).

18. Sankha Ghosh, 'Asambhhaber Chhanda', in *Prastutiparba*, 7, nos 3–4 (October 1982), special issue on Sukumar Ray, 149–57, at 151.

19. See Sukumar's short piece, 'Khukir Lorai Dekha', which was probably derived from a real-life account and describes a little girl found and sheltered by British soldiers in France. She cannot comprehend the differences between the two sides and during a shell-fight, thinks nothing of walking over to the Germans for sweets. See 'Khukir Lorai Dekha', *Sandesh*, 4 (1916–17): 27–8, http://archiv.ub.uni-heidelberg.de/savifadok/volltexte/2010/1118/ (accessed on 28 November 2011).

20. Marie Seton, *Portrait of a Director: Satyajit Ray*, expanded edition (Delhi: Penguin, 2003), 30.

21. Mary Carpenter, for instance, found it deeply puzzling that a people who produced such excellent handicrafts and textiles revealed such a 'remarkable deficiency in the drawing or sculpturing [sic] of the human figure, or even of animals'. See Mary Carpenter, *Six Months in India*, 2 vols (London: Longmans, Green, 1868), 2: 135. Indians themselves did not disagree. In 1854, a 'native' speaker at the Bethune Society—a learned body with European as well as Indian members—asserted that Indian art could offer nothing comparable to 'the specimens left by the genius of Greece and Rome' because Indian artists were so ignorant of human anatomy that they failed to represent bodies and even emotional expressions accurately. See Nabinkrishna Bose [Nobin Kristo Bose], 'The School of Industry and the Arts, &c.', *Selections from the Bethune Society's Papers*, no. 2 (1855): 109–27, at 118.

22. Partha Mitter, *Art and Nationalism in Colonial India, 1850–1922: Occidental Orientations* (Cambridge: Cambridge University Press, 1994), 110–11. See also E.B. Havell, *Indian Sculpture and Painting* (London: John Murray, 1908), 7.

23. Kajri Jain, *Gods in the Bazaar: The Economies of Indian Calendar Art* (Durham, NC: Duke University Press, 2007), 92–3. See also Tapati Guha-Thakurta, *The Making of a New 'Indian' Art: Artists, Aesthetics and Nationalism in Bengal, c. 1850–1920* (Cambridge: Cambridge University Press, 1992), 12–13, 31, 35, 68.

24. Guha-Thakurta, *Making of a New 'Indian' Art*, 110–11.

25. Lord Curzon—who, as Chancellor of Oxford University, would question whether Rabindranath Tagore deserved to receive an honorary degree from the University—was captivated by Varma's 'happy blend of Western technique and Indian subject'. Tagore himself recalled that in his childhood, Varma's paintings reminded him 'how precious our own culture is to us, in restoring to us our inheritance'. See P. Mitter, *Art and Nationalism*, 179–80, 218. For Curzon's views on Tagore, see William Rothenstein, *Men and Memories: Recollections, 1872–1938*, edited by Mary Lago (London: Chatto and Windus, 1978), 170.

26. See Guha-Thakurta, *Making of a New 'Indian' Art*, 137–8, 143; P. Mitter, *Art and Nationalism*, 212; Jain, *Gods in the Bazaar*, 105–7, 114; Geeta Kapur, *When Was Modernism? Essays on Contemporary Cultural Practice in India* (Delhi: Tulika, 2000), 148, 161; and Santa Nag, *Purbasmriti* (Calcutta: Papyrus, 1986), 49.

27. P. Mitter, *Art and Nationalism*, 234–5.

28. See Guha-Thakurta, *Making of a New 'Indian' Art*, 143, 145; and Abanindranath Tagore's tribute to Chatterji in *Probasi*, 26 (1333 BE/1926): 3, http://archiv.ub.uni-heidelberg.de/savifadok/volltexte/2009/984 (accessed on 8 November 2014). For a celebrated artist's opinion that by publicizing the substandard work of some of Abanindranath's followers, Chatterji unwittingly damaged the reputation of the Bengal School, see 'Kathay Kathay', interview of Binodebihari Mukherjee by Satyajit Ray, *Ekshan*, 14, no. 5 (1981): 15–24, at 23. My thanks to Soumen Paul for a copy of this text.

29. P. Mitter, *Art and Nationalism*, 243.

30. Dianne Sachko Macleod, *Art and the Victorian Middle Class: Money and the Making of Cultural Identity* (Cambridge: Cambridge University Press, 1996), 337.

31. See Dhurjati Prasad Mukerji, *Sociology of Indian Culture*, 2nd edn [1948] (Jaipur: Rawat, 1979), 181.

32. Guha-Thakurta, *Making of a New 'Indian' Art*, 178, 192–3. As Aida Yuen Wong has recently argued, this quest for an authentically spiritual Indian art represented 'the internalization of Western clichés about the Orient', even though it 'provided Indians with a sense of pride in their essential difference from the colonizers'. See Aida Yuen Wong, 'Landscapes of Nandalal Bose (1882–1966): Japanism, Nationalism and Populism in Modern India', in *Okakura Tenshin and Pan-Asianism: Shadows of the Past*, edited by Brij Tankha (Folkestone: Global Oriental, 2009), 95–110, at 107.

33. Sumit Sarkar, *Swadeshi Movement in Bengal*, 410–11; and Guha-Thakurta, *Making of a New 'Indian' Art*, 173.

34. On Okakura, who was a Japanese nationalist in his own way and saw his nation as the natural guardian of Asia, see the essays in Tankha, *Okakura Tenshin*, especially Wakakuwa Midori's 'Japanese Cultural Identity and Nineteenth-Century Asian Nationalism: Okakura Tenshin and Swami Vivekananda' (*Okakura Tenshin*, 22–6). Okakura encouraged revolutionary movements against the British and indicated that Japan might provide assistance to Indians in their fight with the British. See Peter Heehs, *The Bomb in Bengal: The Rise of Revolutionary Terrorism in India 1900–1910* (Delhi: Oxford University Press, 2004), 28–9. On his influence on Bengali intellectuals, see Rathindranath Tagore, *On the Edges of Time* (Calcutta: Orient Longman, 1958), 68.

35. See Manu Goswami, *Producing India: From Colonial Economy to National Space* (Chicago: University of Chicago Press, 2004), 254; and Cemil

Aydin, 'A Global Anti-Western Moment? The Russo-Japanese War, Decolonization, and Asian Modernity', in *Competing Visions of World Order: Global Moments and Movements, 1880s–1930s*, edited by Sebastian Conrad and Dominic Sachsenmaier (New York: Palgrave Macmillan, 2007), 213–36. The historian Kalidas Nag (1891–1966), who was in high school at the time, recalled that his generation regarded Japan's victory as 'our own victory'. See Kalidas Nag, *Memoirs*, 2 vols (Calcutta: Writers Workshop, 1991–4), 1 (1991): 19. The children's magazine *Mukul*, while condemning all wars as 'uncivilized', congratulated the Japanese for erasing their reputation of being a primitive race. See 'Rush-Japan Juddha', *Mukul*, 10, no. 10 (1904–5): 152–6. Many swadeshi activists identified so closely with Japan that they explicitly exempted Japanese imports from boycott. See Muzaffar Ahmad, *Amar Jiban o Bharater Communist Party* [1969] (Calcutta: National Book Agency, 1996), 26.

36.   P. Mitter, *Art and Nationalism*, 248–50, 297–300; and Binodebihari Mukhopadhyay, *Adhunik Silpa-Siksha* (1972), in his *Chitrakatha*, edited by Kanchan Chakrabarty (Calcutta: Aruna, 1984), 118. On Havell's contempt for 'Macaulayism', see Osman Jamal, 'E.B. Havell: The Art and Politics of Indianness', *Third Text*, 11, no. 39 (1997): 3–19, at 4, 8.

37.   P. Mitter, *Art and Nationalism*, 281–3, 301.

38.   See Binodebihari Mukhopadhyay, *Chitrakatha*, 120; and E.B. Havell, *Indian Sculpture*, 254. Rabindranath Tagore, incidentally, supported Havell's decision. See R. Siva Kumar, *Santiniketan: The Making of a Contextual Modernism* (Delhi: National Gallery of Modern Art, 1997), [2].

39.   The Indian artist, for Havell, was 'both priest and poet', who saw 'with the mind, not merely with the eye', aiming to 'bring out an essential quality, not the common appearance of things'. See Havell, *Indian Sculpture*, 24, 223. Predictably, he had no patience for Ravi Varma, condemning his paintings for their 'most painful lack of the poetic faculty in illustrating the most imaginative Indian poetry and allegory' (Havell, *Indian Sculpture*, 252). The approved forms of indigenous art, as Tapati Guha-Thakurta has pointed out, 'had to have its "Indian" content defined and specified by the colonial masters, even as its form was improved and modernised by their training' (Guha-Thakurta, *Making of a New 'Indian' Art*, 64–5).

40.   Quoted in Jamal, 'E. B. Havell', 4. Havell even recoiled from swadeshi campaigns to build up India's economy. That, he asserted, would merely 'multiply the evils which the factory system has already inflicted upon India'. See E.B. Havell, *Essays on Indian Art, Industry and Education* (Madras: Natesan, [1910]), preface, unpaginated.

41.   Born of an English mother and a Sri Lankan Tamil father who led a high-profile life in England and counted Disraeli among his friends, Coomaraswamy trained as a geologist but, on his first visit to Sri Lanka as a young man, discovered the destructive impact of colonialism on the indigenous arts and crafts of South Asia. For biographical details, see Roger Lipsey,

Coomaraswamy: His Life and Work (Princeton: Princeton University Press, 1977).

42. See Ananda K. Coomaraswamy, untitled contribution to *The Swadeshi Movement: A Symposium*, 2nd edn (Madras: Natesan, 1919), 243–51, at 248; and Coomaraswamy, *Art and Swadeshi* (Madras: Ganesh, [1912]), 3–4, 6–8, 17, 111. On Coomaraswamy's Indian visits, see Lipsey, *Coomaraswamy: His Life and Work*, 75–93.

43. P. Mitter, *Art and Nationalism*, 235; Guha-Thakurta, *Making of a New 'Indian' Art*, 188. The students of the J.J. School of Art in Bombay, however, do not seem to have been affected by this revaluation and continued to portray indigenous characters and themes in a Western 'academic' style. See Jain, *Gods in the Bazaar*, 145.

44. Rabindranath Tagore, 'Havell and Abanindranath', *Journal of the Indian Society of Oriental Art*, Golden Jubilee Number (November 1961): 92–3.

45. Ananda K. Coomaraswamy, 'The Present State of Indian Art, I: Painting and Sculpture', *The Modern Review*, 2, no. 2 (August 1907): 105–10, at 108. Binodebihari Mukhopadhyay pointed out that what Havell or Coomaraswamy said about Abanindranath's style applied only to a particular period in the artist's career. See Mukhopadhyay, *Chitrakatha*, 238–9, 257–9.

46. Tapati Guha-Thakurta, 'Abanindranath, Known and Unknown: The Artist versus the Art of His Times', in *Art and Visual Culture in India 1857–2007* (Mumbai: Marg Publications, 2009), 84–103, at 99; Abanindranath Tagore and Rani Chanda, *Jorasankor Dharey* (Calcutta: Vishwa Bharati, 1944), 101, 156–9; and O.C. Gangoly, *Bharater Silpa o Amar Katha* (Calcutta: A. Mukherjee, 1969), 143–5.

47. P. Mitter, *Art and Nationalism*, 285; 309. The British eagerly bought Bengal School paintings and the critic O.C. Gangoly recalled that wealthy Indians, hitherto firm in their allegiance to European-style naturalism, began to buy the work of the new indigenist artists only after the British had made it fashionable. See O.C. Gangoly, *Bharater Silpa*, 160, 370. On the sale of Abanindranath's paintings to British royalty and high officials, see Guha-Thakurta, 'Abanindranath, Known and Unknown', 91. The Indian Society of Oriental Art was set up in 1907 on European initiative and with the military hero Lord Kitchener as president. Abanindranath and his students were also involved and the Society was supported by the Landholders' Association, an organization of Bengali zamindars. See O.C. Gangoly, 'Indian Society of Oriental Art: Its Early Days', *Journal of the Indian Society of Oriental Art*: 98–101. After 1917, the new Governor of Bengal Lord Ronaldshay gave a munificent annual grant to the Society to encourage the blossoming of 'the fair flower of an indigenous growth'. Abanindranath and his brother Gaganendranath had no qualms about this but their uncle Rabindranath thought that government support would 'have a baneful effect on the mind and work of the artists'. See *'Essayez': The Memoirs of Lawrence, Second*

Marquess of Zetland (London: John Murray, 1956), 76, 124–6; Gangoly, *Bharater Silpa*, 161–9, 298; and Rathindranath Tagore, *On the Edges of Time* (Calcutta: Orient Longman, 1958), 130.

48. See Akshayakumar Maitreya, *Bharatsilper Katha* [1912–22] (Calcutta: Sahityalok, 1982); and Gurusaday Dutt, *Folk Arts and Crafts of Bengal: The Collected Papers* (Calcutta: Seagull, 1990), 9, 11, 38–9.

49. Quoted by Prodosh Das Gupta, 'The Calcutta Group—Its Aims and Achievements', *Lalit Kala Contemporary*, 31 (April 1981): 5–12, at 6–7. Das Gupta himself, a founding member of the Calcutta Group formed in 1942–3 by eight young artists of an internationalist bent, was even more critical, dismissing the Bengal School art as 'effeminate and wishy-washy, bereft of any inner strength'. See Prodosh Das Gupta, 'The Calcutta Group', 5; and Neelima Vashishtha, *Tradition and Modernity in Indian Arts during the Twentieth Century* (Shimla: Indian Institute of Advanced Study, 2010), 169–70.

50. Guha-Thakurta, *Making of a New 'Indian' Art*, 315–16; and 'Kathay Kathay,' interview of Binodebihari Mukherjee by Satyajit Ray, 23–4. Bose fully complied with Rabindranath's directive and not only gave his students complete liberty to follow their own inclinations but himself transcended the dogmas of the Bengal School, producing a series of new works that were national but not narrowly 'oriental'. See Ratan Parimoo, *Art of Three Tagores: From Revival to Modernity* (Delhi: Kumar Gallery, 2011). As R. Siva Kumar has pointed out, the influence of Rabindranath led Nandalal to appreciate that 'an art that responded to the everyday realities of contemporary life and environment could be a more authentic form of national art than a revivalist art dealing with mythological or historical themes'. See R. Siva Kumar, *Santiniketan: The Making of a Contextual Modernism*, 4, 7.

51. He painted several landscapes of Giridi, Darjeeling, and Puri, and his painting of the Kanchanjangha peak was one of the treasured childhood memories of Satyajit Ray (*Jakhan Chhoto Chhilam* [Calcutta: Ananda, 1982], 48). Upendrakishore presented a signed painting of the Chunar Fort to Rabindranath Tagore, who displayed it prominently in his house at Silaidah in East Bengal. See Jatindranath Basu, 'Silaidahey Rabindrababu', *Sahitya*, 11 (1901 [Ashar 1307]): 144–9, at 146. At an unknown date, Upendrakishore drew a series of pictures to illustrate Tagore's long poem 'Nadi' (The River) which described the long and varied course of a river from the mountains down to the plains and then to the sea. These sketches were reproduced in *Vishwa Bharati Patrika*, 20, no. 2 (Kartik–Poush 1370 [October–December 1963]), between pages 118 and 119.

52. *A Report of the Indian Industrial and Agricultural Exhibition, Calcutta, 1906–07* (Calcutta: 'Industrial India' Office, n.d.), 133.

53. On the Kala Samsad, see 'Bibidha Prasanga o Mantabya', *Silpa o Sahitya*, 5, no. 6 (Ashwin 1312 [September–October 1905]): 120, http://archiv. ub.uni-heidelberg.de/savifadok/volltexte/2011/1681 (accessed on 28 August 2014).

292 THE RAYS BEFORE SATYAJIT

THE RAYS BEFORE SATYAJIT

54. Guha-Thakurta, *Making of a New 'Indian' Art*, 283.

55. Kedarnath Chattopadhyay, 'Satabarshik Sraddhhanjali: Upendra-kishore', *Vishwa Bharati Patrika*, 20, no 2 (1963 [Kartik–Poush 1370 BE]): 108–18, 113.

56. Quoted in S. Ghosh, 'Upendrakishore: Shilpi o Karigar', 63.

57. Abanindranath Tagore, 'The Three Forms of Art', *Modern Review*, 1, no. 4 (April 1907): 392–7.

58. Upendrakisor Ray, 'The Study of Pictorial Art in India', *Modern Review*, 1, no. 6 (June 1907): 545.

59. U. Ray, 'The Study of Pictorial Art in India', 545.

60. P. Mitter, *Art and Nationalism*, 358–67.

61. Kedarnath Chattopadhyay, 'Satabarshik Sraddhhanjali', 114.

62. U. Ray, 'The Study of Pictorial Art in India', 546–7.

63. U. Ray, 'The Study of Pictorial Art in India', 548.

64. The world, Upendrakishore wryly commented, could not do without Mammon and 'even the greatest artists' were to be found among his worshippers. The decline of modern art, if indeed there had been a general decline, was due to the 'want of culture amongst its patrons and followers,' rather than the greed of modern artists (U. Ray, 'The Study of Pictorial Art in India', 548). On the wealthy Abanindranath's conviction that the ideal artist was 'a pure genius, untrammelled by ... the demands of a profession and livelihood', see Guha-Thakurta, 'Abanindranath, Known and Unknown', 87.

65. U. Ray, 'The Study of Pictorial Art in India', 546. On Bengali ideas of European superiority and the quest for emulation, see Ranajit Guha, *Dominance without Hegemony: History and Power in Colonial India* (Cambridge, Mass.: Harvard University Press, 1997), 189–90, 199; and Guha-Thakurta, *Making of a New 'Indian' Art*, 68–9.

66. U. Ray, 'The Study of Pictorial Art in India', 548.

67. Ordhendra Coomar Gangopadhyay, 'The Study of Indian Pictorial Art—A Rejoinder', *Modern Review*, 2, no. 3 (September 1907): 301–7, at 302.

68. O. C. Gangopadhyay, 'The Study of Indian Pictorial Art', 305.

69. O.C. Gangopadhyay, 'The Study of Indian Pictorial Art', 304.

70. O.C. Gangopadhyay, 'The Study of Indian Pictorial Art', 302.

71. 'The Controversy on Indian Art', *Modern Review*, 2, no. 5 (November 1907): 474–5.

72. His son Sukumar, as we shall see, would resume the debate a few years later and with rather greater vigour than his father.

73. Ironically, this comment of Upendrakishore's was recalled by none other than Kedarnath, the son of Ramananda Chatterji, one of the biggest supporters of swadeshi art. See Kedarnath Chattopadhyay, 'Satabarshik Sraddhhanjali', 114.

74. See O.C. Gangoly, 'Indian Society of Oriental Art: Its Early Days', 99; O.C. Gangoly, *Bharater Silpa*, 154, 159, 298, 466; and on photogravure, Anne Kelsey Hammond, 'Aesthetic Aspects of the Photomechanical Print', in

British Photography in the Nineteenth Century: The Fine Art Tradition, edited by Mike Weaver (Cambridge: Cambridge University Press, 1989), 177–9. When naturalistic art re-emerged in Calcutta in the 1920s, a group of young artists led by Hemendranath Mazumdar, a relative of the Rays, launched *Indian Art Academy*, a journal seeking to counter *Rupam*'s Government-funded advocacy for 'oriental' art. The printing of this magazine was entrusted to U. Ray & Sons and the venture was strongly supported by Sukumar Ray. See Partha Mitter, *The Triumph of Modernism: India's Artists and the Avant-garde, 1922–1947* (Delhi: Oxford University Press, 2007), 130. Mazumdar, who had quit the Calcutta Art School in 1911 when its students were asked to help put up street decorations for welcoming King-Emperor George V to Calcutta, was a steadfast nationalist in his political convictions, while Gangoly, Abanindranath and their associates collaborated wholeheartedly with the colonial state. See Kamal Sarkar, *Bharater Bhaskar o Chitrasilpi* (Calcutta: Jogmaya, 1984), 240–2. See also Hemendranath Mazumdar, *Chhabir Chosma* (Calcutta: Ananda, 1991), 135–9, for his views on the inadmissibility of 'oriental' art.

75. On Hemendramohan Bose's multifaceted career, see Siddhartha Ghosh, *Karigari Kalpana o Bangali Udyog* (Calcutta: Dey's, 1988), 170–296; and Siddhartha Ghosh, 'Jantrarasik H. Bose', *Ekshan*, 16, nos 3–4 (1983).

76. Anonymous, *Swargiya Hemendramohan Basu* (Calcutta: Purnachandra Das, 1916), 1–4. The author does not reveal his identity but from references in the text (e.g., 1–2), it is clear that he was a childhood friend of Bose's.

77. When he moved to his own mansion on Amherst Street at the end of his life, cricket matches were a regular event in the garden. Baridbaran Ghosh, 'Bhumika', in *Kuntalin Galpa-Satak*, edited by Baridbaran Ghosh (Calcutta: Ananda, 1989), 11–41, at 15.

78. Anonymous, *Swargiya Hemendramohan Basu*, 1–4.

79. S. Ghosh, 'Jantrarasik H. Bose', 63. One wonders, though, how true the report is. Upendrakishore Ray, in a 1900 article on the violin, remarked that a Stradivarius violin cost about twenty-five thousand rupees and he had never had the good fortune of hearing one being played. See Upendrakishore Ray, 'Behala', pt. 1, *Pradip*, 3, no. 6 (Jaistha 1307 [May–June 1900]): 186–90, at 187–8, http://archiv.ub.uni-heidelberg.de/savifadok/volltexte/2009/877 (accessed on 21 August 2014).

80. Anonymous, *Swargiya Hemendramohan Basu*, 1–4, 6.

81. See *Hindoo Patriot*, 21 March, 1894, 3. Later, Kuntalin was marketed in four different scents—see the advertisement in *Amrita Bazar Patrika*, 26 August 1907, 10.

82. See *The Bengalee*, 19 April 1908, 3.

83. *The Bengalee*, 19 March 1908, 3.

84. *The Bengalee*, 3 August 1909, 4.

85. Anonymous, *Swargiya Hemendramohan Basu*, 6–7; and S. Ghosh, 'Jantrarasik H. Bose', 167.

86. See the advertisement in *Amrita Bazar Patrika*, 9 September 1907, 10.

87. *The Bengalee*, 19 April 1908, 3; and *The Bengalee*, 29 March 1908, 3.

88. See the advertisement in *The Bengalee*, 26 April 1908, 3; and for a complete list of sixteen flower essences, claimed to surpass Indian as well as European rivals in their 'sweetness, delicacy and permanency of fragrance', see the advertisement in *Amrita Bazar Patrika*, 5 November 1906, 7; and for a later division into three categories by price and quality, *The Bengalee*, 1 June 1908, 10. For Bose's range of tooth powder, eau de cologne, pomatum, Tambuline, and lavender water, see *Amrita Bazar Patrika*, 25 June 1906, 8; and *The Bengalee*, 9 February 1908, 13. For the eight kinds of syrups, see *Amrita Bazar Patrika*, 27 May 1907, 9. See also B. Ghosh, *Kuntalin Galpa-Satak*, 17.

89. *The Bengalee*, 30 January 1908, 4.

90. S. Ghosh, 'Jantrarasik H. Bose', 58. Some brief descriptions of Mrinalini and her flair for drawing are available in Leela Majumdar, *Pakdandi* (Calcutta: Ananda, 1986), 112.

91. Saradaranjan may not have been quite as inflexible in such matters as one might imagine. Leela Majumdar recalled that when her father Pramadaranjan married her Brahmo—and Brahmin—mother, Surama (daughter of Ramkumar Vidyaratna, brought up in Upendrakishore's household), in a Brahmo ceremony, Saradaranjan did not oppose the match, although he was far from pleased by it (L. Majumdar, *Pakdandi*, 118). A civil engineer by training, Pramadaranjan worked for the Survey of India and spent much of his life travelling through some of the wildest terrain on the subcontinent. The only Ray of his generation to work for the government, his writings about his travels were published in *Sandesh* and later brought out by Signet Press in 1955 as *Boner Khabar* (News from the Forest) with a cover designed by his great-nephew and soon-to-be famous filmmaker Satyajit Ray. See Bratati Chakravarty, *Bangla Shishu Sahitya Charcha: Ray Paribar* (Calcutta: Dey Book Store, 1997), 105–8; and Hemantakumar Adhya, *Upendrakishore Raychaudhuri* (Delhi: Sahitya Akademi, 1997), 7. Stories about Pramadaranjan Ray, a courageous but somewhat rigid and unbending man who refused to maintain any contact with his daughter after she married a Hindu, are scattered through his daughter Leela Majumdar's two autobiographies, *Aar Konokhaney* (Calcutta: Mitra o Ghosh, 1968) and *Pakdandi*.

92. The children were: Hitendramohan, Jitendramohan, Nitindramohan (Nitin, cinematographer and filmmaker), Sudhindramohan, Manindramohan (Mukul, sound-recordist), Malati (the famous Rabindra-Sangeet singer Malati Ghoshal), Hirendramohan (Ganesh—a celebrated cricketer), Nripendramohan (another famous cricketer, known as Kartik), Manasi, Sailendramohan, Sulata, Somendramohan, Lalita, and Aruna. See B. Chakravarty, *Bangla Shishu Sahitya Charcha*, 35–6. Hitendramohan, who took over the business at the

age of twenty-two in 1916 after his father's untimely death, was an accomplished Arabist and Persianist and the first to translate Omar Khayyam's
Rubaiyat directly from the original Farsi into Bengali. He was also an adept
illustrator and many of Kuladaranjan Ray's works were decorated with
Hitendramohan's illustrations. His interest in music was intense and his
extensive collection of records was well known to connoisseurs of the time.
See B. Ghosh, *Kuntalin Galpa-Satak*, 29–31.

93. Majumdar, *Aar Konokhaney*, 95–6.

94. For a reproduction of a Jabakusum advertisement from the nineteenth
century with an endorsement from a Bengali judge, see Arun Chaudhuri,
Indian Advertising: 1780 to 1950 AD (Delhi: Tata McGraw-Hill, 2007), 143.

95. P.M. Bagchi & Co., who were better known for their almanacs and
their writing ink, also produced many perfumes, ranging from the cheap to
the luxurious. See Amit Bhattacharyya, *Swadeshi Enterprise in Bengal 1880–
1920*, 2nd edn (Calcutta: Readers Service, 2008), 83–99; and Amit
Bhattacharyya, *Business, Politics and Technology: Select Themes in the Economic
History of Modern India* (Calcutta: Readers Service, 2005), 30–51.

96. Bhattacharyya, *Swadeshi Enterprise in Bengal 1880–1920*, 87.

97. See *Amrita Bazar Patrika*, 2 April 1906, 3; and 21 December 1906, 8.

98. One medal was for the 'extensive variety of perfumes manufactured
and the quality of the essences', another for hair wash, lime juice, and glyc-
erine, and a third for syrups. Bose also received a silver medal for his Rose
tooth powder. See *Report of the Indian Industrial and Agricultural Exhibition*,
108–9, 112, 150; and Bose's advertisements of his prize-winning syrups in
Amrita Bazar Patrika, 21 December 1906, 8; and 27 May 1907, 9.

99. *Report of the Indian Industrial and Agricultural Exhibition*, 20.

100. S. Ghosh, 'Jantrarasik H. Bose', 95–6.

101. His successors also advertised in major newspapers elsewhere,
including in distant Lahore. An advertisement carrying the Punjab nationalist
leader Lala Lajpat Rai's endorsement of Kuntalin, for instance, was inserted in
the Lahore newspaper *The Tribune* in 1921. See Prakash Ananda, *A History of
The Tribune* (Delhi: Tribune Trust, 1986), 78–9; and Amitabha Ghosh, 'H.
Bose and the Talking Machine in India', in *Science, Technology, Medicine and
Environment in India: Historical Perspectives*, edited by Chittabrata Palit and
Amit Bhattacharya (Calcutta: Bibhasa, 1998), 99–107, at 101.

102. S. Ghosh, 'Jantrarasik H. Bose', 82–96; and Glyn Barlow, *Industrial
India*, 2nd edn (Madras: Natesan, 1911), 192.

103. Prashant Kidambi, 'Consumption, Domestic Economy, and the Idea
of the "Middle Class" in Late Colonial Bombay', in *The Middle Class in Colonial
India*, edited by Sanjay Joshi (Delhi: Oxford University Press, 2010), 132–53, at
135.

104. Douglas E. Haynes, 'Creating the Consumer? Advertising, Capitalism,
and the Middle Class in Urban Western India, 1914–40', in *Towards a History*

296 THE RAYS BEFORE SATYAJIT

of Consumption in South Asia, edited by Douglas E. Haynes, Abigail McGowan, Tirthankar Roy, and Haruka Yanagisawa (Delhi: Oxford University Press, 2010), 184–223, at 188.

105. Jain, *Gods in the Bazaar*, 124.

106. See S. Ghosh, *Karigari Kalpana*, 198–9; and *The Bengalee*, 30 June 1909, 7. Apart from illustrating Hemendramohan Bose's advertisements, Purnachandra Ghosh joined the advertising agency D.J. Keymer in 1942, the year Satyajit Ray also took up a job at the agency as junior visualizer. Late in his own life, Ray remembered Ghosh as a helpful colleague and 'possibly the first Bengali whose line drawings were so Western that one could not easily tell that they were a Bengali artist's work'. See K. Sarkar, *Bharater Bhaskar*, 106; and Abhijit Dasgupta, 'Political Film Amader Deshey Bodh Hoy Kara Jay Na: Satyajit', *Anandalok*, 25, no. 8 (1 May 1999): 17.

107. S. Ghosh, *Karigari Kalpana*, 198–9.

108. See *Amrita Bazar Patrika*, 9 September 1907, 10.

109. B. Ghosh, *Kuntalin Galpa-Satak*, 18. For one variant omitting Tambulin, see the advertisement in *Amrita Bazar Patrika*, 21 December 1906, 8.

110. For Bhattacharyya's attribution of authorship to Bose, see Amit Bhattacharyya, *Swadeshi Enterprise in Bengal, 1921–47*, 2nd edn (Calcutta: Setu Prakashani, 2007), 165; and on Amritalal Bose's involvement, see Santoshkumar De, *Kabikanthha o Koler Gaan* (Santiniketan: Vishwa-Bharati, 1993), 16 (I am grateful to Debasis Mukhopadhyay for his advice on this issue).

111. See, for instance, the Commercial Agency & Advertising Bureau's announcement in *Amrita Bazar Patrika*, 11 April 1908, 3 (repeated regularly, for example, 21 April 1908, 3.) After the First World War, foreign-owned agencies began to open branches in India. The multinational J. Walter Thomson came to Calcutta in 1926 and then, in 1928, D.J. Keymer. The Bengali firm P.M. Bagchi used two indigenous advertising agencies in the 1930s but virtually nothing seems to be known about their origin, management, range of work, or their other patrons. See M.A. Burghate, *The Study of Advertising Agencies in India* (Delhi: Adhyayan, 2004), 60–3; Arun Chaudhuri, *Indian Advertising*, 152–3, 189–90; and Amit Bhattacharyya, *Business, Politics and Technology*, 48. Incidentally, even in Britain, advertising agencies in their modern form emerged only in the early twentieth century. See J.A.P. Treasure, *The History of British Adveritising Agencies 1875–1939* (Edinburgh: Scottish Academic Press, 1977); Frank Presbrey, *The History and Development of Advertising* (Garden City, NY: Doubleday, 1929), 522–30; and Daniel Pope, *The Making of Modern Advertising* (New York: Basic Books, 1983), 112–83.

112. See B. Ghosh, *Kuntalin Galpa-Satak*, 19. For the use of celebrity endorsements by other firms, see Bhattacharyya, *Swadeshi Enterprise in Bengal, 1921–47*, 169–70.

113. See the Jabakusum advertisement in *The Bengalee*, 21 May 1898, 252 and of Bengal Chemical in *The Bengalee*, 2 April 1898, 165.

114. The history of product placement in India, like many aspects of the history of Indian advertising, remains to be investigated. Even the Western history has been studied adequately only with respect to films. See Jay Newell, Charles T. Salmon, and Susan Chang, 'The Hidden History of Product Placement', *Journal of Broadcasting & Electronic Media*, 50, no. 4 (2006): 575–94.

115. See Michael S. Kinnear, *The Gramophone Company's First Indian Recordings, 1899–1908* (Bombay: Popular Prakashan, 1994), 42. The prize amounts varied but the total prize money was usually around 150 rupees, a considerable sum for that period. See *Kuntalin Puraskar 1309 San* (Calcutta: H. Bose, 1903), 214; and *Kuntalin Puraskar 1310 San* (Calcutta: H Bose, 1904), 185. A different judge was appointed each year. In 1900, it was Rabindranath Tagore and in 1901, Sureshchandra Samajpati, the editor of *Sahitya* magazine and a vocal critic of Tagore. Not all Kuntalin Prize volumes contained multiple stories. In 1904, a 'special' number was published with just one story: 'Karmaphhal' by Rabindranath Tagore. Tagore did not compete for a prize but he did need money to support the Santiniketan school he had founded in 1901. Bose donated 300 rupees to Tagore's school as an honorarium for the story but, cannily, sold it for eight annas instead of distributing it for free. See B. Ghosh, *Kuntalin Galpa-Satak*, 32, 35.

116. See the rules in *Kuntalin Puraskar 1309 San* (Calcutta: H. Bose, 1903), 214–15.

117. B. Ghosh, *Kuntalin Galpa-Satak*, 20, 26.

118. L. Majumdar, *Pakdandi*, 42; S. Ghosh, 'Jantrarasik H. Bose', 63–7.

119. After 1908, however, the collections became quite irregular and although Bose's eldest son, Hitendramohan, attempted to revive them as anthologies of stories by well-known writers, none was published after 1930. See B. Ghosh, *Kuntalin Galpa-Satak*, 31, 34.

120. B. Ghosh, *Kuntalin Galpa-Satak*, 20–1. Hemendramohan Bose taught music at the Sunday School, along with Upendrakishore Ray and his brother Kuladaranjan. See Anonymous, *Swargiya Hemendramohan Basu*, 11; and S. Ghosh, *Karigari Kalpana*, 175–6.

121. See the rules in *Kuntalin Puraskar 1309 San* (Calcutta: H. Bose, 1903), 215; and B. Ghosh, *Kuntalin Galpa-Satak*, 22, 24.

122. The story was titled 'Mandir' and printed in *Kuntalin Puraskar 1309 San* (Calcutta: H. Bose, 1903), 1–27.

123. B. Ghosh, *Kuntalin Galpa-Satak*, 23–5.

124. Haynes, 'Creating the Consumer?', 187.

125. For example, the jingle *bilati sougandhha jata ebe natashir, mahila mahaley keho kachchit adorey, din-din kintu Deb labhichhe prachar, Kuntalin*

puta taila Bangalir ghharey. See Amit Bhattacharyya, *Swadeshi Enterprise in Bengal, 1921–47*, 166.

126. On the prevalence of these themes in indigenous advertisements after 1905, see Bhattacharyya, *Business, Politics and Technology*, 36–40; and Arun Chaudhuri, *Indian Advertising*, 156–7, 173.

127. Arvind Rajagopal, 'Advertising in India: Genealogies of the Consumer Subject', in *Handbook of Modernity in South Asia: Modern Makeovers*, edited by Saurabh Dube (Delhi: Oxford University Press, 2011), 217–28, at 219.

128. Ranabir Ray Choudhury, *Early Calcutta Advertisements 1875–1925* (Bombay: Nachiketa, 1992), 379.

129. This, of course, was long before the Gandhian nationalism of the 1920s and 1930s, when the middle-class Indian consumer, especially if female, would be urged to abstain from conspicuous consumption. See Haynes, 'Creating the Consumer?', 192–3.

130. Anonymous, *Swargiya Hemendramohan Basu*, 11–12.

131. See, for instance, *Amrita Bazar Patrika*, 26 February 1906, 3.

132. S. Ghosh, 'Jantrarasik H. Bose', 161–2.

133. Siddhartha Ghosh, *Chhabi Tola: Bangalir Photography Charcha* (Calcutta: Ananda, 1988), 134.

134. For details of the Autochrome process, see Anthony J. Hamber, *'A Higher Branch of the Art': Photographing the Fine Arts in England, 1839–1880* (Amsterdam: Gordon & Breach, 1996), 90; and 'Gossip: Mostly about Men in the Trade', *Process Work and Electrotyping: Penrose & Co's Monthly Circular*, August–September 1907, 5–6.

135. On the invention of the phonograph and its subsequent improvements, see Oliver Read and Walter L. Welch, *From Tin Foil to Stereo: Evolution of the Phonograph*, 2nd edn (Indianapolis, IN: Howard W Sams/Bobbs-Merrill, 1976).

136. De, *Kabikanthha o Koler Gaan*, 22–3.

137. Ray Choudhury, *Early Calcutta Advertisements*, 16.

138. Kinnear, *Gramophone Company's First Indian Recordings*, x–3. On Berliner and the development of the gramophone, see Frederick William Gaisberg, *The Music Goes Round* [1942] (New York: Arno Press, 1977), especially 9–20; and Read and Welch, *From Tin Foil to Stereo*, 122. The Gramophone Company, when it began to market its disc records in India, recognized that one obstacle to popular acceptance of their technology was that 'the native element like to make their own records'. Many talking machine dealers also took advantage of this functionality of the phonograph and issued their own recordings, perhaps to boost the sales of phonographs. See Christina Lubinski, 'The Global Business with Local Music: Western Gramophone Companies in India before World War I', *Bulletin of the German Historical Institute*, 51 (2012): 67–85, at 80.

139. Amitabha Ghosh, 'Pre-Commercial Era of Sound Recording in India', *Indian Journal of the History of Science*, 34, no. 1 (1999): 47–59. On itinerant film exhibitors in rural India, see Erik Barnouw and S. Krishnaswamy, *Indian Film*, 2nd edn (New York: Oxford University Press, 1980), 9.

140. De, *Kabikanthha o Koler Gaan*, 22–3.

141. O.C. Gangoly, *Bharater Silpa o Amar Katha*, 70–1. Initially, phonographs cost between 25 and 175 rupees and cylinder records were available at two rupees eight annas each. See H. Bose's advertisement in *Amrita Bazar Patrika*, 2 April 1906, 8. The later 'new model' phonograph could cost as much as 800 rupees. See *Amrita Bazar Patrika*, 30 September 1907, 10. Gramophone prices ranged from 26 to 1600 rupees. Disc records, depending on their size, cost from a little more than one rupee to almost four rupees. Once the Gramophone Company had decided to open its own factory in Calcutta, record prices went down significantly, with a 7-inch disc costing one rupee and a 12-inch record available at three rupees. See Ray Choudhury, *Early Calcutta Advertisements 1875–1925*, 2, 4, 16; and the Gramophone and Typewriter Ltd's advertisements, in *Amrita Bazar Patrika*, 3 August 1907, 1; *Amrita Bazar Patrika*, 17 September 1907, 1; and *The Bengalee*, 2 February 1908, 2.

142. Santoshkumar De, *The Gramophone in India: A Brief History* (Calcutta: Uttisthata, 1990), 4.

143. Kinnear, *Gramophone Company's First Indian Recordings*, 36, 42.

144. The brothers Charles and Emile Pathé had set up Pathé Frères in Paris the mid-1890s. In its early days the company manufactured and sold Edison phonographs, cinematographs, and accessories for these machines. See Kinnear, *Gramophone Company's First Indian Recordings*, 54–5; and Read and Welch, *From Tin Foil to Stereo*, 90.

145. See Roberta Pearson, 'Early Cinema', in *The Oxford History of World Cinema*, edited by Geoffrey Nowell-Smith (New York: Oxford University Press, 1996), 13–23, at 14. Pathé-India, established in 1907, was headed by the experienced and well-connected Alex Hague, who not only marketed Pathé films in India but popularized Pathé's film-making equipment among professionals and amateurs wishing to make home movies. See B.D. Garga, *So Many Cinemas: The Motion Picture in India* (Mumbai: Eminence Designs, 1996), 14–15.

146. On Bose's interest in the cinema, see Anonymous, *Swargiya Hemendramohan Basu*, 5–6.

147. Kinnear, *Gramophone Company's First Indian Recordings*, 42, 54–5. On the Madans' pre-eminence in the film business, see Rani Burra, ed., *Looking Back, 1896–1960* (Delhi: Directorate of Film Festivals, 1981), 19; and Garga, *So Many Cinemas*, 25.

148. See 'Profiles of Pioneers: Nitin Bose', in *Indian Motion Picture Almanac 1974–75*, edited by B. Jha (Calcutta: Shot Publications, 1976), 35–48,

at 35–6. Hiralal Sen's life and supposed achievements have been mythified to an extraordinary degree but for a reasoned treatment, see Siddhartha Ghosh, *Chhabi Tola*, 136–8. Despite giving up on the film trade, Bose remained keen on the cinema in a private capacity. Leela Majumdar, at the age of five, was shown Charlie Chaplin films by Bose on his home projector. See L. Majumdar, *Pakdandi*, 120.

149. See Gary Allan Tobin, 'The Bicycle Boom of the 1890s: The Development of Private Transportation and the Birth of the Modern Tourist', *Journal of Popular Culture*, 7 (1974): 838–49.

150. On the history of bicycles in India, see David Arnold, *Everyday Technology: Machines and the Making of India's Modernity* (Chicago: University of Chicago Press, 2013); and Mani Bagchi, *Sudhirkumar Sen: Jiban-Charit* (Calcutta: Shamin Basu, 1964), 36–41, 140–66.

151. Sircar, Bose, and Ray were all taught how to ride a bicycle by Bose himself. See Bagchi, *Sudhirkumar Sen*, 30; and D.M. Bose, 'Abala Bose: Her Life and Times', *Modern Review*, 119, no. 6 (June 1966): 441–56, at 447.

152. Siddhartha Ghosh, 'Jantrarasik H. Bose', 99–103.

153. Arnold, *Everyday Technology*, 103.

154. See *The Bengalee*, 25 January 1908, 8; and 25 December 1908, 7.

155. *The Bengalee*, 12 May 1908, 6.

156. Bagchi, *Sudhirkumar Sen*, 14, 30–1, 77–8; and Arnold, *Everyday Technology*, 104–6.

157. See Kinnear, *Gramophone Company's First Indian Recordings*, 42, 44.

158. It not only sold phonographs and recordings but (imported) electrical and battery-operated equipment of all kinds, including torches, lighters, and electric kettles. See *The Bengalee*, 3 May 1908, 3. Again, Bose showed no interest in manufacturing any of them and electrical equipment would be produced in India only from the 1920s. See S. Ghosh, 'Jantrarasik H. Bose', 160–1.

159. See *Amrita Bazar Patrika*, 26 February 1906, 8.

160. S. Ghosh, 'Jantrarasik H. Bose', 121–4.

161. *Amrita Bazar Patrika*, 2 April 1906, 8. Eight songs were listed for Tagore as well as for Roy but the advertisement stated that other recordings by them were available. On their refusal to record for the Gramophone Company 'or any other foreign-owned company', see Kinnear, *Gramophone Company's First Indian Recordings*, 42. It was only in 1926 that Tagore consented to record for the Gramophone Company. See De, *Kabikanthha o Koler Gaan*, 28–31.

162. Tagore was prominent in the swadeshi movement until 1907 and composed some of his finest patriotic songs to support the cause. The movement's message was also spread across Bengal through songs and musical plays by many others. See Debashish Raychaudhuri, 'Their Indigenous Medium of Popular Contact: The Swadeshi Songs', in *Contesting Colonialism: Partition and Swadeshi Re-Visited*, edited by Tapati Sengupta and Shreela Roy (Delhi: Macmillan, 2007), 65–79.

163. On Tagore recording for Bose at Jagadis Bose's house, see D.M. Bose, 'Abala Bose: Her Life and Times', *Modern Review*, 119, no. 6 (June 1966): 441–56, at 448. Sadly, however, recording on the wax cylinders was simpler than their preservation—Bose's recordings were irreparably damaged by the 1920s and except for a recording of Bande Mataram by Tagore, not one has survived. See S. Ghosh, 'Jantrarasik H. Bose', 109–13.

164. Home, who was a child at the time and whose family was close to Bose's, eagerly attended the recording sessions with his friends. They were particularly delighted when something went wrong with the recording and Tagore had to sing the same song for a second time. See De, *Kabikanthha o Koler Gaan*, 17. As Siddhartha Ghosh points out, early phonograph recordings could not be reproduced more than about twenty-five times. Hence, multiple 'takes' may have been necessary to make a recording commercially viable; slightly later, Edison introduced a new method whereby mass manufacturing of phonograph records became possible (S. Ghosh, 'Jantrarasik H. Bose', 113–14).

165. Boral had also recorded for the Gramophone Company, whose recording engineer Fred Gaisberg sneered at his voice as 'high pitched and effeminate'. But the Company also noted that 'all 300 copies of L.C. Boral's recordings were sold 'within half an hour of the time they were opened'. See Kinnear, *Gramophone Company's First Indian Recordings*, 12; Gerry Farrell, *Indian Music and the West* (Oxford: Oxford University Press, 1997), 128; and Gaisberg, *The Music Goes Round*, 56. According to Raichand Boral, it was Bose who, in 1902, had persuaded his father, Lalchand, to record for the Gramophone Company. See S. Ghosh, 'Jantrarasik H. Bose', 115–16. This was before Bose had launched his own recording business and when Boral eventually recorded for Bose, he provided a testimonial asserting that Bose's recordings of his songs 'were very much superior' to the 'foreign' recordings. See Bose's advertisement in *Amrita Bazar Patrika*, 4 June 1906, 8.

166. On 9 December 1908, the Commissioner of Police proscribed certain stage plays and the singing of and sale of records of 'Bande Mataram', Dwijendralal Roy's 'Amar Desh', and many other popular patriotic songs. See Kinnear, *Gramophone Company's First Indian Recordings*, 63–5.

167. A. Ghosh, 'H. Bose and the Talking Machine in India', 102.

168. *Amrita Bazar Patrika*, 30 April 1906, 8.

169. See *The Bengalee*, 24 January 1908, 3.

170. *Amrita Bazar Patrika*, 17 September 1906, 8. The Gramophone Company was soon advertising its own impressive range of Indian recordings—see *Amrita Bazar Patrika*, 21 March 1907, 1.

171. *Amrita Bazar Patrika*, 5 November 1906, 7.

172. Kinnear, *Gramophone Company's First Indian Recordings*, 42–3; and 'Obituary', *Amrita Bazar Patrika*, 31 August 1916, 8. Many of Bose's customers beyond Bengal were diasporic Bengalis. In Allahabad, for instance, the

celebrated journalist Ramananda Chatterji bought a phonograph and many recordings from Bose and played them at the annual gatherings of Bengalis. Since nobody knew how to operate the machine, Chatterji had to invite a suitably skilled person from Calcutta. See Santa Devi, *Bharat-Muktisadhak Ramananda Chattopadhyay o Ardhasatabdir Bangla* (Calcutta: Dey's, 2005), 169.

173. See *Amrita Bazar Patrika*, 21 May 1907, 7.

174. *Amrita Bazar Patrika*, 17 April 1906, 8; and S. Ghosh, 'Jantrarasik H. Bose', 125. Swadeshi music was not the only area where Bose's patriotism was on display. He was active in organizing exhibitions of swadeshi products and swadeshi-themed melas (fun-fairs) that were regular events after 1910. By 1913, however, these swadeshi melas seem to have made peace with the British. The 1913 mela was inaugurated by the Governor of Bengal, an event that would have been unthinkable at the height of the swadeshi agitation in 1905–7. See S. Ghosh, 'Jantrarasik H. Bose', 79–81.

175. *Amrita Bazar Patrika*, 16 July 1906, 10.

176. *Amrita Bazar Patrika*, 14 August 1906, 8.

177. Lubinski, 'The Global Business with Local Music', 81.

178. It would theoretically have been possible for Bose to get his records manufactured by the Gramophone Company in Europe but collaborating with a British firm (as opposed to Pathé, a French company) may have been ideologically unacceptable for him and, at least for his recordings of swadeshi songs, politically unwise. See S. Ghosh, 'Jantrarasik H. Bose', 114–17.

179. See Kinnear, *Gramophone Company's First Indian Recordings*, 13; Farrell, *Indian Music and the West*, 113, 135; Gaisberg, *The Music Goes Round*, 54; and Vibodh Parthasarathi, 'Not Just Mad Englishmen and a Dog: The Colonial Tuning of "Music on Record", 1900–1908', Working Paper No 02/2008 (Delhi: Centre for Culture, Media and Governance, Jamia Millia Islamia, 2007), http://jmi.ac.in/upload/menuupload/not_vp.pdf (accessed on 23 July 2014).

180. Amitabha Ghosh, 'H. Bose and the Talking Machine in India', 103; and Lubinski, 'The Global Business with Local Music', 82. It is worth noting that the first record factory in the UK was established roughly simultaneously with the one in Calcutta. See De, *The Gramophone in India*, 21. On the volatility of the international shellac trade and India's importance as supplier, see Parthasarathi, 'Not Just Mad Englishmen and a Dog', 29–30.

181. *Amrita Bazar Patrika*, 17 April 1907, 10. A week after this, a new advertisement presented an imaginary dialogue between a father who wanted his son to purchase a disc player, only to be told that the son would 'rather go without any than to buy the inferior things'. See *Amrita Bazar Patrika*, 23 April 1907, 9.

182. *Amrita Bazar Patrika*, 27 May 1907, 9.

183. *Amrita Bazar Patrika*, 12 August 1907, 10.

184. *Amrita Bazar Patrika*, 26 September 1907, 10; and *Amrita Bazar Patrika*, 30 September 1907, 10. The firm also promised to repair any and every kind of talking machine. See *Amrita Bazar Patrika*, 26 August 1907, 10.

185. See the advertisement in *The Bengalee*, 9 February 1908, 13.

186. *The Bengalee*, 23 February 1908, 10; 17 May 1908, 3; 20 September 1908, 3; 1 November 1908, 10; 8 November 1908, 3; and 12 June 1909, 7. See also Read and Welch, *From Tin Foil to Stereo*, 196–7.

187. Kinnear, *Gramophone Company's First Indian Recordings*, 43. For a list of the first transferred recordings (which included Tagore's rendition of 'Vande Mataram',) see *The Bengalee*, 15 March 1908, 11.

188. They used the 'hill and dale' method, originated by Edison. Very different from the 'lateral-cut' technique used for most disc recordings, it was ideal for transferring phonographic recordings to discs. See Amitabha Ghosh, 'H. Bose and the Talking Machine in India', 104; and Read and Welch, *From Tin Foil to Stereo*, 370–1. Because of the different method of recording, Pathé discs played from the centre out, a fact that had caused much amazement to a young Satyajit Ray. See Satyajit Ray, *Jakhan Chhoto Chhilam* (Calcutta: Ananda, 1982), 18.

189. The Pathé-H. Bose Records were also sold in Calcutta under a Pathé label that did not mention Bose. See S. Ghosh, *Karigari Kalpana*, 188, 254–6, 265; Kinnear, *Gramophone Company's First Indian Recordings*, 43.

190. See Madan's advertisement in *The Bengalee*, 20 February 1908, 11; Shaw's in *The Bengalee*, 17 May 1908, 10; and Mullick Brothers' in *The Bengalee*, 30 June 1909, 10. Other European brands (such as Beka) were also trying to corner the Bengali market: see the advertisement of The Talking Machine and Indian Record Co., in *The Bengalee*, 17 May 1908, 10. And, of course, the Gramophone Company was going from strength to strength; by 1909, even Dwijendralal Roy, one of Bose's 'exclusive' phonographic artists, had recorded for it. See *The Bengalee*, 9 May 1909, 2.

191. Kinnear, *Gramophone Company's First Indian Recordings*, 55; and the Pathephone and Cinema Company's advertisement in *The Bengalee*, 20 May 1908, 10. See also their advertisement in *The Bengalee*, 3 May 1908, 10, where Bose is named as one of four agents for 'Calcutta and Darjeeling'.

192. Ironically and no doubt because of the competition offered by the Gramophone Company, Pathé themselves were to lose interest in the Indian record market (while getting ever more deeply involved with the film market in India) by the time of the outbreak of the First World War and had all but withdrawn from it by 1920. See Kinnear, *Gramophone Company's First Indian Recordings*, 43–4, 56.

193. See *The Bengalee*, 1 June 1908, 10; 22 November 1908, 3; and 29 June 1909, 4.

194. *The Bengalee*, 6 December 1908, 10; 8 December 1908, 10; 9 December 1908, 10; 22 June 1909, 4; 24 June 1909, 7; 20 July 1909, 3; and 29 July 1909, 7.

195. In the Industrial and Agricultural Exhibition of 1906, Mukharji and Mukherjee were awarded a First Class Certificate of Merit in the 'Musical Instruments' category for their *'swadeshi* disc records' while Bose received a Gold Medal in the 'Scientific Instruments' category—judged by his good friend Jagadis Bose—for his indigenous phonographic cylinders. See *Report of the Indian Industrial and Agricultural Exhibition*, 126, 128. Not much seems to be known about where these discs were manufactured—or how—and not a single example has survived. All we know is that they were single-sided and carried recordings of some well-known artists like Gauhar Jan. See Micheal S. Kinnear, *The Gramophone Company's Indian Recordings, 1908 to 1910* (Heidelberg, Victoria, Australia: Bajakhana, 2000), 6. Subsequently, Mukharji and Mukherjee also sold equipment for making disc recordings at home. This, says Kinnear, was most likely the Neophone Home Recorder, introduced in 1905 in England and selling for thirty shillings. This technology does not seem to have caught on in India, however. Another indigenous plant for manufacturing disc records was established by Binapani Records in January 1908. It is not known how long it survived but from the end of 1908, the Gramophone Company's own massive record factory in the heart of Calcutta would have offered fierce competition to any indigenous firm. See Kinnear, *Gramophone Company's First Indian Recordings*, 47–9.

196. Indeed, by the time of the First World War, the Gramophone Company had become the market leader in Indian recordings. India was the Company's fourth largest market after Britain, Russia, and Germany. See Lubinski, 'The Global Business with Local Music', 83. It was only in the 1930s that Indian recording companies such as Megaphone or Hindustan established themselves as significant players. See Kinnear, *Gramophone Company's First Indian Recordings*, 47–9, 57–9, 68; and Kinnear, *The Gramophone Company's Indian Recordings, 1908 to 1910*, 5–6, 14.

197. Kinnear, *Gramophone Company's First Indian Recordings*, 44. The exact date of the closure of Bose's sound recording business is not available but the last known advertisement came out in 1911. See S. Ghosh, 'Jantrarasik H. Bose', 146.

198. The first motor race held in Calcutta was in 1904 and there were only eleven competitors, all of them British. Police records show that there were only 110 registered cars in Calcutta in 1904. By the time of the First World War, however, the number had gone up to almost 3,000. See S. Ghosh, 'Jantrarasik H. Bose', 151–5.

199. See D. Warren, *The Motor Car in India* (Bombay: Bennett, Coleman, 1906), 3.

200. Upendrakishore and his descendants, incidentally, never owned a car. See Satyajit Ray, *Jakhan Chhoto Chhilam*, 9.

201. Three-, four-, and six-cylinder cars were also available but Bose is not known to have bought any for himself. A four-cylinder Darracq cost more

than 450 pounds while a four-cylinder Peugeot was priced at 1,000 pounds, which was higher than the price of a six-cylinder Rolls Royce (945 pounds). See Warren, *The Motor Car in India*, Appendix II. Another motor enthusiast of the time was Bose's bicycling companion, the physician Nilratan Sircar. See B. Ghosh, *Kuntalin Galpa-Satak*, 15.

202. S. Ghosh, 'Jantrarasik H. Bose', 101, 156.

203. B. Ghosh, *Kuntalin Galpa-Satak*, 12.

204. See Ghosh, 'Pre-Commercial Era of Sound Recording in India', 54–5; and on the negative impact of the First World War on import trades, see Dwijendra Tripathi, *The Oxford History of Indian Business* (Delhi: Oxford University Press, 2004), 162.

205. Ananda K. Coomaraswamy, *Essays in National Idealism* (Colombo: Colombo Apothecaries, 1909), 204, 206.

206. See the advertisement of Aparajita perfume in *The Bengalee*, 30 December 1908, 6.

207. Arnold, *Everyday Technology*, 102–3.

208. Mukul Bose was also a ham radio pioneer and a dab hand with all kinds of sophisticated technical equipment. Satyajit Ray recalled that Jagadischandra Bose would not allow anybody except Mukul Bose to repair his delicate scientific instruments. See Satyajit Ray, *Jakhan Chhoto Chhilam*, 19.

209. Sheila Parmanand, 'Nitin Bose: Star amidst Stars', *Film World*, 17, no. 1 (January 1980): 23–7, at 23.

210. 'Profiles of Pioneers: Nitin Bose', 35–48, at 36.

211. 'Profiles of Pioneers: Nitin Bose', 36.

212. 'Nitin Bose: Star amidst Stars', 24, 37; and Satyajit Ray, *Jakhan Chhoto Chhilam*, 19. In 1921, Nitin shot a film recording the visit of a Belgian royal couple to Calcutta. Hurford Cowling, the Technical Manager of Kodak India and a family acquaintance, sent it to William Randolph Hearst's International Newsreel Corporation. 'They took 101 feet and paid me at the rate of a dollar per foot,' recalled Bose many decades later. 'The dollar at that time was two rupees, 10 and a half annas, so it was a fantastic sum of money! About 300 rupees!' See 'I Was The Camera, The Camera Was Me', *Cinema Vision India*, 1, no. 2 (1980): 34–41, at 35–6.

213. 'Profiles of Pioneers: Nitin Bose', 37.

214. 'Profiles of Pioneers: Nitin Bose', 38.

215. See Samik Banerji, 'The Early Years of Calcutta Cinema', 297–8; Raha, *Bengali Cinema*, 12; Bagishwar Jha, *B. N. Sircar: A Monograph*, edited by Partha Basu (Calcutta: National Film Archive of India and Seagull Books, 1980); and Sharmistha Gooptu, 'The Glory That Was: An Exploration of the Iconicity of New Theatres', *Comparative Studies of South Asia, Africa and the Middle East*, 23, nos 1–2 (2003): 286–300.

216. 'Profiles of Pioneers: Nitin Bose', 39; and Gooptu, 'The Glory That Was', 290.

306 THE RAYS BEFORE SATYAJIT

217. Wilford E. Deming, 'Talking Pictures in India', *American Cinematographer*, 12, no. 11 (March 1932): 10–12 and 31, at 11.

218. B. Jha, 'Who Had the First Word?' *Cinema Vision India*, 1, no. 2 (1980): 23–4, at 24.

219. See Siddharth Kak, 'The Bombay Talkies School', *Cinema Vision India*, 1, no. 2 (1980): 79–81, at 80.

220. W.M. Khan, 'The First Song', in *Indian Talkie 1931–56: Silver Jubilee Souvenir* (Bombay: Film Federation of India, 1956), 24.

221. Some histories of the playback system assign the credit for its invention to Madhu Bose, in whose Urdu film *Selima* (1934), the heroine's song was actually sung by an artist in the wings while the actress merely made the appropriate lip-movements for the camera. See Gaurangaprasad Ghosh, *Sonar Daag* (Calcutta: Jogmaya Prakasani, 1982), 213–14. Pankajkumar Mallik, the music director of *Bhagyachakra*, reported that Nitin Bose got the idea of playback when he saw Mallik singing along to an English film song playing on the gramophone. See Pankajkumar Mallik, *Amar Jug, Amar Gaan* (Calcutta: Firma KLM, 1980), 97–101. See also Bani Dutt, 'Sound Recording—Then and Now', in *Indian Talkie 1931–56: Silver Jubilee Souvenir* (Bombay: Film Federation of India, 1956), 151–2, at 151; and Bibhuti Laha, 'Motion Picture—Not a Photo of Stage-Play: Free Movement to Represent Life,' in *Indian Talkie 1931–56*, 153–4, at 153.

222. S. Ghosh, *Karigari Kalpana*, 182; 'Profiles of Pioneers: Nitin Bose', 40; 'Nitin Bose: Star amidst Stars', 25.

223. S. Ghosh, 'Jantrarasik H. Bose', 168.

224. Anonymous, *Swargiya Hemendramohan Basu*, 8.

225. S. Ghosh, 'Upendrakishore: Shilpi o Karigar', 93–4.

226. Seton, *Portrait of a Director*, 35.

227. S. Ghosh, 'Jantrarasik H. Bose', 167–9.

228. For an overview, see Suvobrata Sarkar, *The Quest for Technical Knowledge: Bengal in the Nineteeth Century* (Delhi: Manohar, 2012) and for an encyclopaedic history, S.N. Sen, *Scientific and Technical Education in India, 1781–1900* (Delhi: Indian National Science Academy, 1991). For a participant's account of the movement, see Benoy Sarkar, *Education for Industrialization: An Analysis of the Forty Years' Work of Jadavpur College of Engineering and Technology (1905–45)* (Calcutta: Chuckervertty, Chatterjee & Co., 1946)—my thanks to Soumen Paul for a copy of this scarce volume and to Satadru Sen for his advice.

229. On Mahendralal Sircar and the Indian Association for the Cultivation of Science, see Arun Kumar Biswas, ed., *Collected Works of Mahendralal Sircar, Eugene Lafont and the Science Movement (1860–1910)* (Calcutta: Asiatic Society, 2003); and J. Lourdusamy, *Science and National Consciousness in Bengal, 1870–1930* (Hyderabad: Orient Longman, 2004), 56–99.

230. Lourdusamy, *Science and National Consciousness*, 74–82.

231. H.J.S. Cotton, *Technical Education, or the Indian Revolution in Its Economic Aspect* (Calcutta: Canning Library, 1886), 3, 20.

232. B. Sarkar, *Education for Industrialization*, 95.

233. Sumit Sarkar, *Swadeshi Movement in Bengal*, 141.

234. J.G. Cumming, *Technical and Industrial Instruction in Bengal 1888–1908* (Calcutta: Bengal Secretariat Book Depot, 1908), 16–17, 20, 32. The Government's engineering college at Shibpur, established in 1856, was mainly geared towards training engineers and overseers for the Government's Public Works Department—see Cumming, *Technical and Industrial Instruction*, 11–12; and Arun Kumar, 'Colonial Requirements and Engineering Education: The Public Works Department, 1847–1947', in *Technology and the Raj: Western Technology and Technical Transfers to India 1700–1947*, edited by Roy MacLeod and Deepak Kumar (Delhi: SAGE, 1995), 216–32.

235. B. Sarkar, *Education for Industrialization*, 97–100.

236. See H. Mukherjee and U. Mukherjee, *Origins of the National Education Movement*, 39–68, 169–78, 251–314; Sumit Sarkar, *Swadeshi Movement in Bengal*, 140–9; and Chittabrata Palit and Subrata Pahari, *National Council of Education and National Science* (Calcutta: Readers Service, 2005), 10–11.

237. Binaykumar Sarkar, *Naya Banglar Gora Pattan*, 2 vols (Calcutta: Chuckervertty, Chatterjee & Co., 1932), 1: 108–9, 232–4, www.dli.gov.in/ (accessed on 27 June 2014).

238. Benoy Sarkar, *Dominion India in World-Perspectives: Economic and Political* (Calcutta: Chuckervertty, Chatterjee & Co., 1949), 42–4.

239. On this point, see S. Irfan Habib, 'Science, Technical Education and Industrialisation: Contours of a *Bhadralok* Debate, 1890–1915', in *Technology and the Raj*, 235–49; and Amit Bhattacharyya, *Business, Politics and Technology*, 2–3.

240. Donors to the national education movement (and the initially separate technical education movement) were listed in B. Sarkar, *Education for Industrialization*, 339–45.

6

Triumph and Tragedy

In the decade after Upendrakishore's death, his descendants would scale new heights before being engulfed by a sudden and seemingly terminal crisis. Some elements of the Ray 'brand' would, of course, resurface in the 1940s and 1950s with the graphic designs and then the films of Sukumar's son, Satyajit. But despite many continuities with his artisanal, cosmopolitan, and progressive ancestors, Satyajit's career would never be marked by the earlier generations' unique combination of business, art, literature, technology, and progressive values.

The Rays' early twentieth-century glories as well as tragedies were associated with Upendrakishore's eldest son, Sukumar (1887–1923), who revolutionized Bengali literature while also renewing—and redirecting—some of the other projects of his father's generation. It was with his sudden death at the age of thirty-six that the grand saga of the Rays seemed to reach a calamitous end. But while Sukumar was the undisputed star of this period, the quality of his achievements and the disastrous consequences of his early death should not blind us to Upendrakishore's other successors and their less spectacular but far from uninteresting contributions.

Sukhalata Rao: Sweetness and Puritanism

One of the best ways to appreciate the originality of Sukumar's achievements is to contrast them with the work of his elder sister, Sukhalata (1886–1969). Born in consecutive years, each was given a nickname taken from Rabindranath Tagore's novel *Rajarshi*— Sukhalata was called Hasi and Sukumar Tata—and both were to become well-known writers for children.[1] Sukhalata's niece Kalyani Karlekar thought that if Sukumar had inherited Upendrakishore's brilliance (*ojashwita*), then Sukhalata had inherited her father's sweetness and grace (*madhurya*), along with his spirituality and faith. Tall and grave, Sukhalata was encouraged from childhood to write, draw, and compose, and she contributed to *Sandesh* from its very first year.[2] She was also the most openly religious of Upendrakishore's children.[3] In 1906, she married the physician Jayanta Rao, the son of the Oriya Brahmo poet Madhusudan Rao (1853–1912) and like many of the Ray women, proved to be a remarkably competent housewife: 'Whatever she cooked became a work of art ... when she served food, the guests almost forgot to eat as they admired the artistry of her table-setting.'[4] She wrote some thirty books in Bengali and English and was also a painter in the style of the Bengal School, even though it was her father, no uncritical admirer of that style, who had initiated her into art.[5] Recently, Ratan Parimoo has even described her as 'a mature painter of the wash technique worthy of Abanindranath's first generation disciples', a group that included Nandalal Bose.[6]

Today, however, she is remembered mostly on account of her writings for children. She had a particular bent for fantasies and fairy tales, many of them taken from foreign sources. This reliance on foreign sources was quite common at the time, stemming, Buddhadev Bose surmised, from a desire to collect, adapt, and present the riches of world literature to Bengal's children.[7] Sukhalata translated many classic English nursery rhymes from 'Humpty Dumpty' to 'Little Miss Muffet' and adapted many fairy tales from all over the world, including Chinese, Japanese, Turkish, Dutch, and even Maori stories.[8] But the tales of the Brothers Grimm—'The Frog Prince', 'Rapunzel', 'The Little Elves', and 'The Golden Goose'—were her own favourites and proved to be very popular. The narratives were often abridged, the characters given Bengali names and the stories were re-set in a Bengali milieu. The plots remained essentially unaltered, although some of the harsher elements—death of the stepmother in 'Hansel and Gretel', the asphyxiation of the stepdaughter in 'The Little Brother and Sister'—were quietly eliminated.[9] Her style was tailored for very young children and her simple sentences and homespun diction sought to replicate the experience of listening face-to-face to a storyteller.[10]

She also wrote many stories based on indigenous material, often attempting in these to emulate the plain, moralistic style of the traditional folk tale. The good, the true, the ennobling—these were the themes emphasized by a story such as 'Alibhulir Deshey', a story about a voyage to a fantastical land. She also tried her hand at more realistic stories—'Ghulghuli', 'Apar Rahasya', or 'Bandhu', for example—and these were even more explicitly moral in intent.[11] She wrote plays too, but unlike Sukumar's plays, these were less interested in amusing the reader than in emphasizing the importance of kindness, humanity, and sympathy for the downtrodden, and some were unambiguously educational. 'Tarar Ghar', for instance, was a vehicle to teach children the basics of astronomy—an old fascination of her father's—while 'Jatrapathhey', set during the Japanese bombing of Calcutta in 1941–2, was a heartwarming play about human unselfishness.[12]

She wrote a lot of poetry and also an autobiography in poems (*Pather Alo*, 1955)—some of the poems were based on childhood memories whereas others, less suited for a young reader, were concerned with spiritual matters.[13] The family's characteristic interest in science, geography, and natural history was evident in the essays she wrote for *Sandesh* and the textbooks she authored. In the latter, especially the primer *Parasuna* (1920), she rearranged the Bengali alphabet according to the shape of the letters (as opposed to the traditional phonetic classification) and encouraged children to form simple words even before they had learnt the full alphabet. The experiment, inspired by the kindergarten methods that had been so dear to her maternal grandfather, Dwarakanath Ganguli, does not seem to have been very successful, however, with parents and teachers.[14]

Sukhalata was more of an active reformer than her father. She helped establish institutions for the welfare of women and children in Cuttack and received an award for her relief work at the time of the Second World War.[15] Her puritanism, too, was far more explicit than Upendrakishore's. She asserted, for instance, that 'the princes and princesses of fairy tales should be dressed tastefully and in civilized ways (*susabhya suruchisangata saajposhak*)' and just as it was important to avoid the Indian folk tale's demonization of stepmothers and second wives, it was essential not to follow the Western fairy tale's emphasis on love and marriage. 'I am astonished,' she wrote, 'that today, stories involving the sexes meeting in secret are finding a place—and praise—in children's literature. Instead of talking about the love of young men and women in children's stories, it is preferable to highlight the love one feels towards parents, friends, children, siblings or nation (*swadesh-prem*)'.[16]

Even Leela Majumdar (1908–2007), who was hardly free of moralistic convictions herself, found her aunt Sukhalata's opinions to be rather too Victorian and one wonders if Abanindranath Tagore had Sukhalata in mind when he complained that Bengali children's literature was becoming so earnestly didactic that it was beginning to reek of the classroom.[17] Her brother, Sukumar, however, would reveal a dramatically different disposition.

Sukumar Ray: Charisma and Creativity

Sukumar was exceptional right from his childhood and other children accepted him quite naturally as a leader.[18] Happy and boisterous, the boy was constantly thinking up new games and revealing an irrepressible curiosity on technical matters—he used to break open his toys to investigate their inner workings and dismantle musical instruments in the quest to discover where the music originated.[19] He entertained his siblings and their friends with tales of imaginary animals, similar in their nonsensical spirit to those for which he would later win everlasting fame in Bengali literature.[20] His emotional maturity was evident from one of his childhood innovations. When annoyed by somebody, he did not throw a tantrum but played a game of *rag-banano* (literally, manufacturing anger) with his siblings, in which they would act out imaginary scenarios in which the offending person would be placed in stupid or embarrassing situations and ridiculed so consummately that the children's anger would vanish in uproarious laughter.[21] This sublimation of anger into satire would be fundamental to the adult Sukumar's best-known literary creations. He would never write a utopian tract like *Suruchir Kutir* and it is doubtful if he spent much time imagining a perfect world. He was anything but oblivious, however, to the follies and injustices of the less-than-ideal world that he lived in and he skewered them with irony and ridicule.

His interest in drama and poetry emerged early. He enacted Upendrakishore's humorous skit *Kenaram o Becharam* with his siblings and by the time he was eight, he was a published author: his poem 'Nodi' (The River) was published in *Mukul* in 1893 and the next year, 'Tick, Tick, Tong', a translation of 'Hickory Dickory Dock'.[22] He also designed his own puppet show with paper dolls and as he grew older, developed a serious interest in photography.[23] He used to send his photographs to British magazines and in 1904, was awarded a certificate of merit in a competition in the *Boy's Own Paper*.[24] An admirer of the cinema, he once took one of his puritanical, bioscope-hating teachers to a film and at the end of the show, the teacher thanked Sukumar for showing him that films could be wonderful things.[25]

As he grew up, Sukumar revealed an interest in nationalism that was rather more pronounced than Upendrakishore's. Despite being unflinchingly cosmopolitan in his intellectual, social, and cultural attitudes, Sukumar was no admirer of imperialism and during the Boer War, when his sister Punyalata was celebrating a British victory, silenced her by asking her, 'How can you laugh at people being beaten up after having been beaten flat yourselves?'[26] During the swadeshi movement, he would write a short play called 'Ramdhan Badhh', which was about an Englishman called Ramsden who sneered at Indians as 'native niggers'. The play, now lost except for one song, depicted how a bunch of children, chanting 'Vande Mataram' ('Hail Motherland', the battle-cry of the swadeshi movement), taught Ramsden a lesson he would not forget.[27] Sukumar wrote at least one swadeshi song—'Tutilo ki aaj ghumer ghor?' (Are we finally waking from our slumber?)—and Supriya Goswami has even argued that in his nonsense writings, Sukumar produced a literary equivalent of the civil disobedience techniques of swadeshi activists, creating 'a topsy-turvy world which trivializes empire, parodies the laws of the land, and subverts all forms of official power and authority'.[28] But as always with the Rays, Sukumar's nationalism was never blind or uncritical. When brother Subinoy got into the swing of the boycott movement and obtained swadeshi products for use by the family, Sukumar, too, abandoned foreign goods but in a song, teased swadeshi enthusiasts as 'a nation-crazed lot' (*dishipaglar dol*) and indigenous products as 'unattractive, easily-broken, and pricey' (*dekhhte khharap, tnikbe kam, daam-ta ektu beshi*), albeit finishing with the declaration, 'So what? They are good for the nation' (*Ta hokna, tatey desher-i mangal*).[29]

Sukumar was a 'people person' and radiated such charisma that in his presence, remarked Leela Majumdar, one hardly registered anybody else and when he read out his work, listeners were so transfixed by his infinitely expressive voice that they often forgot to laugh.[30] Indeed, he spent so much time with friends that one admiring critic remarked that he could have written much more had he been less gregarious.[31] In fact, for somebody who passed away in his mid-thirties, Sukumar's productivity was impressive, and it is a mistake to see his social and literary activities as mutually exclusive.[32] Around 1905, for example, he founded the Nonsense Club, where, in spite of the name, all kinds of topics were discussed, especially music and drama, enlivened by Sukumar's endlessly inventive and humorous contributions.[33] Sukumar's later masterpieces, remarked one member, were conceived in this 'talk-laboratory' and this was also true for the later Monday Club.[34] Sukumar wrote several humorous plays for performance by the Nonsense Club, including 'Jhhalapala' and 'Lakshmaner Shaktishel', and he played major roles in them, excelling at portraying naive and stupid characters.[35] The Nonsense Club also published a handwritten newsletter called *Sare Batris Bhhaja*, much of which was written by Sukumar and also illustrated by him.[36] Although most issues of this newsletter are lost, one has survived and presages the flights of invention and wit that would characterize Sukumar's mature work. It also had its anticolonial elements: Sukumar's brother Subimal remembered one little poem about 'the villainous Lord Curzon, huffing and puffing against poor, unhappy Bengalis'.[37]

It was not just literature and sociability that kept the young Sukumar busy. His academic career was far from ordinary. After early schooling at the Brahmo Girls' School, he moved in 1895 to the City Collegiate School—another Brahmo institution—from where he passed his entrance examination in 1902 and then, the First Arts in 1904.[38] Like his father, Sukumar chose to go to Presidency College for his undergraduate studies and emerged in 1907 with a second-class double honours in physics and chemistry.[39] He does not seem to have aspired to be a scientist, however, and soon devoted himself to the family trade of printing technology and travelled all the way to Britain for training in photography and photomechanical reproduction on a Calcutta University scholarship.[40] Before that, however, he had an opportunity to spell out his ideas on the identity of the national and the relevance of the foreign in great and polemical detail.

The Foreign and the Indigenous

Two years after his father's intervention on 'authentic' Indian art in *Modern Review*, Sukumar spoke out on the pages of *Probasi* against orientalist 'mystifications'. Ridiculing the alleged spirituality of Bengal School art, he asked whether 'subjects with dreamy eyes, an atmosphere engulfed in mist with a hint of light breaking through, vague expressions, wiry emaciated heroes and heroines that make a mockery of anatomy' could signify genuine spirituality.[41] Every artist from every nation had to learn from nature and even the unreal or the improbable had to be imagined 'in terms of known realities'.[42] Realism and idealism were not polar opposites: one could not succeed without the other.[43] Nor was Sukumar at all impressed by the swadeshi resistance to European art. Should one not try to learn foreign languages because one could never produce great literature in a language that was not one's own? Adopting Upendrakishore's universalism but without his father's linear narrative of artistic progress, he pointed out that 'art was fundamentally and by nature universal' and true artists were driven by their inner creative compulsions, not by the urge to 'produce "Indian art", "Greek art", etc.'[44] National differences in artistic styles were not fundamental differences of language—'the language used by European Pre-Raphaelites,' he asserted, 'was the same as the language of the Impressionists'—but resulted from differences in ornamentation, style, ideals, and subjects.[45]

O.C. Gangoly was as dismissive of the son as he had been of the father. Sukumar's perspective was colonial, he countered, and rooted in the aesthetics of classical Greece and the European Renaissance. It had no relevance to the spiritual concerns of Indian art and artists.[46] Partha Mitter has argued that Sukumar Ray's intervention 'signalled the regrouping of Westernisers who refused to accept Oriental art as the sole national style or jettison the technical advances of academic art'.[47] Sukumar, however, was more of a universalist than a simple-minded Westernizer: his attitude towards the foreign, in the words of Satadru Sen, was one of 'openness without envy'.[48] The so-called Western naturalistic art that was produced in India, he once declared, was neither Western, nor naturalistic and, in most cases, did not even qualify as art.[49] But that did not mean that the so-called Oriental or Indian art being churned out by Abanindranath and his pupils was worthy of much admiration. It was not only Sukumar, but also such active supporters of the swadeshi movement as Binaykumar Sarkar who found the O.C. Gangoly brand of indigenism to be purblind.

A year before Sukumar's death in 1923, Sarkar would speak up for aesthetic cosmopolitanism in *Rupam*, Gangoly's own journal. Although Sarkar's stance was not quite the same as Upendrakishore's or Sukumar's, all three agreed on the need for artists to be open to all the artistic traditions of the world.[50] Urging Indians to paint in a rigid Oriental style was as bad as asking them to stop reading 'Rousseau, Washington, Mill, Mazzini, Treitschke and Lenin' and to stick to Kautilya, Sarkar declared.[51] In that same year, and entirely independently, the historian Jadunath Sarkar declared in a letter to Rabindranath Tagore that the best examples of Bengal School art— with the exception of the work of Abanindranath and Nandalal Bose— were no more than copies of Mughal miniatures or the Ajanta frescoes, and the rest were as crude as the drawings of a child or a 'caveman'. The highest aspiration of these artists, Sarkar charged, was to be praised for their quintessential 'oriental'-ness by Europeans. Had any Dutch master of the past sought praise for being Dutch? Did people like Turner because his art was English? By repudiating universal aesthetic criteria, the Bengal School was encouraging the world to judge the art of 'black folk' (*kala admi*) by a different—and implicitly lower—set of standards.[52]

Some of these critiques would probably have been too acerbic for the gentle Upendrakishore and he may well have disagreed with Binay Sarkar's argument that the universality of art did not inhere in its depiction of nature but in deeper, morphological factors related to mass, volume, and magnitude. But he would surely have applauded the young nationalist's cosmopolitan spirit or the older historian's universalism, and Sukumar—who may have read *The Aesthetics of Young India*—would have agreed with Sarkar that 'the same universal principles of aesthetics' were at play 'in all epochs of art development, no matter whatever be the latitude and longitude, whatever be the subject-matter, the superstition and the *esprit de lois*'.[53] The Rays, in short, were not quite as isolated in their rooted cosmopolitanism as one might imagine. In the maelstrom of the swadeshi movement and its aftermath, many contending forces jostled one another in complex, nuanced ways—the cultural confrontations were not simply between a homogeneous 'nationalist elite' and equally undifferentiated 'Westernizers'.[54] Swadeshi-era debates over the arts and culture were complementary to larger political dissensions about patriotism, indigenism, cosmpolitanism, and the place of religion in nationalist politics.

At the Heart of Empire

Appropriately enough, Sukumar left for Britain shortly after this debate on the relationship of East and West. For all his familiarity with metropolitan printing technologists, Upendrakishore had never been to Britain and when Sukumar left for England in October 1911 on the *SS Arabia*, he was the first Ray to venture abroad. Prior to his departure, all his friends had been invited for a feast and, in the style of the later Monday Club, the invitation was written in untranslatable comic verse by Sukumar himself, alluding, among other things, to buying his first hat and coat.[55] The Rays, for all their cultural cosmopolitanism, had never adopted Western apparel and while on the boat, Sukumar regularly practised putting on his collar and tie, writing to his mother that he was getting so much better at it that he no longer needed half an hour to dress for dinner.[56] Arriving in London at the end of October (via Lyon, Paris, and Calais, where he skilfully used a few French words he had learnt beforehand), he lodged at the students' home run by the Brahmo academic Prasannakumar Ray (1849–1932), husband of Durgamohan and Brahmamoyee Das's eldest daughter, Sarala, and later the first Indian principal of Calcutta's Presidency College.[57] The students' home was located on the bustling and prosperous Cromwell Road in South Kensington, and housed several other Bengali students.[58] Also in Britain were two Calcutta acquaintances, the physicist and future statistician Prasanta Mahalanobis (1893–1972)—who would later graduate from King's College, Cambridge, and become one of Sukumar's closest friends—and Kedarnath, the son of the founder-editor of *Probasi*, Ramananda Chatterji. Sukumar went to 'at homes' at Prasanna Ray's home (where he read out his 'Bhabuk Sabha' and a version of 'Lakshmaner Shaktishel'), sang at the London Maghotsava, visited art galleries, played tennis, billiards, and card games, and followed cricket with great interest.[59] Even food did not pose a problem and Sukumar's parents sent what he could not get in London—pickles, spices, puffed rice, dried mango strips (*amsatta*), and jaggery.[60]

His letters home do not suggest any racial discrimination (except for one encounter on the voyage out with a rude Englishman in the ship's toilet) or loneliness.[61] There are hardly any references to British politics in the letters except for brief descriptions of the 'depredations' (*utpat*) of the suffragette movement and his incredulity at 'gentlewomen' (*bhadraloker meye*), one of them the wife of *Strand* magazine's W.W. Jacobs, throwing stones at Harrods' shop windows.[62] As a young man, he had been so affronted by an attack on educated women in a Christian missionary paper that he had personally forced the editor and his correspondent to apologize in print.[63] In his mature years, he was regarded as being far more supportive of women's rights than many young Sadharan Brahmos.[64] But the suffragettes shocked him by crossing the limits of his (and his family's) progressive ethos, which was consistently liberal and rejected all forms of violent activism.

Being Upendrakishore's son also gave Sukumar considerable access to the artistic and intellectual world of London. Musicologist Arthur H. Fox Strangways (1859–1948), for whose book *The Music of Hindostan* (1914) Upendrakishore had translated several songs of Rabindranath Tagore, introduced Sukumar to the painter William Rothenstein (1872–1945), who would soon play an important role in introducing Rabindranath Tagore (whom he had met on a trip to India in 1911) to the London intelligentsia.[65] Sukumar himself was already close to Tagore and had been a regular visitor to Santiniketan. He would also do his bit for the poet when the latter visited London in 1912 with his translation of *Gitanjali*, which would soon win the Nobel Prize.[66] Tagore's son Rathindranath wrote that while he and his father were in London, 'the one who was the life and soul of the party' was Sukumar Ray.[67] Tagore's admirers, in particular Rothenstein, asked Sukumar to translate some of Tagore's poems and publish them.[68] That does not seem to have come about but Sukumar did give a lecture on Tagore's poetry at the East and West Society in July 1912 which was printed in the magazine *Quest* and was one of the first Indian (and Bengali) discussions of Tagore's work to be published in the West.[69] In this lecture, Andrew Robinson has argued, we can discern 'Sukumar's future clash and disenchantment with the Brahmo Samaj, and even the beginnings of his frightening loss of faith in life'.[70] I do not find such hints in the piece, although it does portray

Tagore, quite justly, as more than merely Brahmo, pointing out not simply his connections to the faith of Rammohan Roy and Debendranath Tagore but also to the work of the great Vaishnava poets of Bengal.[71]

As for work, Britain proved a bit of a mixed bag. William Gamble welcomed Upendrakishore's son warmly and recommended that he study at the London County Council School of Photoengraving and Lithography.[72] Located on Fleet Street, the School had been founded to train enough British print-workers to neutralize growing competition from American printers and process workers.[73] Sukumar enrolled here on courses on collotype and lithography.[74] Although he was fascinated by what he learnt about these and other, newer processes, the School did not live up to Sukumar's expectations.[75] Most of the half-tone and three-colour work being produced there seemed worthless to him, and tired of wasting his time in the regular classes, he arranged for private lessons with one Mr Griggs. Although he liked his tutor very much and admired some of his lithographic work—especially the colour lithographs he had made for a book by E.B. Havell—he learnt much more from visits to commercial presses.[76] As his father's ambassador, he demonstrated Upendrakishore's methods, especially his new technique of using multiple diaphragms, to many of his fellow students and professors.[77] The Principal of the School was deeply impressed by specimens of three-colour half-tone prints done in Calcutta by Upendrakishore with multiple diaphragms. 'He had probably assumed,' Sukumar remarked to his father, 'that we could only produce very crude examples of three-colour work.'[78] Sukumar even tried to get the Penrose Company to manufacture Upendrakishore's Screen Distance Indicator with modifications by Sukumar but despite some interest from Gamble and an offer to pay 'a fair price', nothing seems to have happened.[79]

In October 1912, Sukumar moved to the Manchester Municipal School of Technology, the resources of which he found far more satisfactory than the London school—'why didn't I come here first?', he wondered—although the cold, smoky darkness of Manchester did not appeal to him at all.[80] He was particularly excited by the prospect of conducting a full-scale research project on multiple diaphragms under the supervision of Richard 'Bertie' Fishenden (1880–1956), who seemed relatively well-disposed towards Upendrakishore's innovation.[81] Soon, however, he found that Fishenden—who would

eventually succeed William Gamble as the editor of *Penrose Annual*—
was giving him all kinds of 'useless rubbish' (*ja-taa baajey kaaj*) to
work on and when it became clear that any publications resulting
from the project would carry Fishenden's name as the first author,
Sukumar gave up the idea of working with him.[82]

While in Britain, Sukumar published two articles in *Penrose* on
topics related to half-tone technology and another, which was read out
by Fishenden in one of his classes, in the *British Journal of
Photography*.[83] None, however, was a pace-setter like some of his
father's papers and it is curious that while Sukumar's letters home
were full of references to newer processes like intaglio, offset, or collotype, the articles continued to focus on half-tone, which, even its
earlier champions like Gamble feared, would soon be displaced by the
intaglio process (rotary photogravure), which was not only faster and
less labour-intensive but produced 'an artistic quality and a photographic richness of tone ... that has never been secured in half-tone'.[84]
In fact, the reports of half-tone's death were exaggerated but Sukumar's
interest in the newer processes may have remained muted because he
knew that the family firm would not immediately have the where-
withal to switch to them. Upendrakishore was moving to his own
house, finally getting his own press—which Sukumar ordered from
England, along with a consignment of art paper—and preparing to
launch *Sandesh*. It was not the right time for any dramatic change in
direction.[85]

Sukumar was still in England when the first issue of *Sandesh* was
published but he was very much involved with the project, collecting
material for the magazine and sending illustrations.[86] It was also in
London that Rabindranath Tagore saw the first issue of *Sandesh* and
although he admired it greatly and promised Sukumar to contribute,
he never did write for *Sandesh* during Upendrakishore's editorship
and even the news of his Nobel Prize did not feature on its pages.[87]
But Tagore and Sukumar spent a lot of time together, especially after
Sukumar finished his Manchester course and returned to London in
May 1912.[88] Andrew Robinson has remarked that while in Britain,
Sukumar 'lived in two worlds which seldom overlapped': one of
printing technology and the other of the arts.[89] It might, however, be
more appropriate to regard Sukumar's socializing, his commitment
to printing technology, and his interest in literature as intertwined.
Describing a dinner with Tagore and Rothenstein in a letter to his
father, for instance, he talked about his translations of Tagore's poetry,

and turned, in the very next letter, to a discussion of printing equipment that he wanted to buy for the family business, which ended with
a query about the blocks being made by U. Ray & Sons for the illustrated edition of Tagore's autobiography.[90] For Sukumar, there was
only one world, in which technology and literature, business and
socializing, Calcutta and London, shaded more imperceptibly and
naturally into one another than one might expect. This intertwining
of technology, business, art, and literature, so characteristic of the
Rays, was highly unusual, if not unique, among the other champions
of modernity in India.

Bringing the New Woman Home

Sukumar had long planned to spend some time on the continent on
his way home from England but that does not seem to have tran-
spired.[91] At the end of September 1913, he returned to Calcutta and,
within a couple of months, married Suprabha Das (1892–1960),
granddaughter of the philanthropic zamindar Kalinarayan Gupta
(1830–1903). This was a remarkable alliance with another progressive
East Bengal Brahmo lineage that deserves some discussion.

Rather like Upendrakishore, Kalinarayan Gupta had been adopted
at a young age and his first name had been changed from
Madhabchandra to Kalinarayan.[92] After learning Bengali at home
and, briefly, Sanskrit at a tol, he was trained in Urdu and Farsi, which,
in spite of the victory of the Anglicists in the educational sphere in the
mid-1830s, was still considered by many, especially outside Calcutta,
to be the language of statecraft, law, and administration.[93] Married at
the age of thirteen to the eight-year-old Annadasundari, Gupta was to
have four sons and six daughters.[94] Although an orthodox Hindu,
Gupta gradually developed an interest in Brahmoism after reading
the works of Dwarakanath Ganguli's mentor, Akshaykumar Datta.[95]
His eldest sons—Krishnagovinda, Pyarimohan, and Gangagovinda—
also developed Brahmo leanings while studying in Dhaka but the
family was still Hindu enough for Krishnagovinda to be married
according to Hindu rites at the age of sixteen in 1866.[96] It was only
after they faced social persecution after dining with a Muslim that the
enraged Gupta family ceased to practise the routine rituals of a Hindu
household but their formal initiation into Brahmoism occurred three
years later when Keshab Sen, on a visit to Dhaka, initiated thirty-six

individuals, including the thirty-nine-year-old Kalinarayan Gupta. Gupta's two sons Pyarimohan and Gangagovinda and two servants Madan and Gurudas were initiated with him.[97] Gupta then worked to disseminate Brahmoism among his tenants but made more of an impact with the many Brahmo hymns he composed, his mellifluous singing, and his entirely self-taught mastery of several musical instruments from the violin to the *mridanga*.[98] Musical talent was to run in the Gupta family for several generations.

Gupta was especially active in giving prominence to women in Brahmo worship as well as in secular settings. His wife Annadasundari—who was not a New Woman and had not received much education—wrote hymns, participated fully in the foundation ceremony for the Brahmo temple Gupta established in his estate at Kaoraid, and regularly conducted public worship with her husband.[99] Gupta opposed the contemporary reluctance to permit women to sing during weddings and insisted that all the music at her daughter's wedding be selected and performed by the women in the family.[100] And when Keshab Sen arranged the controversial marriage of his under-age daughter to the Cooch Behar prince, Kalinarayan Gupta was one of the signatories of the letter of protest sent to Sen from the Dhaka Brahmo Samaj and predictably, Gupta joined the radical Sadharans after the split that ensued shortly thereafter.[101]

Perhaps the most famous of Gupta's children was Krishnagovinda (1851–1926), known as K.G. Gupta. In 1873, he succeeded in gaining entry by competitive examination into the 'covenanted' ranks of the Indian Civil Service, which, until the 1850s, had been all-white and remained largely white for long after. When Annette Akroyd decided to go to Calcutta in 1872, he arranged Bengali lessons for her in London and over subsequent decades, served in various important posts and eventually became the first Indian member of the Board of Revenue.[102] In 1908, Gupta was inducted into the Secretary of State for India's advisory council in London as one of the two Indian members provided for by the Minto–Morley reforms and was knighted in 1911.[103] Sukumar Ray would meet Gupta in London and enjoy a home-cooked Bengali-style dinner at his home without, of course, realizing that he would soon be marrying Gupta's niece. This was Suprabha, the daughter of Krishnagovinda Gupta's sister Sarala and Jagatchandra Das, a woman who had not only inherited the musical gifts characterizing her lineage but who would, in the course of a long

322   THE RAYS BEFORE SATYAJIT

and challenging life, surpass the many accomplishments of Dwarakanath Ganguli's utopian heroine, Suruchi.[104]

After finishing her schooling in Dhaka, Suprabha moved to Calcutta and, lodging with Prankrishna Acharya (a very successful doctor of the time, a leading light of the Sadharan Brahmo Samaj and the husband of Kalinarayan Gupta's youngest daughter, Subala), entered Bethune College as an undergraduate.[105] Family tradition holds that Sukumar first grew interested in Suprabha when, on a casual visit to Prankrishna Acharya's home, he heard her singing Tagore songs in the inner quarters of the house and was stunned by her voice.[106] One does not know how exactly the marriage was arranged but there was a formal *koney-dekhha* (an interview and assessment of the potential bride by the groom and his relatives), where Suprabha caused much unwitting amusement by singing Tagore's 'Mamo chittey niti nritye, ke je nachey, tata thoi thoi, tata thoi thoi' without realizing that Sukumar's nickname was Tata.[107] Sukumar and Suprabha were married on 13 December 1913 and Rabindranath Tagore, who had decamped to distant Silaidaha for a respite from the endless tributes and receptions that followed his Nobel Prize, made a special journey to Calcutta to bless the young couple.[108] Tagore's links with the Rays are often exaggerated but his affection for Sukumar was deep and genuine and he grew to admire Suprabha so much that he taught her many of his songs himself.[109]

Suprabha, whose nickname was Tulu, was not just a good singer, she was a superb cook, a dab hand at sewing and embroidery, and an omnicompetent housekeeper.[110] Her perfectionism was legendary. The twelve-year-old Leela Majumdar was once entrusted to Suprabha Ray for some training in cooking. 'I broke into a sweat within half an hour,' recalled Majumdar. 'Every action had to be totally flawless.'[111] Bijoya Ray, who was not only Satyajit Ray's wife but also his cousin and intimately familiar with the milieu of Satyajit's upbringing, recalled that her mother-in-law was so skilled at so many different kinds of activity that she was rarely satisfied by other people's work and very blunt in pointing out their shortcomings.[112] But Suprabha could also be very traditional and 'soft' when needed. When she went to Masua with Sukumar after their marriage, she behaved exactly as a new bride was supposed to, always keeping one step behind Narendrakishore's wife and covering her head with the end of her sari.[113] Everything Suprabha Ray ever did was marked by this ability to navigate effortlessly through the thickets of tradition without losing her moorings in the modern universe.

The End of the Old Order

In 1914, shortly after Sukumar's marriage, the family moved to their large new house on Garpar Road in north Calcutta. Upendrakishore had designed the house himself but he could barely live in it.[114] He had been suffering from diabetes for some years and in this pre-insulin period, treatment was far from reliable.[115] He had already 'practically retired from his half-tone business'; leaving it in the hands of Sukumar and Subinoy Ray, he concentrated on music and *Sandesh*.[116] His condition worsened after 1914, supposedly because the import of a particular European medicine had ceased because of the war.[117] He was taken to Giridi, a traditional upcountry vacation spot famed for its restorative climate and particularly popular among Brahmos. But the climate failed to work its magic and a desperately ill Upendrakishore was brought back to Calcutta.[118] Even though he was in pain and no doubt conscious of the many projects he was leaving unfinished, Sukumar thought his father had been at peace with himself, with his God, and with the world.[119] Only fifty-two when he died on 20 December 1915, he left his family bereft and although he had always avoided positions of prominence in the Brahmo Samaj, his death was regarded as a grievous loss for the entire Brahmo community, and not just the Sadharan Brahmos.[120] In Britain, Upendrakishore's admirers at the Penrose Company were understandably more concerned with his half-tone research and hoped that the 'voluminous notes he had left behind' would be edited and published by Sukumar.[121]

Sukumar did not, in fact, do that, but he took over the family business and the standards of process-work not only remained high but, in some cases, may even have surpassed those of Upendrakishore's era.[122] The publishing side of the business, which Upendrakishore had inaugurated, also flourished. Upendrakishore's books, hitherto published privately or by the City Book Society, were now brought out under the imprint of U. Ray & Sons, and the list soon expanded to include Kuladaranjan Ray, Sukhalata Rao, and a range of authors from outside the family. The firm also handled printing assignments from other publishers, including the City Book Society; even the magazine *Mukul* would be printed, during its final days, at the press where its greatest rival, *Sandesh*, was produced.[123] Sukumar also took over the editorship of *Sandesh*, transforming that magazine's character.

Although he had contributed to *Sandesh* before his father's death, he had then been rather keener on writing on serious themes for the readers of *Probasi* or similar magazines. In those important essays—most notably, in his essays on the fallacies of swadeshi art—we get a glimpse of Sukumar the all-round intellectual, a witty polemicist with an independent mind and irreverent attitude. After Upendrakishore's death, however, he hardly ever wrote such essays. The Sukumar Ray that most Bengalis remember today emerged on the pages of *Sandesh* after 1915, in poetry, prose, riddles, and illustrations that operated at many levels but were addressed primarily to the young.[124] But not quite as young as the readers Upendrakishore or Sukhalata catered to. Sukumar changed *Sandesh*, as Leela Majumdar and Satyajit Ray remarked, from a magazine for young children to one for children between eight and thirteen, an age group called *kishor* in Bengali.[125]

There was much more poetry in the new *Sandesh* and Sukumar's illustrations complemented the wit and imagination of his writings.[126] 'He possessed a sixth sense of the absurd,' says art historian Partha Mitter, 'and an imagination which could parody almost any serious statement.'[127] Unlike Upendrakishore, Sukumar was not a prolific painter and used sketches almost like stage props, leaving some incomplete to create the illusion of a partly illuminated stage.[128] The poetry that went with the pictures mixed the real and the outlandish with abandon but without sacrificing either their value as poetry or their Bengaliness. The Bengali language, as Mitter explains, 'lends itself to *double entendres* and wordplay. Its speakers have always been captivated by puns, onomatopoeia, alliteration and repetition of sounds'.[129] This was the tradition that Sukumar would mark out as his own and immortalize, but as Satadru Sen has rightly pointed out, Sukumar's language reflected the contemporary revolution in Bengali speech and writing, when the previous demarcation between the formal sadhu bhasha and the spoken chalit bhasa was breaking down. Mixing sadhu and chalit, serious and profane, and Bengali and English with great panache, Sukumar's language games celebrated as well as derided the 'mongrel, heterotemporaneous nature of colonial society'. His nonsense combined the 'irrational substance of colonial reality, and the rational response to it'.[130]

Sukumar's achievement is all the more noteworthy because not all his best works were completely original. He was undoubtedly influenced by Edward Lear and Lewis Carroll and, as Siddhartha Ghosh has shown, his illustrations suggest a 'familiarity with the work of W.W. Denslow, Arthur Rackham, Winsor McCay and Rudolf Dirks who created the Katzenjammer Kids'.[131] While the stimuli might have come from abroad, the results were entirely unique to Sukumar and to Bengal. His seemingly endless capacity to imagine incongruous situations, his passion for playing with words, his ebullient humour, and the critiques of contemporary mores that he subtly injected into his work brought something new to Bengali literature. Translators, including his son, Satyajit, have not entirely succeeded in capturing the true flavour of Sukumar in English, perhaps because the characters and situations, despite being obviously fantastical, are so emphatically of Bengal in their characteristics that they remain virtually untranslatable.[132]

Certain fundamental concerns of *Sandesh*, however, remained unchanged. There was, of course, no loosening of the puritanical avoidance of male–female relations and edutainment continued to be a major goal. Although there were no more tributes to emperors on its pages, *Sandesh* was equally silent on nationalists.[133] And although not as keen on mythology and the classical epics as his father or uncle Kuladaranjan, Sukumar fully shared Upendrakishore's interest in science, writing countless factual pieces for *Sandesh* on scientific discoveries, natural history, cultural events, and technological advances, and many biographical essays on scientists, scholars and philosophers.[134] He was remarkably up-to-date in his choice of topics. A man who would die before the end of 1923 wrote, among other things, about radio transmission and rockets, even speculating about what a trip to the moon might be like.[135] The essays were mostly derived from foreign sources and pervaded by the uncritical reverence for scientific progress—the scientism—that was and is so characteristic of Bengali intellectuals but there was another side to Sukumar. In poems such as 'Haturey' (The Quack) or 'Biggyan Siksha' (Teaching Science) and in prose pieces like 'Heshoram Hushiyarer Diary' (The Diary of Heshoram Hushiyar), he poked fun at scientists with the same abandon with which he lampooned classical heroes or everyday eccentrics.[136] Sukumar never lost sight of the distinction between science—which he revered—and the scientist, who could be as petty or as risible as any other human being.

Although some of his masterpieces were inspired by foreign sources, Sukumar left quite a few works that had no discernible model, especially the classic school stories later collected as *Pagla Dashu*, which have been compared to Mark Twain's *Tom Sawyer* by a

historian of Bengali humorous literature.[137] Dasarathi (Dashu)'s
exploits, apart from providing some of the most entertaining examples of a genre that has never been particularly popular in Bengali
literature, also moved beyond the simple-minded championing of
'good boys' in earlier children's literature.[138] Sukumar's schoolboy
protagonist Dashu is not evil but incorrigibly mischievous and more
than a little eccentric. He plays countless tricks on the goodie-goodies
and often treats teachers quite disrespectfully. He is constantly upset-
ting the settled order of school life and is, therefore, disparaged as
'crazy' but the point about Dashu is not that he is insane, but honest
and totally instinctive.

Buddhadev Bose found *Pagla Dashu* to be the only work of
Sukumar that had become dated.[139] While that may well be true for
the empirical details of school life, Dashu himself and his antics are
as timeless as the eccentrics who populate *Abol Tabol*. Whether Dashu
is mad, childishly instinctive, or just mischievous, it is clear that he is
unlikely to grow up to be a docile cog in the wheel of bhadralok society
or stoically satisfy the colonial economy's demand for tractable,
disciplined but none too ambitious workers.[140] The humour of the
stories, as Satadru Sen has put it, stems from the 'sharply observed,
and keenly felt, incongruity between native society and the Macaulayan
curriculum' and Dashu's supposed lunacy is in fact 'a native-ness that
resists Macaulay'.[141] But some of Dashu's antics also resist the social
code of the bhadralok and its insistence on respectful behaviour
towards elders and particularly towards teachers. Ironically but revealingly, Satyajit Ray, who revived *Sandesh* in 1961 and co-edited it until
his death, confessed that the tricks Dashu played on his teachers were
so irreverent that the editors today would not dare to publish such
stories in the magazine.[142]

'All My Singing Ends in Sleep'

The 1920s began on a high note for Suprabha and Sukumar, with the
birth of a son, delivered by the famous Dr Kadambini Ganguli. The
boy was initially named Prasad but Sukumar, disregarding
Rabindranath Tagore's suggestion of Saritkumar, changed it to
Satyajit.[143] The new name was formalized at a traditional Brahmo
namkaran ceremony on the boy's second birthday on 2 May 1923, the
naming deed being signed, among others, by Kadambini Ganguli.[144]

By the time of that ceremony, Sukumar was already ill, having contracted the tropical disease kala-azar on a trip to Masua in 1921, and the fever had started soon after his son's birth on 2 May.[145] It is not known precisely what kind of treatment Sukumar Ray received, but his first physician was Dwijendranath Maitra (a member of the Monday Club) and family tradition holds that Sukumar's condition was not initially diagnosed as kala-azar.[146]

Kala-azar, an infectious disease caused by the parasite *Leishmania donovanii* and spread by sand-flies, used to be endemic in eastern India. Characterized by prolonged fever, anaemia, and emaciation, it killed nearly 95 per cent of patients. The causal organism was unknown until 1903 and there was no treatment for it until 1915, when antimony derivatives began to be used with some benefit. Not all patients responded to them, however, and the injections were not only very painful but produced severe side-effects. In 1921, the Calcutta physician Upendranath Brahmachari (1875–1946) introduced a new antimony derivative called urea stibamine, which gave better results.[147] Although we have no definitive information on Sukumar's treatment, he must have received antimony treatment and Satyajit Ray recalled that he was also treated with Brahmachari's urea stibamine, but nothing, unfortunately, worked.[148] As was common at the time, the ailing Sukumar was taken to various resorts, including two of the family's favourite places, Giridi and Darjeeling, but to little obvious benefit.

Despite his worsening physical condition, Sukumar remained resolute, cheerful and, as his sister Punyalata recalled, unshakeable in his religious faith.[149] There was no change as far as *Sandesh* was concerned—Sukumar continued to fill it with sketches, poems, and stories that count among his best work.[150] While confined to a sanatorium in Darjeeling, for instance, he wrote the memorable poem 'Baburam Sapurey', and *Haw-Jaw-Baw-Raw-Law* was written during one of his recuperative stays at Gaganchandra Home's house in Giridi.[151] Another inspired work was *Heshoram Hushiyarer Diary*. Although inspired by Arthur Conan Doyle's novel *The Lost World*, in which a team led by the cantankerous Professor Challenger finds live dinosaurs in a remote part of the Amazon rainforest, Sukumar's dinosaurs had nothing to do with science. Graced with names like Gomratherium or Chillanosaurus (approximate translations would be Grumpytherium and Screamosaurus), these animals belonged to Sukumar's own private menagerie and the leader of the expedition,

Professor Hushiyar, seems to have stepped out of one of Sukumar's nonsense poems in *Abol-Tabol*.

That classic collection, too, was put together, illustrated, and designed by Sukumar on his deathbed with the young Satyajit often sitting on his stomach and playing with his paints.[152] On the last pages of the dummy itself, Sukumar wrote his very last poem.[153] Full of high-spirited whimsy, its final lines bid an incomparable adieu to the world: 'A keen primordial lunar chill/The nightmare's nest with bunchy frill/My drowsy brain such glimpses steep/And all my singing ends in sleep.'[154] These flights of the imagination, however, were complemented by a calm, devout acceptance of his approaching death. The true depth of Sukumar's religiosity became evident to his friends only during his last days. An anonymous obituarist, who was evidently a close friend, wrote that Sukumar 'had learnt to realise God as Beauty, Joy and Love', remarking shortly before his death: 'The blossoming of the soul by giving and receiving love, both human and Divine—this is the supreme end and fulfilment of life.'[155] When Rabindranath Tagore came to see him for the last time, Sukumar requested him to sing 'songs of fulfilment, songs of bliss' (*purnatar gaan, anander gaan*).[156] One of them, 'Dukhho e nahe, sukh nahe go, gabhhira santi e je' ('Not grief, nor happiness, this is profound peace'), had never been set to tune and when Sukumar requested it, Tagore sang it twice on a tune he improvised then and there. It was never noted down, however, and the lyric has remained without a tune ever since. It is almost as if the dying Sukumar not only coaxed the song into existence but took it away with him for all eternity.[157]

On the morning of 10 September 1923, as Calcutta was shaken by an earthquake, Sukumar Ray passed away, leaving his twenty-nine-year-old widow and a son who was not even three. Nine days later, *Abol Tabol* was published by U. Ray & Sons.[158] Nobody, Leela Majumdar recalls, cried loudly—Brahmos were famous for their command over their emotions—but an air of devastation hung over the household. 'That Garpar was not the Garpar of yore,' she found. 'Now there was no laughter, no talk, no work, no joy.'[159]

The Sense of Nonsense

Although usually categorized as 'nonsense', Sukumar's best work was far more complex and best approached, at least by grown-ups, as a series of commentaries, by turns satirical, philosophical, and farcical, on the world around him and 'the nonsensical nature of the colonial everyday, with its yawning gaps between aspiration and reality'.[160] This extraordinary ability to elevate farce to satire and satire to philosophy is most obvious in his plays. Sukumar's dramatic interests emerged early, with a childhood dramatization of his father's story 'Kenaram o Becharam' and the lost anti-colonial skit 'Ramdhan Badhh'. His earliest extant play is 'Jhhalapala' (1911), which depicts how a rich landowner, with the help of his old servant and a lawyer uncle, gets rid of favour-seekers and flatterers by unmalicious trickery.[161] Even though the play is almost pure farce, the author of 'Ramdhan Badhh' makes a cameo appearance in it, when a patriotic singer is beaten up by an entirely Indian audience because his anti-British song was obviously 'seditious'.[162] Here, of course, Sukumar's critique was directed not against the British but those innumerable law-abiding Indians who did their dirty work for the British purely out of unreasoning, unpatriotic fear.[163]

Another play written around the same time, 'Lakshmaner Shaktishel', was more innovative.[164] Unlike his father, he never tried his hand at a straightforward adaptation of the Ramayana but in 'Shaktishel', he turned that epic into a hilarious spoof.[165] The play was largely based on one specific chapter—the Lankakanda—where Lakshmana is fatally injured by Ravana's wonder-weapon (the shaktishel of the title), and Hanuman saves his life by uprooting and transporting a whole mountain containing the one magic herb that would cure Lakshmana. Again a one-act play with four scenes, 'Shaktishel' turned these deadly serious events into wonderfully comic vignettes. When Lakshman collapses after being hit with the shaktishel, Ravana picks his pocket and runs away.[166] Hanuman, reluctant to travel so many miles to get the mountain, first suggests that they try homoeopathy instead and when he does finally bring the mountain, he dumps it on Yama, the god of death, who has come to take Lakshman away.[167] As the medicine works and Lakshmana recovers, everybody remarks that it is so potent because it is a swadeshi drug.[168]

In 'Bhabuk Sabha', published in *Probasi* in 1914 but written earlier—Sukumar had read it out to some friends while he was in Britain—and the 1915 play 'Shabdakalpadrum' (which was performed in Santiniketan by Sukumar on the occasion of Rabindranath Tagore's birthday in 1917), Sukumar turned to one of his enduring interests: the bond between words (the signifier, in today's academic jargon) and meanings (the signified).[169] This play and 'Shabdakalpadrum' both argued that language itself would be destroyed and chaos ensue if words themselves were treated as more important than their meanings. Sukumar explored this theme at greater depth in his essay 'Bhasar Atyachar' (The Tyranny of Language, also written around 1915). Did all those who used the word 'evolution' have an adequate understanding of Darwin's theory? he wondered. Did those Englishmen who so complacently pigeon-holed Tagore's *Gitanjali* as a work of 'mystic idealism' understand the complexity of Tagore's poetry?[170] Words, when detached from their complex significations, clouded people's minds and beliefs, obstructing real knowledge and inspiring rash actions.[171] 'Half the battles of the world are wars of mere words,' declared Sukumar, illustrating his contention with the battles between Hindus and non-Hindus, or between 'moderate' and 'extremist' nationalists.[172] The true value of language, he asserted, lay in *meanings*, and not, as so many people imagined, in the words themselves.[173]

Around the time of 'Shabdakalpadrum', Sukumar wrote another play, 'Chalachittachanchari'.[174] Dealing with the outwardly polite but actually petty rivalry between two groups of spiritually inclined intellectuals, the play was often regarded as a roman à clef and many tried to determine the real-life equivalents of the two opposed groups. One of the groups was reminiscent of Rabindranath Tagore's ashram school at Santiniketan but for some, the two warring camps were more akin to the different sects of the Brahmo Samaj or, alternatively, the Brahmo Samaj and its Hindu revivalist opponents.[175] But even for those who know little and care less about any of those institutions, the play is richly rewarding for the sheer comic gusto with which it sends up pseudo-intellectualism of all kinds through the apparently imbecilic responses of the central character, the apparently naive Bhabadulal, who, the play occasionally suggests, might actually be rather sharper than he seems to be.[176] Indeed, some of Bhabadulal's behaviour mirrored Sukumar's own childhood trick of pretending to be stupid in order to protect himself from unwelcome attention.[177]

An odd feature of Sukumar's plays (with the exception of 'Hingshuti') was the absence of female characters.[178] This elimination of the feminine was also characteristic of most of his other work and might suggest that Sukumar was not merely opposed to the professional stage and its courtesan-actresses but objected to the very notion of women acting on stage or even appearing in literary works.

But despite this lacuna, Sukumar's best work has a timeless appeal but *not* because they were located in a topsy-turvy universe far removed from the turbulence of early-twentieth-century India. Sukumar's life spanned the Boer War, the Russo-Japanese War, the swadeshi movement, the First World War, the Jallianwallah Bagh massacre, and Gandhi's Non-cooperation Movement—years that Satadru Sen has described as 'the most formative decades of middle-class Bengaliness'.[179] Although Sukumar was no demagogue, these events left indirect, stylized imprints on his work, especially during the First World War and the immediate post-war years, when Bengal went through a particularly turbulent period.[180]

The oft-repeated British claims for their own fairness, liberality, and broadmindedness—believed so ardently for so long by so many Indians—was lampooned in 'Bhoy Peo Na' a poem about a fierce-looking animal with a huge club who tries to lure a dhoti-clad Bengali into his cave with claims of his benevolent disposition.[181] The poem 'Baburam Sapurey', written in 1921, relating the strange saga of a man wanting to demonstrate his courage by beating up snakes that did not move, bite, or run, was poking fun at the spinelessness of the new non-violent (Gandhian) nationalists.[182] Another poem, 'Ekushey Ain' (1922), which detailed examples of bizarre laws including one providing for the arrest of poets, must have reminded contemporary adult readers of the torrent of new laws with which the Raj sought to stifle Indian dissent in the 1920s. Just at the time that this poem was written, the poet Nazrul Islam and his 'seditious' magazines, *Jugabani* and *Dhumketu*, were attracting police attention and Nazrul was arrested within a month of the publication of 'Ekushey Ain'.[183] As Sibaji Bandyopadhyay has suggested, there is every reason to regard *Abol Tabol* and, indeed, all of Sukumar's best-known works as attempts to construct a 'counter-discourse' satirizing the incongruities of colonial Bengali life through portrayals of virtually every social type populating the period, from moderate Congress politicians and radical nationalists to clerks, policemen, and other cogs in the wheel of the colonial state.[184]

The 1922 skit *Haw-Jaw-Baw-Raw-Law* (Abracadabra), serialized in four issues of *Sandesh*, provides more support for such contentions. It is also a great illustration of the family's talent for taking something European and transforming it into an utterly original and all but untranslatable work.[185] Based on *Alice in Wonderland*, it retains, as Satyajit Ray pointed out, all of Carroll's devices (a child falling asleep and dreaming the whole story, talking animals, a trial) but transmutes them into a thoroughly Bengali romp crammed with quirky new characters, bizarre ideas, and manic witticisms.[186] And, as critics have been discovering of late, Sukumar's masterpiece contains much that is uniquely of its time and place. As in some of the poems of *Abol Tabol*, Sukumar excelled in lightly veiled depictions of absurd colonial rules and anglicized Indians who followed them unthinkingly or, conversely, of children subversive of all authority.[187]

English education and the much-hyped mental awakening of the Bengali bourgeoisie in the nineteenth century is shown by Sukumar to have created a stunted, semi-modern, and semi-bourgeois class, epitomized by the goat named Byakaran (Grammar) Singh, who appears with the sign 'BA' around its neck (indicating both the cherished university degree and the *bya-bya* call of the goat). The trial presided over by a sleepy owl in dark glasses and populated by corrupt pleaders mouthing meaningless legal phrases ridiculed the proliferation of lawyers, many of them incompetent and dishonest, that, as we saw earlier, was another outcome of the spread of English education in colonial Bengal.[188] And that extraordinary song—'Aajkey hethhaye chamchikey aar penchara, Aashbe sabai, morbey indur bechara'—is not just astoundingly inventive in its word play, but invokes the reign of terror in post-Great War India represented by the Rowlatt Acts, the Jallianwallah Bag massacre, and the prospect of further coercive laws.[189]

But *Haw-Jaw-Baw-Raw-Law* was not simply a work of socio-political critique. Written just after the award of the Nobel Prize to Albert Einstein, it was also full of allusions to the new physics, to the collapse of the clockwork universe and linear time. An exchange, where we learn that seven multiplied by two gives fourteen only at one particular moment and other results at other times, or the idea of reversing one's age once one reached forty, then aging back to it and growing young again *ad infinitum* are, of course, hilarious but their scientific and philosophical allusions are unmistakable.[190] The same applies to the episode where we are told that one could find the present location of a character called Gechhodada only by calculating where he was *not* and all the places where he *could* be. If one wanted to see him, one would need to do a further set of sums and determine where he *would* be by the time one got to him. This description has been regarded as an anticipation of Heisenberg's uncertainty principle by one commentator, although it could well have been influenced by a passage in Trailokyanath Mukhopadhyay's 1892 fantasy *Kankabati*, where a Westernized frog suggests a similar procedure to the heroine asking for directions to a mountain-palace guarded by a demoness.[191] But what was no more than a way to lampoon a Westernized Bengali for Trailokyanath was elevated by Sukumar into the realm of philosophy, communicating the uncertainty of time and space, and the absence of anything like absolute truth.[192] *Haw-Jaw-Baw-Raw-Law*, we should not forget, was the work of an author who was not only battling a deadly illness but whose private faith, hope, and ideological certainties, as we shall see, were under severe and possibly terminal strain.[193]

Bon Viveur, Reformer—and Melancholic?

Sukumar's long-defunct Nonsense Club was revived after his return from England as the vastly more serious Monday Club, set up on 31 July 1915 with nineteen members from diverse backgrounds.[194] Gradually, the number of members rose to thirty or thereabouts, and many of them would later attain a great deal of fame for their contributions to their own fields.[195] Unlike the Nonsense Club, this was a real club with a membership list and a monthly subscription.[196] It met once a week at the house of a member and although the host was permitted to invite non-members whose contributions might be relevant to the club's concerns, it was not acted upon too often because the Club was already full of stars.[197] Poet Satyendranath Dutta, linguist Sunitikumar Chattopadhyay, barrister and composer Atulprasad Sen, German-trained philosopher Srischandra Sen, and physicist and statistician Prasantachandra Mahalanobis were all members, and their unquestioned leader was Sukumar Ray.[198] The invitations to sessions of the Club were issued in the name of the secretary Sisirkumar Dutta but composed by Sukumar, poking fun at members' appearances and appetites in characteristically inventive—and hilarious—rhyme.[199] The Monday Club also had its own anthem— Satyendranath Dutta's parody of Rabindranath Tagore's 'Amader Santiniketan'—and the members sometimes sang it so raucously that neighbours mistook them for drunken louts singing theatre songs.[200]

The club's discussions were miscellaneous and often very high-minded. Plato, Nietzsche, the laws of Manu, the relationship of Brahmoism to Hinduism, philological science, the novels of

Bankimchandra Chatterji, the work of Rammohan Roy, Kipling's
Barrack-Room Ballads, the jute industry, the poetry of Rabindranath
Tagore, and the plays of August Strindberg—all of these and more
featured on the agenda at various times. Some topics could, however,
be impossibly abstruse: a talk given on statistics by Prasanta
Mahalanobis was found completely incomprehensible by most members. But the talks merely represented the serious elements of the
Club's business; the sessions also included humorous entertainment, music, the rambling, open-ended talkfests that Bengalis call
adda, and, as one would expect in any gathering of middle-class
Bengalis, toothsome feasts.[201] (There was no alcohol, however—the
members, for all their high spirits, were staunch Bengali bhadralok
and although not all of them were Brahmos, the ethos of the Club
was at least partly influenced by Brahmo ideals on temperance.)[202]
The Club also organized excursions. One member recalled a magical
trip to Kolaghat, where they dined on the fabulous recipes of
Suprabha Ray—who, as we shall see, could not join the Club because
of her gender—and listened enraptured to Atulprasad Sen singing
his own compositions.[203]

Sukumar himself referred to the Monday Club as the Monda
Club, *monda* being a generic Bengali term for a large, spherical sweet.
It was really a literary and gastronomic club, explained Prabhatchandra
Ganguli, and each session culminated in a fairly lavish feast. The
delectable food was prepared by the womenfolk of the host's household
and the culinary skills of Sukumar's wife were particularly noteworthy. Items served at sessions often acquired considerable renown
among the members—some, such as the *sharbat* (cooling, non-alco-
holic drinks made from various fruits or syrups) served at Prabhat
Ganguli's house were hailed in Satyendranath Dutta's club-song
'Amader Manda-Sammilan'. The credit for these items went always to
the male host, not to the women of the household who had actually
prepared them. It was Charubabu's yogurt or Jangli's sharbat that was
praised, not their mother's or wife's or sister-in-law's.[204] Once,
Prasanta Mahalanobis, arguing that the Club was becoming a virtual
excuse for feasts, served only tea and cheap biscuits at a session. The
members were not amused, but after Sukumar had quietly sent a distress call to Prasanta's sister, the lavish viands that the Club was used
to arrived in about fifteen minutes.[205] Although women took care of
this vital business on the Club's agenda at every session regardless of
venue, women could not formally join it. They could only be invited

on special occasions.[206] That a group led by the grandson of Dwarakanath Ganguli and with many Brahmo members (of whom one, Prabhatchandra, was Dwarakanath and Kadambini's son) followed such a policy demonstrates how, even in progressive circles, the question of women's place in civil society had not been fully resolved despite more than half a century of activism by some of those same progressives and their ancestors.

The Monday Club, although it seems to have been hugely popular with its members, did not survive for very long. There was no formal decision to disband but after about four years of uproarious existence, the Club faded away slowly around 1919, almost like Lewis Carroll's Cheshire Cat.[207] Although its temper had been distinctive, semi-institutionalized literary groups were anything but uncommon at the time. Modern Bengali 'sociality', as Dipesh Chakrabarty has pointed out in his oft-cited essay on adda, typically adopted this form in the early twentieth century.[208] Sukumar's Monday Club, as Debashis Chattopadhyay has shown, was analogous to the Khamkheyali Sabha (Eccentric Association) set up in 1896 by none other than Rabindranath Tagore.[209] This 'club' met every month at the residences of its members by turn, a pattern that was exactly similar to that of the Monday Club, and members had to read something at every meeting.[210] Tagore himself wrote down a record of each meeting at its end (which, as far as we know, Sukumar never did) and the invitations to the meetings were composed in verse by Rabindranath himself. It, too, was full of the period's cultural stars—not only poets, writers, and composers but also figures like scientist Jagadischandra Bose and the later nationalist leader Chittaranjan Das. It even had one member in common with Sukumar's Monday Club: Atulprasad Sen.[211]

Rabindranath was writing many short stories then and he would often read these out to the club.[212] It was also for the Khamkheyali Sabha that Tagore wrote his play 'Baikunther Khata' and the play was performed by the members.[213] But again, the club was not only concerned with intellectual feasts. Food was of cardinal importance and although provided, obviously, by the women, Tagore was far more interventionist about the menu than the members of the Monday Club and caused many headaches for his wife.[214] From 1909 until 1918, another club called Bichitra met regularly at the Tagore house and many members of the Monday Club, including Sukumar himself, would often attend its sessions.[215] The star turn of the weekly meetings was Rabindranath Tagore reading from his unpublished

works, an experience that was outclassed only when the poet staged—
and acted in—plays for the club. All this, inevitably, was followed by a
'sumptuous banquet'.[216]

If the Monday Club and, to a smaller extent, Bichitra represented
the 'literary and gastronomic' side of Sukumar Ray's character, then
the Brahmo Samaj provided the arena for the reformer and activist in
him. Although Upendrakishore was deeply devout, he had served the
Samaj relatively silently, generally keeping himself away from the
internal politics of the community.[217] Sukumar, however, was far
more of a reformer. From 1902, long before the establishment of the
Monday Club, Sukumar had been prominent in the Students' Weekly
Service, the youth wing of the Brahmo Samaj founded in 1879 by
Sivanath Sastri, serving on its Executive Committee and subsequently
becoming its President.[218] Meeting every Sunday morning at seven,
the aim of this body was to guide the physical and spiritual development
of Brahmo youth and help integrate them fully with the Brahmo
community.[219] By Sukumar's time, the student movement had begun
to wane and he tried to revitalize it. A new Brahmo Youth Committee
was formed; it met on Wednesdays at the Sadharan Brahmo Samaj
temple and, rather like the members of the later Monday Club, the
Brahmo Youth Committee went on excursions every month to various
places within or slightly beyond Calcutta.[220] Sukumar also founded
Alok, a magazine for Brahmo youth, and tried to integrate younger
people into the regular work and worship of the Sadharan Brahmo
Samaj.[221] All of this came to an abrupt end when Sukumar left for
England in 1911, but after his return to Calcutta, he resumed his role,
reorganizing the youth wing and becoming its Assistant Secretary in
1916.[222]

Sukumar's Monday Club associate Sunitikumar Chattopadhyay
once remarked that although many insiders thought that Prasanta
Mahalanobis would be the leader of the coming generation of
Brahmos, there was never any doubt in his own mind that Sukumar
was the 'brightest of all and a unique personality'.[223] Unlike others,
Sukumar was a thoroughgoing reformist, never afraid of challenging
elders when he disagreed with their decisions. An obituarist remarked
that he had inherited not only Upendrakishore's 'artistic temperament', but also Dwarakanath Ganguli's 'courage to stand up boldly for
what he believed to be true or right'.[224] He was also devout without
being ostentatious about it and he certainly did not consider
Brahmoism or the Sadharan Brahmo Samaj to have attained a state of

perfection.[225] The historian Susobhan Sarkar, an acolyte of Sukumar's, recalled how Sukumar, although profoundly religious and committed to the Brahmo movement, had rebelled against the relentlessly negative spirit of the regulations that the elders had formulated for the student wing: 'You must not go to the theatre, must not smoke, there were so many "mustn'ts".'[226] Sukumar himself, as we have seen, shared the elders' distaste for the professional stage; he was offended not by the puritanism of the regulations but by their negativity.[227] Ably assisted by Prasanta Mahalanobis and others, he drew up a positive programme emphasizing cultural activities and social service and opened the student wing to non-Brahmos.[228] Three 'fraternities'—Devotional, Educational, and Literary—were established within the student wing in 1919 to facilitate these activities. Around 1921, a new social fraternity was formed to facilitate informal interactions of young people—and not just of men, as with the Monday Club. Hirankumar Sanyal recalled the blissful as well as intellectually stimulating addas at fraternity meetings, where Ramananda Chatterji's daughters, Santa and Sita, participated regularly.[229]

One old and controversial question on which Sukumar took a radical, even a seemingly dogmatic stance was the 'Hinduness' of Brahmos.[230] The traditional position, associated with the earliest incarnations of the Brahmo Samaj, was that Brahmoism was merely reformed, monotheistic Hinduism, not a separate faith.[231] That changed from the days of Keshab Sen and by Sukumar's time, many Brahmos considered themselves not to be Hindus. Sukumar's friend Ajitkumar Chakrabarty—a member of the Adi Brahmo Samaj— argued in 1914 in the *Tattvabodhini Patrika* that it was crass and self-destructive of Brahmos to cut themselves off from the parent Hindu tradition, calling upon all Brahmos to embrace their identity as Hindus and to reform the evils of Hinduism from within.[232] Rabindranath Tagore, too, wanted Brahmos to accept their identity as reforming and reformed Hindus. In any case, Tagore pointed out, Hinduism was not simply a religion but the way of life of an entire civilization: while one could change one's religion at will, trying to change one's civilizational identity was futile.[233]

Such opinions were predictably controversial with Sadharan Brahmos. Responding to Chakrabarty's article, his friend Sukumar Ray accepted that there were many problems with the Sadharan Brahmo Samaj, especially its narrow outlook and lack of imagination. But those problems could not be resolved by yoking the Samaj to the even narrower Hinduism of the early twentieth century.[234] Instead of wasting their time pondering whether they were Hindus or to what extent, Brahmos should seek to rekindle their revolutionary fervour, which had once energized the entire nation.[235] Sukumar's position in this particular debate was far from Tagorean but Sukumar, of course, was an ardent admirer of Tagore and he would lead an ill-tempered and long-running battle to induct Tagore as an honorary member of the Sadharan Brahmo Samaj.

For all the controversy surrounding the discussion of Hindu–Brahmo links in *Tattvabodhhini*, Rabindranath Tagore was neither an orthodox Hindu nor an orthodox Brahmo. That is why the young of both communities found him inspirational and in January 1917, Sukumar and his Monday Club friends—Kalidas Nag, Prasanta Mahalanobis, Hiran Sanyal, Susobhan Sarkar—proposed to invite Tagore to be an honorary member of the Sadharan Brahmo Samaj.[236] Powerful figures within the Samaj, including Krishnakumar Mitra (the chairman of the executive committee) strongly objected to the proposal and some of them resigned from their posts.[237] No official reason was ever given for their opposition and it is usually speculated that Tagore's romantic poetry was offensive to puritanical Sadharan Brahmo elders or that they found the poet to be too frivolous in temperament.[238] Not every objection to Tagore's induction may have been quite so 'Victorian', however. For radical Brahmos, it was problematic that non-Brahmins were rarely allowed to conduct formal worship at the Adi Brahmo Samaj and Tagore had never raised his voice against this. Also, Rabindranath had married off his own daughters when they were still children and this was unacceptable to the Sadharan Brahmos, the very formation of whose church was an act of protest against Keshab Sen's decision to give his underage daughter in marriage to an idolatrous Hindu.[239] But perhaps the greatest problem with Tagore's induction was the poet's repeated affirmations of his Hindu identity.[240] For a time during the swadeshi movement, Tagore had even flirted with Hindu revivalist ideas, coming close to endorsing caste distinctions and even sati. Tagore later jettisoned those ideas and embraced the universalism with which he would come to be associated but his earlier views had not been forgotten or forgiven by many of his Brahmo contemporaries.[241]

Contrary to their portrayal in the hagiographic literature on Sukumar as benighted conservatives, some Sadharan Brahmo elders, in spite of their moral puritanism and other Victorian quirks, could be rather more radical in their sociopolitical views than Tagore. When the movement against the partition of Bengal started in 1905, it was Krishnakumar Mitra who had first proposed to boycott British products and he remained a steadfast supporter of the movement long after Tagore himself had retreated from it.[242] A longstanding supporter of women's rights, Mitra would found the Women's Protection League in 1924, which devoted itself to the prevention of sexual abuse and crimes against women but also helped women victims of sexual crimes to prosecute their attackers in court.[243] Describing him as 'one of the worthiest and most selfless' men of his generation, Surendranath Banerjea observed: 'He reminds one of the old Puritans. Ascetic in his temperament, unbending in his convictions, careless of the good things of life, and remorseless in his hatred of shams and shows.'[244] It is not unlikely, in fact, that Mitra found Tagore to be too socially *illiberal* to be an honorary member of the Sadharan Brahmo Samaj.

Despite the elders' refusal to admit Tagore, the discontent among Tagore's supporters refused to die down, leading almost to another split in the Brahmo movement. 'Prasanta Mahalanobis was the strategist of this rebellion, but Sukumar was its heart and soul (*prankendra*),' recalled Hiran Sanyal.[245] The dispute did not simply represent a generational clash: although Krishnakumar Mitra, Herambachandra Maitra (1857–1938), Prankrishna Acharya, and Nabadwipchandra Das were against admitting Tagore, other senior members like Ramananda Chatterji, Prafullachandra Ray, Jagadischandra Bose, Nilratan Sircar, and Brajendranath Seal were in favour of Sukumar's motion.[246] In 1921, the protesters even organized their own Maghotsava and stayed away from the main event at the Samaj but the elders gave way before the end of the festival. On the advice of senior jurists in the community, it was decided to lance the boil by polling the entire Sadharan Brahmo community on the issue of Tagore's membership.[247]

Days before the referendum, Mahalanobis published a booklet titled *Keno Rabindranathkey Chai* (Why We Want Rabindranath) with, reportedly, a lot of input by Sukumar Ray.[248] Denying the relevance of Tagore's older views, it emphasized that in his religious principles, Tagore was as universalist as any Brahmo but wanted this universalism to be expressed in an authentically 'national' (that is, Hindu) form, a view that had also been held by Brahmo greats from Rammohan Roy to Sivanath Sastri. Debendranath Tagore, Mahalanobis added, had put up with caste distinctions and married off his underage daughters but had nonetheless been welcomed by the Sadharan Brahmo Samaj as an honorary member years ago. Why then the controversy over according the same honour to his son, who, in his works as well as in his present life, called incessantly for the brotherhood of man and the universality of the one true God?[249] The referendum was held in March 1921 and the poet was admitted with 496 votes in his favour and 232 against.[250]

Strikingly, the personal affection and even admiration that the conservatives had long had for the young Sukumar remained undiminished throughout this protracted row. Once, at its height, the arch-conservative Heramba Maitra asked Sukumar what the ideal of existence was. 'A serious interest in life,' Sukumar responded. Maitra was so delighted by the answer that he immediately ordered sweets for everybody present. When the young turks organized their own Maghotsava, Krishnakumar Mitra went to see Sukumar almost every day in order to persuade him to return to the Samaj with his associates.[251] Nabadwipchandra Das, who had resigned from the Sadharan Brahmo Samaj in protest against the induction of Tagore, remained so fond of Sukumar that although himself ailing and infirm, he undertook a long journey to Calcutta in 1923 to see Sukumar when he was close to death.[252]

Sukumar's vision of a revitalized Brahmo Samaj, in any case, was not to be fulfilled, but perhaps not only because of his early death. Even before his fatal illness, he seems to have been afflicted by a mysterious psychological malaise. In a confidential letter written on 23 August 1920 to Prasanta Mahalanobis, he confessed that for 'a long time', he had been conscious of his acute lack of empathy with the activities of the Brahmo Samaj.[253] 'Words of hope, words of joy, words of optimism—I do not really believe in any of them in the slightest ... What I really believe in are their exact opposites: rampant, morbid, out and out pessimism.' For some time, the thirty-three-year-old Sukumar revealed, he had felt that he was heading for a crisis and he was sure that it was 'nothing other than death'. It was essential now to arrange his affairs and to fulfil his remaining aspirations; all Brahmo Samaj commitments, therefore, had to be given up, including any involvement in the ongoing dispute over Tagore's membership.[254]

In personal life, few of his friends seem to have noticed any mental agony during this period. Sukumar continued to be active as editor and writer and even as the kala-azar began to wreak havoc on his body, he filled *Sandesh* with his best work and, maintaining the family tradition of versatility, designed several new printing processes, which he wanted to patent.[255] The historian Susobhan Sarkar recalled that in mid-1921, he had spent a week with the ailing Sukumar at a sanatorium in Darjeeling, where Sukumar was almost his old voluble self and even recited 'Baburam Sapurey' with enthusiasm. 'I did not detect a trace of bitterness in him then,' remarked Sarkar, and was surprised to hear about the confidential letter.[256] There was no perceptible waning of Sukumar's Brahmo faith either; indeed, as we saw earlier, his friends remarked how the ravages of his illness seemed to have deepened his already profound faith in God. We simply do not know enough about Sukumar's thoughts, feelings, and experiences to identify what precipitated his dark night of the soul and whether it was permanent. A contemporary psychiatrist might regard it as a manifestation of severe depression, some might assume that Sukumar's mental turbulence had resulted from a premonition of his own death, and others still might blame it on psychological exhaustion precipitated by his battles with the Brahmo elders. If one reads the letter carefully, however, one notes that Sukumar was more concerned with his private disappointments, loss of religious conviction, and unfulfilled aspirations; the dispute with the Samaj over Tagore was only of marginal import. But although we cannot explain the letter any more definitively than that, it warns us not to regard Sukumar, as his hagiographers and admirers so often do, as incessantly brilliant, self-possessed, charismatic, gregarious, and insouciant. Behind and beneath those eye-catching personae, there was another Sukumar, one who was vulnerable and fragile, subject to corrosive religious doubt, filled with trepidation about his own future and radically unsure about the meaning of his life and work.[257]

Notes

1. Hemantakumar Adhya, *Sukumar Ray: Jibankatha* (Calcutta: Pustak Bipani, 1990), 5. 'Hasi' is not just a name, it also means 'smile' or 'laugh' in Bengali—but Sukhalata turned out to be such a serious, unsmiling person that people found her intimidating. See Leela Majumdar, 'Sukhalata Rao', *Sandesh*, Annual Puja Number (1986): 500–2, at 500. My thanks to Riddhi Goswami for this article.

2. Kalyani Karlekar, 'Amar Mashima Sukhalata Rao', in *Sukhalata Rao: Rachanasangraha 1*, edited by Jayita Bagchi (Calcutta: Thema, 1999), 3–7, at 3, 7.

3. Karlekar, 'Amar Mashima', 7.

4. Karlekar, 'Amar Mashima', 4. Madhusudan Rao 'was practically a pioneer of the Brahmo Samaj in Orissa, being among the very first domiciled Brahmos in Cuttack who discarded the Brahminical thread, educated his daughters and when they were of age gave them in marriage in accordance with the Brahmo ritual'. See Bipinchandra Pal, *Memories of My Life and Times* (Calcutta: Bipinchandra Pal Institute, 1973), 293–4.

5. See Partha Basu, *Satyajit Ray* (Calcutta: Paschimbanga Bangla Akademi, 2006), 18; Bratati Chakravarty, *Bangla Shishu Sahitya Charcha: Ray Paribar* (Calcutta: Dey Book Store, 1997), 109–33; and Kamal Sarkar, *Bharater Bhaskar o Chitrasilpi* (Calcutta: Jogmaya, 1984), 216–17. She illustrated many of her own books but some of her paintings also featured in *Probasi* and *Modern Review* and were later collected in issues of *Chatterjee's Picture Album*. For full-colour plates of some of her paintings (most of them printed by her father's company), see 'Shrimati the Martyr', in *Chatterjee's Picture Albums*, no. 1 (undated), 12; 'Behula on the Raft', *Chatterjee's Picture Albums*, no. 2, 4; 'Behula at the Court of Indra', *Chatterjee's Picture Albums*, no. 3, 5; 'Sachi and Aindrila', *Chatterjee's Picture Albums*, no. 4, 16.

6. Ratan Parimoo, *Art of Three Tagores: From Revival to Modernity* (Delhi: Kumar Gallery, 2011), 290–2.

7. Buddhadev Bose, 'Bangla Shishusahitya' (1952), in Buddhadev Bose, *Sahityacharcha* (Calcutta: Dey's, 1976), 38–64, at 41–2.

8. B. Chakravarty, *Bangla Shishu Sahitya*, 122–7.

9. B. Chakravarty, *Bangla Shishu Sahitya*, 112–15.

10. Buddhadev Bose, 'Bangla Shishusahitya', 41.

11. B. Chakravarty, *Bangla Shishu Sahitya*, 117–21.

12. B. Chakravarty, *Bangla Shishu Sahitya*, 129–31.

13. B. Chakravarty, *Bangla Shishu Sahitya*, 127–8.

14. Siddhartha Ghosh, *Karigari Kalpana o Bangali Udyog* (Calcutta: Dey's, 1988), 114–15.

15. B. Chakravarty, *Bangla Shishu Sahitya*, 110, 132–3.

16. 'Sisusahitye Suruchi' [1933], in *Sukhalata Rao: Rachanasangraha*, I, edited by Jayeeta Bagchi (Calcutta: Thema, 1999), 19–20. Children's literature, for her, had to be 'pure' (*nirmal*)—it must not encourage disrespect for elders or social resentment of any kind, and should strive to sow the seeds of morality (*nyay*) and truthfulness. See 'Probasi Banga Sahitya Sammelan', in *Sukhalata Rao*, 29–38, at 37.

17. Leela Majumdar, 'Sukhalata Rao' (1986), 502; and Abanindranath Tagore and Rani Chanda, *Gharoa*, 2nd edn (Calcutta: Vishwa Bharati, 1943), 3. Majumdar held that the 'right' kind of children's literature must not only be free of sexual and bawdy elements but reinforce the child's faith in the creator's benevolence (*srishtikartar mangalbidhhan*). Sukumar Ray had printed a story by Majumdar in *Sandesh* depicting a mischievous boy who gains from his mischief but Majumdar came to realize later that she had been wrong to

imply that one could profit from malice and misbehaviour. Decades later, when *Sandesh* had been revived and she was one of the co-editors, she never approved stories like that. See Leela Majumdar, *Pakdandi* (Calcutta: Ananda, 1986), 125–6, 349, 350–1, 422–3.

18. Punyalata Chakrabarti, *Chhelebelar Dinguli* (1958; reprint, Calcutta: Newscript, 1981, 112.

19. P. Chakrabarti, *Chhelebelar Dinguli*, 7, 9.

20. P. Chakrabarti, *Chhelebelar Dinguli*, 12.

21. P. Chakrabarti, *Chhelebelar Dinguli*, 55.

22. B. Chakravarty, *Bangla Shishu Sahitya*, 135. The poems are available in Satyajit Ray and Partha Basu, eds, *Sukumar Sahityasamagra*, 3 vols (Calcutta: Ananda Publishers, 1989), 2: 327.

23. Marie Seton, *Portrait of a Director: Satyajit Ray*, expanded edition (Delhi: Penguin, 2003), 31. In 1911, he would contribute an article on photography to *Probasi* in which he urged his readers to appreciate that cameras were not simply playthings for the curious, but tools of scientific investigation and also of artistic experimentation. See 'Photography', in *Sukumar Sahityasamagra*, 3: 93–4.

24. The photograph competed in the category 'Indoor and Outdoor Pets'; where the one guinea prize was won by R.W. Copeman of Wincanton, while Sukumar, along with 11 others from England, South Africa, Spain, and Australia, received certificates. None of the photographs was printed and Sukumar's entry is unavailable with the Ray family. For the prize announcement, see *Boy's Own Paper*, 27 (22 October 1904), 63.

25. P. Chakrabarti, *Chhelebelar Dinguli*, 112–13. Where professional theatre was concerned, however, Sukumar, despite writing and staging plays, was as inflexible an opponent as any old Brahmo and remained so for his whole life. His wife, Suprabha, shared his opposition and did not permit the young Satyajit to accompany his uncle and cousins on family trips to the theatre. See Bijoya Ray, *Amader Katha* (Calcutta: Ananda, 2008), 50.

26. P. Chakrabarti, *Chhelebelar Dinguli*, 118.

27. P. Chakrabarti, *Chhelebelar Dinguli*, 117–18.

28. See Ray and Basu, *Sukumar Sahityasamagra*, 3: 153; and Supriya Goswami, *Colonial India in Children's Literature* (New York: Routledge, 2012), 151, 153.

29. P. Chakrabarti, *Chhelebelar Dinguli*, 120; Leela Majumdar, *Upendrakishore* (Calcutta: Newscript, 1963), 78. Subinoy once got some locally made cups and saucers that were not only misshapen but absorbent. When served tea in those cups, one had to drink up quickly, or most of the tea would be sucked into the china. See Leela Majumdar, *Aar Konokhaney* (Calcutta: Mitra o Ghosh, 1968), 51.

30. L. Majumdar, *Aar Konokhaney*, 49; L. Majumdar, *Pakdandi*, 60. Later in his life, when he acted in an impropmptu skit at a picnic, his performance

was so captivating that the audience forgot all about eating—a major achieve-
ment with a Bengali middle-class audience. See Punyalata Chakrabarti,
'Sukumar Ray' (1961), in *Sukumar Ray: Chirokaler Sera*, edited by Debasis
Mukhopadhyay (Calcutta: Shishu Sahitya Samsad, 1996), vii–xi, at, ix–x.

31.   Ajit Dutta, *Bangla Sahitye Hasyaras* (Calcutta: Jignasa, 1960), 445.

32.   Virtually all of Sukumar's enduring fame stems from the poetry,
illustrations, and prose that he published in *Sandesh* between Upendrakishore's
death in 1915 and his own passing in 1923.

33.   For a rather superficial account of the Club and its more serious successor, the Monday Club, see Debasish Chattopadhyay, 'Nonsense Club and
Monday Club: The Cultural Utopias of Sukumar Ray', in *The Literary Utopias
of Cultural Communities*, edited by Marguérite Corporaal and Evert Jan van
Leeuwen (Amsterdam: Rodopi, 2010), 243–52. The Nonsense Club disbanded
when Sukumar left for England in 1911.

34.   Bimalangsuprakash Ray, 'Sukumar Ray-er Smriti', *Dainik Kabita*, 25
Baisakh 1380 (8 May 1973), unpaginated. Many thanks to Soumen Paul for a
copy of this essay.

35.   It is not known exactly when these plays were written but the best
guess seems to be between 1907 and 1911. See Pulak Chanda, 'Sukumarer
Natak', in *Prastutiparba*, 7, nos 3–4 (October 1982)—special issue on Sukumar
Ray, 161–77, at 162. As director, Sukumar avoided using props or costumes or
make-up—all roles, including that of animals or monsters, were performed
by actors in their usual clothes. The intention was to compel the audience to
focus on the content. See Hitendrakishore Raychaudhuri, *Upendrakishore o
Masua Ray Paribarer Galpasalpa* (Calcutta: Firma KLM, 1984), 94.

36.   P. Chakrabarti, *Chhelebelar Dinguli*, 120–1. Sare Batris Bhhaja was a
savoury mix sold on the streets of Calcutta, which claimed to be made from
thirty-two types of ingredients and had half a chilli on top. See P. Chakrabarti,
Chhelebelar Dinguli. The one extant copy of the magazine is reproduced in Ray
and Basu, *Sukumar Sahityasamagra*, 3: 341–9; see also Ray and Basu, *Sukumar
Sahityasamagra*, 3: 422.

37.   The poem, as reported by Subimal Ray, was: *Lord Curzon, ati durjan,
tarjan-garjan saar/Deen Bangali, sukhera kangali, bhunjichhey ganjana taar.*
Quoted in Ajit Dutta, *Bangla Sahitye Hasyaras*, 434.

38.   Leela Majumdar, *Sukumar*, 2nd edn (Calcutta: Paschimbanga Bangla
Akademi, 2001), 12; and S. Ghosh, 'Upendrakishore: Shilpi o Karigar', *Ekshan*,
16, no. 6 (1984): 53. The City Collegiate School, established in January 1879 by
Sivanath Sastri, Anandamohan Bose, and that non-Brahmo supporter of so
many Brahmo causes, Surendranath Banerjea, was intended to disseminate
Brahmo ideals among children and also to provide employment to young
Brahmo schoolteachers. The student body was diverse and included Jews,
Muslims, and Sikhs. From 1881, it started a college division that offered the
'First Arts' qualification and, subsequently, legal training as well as the full

BA course. Along with many others, Upendrakishore and his adoptive brother, Narendrakishore, contributed generously to the school, donating a thousand rupees towards the construction of a new building in 1884. See Sivanath Sastri, *Atmacharit*, edited by Gautam Neogy (Calcutta: Sadharan Brahmo Samaj, 1982), 235–6; and Umeschandra Dutta, 'Brief History of the City College' (1904), reprinted in Srikumar Bandyopadhyay and Tapasya Ghosh, eds, *City College Smaranika: 125 Bachhar, 1881–2006* (Calcutta: City College, 2007), 419–23; Sophia Dobson Collet, ed., *The Brahmo Year-Book for 1881* (London: Williams and Norgate, 1882), 21–3; and Krishnakumar Mitra, *Atmacharit*, 2nd edn (Calcutta: Sadharan Brahmo Samaj, 1975), 142–4, 147–53.

39. Adhya, *Sukumar Ray*, 29–30. Only one student got a first class honours in physics that year and none in chemistry—Sukumar, therefore, was awarded the Rai Amritanath Mitra Bahadur Prize, a cash award given annually from 1901 to the Hindu student who had secured 'the highest percentage of marks in Honours in the combined subjects of Physical Science and Chemistry' and had undertaken to 'proceed to the higher degree of MA or MSc'. See *University of Calcutta: Calendar*, 1908, 2: 422, 700. Sukumar must, therefore, have undertaken to do a Masters degree but did not fulfil it. See *University of Calcutta: Calendar*, 1909, 2: 743–4; *University of Calcutta: Calendar*, 1911, 2: 813; and *University of Calcutta: Calendar*, 1912, 2: 891.

40. Funded by a bequest from the businessman Guruprasanna Ghosh, this award was available only to Hindus who were 'pure natives of Bengal' and wished to 'study in Europe, America or Japan'. There was a strong preference for those wanting to specialize in fields of agricultural or industrial relevance and 'the sons of artisans and mechanics' were welcome to compete. The annual amount (payable quarterly in advance) of the scholarship was lavish by the standards of the time: two thousand rupees for those going to Europe or the United States and one thousand for those studying in Japan. See *University of Calcutta: Calendar*, 1909, 2: 742–4. For provisions for those without university qualifications, see *University of Calcutta: Calendar*, 1911, 2: 812.

41. Sukumar's contribution was not explicitly linked to Upendrakishore's earlier essay and was ostensibly in response to a piece by O.C. Gangoly in the Ashar 1307 issue of *Probasi*. See Sukumar Ray, 'Bharatiya Chitrasilpa' [1910], reprinted in Shovon Som and Anil Acharya, eds, *Bangla Shilpa Samalochonar Dhhara* (Calcutta: Anustup, 1986), 86–9, at 87. Translation from Partha Mitter, *Art and Nationalism in Colonial India, 1850–1922: Occidental Orientations* (Cambridge: Cambridge University Press, 1994), 368.

42. Sukumar Ray, 'Bharatiya Chitrasilpa' [1910], 87–8; and 'Bharatiya Chitrakala' [1910], reprinted in Som and Acharya, eds, *Bangla Shilpa Samalochonar Dhhara*, 90–3, at 93. The phrase 'in terms of known realities' was used in English. Some years later, in a session of the Monday Club, Sukumar demonstrated how the landscapes of John Constable had followed nature while subtly redefining it. See Hirankumar Sanyal, *Parichoy-er Kuri*

Bachhar o Anyanya Smritichitra (Calcutta: Papyrus, 1978), 161–2. Sukumar would follow the same principle in his nonsense writings. See Siddhartha Ghosh, 'Ujhhyanam Panditer Soja Kathha', 15–16; and Anupam Majumdar, 'Samoyer Aynaye *Abol Tabol*', 60.

43. Sukumar Ray, 'Bharatiya Chitrashilpa' [1910], 88.

44. Sukumar Ray, 'Bharatiya Chitrashilpa' [1910], 88–9.

45. Sukumar Ray, 'Bharatiya Chitrakala' [1910], 93.

46. Sukumar Ray, 'Bharatiya Chitrakala' [1910], 92. Such debates between Bengali intellectuals, Partha Mitter has emphasized, were ultimately arguments between friends, 'a game that continued the unresolved internal debate among Bengalis on cultural identity'. See P. Mitter, *Art and Nationalism in Colonial India*, 172. It was, in fact, none other than Sukumar Ray who was to translate a 1913 piece by Abanindranath on the classical–textual justifications for distortions of normal anatomy in Indian art. See Abanindranath Tagore, *Some Notes on Indian Artistic Anatomy* (Calcutta: Indian Society of Oriental Art, 1914). One must not overestimate the friendliness, however. In his long autobiography, Gangoly often discussed the opposition to 'Indian art', but never once mentioned Upendrakishore or Sukumar, preferring instead to focus on the far less intelligent and patently reactionary objections of Sureshchandra Samajpati, the editor of the periodical *Sahitya*. See O.C. Gangoly, *Bharater Shilpa o Amar Katha* (Calcutta: A. Mukherjee, 1969), especially 154–9, 170–80. Also, as we saw earlier, Gangoly never patronized the printing and block-making services of U. Ray & Sons, preferring to use European firms.

47. P. Mitter, *Art and Nationalism in Colonial India*, 369.

48. Satadru Sen, *Traces of Empire: India, America and Postcolonial Cultures* (Delhi: Primus, 2014), 40.

49. See his essay 'Silpey Atyukti' [1914], in *Sukumar Sahityasamagra*, 3: 84–92, at 85.

50. Benoy Kumar Sarkar, *The Aesthetics of Young India* (Calcutta: Kar, Majumder, 1922), 7–10, 24–5. In addition to Sarkar's article, this volume includes the responses to it in *Rupam* and other periodicals. See also Tapati Guha-Thakurta, *The Making of a New 'Indian' Art: Artists, Aesthetics and Nationalism in Bengal, c. 1850–1920* (Cambridge: Cambridge University Press, 1992), 222–3.

51. B.K. Sarkar, *Aesthetics of Young India*, 7–10, 24–5. See also the response by Agastya (pseudonym of O.C. Gangoly) pointing out that India 'must recover her own self before she is fit to enrich and develop herself by exchanging thoughts with her Western mate' and that it was 'the racial flavour, the provincial accent' in art that constituted 'the peculiar contribution of the artist'. If the artist somehow managed to extirpate this racial individuality, then 'he could produce no Art ... an aesthetic Esperanto is a contradiction in terms' (B.K. Sarkar, *Aesthetics of Young India*, 78, 81).

52. Jadunath Sarkar, letter to Rabindranath Tagore, dated 31 May 1922, in *Rabindranath Thakur: Chithhipatra* (Calcutta: Viswa Bharati, 1995), 15: 85–95, at 91–2. I owe this reference to Arnab Dutta.

53. See B.K. Sarkar, *Aesthetics of Young India*, 56; and Guha-Thakurta, *Making of a New 'Indian' Art*, 223.

54. As Sumit Sarkar has recently speculated, the disputes over Indian art may have been an 'arts theory counterpart' for the political differences between 'moderate' and 'extremist' nationalists, and the interventions of Upendrakishore and Sukumar, he suggests, 'were in tandem with Rabindranath's contemporary denunciations of Extremist methods and values'. See Sumit Sarkar, *Modern Times: India, 1880s–1950s—Environment, Economy, Culture* (Ranikhet: Permanent Black, 2014), 426–7.

55. The original reads: *Kore tarahuro bisham chot/Kinechi hat, kinechi coat/Peyechhi passage, esechhe boat/Bendhechhi talpi, tulechhi mot/Bolechhe sabai, ta hole oth/Asan ebar Biletey chhot/Tai sabha habey biday vote/Knado knado bhhab fuliye thhont/Hethay sakaley koribey jot/(Programme-tuku korio note)/Programme—Sukra sandhya sathik saat/Ahar, amod, ulkapat*. See Ray and Basu, *Sukumar Sahityasamagra*, 3: 161–2.

56. On neckties and cutlery and his growing proficiency with them, see S. Ray and P. Basu, *Sukumar Sahityasamagra*, 3: 166–7, 170. But when in London, he found that his hat would often blow away and so he wore a turban instead. See Ray and Basu, *Sukumar Sahityasamagra*, 171. En route to Britain, he did some sketching, including a landscape, titled 'Off Suez', which was dated October 1911. This is available in a small, untitled, green-covered sketchbook in possession of the Ray family (hereafter cited as Sukumar Ray, Sketch-Book).

57. See Ray and Basu, *Sukumar Sahityasamagra*, 3: 169; and Punyalata Chakrabarti, *Ekal Jakhhan Shuru Holo* [1964], edited by Jayeeta Bagchi, Abhijit Sen, and Anindita Bhaduri (Calcutta: Dey's, 2007), 82.

58. The building was the headquarters of the National Indian Association, which had emerged from the 1872 merger of Mary Carpenter's Bristol Indian Association and another closely associated body in London. See Ray and Basu, *Sukumar Sahityasamagra*, 3: 168, 408; and Shompa Lahiri, *Indians in Britain: Anglo-Indian Encounters, Race and Identity, 1880–1930* (London: Frank Cass, 2000), 14–15, 73, 198.

59. The Maghotsava celebrates the foundation of the Brahmo Samaj by Rammohan Roy on 11 Magh (a date that falls around 23 January). Although 11 Magh is the high point of the festival, the Maghotsava continues for a week. See Collet, *Brahmo Year-Book for 1876*, 14–15. On Sukumar's London experiences, see Ray and Basu, *Sukumar Sahityasamagra*, 3: 169, 170–1, 173, 176, 179–81, 189, 190, 194, 201. After his return to Calcutta, he would write an essay titled 'Shilpey Atyukti' (Exaggeration in Art [1914]), which his son, Satyajit, attributed to Sukumar's visit to the first exhibition of post-impressionist

paintings in London in 1912. Although not entirely critical of trends like futurism or cubism, the essay is ambivalent about them and concludes with warnings about the need for artists to integrate their feelings with their sense of the real. For the essay and Satyajit Ray's comment, see Ray and Basu, *Sukumar Sahityasamagra*, 84–92 and 403, respectively.

60. See Ray and Basu, *Sukumar Sahityasamagra*, 3: 206, 213, 228, 247.

61. For the encounter in the toilet, see Ray and Basu, *Sukumar Sahityasamagra*, 3: 262. He was much amused that while in Manchester later, a child was disappointed that he and some of his friends were just Indians, and not, as he had expected, 'Red' Indians 'with their feathers on'. See Ray and Basu, *Sukumar Sahityasamagra*, 3: 220.

62. Ray and Basu, *Sukumar Sahityasamagra*, 3: 194. Rabindranath Tagore's daughter-in-law, Protima, however, was very supportive of the suffragettes and one day, when she was unexpectedly late, her husband Rathindranath speculated that she might have been arrested after breaking shop windows with the activists. See Rathindranath Tagore, *On the Edges of Time* (Calcutta: Orient Longman, 1958), 121–2.

63. See P. Chakrabarti, *Chhelebelar Dinguli*, 114.

64. Ramananda Chatterji's daughter Sita Devi recalled that only Sukumar Ray had spoken in support of women at a meeting of young Sadharan Brahmos with Rabindranath Tagore. See Sita Devi, *Punyasmriti* (Calcutta: Jignasa, 1964), 92–3.

65. Rothenstein even asked Sukumar to serve as a model in Oriental costume for one of his paintings, but it is not known whether Sukumar actually did so. See Ray and Basu, *Sukumar Sahityasamagra*, 3: 175, 200–1, 409.

66. Amitabha Chaudhuri, *Ekatrey Rabindranath* (Calcutta: Dey's, 1983), 496.

67. Rathindranath Tagore, *On the Edges of Time*, 118.

68. Ray and Basu, *Sukumar Sahityasamagra*, 3: 205.

69. Ray and Basu, *Sukumar Sahityasamagra*, 3: 248. Before this, Sukumar had also presented a paper on Bengali literature—which had called for a lot of research and included some translations of Tagore's poetry—but it has not survived. See Ray and Basu, *Sukumar Sahityasamagra*, 202–3. Incidentally, Sukumar's friend Ajitkumar Chakrabarty (who had come to Britain two years before Sukumar as a student sponsored for Manchester College, Oxford, by the British and Foreign Unitarian Association) had spoken about Tagore in the British press in 1910, describing him as the 'greatest living poet of Bengal today, and one of the great thought-forces of Bengal too' and providing a brief account of the poet's educational ideas. See 'New B & F U A Indian Student: Interview with Mr A. Kumar Chakraverti', *The Christian Life and Unitarian Herald*, 1 October 1910, 497. The first mention of Tagore in the mainstream British press appears to have been in a report in

the *Times* of the dinner given to Tagore by the India Society in London on 10 July 1912. See Kalyan Kundu, Sakti Bhattacharya, and Kalyan Sircar, eds, *Imagining Tagore: Rabindranath and the British Press (1912–1941)* (Calcutta: Sahitya Samsad, 2000), 5–6.

70. Andrew Robinson, 'Selected Letters of Sukumar Ray', *South Asia Research*, 7, no. 2 (1987): 169–236, at 176.

71. 'The Spirit of Rabindranath Tagore', in *Sukumar Sahityasamagra*, 3: 112–21, at 115–16. In a letter to his mother, Sukumar remarked that in his talk, he was going to use Tagore's poetry to launch into discussions of religious and other movements in Bengali life, including the Brahmo Samaj (Ray and Basu, *Sukumar Sahityasamagra*, 3: 246). Sukumar did discuss Vedantc monism, the cult of bhakti (devotion), Rammohan Roy, and Debendranath Tagore in the article, but he did not discuss the Brahmo Samaj directly.

72. Ray and Basu, *Sukumar Sahityasamagra*, 3: 168–9, 408. Originating from the Guild and Technical School founded in 1893 by the National Society of Lithographic Artists, Designers, and Engravers to train their members in the latest technical advances in photomechanical reproduction, the institution became the Bolt Court Technical School in 1895 and, after being taken over by the London County Council in 1898, the LCC School of Photoengraving and Lithography. In the early 1950s, the School was merged with the London School of Printing to form the London School of Printing and Graphic Arts. See Rupert Cannon, *The Bolt Court Connection: A History of the LCC School of Photoengraving and Lithography 1893–1949* (London: London College of Printing, 1985), 5–25, 102–3.

73. By the time Sukumar arrived, it had more than six hundred students on its rolls and had built up an international reputation, especially for its classes on photomechanical reproduction, and usually had a substantial contingent of foreign students from the Commonwealth and beyond. On the history of this School, the involvement of local government bodies in Britain in technical education, and overseas competition in the printing trades, see Gerry Beegan, *The Mass Image: A Social History of Photomechanical Reproduction in Victorian London* (Basingstoke: Palgrave, 2008), 94–6; and Cannon, *The Bolt Court Connection*, 24–5, 90–1.

74. He suggested to his father that he should consider setting up a lithographic department with a rotary press, which would make it easier to print large quantities quickly. See Ray and Basu, *Sukumar Sahityasamagra*, 3: 172, 233, 234–5. He even recommended that *Sandesh* be printed by lithography, since it allowed for printing illustrations without the cost and complexities of making half-tone blocks, and told Upendrakishore that he was going to look for a good lithographic handpress. See Ray and Basu, *Sukumar Sahityasamagra*, 241, 253.

75. He was especially impressed by the results of intaglio techniques and the excellent results of combining them with lithography and offset printing. See Ray and Basu, *Sukumar Sahityasamagra*, 3: 187–8, 191. In a few years, he told his father, the cost of the machinery needed for photogravure (an intaglio process) would probably go down considerably, making it practicable for the family business to invest in it. See Ray and Basu, *Sukumar Sahityasamagra*, 237.

76. Ray and Basu, *Sukumar Sahityasamagra*, 3: 168, 170–1, 173, 175, 181, 191. The principal's introductions helped overcome the reluctance of commercial firms to allow a stranger to study their processes. Sukumar was especially impressed by offset printing. See Ray and Basu, *Sukumar Sahityasamagra*, 182–3, 188, 191, 252–3.

77. Ray and Basu, *Sukumar Sahityasamagra*, 3: 176, 198.

78. Ray and Basu, *Sukumar Sahityasamagra*, 3: 193, 195.

79. Ray and Basu, *Sukumar Sahityasamagra*, 3: 208, 209.

80. Ray and Basu, *Sukumar Sahityasamagra*, 3: 212–13, 215, 218, 224. The Manchester Municipal School of Technology was established in 1902, offering training in a wide variety of artisanal and technological fields. There were many Indian students there in Sukumar's time, but all working in the engineering or textile departments (see Ray and Basu, *Sukumar Sahityasamagra*, 3: 218). The Department of Photographic and Printing Crafts, where Sukumar enrolled, was particularly well-resourced. For a detailed description of the Department, see [William Gamble], 'A Visit to the Municipal School of Technology, Manchester', *Penrose's Pictorial Annual* (1903–4): 129–36. Socially, Sukumar felt very comfortable, with several Bengalis in the same house and other Indians nearby. See Ray and Basu, *Sukumar Sahityasamagra*, 3: 229. He also greatly liked a Japanese classmate and mentioned him often in his letters. See, for example, Ray and Basu, *Sukumar Sahityasamagra*, 3: 218, 236, 239.

81. Ray and Basu, *Sukumar Sahityasamagra*, 3: 214, 216, 219. R.B. Fishenden's life and career, remarked an obituarist, 'epitomized the most momentous period of change and development which had ever been known in the history of the graphic arts'. See Beatrice Warde, 'In Memoriam Richard Bertram Fishenden 1880–1956', *The Penrose Annual*, 1957, unpaginated.

82. Ray and Basu, *Sukumar Sahityasamagra*, 3: 221, 238. Sukumar was also greatly annoyed by the School forcing him to enrol on expensive lecture courses that he had no interest in and sneered almost in a Napoleonic vein about the shopkeeper-like mentality of the British. See Ray and Basu, *Sukumar Sahityasamagra*, 3: 221. He was also irritated when his teachers persuaded him to take the City and Guilds examination (which he found 'absolutely childish'), not because they thought he would gain from it, but because he was likely to be a 'brilliant success' and would thus do the School's reputation a lot of good. As expected by his instructors, he received a

first class mark and a medal but he was not exactly overwhelmed by his success. Ray and Basu, *Sukumar Sahityasamagra*, 3: 238, 249.

83. Sukumar Ray, 'Half-Tone Facts Summarized', *Penrose's Pictorial Annual*, 18 (1912–13): 121–4; 'Standardizing the Original', *Penrose's Pictorial Annual*, 19 (1913–14): 65–7; and 'The Half-Tone Dot', *British Journal of Photography*, 60 (18 July 1913): 554–5. On Fishenden's admiration for the last article, see Ray and Basu, *Sukumar Sahityasamagra*, 3: 252–3.

84. 'The half-tone is a flat-surfaced print at its best,' wrote Gamble, 'while the intaglio has the relievo effect of colour piled up in proportion to light and shade, which is just what an artist desires to see as the counterpart of the methods he adopts in painting a picture'. See [William Gamble], 'The Year's Progress in Process Work', *Penrose's Pictorial Annual*, 19 (1913–14): 1–9, at 1–2.

85. Ray and Basu, *Sukumar Sahityasamagra*, 3: 192, 195, 221, 235.

86. 'Bhabam Hajam', Kedarnath Chatterji's contribution to the fourth issue of *Sandesh* (Sraban 1320) was accompanied by Sukumar's illustration—the author and the illustrator both sent their contributions from Britain. See Ray and Basu, *Sukumar Sahityasamagra*, 3: 237, 243–4, 249. Two preliminary versions of Sukumar's drawing are available in Sukumar Ray, Sketch-Book.

87. On Tagore's praise for *Sandesh* and his promise to write for it, see Ray and Basu, *Sukumar Sahityasamagra*, 3: 244. Tagore's first contribution to *Sandesh* was the poem 'Bristi o Roudra' (Rain and Sunshine), published in the Bhadra 1328 issue, when Sukumar was the editor. Another brief poem, 'Samoy Hara' (Free of time) was published the next year with illustrations by Sukumar himself. See Adhya, *Sukumar Ray*, 83–4; and *Sandesh*, 11 (1922–3): 32, http://archiv.ub.uni-heidelberg.de/savifadok/volltexte/2010/1124 (accessed on 18 January 2015).

88. Ray and Basu, *Sukumar Sahityasamagra*, 3: 240–3, 248–51, 265. He also thought of taking an art class but did not ultimately do so. He did, however, spend a lot of time practising drawing and observing Rothenstein at work. See Ray and Basu, *Sukumar Sahityasamagra*, 3: 246–7.

89. Robinson, 'Selected Letters of Sukumar Ray', 175–6.

90. Ray and Basu, *Sukumar Sahityasamagra*, 3: 204–7.

91. See Ray and Basu, *Sukumar Sahityasamagra*, 3: 199, 248, 251, 253; and Adhya, *Sukumar Ray*, 58.

92. Bankabihari Kar, *Bhakta Kalinarayan Gupta-r Jibanbrittanta* (Calcutta: Brahmo Mission Press, 1925), 3–4.

93. Kar, *Bhakta Kalinarayan*, 7–8. In his autobiography, Kartikeyachandra Roy (1820–1885) recalled that in his childhood, children from better-off or aspirational families were taught Farsi rather than English. See Mohit Roy, ed., *Diwan Kartikeyachandra Roy-er Atmajibancharit* (Calcutta: Pragnya, 1990), 7, 30–2.

94. The four sons were Krishnagovinda, Pyarimohan, Gangagovinda, and Binoychandra. The daughters were Hemantasasi, Soudamini, Chapala, Sarala, Bimala, and Subala (Kar, *Bhakta Kalinarayan*, 19–20).

95. Kar, *Bhakta Kalinarayan*, 12–15.

96. Gupta is supposed to have been so free of caste prejudices that he took personal charge of a low-caste man in his village who had been ostracized because of mental illness. Once the man had recovered, Gupta appointed him and his family members as servants in his own household. When the man finally died, the villagers refused to help in his last rites because he was still ostracized as far as they were concerned. Gupta bathed the corpse, draped it for the last rites, and personally carried it to the cremation ground. One does not know where the dead man's family members were at the time but even if the story is taken as true, it is worth remembering that this obliviousness to caste had developed gradually. In fact, Gupta, even after becoming a Brahmo, had maintained the rules of caste for a long time and it was only at the time of the wedding of his youngest child Subala to Prankrishna Acharya that he had chosen a groom from another caste. See Kar, *Bhakta Kalinarayan*, 28, 81, 89–90, 148–9.

97. Kar, *Bhakta Kalinarayan*, 28, 81; and Srinath Chanda, *Brahmo Samajey Challis Batsar* (Dhaka: Bharat Mahila Press, 1913), 59.

98. See Sivanath Sastri, *History of the Brahmo Samaj* [1911–12], 2nd edn, 2 vols in 1 (Calcutta: Sadharan Brahmo Samaj, 1974), 351–2, 401, 405–6; Kar, *Bhakta Kalinarayan*, 101–11, 156; and Gaganchandra Home, *Jiban-Smriti* (Calcutta: Privately Published, 1929), 22.

99. Kar, *Bhakta Kalinarayan*, 99–101.

100. Kar, *Bhakta Kalinarayan*, 51–3.

101. For the letter, see 'Protest of the Anusthanic Brahmos of Dacca', in *Brahmo Year-Book for 1878*, 17.

102. Lord Beveridge [William Beveridge], *India Called Them* (London: George Allen & Unwin, 1947), 87.

103. The nomination of one Hindu and one Muslim 'native'—Gupta and Syed Husain Bilgrami, respectively—to the Council was largely a token affair and Morley, the Secretary of State for India, admitted that 'their colour is more important than their brains'. On the reforms and the career of K.G. Gupta, see M.N. Das, *India under Morley and Minto: Politics behind Revolution, Repression and Reforms* (London: George Allen & Unwin, 1964), 218–21.

104. Ray and Basu, *Sukumar Sahityasamagra*, 3: 251. Jagatchandra Das, a mid-level functionary in the Raj's revenue and judicial administration, had first married Kalinarayan Gupta's second daughter Soudamini in 1876. See 'Brahmo Marriages from January 1876 to July 1877', in *Brahmo Year-Book for 1877*, 54. Soudamini died young and Jagatchandra then married her younger sister, Sarala. The couple had six children, the second of whom was Suprabha. Without naming names, Kalinarayan Gupta's biographer states

that once, Gupta had refused to attend the wedding of one of his own daughters because she was marrying a widower and he disapproved of anybody marrying twice. This may have been the wedding of Sarala and Jagatchandra or the marriage of Hemantasasi, another widowed daughter of Gupta's, to the widower Durgamohan Das. See Kar, *Bhakta Kalinarayan*, 146–7; Sarala Devi Chaudhurani, *Jibaner Jharapata* (Calcutta: Sahitya Sansad, 1957), 83; Sivanath Sastri, *Ramtonu Lahiri o Tatkalin Bangasamaj*, edited and annotated by Jyotirmoy Ghosh (Calcutta: Punascha, 2007), 69; and Subalchandra Mitra, *Isvar Chandra Vidyasagar: A Story of His Life and Work* (Calcutta: New Bengal Press, 1902), 655. Many thanks to Sourit Dey for his help with this material.

105. Santa Nag, *Purbasmriti* (Calcutta: Papyrus, 1986), 63; Madhurilata Mahalanobis, 'Dada Sukumar Ray', [1987], *Korak*, Special issue on Sukumar Ray (2003): 206–9, at 207.

106. Nalini Das, *Sat Rajar Dhon Ek Manik: Satyajit Ray-er Chhelebela*, 2nd edn (Calcutta: Newscript, 2005), 80–1; and P. Basu, *Satyajit Ray*, 22.

107. The amusement was intensified by the fact that Bengali women of the period, even among Brahmos, were not supposed to address their husbands by name. See Madhurilata Mahalanobis, 'Dada Sukumar Ray', 207.

108. Sita Devi, *Punyasmriti*, 68.

109. Sukumar, sometimes accompanied by his Monday Club friends or his wife, would often visit the poet in Santiniketan as well as Calcutta. During these visits, he would organize various events and performances of some of his own work. In 1935, twelve years after Sukumar's death, Tagore would set one of his nonsense poems to music. See Amitabha Chaudhuri, *Ekatrey Rabindranath* (Calcutta: Dey's, 1983), 496–9; Adhya, *Sukumar Ray*, 61; Sita Devi, *Punyasmriti*, 97, 98–9; and Subhas Chowdhury, 'Surakar Sukumar Ray', in *Prastutiparba*, 186–94, at 189.

110. L. Majumdar, *Pakdandi*, 96.

111. L. Majumdar, *Aar Konokhaney*, 53.

112. Bijoya herself rarely agreed with Suprabha's opinions but never had the courage to express her disagreement. Everybody in the household, including Satyajit, feared Suprabha, she wrote. After the birth of Sandip in 1953, however, Suprabha Ray's personality is said to have undergone a transformation; she not only doted on her grandson but became far more relaxed and openly affectionate with others. See Bijoya Ray, *Amader Katha*, 89, 209.

113. In private, however, the two women were great friends and spent hours chatting and laughing. See Hitendrakishore Raychaudhuri, *Upendrakishore*, 90.

114. Shortly after Upendrakishore moved to his Garpar house, his brother-in-law, Hemendramohan Bose, also moved into his grand new house on Amherst Street but he, too, died shortly after moving in there. Both men were 52 at the time of death. See S. Ghosh, 'Jantrarasik H. Bose', *Ekshan*, 16, nos 3–4 (1983): 62.

115.   Many of his contemporaries thought that he had contracted diabetes simply because he worked too hard. See, for instance, Kedarnath Chattopadhyay, 'Satabarshik Sraddhhanjali: Upendrakishore', *Vishwa Bharati Patrika*, 20, no. 2 (1963 [Kartik–Poush 1370 BE]): 118. The causal relationship between overwork, strain, and diabetes seems to have been widely accepted at the time. His wife as well as he had contracted diabetes during a period of acute strain, declared Sivanath Sastri. See Sastri, *Atmacharit*, 390.

116.   'The Late Mr U. Ray', *Modern Review*, 19, no. 1 (January 1916): 105. In an obvious reference to Sukumar's stint in Britain, the firm's advertisements now offered 'the unique results of twenty years' experience and research and two years' intimate study of European methods'. See Siddhartha Ghosh, '*Abol Tabol*: The Making of a Book', in *Print Areas: Book History in India*, edited by Abhijit Gupta and Swapan Chakravorty (Delhi: Permanent Black, 2004), 247.

117.   L. Majumdar, *Pakdandi*, 42. The identity of the medicine is unknown but it could well have been a crude pancreatic extract called acomatol, which was in vogue for the treatment of diabetes in Europe before the coming of insulin. Its efficacy was doubtful, however, and it is unlikely that Upendrakishore's life could have been saved by it. See Michael Bliss, *The Discovery of Insulin* (Edinburgh: Paul Harris, 1983), 28–33. My thanks to Roberta Bivins for her help on this question.

118.   About two hundred miles from Calcutta, situated a thousand feet above sea level and on the banks of the Usri River, Giridi became a favourite vacationing spot for Bengalis from the 1890s and was much liked for its dry, invigorating climate and cheap, plentiful food. Many Brahmos, including Hemendramohan Bose, Gaganchandra Home, and Dwijendranath Maitra, owned houses there, although Upendrakishore's family never did. See Sunirmal Basu, *Jiban Khatar Kayek Pata* (1955), in *Sunirmal Rachana Sambhar*, 3 vols, edited by Nirmalendu Goutam and Haribandhu Mukhoti (Calcutta: Forward, 1973–5), 3 (1975): 161–340, at 220–2 and 224–6; L. Majumdar, *Pakdandi*, 198–9; Siddhartha Ghosh, 'Sukumar Ray: Jibaner Kalanukramik Ghatanapanji', *Ekshan*, 17, no. 6 (1986): 245–69, at 249; and Arati Sen, *Smritir Aloye Giridi* (Calcutta: Subarnarekha, 2005), 9–10, 14–17, 21–2, 60–2, 76–9, 141–3, 222. In the second half of the twentieth century, memories of those days of Bengali prominence in Giridi would be revived by Satyajit Ray's stories about Trilokeswar Shonku, an internationally acclaimed Bengali scientist-inventor who lived and worked in Giridi.

119.   See Sukumar Ray, 'Upendrakishore Ray' [1916], in *Sukumar Sahityasamagra*, 3: 81. As we know, he had wanted to write a scholarly work on the evolution of the tales in the Puranas and he also seems to have left behind an unfinished work on astronomy, which, Ramananda Chatterji hoped, would be completed by Sukumar. He had also had plans to reform Bengali typography, so as to make it easier as well as cheaper to cast and compose types. A Bengali typewriter was another project that he had contemplated. See the

obituary in *Probasi*, Magh 1322 (January 1916), reprinted in Hemantakumar Adhya, *Upendrakishore Raychaudhuri* (Delhi: Sahitya Akademi, 1997), 46–7.

120. Upendrakishore's body lay at the Sadharan Brahmo Samaj temple for some time, where Krishnakumar Mitra led the prayer service, and crowds of Brahmos followed the body as it was taken for cremation. See the anonymous obiturary in *Tattvakaumudi*, Poush 1322 (January 1916), reprinted in Adhya, *Upendrakishore Raychaudhuri*, 44–5. The *Tattvabodhini Patrika*, the mouthpiece of the Adi Brahmo Samaj, hailed his refusal to behave in narrow, sectarian ways. See anonymous obituary in *Tattvabodhini Patrika*, Falgun 1322 (February 1916), reprinted in Adhya, *Upendrakishore Raychaudhuri*, 43.

121. See 'Death of Mr U. K. Ray', *Process Work and Electrotyping: Penrose's Monthly*, January 1917, 77. A second obituary note, published a few years later with a photograph, also mentioned Upendrakishore's 'unpublished manuscripts on process work as well as other subjects'. See 'The Late Mr U. K. Ray', December 1919–February 1920, 122.

122. See, for instance, the superb reproductions in Mukul C. Dey, *Twelve Portraits* (Calcutta: Amal Home, 1917) and the plates in Rakhaldas Bandyopadhyay, *Bangalar Itihas: Pratham Bhag* (Calcutta: Gurudas Chattopadhyay, 1914).

123. Ghosh, *Karigari Kalpana*, 114–15; and on the printing of *Mukul*, *Bengal Library Catalogue of Books Registered in the Presidency of Bengal: Appendix to the Calcutta Gazette*, 4th quarter (1915): 83, 86; 2nd quarter (1916): 89; 3rd quarter (1916): 111; 2nd quarter (1917): 103.

124. Ajit Dutta, *Bangla Sahitye Hasyaras*, 445–6. The best overview in English of Sukumar Ray's literary work is Sukanta Chaudhuri, 'The World of Sukumar Ray', in *Telling Tales: Children's Literature in India*, edited by Amit Dasgupta (Delhi: Indian Council for Cultural Relations/Wiley Eastern, 1995), 88–96. Among the few pieces Sukumar wrote for grown-ups after taking over as the editor of *Sandesh* was 'Kyabaler Patra' (Ray and Basu, *Sukumar Sahityasamagra*, 3: 45–7) in which he poked fun at the celebrated litterateur Pramatha Chaudhuri, and the incomplete epic in alliterative verse, 'Sri Sri Barnamalatattva' (Ray and Basu, *Sukumar Sahityasamagra*, 3: 154–8), which was published in the magazine *Bichitra* four years after his death. See also Sanyal, *Parichoy-er Kuri Bachhar*, 163; and B. Chakravarty, *Bangla Shishu Sahitya*, 165–6.

125. L. Majumdar, *Sukumar*, 92. Satyajit Ray's 1986 comment in a lecture is quoted in Adhya, *Sukumar Ray*, 85. There were many changes in the magazine's price and print order during Sukumar's editorship. The print order for *Sandesh* came down to 2,500 from the Jaistha 1323 (May–June 1916) issue, the third issue to be edited by Sukumar, and the price went up to 2 annas 6 pice from the Baisakh 1325 (April–May 1918) issue. See *Bengal Library Catalogue of Books*, 2nd quarter (1916): 94; 3rd quarter (1916): 117; 4th quarter (1916): 66; 1st

quarter (1917): 139; 4th quarter (1917): 94; 2nd quarter (1918): 99; and 1st quarter (1922): 149. The price was lowered from Sraban 1330 (July–August 1923) issue (*Bengal Library Catalogue of Books*, 3rd quarter (1923): 128), possibly because of growing competition from *Mouchak*, a children's magazine established by the publishing firm of M.C. Sirkar. See *Bengal Library Catalogue of Books*, 2nd quarter (1920): 96.

126. B. Chakravarty, *Bangla Shishu Sahitya*, 216–17; Krishnarup Chakravarti, *Sukumar Rayer Ashcharya Jagat* (Calcutta: Ananda, 1983), 27; and Satyajit Ray, 'Bhumika', in *Sukumar Sahityasamagra*, 1: ii–iii. During Sukumar's editorship of *Sandesh*, his siblings, Sukhalata and Subinoy, also contributed illustrations, apart from well-known illustrators of the time like Jatindrakumar Sen, Asitkumar Haldar, Purnachandra Ghosh, and Hemendramohan Bose's son Hitendramohan. See B. Chakravarty, *Bangla Shishu Sahitya*, 223.

127. P. Mitter, *Art and Nationalism in Colonial India*, 134.

128. Sukumar did paint a few watercolour landscapes, including one of the Ganga at sunset at the very end of his life. It was reproduced in *Sandesh* after his death. See the frontispiece in *Sandesh*, Kartik 1330 [11, no. 7 (1922–3)] and 'Surjyastey Ganga', a note on the picture in *Sandesh*, 222, http://archiv. ub.uni-heidelberg.de/savifadok/volltexte/2010/1124/ (accessed on 24 November 2011). See also Samir Mondal, 'Sukumar-Silpa', in *Prastutiparba*, 82–4. Critic Sovon Som has even speculated that at least for some of the poems, the idea for the illustration may have come before the words. See Sovon Som, 'Sukumar Ray-er Silpabhhabna', in *Prastutiparba*, 85–97, at 94. For a comprehensive analysis of Sukumar's illustrations, see Pranabranjan Roy, 'Kheyal Rash-er Chhabi', in *Sukumar: Silpa o Sahitya*, edited by Bishnu Basu (Calcutta: Pratibhas, 1989), 89–104.

129. P. Mitter, *Art and Nationalism in Colonial India*, 133.

130. S. Sen, *Traces of Empire*, 54, 57.

131. S. Ghosh, *'Abol Tabol'*, 247.

132. Talking to Ved Mehta in 1966, Satyajit Ray remarked: 'At present, I am trying to translate my father's nonsense rhymes into English, but I am having a great deal of difficulty with this'. See Ved Mehta, *Portrait of India* (London: Weidenfeld and Nicolson, 1970), 411. For Ray's translations, see Sukumar Ray, *Nonsense Rhymes* (Calcutta: Writers Workshop, 1970). Other versions are available in Sukanta Chaudhuri, *The Select Nonsense of Sukumar Ray* (Calcutta: Oxford University Press, 1987).

133. It was only during Subinoy's editorship that the magazine published obituaries of Chittaranjan Das and Surendranath Banerjea. For the tribute to Chittaranjan Das (based on a lecture by Lalitmohan Das), see *Sandesh*, 13 (1925): 122–6 and for that on Banerjea (by Amal Home), *Sandesh*, 167–71, http://archiv.ub.uni-heidelberg.de/savifadok/volltexte/2010/1128 (accessed on 18 January 2015). Most children's magazines and books of that era seem to

have maintained a careful distance from nationalism, including such cultural manifestations of it as the movement for national education, or for education in the mother-tongue. See Khagendranath Mitra, *Satabdir Sisu-Sahitya, 1818–1960*, 2nd edn (Calcutta: Vidyodaya, 1967), 207.

134. Ray and Basu, *Sukumar Sahityasamagra*, 2: vii–viii, at vii; and B. Chakravarty, *Bangla Shishu Sahitya*, 167–8. He also devised many puzzles, riddles, and logic games. In all, Sukumar wrote 16 biographical articles, 47 pieces on different aspects of natural history, 40 on science and technology, and 13 on history and culture for *Sandesh*. See Siddhartha Ghosh, 'Ujhyanam Panditer Soja Katha', in *Prastutiparba*, 15–26, at 21–2, 23–5. Upendrakishore and Sukumar, however, were not the only Bengalis to write about science in child-friendly prose. Indeed, the works of Jagadananda Roy were probably more notable in this regard than anything published in *Sandesh*. Roy's works commenced with a treatise on astronomy (*Graha-Nakshatra*) in 1915—despite Upendrakishore's personal interest in astronomy, it was Roy who wrote the first book on the subject for children—and he was to write extensively on virtually every area of science for children. Unlike Upendrakishore or Sukumar, however, Jagadananda Roy wrote little else. See Mitra, *Satabdir Shishu-Sahitya*, 205–6, 208.

135. See, for instance, the 1922 'Akashbanir Kol' (Ray and Basu, *Sukumar Sahityasamagra*, 2: 310–13) discussing telephone and radio technology and the 1920 'Chandmari' (Ray and Basu, *Sukumar Sahityasamagra*, 2: 290–1) on the possible use of rockets for exploring the moon.

136. See, for these texts, Ray and Basu, *Sukumar Sahityasamagra*, 1: 14, 23 and 161–7, respectively.

137. Ajit Dutta, *Bangla Sahitye Hasyaras*, 458.

138. On the 'good boy' ideal in Bengali children's literature, see Sibaji Bandyopadhyay, *Gopal-Rakhal Dwandasamas: Upanibesbad o Bangla Sisusahitya* (Calcutta: Papyrus, 1991), 176–9. The school story does not seem to have attracted too many Bengali authors, one of the few exceptions being Dakshinaranjan Mitra Majumdar. See, for instance, 'Charu o Haru' (1912), in *Dakshinaranjan Rachana Samagra* (Calcutta: Mitra o Ghosh, 1981), 2 vols, 2: 200–24. The situation in early-twentieth-century Britain was very different, with the public school story being a staple of children's literature. See Kirsten Drotner, *English Children and Their Magazines, 1751–1945* (New Haven: Yale University Press, 1988), 128–9.

139. Buddhadev Bose, 'Bangla Sisusahitya' (1952), 40.

140. See Sibaji Bandyopadhyay, *Gopal-Rakhal Dwandasamas*, 170–1.

141. S. Sen, *Traces of Empire*, 42, 49.

142. See Siddhartha Ghosh, 'Sir, Sahapathi o Satyajit Ray', in *Sandesher Satyajit*, edited by Prasadranjan Ray and Debasis Sen (Calcutta: Saibya, 2007), 44–6, at 45.

143. See Debasis Mukhopadhyay, *Satyajit Ray: Tathyapanji* (Calcutta: Sristi, 2001), 15.

144. Since Sukumar was looking for a 'simple' name for his son, Tagore is said to have jokingly suggested the name Sahajkumar and, more seriously, Saritkumar. Tagore's whimsical suggestion of Sahajkumar had been inspired by the actual name of Subinoy Ray's son: Saralkumar. (Both *sahaj* and *saral* mean simple or clear in Bengali, although *sahaj* would not be used in a name.) See Kalyani Karlekar, 'Chhelemanush Satyajit', in *Sandesher Satyajit*, 84–7, at 85; and Madhuri Mahalanobis, 'Maniker Chhelebela', in *Sandesher Satyajit*, 88–91, at 88. See also Kalyani Karlekar, 'Satyajit's Childhood and the Child in Satyajit', in *Satyajit Ray: An Intimate Master*, edited by Santi Das (Delhi: Allied, 1998), 1–5, at 1. The naming deed of Satyajit 'Raychaudhuri' [sic] is reproduced in a facsimile pullout in Satyajit Ray, *Jakhan Chhoto Chhilam* (Calcutta: Ananda, 1982).

145. See Madhurilata Mahalanobis, 'Dada Sukumar Ray', 208 and Adhya, *Sukumar Ray*, 89–90.

146. Adhya, *Sukumar Ray*, 90; and Madhurilata Mahalanobis, 'Dada Sukumar Ray', 208–9.

147. On the history of kala-azar and its treatment, see Achintya Kumar Dutta, 'Upendranath Brahmachari in Pursuit of Kala-Azar', in *History of Medicine in India: The Medical Encounter*, edited by Chittabrata Palit and Achintya Kumar Datta (Delhi: Kalpaz, 2005), 133–55.

148. Urea stibamine *was* being used in clinical trials by Brahmachari by 1923 but available only in very small quantities. Brahmachari told the Calcutta Medical Club on 20 September 1923 (that is, ten days after Sukumar Ray's death) that he was still conducting scientific trials of the drug and could not predict when it would be available in larger amounts. See U.N. Brahmachari, *Gleanings from My Researches*, 2 vols (Calcutta: University of Calcutta, 1940), 1: 351. At the time of Sukumar's birth centenary in 1987, Satyajit Ray told Debasis Mukhopadhyay that Sukumar was known to have been treated with urea stibamine. Debasis Mukhopadhyay, personal communication.

149. Adhya, *Sukumar Ray*, 90–1; and Punyalata Chakrabarti, 'Sukumar Ray' (1961), xi.

150. Kalyani Karlekar, 'Sukumar Ray', in Punyalata Chakrabarti and Kalyani Karlekar, eds, *Sukumar Samagra Rachanabali*, 2 vols (Calcutta: Asia Publishing, 1960), 1: 1–18, at 17–18. The poems and articles were often dictated to Suprabha Ray, while Suprabha as well as Kuladaranjan's daughter Madhurilata helped him with his drawings. See Madhurilata Mahalanobis, 'Dada Sukumar Ray', 209.

151. Adhya, *Sukumar Ray*, 90–1; and Ajay Home, 'Tatakaka', *Ekshan*, 16, no. 5 (1984): 87–90, at 90.

152. See Madhurilata Mahalanobis, 'Maniker Chhelebela', 88. Although most of the poems of *Abol Tabol* had been published in *Sandesh* with Sukumar's own illustrations, he replaced the latter (which had been printed by half-tone blocks and had some photographic characteristics) with new,

more two-dimensional sketches printed by line blocks, which were more appropriate than half-tone blocks for the antique paper used in the book. See Sovon Som, 'Sukumar Ray-er Chhabi', in *Satayu Sukumar*, edited by Sisirkumar Das (Calcutta: Karigar, 2012), 94–106, at 103; and Siddhartha Ghosh, 'Mudran-Bisarad Sukumar', in *Satayu Sukumar*, 111–18, at 118.

153. Many of the shorter poems, too, were added directly to the dummy copy. The format of the book, as designed by Sukumar, was unique in the history of Bengali print culture. He wanted it to be bound at the top, so that the pages would have to be turned in a vertical direction, just like a handwritten *punthhi* of bygone days. See S. Ghosh, '*Abol Tabol*', 248–450. This layout, however, was followed only in the first edition.

154. Translation from Sukanta Chaudhuri, *The Select Nonsense of Sukumar Ray*, 44.

155. *Indian Messenger*, 16 September 1923, cutting in a notebook collecting obituaries of Sukumar, in the possession of the Ray family.

156. Reported by Tagore himself in his sermon at the Santiniketan temple three days after Sukumar's death. This sermon is available in Adhya, *Sukumar Ray*, 108–11.

157. See http://www.gitabitan.net/top.asp?songid=1606 (accessed on 12 September 2011); and Susobhan Sarkar, *Prasanga Rabindranath* (Calcutta: Ananda, 1982), 8. I am grateful to Biswajit Mitra for his help in researching this issue.

158. See S. Ghosh, 'Sukumar Ray: Jibaner Kalanukramik Ghatanapanji', 268.

159. L. Majumdar, *Pakdandi*, 140–1.

160. Ajay Home, 'Tatakaka', 88–9; and Satadru Sen, *Traces of Empire*, 39.

161. 'Jhhalapala', in *Sukumar Sahityasamagra*, 2: 1–19.

162. Ray and Basu, *Sukumar Sahityasamagra*, 2: 10.

163. See Pulak Chanda, 'Sukumarer Natak', in *Prastutiparba*, 161–77, at 165.

164. This play, too, was serialized in *Sandesh* after Sukumar's death and is available in *Sukumar Sahityasamagra*, 2: 20–33. 'Shaktishel' was probably based, at least in part, on an earlier work of Sukumar's called 'Adbhhut Ramayana' (Bizarre Ramayana). The latter seems to have been something like a musical and Sukumar is known to have performed it at Santiniketan in May 1911 on the occasion of Tagore's birthday. See Sita Devi, *Punyasmriti* (Calcutta: Jignasa, 1964), 10, 21.

165. Sukumar did have a plan to retell the Mahabharata in verse but barely started on the project. See Ray and Basu, *Sukumar Sahityasamagra*, 2: 329–30, 365.

166. 'Lakshmaner Shaktishel', in *Sukumar Sahityasamagra*, 2: 20–33.

167. Ray and Basu, *Sukumar Sahityasamagra*, 2: 27–8.

168. Ray and Basu, *Sukumar Sahityasamagra*, 2: 33. Pulak Chanda has even suggested that the entire play can be read as a comic parable on the

internal divisions and contradictions within the swadeshi movement, with the latter being represented by Rama and his followers and the British by Ravana and his army. See P. Chanda, 'Sukumarer Natak', 163–4.

169. B. Chakravarty, *Bangla Shishu Sahitya*, 161–2. The targets of the satire were those intellectuals who denied that the signified was more important than the signifier. Some suspected Sukumar of aiming at his friend Satyendranath Dutta, a poet who allegedly elevated 'feeling' above mere meaning. Even Rabindranath Tagore, it is rumoured, had suspected Sukumar of lampooning him in *Bhabuk Sabha*. See P. Chanda, 'Sukumarer Natak', 166–7.

170. Sukumar Ray, 'Bhasar Atyachar', in *Sukumar Sahityasamagra*, 3: 39–40.

171. Ray and Basu, *Sukumar Sahityasamagra*, 3: 39–40, 42–3.

172. Ray and Basu, *Sukumar Sahityasamagra*, 3: 43.

173. Ray and Basu, *Sukumar Sahityasamagra*, 3: 44.

174. Published only after his death in the magazine *Bichitra*, the play became widely known only in the early 1960s when it was staged by the Rupakar theatre group in Calcutta. See Bishnu Basu, 'Chalachittachanchari', in *Prastutiparba*, 116–24, at 116. The text of the play is available in Ray and Basu, *Sukumar Sahityasamagra*, 2: 43–63.

175. See Manabendra Bandyopadhyay, 'Shake the Bottle! Shake the Bottle!', in *Prastutiparba*, 139–48, at 147; 'Smriticharan: Susobhan Sarkar', *Prastutiparba*, 122–4, at 124; Bishnu Basu, 'Chalachittachanchari', in *Prastutiparba*, 116–24, at 116–17; and K. Chakravarti, *Sukumar Rayer Ashcharya Jagat*, 96.

176. K. Chakravarti, *Sukumar Rayer Ashcharya Jagat*, 102–3.

177. When an aunt tried to teach him to sit straight and eat 'properly' with cutlery, for instance, the child Sukumar pretended to be so stupid and clumsy that the aunt soon ended her civilizing mission. See P. Chakrabarti, *Chhelebelar Dinguli*, 82.

178. In *Hingshuti*, first published in *Sandesh* in the Bhadra 1327 issue, Sukumar dealt with jealousy between five young girls and how that was resolved with the assistance of two wise old women. See B. Chakravarty, *Bangla Shishu Sahitya*, 160.

179. S. Sen, *Traces of Empire*, 39.

180. See Anupam Majumdar, 'Samoyer Aynaye *Abol Tabol*', in *Prastutiparba*, 55–74; and Ashis Lahiri, 'Asangatir Unish-Bish', in *Prastutiparba*, 13–14. Susobhan Sarkar, who later became a communist, could not recall Sukumar ever discussing politics ('Smriticharan: Susobhan Sarkar', 124) and Hiran Sanyal, another communist, did not think that Sukumar's political views were 'progressive' in the modern (that is, leftist) sense. See Sanyal, *Parichoy-er Kuri Bachhar*, 161. For the impact of the First World War on Bengal, see J.H. Broomfield, *Elite Conflict in a Plural Society: Twentieth-Century Bengal* (Berkeley: University of California Press, 1968), 155. The historian Rajat Ray has even argued that a 'revolutionary mentality' was born in Bengal

during the First World War, sustained by 'unprecedented social distress'. See Rajat Kanta Ray, *Social Conflict and Political Unrest in Bengal, 1875–1927* (Delhi: Oxford University Press, 1984), 206–10. See also Ranajit Guha, *Dominance without Hegemony: History and Power in Colonial India* (Cambridge, Mass.: Harvard University Press, 1997), 136–7.

181. Anupam Majumdar, 'Samoyer Aynaye *Abol Tabol*', 60–6.

182. Sadhan Chattopadhyay, '*Abol Tabol*-er Tinti Kabita', in *Prastutiparba*, 112–15, at 113.

183. S. Chattopadhyay, '*Abol Tabol*-er Tinti Kabita', 114.

184. As Bandyopadhyay (*Gopal-Rakhal Dwandasamas*, 309–13) has also emphasized, however, Sukumar had not transcended all the myths the bhadralok had created about their history. In *Ateeter Chhabi* (1922), a history of the Brahmo movement in verse and the only book Sukumar was to publish in his lifetime, Sukumar endorses the linear vision of Indian history widely held by modern Bengalis, in which the glories of classical Hindu antiquity were succeeded by medieval gloom, which lifted only with the entirely Hindu 'renaissance' of the nineteenth century. The long poem is free of any allusions to Islam or even to Buddhism and the West appears only as the source of new knowledge, not of colonial subjection. See Ray and Basu, *Sukumar Sahityasamagra*, 1: 83–9.

185. *Haw-Jaw-Baw-Raw-Law* was published as a book in September 1924 by U. Ray & Sons. See B. Chakravarty, *Bangla Shishu Sahitya*, 148. The work is available in Ray and Basu, *Sukumar Sahityasamagra*, 1: 128–46.

186. For Satyajit Ray's comment, see Ray and Basu, *Sukumar Sahityasamagra*, 1: vii.

187. Goswami, *Colonial India in Children's Literature*, 153–60.

188. Goswami, *Colonial India in Children's Literature*, 163.

189. Lahiri, 'Asangatir Unish-Bish', 9–11.

190. Lahiri, 'Asangatir Unish-Bish', 7–8. For Sukumar's 'serious' reflections on the fundamental uncertainties of life that had been revealed by philosophy, evolutionary biology, and modern physics, see his essay 'Chirantan Prasna' (1905), in *Sukumar Sahityasamagra*, 3: 48–55.

191. Gouriprasad Ghosh, 'Sisu Swapnalokey Notun Biggyaner Chhaya', in *Prastutiparba*, 27–43, at 34; and 'Kankabati' in *Trailokya Rachanasamagra*, 2 vols, edited by Satyanarayan Bhattacharya, Nirmal Das, Shyamal Sengupta, Dibyajyoti Majumdar, and Nepalpada Das (Calcutta: Granthamela, 1973–4), 1 (1973): 1–154, at 106–8. On the life and work of Trailokyanath, who is often regarded as the greatest Bengali satirist before Sukumar, see *Trailokya Rachanasamagra*, xxv–lxiv, 523–6, 551–75; and Debnarayan Roy, *Trailokyanath: Jiban o Sahitya* (Calcutta: Pustak Bipani, 1996).

192. Lahiri, 'Asangatir Unish-Bish', 4–5.

193. Lahiri, 'Asangatir Unish-Bish', 4.

194. On the foundation of the Monday Club, see *Biswapathik Kalidas Nag* (Calcutta: Writers Workshop, 1986), 229. For a complete list of founding

members, see Prabhatchandra Gangopadhyay, 'Amader Monday Club' [1963], in *Sukumar Mela* (Calcutta: Patha Bhavan Primary Section, 1987), 41–52, at 46. My thanks to Sumonjit Sarkar and Debasis Mukhopadhyay for providing me with a copy of the latter.

195. For a complete list of all twenty-eight who joined the Club over its three active years, see Ray and Basu, *Sukumar Sahityasamagra*, 3: 419–20.

196. Sanyal, *Parichoy-er Kuri Bachhar*, 145.

197. For instance, Dwarakanath Ganguli's son Prabhatchandra (Jangli) invited the popular writer Saratchandra Chattopadhyay, the poet and composer Kazi Nazrul Islam, and the blind singer Krishnachandra Dey to different sessions of the Club. See Prabhatchandra Gangopadhyay, 'Amader Monday Club', 46.

198. 'We always gathered around him,' recalled Hiran Sanyal. 'He possessed a magnetic ability to draw people to himself' (see Sanyal, *Parichoy-er Kuri Bachhar*, 160).

199. All the existing invitations have been reprinted, some in facsimile, in *Sukumar Sahityasamagra*, 3: 268–78.

200. Ajit Dutta, *Bangla Sahitye Hasyaras*, 440–1.

201. P.Gangopadhyay, 'Amader Monday Club', 46.

202. See Ray and Basu, *Sukumar Sahityasamagra*, 3: 268–90, 418–22; and P. Gangopadhyay, 'Amader Monday Club', 46. It was not only for members of the Monday Club that Sukumar composed rhymed invitations. He would often resort to rhyme even for inviting a guest to tea. For one sample of such an invitation, see Santa Nag, *Purbasmriti* (Calcutta: Papyrus, 1986), 83–4.

203. Leela Majumdar, *Sukumar*, 2nd edn (Calcutta: Paschimbanga Bangla Akademi, 2001), 72.

204. P. Gangopadhyay, 'Amader Monday Club', 41, 48.

205. Sanyal, *Parichoy-er Kuri Bachhar*, 133–4.

206. See Ray and Basu, *Sukumar Sahityasamagra*, 3: 420.

207. Apart from the departure of some prominent members from Calcutta around that time, Sukumar's growing involvement with the Brahmo Samaj after 1919 might have expedited the end of the Monday Club. See Sanyal, *Parichoy-er Kuri Bachhar*, 166.

208. Dipesh Chakrabarty, 'Adda: A History of Sociality', in *Provincializing Europe: Postcolonial Thought and Historical Difference* (Chicago: University of Chicago Press, 2000), 180–213. In arguing that the adda is fundamentally characterized by its lack of concrete goals and purposes (*Provincializing Europe*, 204), Chakrabarty may be underestimating the indirect stimulation of literary and other production by addas. As we saw earlier, Sukumar's own early work was shaped to a considerable degree by conversations at the Nonsense Club and the same argument may well apply to the Monday Club.

209. Debasish Chattopadhyay, 'Nonsense Club and Monday Club: The Cultural Utopias of Sukumar Ray', in *The Literary Utopias of Cultural Communities*, edited by Marguérite Corporaal and Evert Jan van Leeuwen (Amsterdam: Rodopi, 2010), 243–52. The best description of the Khamkheyali Sabha is in Abanindranath Tagore and Rani Chanda, *Gharoa*, 2nd edn (Calcutta: Vishwa Bharati, 1943), 9, 97–102. The agenda for the very first session of the club on 24 Magh 1303 included, apart from the expected mix of music, recitations, readings, and dinner, 'listening to the phonograph'. See Santoshkumar De, *Kabikanthha o Koler Gaan* (Santiniketan: Vishwa-Bharati, 1993), 62. Siddhartha Ghosh has suggested that this phonograph may have been obtained from Hemendramohan Bose. See S. Ghosh, *Karigari Kalpana*, 226–7.

210. Not all literary 'clubs' were so expansive in vision or sticklers for regular weekly sessions. For examples of less formal associations, see Ajit Dutta, *Bangla Sahitye Hasyaras*, 395; and two volumes of reminiscences by Hemendrakumar Roy: *Jnader Dekhechhi* (Calcutta: New Age, 1951); and *Ekhon Jnader Dekhchhi* (Calcutta: Indian Associated Publishing, 1955). My thanks to Sourav Bagchi and Sarbajit Mitra for these references.

211. Rathindranath Tagore, *On the Edges of Time*, 16, 18.

212. Rathindranath Tagore, *On the Edges of Time*, 16–17.

213. See Prabhatkumar Mukhopadhyay, *Rabindrajibani o Rabindra-Sahitya Prabeshak*, 4th edn, 4 vols (Calcutta: Vishwa Bharati, 1970), 1: 450.

214. 'Father's imagination would run riot on these occasions and he would suggest all sorts of strange dishes which had never been attempted before, and Mother had to rack her brains to achieve the impossible,' recalled Rathindranath Tagore. See Rathindranath Tagore, *On the Edges of Time*, 16, 18.

215. Adhya, *Sukumar Ray*, 73–5. Sukumar's participation in Bichitra could be enthusiastic but there was no question about his commitment to the Monday Club. Once, when Bichitra met on a Monday but a couple of Monday Club members still chose to attend it, they were formally censured, and only partly in jest. See Sanyal, *Parichoy-er Kuri Bachhar*, 161. Founded by Rathindranath Tagore in 1909, Bichitra ran as an art school and studio in the daytime, presided over by Gaganendranath and Abanindranath Tagore. See Guha-Thakurta, *Making of a New 'Indian' Art*, 275–6; and Ratan Parimoo, *Art of Three Tagores: From Revival to Modernity* (Delhi: Kumar Gallery, 2011), 121.

216. Rathindranath Tagore, *On the Edges of Time*, 92–3, 104–5.

217. See the anonymous obiturary in *Tattvakaumudi*, Poush 1322 (January 1916), reprinted in Adhya, *Upendrakishore Raychaudhuri*, 44–5.

218. See Collet, *Brahmo Year-Book for 1879*, 76; and Sastri, *History of the Brahmo Samaj*, 286–7. On the roles played by Sukumar, see his obituary in

Indian Messenger, 16 September 1923, cutting in an untitled notebook collecting all obituaries of Sukumar, in the possession of the Ray family.

219. An associated body called the Young Men's Theistic Society was also established—it met once a month to discuss theological and ethical questions. In addition, the younger teachers ran a Sunday Moral Training School for the schoolchildren. See Sastri, *History of the Brahmo Samaj*, 287. Prominent Brahmos such as Sastri himself or Anandamohan Bose (1847–1906) would often speak at the Students' Weekly Service and the student members eventually started a night school for the working classes and organized a temperance campaign. See Collet, *Brahmo Year-Book for 1880*, 97; and Krishnakumar Mitra, *Atmacharit*, 144–6.

220. Adhya, *Sukumar Ray*, 40–1.

221. See Santa Nag, *Purbasmriti*, 66–7, 72; and *Indian Messenger*, 16 September 1923, cutting in an untitled notebook collecting all obituaries of Sukumar, in the possession of the Ray family. On *Alok*, see Bimalangsuprakash Ray, 'Sukumar Ray-er Smriti', unpaginated.

222. *Alok*, however, was not relaunched. See Bimalangsuprakash Ray, 'Sukumar Ray-er Smriti'; and Ashok Rudra, *Prasanta Chandra Mahalanobis: A Biography* (Delhi: Oxford University Press, 1996), 66–7. Sukumar inquired regularly about the group's activities from England but nothing, it seems, could keep the movement alive in his absence. See, for instance, Ray and Basu, *Sukumar Sahityasamagra*, 3: 190, 206.

223. Gopal Haldar, 'Sukumar Ray', in *Sukumar Mela*, 33–4. My thanks to Soumen Paul for a copy of this essay.

224. *Indian Messenger*, 16 September 1923.

225. *Indian Messenger*, 16 September 1923.

226. 'Smriticharan: Susobhan Sarkar', 122. On Sukumar's religiosity, see also Susobhan Sarkar, 'Sukumar Ray: Ja Mone Porey', *Baromas*, Special Puja Annual (1982), 1–5. My thanks to Soumen Paul for a copy of this essay.

227. This was a Sadharan Brahmo tendency that had bothered Rabindranath Tagore too: 'Their prohibitions do not work, because they simply announce what kind of entertainment is unacceptable. They never say what *is* permissible', he had complained. See Sita Devi, *Punyasmriti*, 131.

228. 'Smriticharan: Susobhan Sarkar', in *Prastutiparba*, 122; and a June 1981 interview with Sarkar, available in Adhya, *Sukumar Ray*, 126. Prasanta Mahalanobis's grandfather Gurucharan (1833–1916) had been on the radical side on most Brahmo issues—converting to Brahmoism in 1861, he had married a widow in 1864 (uncommon even among Brahmos at the time), left Debendranath Tagore's Brahmo Samaj to join Keshab Sen's Brahmo Samaj of India and then left Sen's group to be the first treasurer of the Sadharan Brahmo Samaj in 1878. The founder of the pharmaceutical firm Mahalanobis and Company, he was regarded as epitomizing the Brahmo ideal of honesty in business and became known for his fair prices and reliable products. See

Gurucharan Mahalanobis, *Atmakatha*; Sanyal, *Parichoy-er Kuri Bachhar*, 189–90; and Krishnakumar Mitra, *Atmacharit*, 157.

229. They met regularly at Mahalanobis's house and discussed varied topics, including such potentially controversial ones as the ideals of marriage and their evolution through history, Bolshevism and Lenin, Einstein and relativity and, inevitably, Tagore and his creations. Sanyal, *Parichoy-er Kuri Bachhar*, 31–2. In 1923, Sita married Sudhirkumar Chaudhuri (the secretary of the literary fraternity) and the couple moved to Rangoon; Sukumar Ray died that same year and Prasanta Mahalanobis became preoccupied with other matters. The Social Fraternity, therefore, folded up. See Madhabi De, *Santa Devi o Sita Devi: Jiban, Sahitya, Adhunikata* (Calcutta: Sahityalok, 2003), 54.

230. The controversy went back to the time of Debendranath Tagore, who had insisted that Brahmos were Hindus and not members of some new faith. See Adhya, *Sukumar Ray*, 63.

231. Sophia Dobson Collet had found Brahmoism's intermediate identity and sympathy for other faiths to be 'gracious' but also a barrier to the formulation of an independent ideal of faith and life. See Collet, *Brahmo Year-Book for 1879*, 65.

232. Chakrabarty's article was a response to a call by the New Dispensation wing of the Brahmo Samaj for the re-unification of the Brahmo denominations but leaving out the Adi Brahmo Samaj because of its closeness to conventional Hinduism. See Adhya, *Sukumar Ray*, 63; and Abhra Ghosh, 'Sukumar Ray-er Brahmo-mat', in *Prastutiparba*, 125–38, at 130.

233. See Rabindranath Tagore, 'Atmaparichay', in *Rabindra Rachanabali*, Sulabh Sanskaran, 18 vols (Calcutta: Vishwa-Bharati, 1990), 9: 592–603. See also Rabindranath Tagore, 'Hindu-Brahmo', in *Rabindra Rachanabali*, 9: 724–30. Predictably, Tagore's views on the Hindu identity of Brahmos were strongly contested in *Tattvakaumudi*, the organ of the Sadharan Brahmo Samaj. See Abhra Ghosh, 'Sukumar Ray-er Brahmo-mat', 128–9. A concrete example of the attitude of some Sadharan Brahmos was their criticism of the reformer Sasipada Banerji (who had faced much persecution after his conversion to Brahmoism) for his refusal to stop describing himself as Hindu. See Kuladaprasad Mallik, *Nabajuger Sadhana* (Calcutta: A.C. Sarkar, 1913), 89–91.

234. Sukumar Ray, 'Brahmo-Hindu Samasya', in *Sukumar Sahityasamagra*, 3: 103–9, especially 105–6.

235. Sukumar Ray, '"Brahmo o Hindu" Prabandher Pratibad', in *Sukumar Sahityasamagra*, 3: 101–2. In *Ateeter Chhabi*, he would make the same points, contrasting the dispiriting state of the Brahmo movement of his time with its glorious past. Whatever one thinks of spiritualism, it may be worth noting that, in reply to a question asked by Rabindranath Tagore on the Brahmo Samaj at a seance, the supposed spirit of Sukumar Ray declared: 'No, that's

not the right path.' The entire conversation is reproduced in Amitabha Chaudhuri, *Ekatrey Rabindranath* (Calcutta: Dey's, 1983), 503–9. On Tagore's seances, see *Ekatrey Rabindranath*, 5–117.

236. It is not known whether Tagore himself was greatly interested in the question and Leela Majumdar thinks that he was not. See Robinson, 'Selected Letters of Sukumar Ray', 182–3; L. Majumdar, *Sukumar*, 101.

237. Adhya, *Sukumar Ray*, 76. Although it is only the proposal for Tagore's membership that we still remember, Sukumar Ray and Prasanta Mahalanobis had also ruffled feathers by proposing several changes in the regulations that would have made the administration of the Samaj less dependent on a handful of elders. See Abhra Ghosh, 'Sukumar Ray-er Brahmo-mat', 133–5.

238. See, for instance, Susobhan Sarkar, *Prasanga Rabindranath*, 9.

239. Abhra Ghosh, 'Sukumar Ray-er Brahmo-mat', 135.

240. The importance of this objection is attested by the efforts of Prasanta Mahalanobis to portray Tagore as a supporter of universalist (that is, Brahmo) *principles* and national (that is, Hindu) *forms* in religion. See Mahalanobis, *Keno Rabindranathkey Chai* (Calcutta: Privately Published, 1921). I am indebted to Amit Das for providing me with a copy of this pamphlet.

241. Sumit Sarkar, *The Swadeshi Movement in Bengal, 1903–1908*, new edn (Ranikhet: Permanent Black, 2010), 44–51 and on Tagore's repudiation of revivalist ideas after 1907, 52, 69–72, 296.

242. He threw himself into the movement, travelling all over Bengal, often with Surendranath Banerjea. Along with several other leading figures (but not Banerjea), Mitra was deported from Bengal and imprisoned without trial for alleged links with terrorists. See Krishnakumar Mitra, *Atmacharit*, especially the appendix by Kanailal Chattopadhyay (280–351); Bipinchandra Pal, 'Krishna Kumar Mitra', in B.C. Pal, *Character Sketches* (Calcutta: Yugajatri, 1957), 234–43, especially 235; and Surendranath Banerjea, *A Nation in Making: Being the Reminiscences of Fifty Years of Public Life* (London: Oxford University Press, 1927), 249. Brahmo 'economic nationalism' long predated the swadeshi movement. Rajanikanta Guha recalled in his autobiography that some twenty years before the partition of Bengal, he and his schoolmates had stopped using foreign products, including footwear and steel pens. See Rajanikanta Guha, *Atmacharit* (Calcutta: Jatindranath Roy, 1949), 132–3. Dwarakanath Ganguli, too, supported these initiatives. In 1896, an exhibition of Indian handicrafts and industrial products accompanied the Calcutta session of the Indian National Congress. Dwarakanath, then only two years away from death, had travelled across the country to collect suitable exhibits. See Prabhatchandra Gangopadhyay, *Bharater Rastriya Itihaser Khasra*, 2nd edn (Calcutta: Jignasa, 1965), 130–4, especially 132.

243. Lotika Ghose, 'Social and Educational Movements for Women and by Women, 1820–1950', in *Bethune School & College Centenary Volume*, edited by Kalidas Nag (Calcutta: no pub., 1951), 139–40.

244. Banerjea, *A Nation in Making*, 95.

245. Sanyal, *Parichoy-er Kuri Bachhar*, 166. Prasantachandra is said to have been 'a natural leader' in childhood (rather like Sukumar) and a 'great dictator' in his mature years, but as a young adult, he seems to have deferred willingly to Sukumar. On Mahalanobis's personality, see Rudra, *Prasanta Chandra Mahalanobis*, 24–5 and 332–55.

246. Adhya, *Sukumar Ray*, 76. Ramananda Chatterji generally sided with the young in most generational disagreements, recalled his daughter Santa. See Santa Nag, *Purbasmriti*, 66.

247. Susobhan Sarkar, *Prasanga Rabindranath*, 9.

248. Adhya, *Sukumar Ray*, 76–7.

249. Mahalanobis, *Keno Rabindranathkey Chai*.

250. Susobhan Sarkar, *Prasanga Rabindranath*, 9. Had there been no controversy, Mahalanobis thought, more than 95 per cent of the votes would have been in favour of admitting Tagore. See Abhra Ghosh, 'Sukumar Ray-er Brahmo-mat', 135.

251. Sanyal, *Parichoy-er Kuri Bachhar*, 193.

252. Unfortunately, Sukumar had passed away by the time Das reached Calcutta. See Bankabihari Kar, *Brahmarpitachitta Swargiya Nabadwipchandra Daser Jibanbrittanta* (Dhaka: Purba-Bangla Brahmo Samaj, 1926), 91–2, 101–2. In 1923, Prasanta Mahalanobis would marry Nirmalkumari, the daughter of Heramba Maitra, albeit not with the approval of his stern father-in-law. Maitra and his wife refused to attend the wedding and it was held in the presence of Rabindranath Tagore and in the house of physician Nilratan Sircar, who was Prasanta's maternal uncle. See Rudra, *Prasanta Chandra Mahalanobis*, 37–63.

253. Ray and Basu, *Sukumar Sahityasamagra*, 3: 254–7. This letter, Satyajit Ray wrote, was given by Mahalanobis to Suprabha Ray after Sukumar's death and remained known only within the immediate family until its publication in 1982 (see Ray and Basu, *Sukumar Sahityasamagra*, 403–4). Sukumar's youngest brother, Subimal, however, recalled that parts of the letter were read out by Mahalanobis at the memorial service for Sukumar at the Sadharan Brahmo Samaj temple on 29 September 1923, which was organized by the Brahmo youth wing and at which Rabindranath Tagore, now an honorary member of the Sadharan Brahmo Samaj, presided. For a brief report of the service mentioning a speech by Mahalanobis but not giving further details, reproduced from the Sadharan Brahmo Samaj paper *Tattvakaumudi*, see Adhya, *Sukumar Ray*, 118 and for Subimal Ray's recollections of the evening, see his *Pretsiddher Kahini o Anyanya Rachana* (Calcutta: Asha Prakasani, 1978), 93. The letter was also mentioned and its essential points quoted in Seton, *Portrait of a Director*, 35, the first edition of which was published in 1970.

254. Ray and Basu, *Sukumar Sahityasamagra*, 3: 254–7. For a different translation, see Robinson, 'Selected Letters of Sukumar Ray', 224–6. The

phrase 'rampant, morbid, out and out pessimism' was given in English in the original; so was the word 'death' and it was underlined.

255. Satyajit Ray, 'Bhumika', in *Sukumar Sahityasamagra*, 1: vii.

256. 'Smriticharan: Susobhan Sarkar', 123.

257. Up to a point, the same was true of the outwardly dynamic and self-assured Prasanta Mahalanobis himself. See Rudra, *Prasanta Chandra Mahalanobis*, 406–9, for examples of his profound depression and hopelessness, including but by no means limited to the struggles around Tagore's election.

Epilogue

New Challenges, Old Values

After Sukumar passed away in 1923, the management of U. Ray & Sons as well as the editorship of *Sandesh* were taken over by Subinoy Ray (1890–1941), a rather orthodox Brahmo who was a talented writer in his own right.[1] Neither he nor Sukumar, however, was a particularly gifted businessman. As early as in 1919, when Sukumar was healthy and at the helm of affairs, goods were being stolen and jobs done so unsatisfactorily that even Ramananda Chatterji, one of the Ray firm's oldest and most loyal clients, had threatened to take his work elsewhere. Sukumar charged the office manager Karunabindu Biswas with neglecting the Rays' work in order to develop his own (unspecified) business and proposed that he retire.[2] Biswas stayed on, however—we do not know why or how—and after Sukumar's death in 1923, the situation worsened rapidly. Leela Majumdar heard that the company had debts of 150,000 rupees and outstanding bills worth more than 200,000 rupees.[3] If Majumdar's information was correct, then the firm failed to collect what was owing to it, for Subinoy borrowed a hundred thousand rupees by mortgaging the house, the press, and the remaining land in Mymensingh to the wealthy Kundu family of Bhagyakul.[4]

Even that loan did not help clear the firm's debts and the creditors refused to wait any longer. They even called in the police, who, mistaking Upendrakishore's youngest son, Subimal, for Subinoy, arrested the hapless young man, who had to spend the night in gaol.[5] Finally, in 1927—a mere twelve years after founder Upendrakishore's death—U. Ray & Sons declared bankruptcy.[6] The family mansion at 100A, Garpar Road, was purchased by the Athenaeum Institution, a nearby boys' school, and Suprabha Ray was awarded a monthly sum for the education of her son as long as he was a minor.[7] Every single object in the house—except the women's jewellery—was put up for auction, with the young Satyajit, totally uncomprehending of the crisis, playing amidst the clutter with great enjoyment.[8] The business, along with its trading name, was purchased by the same Karunabindu Biswas whom Sukumar had tried to remove. Biswas was a Brahmo and is said to have assured the Rays that he was purchasing the firm so as to allow the family to continue running it. He did not keep his promise. He continued to publish Upendrakishore's books and those by other members of the family but did not pay any royalties. Old blocks continued to be used long beyond their lifetime and Biswas did not make any effort to maintain, let alone improve, the firm's prowess in block-making.[9]

The passing of Sukumar and the collapse of the business could have crushed the Rays forever. (Problems with the East Bengal zamindari may also have contributed to this toxic mix but nothing seems to be known about this aspect. We do not even know who purchased the land that Upendrakishore had retained.) Members of the family scattered in all directions, moving in with relatives. Amazed by the fact that the celebrated filmmaker Satyajit Ray's household comprised not only his own wife and son, but also his uncle Subimal and mother-in-law (who had moved in after the death of Suprabha Ray in 1960), Marie Seton remarked that such a living arrangement was 'almost unknown as a setting for the life and work of most internationally known artists in the West'.[10] What Seton did not understand was that it was not unique for Satyajit but characteristic of his clan. At times of crisis or loss, the family organism would always gather traumatized members into its protective embrace and if the hosts felt any resentment at having to shelter their homeless kin, then history has not recorded any trace of it.

Long ago, when Kuladaranjan Ray had lost his wife, he and his children had moved in with Upendrakishore and now that Upendrakishore's descendants were in crisis, other relatives opened their doors to them. Subinoy's wife, Pushpalata, and son, Saralkumar, went to live with Pushpalata's parents, who lived in a small town in distant Madhya Pradesh.[11] Subimal Ray (1897–1975), who had never had any interest in the family business and had originally planned to compete for the Indian Civil Service, got a schoolmaster's job and moved in with uncle Muktidaranjan, taking his elderly mother Bidhumukhi with him.[12] None of them, however, faced Suprabha Ray's challenge of bringing up a fatherless child and the courage, energy, and imagination with which she confronted it have not always been appreciated adequately. When Satyajit Ray's admirers examine his roots, they usually focus on Upendrakishore and Sukumar Ray. In their drive to set up a genealogy of (male) genius, they forget that Satyajit never had an opportunity to imbibe their ideals or creative instincts directly. Upendrakishore had died six years before his birth and his father had passed away when he was not even three years old. Apart from figures like Kuladaranjan or Subimal Ray, it was his mother who communicated their legacy to him, while being a role model in her own right.

Mother and Son

Outwardly, Suprabha Ray was an entirely traditional Bengali woman dressed in the borderless white sari (thaan) of the conventional Hindu widow. Brahmo widows were under no compulsion to follow that practice and Kadambini Ganguli, then nearing the end of her life, told Suprabha that Upendrakishore, who had urged Kadambini not to wear a thaan after she was widowed in 1898, would not have approved of his daughter-in-law's choice.[13] Suprabha Ray did not pay any heed to that admonition but in spite of her traditional apparel, she was no helpless, grieving widow. She confronted her many challenges with an indomitable courage that even Dwarakanath Ganguli's Suruchi could not have matched.

Almost immediately after Sukumar's death, Suprabha's mother Sarala Das fell ill and she had to go off to nurse her, leaving her young son with Kuladaranjan Ray's daughter Madhuri (Bulu) at the household of Upendrakishore's brother Pramadaranjan.[14] After a few months, Suprabha returned and along with Satyajit, went to live with her brother Prasantakumar Das (1900–1981). Although Suprabha Ray's other brothers were more or less Anglicized barristers, Prasanta Das had never been abroad and worked for an insurance company owned by a relative. He had not married yet, led a very traditional Bengali life, spoke unashamedly in the Bangal dialect, and had few intellectual or artistic pretensions, preferring to spend his free time playing ludo or flying kites. Although Satyajit later felt that he had been 'cut off from everything intellectual' at the Das household, he was eternally grateful for Das's 'extreme generosity' in saving him and his mother 'from a fate that could have been catastrophic'. It was not just Suprabha and her son to whom Das was generous. Suprabha's sister, the celebrated singer Kanak Das (1903–1988), also lived in the same household and from 1932, Madhuri Das, the widow of Suprabha Ray's half-brother Charuchandra Das (1880–1931), and three of Madhuri's four daughters—Gauri, Joya, and Bijoya—came to live with him.[15] Various other people, some not even directly related, drifted in and out over the years. A huge new dining table had to be ordered to enable the entire 'family' to eat together and Das had to move into another house twice to accommodate everybody.[16] Das's last move was to his own three-storeyed house behind Triangular Park in south Calcutta, where he set aside the best room in the house for Suprabha and Satyajit, along with a terrace for his sister's potted plants.[17] Suprabha Ray, predictably, was no freeloader. As her son was to recall, she 'looked after the household affairs, the day-to-day expenses, and took charge of the kitchen' at her brother's house. Her cooking was legendary and her domestic management no less perfect. Few Bengali women of her generation and class would have aspired to do more but Suprabha also took up a full-time job.[18] Except for Kadambini Ganguli, none of the Ray women had ever worked for a living and Suprabha's example taught her son more about the New Woman than a hundred tracts or lectures could have.

The Vidyasagar Bani Bhavan in north Calcutta, where Suprabha worked, was established in 1922 by the Nari Siksha Samiti, an organization founded in 1919 by Abala Bose (1864–1951), daughter of Brahmamoyee and Durgamohan Das and wife of Jagadischandra Bose, with the participation of, among others, Jyotirmoyee Ganguli, the daughter of Kadambini and Dwarakanath Ganguli.[19] As Ghulam Murshid has shown, after it became clear that Vidyasagar's campaign for the remarriage of widows was never going to find wide enough support, progressives had turned to the simpler task of making widows self-sufficient.[20] The Nari Siksha Samiti was one such pragmatic initiative and after establishing several schools in Calcutta and the rural hinterland, it set up the Vidyasagar Bani Bhavan in 1922 for training widows for employment as teachers in those schools. The trainees were given an ordinary school education and then offered courses on

sewing, weaving, tailoring, clay-modelling, leather work, and embroidery. Every student received a portion of the profit accruing from the
sale of the products.[21] Suprabha Ray was the Superintendent of the
handicraft department and commuted by bus every day from south
Calcutta to the school, which, ironically, was located close to
Upendrakishore's old Garpar house.[22]

She also learnt leatherwork from a family acquaintance and spent
much time making bags, purses, and spectacle cases, some of which
she sold. Decades later, her son could still remember the reek of spirit
(which had to be mixed with the paint used on leather) that used to
pervade their room.[23] She also learnt sculpture from Nitai Pal, a
well-known sculptor of the time, and made a number of heads.[24]
Marie Seton found them to be 'beautifully modelled' and possessing
'a concentrated serenity'. She was even more struck by Suprabha herself, whom she encountered even before she had met her son. An
'unusually tall' woman, she had a presence that was 'commanding
without being formidable. Her manner had warmth'. She explained
to Seton that sculpting was a whim that had come upon her suddenly
and then dissipated after a few years.[25] It had not been a purely
aesthetic venture, however. Seton was unaware that the cash-strapped
single mother had sold many of her sculpted heads for about fifty
rupees each, which was a very decent sum in the 1930s.[26]

Sharmila Tagore, who met Suprabha only when she was quite
elderly and her son a famous filmmaker, was struck by her strength of
character and convinced that the respect for women that was evident
in Ray's films had stemmed from his relationship with his mother.[27]
Satyajit himself acknowledged that his mother's indefatigability had
inspired him to work hard for eighteen hours a day.[28] This was not
simply an expression of filial piety. For, in addition to all her work at
home and in the world, Suprabha single-handedly taught Satyajit at
home, sending him to school only when he was about eight. 'She was
a very good teacher,' Ray would later observe, 'and taught me English,
Bengali, arithmetic, history and geography.'[29] For entertainment, she
read him various English stories, of which Ray remembered two by
Arthur Conan Doyle: 'Blue John Gap' and 'The Brazilian Cat'. Both of
these he would later translate into Bengali.[30] One does not know if
she also taught him to sing—Suprabha was a talented singer, especially of Tagore's songs—but the boy, although known to possess a
good singing voice like the other members of the Das clan, was always
reluctant to sing in public.[31] But Satyajit's relationship with his

mother had its ambivalent aspects. He would always admit that his portrayal of the growing distance between the adolescent Apu and his widowed mother in *Aparajito* (The Unvanquished, 1956) had been psychologically influenced by his own experience with his widowed mother.[32]

Satyajit was always a quiet child and, as Marie Seton would write, 'so little at odds with the world that like his grandfather, no one ever saw him lose his temper'.[33] The boy was not a fussy eater and cared little for clothes. He did not like strict routines and although inter-ested in sport, it was not his primary passion.[34] He would sit quietly for hours, gazing at the world outside—at the sky, at trees, or birds. When taken out for drives by relatives, he would always want to go to the then-new Dhakuria Lakes, which was full of trees and birds and the same love for nature was expressed during a slightly later trip to Santiniketan with his mother and Madhuri Mahalanobis.[35] But the young Ray was not simply a nature-worshipper. In the Garpar house, he would spend his afternoons in the press on the ground floor and in the compositors' room, watching type being composed, blocks being made with a huge process camera, or covers of *Sandesh* being printed in colour. He would often scribble something and hand it to the oper-ator of the process camera for inclusion in the next issue of *Sandesh*. The operator would play along, holding the scribble under the lens, and showing the delighted child the inverted image of his drawing.[36] 'Whenever I smell oil of turpentine, the vision of the block-making department of U. Ray & Sons rises before my eyes,' Satyajit was to write more than five decades later.[37]

And of course, there were other children and relatives at Garpar with whom he could spend time. His uncle's house, although crammed with people, lacked anybody of Satyajit's age.[38] Perhaps his greatest friend at this time was Chhedi, the son of the Bihari maid Shyama. Chhedi was about five years older than Satyajit and always called him Raychaudhuri. Late in life, Ray still remembered Chhedi's skill with kites and ability to improvise toys out of unlikely objects. He would make an intriguing firecracker out of a key and a lantern with the earthenware pots in which yogurt is sold in Calcutta.[39] Generous as ever, Prasanta Das would later help Chhedi establish his own tai-loring business and when *Pather Panchali* was the talk of the town, Chhedi would jokingly announce to gatherings at the Das household that today's celebrity, 'my friend Raychaudhuri', was once his humble assistant at kite-flying.[40]

Some of Satyajit's favourite relatives, despite being scattered all over Calcutta, still kept in touch and added much to his life. Uncle Subimal would often visit with news from the mini-diaspora of their relatives and Kuladaranjan, who had once intrigued Satyajit by showing him how faded photographs were enlarged and finished with an airbrush, now came regularly to regale the growing boy with stories from the classical epics.[41] Satyajit was so taken with one episode from the Mahabharata—the grim and grisly death of Jayadrath—that he made Kuladaranjan recount it four times.[42] But despite all of this, much of the boy's time was spent alone and it was during these years that he developed what Marie Seton called an ability to be 'part of, yet apart from, his immediate surroundings', to work with 'complete concentration though the greatest hubbub may be going on around him'.[43]

After Satyajit's death in 1992, his aunt and first teacher, Madhuri, said that whenever she thought of Satyajit, she saw 'a quiet boy, sitting alone, hand on cheek, thinking—or drawing or listening to music'.[44] His musical ear had developed early. Even as an infant, he had noticed that if one rolled a marble over the stone slabs of the Garpar sitting room floor, the sound of the rolling marble changed as it passed from slab to slab.[45] His lifelong passion for Western classical music was kindled in childhood by presents from Prasanta Mahalanobis's younger brother Prafulla.[46] Mahalanobis, whom Ray called Uncle Bula and who married his Aunt Madhuri, ran a shop called Carr and Mahalanobis (founded by his father Prabodh Mahalanobis and physician Nilratan Sircar, whose surname had provided the Carr), which specialized in gramophones and sporting equipment.[47] The presents were two toy gramophones (Kiddyphone, produced in the UK, and Pigmyphone, a German import) with about forty tiny records of marches and waltzes which Satyajit came to love as much as the Tagore songs he heard so often from his mother or his aunt Kanak Das.[48] (Incidentally, Uncle Bula also introduced the boy to the rather more mundane pleasures of ice cream, which the boy thought was too cold and asked for it to be warmed.)[49] The Blue Danube waltz was a particular favourite and he then discovered a Berlin State Opera Orchestra recording of one movement—the rondo—of Fritz Kreisler playing Beethoven's violin concerto and was entranced by it. 'It seemed a type of music I was totally familiar with; it didn't seem alien,' he would later declare.[50]

There was more conventional entertainment too. The young Satyajit greatly enjoyed going to the circus and also to carnivals. He was struck by the Ferris wheels at the latter but especially intrigued by stalls offering numerous ways of gambling.[51] Magic shows were also of great interest to the boy and once, watching a Bengali magician doing remarkable tricks at a wedding feast, he developed the ambition of becoming a magician himself.[52] Until the time he went to college, Ray would buy books on magic and practise tricks standing before a mirror.[53] And, of course, like most solitary children, he also loved to lose himself in books, often spending his afternoons leafing through the ten-volume *Book of Knowledge*, a British encyclopaedia for children that was very popular in Bengali middle-class households not only in Ray's time but well into the 1960s. Another favourite was the four-volume *Romance of Famous Lives*—the famous lives, as he remarked later, were all of Westerners but he enjoyed them nonetheless, especially the illustrations.[54] He also read a lot of fiction, especially detective stories—Agatha Christie, S.S. Van Dine, Ellery Queen, Arthur Conan Doyle—and the humorous novels of P.G. Wodehouse.[55] Later in life, he would go to the National Library every Saturday and read 'everything, from the *Encyclopaedia Britannica* to biographies', taking copious notes. Little of this voracious reading, however, was in Bengali. The filmmaker whose stellar career would be indebted to Bengali literature remained almost ignorant of Bengali literature until he began to design book covers for the publisher Signet Press in the 1940s.

Although Ray, arguably, shared many Brahmo moral and social ideals, he had reacted very negatively to Brahmo religious ceremonies as a child and never participated in Brahmo Samaj activities in his adult life.[56] When he was a child, his mother would drag him to the Maghotsava every year but he was bored stiff by the endless sermons and prayers.[57] The only things he did enjoy were some of the hymns and songs, especially those with 'a Western tinge to them'. Two compositions by Rabindranath Tagore, '*Anandalokay Mangalalokay* or the stately chorus, *Padoprantay rakho shebokey*,' he recalled, 'came as a wonderful relief after three exhausting hours of sermon'.[58] Brahmoism, he felt, suffered from the lack of a truly joyous, all-inclusive festival like the Durga Puja or Christmas.[59] He was particularly fascinated by Christmas, becoming so obsessed with Father Christmas after beholding his portly form at the toy department of Calcutta's poshest department store that once, when he was nine, a cousin dressed up as Father Christmas in the middle of June and put presents into the stocking waiting on Satyajit's bedpost, while the boy, pretending to be asleep, watched this unfolding drama with great delight through half-open eyes.[60]

The Family and the World

Even though Satyajit never experienced the stable, prosperous, and creative family environment that his father had enjoyed, he was not deprived of the sense of belonging to a particular clan with a particular heritage. Much of this was transmitted to him by his mother, uncle Subimal or great-uncle Kuladaranjan, but some of it was also conveyed less directly through the revival of *Sandesh* in October 1931 under the joint editorship of Sudhabindu Biswas—Karunabindu's brother—and Subinoy Ray.[61] Leela Majumdar (then Leela Ray), who had debuted in the magazine during Sukumar's editorship, now became a regular writer and illustrator but Subinoy's greatest coup was to serialize Rabindranath Tagore's fantasy *Shey* (He) with the poet's own enigmatic drawings. Apart from two poems published in Sukumar's time, this was Tagore's only contribution to *Sandesh*.[62] Although Satyajit loved the revived *Sandesh*, other children probably did not and sales were too disappointing for the venture to continue.[63] Buddhadev Bose opined that the new *Sandesh*, rather like Sherlock Holmes after his return from the dead, lacked the flavour and character of the first incarnation, but the problem may have been quite the opposite.[64] The new series may have stuck far too closely to Upendrakishore's original programme instead of reinventing it for the 1930s. 'Everything beautiful, everything innocent, everything instructive—using them to entertain and through entertaining, educate—that is the main objective of *Sandesh*,' announced the first editorial of Subinoy's version, and that, clearly, proved to be too little or too staid for the new age.[65]

Fortunately, Satyajit did not have to rely only on the revived *Sandesh* for experiencing his family heritage. Apart from the regular visits of Kuladaranjan and Subimal, the boy also loved visiting the numerous talented children of Hemendramohan Bose, the great-uncle who had passed away five years before Satyajit's birth.[66] The Bose house was a fun place and full of high-spirited activity, the like of which, Ray wrote, he had never found elsewhere.[67] One of Bose's sons, Nitindramohan (Nitin) was already dabbling in films and the young Satyajit recalled seeing one of Uncle Nitin's early successes—a film of a wild elephant hunt in Tripura, which he had sold to the Fox studio in America for more than a thousand dollars—on the Bose family projector.[68] Satyajit would never be a big fan of Nitin Bose's films, praising their technical qualities but finding them 'a strange concoction' otherwise.[69] Still, it was an unusual experience for a middle-class Bengali boy of that period to have a real live filmmaker in the family and the experience, at the very least, made the film industry seem a little less alien to him.

During the summer and autumn vacations at Vidyasagar Bani Bhavan, Suprabha Ray took her son to visit her own and the Rays' many relatives scattered across Bengal and India. One trip was to Lucknow, where lived Suprabha's cousin, the barrister, lyricist, composer, and former member of Sukumar Ray's Monday Club, Atulprasad Sen. Much to the delight of the musical Satyajit, Sen's house was always full of music and musicians. Once, the classical singer Shrikrishna Narayan Ratanjankar came and sang a piece in the early-morning raga of Bhairavi, from which Atulprasad Sen derived his own Bengali song 'Suno, sey dakey aamare' (Hark, he calls me). The experience imprinted itself on Satyajit's mind and he would use Sen's song with haunting effect in his 1969 film *Aranyer Din Ratri* (Days and Nights in the Forest). Of course, there were limits to the boy's musical sensibility. When Sen and Suprabha Ray dragged him to a lecture on Indian classical music in English—a language he did not yet follow with ease—he kept nodding off and later lamented, 'I wish I had known then that the lecturer was Vishnu Narayan Bhatkhande, whose erudition and musical expertise were virtually unequalled in India.'[70]

The family had other relatives in Lucknow and some of them had children of Satyajit's age. In their company, Ray got to see many of Lucknow's glorious old monuments, so different in their style from what he had seen in Calcutta. They reminded him of the Arabian Nights and he was captivated by the great labyrinth (the *bhulbhulaiya*) in the Bara Imambara—a maze so complicated that many people foolhardy enough to enter it without a guide were reputed to have died inside. The cannon damage on the walls of the ruined British Residency or the plaque commemorating the death of Sir Henry Lawrence brought history alive for him, and some of that childhood excitement was evident in his recreations of historic Lucknow in several stories and one film—*Shatranj ke Khilari* (The Chess Players, 1977).[71]

On another trip with his mother to see relatives in the hill resort of Darjeeling, the seven-year-old Ray had his first experience of school. The eldest daughter of Sivanath Sastri, Hemlata Sarkar, had set up a school in Darjeeling and Suprabha Ray taught there during her visit. She took her son with her and because the whole school was assembled in one large hall, the boy could see his mother teaching at one end of the room while he was studying at another end.[72] Far more memorable was the peak of Kanchanjangha, which he had previously known only from a painting by Upendrakishore. Kanchanjangha at dawn would always be the world's most beautiful scene, bar none, for Satyajit and he would use the peak symbolically in *Kanchanjangha* (1962), his first colour film and his first original screenplay. As a child, however, he was deeply embarrassed when, in the middle of a large crowd (including some Europeans) admiring the peak revealing itself gradually at sunrise, his mother had burst into a full-throated rendition of *Jaya Hok, Jaya Hok, Naba Arunodaya*, Tagore's rousing invocation of a new dawn.[73]

The young Ray and his mother also went periodically to Bihar, to visit Aunt Punyalata and her husband, Arunnath Chakrabarti. The latter worked in the Bihar Civil Service and moved around with his family all over the province; most often, however, he was posted in the town of Hazaribag. They had two daughters—Ruby (Kalyani) and Nini (Nalini)—but as was usual in the Ray family, the household also included the three children of Arunnath's younger brother, Kirannath, of whom one, Kalyan Chakrabarti, shared the young Satyajit's dawning interest in photography, stamp collecting, and solving crossword puzzles. (It was also Kalyan who dressed up as Father Christmas in midsummer to entertain Satyajit.)[74] The two were so competitive and disputatious over photography that their exchanges came to be known to the family as the 'Ray–Chakrabarty fight'.[75] Often, other members of the Ray clan—Kuladaranjan Ray and his two daughters, Pramadaranjan Ray and members of his large family, Subinoy Ray and his son, or the unmarried Subimal Ray—would be visiting the Chakrabartys at the same time and they would spend their evenings playing indoor games.[76]

Not all of Suprabha Ray's visits were to relatives. When Satyajit was eight, she took him to Santiniketan and at his first meeting with Nandalal Bose, who would later be one of his major mentors, he asked the artist to draw something in his autograph book and got four little sketches. Then it was the turn of Tagore himself, who obliged with an eight-line poem but warned him that he would not fully appreciate its meaning until he had grown up: 'I have travelled all round the world to see rivers and mountains but forgot to look at the dewdrop on the little blade of grass just outside my door.'[77] Decades later, Ray declared that Tagore's poem was not only 'one of the best things he ever wrote in a small manner', but summed up the entire Indian aesthetic tradition: 'The presence of the essential thing in a very small detail, which you must catch in order to express the larger thing; and this is in Indian art, this is in Rajput miniatures, this is in Ajanta, this is in Ellora, this is in the classics, in Kalidasa, in *Sakuntala*, in folk-poetry, in folk-singing.'[78] And, he might well have added, in his own films.

The Schoolboy

Satyajit was sent to school quite late but did not experience any difficulties in adjusting to it. Ashis Nandy has claimed that Ray went to a 'quasi-Edwardian, élite public school'.[79] Although the young Ray's tastes were Western, Nandy's description of his school is wildly inaccurate. The curriculum of the Ballygunge Government School did emphasize the study of English, some of its teachers did wear suits, and a few students did come from the Westernized upper middle classes with attitudes to match.[80] That, however, was all that was Western about it. It was an entirely Bengali institution and very different in curriculum, medium of instruction, and general tone from what Nandy seems to imagine.[81]

Satyajit was good at his studies, often ranking near the top of his class, and passed his Matriculation examination in the first division. Members of his family all noted his intelligence and depth of knowledge.[82] His memoirs are full of deft, richly observed portraits of his quirky teachers, but whether then or later in college, Satyajit—unlike Apu in his film *Aparajito*—would never find much excitement in formal education.[83] The one skill which Ray excelled in at school was drawing but he was too shy to show it off. During prize day at Ray's school, there was an event called 'music drawing'. One student sang while another illustrated that song by concurrently drawing a picture on a blackboard with coloured chalk—all of this, of course, while the assembled parents and students watched. When asked to perform this task Satyajit declined simply because of his intense shyness and stage-fright. (He even hated to win prizes, because he found it terrifying to walk up to the stage in front of so many people.)[84] Despite his shyness, Satyajit was liked by his classmates, though often teased about his family connections. Once the boys discovered that he was the son of Sukumar Ray and the nephew of singer Kanak Das and cricketing hero Kartik Bose, they inquired whether King George V was his grandfather.[85] Ray, however, was not the only boy with celebrity connections—there was also Anil Gupta, a grandson of Lord (Satyendra Prasanna) Sinha (1863–1928), a very wealthy barrister who, after serving as the Government of India's standing counsel, Advocate General, and the Law member of the Viceroy's Executive Council over the first decade of the twentieth century, had been elevated to the British peerage after the First World War and appointed the Under-Secretary of State for India.[86]

Anil Gupta dazzled the boys with all kinds of luxuries that they could not dream of owning and although a very different kind of person from Satyajit, he would play an important role by deepening Satyajit's already strong interest in Western classical music.[87] The two friends would go on record hunts together and their first great buy was one movement of Beethoven's Fifth Symphony. Satyajit, of course, could not buy records with the abandon of his wealthy frien' Once, he found a nine-disc set of Beethoven's Ninth Symphony had to save up his pocket money and buy one disc a month.[88], then chanced upon Mozart's 'Eine kleine Nachtmusik', and d Gupta reminisced, 'lost his sleep that night'.[89] By the time tl[90] out of school, Gupta had become one of Satyajit's close cal Along with a few others, they would play games to test m a proficiency. A random section, for example, would b, the record and the listeners asked to identify the work, first movement being played, and the conductor. Wh music and got all the points right won the game.[91] We was my became an obsession for Ray. 'For about ten with the doing nothing but buying records and buy would all bedside reading,' he recalled. 'I would list with staff scores and then when I read them again, an entire come back. And that is when I started identify any notation.'[92] He also discovered that nd.[93] Oddly, symphony after listening to it a few ent, whether musical work he knew after hea though, Satyajit would never le Indian or Western.[94]

Although music was his first passion, images, too, were dear to the young Satyajit. When a boy of six, he had discovered that the light filtering through shutters cast inverted pictures of street scenes on the walls of his bedroom at a particular time of the afternoon. He spent many hours lying in bed watching this 'free bioscope' of people and traffic moving on the wall of the room. He also found that he could observe miniaturized and inverted scenes of life on the street by holding a piece of frosted glass to a hole in the front door.[95] The images impressed him even more when they were accompanied by sounds.[96] The joys of turning two-dimensional photographs into three-dimensional scenes with a Victorian stereoscope also kept him occupied during the long, solitary afternoons when his mother was away working. He had a magic lantern as well and was so fascinated by it that in middle age, he suspected that it may well have triggered his interest in films.[97]

That interest did not in fact develop very early but there were some interesting pointers towards what was to come. Once, during a game of doctors and patients, his cousin Ruby (Kalyani, daughter of Punyalata) presented him with a professional-looking doctor's bag with the label 'Dr Satyajit Ray, MD, FRCS, MRCP'. Satyajit, however, shook his head gravely and said he would never be a doctor. 'I'll go to Germany, learn how to make films, and come back and make films here,' he announced.[98] On the face of it, this was an unusual ambition for the son of a family and a community that frowned so severely upon the 'immoral' character of the professional stage. Film actresses hailed from the same morally dubious backgrounds as stage actresses and the atmosphere of the film industry had never aroused any admiration among puritans. But it is one of the paradoxes of Brahmo history that the community was rather less opposed to the cinema than to the stage. Apart from Satyajit Ray himself and his uncle Nitin Bose, such film pioneers as Himansu Rai, Niranjan Pal, Dhirendranath Ganguly and Madhu Bose were all Brahmos and the list would be easily be included technical personnel.[99] For many years, however, the Rays could hardly be a viewer of films. As long as he was at Garpar, the cinema halls were too far for regular visits but once he had moved with his mother to the household of the fun-loving Prasanta Das Gupta, cinema became one of his regular entertainments, although the theatre, needless to say, was strictly forbidden.[100] Only morally wholesome products were permitted and cinema and family went together.[101] Ray's film viewing commenced with Chaplin, Buster Keaton, and Harold Lloyd but the films he recalled most fondly in adult life were Ben Hur, The Count of Monte Cristo, The Thief of Baghdad, and Uncle Tom's Cabin.[102] While seeing Uncle Tom's Cabin with the Das family, he had had his first experience of the power of images over emotions. When, in the last scene of the film, the ghost of Tom visits Simon Legree and Legree lashes at him with his whip, one member of the Das party leapt up from his seat, screaming loudly in Bangal dialect: 'You whip him still, you swine, you *still* whip him? Just you wait, you satan, you'll soon get your just deserts!'[103] Fortunately, perhaps, this was an isolated incident and the only sounds in Ray's earliest viewing experience were those of the live piano music accompanying silent films in the better cinemas and he was to become a profound admirer of this lost art.[104]

When the talkies came, Ray went through 'a Laurel-and-Hardy phase, a Tarzan phase and a swashbuckling adventure phase'.[105] He also had his first, traumatic exposure to Bengali commercial cinema, a memory that he never managed to exorcise. A cousin of his mother's took him once to see Tarzan the Ape Man (starring Johnnie Weissmuller) but the show was sold out and noting the nine-year-old's evident disappointment, the uncle took him instead to a nearby cinema showing the Bengali silent Kaal Parinoy (The Doomed Marriage, 1930).[106] Ray described the film as an 'early example of Indian soft porn' and pushing sixty, he could still recall the unsettling mixture of disgust and fascination that the film had evoked: 'The hero and the heroine—or was it the vamp?—newly married, were in bed, and a close-up showed the woman's leg rubbing against the man's. I was only nine then, but old enough to realise that I had strayed into forbidden territory.' The uncle was no less conscious of the inappropriateness of the film but the boy met his whispered urgings to leave 'with a stony silence'.[107] A psychoanalyst might find in this incident the origin of the sexual puritanism that allegedly marked Satyajit's own films, but it is worth contrasting his revulsion at Kaal Parinoy with his reactions to Ernst Lubitsch's Love Parade, The Smiling Lieutenant, and One Hour With You, erotic comedies that he had somehow managed to see despite strict family supervision and which had opened 'a forbidden world' to him, 'only half understood, but observed with a tingling curiosity'.[108] In other words, it may not simply have been his puritanism that led to his horror at Kaal Parinoy, but its lack of style, urbanity, and wit. There was nothing in the Bengali cinema of his boyhood that Ray found sophisticated enough to satisfy him—and precious little in his adult years. *Indian* cinema he could sometimes praise but mainstream Bengali cinema remained entirely and forever beyond redemption.[109]

When he was about fifteen, Ray was allowed to choose his own films and went wild: 'Westerns, gangster films, horror films, musicals, comedies, dramas and all those other species which Hollywood served up with such expertise, came tumbling my way to be lapped up with ever-increasing appetite.'[110] Virtually all the films he saw were American and initially at least, he was more a film-fan than a critical cinephile.[111] The entire Hollywood 'package'—stars of course, but also good scripts and sleek production values—greatly appealed to him and he candidly disclaimed any highbrow or avant-garde elements in his love for Hollywood.[112] As he recalled while accepting his Oscar from his deathbed in 1992, he even wrote fan mail to Hollywood glitterati. The actress Deanna Durbin, whom Ray adored 'not only because of her looks and her obvious gift as an actress, but because of her lovely soprano voice', sent a reply but Ginger Rogers, another of Ray's icons, did not.[113] As he grew older, however, he became more of a serious student of the art: 'I noted each title in a little pocket diary, adding brief critical comments, and my own star rating.' One of the few films that got a four-star rating (the highest) was *David Copperfield* and no Bengali film ever received more than two.[114] If he liked a film, he *had* to see it again and again until he had the whole film in his head, just as he listened to a symphony repeatedly until he had 'mastered every detail' of the entire work.[115] The fan mail now went to directors, not stars, but not to much avail. An effusive twelve-page letter to Billy Wilder, written after seeing *Double Indemnity*, was ignored.[116]

Towards the Modern and the Cosmopolitan

The young Satyajit might have been fairly Bengali in his everyday life but his cultural preferences, it should be obvious from the foregoing, were almost entirely Western.

He may have asked Nandalal Bose for sketches but his attitude towards Santiniketan, Santiniketanites, and their art long remained ill-informed and anything but respectful.[117] The few Santiniketanites he knew had made a poor impression on him. They 'all had long hair, and spoke Bengali in a strange affected sing-song', he wrote, and, although he is unlikely to have read his father's and grandfather's critiques of Bengal School art at that point, he shared their dislike of Bengal School art.[118] 'My mind rebelled against the effete style and content,' he was to declare.[119] His own youthful taste in art, he confessed, 'had been formed by the same ten-volume *Book of Knowledge* which had told me about Beethoven' and his favourite paintings and sculptures were 'Gainsborough's *Blue Boy*, Franz Hals's *Laughing Cavalier*, Michelangelo's *David*, Rodin's *Thinker*, Landseer's proud stag with the spreading antlers, and Joshua Reynolds's *Bubbles*, which, in those days, was used in advertisements for Pears Soap'.[120]

This one-dimensional Europhilia would begin to leave him only after Suprabha Ray persuaded him to train in art at Santiniketan. It was under the tutelage of Nandalal Bose, Binodebihari Mukherjee, and Ramkinkar Baij, and in the company of his talented friends Prithwish Neogy, Dinkar Kowshik, and Asesh Bandyopadhyay—not Rabindranath Tagore, as imagined by so many—that Satyajit Ray would discover the true diversity and profundity of Indian art and music, while the Santiniketan library and the friendship of the music-loving German-Jewish professor Alex Aronson would deepen his old love for European music, literature, and culture. Familiarity with modern Bengali literature would come even later. Satyajit, to be sure, would perpetuate his family's tradition of being at once Bengali, Indian, global, traditional, and modern but it would take years of preparation and many serendipitous encounters for him to reach that point.

In one respect, however, Satyajit would not follow the path of his forefathers: the story of the Rays would never again be an entrepreneurial one after the collapse of U. Ray & Sons. 'My father and grandfather', Satyajit once asserted, 'were idealists. They wanted to change so many things ... they were not practical men.'[121] He was right—but only up to a point. Upendrakishore Ray, to be sure, was not a ruthless businessman and Sukumar was even less of one. Even Hemendramohan Bose, despite being so dynamic an entrepreneur, failed to achieve as much as he might have. But neither Upendrakishore nor Hemendramohan had gone into business simply to acquire wealth. Trade and enterprise, for them, were the means to bring about technological and social modernity and this combination of business, technology, and reformism was distinctive for the late nineteenth century, when Indian reformers and modernists hailed mostly from the ranks of lawyers, journalists, teachers, government officers, or zamindars. Satyajit Ray was being unfair in dismissing his ancestors' entrepreneurial interests as impractical idealism.

Sukumar's untimely death, the failure of the family business, and, not least, changes in Bengali society in the 1930s and beyond made the old combination unsustainable, however. The Rays now retreated permanently from the uncertain world of business and even on the question of modernism, attempted few original initiatives. Subinoy, Subimal, and Sukhalata carried on with children's literature alone—which had been just one of the family's many interests—and that mostly on Upendrakishore's aging model. With his graphic designs and, subsequently, his films and literary work, Satyajit would recapture some of the rooted cosmopolitanism of Upendrakishore and Sukumar but he would not practise their entrepreneurialism. Indeed, he would develop an antipathy to businesspeople, confessing that he considered all of them to be at least 'slightly immoral'.[122] In his films, there would be many indications of his endorsement of his ancestors' progressive social ideals but he would never be involved in any reformist organization, least of all the Brahmo Samaj, which, by his time, had admittedly lost much of its original reformist fervour. So, although some of the progressive, modernist projects of the nineteenth-century Rays would flourish again, albeit in transformed versions, in Satyajit's polymathic career, their distinctive blend of modernism, reformism, trade and enterprise would never again be seen after the 1920s.

Notes

1. Subinoy, who consistently used the original family surname, Raychaudhuri, edited *Sandesh* from October 1923 to October 1924. See *Bengal Library Catalogue of Books Registered in the Presidency of Bengal: Appendix to the Calcutta Gazette*, 4th quarter (1923): 53. He had a tragic life. A diabetic like his father, he worked for the Geological Survey of India after the collapse of the family business, later contracting tuberculosis and dying at the age of fifty-seven. His widow, Pushpalata, ended her life at a home for elderly women at a date that seems not to have been recorded, and their only son, Saralkumar, developed an intractable mental illness and spent most of his life at the Mental Hospital in Ranchi. See Bratati Chakravarty, *Bangla Shishu Sahitya Charcha: Ray Paribar* (Calcutta: Dey Book Store, 1997), 187–8; and Leela Majumdar, *Pakdandi* (Calcutta: Ananda, 1986), 99–100, 200. Subinoy wrote many humorous stories and science articles and also devised numerous

riddles for *Sandesh* as well as other children's magazines. For a selection of these, see Parthajit Gangopadhyay, ed., *Subinoy Raychaudhuri: Rachana Sangraha* (Calcutta: Dey's, 2013).

2. Satyajit Ray and Partha Basu, eds, *Sukumar Sahityasamagra*, 3 vols (Calcutta: Ananda Publishers, 1989), 3: 257–61.

3. L. Majumdar, *Pakdandi*, 99–100, 149, 200, 205.

4. Siddhartha Ghosh, 'Upendrakishore: Shilpi o Karigar', *Ekshan*, 16, no. 6 (1984): 100–2; Partha Basu, *Satyajit Ray* (Calcutta: Paschimbanga Bangla Akademi, 2006), 44.

5. After spending a night behind bars, Subimal came home gleefully, recounting how he had dined well at 'their' expense and impressed every inmate and warder with his 'yogic' trick of taking in water through the nostrils and expelling it through the mouth. See B. Chakravarty, *Bangla Shishu Sahitya*, 198.

6. Lalitmohan Gupta and other old associates of Upendrakishore left to start their own photoengraving companies. See Siddhartha Ghosh, *Karigari Kalpana o Bangali Udyog* (Calcutta: Dey's, 1988), 119–21.

7. P. Basu, *Satyajit Ray*, 44–5.

8. Leela Majumdar, *Aar Konokhaney* (Calcutta: Mitra o Ghosh, 1968), 124; L. Majumdar, *Pakdandi*, 149, 180. When he took his biographer Marie Seton to the Garpar house in the 1960s, Ray noticed that the room in which he was born was now the headmaster's office. See *Nijer Aynaye Satyajit: Dirghatama o Shesh Sakshatkar* (Calcutta: Badwip, 1993), 2.

9. See S. Ghosh, 'Upendrakishore: Shilpi o Karigar', 47–144. In 1943, when Satyajit Ray's advertising colleague Dilip Gupta proposed republishing Sukumar Ray's *Abol-Tabol* and *Haw-Jaw-Baw-Raw-Law* with new illustrations by Satyajit Ray, a whole generation had grown up without seeing the books in their intended form and Sukumar's heirs had not received any royalty for almost two decades. The cautious Gupta inserted a lawyer's notice in newspapers before publishing the books just in case Karunabindu Biswas claimed copyright; Biswas ignored it and for some years, the Signet editions were available concurrently with Biswas's. See *Nijer Aynaye Satyajit*, 4.

10. Marie Seton, *Portrait of a Director: Satyajit Ray*, expanded edition (New Delhi: Penguin Books, 2003), 91.

11. They returned to Calcutta only after Subinoy had found a job in the Geological Survey of India. See Manasi Dasgupta, *Upendrakishore Raychaudhuri (1863–1915)* (Calcutta: Bangiya Sahitya Parishad, 2004), 54.

12. When Bidhumukhi died in 1927, Subimal moved again, this time to his brother Pramadaranjan's home and, in his final years, he lived with Satyajit and his family. See P. Basu, *Satyajit Ray*, 47; B. Chakravarty, *Bangla Shishu Sahitya*, 196. Possessing a warm and whimsical imagination, Subimal was particularly fond of recounting long, often nonsensical stories to children, and coining bizarre nicknames for relatives. Satyajit became Nulmuli,

388 THE RAYS BEFORE SATYAJIT

Kuladaranjan's daughter Ila became Wang, whilst Ila's father was named Dedux. The steely Suprabha Ray was revealingly named Bajra-Bouthan (Thunder Sister-in-Law). See Satyajit Ray, *Jakhan Chhoto Chhilam* (Calcutta: Ananda, 1982), 41. Subimal never married and over his peripatetic life, kept in touch with all the scattered members of the vast Ray family and served as a liaison man. See B. Chakravarty, *Bangla Shishu Sahitya*, 199. He wrote quite a bit for *Sandesh* in its later incarnations and for many years, maintained a diary with extraordinary colour-coded entries that meticulously listed his daily activities but without revealing anything too personal. A simple, bookish, and devout man, he seemed to Marie Seton (who had obtained virtually all her information on the history of the Ray family from him) to 'embody the family ideal of restrained probity'. See Seton, *Portrait of a Director*, 225–6. One of Subimal Ray's diaries (for 1968) is available in the Ray family collection.

13. P. Basu, *Satyajit Ray*, 36. On the practices of Brahmo widows, see Meredith Borthwick, *The Changing Role of Women in Bengal, 1849–1905* (Princeton: Princeton University Press, 1984), 148. Kadambini Ganguli's undated letter is available in the collections of the Ray family.

14. Madhuri, who was a schoolteacher for a while, was Satyajit's first teacher. She taught him the English and Bengali alphabets and then read some simple stories with him, drawing pictures (which were found clumsy by the future commercial artist) to illustrate them. See Madhuri Mahalanobis, 'Maniker Chhelebela', in *Sandesher Satyajit*, edited by Prasadranjan Ray and Debashis Sen (Calcutta: Shaibya, 2007), 88–91, at 88–9. Satyajit was a skilled artist from childhood; he had drawn such an excellent pencil portrait of Rammohan Roy that his cousin Nini (Nalini Das) had had it framed. See Nalini Das, *Sat Rajar Dhon Ek Manik: Satyajit Ray-er Chhelebela*, 2nd edn (Calcutta: Newscript, 2005), 95–6.

15. Seton, *Portrait of a Director*, 39 and Satyajit Ray, *Jakhan Chhoto Chhilam*, 25. Das married shortly afterwards and was to have two sons and two daughters. See Satyajit Ray, *My Years with Apu* (London: Faber & Faber, 1994), 4, 8; and Bijoya Ray, *Amader Katha* (Calcutta: Ananda, 2008), 67.

16. Two such 'guests' were Suprabha Ray's cousins Hirendranath Dasgupta, who had come from Dhaka in East Bengal to look for a job in Calcutta, and the man Satyajit called Nanimama (Uncle Nani), whose formal name is unknown. The latter was unmarried and very proficient in what Ray, perhaps wishing to be delicate, called 'feminine skills'. Adept at sewing and cooking, he later mastered leatherwork and even wrote a book on it. It was from him that Suprabha Ray learnt leatherwork. See B. Ray, *Amader Kathha*, 66; and Satyajit Ray, *Jakhan Chhoto Chhilam*, 30–1.

17. B. Ray, *Amader Katha*, 64.

18. Satyajit Ray, *My Years with Apu*, 4.

19. See D.M. Bose, 'Abala Bose: Her Life and Times', *Modern Review*, 119, no. 6 (June 1966): 441–56, at 455–6; Tanika Sarkar, Foreword to Abhijit Sen

and Anindita Bhaduri, eds, *Jyotirmoyee Gangopadhyayer Rachana Sankalan* (Calcutta: Dey's/Jadavpur University, 2007), 5–14; and Abala Bose, 'Vidyasagar Bani Bhavan', *Udayan*, 1, no. 8 (Agrahayan 1340 [December 1933]): 939–45 (my warm thanks to Debasis Mukhopadhyay for presenting me with the last article).

20. In the 1880s, Pandita Ramabai had founded such a home in the Bombay Presidency and in Bengal, the Brahmo reformer Sasipada Banerji had followed suit. See Ghulam Murshid, *Reluctant Debutante: Response of Bengali Women to Modernization, 1849–1905* (Rajshahi: Rajshahi University Sahitya Samsad, 1983), 190–1; and Abala Bose, 'Vidyasagar Bani Bhavan', 939.

21. Abala Bose, 'Vidyasagar Bani Bhavan', 942–3.

22. On Suprabha Ray's post at the Bani Bhavan, see Abala Bose, 'Vidyasagar Bani Bhavan', 941.

23. Satyajit Ray, *Jakhan Chhoto Chhilam*, 30–1.

24. Satyajit Ray, *Jakhan Chhoto Chhilam*, 31.

25. Seton, *Portrait of a Director*, 6–7, 41.

26. Satyajit Ray, *Jakhan Chhoto Chhilam*, 31.

27. Sharmila Tagore, 'Manikda' [1992], in Subrata Rudra, ed., *Satyajit: Jiban aar Silpa* (Calcutta: Pratibhas, 1996), 116–23, at 121.

28. Andrew Robinson, 'The Years before Apu: A Biographical Sketch', in *Satyajit Ray: A Vision of Cinema* (London: I. B. Tauris, 2005), 25–63, at 26; and P. Basu, *Satyajit Ray*, 50.

29. Satyajit Ray, *Jakhan Chhoto Chhilam*, 44, 59; Robinson, 'The Years before Apu', 26.

30. P. Basu, *Satyajit Ray*, 57.

31. Seton, *Portrait of a Director*, 41. Ray did occasionally use his voice in his films—the most famous being the artificially distorted chant of the King of the Ghosts in *Goopy Gyne Bagha Byne* (The Adventures of Goopy and Bagha, 1968)—but he never actually sang until his final film *Agantuk* (The Stranger, 1991), where he lent his voice for three brief songs, all performed on screen by Utpal Dutt.

32. Andrew Robinson, *Satyajit Ray: The Inner Eye*, 2nd edn (London: I. B. Tauris, 2003), 42.

33. Seton, *Portrait of a Director*, 40.

34. Nor was he very keen on physical exercise, as he discovered when the sturdy Pramadaranjan Ray made him join his own sons for callisthenics. Swimming was more attractive, partly because Ray was awed by Johnny Weissmuller's performance as Tarzan and the swimming club he joined had an autographed portrait of the great man hanging in its office. See Satyajit Ray, *Jakhan Chhoto Chhilam*, 35–9.

35. Madhuri Mahalanobis, 'Maniker Chhelebela', 89.

36. *Nijer Aynaye Satyajit*, 1.

37. Satyajit Ray, *Jakhan Chhoto Chhilam*, 13–15.

38.   See Robinson, 'The Years before Apu', 28.

39.   See the description of these (with Ray's own illustrations), in Satyajit Ray, *Jakhan Chhoto Chhilam*, 16–18.

40.   Somewhat more barbed was his recollection that the young 'Raychaudhuri' had a habit of complaining to his aunt Kanak Das about Chhedi, at which Das, without bothering to ascertain the truth of the charges, would give Chhedi a beating or lock him up in a bathroom. When such things happened, Chhedi would stop speaking to 'Raychaudhuri' but the rift would soon be healed. See Amiya Sanyal, *Prasanga Satyajit* (Calcutta: M.C. Sarkar, 2004), 10–11.

41.   Satyajit Ray, *Jakhan Chhoto Chhilam*, 39. Kuladaranjan was an excellent photographic technician and won a gold medal at the Indian Industrial and Agricultural Exhibition of 1906–7 for 'bromide paintings'. See *A Report of the Indian Industrial and Agricultural Exhibition, Calcutta, 1906–07* (Calcutta: 'Industrial India' Office, n.d.), 136.

42.   Arjun had resolved to burn himself to death if he could not slay Jayadrath but found it very hard to vanquish his adversary. So, Arjun's charioteer, the god Krishna, cast a spell that made the sky go dark, at which everybody thought that the sun had set and the battle was over for the day. Taking advantage of his adversary's inattention, Arjun now blew away Jayadrath's head, but that only led to a new problem. There was a curse (laid by Jayadrath's father) that the moment Jayadrath's head fell on the ground, the head of his killer would immediately explode. So, Arjun shot one arrow after another, transporting the cut head all the way to the lap of Jayadrath's aged father. Startled, the old man leapt up, his son's head fell to the ground and his own head exploded. Satyajit Ray, *Jakhan Chhoto Chhilam*, 39–40.

43.   Seton, *Portrait of a Director*, 40, 41.

44.   Madhuri Mahalanobis, 'Maniker Chhelebela', 91.

45.   *Nijer Aynaye Satyajit*, 2. Madhuri Mahalanobis also played the piano to entertain Manik but foreshadowing his later catholicity of musical taste, he would ask her to play the Tagore song 'Hyade go Nandarani, aamader Shyamke chhere dao'. He would occasionally try to play the piano but his grandfather's violin he never apparently touched. See Madhuri Mahalanobis, 'Maniker Chhelebela', 89.

46.   A skilled photographer and a good enough flautist to have played for plays directed by Rabindranath Tagore, Prafulla Mahalanobis also made many recordings of Tagore songs by Santiniketan artists and even the poet himself. Leela Majumdar remembered Mahalanobis as an extraordinarily generous soul, who felt genuinely happy to help people and volunteered to take up burdens others might shirk. See Hitendrakishore Raychaudhuri, *Upendrakishore o Masua Ray Paribarer Galpasalpa* (Calcutta: Firma KLM, 1984), 18; Sunirmal Basu, *Jiban KhatarKayek Pata* (1955), in *Sunirmal Rachana Sambhar*, 3 vols, edited by Nirmalendu Goutam and Haribandhu Mukhoti (Calcutta: Forward,

1973–75), 3 (1975): 161–340, at 256–7; Nalini Das, *Sat Rajar Dhon Ek Manik*, 65; Susobhan Sarkar, *Prasanga Rabindranath* (Calcutta: Ananda, 1982), 19; and L. Majumdar, *Pakdandi*, 173.

47. See Hirankumar Sanyal, *Parichoy-er Kuri Bachhar o Anyanya Smritichitra* (Calcutta: Papyrus, 1978), 190–1.

48. Later, Mahalanobis presented Ray with a crystal radio set. See Satyajit Ray, *Jakhan Chhoto Chhilam*, 21–2; Satyajit Ray, 'The Education of a Film-Maker', *New Left Review*, I/141 (September–October 1983): 79–94, at 81; 'Satyajit Ray', in *Talking Films: The Best of the Guardian Film Lectures*, edited by Andrew Britton (London: Fourth Estate, 1991), 81–102, at 93; Abhijit Dasgupta, 'Political Film Amader Deshey Bodh Hoy Kara Jay Na: Satyajit', *Anandalok*, 25, no. 8 (1 May 1999): 72.

49. Satyajit Ray, *Jakhan Chhoto Chhilam*, 15.

50. 'Satyajit Ray', in *Talking Films*, 93; A. Dasgupta, 'Political Film Amader Deshey Bodh Hoy Kara Jay Na', 72.

51. Satyajit Ray, *Jakhan Chhoto Chhilam*, 28. Very late in life and during a period of debilitating physical illness, Satyajit would become, in the words of his son, Sandip, a slot-machine freak, taking frequent trips to Nepal where gambling was legal and where he would spend much time in the casinos. See Robinson, *Satyajit Ray: The Inner Eye*, 10. The seeds of this interest may well have been planted at the carnivals of his childhood, although one presumes that his strict Brahmo guardians did not permit him to indulge in it then.

52. Encountering the magician on the street one day, he told him he wanted to learn magic from him—the magician immediately took out a pack of cards and taught him a simple card trick. The excited disciple, however, forgot to take the master's address and could not find him later. See Satyajit Ray, *Jakhan Chhoto Chhilam*, 27–8.

53. Satyajit Ray, *Jakhan Chhoto Chhilam*, 27–8.

54. Satyajit Ray, *Jakhan Chhoto Chhilam*, 25.

55. A. Dasgupta, 'Political Film Amader Deshey Bodh Hoy Kara Jay Na', 11.

56. 'As a child', Ray told Andrew Robinson, 'I found Hinduism much more exciting than Brahmoism, and Christianity too. When I think of Brahmoism I think of solemn sermons mainly. I don't think of being free from the shackles of orthodoxy.' See Robinson, 'The Years before Apu', 25.

57. 'After sitting on the same rug year after year and listening to the prayers with head lowered, I came to know the design of the rug by heart,' he wrote when he was almost sixty. See Satyajit Ray, *Jakhan Chhoto Chhilam*, 19–20.

58. Satyajit Ray, 'The Education of a Film-Maker', 81. Rajnarayan Basu, an associate of Debendranath Tagore's and one of the prominent members of the Adi Brahmo Samaj, had remarked in his autobiography that the Brahmo faith had two dimensions: one sweet and the other austere; the Brahmo hymns

constituted the former and the services the latter. See Rajnarayan Basu, *Atmacharit* (Calcutta: P.C. Dass, 1909), 79. Ray, obviously, had no patience for the austere.

59. Satyajit Ray, *Jakhan Chhoto Chhilam*, 19–21. As a child, Leela Majumdar too regretted that her family's Brahmoism excluded them from the festivities of the Durga Puja. See L. Majumdar, *Aar Konokhaney*, 22–3; and L. Majumdar, *Pakdandi*, 19, 33, 36. For another complaint about the lack of festivity in Brahmoism, see Saraladevi Chaudhurani, *Jibaner Jharapata* (Calcutta: Sahitya Sansad, 1957), 63–6.

60. Satyajit Ray, *Jakhan Chhoto Chhilam*, 21. 'When Manik showed no interest in Father Christmas one year, we realized that he had grown up,' recalled his cousin Nalini Das. See N. Das, *Sat Rajar Dhon Ek Manik*, 90.

61. Nalini Das, '*Sandesh* Sampadak Satyajit Ray', in *Nana Rupey Satyajit*, edited by Bijit Ghosh (Calcutta: Punascha, 2003), 183–8, at 185. For the complete three-volume collection (1931–3) of the second series of *Sandesh*, see http://www.savifa.uni-hd.de/thematicportals/periodicals/sandesa.html (accessed on 15 November 2011).

62. Hemantakumar Adhya, *Sukumar Ray: Jibankatha* (Calcutta: Pustak Bipani, 1990), 84.

63. Satyajit Ray, *Jakhan Chhoto Chhilam*, 35; Nalini Das, '*Sandesh* Sampadak Satyajit Ray', 185. On the persistence of this ideal even in the third (and still continuing) series of *Sandesh*, see Shyamasree Lal, '"*Sandesh*" and the Child's World of Imagination', *India International Centre Quarterly*, 10, no. 4 (1983): 433–42, at 440–1. Although Satyajit Ray's detective stories or his tales featuring ghosts, crooked scientists, and extra-sensory events would repeatedly undermine the straightlaced, positivistic rationalism of his co-editors Nalini Das and Leela Majumdar and win the hearts of countless readers of all ages, the magazine, as a whole, showed no inclination to rethink Upendrakishore's model.

64. Buddhadev Bose, 'Bangla Shishusahitya' (1952), in Buddhadev Bose, *Sahityacharcha* (Calcutta: Dey's, 1976), 38–64, at 46.

65. See the untitled, unsigned, and unpaginated introduction to the first volume of *Sandesh*, new ser., 1, no. 1 (September 1931). Available at http://archiv.ub.uni-heidelberg.de/savifadok/volltexte/2010/1130 (accessed on 10 November 2011).

66. Satyajit Ray, 'Bhumika' [Foreword] to Siddhartha Ghosh, 'Jantrarasik H. Bose', 54.

67. Satyajit Ray, *Jakhan Chhoto Chhilam*, 19.

68. Parmanand, 'Nitin Bose: Star amidst Stars', 24; 'Profiles of Pioneers: Nitin Bose', in *Indian Motion Picture Almanac 1974–75*, edited by B. Jha (Calcutta: Shot Publications, 1976) 37; and Satyajit Ray, *Jakhan Chhoto Chhilam*, 19.

69. *Benegal on Ray—Satyajit Ray, a film by Shyam Benegal*, script reconstructed by Alakananda Datta and Samik Bandyopadhyay (Calcutta: Seagull,

1988), 108. Nevertheless, it is worth noting that much of Nitin Bose's 1938 film *Desher Mati* (Hindi version: *Dharti Mata*) was shot on location, using natural light and Satyajit Ray saw it at least twice. It may have inspired his own naturalistic approach in *Pather Panchali*. See 'Profiles of Pioneers: Nitin Bose', 40; Ujjal Chakraborty, Aniruddha Dhar, and Atanu Chakraborty, *Panchali theke Oscar*, 2 vols (Calcutta: Pratibhas, 2010), 1: 21; and *Nijer Aynaye Satyajit*, 16.

70. Satyajit Ray, *Jakhan Chhoto Chhilam*, 44.

71. Satyajit Ray, *Jakhan Chhoto Chhilam*, 45.

72. Satyajit Ray, *Jakhan Chhoto Chhilam*, 48.

73. Satyajit Ray, *Jakhan Chhoto Chhilam*, 48–9. Ray would use this song evocatively in his 1961 documentary, *Rabindranath Tagore*.

74. Nalini Das, *Sat Rajar Dhon Ek Manik*, 83–4, 106–8. At the age of fifteen, Ray would send a photograph of Kashmir to the *Boy's Own Paper* and outdo his father by winning a prize of one pound. Kashmir itself, where Suprabha had taken him as a special treat, he did not greatly enjoy. To the horror of his mother, the boy, instead of being captivated by the scenic beauty of the valley, kept complaining about the absence of cinemas. See P. Basu, *Satyajit Ray*, 64; and Robinson, *Satyajit Ray: The Inner Eye*, 36.

75. Nalini Das, *Sat Rajar Dhon Ek Manik*, 84–5, 96. Seton (*Portrait of a Director*, 41) opined that Ray's 'early photographs, like his drawings, revealed no conspicuous talent' but such assessments are not necessarily valid. At least one photograph taken in Calcutta with a sitting teenage Ray and his mother standing behind his chair, facing the camera somewhat obliquely, was brilliantly composed and has an added interest in that it was, in twenty-first-century terminology, a selfie. He had tied a string to the camera's shutter and pulled it while posing for the photograph. The picture is reproduced with an explanatory caption in Satyajit Ray, *Jakhan Chhoto Chhilam*, unnumbered plate between pages 40 and 41. The same has also been used on the back-cover of the present volume.

76. Apart from old reliables like cards, snakes and ladders, or ludo, they played a whispering game in which one player would whisper something into the ears of the adjacent player and the words would be passed around in a circle, undergoing amusing and unpredictable transformations. The memory game that featured so prominently in Ray's film *Aranyer Din Ratri* (Days and Nights in the Forest, 1969) surely carried some of the flavour of these childhood experiences. See Nalini Das, *Sat Rajar Dhon Ek Manik*, 91–2.

77. Satyajit Ray, *Jakhan Chhoto Chhilam*, 36–7 (where the original poem from Ray's autograph book is reproduced in facsimile).

78. Bert Cardullo, ed., *Satyajit Ray: Interviews* (Jackson: University Press of Mississippi, 2007), 51; Satyajit Ray, *Jakhan Chhoto Chhilam*, 37.

79. Ashis Nandy, *An Ambiguous Journey to the City: The Village and Other Odd Ruins of the Self in the Indian Imagination* (Delhi: Oxford University Press, 2001), 18.

80. See the description of the school in Tapan Raychaudhuri, *Bangal-Nama* (Calcutta: Ananda, 2007), 65–7.

81. As Ray explained once to a French interviewer, '[Y]ou could go to an English school, a religious school run by the Jesuits [he obviously meant St Xavier's], but that's not what I did. I went to a Bengali school, but there, too, we learned English, we read English books, English literature, and even popular English novels, cartoons and all that.' See his interview with Michel Ciment (1978), in Ciment, *Film World: Interviews with Cinema's Leading Directors*, translated by Julie Rose (Oxford: Berg, 2009), 277–99, at 283.

82. P. Basu, *Satyajit Ray*, 61–2, 68.

83. The only exception was one lesson, where the headmaster (filling in for an absent teacher) demonstrated a bit of graphic magic. He first wrote out the Bengali numerals as words on the blackboard. Then, as he rubbed out some parts of the words, there emerged the numerals themselves. 'I never learnt so many new things or enjoyed a lesson more than that one', Ray declared. See the description (with illustration) in Satyajit Ray, *Jakhan Chhoto Chhilam*, 63–4.

84. Satyajit Ray, *Jakhan Chhoto Chhilam*, 70. Throughout his life, he would win many prizes and speak many times before large audiences. Although he was a witty and articulate speaker, his rigid comportment and stern demeanour suggested that the adult Ray had not entirely lost his childhood stage-fright.

85. Satyajit Ray, *Jakhan Chhoto Chhilam*, 67.

86. Sinha's induction into the higher levels of government was one of the outcomes of the Morley–Minto Reforms that sought to involve a greater number of 'natives' in the administration of India. On Sinha's career, see Sibratan Mitra, 'Satyendra Prasanna Sinha', *Probasi*, 9 (1909): 57–65, available at http://archiv.ub.uni-heidelberg.de/savifadok/volltexte/2009/953 (accessed on 25 August 2014).

87. Satyajit Ray, *Jakhan Chhoto Chhilam*, 67, 72–3.

88. See Joydeb Mukhopadhyay, 'Jemon Dekhechhi Satyajit Ray-ke', *Pratibesh Sahitya* (Calcutta), 1, nos 9–10 (November–December 1996), 7–13, at 8, 13; Satyajit Ray, *My Years with Apu*, 5; and Ciment, *Film World: Interviews with Cinema's Leading Directors*, 284. In 1970, in a radio lecture titled 'What Beethoven Means to Me', Ray declared: 'I knew music before I knew the cinema and the first piece of Western classical music I got to know and love was Beethoven's. I can therefore say with complete honesty that I owe an immeasurable debt of gratitude to Beethoven.' Quoted in Adi Gazdar, 'Manik and His Music', in *Satyajit Ray: An Intimate Master*, edited by Santi Das (Delhi: Allied, 1998), 36–9, at 39. That same year, Ray told an interviewer that he would love to make a biographical film on Beethoven and might one day seriously propose the idea to East or West German sponsors. See *Nijer Aynaye Satyajit*, 12.

89. Gupta added that Ray's films, at their best, were as 'beautiful, logical, symmetrical and inevitable' as Mozart's music, not one note of which could be improved by anybody. See Mitra, 'The Genius of Satyajit Ray', 53.

90. It was not just music that had drawn them together; Ray also greatly admired his friend's proficiency in English. Gupta had spent some time in Switzerland when very young and was far more fluent in English than the average Bengali. Late in life, Ray thought it odd that a boy like Anil, hailing from such a Westernized family, had been sent to a Bengali-medium school. See A. Dasgupta, 'Political Film Amader Deshey Bodh Hoy Kara Jay Na', 71.

91. Radhaprasad Gupta, 'Satyajit Ray aar Kichhu Purano Diner Kathha', *Desh*, 59, no. 27 (2 May 1992): 7–15, at 7.

92. Wendy Allen and Roger Spikes, 'Satyajit Ray', *Stills*, 1, no. 3 (Autumn 1981): 40–8, at 45; and 'Towards an Invisible Soundtrack? Interview with Dhritiman Chatterjee', *Cinema Vision India*, 1, no. 4 (October 1980): 12–19, at 14.

93. *Nijer Aynaye Satyajit*, 17.

94. 'I have never played an instrument, except the gramophone,' he once quipped. See *Nijer Aynaye Satyajit*, 17. For about a year in the early 1960s, however, he had learnt to play the pakhwaj but could not continue because of the pressure of film work. See A. Dasgupta, 'Political Film Amader Deshey Bodh Hoy Kara Jay Na', 72. Although he composed music for his films on the piano (and later, the synthesizer), his piano-playing was entirely functional. 'I don't play it in a very orthodox way. It is just a base to compose with,' he said. See Ciment, *Film World*, 297. He would often whistle or sing the tunes to explain what he needed to the players. See *Nijer Aynaye Satyajit*, 12–13.

95. Satyajit Ray, *Jakhan Chhoto Chhilam*, 24.

96. Seton, *Portrait of a Director*, 41.

97. Satyajit Ray, *Jakhan Chhoto Chhilam*, 24–6. The magic lantern, of course, also played a vital role in the childhood of Ingmar Bergman, and has an important place in the history of Indian cinema. Quite some time before the advent of cinema with the films of the Lumière brothers in 1896, the Patwardhan family regaled Bombay audiences with magic lantern shows that mimicked the movies. The slides shown were accompanied with dialogue, which was delivered by concealed 'actors'. See Bergman, *The Magic Lantern*, translated by Joan Tate (London: Hamish Hamilton, 1988), especially p. 16; Bapu Watve, *Dadasaheb Phalke: The Father of Indian Cinema*, translated by S.A. Virkar (Delhi: National Book Trust, 2004), 2–6; and Jayantakumar Ghosh, *Bratyajaner Bioscope* (Calcutta: Dey's, 2008), 33–5.

98. Kalyani Karlekar, 'Chhelemanush Satyajit', in *Sandesher Satyajit*, 86; and Nalini Das, *Sat Rajar Dhon Ek Manik*, 88–9. Marie Seton, who heard this anecdote from Kalyani Karlekar herself, suggested that Satyajit had thought of Germany because Nitin Bose had trained there. See Seton, *Portrait of a Director*, 40. In fact, however, Nitin Bose had never been to Germany. The German connection may have stemmed from Subinoy Ray's short-lived attempt in the dying days of U. Ray & Sons to start an import–export business with German firms. See Kalyani Karlekar, 'Chhelemanush Satyajit', 86.

99. P. Basu, *Satyajit Ray*, 124. Even more strikingly, Satyajit's cousin and future wife, Bijoya, acted during the 1940s in a couple of minor films in Calcutta and then in a Hindi film directed by Nitin Bose. It is true that she did it only because she and her widowed mother were in acute financial need and it is also a matter of record that neither she nor her future husband was happy about it. The very fact that she did it, however, is noteworthy, because few contemporary women from respectable Hindu families, no matter how needy, would have made such a choice. See B. Ray, *Amader Kathha*, 70–86.

100. See A. Dasgupta, 'Political Film Amader Deshey Bodh Hoy Kara Jay Na', 11.

101. B. Ray, *Amader Kathha*, 50. 'Newspapers in those days,' Ray later reminisced, 'carried large pictorial ads of the foreign films. One look at them, and a glance at the headlines were enough to tell the elders whether or not the films were likely to tarnish innocent minds. Those were the days of the flamboyant Hollywood stars, and what they were good at was not considered particularly suitable for a boy barely in his teens'. See Satyajit Ray, 'The Education of a Film-Maker', 81.

102. Satyajit Ray, *Our Films, Their Films* (Calcutta: Orient Longman, 1976), 4, 128.

103. Satyajit Ray, *Jakhan Chhoto Chhilam*, 29.

104. He was never to forget the skills of Byron Hopper, who played the Wurlitzer at the Palace of Varieties, one of the swankiest cinemas in Calcutta. See Satyajit Ray, *Jakhan Chhoto Chhilam*, 28–9.

105. Satyajit Ray, *Our Films, Their Films*, 4.

106. A Madan production of 1930, this ten-reel silent film was directed by Priyanath Ganguly and starred Naresh Mitra, Dhiraj Bhattacharya, and Patience Cooper. See Gaurangaprasad Ghosh, *Sonar Daag* (Calcutta: Jogmaya Prakasani, 1982), 128, 196.

107. Satyajit Ray, 'I Wish I Could Have Shown Them to You', *Cinema Vision India*, 1, no 1 (1980): 6–7, at 7; Satyajit Ray, *Jakhan Chhoto Chhilam*, 30.

108. Satyajit Ray, 'The Education of a Film-Maker', 81.

109. He praised *Dharti ke Lal*, a Hindi film about the consequences of the 1943 Bengal famine produced by the communist-affiliated Indian People's Theatre Association; Uday Shankar's *Kalpana*; and the Marathi films made by the Prabhat Studio in its earlier period. See Satyajit Ray, 'What Is Wrong with Indian Films?' [1948], in *Our Films, Their Films*, 19–24, at 23–4; and *Benegal on Ray*, 108.

110. Satyajit Ray, *Our Films, Their Films*, 4.

111. 'I was keen on some of the personalities, some of the songs—I loved the singing and dancing of Astaire and Rogers. I went to see films purely as a fan,' he said. See *Nijer Aynaye Satyajit*, 7, 15.

112. A. Dasgupta, 'Political Film Amader Deshey Bodh Hoy Kara Jay Na', 11.

113. See Satyajit Ray, *My Years with Apu*, 4; Robinson, *Satyajit Ray: The Inner Eye*, 38; P. Basu, *Satyajit Ray*, 325; and B. Ray, *Amader Kathha*, 548. Apparently, a lot of Indians wrote such fan mail to Hollywood stars. Alex Hague, the proprietor of Pathé India, told the Indian Cinematograph Committee that 'every mail boat from India takes packets of letters to Hollywood appreciating the stars'. See *Indian Cinematograph Committee 1927–1928: Evidence*, 5 vols (Calcutta: Government of India Central Publications Branch, 1928), 1: 521.

114. *Nijer Aynaye Satyajit*, 16.

115. A. Dasgupta, 'Political Film Amader Deshey Bodh Hoy Kara Jay Na', 12.

116. When the elderly Wilder heard this in the Oscar telecast, he sent a cable to Ray apologizing for his discourtesy. See B. Ray, *Amader Kathha*, 548.

117. A. Dasgupta, 'Political Film Amader Deshey Bodh Hoy Kara Jay Na', 12.

118. Satyajit Ray, 'The Education of a Film-Maker', 82. Ray's aunt Leela Majumdar, who taught English and mathematics for about a year at Santiniketan in the early 1930s, recalled that her father—Upendrakishore's brother Pramadaranjan—was also very critical of the 'effeminate' milieu of Santiniketan and objected to Tagore's own flowing manes. See L. Majumdar, *Aar Konokhaney*, 145; L. Majumdar, *Pakdandi*, 243; and Satyajit Ray, *Jakhan Chhoto Chhilam*, 36.

119. Satyajit Ray, 'Binode-da' [1971], in Ray, *Bishoy Chalachchitra* (Calcutta: Ananda, 1982), 118–23, at 118, 121.

120. Satyajit Ray, 'The Education of a Film-Maker', 82.

121. Seton, *Portrait of a Director*, 35.

122. Robinson, *Satyajit Ray: The Inner Eye*, 214.

Index

Ives, Frederic Eugene, 205

Jabakusum (hair oil), 264, 267,
    295n94, 296n113
Jacobs, W. W., 317
Jadavpur University, 283
Jain, Kajri, 2, 24, 26n3, 265,
    290n43
jauhar, 151, 183n42
Jex-Blake, Sophia, 97, 100, 132–
    3n124, 134n136
Johns Hopkins University Medical
    School (Baltimore, USA), 97
Joshi, Anandibai, 29n34, 83, 100,
    119n3, 134n142
Joshi, Sanjay, 13, 30nn35–7, 64n10,
    125n43, 140n216
Juvenile Magazine, 226

Kaal Parinoy, 383, 396n106
kala-azar, 327, 340, 358n147
Kankabati, 333, 361n191
Karlekar, Kalyani (née Chakrabarti),
    197n236, 243–4n137, 309, 341n2,
    379, 382, 395n98
Karlekar, Malavika, 109, 122n26,
    131n108, 134n141
Karve, Dhondo Keshav, 62
Keay, John Seymour, 155, 186n79
Keno Rabindranathkey Chai, 339–40,
    366n240
Keshranjan (hair oil), 264
Khan, Sir Syed Ahmed, 44
Kidambi, Prashant, 265, 295n103
kindergarten, 229n7, 309
Kinnear, Michael S., 76–7n135,
    297n115, 304n195
Kolsky, Elizabeth, 187n87, 285–6n11
Kopf, David, 23, 35–6n86, 36–7n91,
    123–4n35
Kowshik, Dinkar, 385
kulin Brahmins, 85, 86, 109, 113,
    122nn22–4, 175

Lafont, Father Eugene, 270
Lear, Edward, 7, 324
Levy, Louis, 206
Levy, Max, 206, 238n85
lithography, 205, 234n52, 255, 318,
    349n74
Locke, John, 223, 241–2n118,
    243n128
London County Council School of
    Photoengraving and Lithography,
    318, 349nn72–3
London Missionary Society, 89
London School of Medicine for
    Women, 132–3n124
Loreto Convent (Calcutta), 108,
    229n7
Lubinski, Christina, 274, 298n138
Lubitsch, Ernst, 383
Lytton, 2nd Baron (Viceroy), 146

'Macaulayism', 256, 289n36
Macleod, Dianne Sachko, 255,
    288n30
Madan family, 271, 278, 299n147,
    396n106
Madras Medical School, 98
Mahakali Pathshala, 107, 138n190
Mahalanobis, Gurucharan, 32n57,
    364–5n228
Mahalanobis, Madhurilata (née
    Ray), 230–1n16, 358n150, 371, 374,
    388n14, 390n45
Mahalanobis, Prabodhchandra,
    32n57, 375
Mahalanobis, Prafullachandra
    (Bula), 32n57, 375, 390–1n46,
    391n48
Mahalanobis, Prasantachandra,
    32n57, 138n188, 231–2n26, 316,
    333, 334, 336, 338, 339, 340,
    366n237, 366n240, 367n245,
    367n250, 367nn252–3,
    368n257

201; children of, 199; and children's literature, 6, 59, 61, 79n151, 198, 216–23, 225–6; and colonial violence, 285–6n11; cosmopolitanism, 226; cricket, 46, 47, 69n68; death, 323, 353n114, 355n120; diabetes, 354n115, 354n117; and Dwarkin's, 76–7n135, 203; education, 52, 55–8, 74n122, 75–6n132; as educator, 201; as employer, 212, 239–40n106, 240n107; entrepreneurial initiatives, 18–19, 32–3n58; family relationships, 57–8, 76n134, 77n137, 201; and Dwarakanath Ganguli, 59, 62, 114, 199; and Kadambini Ganguli, 371; and Hinduism, 55, 77n137, 223, 227, 245n152, 259; humour, 223; idealism, 281; imperial loyalty, 253, 286n12; as innovator, 208–9; *Kenaram o Becharam*, 329; as landowner, 200, 230n11; lifestyle, 252; literary style, 79n151, 217, 218–19, 222, 245n153, 247n176; marriage, 62, 199, 228nn2–3; and modernity, 222; as musician, lyricist and composer, 51, 201–3, 232n31, 232nn34–5, 233n39, 285n10, 293n79, 297n120; and national education movement, 281–4; and nationalism, 7, 221, 226–7, 233n39, 252, 259–60, 285–6n11; on naturalism, 259; patenting, 239n101; personality, 77n137, 200, 223, 281; photography and half-tone process, 4–5, 18, 77n138, 204, 207–13, 233n43, 237n77, 238–9n95, 239n101, 240n108, 269, 278, 318; as poet, 218; political orientation, 61, 252–3; printing and publishing,

244n143, 249n194, 319; prizes won, 212; and Puranas, 250n208, 354–5n119; puritanism, 200; as reformer, 200; residences, 199, 204, 229n5, 249n194, 281, 319, 323, 353n114; and Sashi Hesh, 201, 231n20; scientific interests, 217, 222, 228n1, 247n172, 354–5n119, 357n134; 'Saatmaar Paloan', 221; *Sandesh*, 7, 223–8, 281, 319; *Sekaler Katha*, 217–18, 244nn139–42; surname, 58, 77–8n139; and *swadeshi*, 220, 221, 225–7, 251, 252, 254, 277–8, 285n10; and Rabindranath Tagore, 202, 203, 205, 218, 232n29, 234n47, 234n51, 291n51, 320; as translator, 202; tributes to, 198, 208, 209, 210, 211, 212, 216–17, 220–1, 232–3n36, 239n102, 355nn120–1; *Tuntunir Boi*, 220, 244n143; unfinished projects, 354–5n119, 355n121; Ramayana and Mahabharata, 5, 204, 217, 218–20, 222, 234n47, 244n146, 244–5n147, 245n149, 245n152, 247nn175–6; Western reputation, 211–12

Ray, Vishnuram, 40, 50

Raychaudhuri, Brajendrakishore, 46

Raychaudhuri, Harikishore, 2, 50–1, 55, 57, 58, 59, 71n90, 73–4n115

Raychaudhuri, Hitendrakishore, 45, 68n49, 201, 225–6

Raychaudhuri, Manorama, 51

Raychaudhuri, Narendrakishore, 51, 57, 58, 74n116, 77n137, 200, 201, 230n11, 252, 322, 344–5n138

Raychaudhuri, Rajlakshmi, 51, 76n134

Raychaudhuri, Surobala, 51

Raychaudhuri, Tapan, 30n40, 230n10, 394n80

About the Author

Chandak Sengoopta is Professor of History at Birkbeck College, University of London, UK. He has also taught at University College London and the University of Manchester. His previously published works include *Imprint of the Raj: How Fingerprinting Was Born in Colonial India* (2003). He is currently working on a new and comprehensive biography of Satyajit Ray.